DATSUN
2-WHEEL DRIVE PICKUPS
1970-1983
SHOP MANUAL

ALAN AHLSTRAND
Editor

CLYMER PUBLICATIONS

World's largest publisher of books
devoted exclusively to automobiles and motorcycles.

A division of INTERTEC PUBLISHING CORPORATION
P.O. Box 12901, Overland Park, Kansas 66212

FIRST EDITION
First Printing February, 1977

SECOND EDITION
Revised by Alan Ahlstrand to include 1978-1979 models
First Printing December, 1979

THIRD EDITION
Revised by Alan Ahlstrand to include 1980 models
First Printing November, 1980

FOURTH EDITION
Revised by Alan Ahlstrand to include 1981 models
First Printing September, 1981

FIFTH EDITION
Revised by Alan Ahlstrand to include 1982 models
First Printing October, 1982

SIXTH EDITION
Revised by Alan Ahlstrand to include 1983 models
First Printing August, 1983
Second Printing February, 1984
Third Printing November, 1984
Fourth Printing September, 1985
Fifth Printing February, 1986
Sixth Printing January, 1987
Seventh Printing September, 1987
Eighth Printing June, 1988
Ninth Printing April, 1989

Printed in U.S.A.

ISBN: 0-89287-151-2

Illustrations courtesy of Nissan Motor Corporation in U.S.A.

COVER: Photographed by Michael Brown Photographic Productions, Los Angeles, California.

CONTENTS

DATSUN
2-WHEEL DRIVE PICKUPS
1970-1983
SHOP MANUAL

QUICK REFERENCE DATA

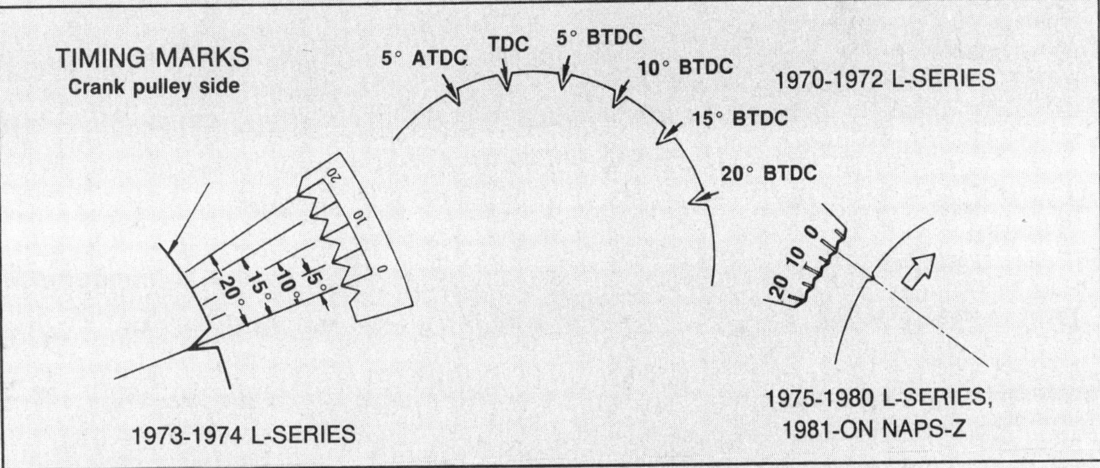

RECOMMENDED LUBRICANTS

Engine	API Service SF or SE
Manual transmission	API GL-4
Automatic transmission	Dexron
Differential	API GL-5
Brake and clutch fluid	DOT 3

APPROXIMATE REFILL CAPACITIES

Engine oil	
1970-1973 and 1975-1980	
With filter change	4 1/2 qt. (4.3 liters)
Without filter change	4 qt. (3.8 liters)
1974	
With filter change	5 1/8 qt. (4.8 liters)
Without filter change	4 3/8 qt. (4.1 liters)
1981-on	
With filter change	4 5/8 qt. (4.4 liters)
Without filter change	4 1/8 qt. (3.9 liters)
Manual transmission oil	
1970-1973	2 1/8 qt. (2.0 liters)
1974 and later 4-speed	3 5/8 pt. (1.7 liters)
1977 and later 5-speed	4 1/4 pt. (2 liters)
Automatic transmission fluid	5 7/8 qt. (5.5 liters)
Differential oil	
521 pickup	1 3/4 pt. (0.8 liter)
620 pickup	2 1/8 pt. (1.0 liter)
720 pickup	2 5/8 pt. (1.25 liters)

Cooling system	
521 pickup	7 qt. (6.6 liters)
620 pickup	
1972-1974	6 3/8 qt. (6.0 liters)
1975-1977 (manual)	8 1/2 qt. (8 liters)
1975-1977 (automatic)	8 1/4 qt. (7.8 liters)
1978-1979 manual (including reservoir tank)	9 3/8 qt. (8.9 liters)
1978-1979 automatic (including reservoir tank)	9 1/8 qt. (8.7 liters)
720 pickup	
1980 manual (including reservoir tank)	9 3/8 qt. (8.9 liters)
1980 automatic (including reservoir tank)	9 1/8 qt. (8.9 liters)
1981-on manual (including reservoir tank)	10 3/4 qt. (10.2 liters)
1981-on automatic (including reservoir tank)	10 5/8 qt. (10.1 liters)

TUNE-UP SPECIFICATIONS

Compression pressure	
Standard	171 psi (12 kg/cm^2)
Minimum	128 psi (9 kg/cm^2)
Valve clearance	
L-series engines	
Intake, hot	0.010 in. (0.25 mm)
Exhaust, hot	0.012 in. (0.30 mm)
Intake, cold	0.008 in. (0.20 mm)
Exhaust, cold	0.010 in. (0.25 mm)
NAPS-Z engine	
Intake, hot	0.012 in. (0.30 mm)
Exhaust, hot	0.012 in. (0.30 mm)
Intake, cold	0.008 in. (0.21 mm)
Exhaust, cold	0.009 in. (0.23 mm)
Firing order	1-3-4-2
Distributor rotation	Counterclockwise
Spark plug type (NGK brand)	
1970-1971	BP6E
1972	BP5ES
1973-1974	B6ES
1975-1976	BP6ES
1977 California, all 1978	
Standard type	BP6ES-11
Hot type	BP4E-11, BP5ES-11
Cold type	BP7ES-11
1977 non-California	
Standard type	BP6ES-11
Hot type	BP4E, BP5ES
Cold type	BP7ES
1979	
Standard type	BP6ES-11, BPR63S-11*
Hot type	BP4E-11, BP5ES-11, BPR4E-11*, BPR5ES-11*
Cold type	BP7ES-11, BPR7ES-11*
1980 U.S.	
Standard type	BP6ES-11, BPR6ES-11*
Hot type	BP4ES-11, BP5ES-11, BPR4ES-11,* BPR5ES-11*
Cold type	BP7ES-11, BPR7ES-11*
1980 Canada	
Standard type	BPR6ES
Hot type	BPR4ES, BPR5ES
Cold type	BPR7ES
1981 U.S.	
Standard type	BP6ES, BPR6ES*
Hot type	BP5ES, BPR5ES*
Cold type	BP7ES, BPR7ES*
1981 Canada	
Standard type	BPR6ES
Hot type	BPR5ES
Cold type	BPR7ES
1982-on intake side	
Standard	BPR6ES
Hot type	BPR5ES
Cold type	BPR7ES
1982-on exhaust side	
Standard and hot type	BPR5ES
Cold type	BPR6ES, BPR7ES
Spark plug gap	
1970-1972	0.031-0.035 in. (0.8-0.9 mm)

(continued)

TUNE-UP SPECIFICATIONS (continued)

1973-1974	0.028-0.031 in. (0.7-0.8 mm)
1975 California, 1975-1977 non-California	0.031-0.035 in. (0.8-0.9 mm)
1976-1977 California	0.039-0.043 in. (1.0-1.1 mm)
1978-1979	0.039-0.043 in. (1.0-1.1 mm)
1980	
U.S.	0.039-0.043 in. (1.0-1.1 mm)
Canada	0.031-0.035 in. (0.8-0.9 mm)
1981-on	0.031-0.035 in. (0.8-0.9 mm)
Points gap (breaker point ignition)	0.018-0.022 in. (0.45-0.55 mm)
Dwell angle (breaker point ignition)	49-55°
Ignition timing (at idle speed,° BTDC)	
1970-1971 (advanced)	10
1970-1971 (retarded)	0 (top dead center)
1972 (advanced)	7
1972 (retarded)	0 (top dead center)
1973 (advanced)	12
1973 (retarded)	
Through chassis No. PL620-141296	5
From chassis No. PL620-141297	8
1974	12
1975-1977	
California	10
Non-California	12
1978-1979	12
1980	
California	
Standard**	12 ±2
Heavy duty**	10 ±2
49-state	12 ±2
Canada	
Standard**	12
Heavy duty**	12 ±2
1981	5 ±2
1982-on	3 ±2
Idle speed	
1970-1972	700 rpm
1973-1974	
Manual	800 rpm
Automatic	650 rpm in DRIVE
1975-1979	See text
1980	
All except Canadian standard models**	600 ±100 rpm (automatics in DRIVE)
Canadian standard models**	600 rpm (automatics in DRIVE)
1981-on	650 ±100 rpm (automatics in DRIVE)

* Optional resistor type.

** Heavy duty models include the letter "E" in the vehicle identification number. Standard models do not. King Cabs and long beds are standard models.

BULB SPECIFICATIONS

Application	Wattage	Trade number
1970-1979		
Headlights		
High beams	37.5	4001
Low beams	37.5/50	4002
Front parking/turn signal lights	23/8	1034
Side marker lights	8	67
Rear combination lights (521 pickup)		
Stop/tail lights	23/8	1034
Rear turn signals	23	1073
Backup lights	23	1073
Rear combination lights (620 pickup)		
Turn/stop lights	23	1073
Tail, stop, and turn lights	23/8	1034
Tail lights	8	67
Backup lights	23	1073
License plate light	7.5	89
Interior light		
521 pickup	6	—
620 pickup	5	—
Engine compartment	6	—
Gauge illumination lights		
521 pickup	3.4	158
620 pickup	1.7	161
Indicator and warning lights		161
Knob and control illumination	3.4	158
1980-on		
Headlights		
Inner	50	4651
Outer	40/60	4652
Front turn signals	27	1156
Front parking lights	5	—
Front side marker lights	5	—
Rear side marker lights	3.8	—
Stop/tail lights	27/8	1157
Rear turn signals	27	1156
Back-up lights	27	1156
License plate lights	10	—
Interior light		
Standard cab	5	—
King Cab	10	—
Oil pressure gauge illumination	3.4	158
Voltmeter illumination	3.4	158
Other gauge illumination	1.7	—
Warning lamps	3.4	158
Cigarette lighter illumination	1.4	—
Heater A/C illumination	3.4	158
Radio illumination	3.4	158
Rear defogger indicator lamp	1.4	—
Rear defogger switch illumination	3	158

INTRODUCTION

This detailed, comprehensive manual covers all 1970-1983 Datsun pickups. The expert text gives complete information on maintenance, repair, and overhaul. Hundreds of drawings guide you through every step. The book includes all you need to know to keep your car running right.

Specific information for 1970-1981 models is contained in Chapters One through Fourteen. The Supplement at the back of the book contains information on 1982 and later models that differs from that in the main body of the book.

Where repairs are practical for the owner/mechanic, complete procedures are given. Equally important, difficult jobs are pointed out. Such operations are usually more economically performed by a dealer or independent garage.

A shop manual is a reference. You want to be able to find information fast. As in all Clymer books, this one is designed with this in mind. All chapters are thumb tabbed. Important items are indexed at the rear of the book. All the most frequently used specifications and capacities are summarized on the *Quick Reference* pages at the front of the book.

Keep the book handy. Carry it in your glove box. It will help you to better understand your Datsun Pickup, lower repair and maintenance costs, and generally improve your satisfaction with your vehicle.

1

CHAPTER ONE

GENERAL INFORMATION

The troubleshooting, tune-up, maintenance, and step-by-step repair procedures in this book are written for the owner and home mechanic. The text is accompanied by useful photos and diagrams to make the job as clear and correct as possible.

Troubleshooting, tune-up, maintenance, and repair are not difficult if you know what tools and equipment to use and what to do. Anyone not afraid to get their hands dirty, of average intelligence, and with some mechanical ability can perform most of the procedures in this book.

In some cases, a repair job may require tools or skills not reasonably expected of the home mechanic. These procedures are noted in each chapter and it is recommended that you take the job to your dealer, a competent mechanic, or machine shop.

MANUAL ORGANIZATION

This chapter provides general information and safety and service hints. Also included are lists of recommended shop and emergency tools as well as a brief description of troubleshooting and tune-up equipment.

Chapter Two provides methods and suggestions for quick and accurate diagnosis and repair of problems. Troubleshooting procedures discuss typical symptoms and logical methods to pinpoint the trouble.

Chapter Three explains all periodic lubrication and routine maintenance necessary to keep your vehicle running well. Chapter Three also includes recommended tune-up procedures, eliminating the need to constantly consult chapters on the various subassemblies.

Subsequent chapters cover specific systems such as the engine, transmission, and electrical systems. Each of these chapters provides disassembly, repair, and assembly procedures in a simple step-by-step format. If a repair requires special skills or tools, or is otherwise impractical for the home mechanic, it is so indicated. In these cases it is usually faster and less expensive to have the repairs made by a dealer or competent repair shop. Necessary specifications concerning a particular system are included at the end of the appropriate chapter.

When special tools are required to perform a procedure included in this manual, the tool is illustrated either in actual use or alone. It may be possible to rent or borrow these tools. The inventive mechanic may also be able to find a suitable substitute in his tool box, or to fabricate one.

The terms NOTE, CAUTION, and WARNING have specific meanings in this manual. A NOTE provides additional or explanatory information. A CAUTION is used to emphasize areas where equipment damage could result if proper precautions are not taken. A WARNING is used to stress those areas where personal injury or death could result from negligence, in addition to possible mechanical damage.

SERVICE HINTS

Observing the following practices will save time, effort, and frustration, as well as prevent possible injury.

Throughout this manual keep in mind two conventions. "Front" refers to the front of the vehicle. The front of any component, such as the transmission, is that end which faces toward the front of the vehicle. The "left" and "right" sides of the vehicle refer to the orientation of a person sitting in the vehicle facing forward. For example, the steering wheel is on the left side. These rules are simple, but even experienced mechanics occasionally become disoriented.

Most of the service procedures covered are straightforward and can be performed by anyone reasonably handy with tools. It is suggested, however, that you consider your own capabilities carefully before attempting any operation involving major disassembly of the engine.

Some operations, for example, require the use of a press. It would be wiser to have these performed by a shop equipped for such work, rather than to try to do the job yourself with makeshift equipment. Other procedures require precision measurements. Unless you have the skills and equipment required, it would be better to have a qualified repair shop make the measurements for you.

Repairs go much faster and easier if the parts that will be worked on are clean before you begin. There are special cleaners for washing the engine and related parts. Brush or spray on the cleaning solution, let it stand, then rinse it away with a garden hose. Clean all oily or greasy parts with cleaning solvent as you remove them.

WARNING

Never use gasoline as a cleaning agent. It presents an extreme fire hazard. Be sure to work in a well-ventilated area when using cleaning solvent. Keep a fire extinguisher, rated for gasoline fires, handy in any case.

Much of the labor charge for repairs made by dealers is for the removal and disassembly of other parts to reach the defective unit. It is frequently possible to perform the preliminary operations yourself and then take the defective unit in to the dealer for repair, at considerable savings.

Once you have decided to tackle the job yourself, make sure you locate the appropriate section in this manual, and read it entirely. Study the illustrations and text until you have a good idea of what is involved in completing the job satisfactorily. If special tools are required, make arrangements to get them before you start. Also, purchase any known defective parts prior to starting on the procedure. It is frustrating and time-consuming to get partially into a job and then be unable to complete it.

Simple wiring checks can be easily made at home, but knowledge of electronics is almost a necessity for performing tests with complicated electronic testing gear.

During disassembly of parts keep a few general cautions in mind. Force is rarely needed to get things apart. If parts are a tight fit, like a bearing in a case, there is usually a tool designed to separate them. Never use a screwdriver to pry apart parts with machined surfaces such as cylinder head and valve cover. You will mar the surfaces and end up with leaks.

Make diagrams wherever similar-appearing parts are found. You may think you can remember where everything came from — but mistakes are costly. There is also the possibility you may get sidetracked and not return to work for days or even weeks — in which interval, carefully laid out parts may have become disturbed.

Tag all similar internal parts for location, and mark all mating parts for position. Record number and thickness of any shims as they are removed. Small parts such as bolts can be identified by placing them in plastic sandwich bags that are sealed and labeled with masking tape.

Wiring should be tagged with masking tape and marked as each wire is removed. Again, do not rely on memory alone.

When working under the vehicle, do not trust a hydraulic or mechanical jack to hold the vehicle up by itself. Always use jackstands. See **Figure 1**.

Disconnect battery ground cable before working near electrical connections and before disconnecting wires. Never run the engine with the battery disconnected; the alternator could be seriously damaged.

Protect finished surfaces from physical damage or corrosion. Keep gasoline and brake fluid off painted surfaces.

Frozen or very tight bolts and screws can often be loosened by soaking with penetrating oil like Liquid Wrench or WD-40, then sharply striking the bolt head a few times with a hammer and punch (or screwdriver for screws). Avoid heat unless absolutely necessary, since it may melt, warp, or remove the temper from many parts.

Avoid flames or sparks when working near a charging battery or flammable liquids, such as brake fluid or gasoline.

No parts, except those assembled with a press fit, require unusual force during assembly. If a part is hard to remove or install, find out why before proceeding.

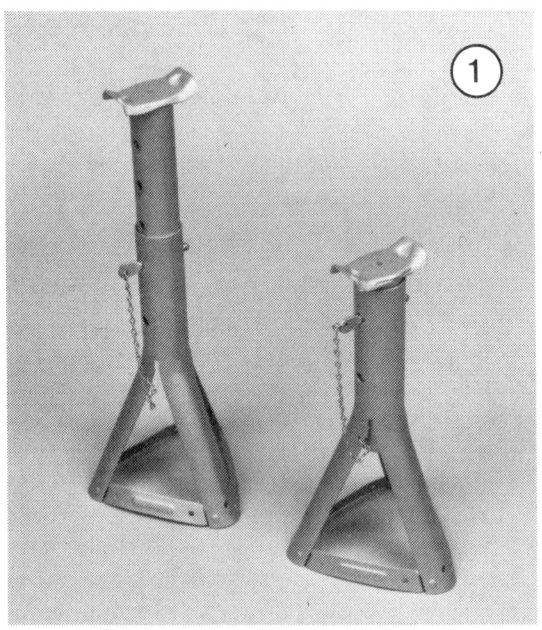

Cover all openings after removing parts to keep dirt, small tools, etc., from falling in.

When assembling two parts, start all fasteners, then tighten evenly.

The clutch plate, wiring connections, brake shoes, drums, pads, and discs should be kept clean and free of grease and oil.

When assembling parts, be sure all shims and washers are replaced exactly as they came out.

Whenever a rotating part butts against a stationary part, look for a shim or washer. Use new gaskets if there is any doubt about the condition of old ones. Generally, you should apply gasket cement to one mating surface only, so the parts may be easily disassembled in the future. A thin coat of oil on gaskets helps them seal effectively.

Heavy grease can be used to hold small parts in place if they tend to fall out during assembly. However, keep grease and oil away from electrical, clutch, and brake components.

High spots may be sanded off a piston with sandpaper, but emery cloth and oil do a much more professional job.

Carburetors are best cleaned by disassembling them and soaking the parts in a commercial carburetor cleaner. Never soak gaskets and rubber parts in these cleaners. Never use wire to clean out jets and air passages; they are easily damaged. Use compressed air to blow out the carburetor, but only if the float has been removed first.

Take your time and do the job right. Do not forget that a newly rebuilt engine must be broken in the same as a new one. Refer to your owner's manual for the proper break-in procedures.

SAFETY FIRST

Professional mechanics can work for years and never sustain a serious injury. If you observe a few rules of common sense and safety, you can enjoy many safe hours servicing your vehicle. You could hurt yourself or damage the vehicle if you ignore these rules.

1. Never use gasoline as a cleaning solvent.

2. Never smoke or use a torch in the vicinity of flammable liquids such as cleaning solvent in open containers.

3. Never smoke or use a torch in an area where batteries are being charged. Highly explosive hydrogen gas is formed during the charging process.

4. Use the proper sized wrenches to avoid damage to nuts and injury to yourself.

5. When loosening a tight or stuck nut, be guided by what would happen if the wrench should slip. Protect yourself accordingly.

6. Keep your work area clean and uncluttered.

7. Wear safety goggles during all operations involving drilling, grinding, or use of a cold chisel.

8. Never use worn tools.

9. Keep a fire extinguisher handy and be sure it is rated for gasoline (Class B) and electrical (Class C) fires.

EXPENDABLE SUPPLIES

Certain expendable supplies are necessary. These include grease, oil, gasket cement, wiping rags, cleaning solvent, and distilled water. Also, special locking compounds, silicone lubricants, and engine cleaners may be useful. Cleaning solvent is available at most service stations and distilled water for the battery is available at most supermarkets.

SHOP TOOLS

For proper servicing, you will need an assortment of ordinary hand tools (**Figure 2**).

As a minimum, these include:

a. Combination wrenches
b. Sockets
c. Plastic mallet
d. Small hammer
e. Snap ring pliers
f. Gas pliers
g. Phillips screwdrivers
h. Slot (common) screwdrivers
i. Feeler gauges
j. Spark plug gauge
k. Spark plug wrench

Special tools necessary are shown in the chapters covering the particular repair in which they are used.

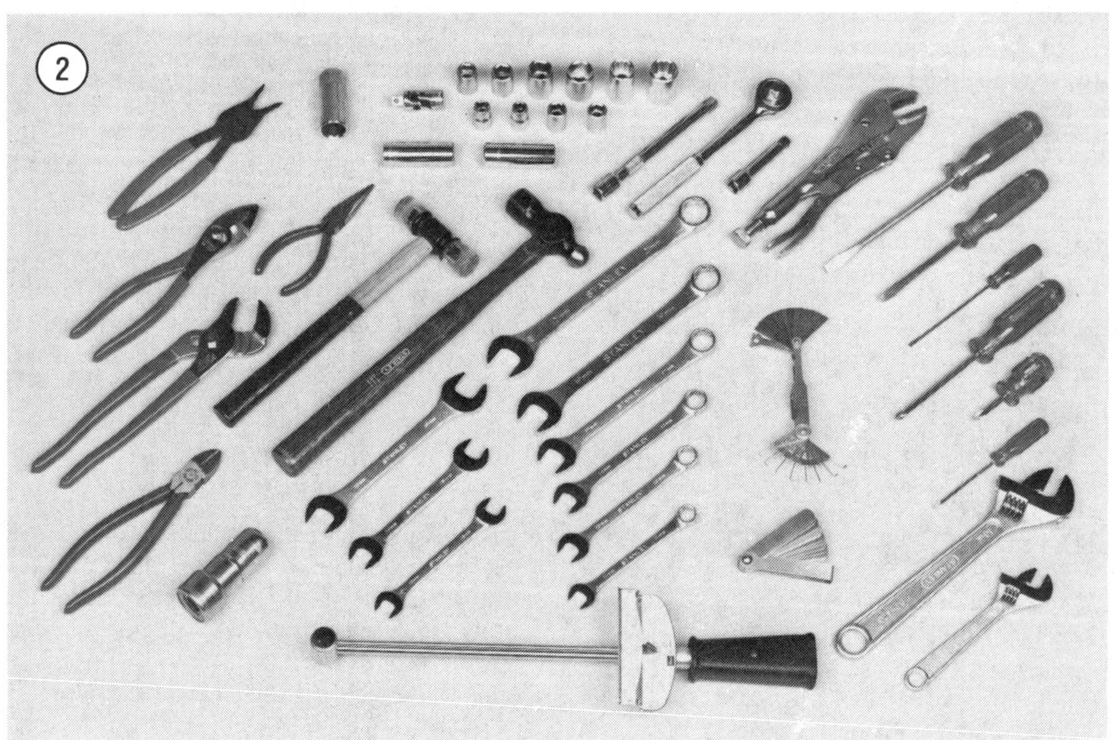

Engine tune-up and troubleshooting procedures require other special tools and equipment. These are described in detail in the following sections.

EMERGENCY TOOL KIT

A small emergency tool kit kept in the trunk is handy for road emergencies which otherwise could leave you stranded. The tools listed below and shown in **Figure 3** will let you handle most roadside repairs.

a. Combination wrenches
b. Crescent (adjustable) wrench
c. Screwdrivers — common and Phillips
d. Pliers — conventional (gas) and needle nose
e. Vise Grips
f. Hammer — plastic and metal
g. Small container of waterless hand cleaner
h. Rags for clean up
i. Silver waterproof sealing tape (duct tape)
j. Flashlight
k. Emergency road flares — at least four
l. Spare drive belts (water pump, alternator, etc.)

TROUBLESHOOTING AND TUNE-UP EQUIPMENT

Voltmeter, Ohmmeter, and Ammeter

For testing the ignition or electrical system, a good voltmeter is required. For automotive use, an instrument covering 0-20 volts is satisfac-

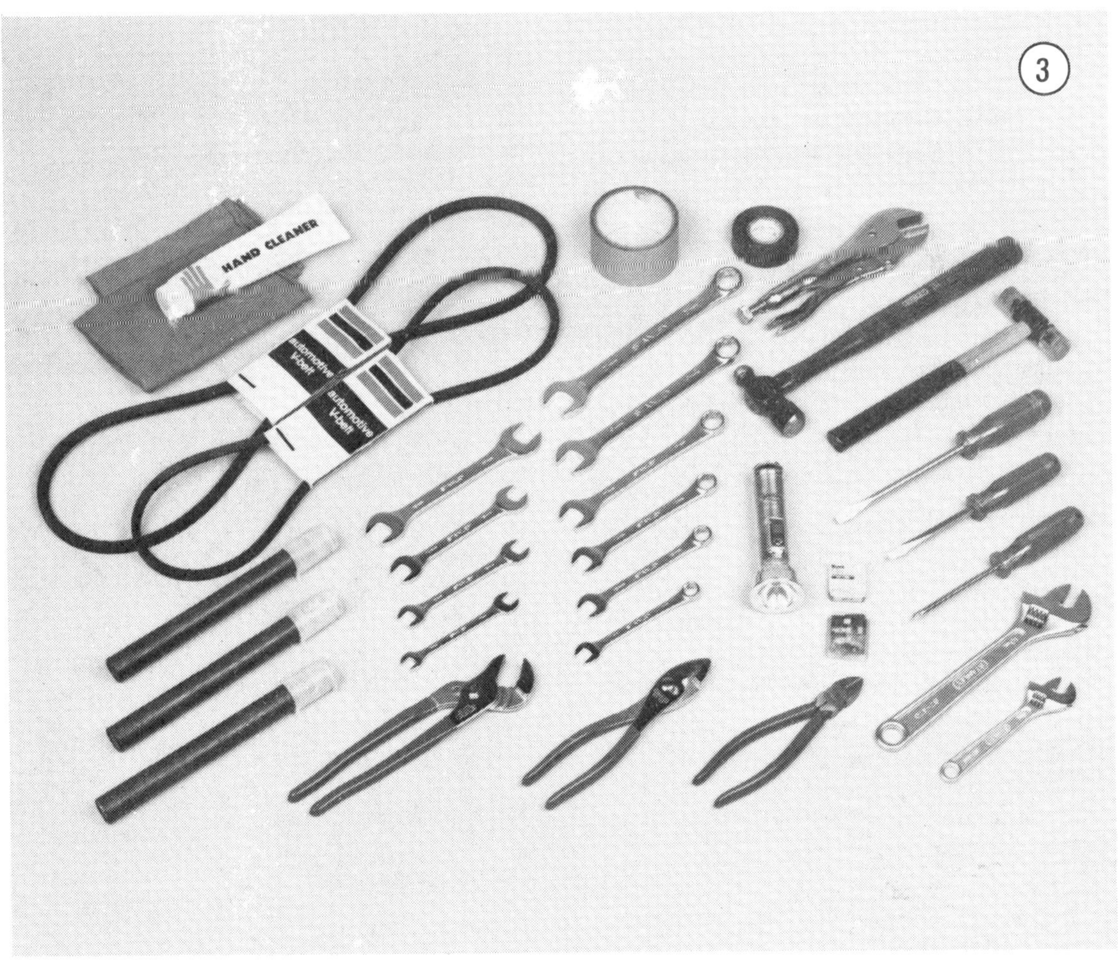

tory. One which also has a 0-2 volt scale is necessary for testing relays, points, or individual contacts where voltage drops are much smaller. Accuracy should be ± ½ volt.

An ohmmeter measures electrical resistance. This instrument is useful for checking continuity (open and short circuits), and testing fuses and lights.

The ammeter measures electrical current. Ammeters for automotive use should cover 0-50 amperes and 0-250 amperes. These are useful for checking battery charging and starting current.

Several inexpensive VOM's (volt-ohm-milliammeter) combine all three instruments into one which fits easily in any tool box. See **Figure 4**. However, the ammeter ranges are usually too small for automotive work.

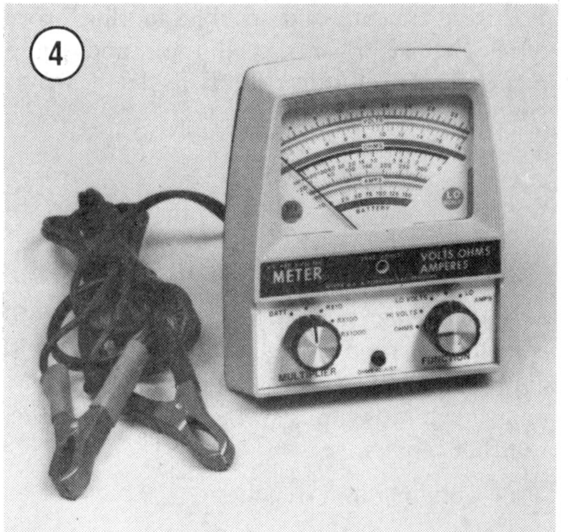

4

Hydrometer

The hydrometer gives a useful indication of battery condition and charge by measuring the specific gravity of the electrolyte in each cell. See **Figure 5**. Complete details on use and interpretation of readings are provided in the electrical chapter.

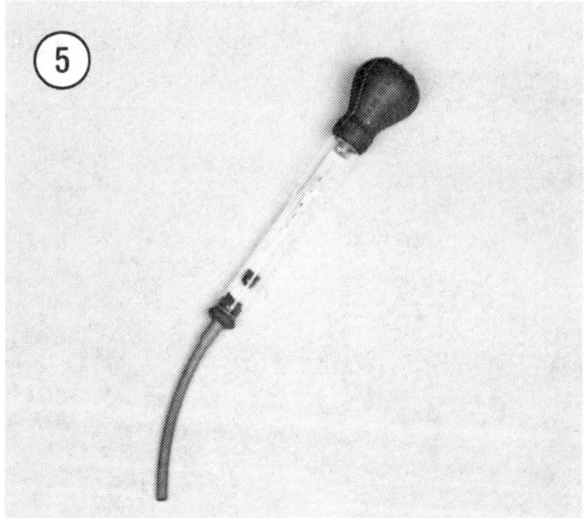
5

Compression Tester

The compression tester measures the compression pressure built up in each cylinder. The results, when properly interpreted, can indicate general cylinder and valve condition. See **Figure 6**.

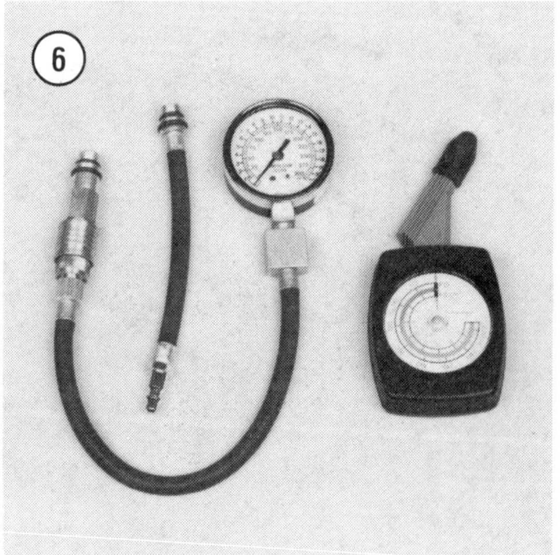
6

Vacuum Gauge

The vacuum gauge (**Figure 7**) is one of the easiest instruments to use, but one of the most difficult for the inexperienced mechanic to interpret. The results, when interpreted with other findings, can provide valuable clues to possible trouble.

To use the vacuum gauge, connect it to a vacuum hose that goes to the intake manifold. Attach it either directly to the hose or to a T-fitting installed into the hose.

> NOTE: *Subtract one inch from the reading for every 1,000 ft. elevation.*

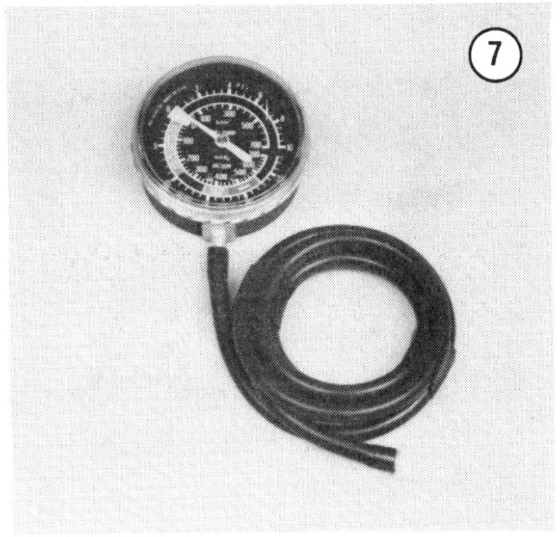

7

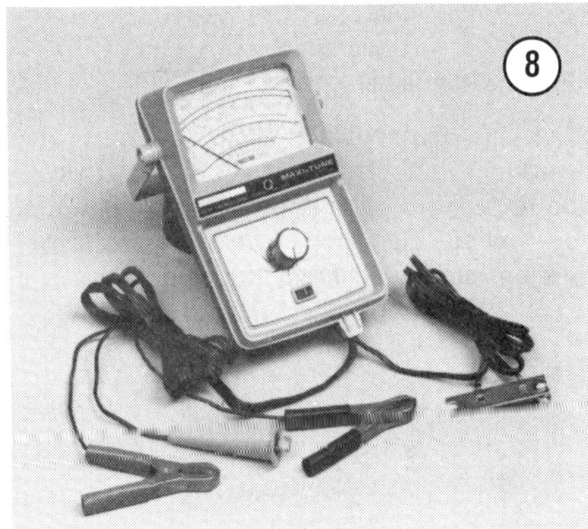

8

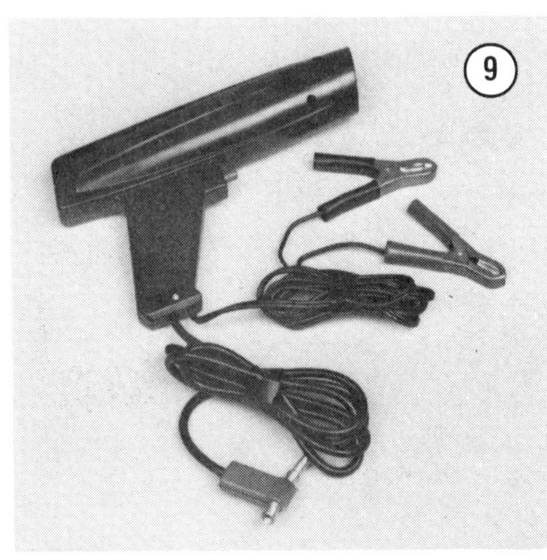

9

Fuel Pressure Gauge

This instrument is invaluable for evaluating fuel pump performance. Fuel system troubleshooting procedures in this manual use a fuel pressure gauge. Usually a vacuum gauge and fuel pressure gauge are combined.

Dwell Meter (Contact Breaker Point Ignition Only)

A dwell meter measures the distance in degrees of cam rotation that the breaker points remain closed while the engine is running. Since this angle is determined by breaker point gap, dwell angle is an accurate indication of breaker point gap.

Many tachometers intended for tuning and testing incorporate a dwell meter as well. See **Figure 8**. Follow the manufacturer's instructions to measure dwell.

Tachometer

A tachometer is necessary for tuning. See **Figure 8**. Ignition timing and carburetor adjustments must be performed at the specified idle speed. The best instrument for this purpose is one with a low range of 0-1,000 or 0-2,000 rpm for setting idle, and a high range of 0-4,000 or more for setting ignition timing at 3,000 rpm. Extended range (0-6,000 or 0-8,000 rpm) instruments lack accuracy at lower speeds. The instrument should be capable of detecting changes of 25 rpm on the low range.

Strobe Timing Light

This instrument is necessary for tuning, as it permits very accurate ignition timing. The light flashes at precisely the same instant that No. 1 cylinder fires, at which time the timing marks on the engine should align. Refer to Chapter Three for exact location of the timing marks for your engine.

Suitable lights range from inexpensive neon bulb types ($2-3) to powerful xenon strobe lights ($20-40). See **Figure 9**. Neon timing lights are difficult to see and must be used in dimly lit areas. Xenon strobe timing lights can be used outside in bright sunlight. Both types work on this vehicle; use according to the manufacturer's instructions.

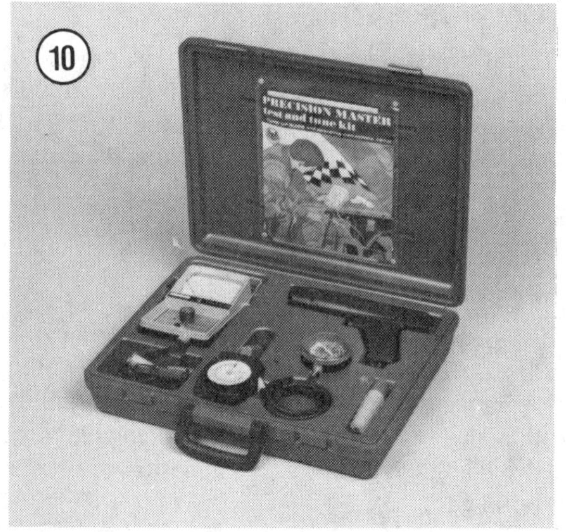

Tune-up Kits

Many manufacturer's offer kits that combine several useful instruments. Some come in a convenient carry case and are usally less expensive than purchasing one instrument at a time. **Figure 10** shows one of the kits that is available. The prices vary with the number of instruments included in the kit.

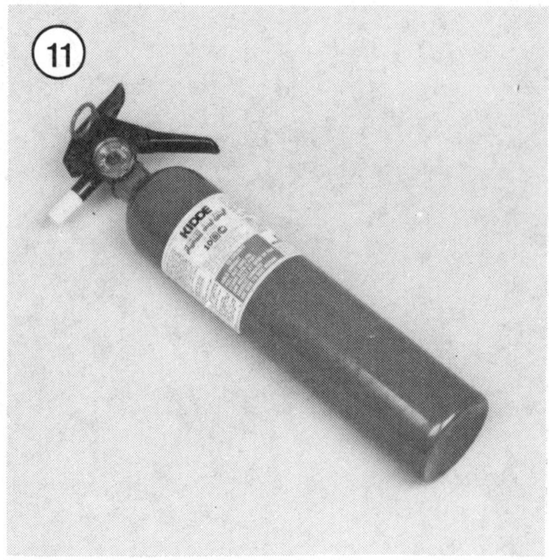

Fire Extinguisher

A fire extinguisher is a necessity when working on a vehicle. It should be rated for both *Class B* (flammable liquids—gasoline, oil, paint, etc.) and *Class C* (electrical—wiring, etc.) type fires. It should always be kept within reach. See **Figure 11**.

CHAPTER TWO

TROUBLESHOOTING

Troubleshooting can be a relatively simple matter if it is done logically. The first step in any troubleshooting procedure must be defining the symptoms as closely as possible. Subsequent steps involve testing and analyzing areas which could cause the symptoms. A haphazard approach may eventually find the trouble, but in terms of wasted time and unnecessary parts replacement, it can be very costly.

The troubleshooting procedures in this chapter analyze typical symptoms and show logical methods of isolation. These are not the only methods. There may be several approaches to a problem, but all methods must have one thing in common — a logical, systematic approach.

STARTING SYSTEM

The starting system consists of the starter motor and the starter solenoid. The ignition key controls the starter solenoid, which mechanically engages the starter with the engine flywheel, and supplies electrical current to turn the starter motor.

Starting system troubles are relatively easy to find. In most cases, the trouble is a loose or dirty electrical connection. **Figures 1 and 2** provide routines for finding the trouble.

CHARGING SYSTEM

The charging system consists of the alternator (or generator on older vehicles), voltage regulator, and battery. A drive belt driven by the engine crankshaft turns the alternator which produces electrical energy to charge the battery. As engine speed varies, the voltage from the alternator varies. A voltage regulator controls the charging current to the battery and maintains the voltage to the vehicle's electrical system at safe levels. A warning light or gauge on the instrument panel signals the driver when charging is not taking place. Refer to **Figure 3** for a typical charging system.

Complete troubleshooting of the charging system requires test equipment and skills which the average home mechanic does not possess. However, there are a few tests which can be done to pinpoint most troubles.

Charging system trouble may stem from a defective alternator (or generator), voltage regulator, battery, or drive belt. It may also be caused by something as simple as incorrect drive belt tension. The following are symptoms of typical problems you may encounter.

1. ***Battery dies frequently, even though the warning lamp indicates no discharge*** — This can be caused by a drive belt that is slightly too

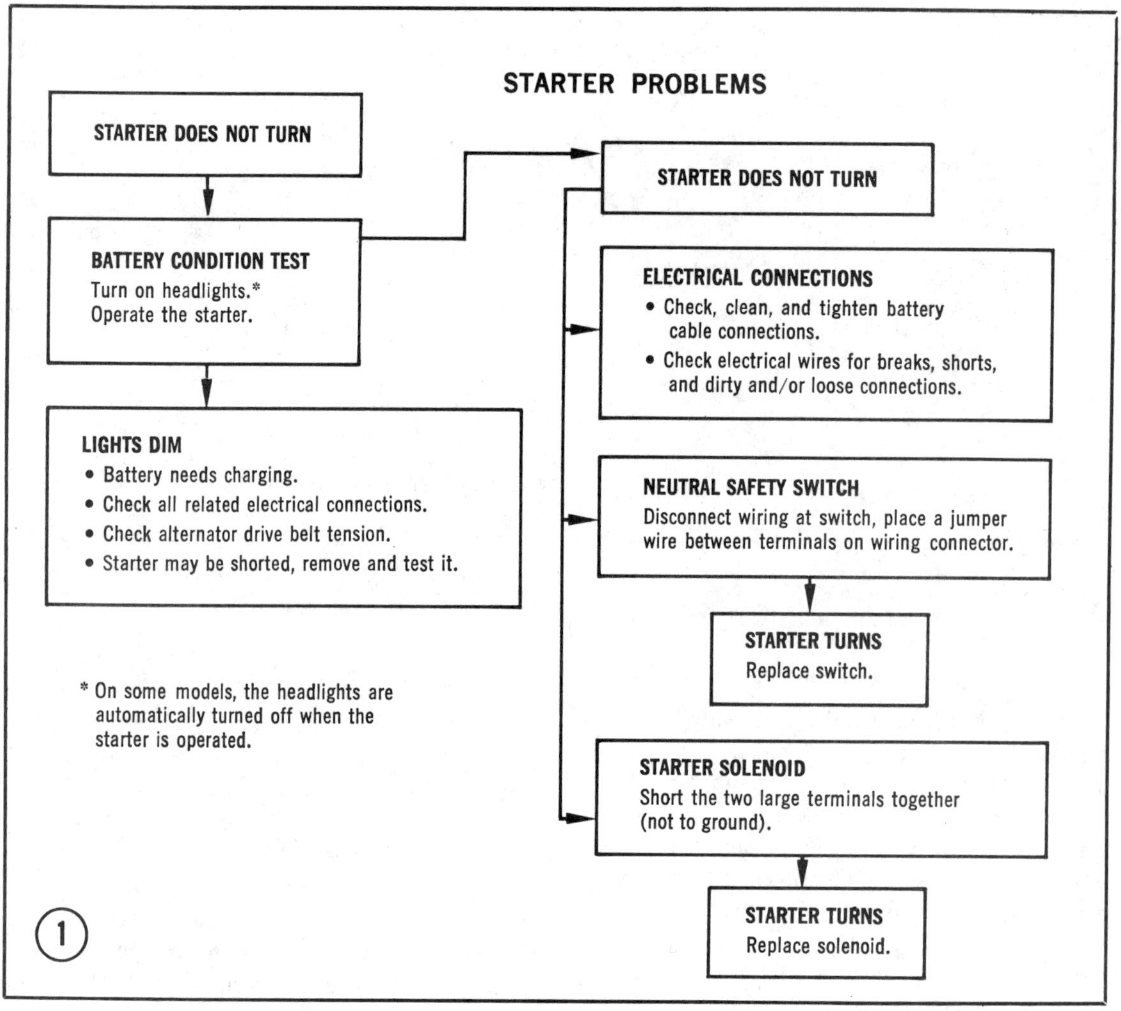

STARTER PROBLEMS
STARTER DOES NOT TURN
BATTERY CONDITION TEST
Turn on headlights.*
Operate the starter.
LIGHTS DIM
• Battery needs charging.
• Check all related electrical connections.
• Check alternator drive belt tension.
• Starter may be shorted, remove and test it.
* On some models, the headlights are automatically turned off when the starter is operated.
STARTER DOES NOT TURN
ELECTRICAL CONNECTIONS
• Check, clean, and tighten battery cable connections.
• Check electrical wires for breaks, shorts, and dirty and/or loose connections.
NEUTRAL SAFETY SWITCH
Disconnect wiring at switch, place a jumper wire between terminals on wiring connector.
STARTER TURNS
Replace switch.
STARTER SOLENOID
Short the two large terminals together (not to ground).
STARTER TURNS
Replace solenoid.
1

STARTER PROBLEMS
STARTER TURNS
DOES NOT ENGAGE WITH ENGINE
Check pinion or solenoid shifting fork and teeth on flywheel gear.
ENGAGES WITH ENGINE — WILL NOT RELEASE
Check for sticking solenoid or jammed pinion onto flywheel.
LOUD GRINDING NOISE
Check flywheel to pinion alignment. The overrunning clutch may be broken.
Remove the starter and examine the gear teeth; replace if necessary.
2

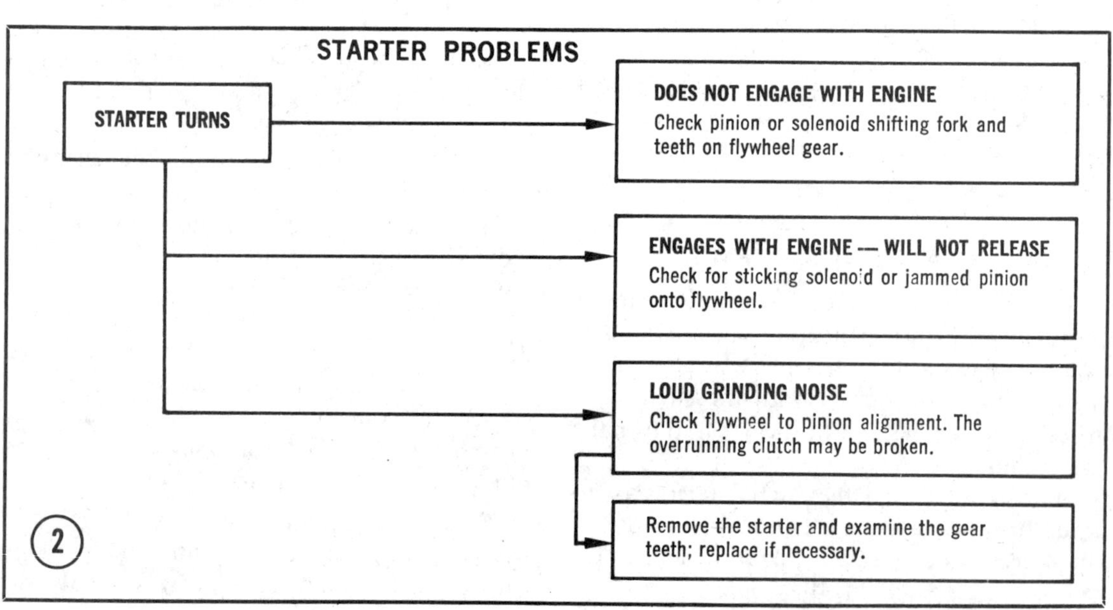

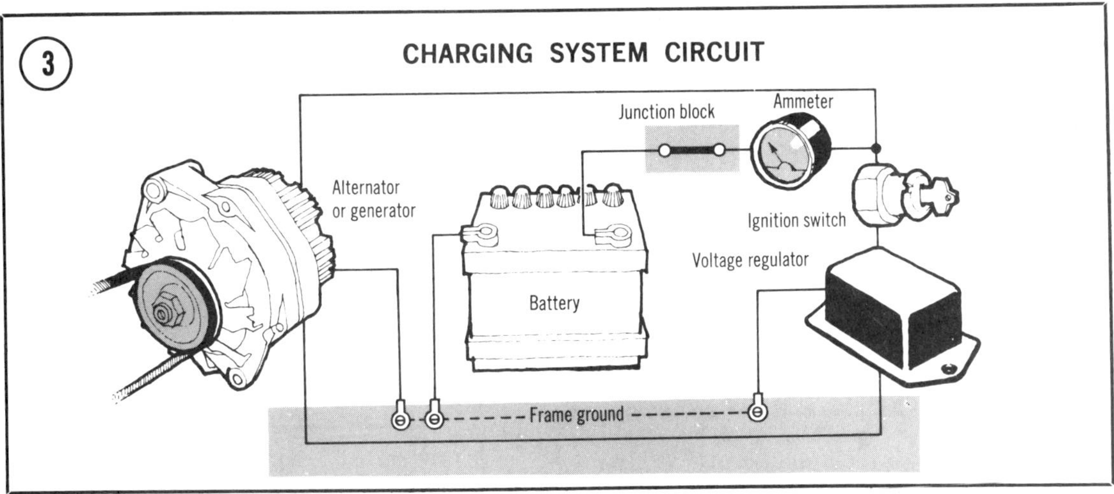

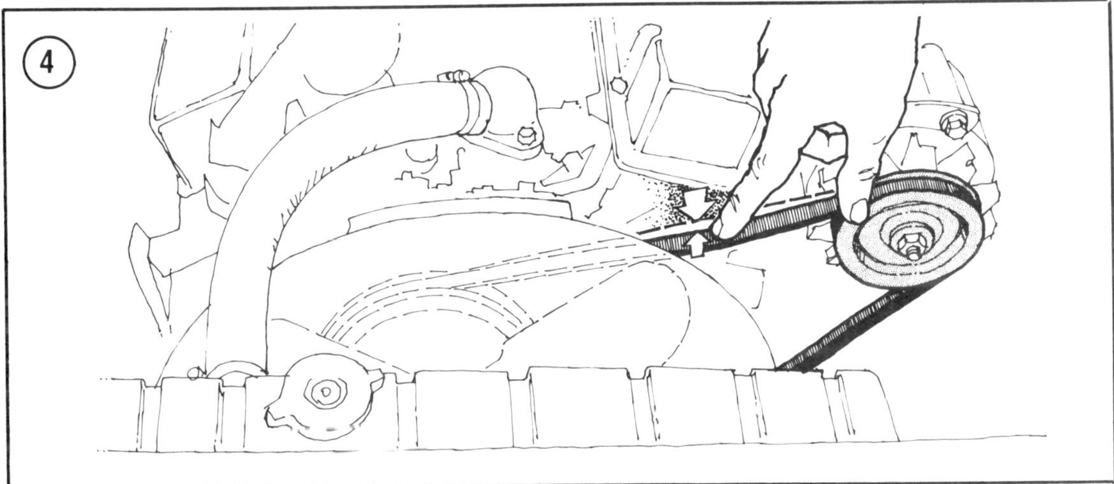

loose. Grasp the alternator (or generator) pulley and try to turn it. If the pulley can be turned without moving the belt, the drive belt is too loose. As a rule, keep the belt tight enough that it can be deflected about ½ in. under moderate thumb pressure between the pulleys (**Figure 4**). The battery may also be at fault; test the battery condition.

2. ***Charging system warning lamp does not come on when ignition switch is turned on*** — This may indicate a defective ignition switch, battery, voltage regulator, or lamp. First try to start the vehicle. If it doesn't start, check the ignition switch and battery. If the car starts, remove the warning lamp; test it for continuity with an ohmmeter or substitute a new lamp. If the lamp is good, locate the voltage regulator and make sure it is properly grounded (try tightening the mounting screws). Also the alternator (or generator) brushes may not be making contact. Test the alternator (or generator) and voltage regulator.

3. ***Alternator (or generator) warning lamp comes on and stays on*** — This usually indicates that no charging is taking place. First check drive belt tension (**Figure 4**). Then check battery condition, and check all wiring connections in the charging system. If this does not locate the trouble, check the alternator (or generator) and voltage regulator.

4. ***Charging system warning lamp flashes on and off intermittently*** — This usually indicates the charging system is working intermittently.

Check the drive belt tension (**Figure 4**), and check all electrical connections in the charging system. Check the alternator (or generator). *On generators only*, check the condition of the commutator.

5. ***Battery requires frequent additions of water, or lamps require frequent replacement*** — The alternator (or generator) is probably overcharging the battery. The voltage regulator is probably at fault.

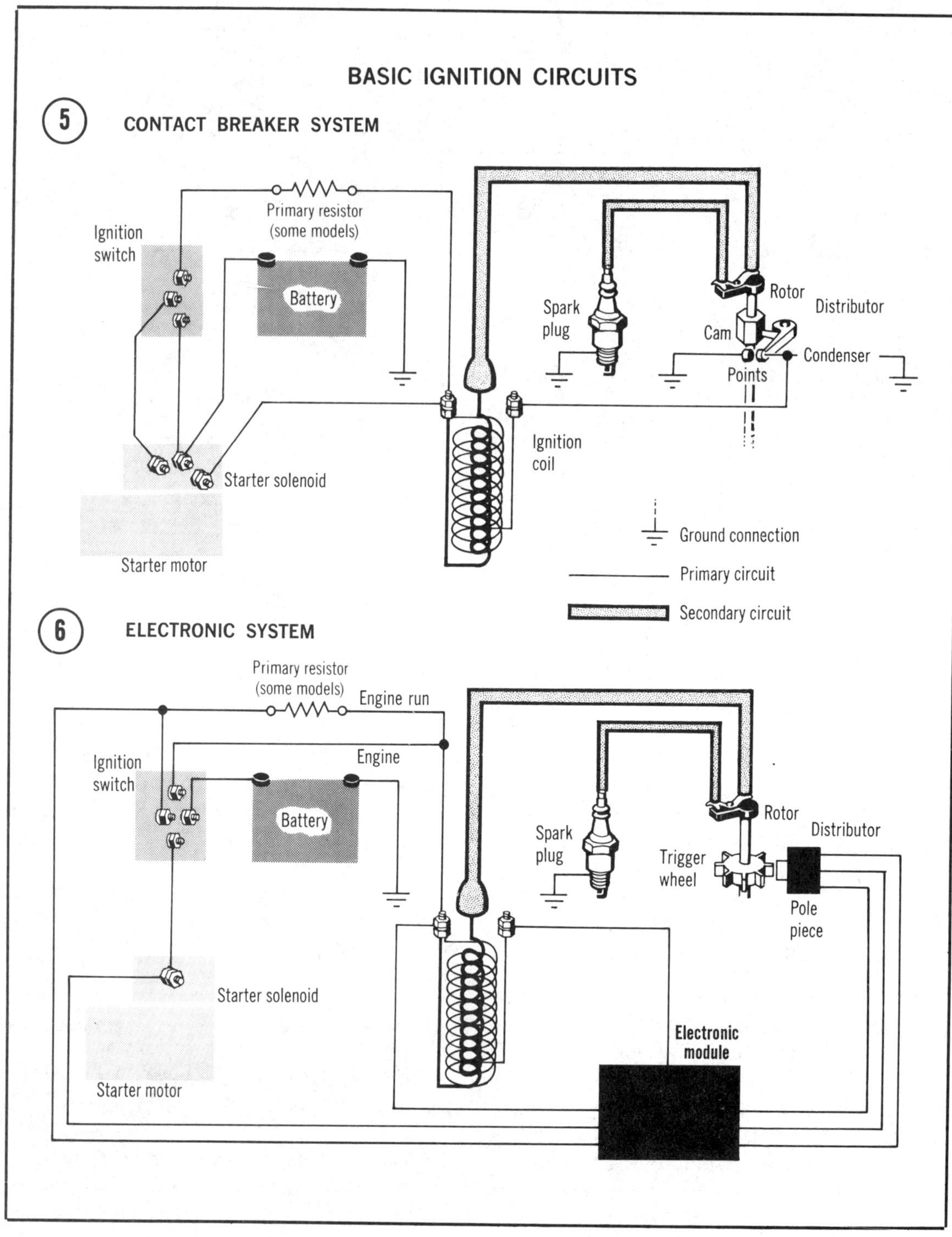

6. ***Excessive noise from the alternator (or generator)*** — Check for loose mounting brackets and bolts. The problem may also be worn bearings or the need of lubrication in some cases. If an alternator whines, a shorted diode may be indicated.

IGNITION SYSTEM

The ignition system may be either a conventional contact breaker type or an electronic ignition. See electrical chapter to determine which type you have. **Figures 5 and 6** show simplified diagrams of each type.

Most problems involving failure to start, poor performance, or rough running stem from trouble in the ignition system, particularly in contact breaker systems. Many novice troubleshooters get into trouble when they assume that these symptoms point to the fuel system instead of the ignition system.

Ignition system troubles may be roughly divided between those affecting only one cylinder and those affecting all cylinders. If the trouble affects only one cylinder, it can only be in the spark plug, spark plug wire, or portion of the distributor associated with that cylinder. If the trouble affects all cylinders (weak spark or no spark), then the trouble is in the ignition coil, rotor, distributor, or associated wiring.

The troubleshooting procedures outlined in **Figure 7** (breaker point ignition) or **Figure 8**

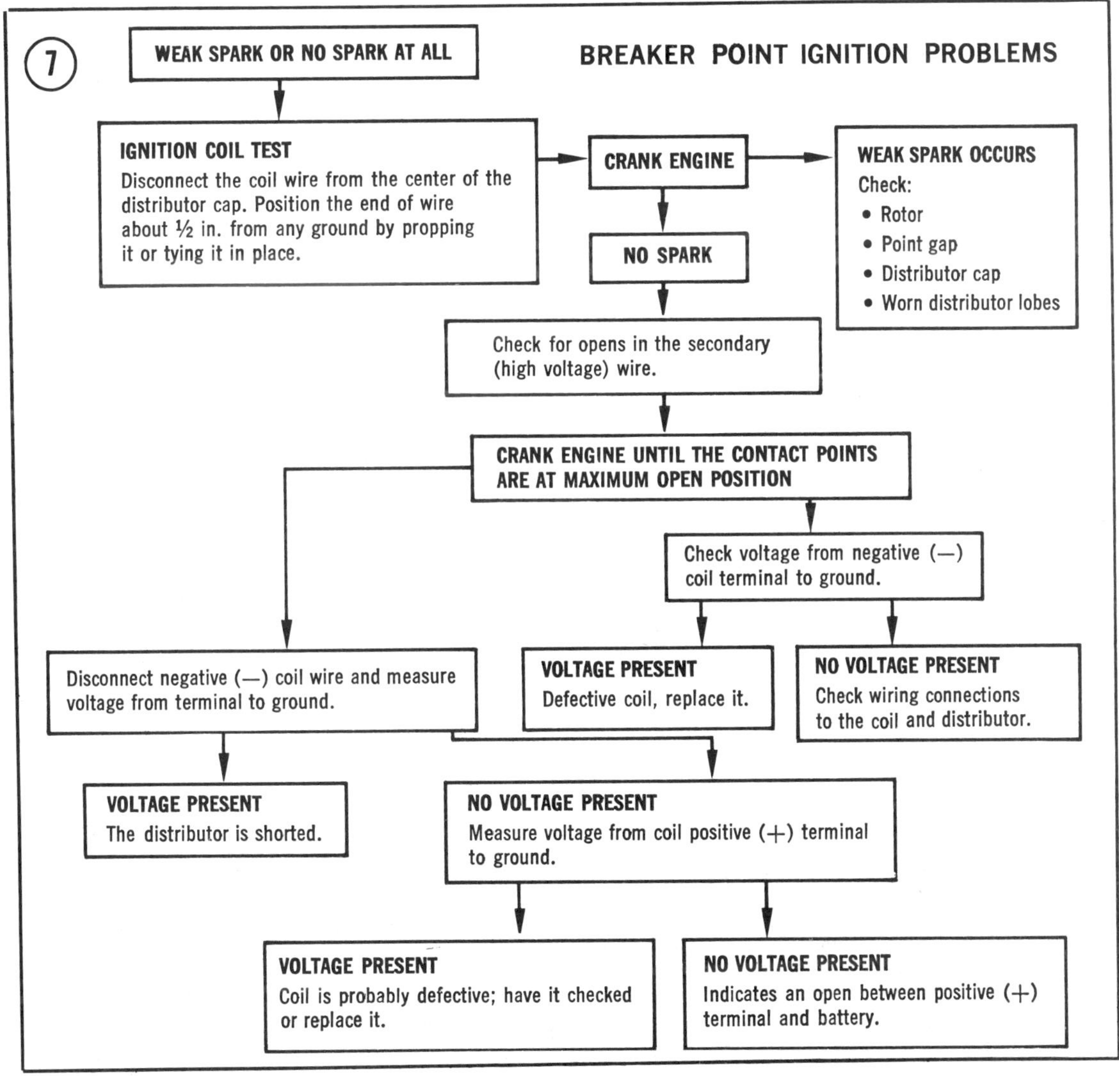

(electronic ignition) will help you isolate ignition problems fast. Of course, they assume that the battery is in good enough condition to crank the engine over at its normal rate.

ENGINE PERFORMANCE

A number of factors can make the engine difficult or impossible to start, or cause rough running, poor performance and so on. The majority of novice troubleshooters immediately suspect the carburetor or fuel injection system. In the majority of cases, though, the trouble exists in the ignition system.

The troubleshooting procedures outlined in **Figures 9 through 14** will help you solve the majority of engine starting troubles in a systematic manner.

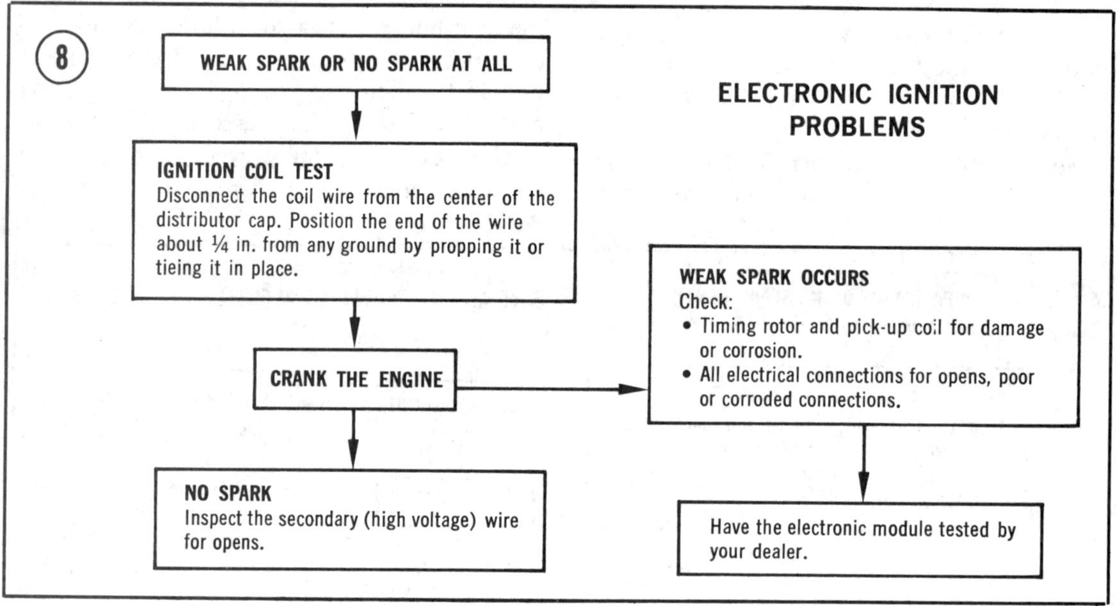

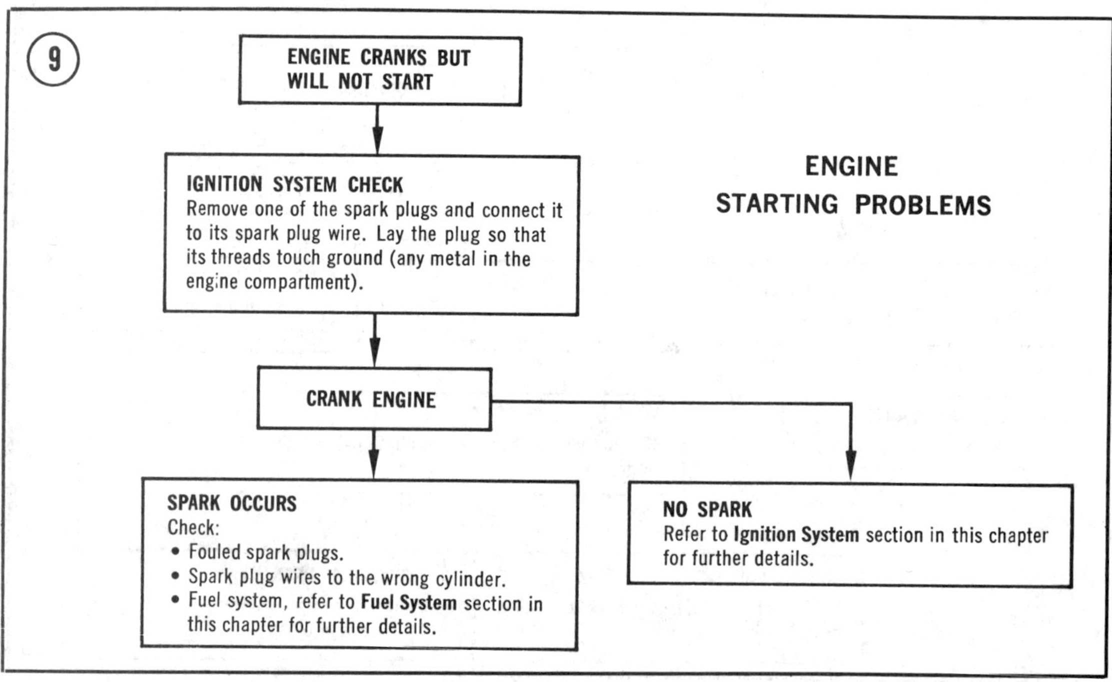

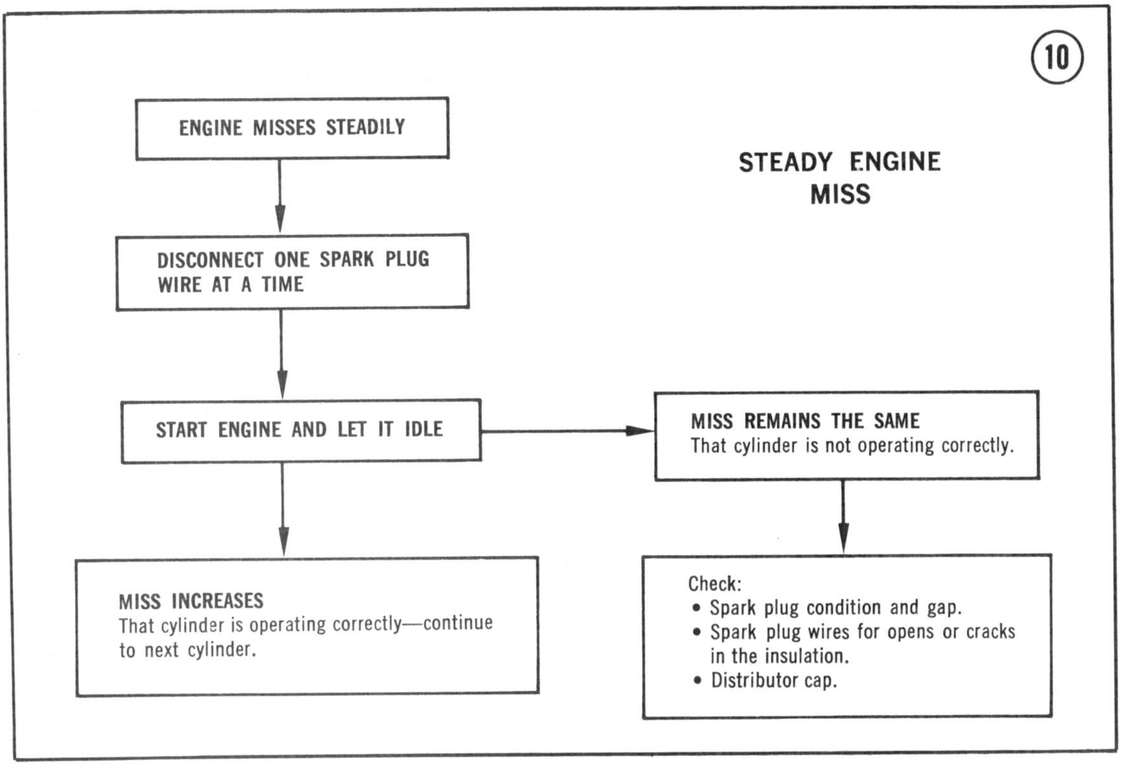

2

(10)

STEADY ENGINE MISS

ENGINE MISSES STEADILY

↓

DISCONNECT ONE SPARK PLUG WIRE AT A TIME

↓

START ENGINE AND LET IT IDLE

↓

MISS INCREASES
That cylinder is operating correctly—continue to next cylinder.

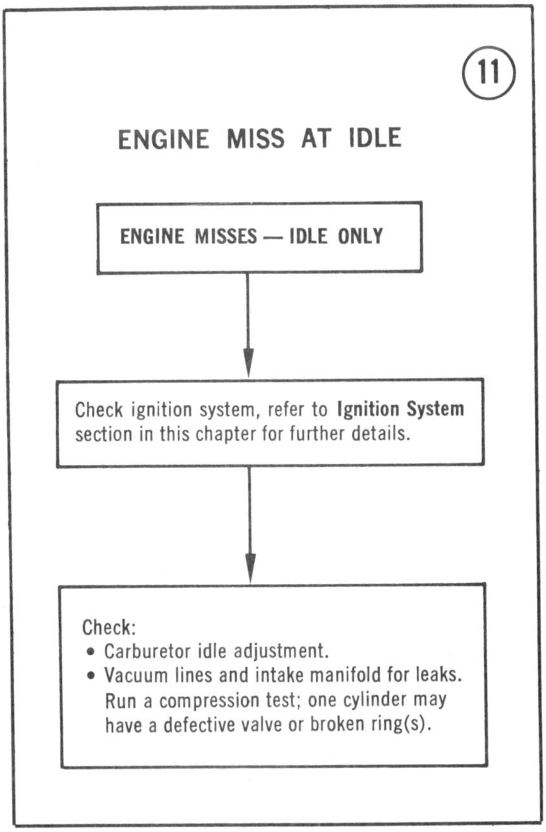

→

MISS REMAINS THE SAME
That cylinder is not operating correctly.

↓

Check:
- Spark plug condition and gap.
- Spark plug wires for opens or cracks in the insulation.
- Distributor cap.

(11)

ENGINE MISS AT IDLE

ENGINE MISSES — IDLE ONLY

↓

Check ignition system, refer to **Ignition System** section in this chapter for further details.

↓

Check:
- Carburetor idle adjustment.
- Vacuum lines and intake manifold for leaks. Run a compression test; one cylinder may have a defective valve or broken ring(s).

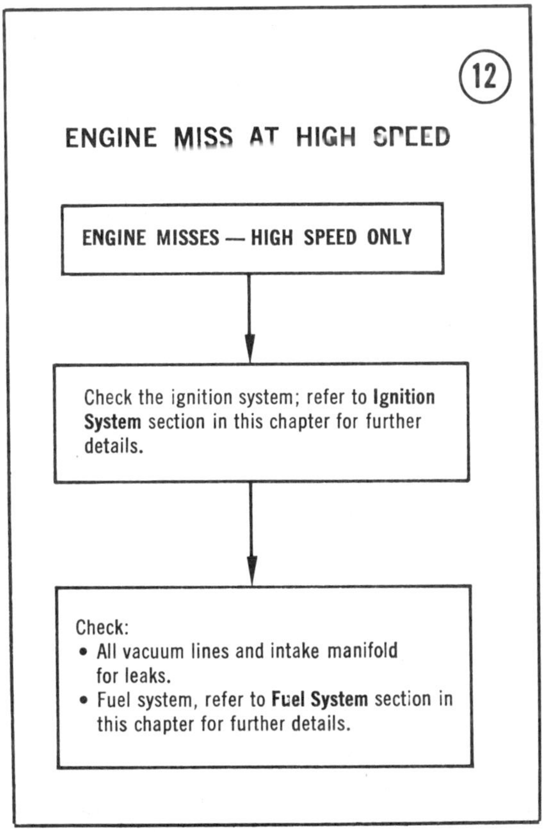

(12)

ENGINE MISS AT HIGH SPEED

ENGINE MISSES — HIGH SPEED ONLY

↓

Check the ignition system; refer to **Ignition System** section in this chapter for further details.

↓

Check:
- All vacuum lines and intake manifold for leaks.
- Fuel system, refer to **Fuel System** section in this chapter for further details.

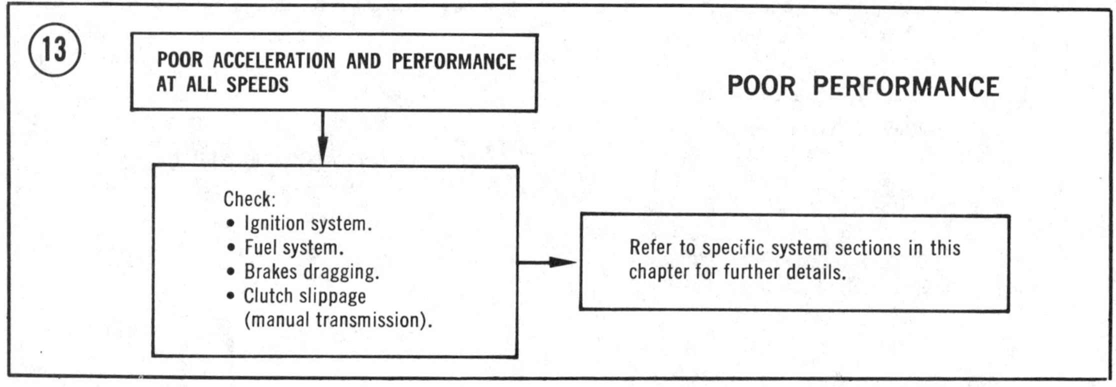

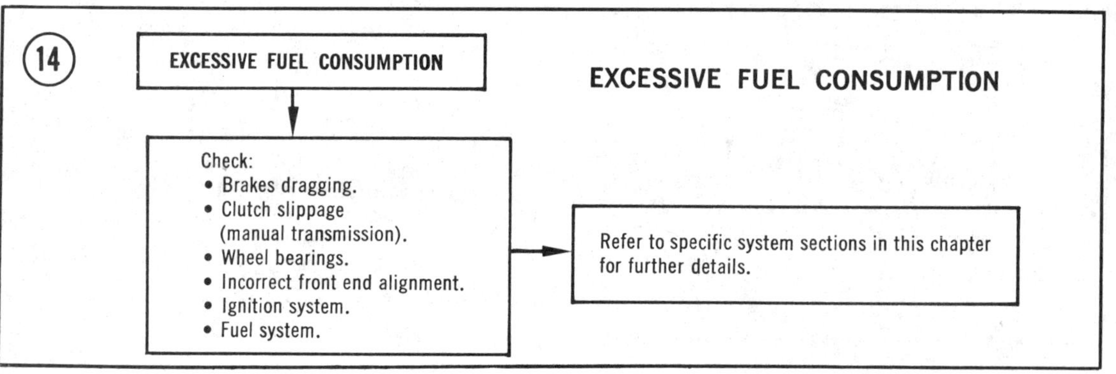

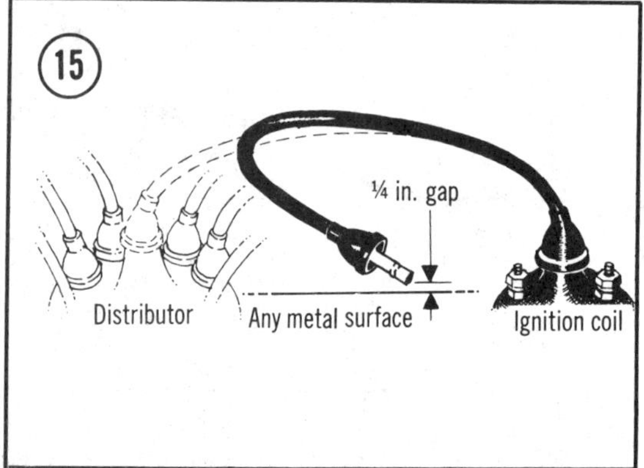

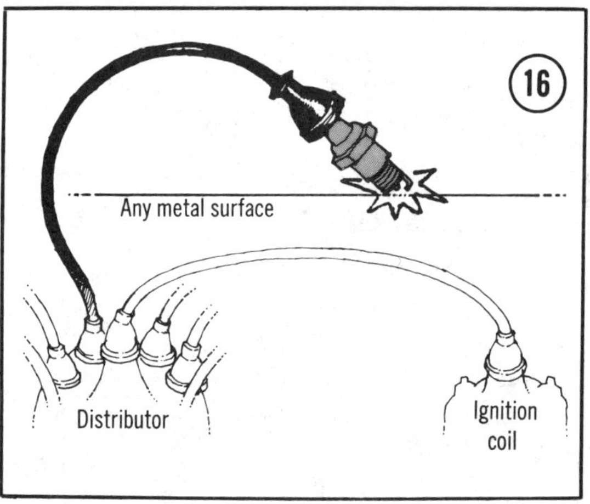

Some tests of the ignition system require running the engine with a spark plug or ignition coil wire disconnected. The safest way to do this is to disconnect the wire with the engine stopped, then prop the end of the wire next to a metal surface as shown in **Figures 15 and 16**.

WARNING

Never disconnect a spark plug or ignition coil wire while the engine is running. The high voltage in an ignition system, particularly the newer high-energy electronic ignition systems could cause serious injury or even death.

Spark plug condition is an important indication of engine performance. Spark plugs in a properly operating engine will have slightly pitted electrodes, and a light tan insulator tip. **Figure 17** shows a normal plug, and a number of others which indicate trouble in their respective cylinders.

• Appearance—Firing tip has deposits of light gray to light tan.
• Can be cleaned, regapped and reused.

• Appearance—Dull, dry black with fluffy carbon deposits on the insulator tip, electrode and exposed shell.
• Caused by—Fuel/air mixture too rich, plug heat range too cold, weak ignition system, dirty air cleaner, faulty automatic choke or excessive idling.
• Can be cleaned, regapped and reused.

• Appearance—Wet black deposits on insulator and exposed shell.
• Caused by—Excessive oil entering the combustion chamber through worn rings, pistons, valve guides or bearings.
• Replace with new plugs (use a hotter plug if engine is not repaired).

• Appearance — Yellow insulator deposits (may sometimes be dark gray, black or tan in color) on the insulator tip.
• Caused by—Highly leaded gasoline.
• Replace with new plugs.

• Appearance—Yellow glazed deposits indicating melted lead deposits due to hard acceleration.
• Caused by—Highly leaded gasoline.
• Replace with new plugs.

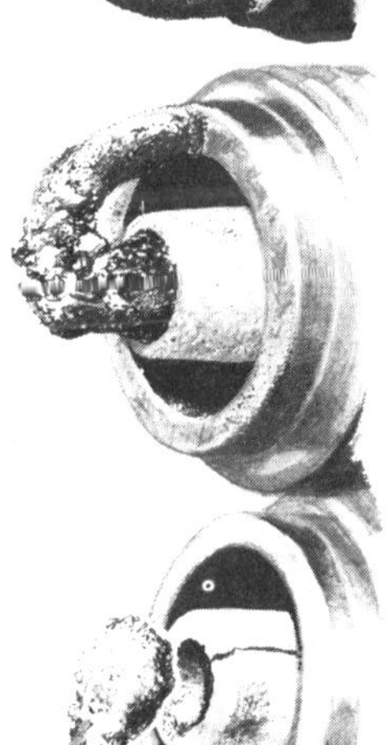

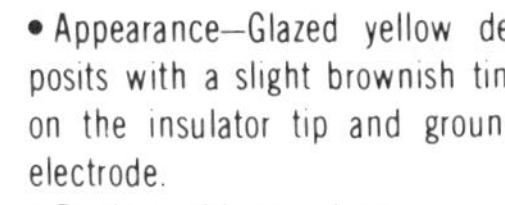

• Appearance—Glazed yellow deposits with a slight brownish tint on the insulator tip and ground electrode.
• Replace with new plugs.

• Appearance — Brown colored hardened ash deposits on the insulator tip and ground electrode.
• Caused by—Fuel and/or oil additives.
• Replace with new plugs.

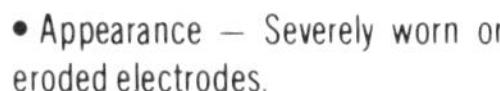

• Appearance — Severely worn or eroded electrodes.
• Caused by—Normal wear or unusual oil and/or fuel additives.
• Replace with new plugs.

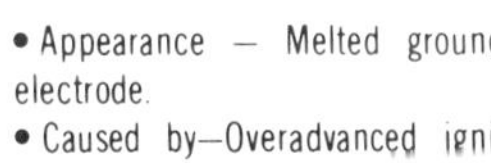

• Appearance — Melted ground electrode.
• Caused by—Overadvanced ignition timing, inoperative ignition advance mechanism, too low of a fuel octane rating, lean fuel/air mixture or carbon deposits in combustion chamber.

• Appearance—Melted center electrode.
• Caused by—Abnormal combustion due to overadvanced ignition timing or incorrect advance, too low of a fuel octane rating, lean fuel/air mixture, or carbon deposits in combustion chamber.
• Correct engine problem and replace with new plugs.

• Appearance—Melted center electrode and white blistered insulator tip.
• Caused by—Incorrect plug heat range selection.
• Replace with new plugs.

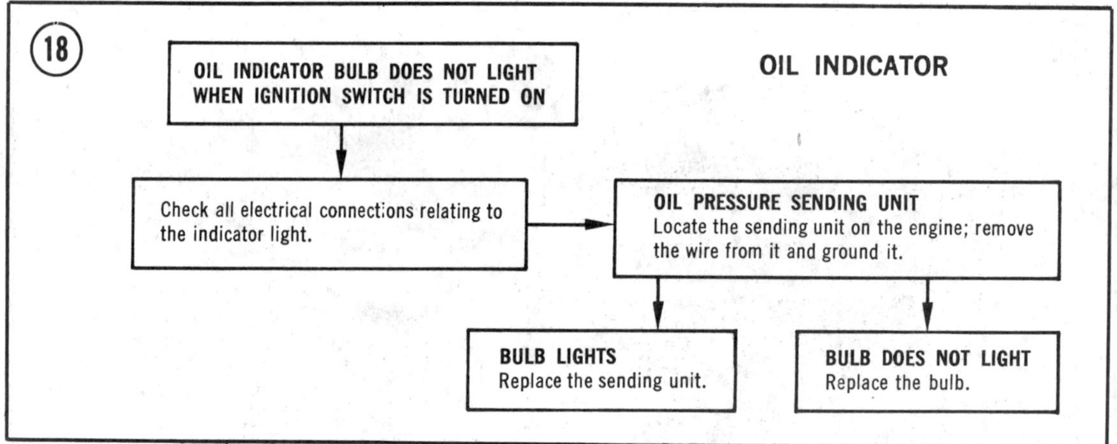

ENGINE OIL PRESSURE LIGHT

Proper oil pressure to the engine is vital. If oil pressure is insufficient, the engine can destroy itself in a comparatively short time.

The oil pressure warning circuit monitors oil pressure constantly. If pressure drops below a predetermined level, the light comes on.

Obviously, it is vital for the warning circuit to be working to signal low oil pressure. Each time you turn on the ignition, but before you start the car, the warning light should come on. If it doesn't, there is trouble in the warning circuit, not the oil pressure system. See **Figure 18** to troubleshoot the warning circuit.

Once the engine is running, the warning light should stay off. If the warning light comes on or acts erratically while the engine is running there is trouble with the engine oil pressure system. *Stop the engine immediately*. Refer to **Figure 19** for possible causes of the problem.

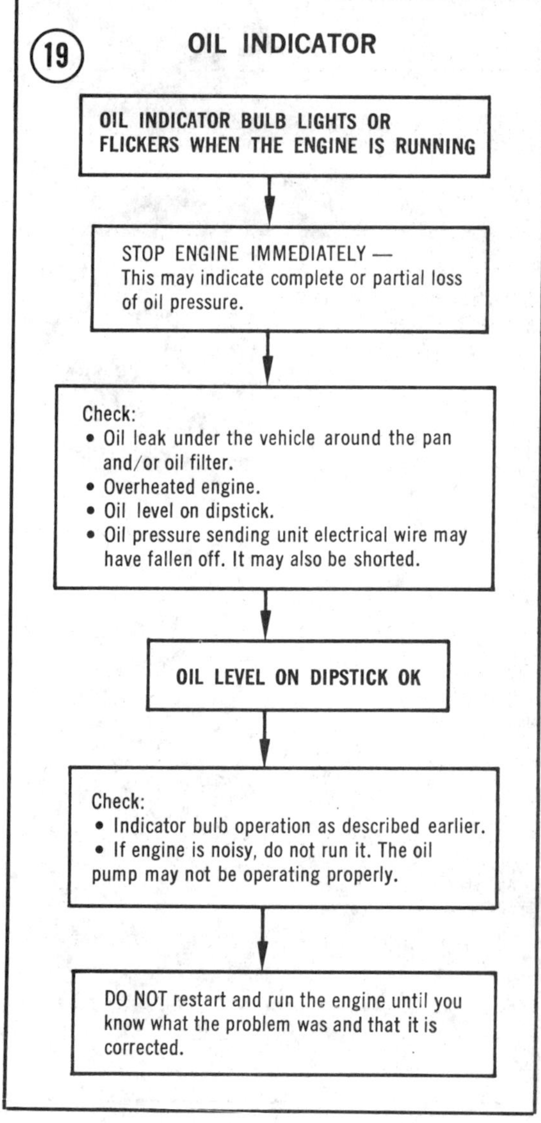

FUEL SYSTEM (CARBURETTED)

Fuel system problems must be isolated to the fuel pump (mechanical or electric), fuel lines, fuel filter, or carburetor. These procedures assume the ignition system is working properly and is correctly adjusted.

1. ***Engine will not start*** — First make sure that fuel is being delivered to the carburetor. Remove the air cleaner, look into the carburetor throat, and operate the accelerator

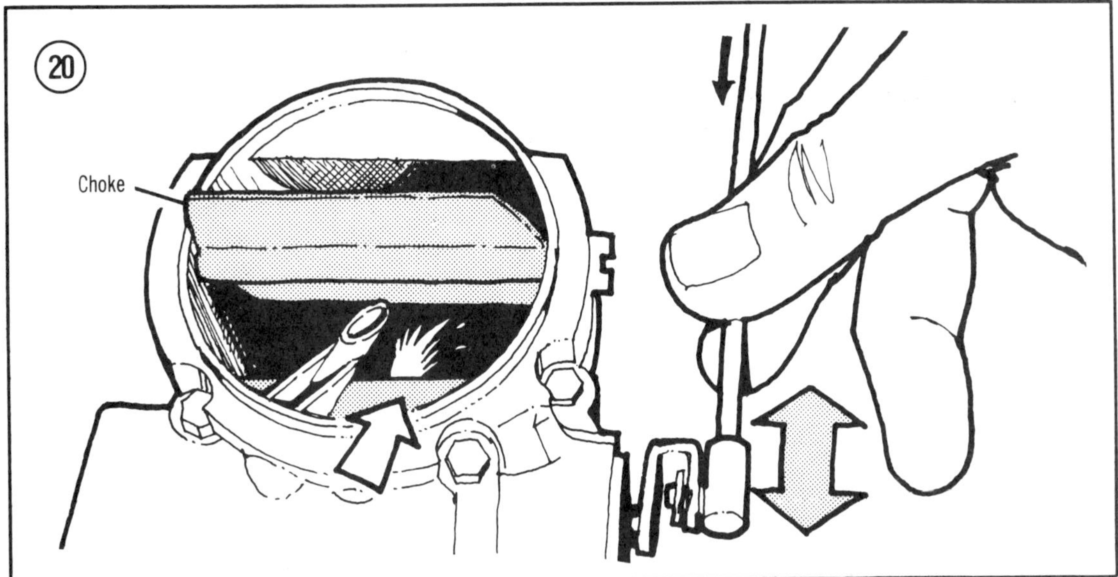

linkage several times. There should be a stream of fuel from the accelerator pump discharge tube each time the accelerator linkage is depressed (**Figure 20**). If not, check fuel pump delivery (described later), float valve, and float adjustment. If the engine will not start, check the automatic choke parts for sticking or damage. If necessary, rebuild or replace the carburetor.

2. ***Engine runs at fast idle*** — Check the choke setting. Check the idle speed, idle mixture, and decel valve (if equipped) adjustment.

3. ***Rough idle or engine miss with frequent stalling*** — Check idle mixture and idle speed adjustments.

4. ***Engine "diesels" (continues to run) when ignition is switched off*** — Check idle mixture (probably too rich), ignition timing, and idle speed (probably too fast). Check the throttle solenoid (if equipped) for proper operation. Check for overheated engine.

5. ***Stumbling when accelerating from idle*** — Check the idle speed and mixture adjustments. Check the accelerator pump.

6. ***Engine misses at high speed or lacks power*** — This indicates possible fuel starvation. Check fuel pump pressure and capacity as described in this chapter. Check float needle valves. Check for a clogged fuel filter or air cleaner.

7. ***Black exhaust smoke*** — This indicates a badly overrich mixture. Check idle mixture and idle speed adjustment. Check choke setting. Check for excessive fuel pump pressure, leaky floats, or worn needle valves.

8. ***Excessive fuel consumption*** — Check for overrich mixture. Make sure choke mechanism works properly. Check idle mixture and idle speed. Check for excessive fuel pump pressure, leaky floats, or worn float needle valves.

FUEL SYSTEM (FUEL INJECTED)

Troubleshooting a fuel injection system requires more thought, experience, and know-how than any other part of the vehicle. A logical approach and proper test equipment are essential in order to successfully find and fix these troubles.

It is best to leave fuel injection troubles to your dealer. In order to isolate a problem to the injection system make sure that the fuel pump is operating properly. Check its performance as described later in this section. Also make sure that fuel filter and air cleaner are not clogged.

FUEL PUMP TEST (MECHANICAL AND ELECTRIC)

1. Disconnect the fuel inlet line where it enters the carburetor or fuel injection system.

2. Fit a rubber hose over the fuel line so fuel can be directed into a graduated container with about one quart capacity. See **Figure 21**.

3. To avoid accidental starting of the engine, disconnect the secondary coil wire from the coil or disconnect and insulate the coil primary wire.

4. Crank the engine for about 30 seconds.

5. If the fuel pump supplies the specified amount (refer to the fuel chapter later in this book), the trouble may be in the carburetor or fuel injection system. The fuel injection system should be tested by your dealer.

6. If there is no fuel present or the pump cannot supply the specified amount, either the fuel pump is defective or there is an obstruction in the fuel line. Replace the fuel pump and/or inspect the fuel lines for air leaks or obstructions.

7. Also pressure test the fuel pump by installing a T-fitting in the fuel line between the fuel pump and the carburetor. Connect a fuel pressure gauge to the fitting with a short tube (**Figure 22**).

8. Reconnect the coil wire, start the engine, and record the pressure. Refer to the fuel chapter later in this book for the correct pressure. If the pressure varies from that specified, the pump should be replaced.

9. Stop the engine. The pressure should drop off very slowly. If it drops off rapidly, the outlet valve in the pump is leaking and the pump should be replaced.

EMISSION CONTROL SYSTEMS

Major emission control systems used on nearly all U.S. models include the following:

a. Positive crankcase ventilation (PCV)
b. Thermostatic air cleaner
c. Air injection reaction (AIR)
d. Fuel evaporation control
e. Exhaust gas recirculation (EGR)

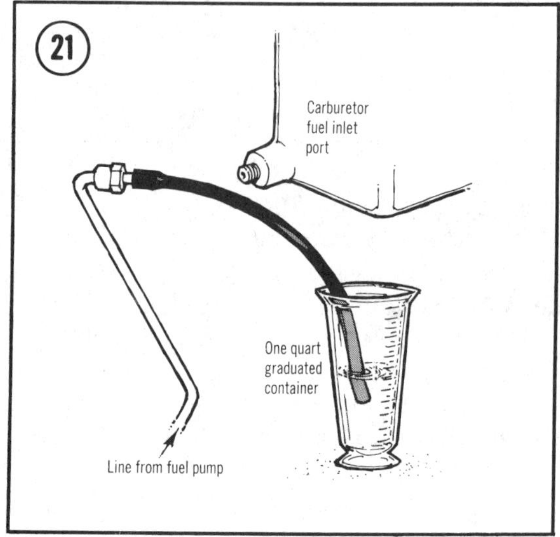

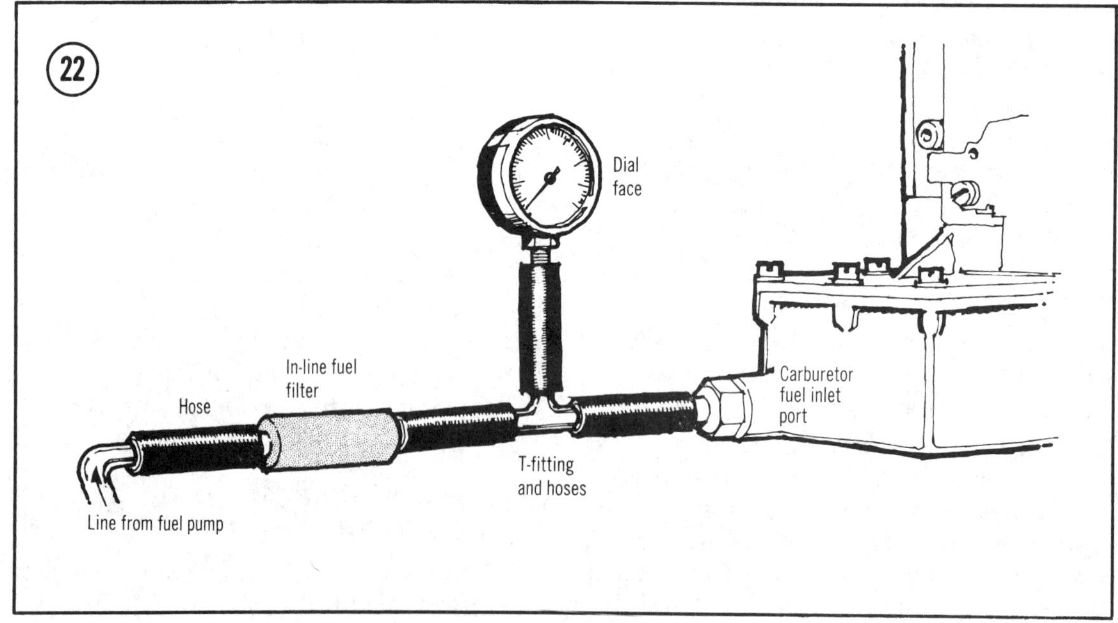

Emission control systems vary considerably from model to model. Individual models contain variations of the four systems described here. In addition, they may include other special systems. Use the index to find specific emission control components in other chapters.

Many of the systems and components are factory set and sealed. Without special expensive test equipment, it is impossible to adjust the systems to meet state and federal requirements.

Troubleshooting can also be difficult without special equipment. The procedures described below will help you find emission control parts which have failed, but repairs may have to be entrusted to a dealer or other properly equipped repair shop.

With the proper equipment, you can test the carbon monoxide and hydrocarbon levels. **Figure 23** provides some sources of trouble if the readings are not correct.

Positive Crankcase Ventilation

Fresh air drawn from the air cleaner housing scavenges emissions (e.g., piston blow-by) from the crankcase, then the intake manifold vacuum draws emissions into the intake manifold. They can then be reburned in the normal combustion process. **Figure 24** shows a typical system. **Figure 25** provides a testing procedure.

Thermostatic Air Cleaner

The thermostatically controlled air cleaner maintains incoming air to the engine at a predetermined level, usually about 100°F or higher. It mixes cold air with heated air from the exhaust manifold region. The air cleaner in-

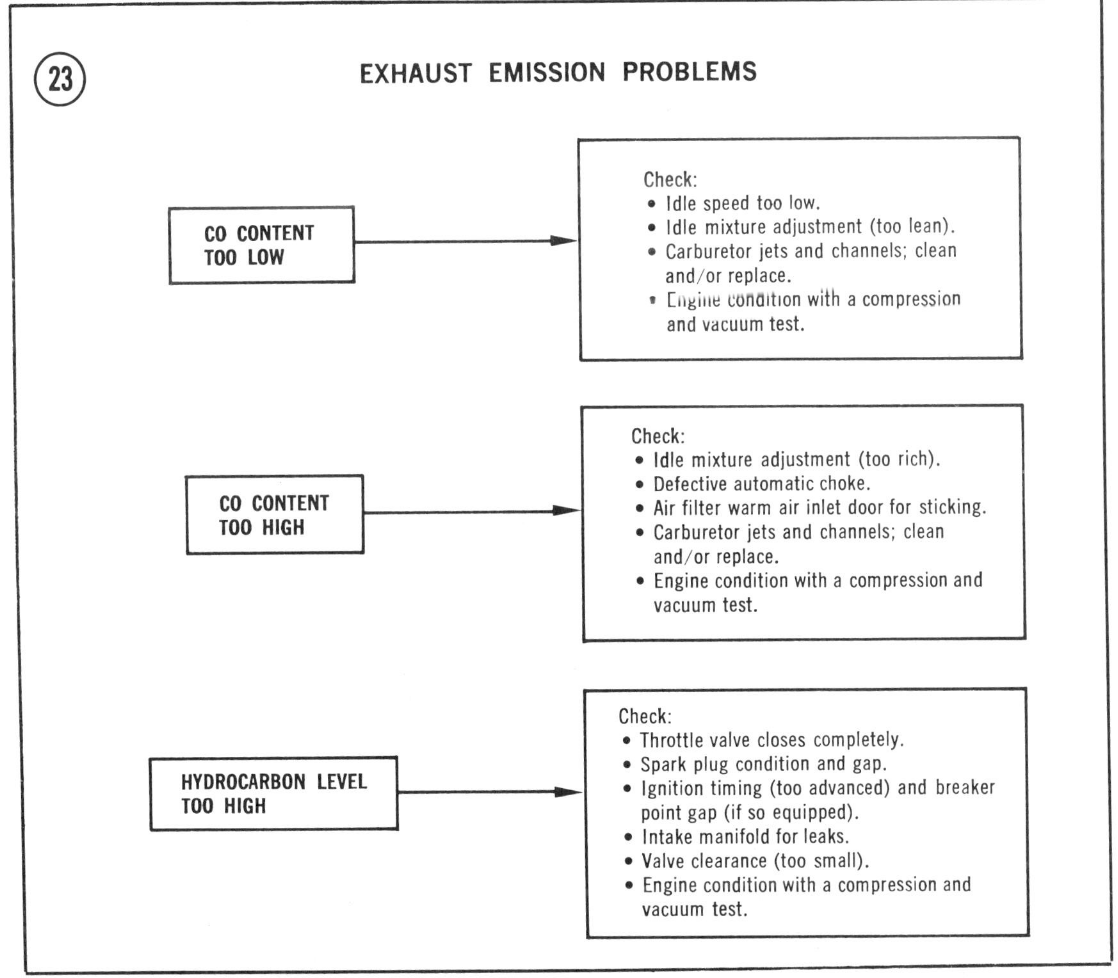

cludes a temperature sensor, vacuum motor, and a hinged door. See **Figure 26**.

The system is comparatively easy to test. See **Figure 27** for the procedure.

Air Injection Reaction System

The air injection reaction system reduces air pollution by oxidizing hydrocarbons and carbon monoxide as they leave the combustion chamber. See **Figure 28**.

The air injection pump, driven by the engine, compresses filtered air and injects it at the exhaust port of each cylinder. The fresh air mixes with the unburned gases in the exhaust and promotes further burning. A check valve prevents exhaust gases from entering and damaging the air pump if the pump becomes inoperative, e.g., from a fan belt failure.

Figure 29 explains the testing procedure for this system.

Fuel Evaporation Control

Fuel vapor from the fuel tank passes through the liquid/vapor separator to the carbon canister. See **Figure 30**. The carbon absorbs and

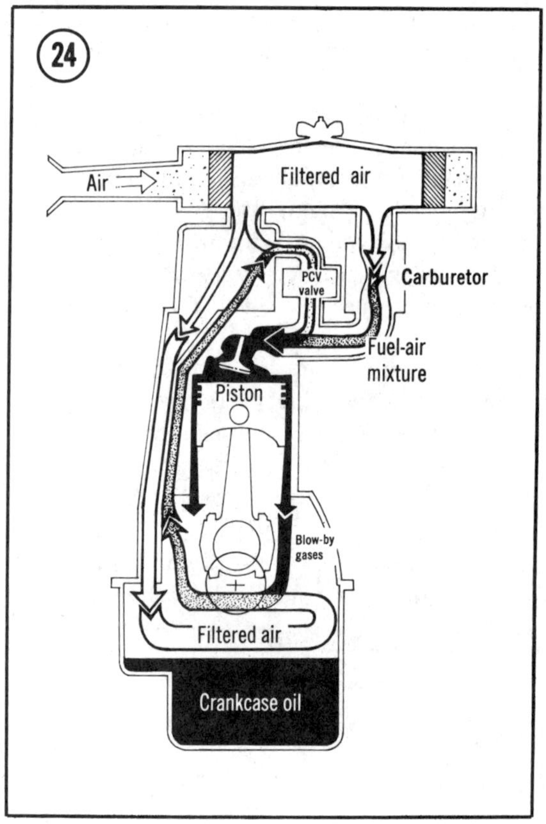

24

Air
Filtered air
PCV valve
Carburetor
Fuel-air mixture
Piston
Blow-by gases
Filtered air
Crankcase oil

25

PCV VALVE TEST
START ENGINE
Let it idle, remove oil fill cap and place a piece of paper over the opening. The paper should be sucked onto the opening by vacuum.
VACUUM PRESENT
Valve is operating correctly.
NO VACUUM PRESENT
Valve is stuck closed.
Remove PCV valve and shake it, it should rattle.
VALVE RATTLES
Check hose from valve for obstructions. Clean out or replace it.
VALVE DOES NOT RATTLE
Take it apart and clean or replace it.

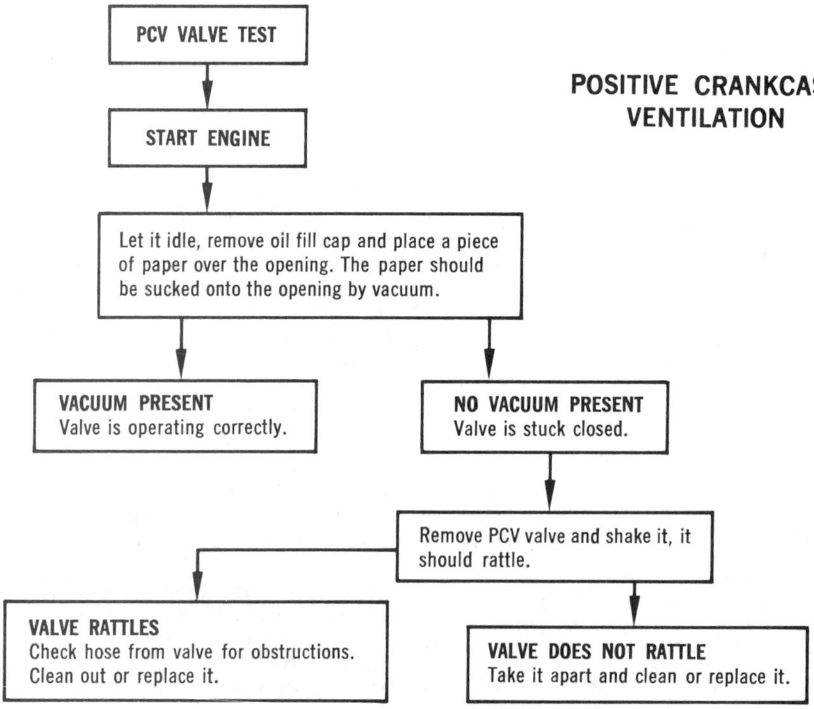

POSITIVE CRANKCASE VENTILATION

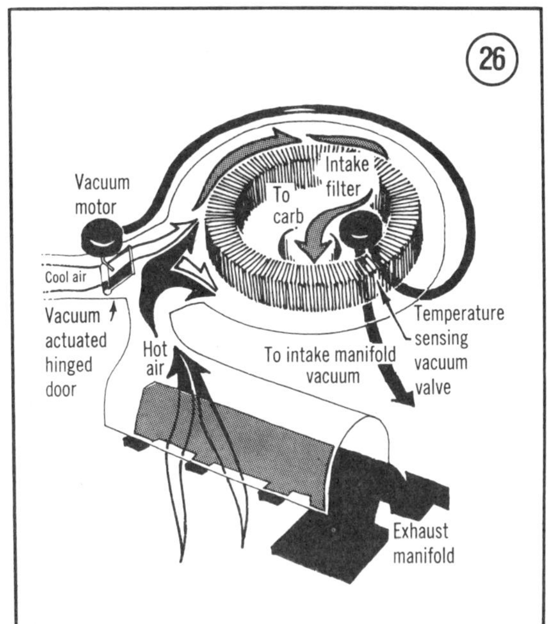
26
Vacuum motor
Intake filter
To carb
Cool air
Vacuum actuated hinged door
Hot air
To intake manifold vacuum
Temperature sensing vacuum valve
Exhaust manifold

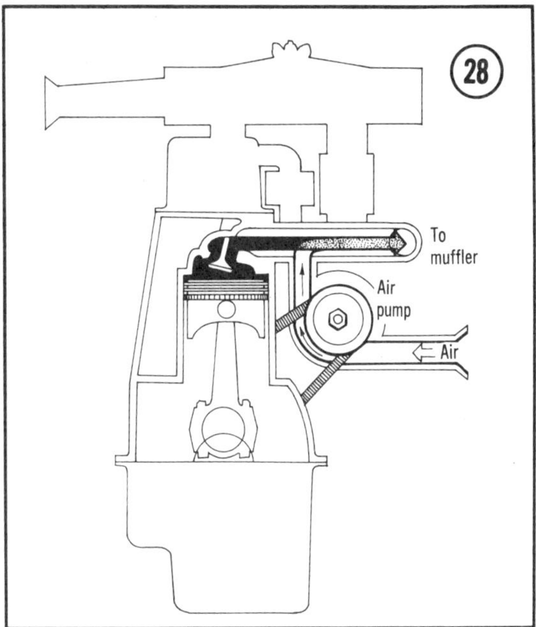
28
To muffler
Air pump
Air

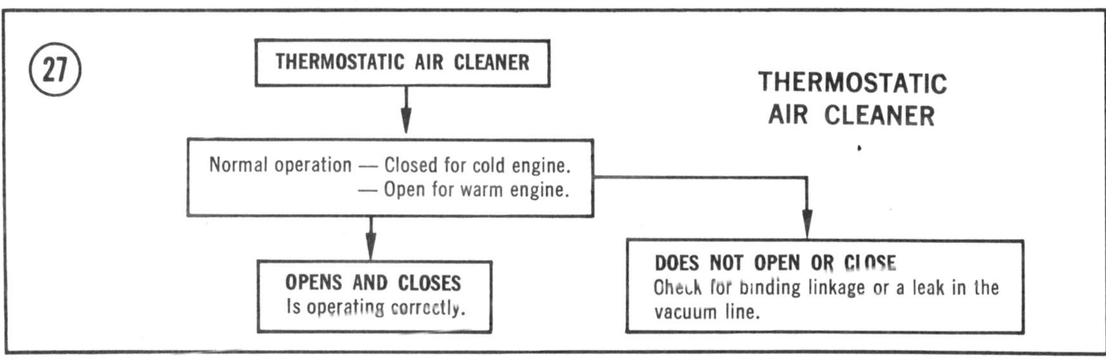
27
THERMOSTATIC AIR CLEANER
THERMOSTATIC AIR CLEANER
Normal operation — Closed for cold engine.
— Open for warm engine.
OPENS AND CLOSES
Is operating correctly.
DOES NOT OPEN OR CLOSE
Check for binding linkage or a leak in the vacuum line.

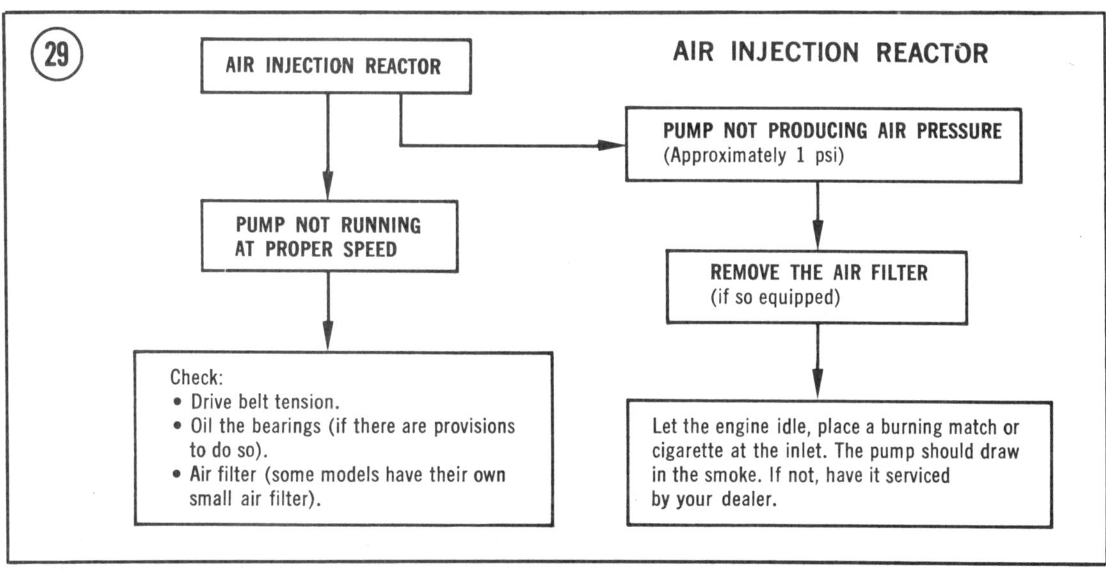
29
AIR INJECTION REACTOR
AIR INJECTION REACTOR
PUMP NOT PRODUCING AIR PRESSURE
(Approximately 1 psi)
PUMP NOT RUNNING AT PROPER SPEED
REMOVE THE AIR FILTER
(if so equipped)
Check:
• Drive belt tension.
• Oil the bearings (if there are provisions to do so).
• Air filter (some models have their own small air filter).
Let the engine idle, place a burning match or cigarette at the inlet. The pump should draw in the smoke. If not, have it serviced by your dealer.

stores the vapor when the engine is stopped. When the engine runs, manifold vacuum draws the vapor from the canister. Instead of being released into the atmosphere, the fuel vapor takes part in the normal combustion process.

Exhaust Gas Recirculation

The exhaust gas recirculation (EGR) system is used to reduce the emission of nitrogen oxides (NO_x). Relatively inert exhaust gases are introduced into the combustion process to slightly reduce peak temperatures. This reduction in temperature reduces the formation of NO_x.

Figure 31 provides a simple test of this system.

ENGINE NOISES

Often the first evidence of an internal engine trouble is a strange noise. That knocking, clicking, or tapping which you never heard before may be warning you of impending trouble.

While engine noises can indicate problems, they are sometimes difficult to interpret correctly; inexperienced mechanics can be seriously misled by them.

Professional mechanics often use a special stethoscope which looks similar to a doctor's stethoscope for isolating engine noises. You can do nearly as well with a "sounding stick" which can be an ordinary piece of doweling or a section of small hose. By placing one end in contact with the area to which you want to listen and the other end near your ear, you can hear

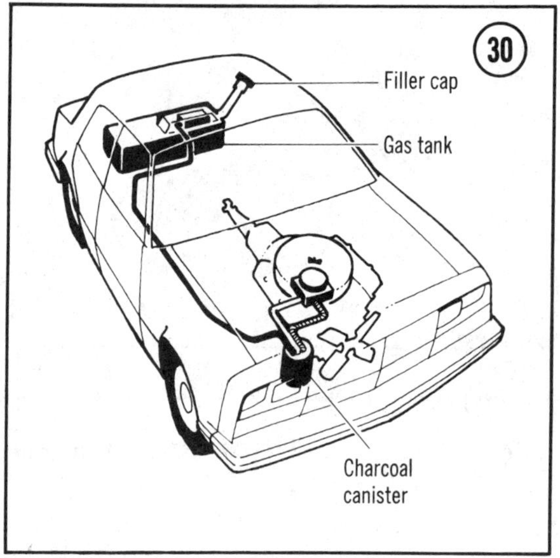

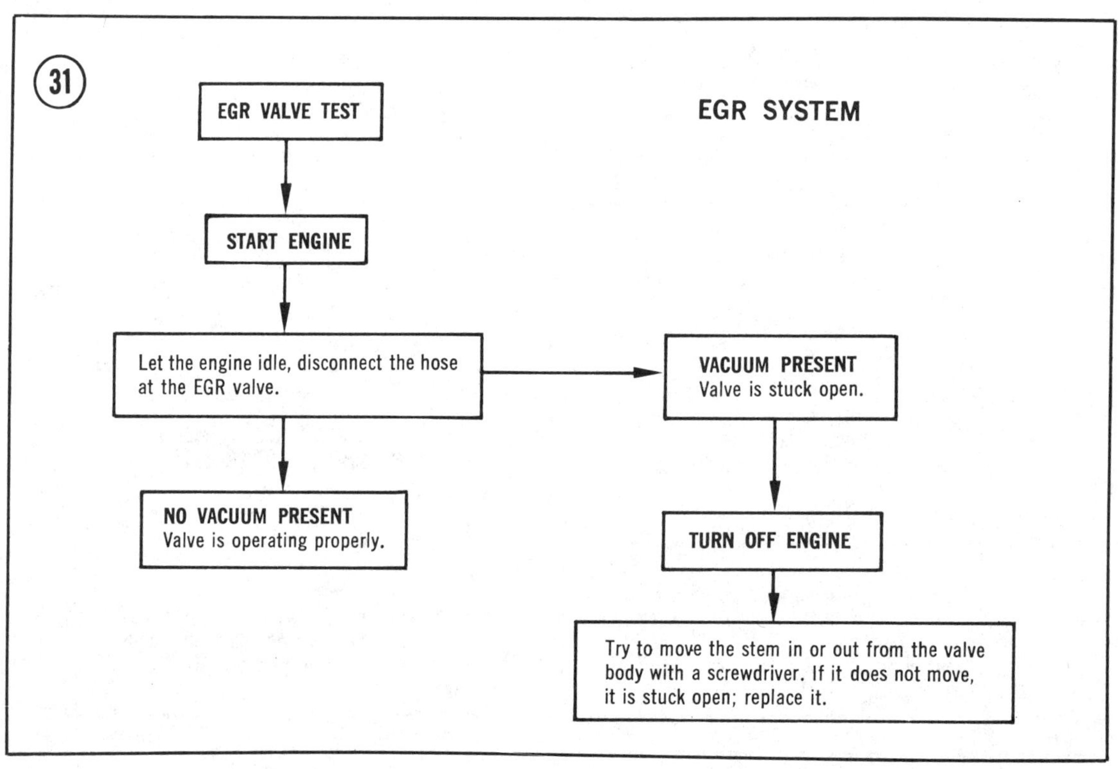

sounds emanating from that area. The first time you do this, you may be horrified at the strange noises coming from even a normal engine. If you can, have an experienced friend or mechanic help you sort the noises out.

Clicking or Tapping Noises

Clicking or tapping noises usually come from the valve train, and indicate excessive valve clearance.

If your vehicle has adjustable valves, the procedure for adjusting the valve clearance is explained in Chapter Three. If your vehicle has hydraulic lifters, the clearance may not be adjustable. The noise may be coming from a collapsed lifter. These may be cleaned or replaced as described in the engine chapter.

A sticking valve may also sound like a valve with excessive clearance. In addition, excessive wear in valve train components can cause similar engine noises.

Knocking Noises

A heavy, dull knocking is usually caused by a worn main bearing. The noise is loudest when the engine is working hard, i.e., accelerating hard at low speed. You may be able to isolate the trouble to a single bearing by disconnecting the spark plugs one at a time. When you reach the spark plug nearest the bearing, the knock will be reduced or disappear.

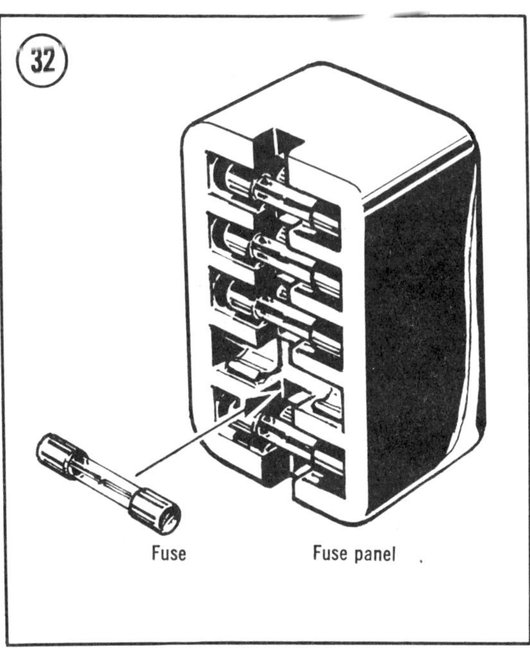

Worn connecting rod bearings may also produce a knock, but the sound is usually more "metallic." As with a main bearing, the noise is worse when accelerating. It may even increase further just as you go from accelerating to coasting. Disconnecting spark plugs will help isolate this knock as well.

A double knock or clicking usually indicates a worn piston pin. Disconnecting spark plugs will isolate this to a particular piston, however, the noise will *increase* when you reach the affected piston.

A loose flywheel and excessive crankshaft end play also produce knocking noises. While similar to main bearing noises, these are usually intermittent, not constant, and they do not change when spark plugs are disconnected.

Some mechanics confuse piston pin noise with piston slap. The double knock will distinguish the piston pin noise. Piston slap is identified by the fact that it is always louder when the engine is cold.

ELECTRICAL ACCESSORIES

Lights and Switches (Interior and Exterior)

1. ***Bulb does not light*** — Remove the bulb and check for a broken element. Also check the inside of the socket; make sure the contacts are clean and free of corrosion. If the bulb and socket are OK, check to see if a fuse has blown or a circuit breaker has tripped. The fuse panel (**Figure 32**) is usually located under the instrument panel. Replace the blown fuse or reset the circuit breaker. If the fuse blows or the breaker trips again, there is a short in that circuit. Check that circuit all the way to the battery. Look for worn wire insulation or burned wires.

If all the above are all right, check the switch controlling the bulb for continuity with an ohmmeter at the switch terminals. Check the switch contact terminals for loose or dirty electrical connections.

2. ***Headlights work but will not switch from either high or low beam*** — Check the beam selector switch for continuity with an ohmmeter

at the switch terminals. Check the switch contact terminals for loose or dirty electrical connections.

3. ***Brake light switch inoperative*** — On mechanically operated switches, usually mounted near the brake pedal arm, adjust the switch to achieve correct mechanical operation. Check the switch for continuity with an ohmmeter at the switch terminals. Check the switch contact terminals for loose or dirty electrical connections.

4. ***Back-up lights do not operate*** — Check light bulb as described earlier. Locate the switch, normally located near the shift lever. Adjust switch to achieve correct mechanical operation. Check the switch for continuity with an ohmmeter at the switch terminals. Bypass the switch with a jumper wire; if the lights work, replace the switch.

Directional Signals

1. ***Directional signals do not operate*** — If the indicator light on the instrument panel burns steadily instead of flashing, this usually indicates that one of the exterior lights is burned out. Check all lamps that normally flash. If all are all right, the flasher unit may be defective. Replace it with a good one.

2. ***Directional signal indicator light on instrument panel does not light up*** — Check the light bulbs as described earlier. Check all electrical connections and check the flasher unit.

3. ***Directional signals will not self-cancel*** — Check the self-cancelling mechanism located inside the steering column.

4. ***Directional signals flash slowly*** — Check the condition of the battery and the alternator (or generator) drive belt tension (**Figure 4**). Check the flasher unit and all related electrical connections.

Windshield Wipers

1. ***Wipers do not operate*** — Check for a blown fuse or circuit breaker that has tripped; replace or reset. Check all related terminals for loose or dirty electrical connections. Check continuity of the control switch with an ohmmeter at the switch terminals. Check the linkage and arms for loose, broken, or binding parts. Straighten out or replace where necessary.

2. ***Wiper motor hums but will not operate*** — The motor may be shorted out internally; check and/or replace the motor. Also check for broken or binding linkage and arms.

3. ***Wiper arms will not return to the stowed position when turned off*** — The motor has a special internal switch for this purpose. Have it inspected by your dealer. Do not attempt this yourself.

Interior Heater

1. ***Heater fan does not operate*** — Check for a blown fuse or circuit breaker that has tripped. Check the switch for continuity with an ohmmeter at the switch terminals. Check the switch contact terminals for loose or dirty electrical connections.

2. ***Heat output is insufficient*** — Check the heater hose/engine coolant control valve usually located in the engine compartment; make sure it is in the open position. Ensure that the heater door(s) and cable(s) are operating correctly and are in the open position. Inspect the heat ducts; make sure that they are not crimped or blocked.

COOLING SYSTEM

The temperature gauge or warning light usually signals cooling system troubles before there is any damage. As long as you stop the vehicle at the first indication of trouble, serious damage is unlikely.

In most cases, the trouble will be obvious as soon as you open the hood. If there is coolant or steam leaking, look for a defective radiator, radiator hose, or heater hose. If there is no evidence of leakage, make sure that the fan belt is in good condition. If the trouble is not obvious, refer to **Figures 33 and 34** to help isolate the trouble.

Automotive cooling systems operate under pressure to permit higher operating temperatures without boil-over. The system should be checked periodically to make sure it can withstand normal pressure. **Figure 35** shows the equipment which nearly any service station has for testing the system pressure.

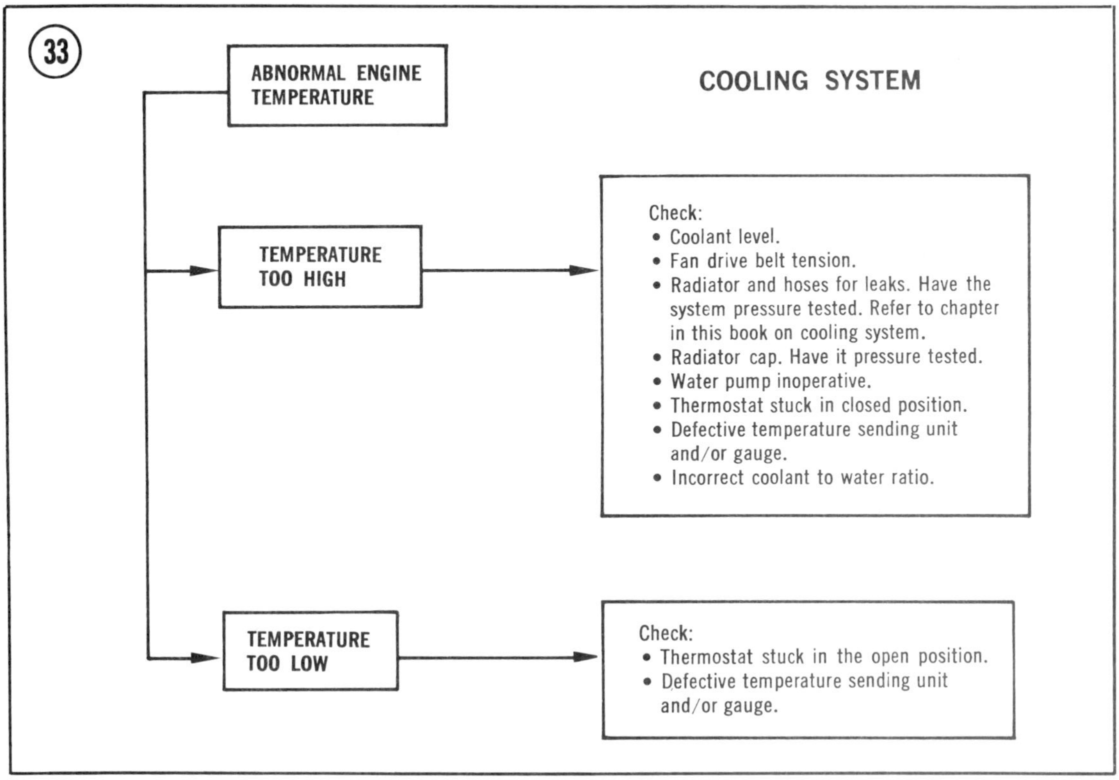

33
COOLING SYSTEM
ABNORMAL ENGINE TEMPERATURE
TEMPERATURE TOO HIGH
Check:
• Coolant level.
• Fan drive belt tension.
• Radiator and hoses for leaks. Have the system pressure tested. Refer to chapter in this book on cooling system.
• Radiator cap. Have it pressure tested.
• Water pump inoperative.
• Thermostat stuck in closed position.
• Defective temperature sending unit and/or gauge.
• Incorrect coolant to water ratio.
TEMPERATURE TOO LOW
Check:
• Thermostat stuck in the open position.
• Defective temperature sending unit and/or gauge.

34
COOLING SYSTEM
CONTINUED LOSS OF COOLANT
Check:
• Radiator and hoses for leaks. Have the system pressure tested.
• Radiator cap. Have it pressure tested.
• Water pump for leaks.

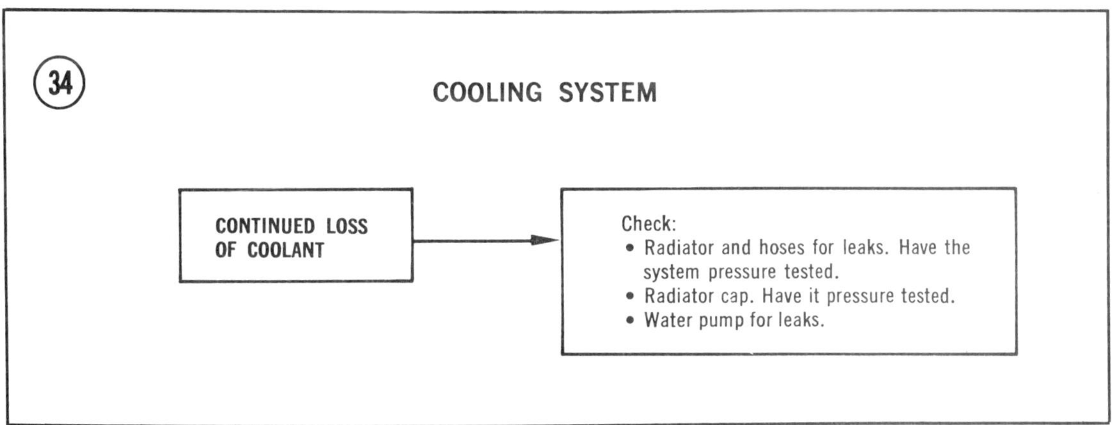

CLUTCH

All clutch troubles except adjustments require transmission removal to identify and cure the problem.

1. ***Slippage*** — This is most noticeable when accelerating in a high gear at relatively low speed. To check slippage, park the vehicle on a level surface with the handbrake set. Shift to 2nd gear and release the clutch as if driving off. If the clutch is good, the engine will slow and stall. If the clutch slips, continued engine speed will give it away.

Slippage results from insufficient clutch pedal free play, oil or grease on the clutch disc, worn pressure plate, or weak springs.

2. ***Drag or failure to release*** — This trouble usually causes difficult shifting and gear clash, especially when downshifting. The cause may be excessive clutch pedal free play, warped or bent pressure plate or clutch disc, broken or

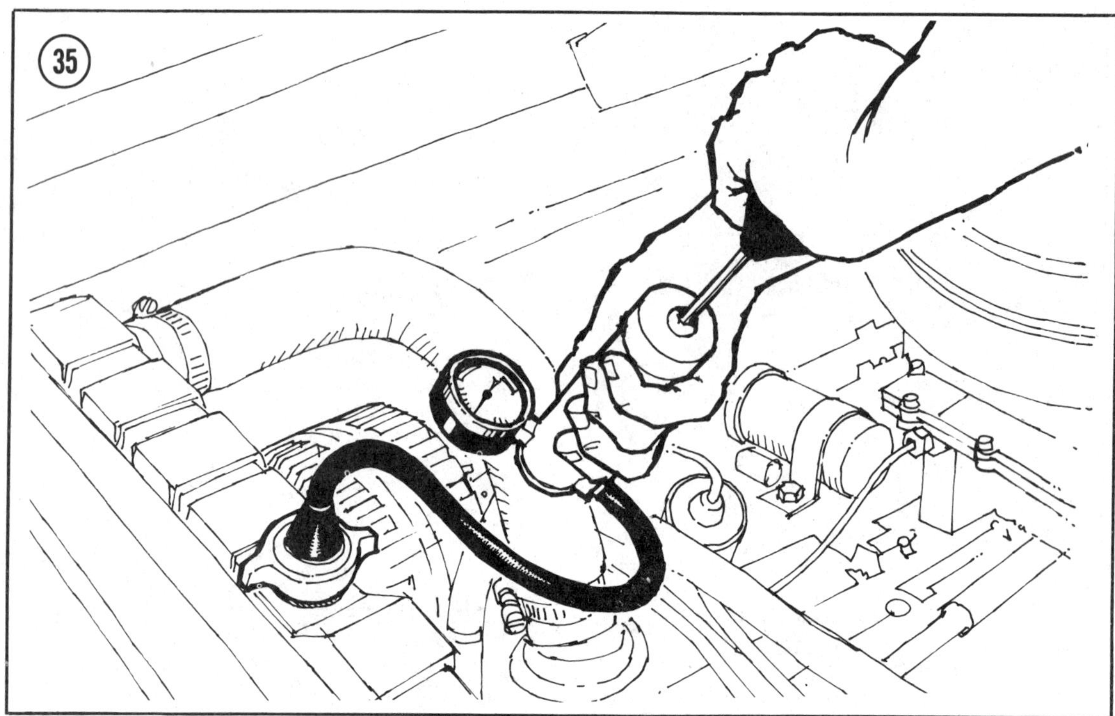

loose linings, or lack of lubrication in pilot bearing. Also check condition of transmission main shaft splines.

3. ***Chatter or grabbing*** — A number of things can cause this trouble. Check tightness of engine mounts and engine-to-transmission mounting bolts. Check for worn or misaligned pressure plate and misaligned release plate.

4. ***Other noises*** — Noise usually indicates a dry or defective release or pilot bearing. Check the bearings and replace if necessary. Also check all parts for misalignment and uneven wear.

MANUAL TRANSMISSION/TRANSAXLE

Transmission and transaxle troubles are evident when one or more of the following symptoms appear:

a. Difficulty changing gears
b. Gears clash when downshifting
c. Slipping out of gear
d. Excessive noise in NEUTRAL
e. Excessive noise in gear
f. Oil leaks

Transmission and transaxle repairs are not recommended unless the many special tools required are available.

Transmission and transaxle troubles are sometimes difficult to distinguish from clutch troubles. Eliminate the clutch as a source of trouble before installing a new or rebuilt transmission or transaxle.

AUTOMATIC TRANSMISSION

Most automatic transmission repairs require considerable specialized knowledge and tools. It is impractical for the home mechanic to invest in the tools, since they cost more than a properly rebuilt transmission.

Check fluid level and condition frequently to help prevent future problems. If the fluid is orange or black in color or smells like varnish, it is an indication of some type of damage or failure within the transmission. Have the transmission serviced by your dealer or competent automatic transmission service facility.

BRAKES

Good brakes are vital to the safe operation of the vehicle. Performing the maintenance speci-

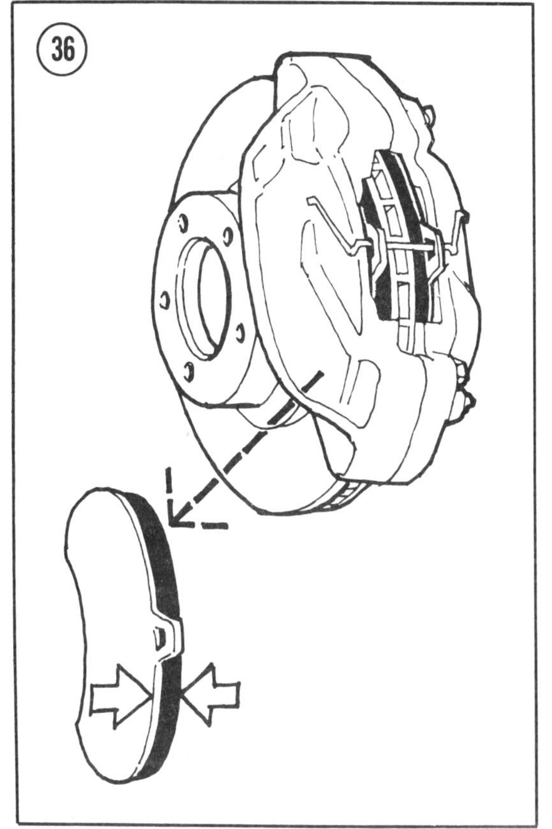

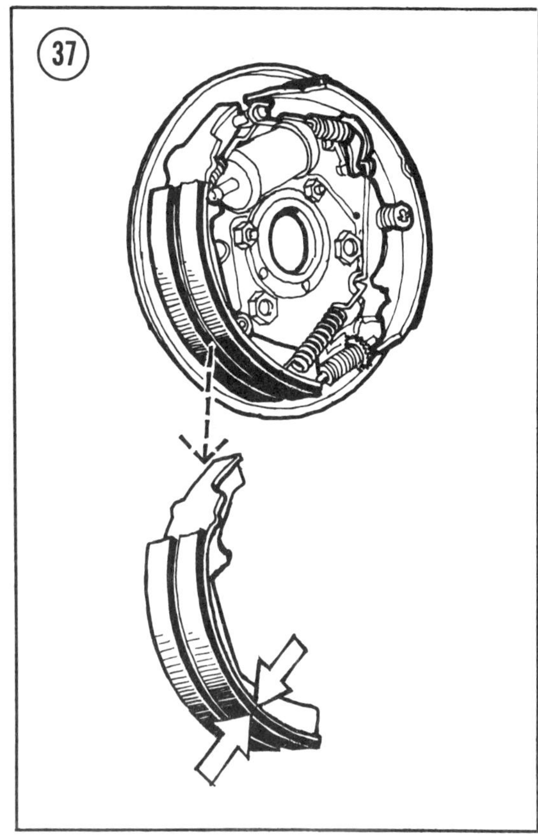

fied in Chapter Three will minimize problems with the brakes. Most importantly, check and maintain the level of fluid in the master cylinder, and check the thickness of the linings on the disc brake pads (**Figure 36**) or drum brake shoes (**Figure 37**).

If trouble develops, **Figures 38 through 40** will help you locate the problem. Refer to the brake chapter for actual repair procedures.

STEERING AND SUSPENSION

Trouble in the suspension or steering is evident when the following occur:

a. Steering is hard
b. Car pulls to one side
c. Car wanders or front wheels wobble
d. Steering has excessive play
e. Tire wear is abnormal

Unusual steering, pulling, or wandering is usually caused by bent or otherwise misaligned suspension parts. This is difficult to check without proper alignment equipment. Refer to the suspension chapter in this book for repairs that you can perform and those that must be left to a dealer or suspension specialist.

If your trouble seems to be excessive play, check wheel bearing adjustment first. This is the most frequent cause. Then check ball-joints (refer to Suspension chapter). Finally, check tie rod end ball-joints by shaking each tie rod. Also check steering gear, or rack-and-pinion assembly to see that it is securely bolted down.

TIRE WEAR ANALYSIS

Abnormal tire wear should be analyzed to determine its causes. The most common causes are the following:

a. Incorrect tire pressure
b. Improper driving
c. Overloading
d. Bad road surfaces
e. Incorrect wheel alignment

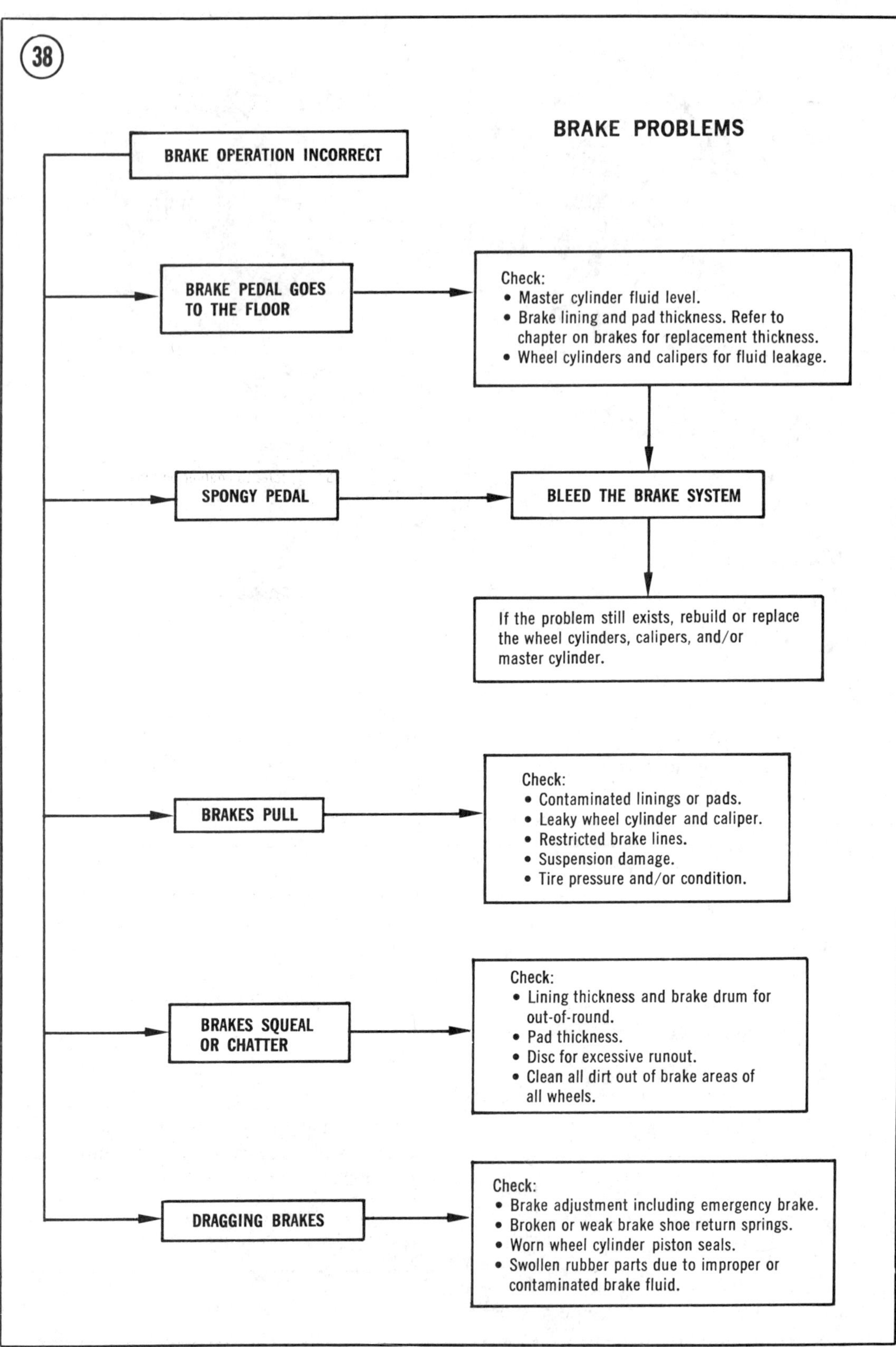
38
BRAKE PROBLEMS
BRAKE OPERATION INCORRECT
BRAKE PEDAL GOES TO THE FLOOR
Check:
• Master cylinder fluid level.
• Brake lining and pad thickness. Refer to chapter on brakes for replacement thickness.
• Wheel cylinders and calipers for fluid leakage.
SPONGY PEDAL
BLEED THE BRAKE SYSTEM
If the problem still exists, rebuild or replace the wheel cylinders, calipers, and/or master cylinder.
BRAKES PULL
Check:
• Contaminated linings or pads.
• Leaky wheel cylinder and caliper.
• Restricted brake lines.
• Suspension damage.
• Tire pressure and/or condition.
BRAKES SQUEAL OR CHATTER
Check:
• Lining thickness and brake drum for out-of-round.
• Pad thickness.
• Disc for excessive runout.
• Clean all dirt out of brake areas of all wheels.
DRAGGING BRAKES
Check:
• Brake adjustment including emergency brake.
• Broken or weak brake shoe return springs.
• Worn wheel cylinder piston seals.
• Swollen rubber parts due to improper or contaminated brake fluid.

(39)

BRAKE PROBLEMS

BRAKE OPERATION INCORRECT

HARD PEDAL → Check:
- Contaminated linings or pads.
- Brake line restriction.

HIGH SPEED FADE → Check:
- Drum distortion and out-of-round.
- Disc for excessive runout.
- Brake fluid for recommended type.

Drain the entire system and refill with correct type; if in doubt, refer to chapter on brakes in this book for specific details.

→ **BLEED THE BRAKE SYSTEM**

PULSATING PEDAL → Check:
- Drum distortion and out-of-round.
- Disc for excessive runout.
- Suspension damage.

(40)

BRAKE PROBLEMS

BRAKE LIGHT ON INSTRUMENT PANEL COMES ON AND STAYS ON (1968 and later models)

→ **PARTIAL OR COMPLETE BRAKE SYSTEM FAILURE**

→ Check the entire brake system for signs of brake fluid leakage and/or damage. Thoroughly inspect the master cylinder, wheel cylinders, calipers, brake lines, and flexible hoses.
DO NOT drive the vehicle until you know what the problem was and that it is corrected.

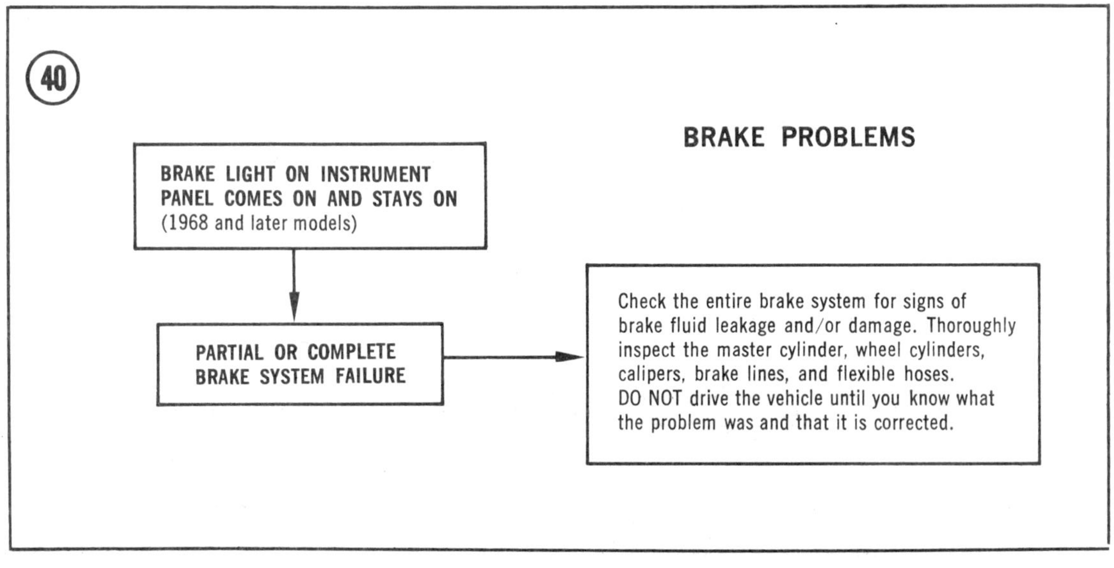

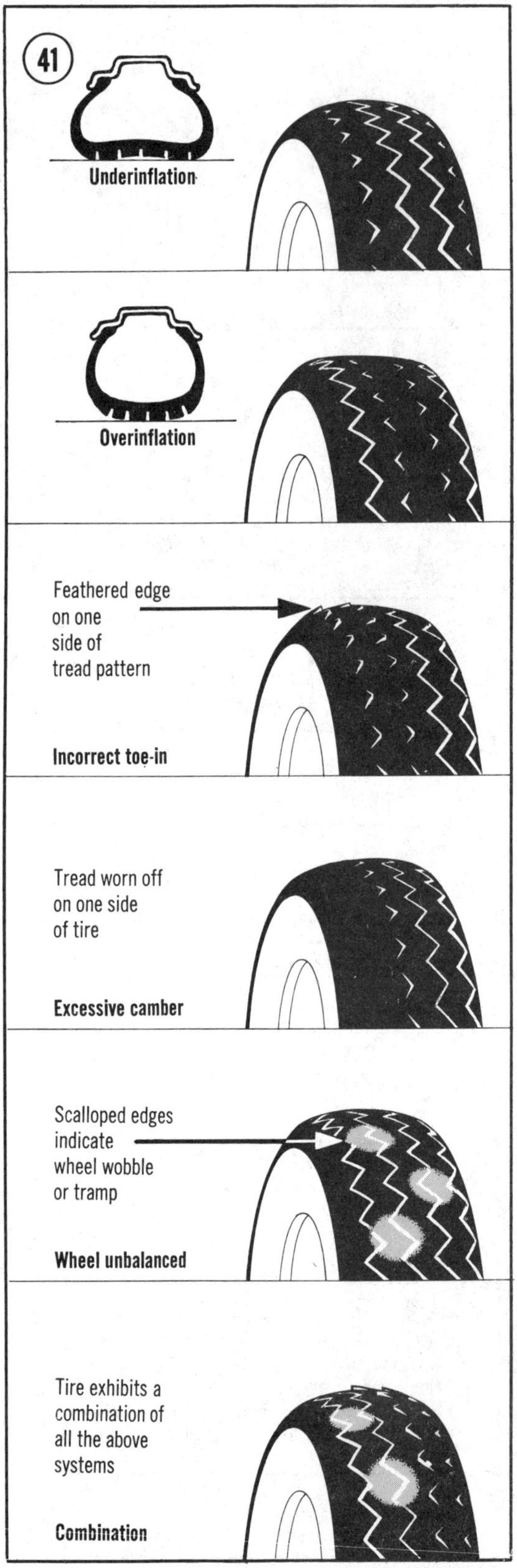

41

Underinflation

Overinflation

Feathered edge on one side of tread pattern

Incorrect toe-in

Tread worn off on one side of tire

Excessive camber

Scalloped edges indicate wheel wobble or tramp

Wheel unbalanced

Tire exhibits a combination of all the above systems

Combination

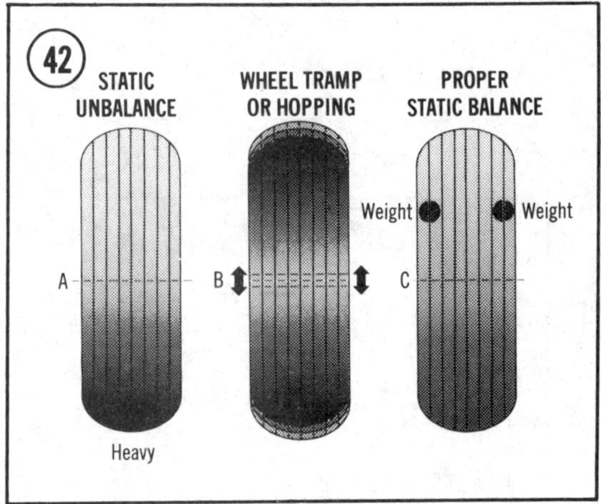

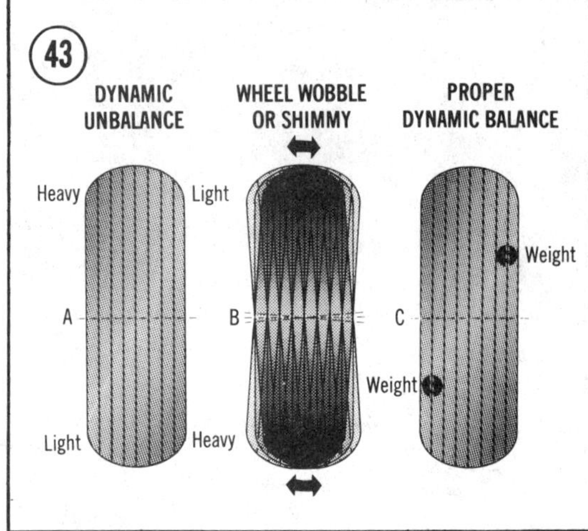

Figure 41 identifies wear patterns and indicates the most probable causes.

WHEEL BALANCING

All four wheels and tires must be in balance along two axes. To be in static balance (**Figure 42**), weight must be evenly distributed around the axis of rotation. (A) shows a statically unbalanced wheel; (B) shows the result — wheel tramp or hopping; (C) shows proper static balance.

To be in dynamic balance (**Figure 43**), the centerline of the weight must coincide with the centerline of the wheel. (A) shows a dynamically unbalanced wheel; (B) shows the result — wheel wobble or shimmy; (C) shows proper dynamic balance.

NOTE: If you own a 1982 or later model, first check the Supplement at the back of the book for any new service information.

3

CHAPTER THREE

LUBRICATION, MAINTENANCE, AND TUNE-UP

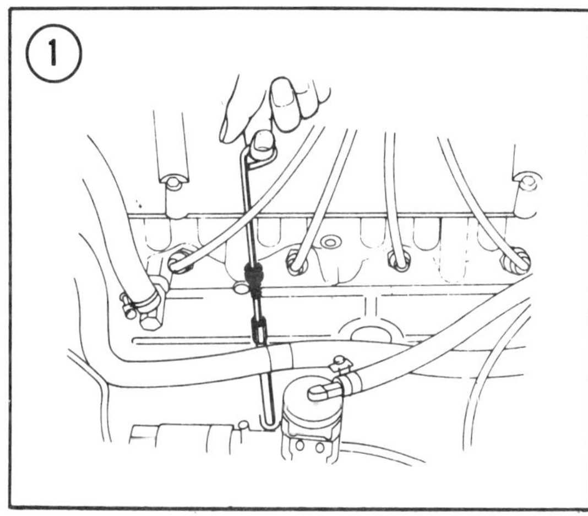

This chapter deals with the normal maintenance necessary to keep your truck running properly. **Tables 1-7** list service intervals. **Tables 1-12** are at the end of the chapter.

ROUTINE CHECKS

The following checks should be done at each stop for gas.

1. With the engine off, check oil level on the dipstick. See **Figure 1** (1970-1980) or **Figure 2** (1981).
2. Check coolant level in the expansion tank (if so equipped). See **Figure 3**. If the truck doesn't have an expansion tank, check coolant level in the radiator.

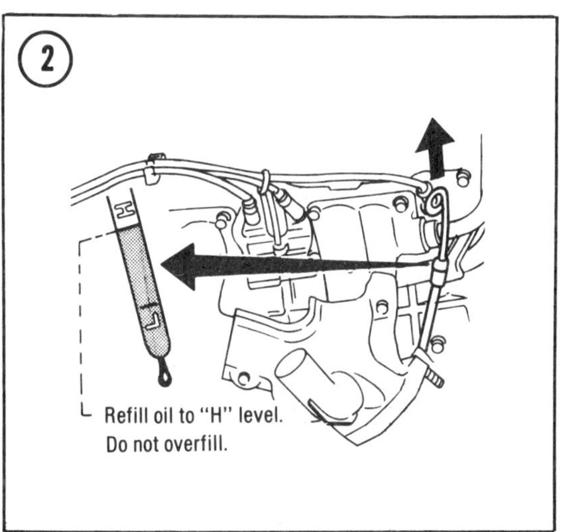

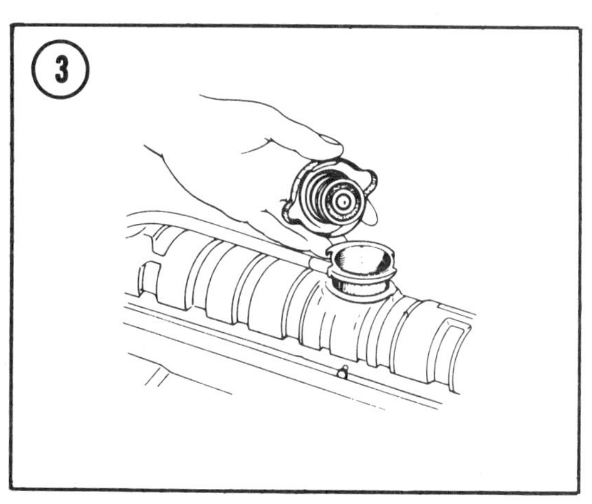

WARNING

Do not remove the radiator cap quickly when the engine is hot. Cover the cap with a rag and turn it 1/4 turn counterclockwise. After cooling system pressure has been released, press the cap down, turn counterclockwise, and remove.

3. Remove the battery filler caps and check electrolyte level (**Figure 4**). It should be approximately 1/4 in. above the plates inside the battery. If low, top up with distilled water. Do not overfill.
4. Check the level of the windshield washer container. It should be kept full.

CAUTION

Do not use radiator anti-freeze in the windshield washer container. The runoff may damage the vehicle's paint.

5. Check fluid level in the brake and clutch master cylinders. **Figure 5** shows the 1970-1980 cylinders. The 1981 brake master cylinder uses a single reservoir (**Figure 6**). Fluid should be between the lines on the reservoirs. If low, top up with brake fluid marked DOT 3. The same fluid is used for clutch and brakes.

CAUTION

Do not remove reservoir caps unless topping up fluid. Clean the area around the caps before removing.

6. Check tire pressures. This should be done when the tires are cold. Recommended pressures are listed in **Table 10**.

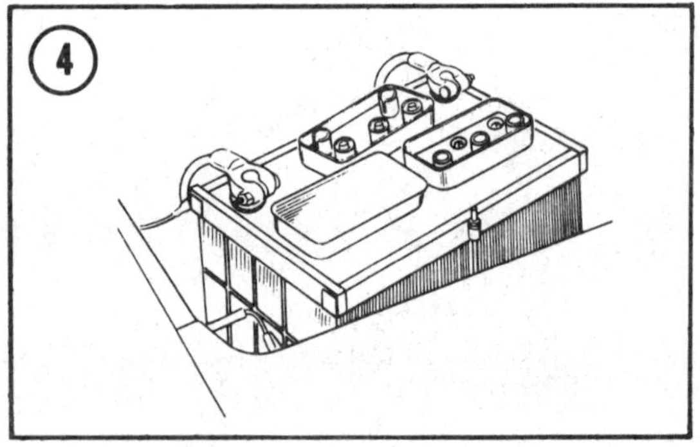

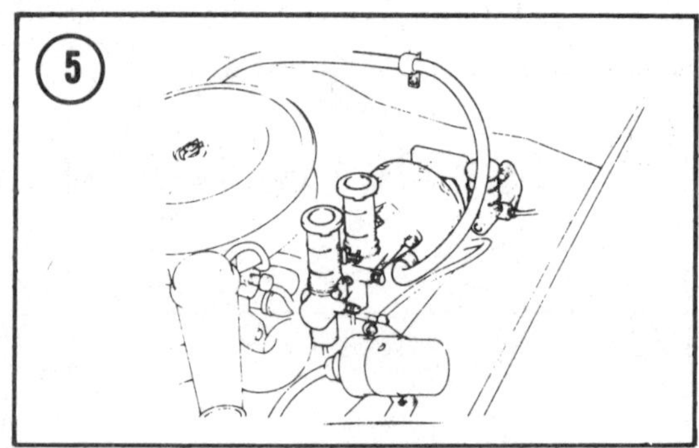

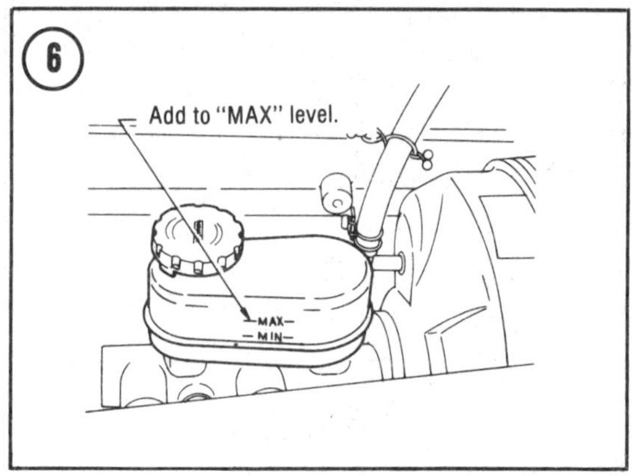

Engine Oil and Filter

If the truck is given normal use, change the oil when recommended in **Tables 2-7**. If it is used for stop-and-go driving, in dusty areas or left idling for long periods, change the oil every 3,000 miles or 3 months.

Use an oil recommended in **Table 5** and **Table 6**. The rating (SE) is usually printed on top of the can (**Figure 7**).

To drain the oil and change the filter, you will need:

a. Drain pan
b. Oil can spout or can opener and funnel
c. Filter wrench
d. 5 quarts of oil
e. Oil filter

There are several ways to discard the old oil safely. The easiest is to pour it from the drain pan into a gallon bleach or milk bottle. The oil can be taken to a service station for dumping or, where permitted, thrown in your household trash.

1. Warm the engine to operating temperature, then shut it off.
2. Put the drain pan under the drain plug (**Figure 8**). Remove the plug and let the oil drain for at least 10 minutes.

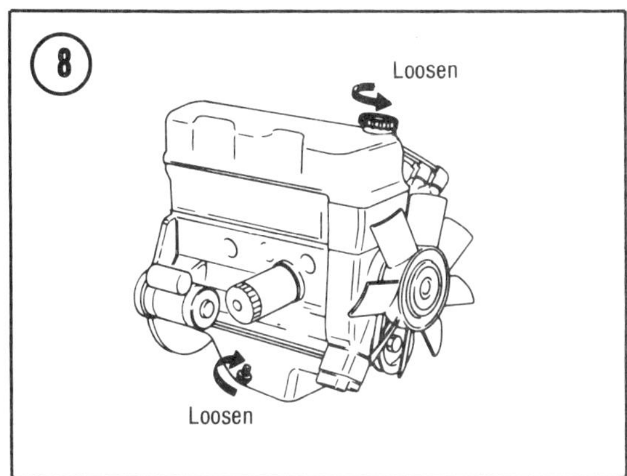

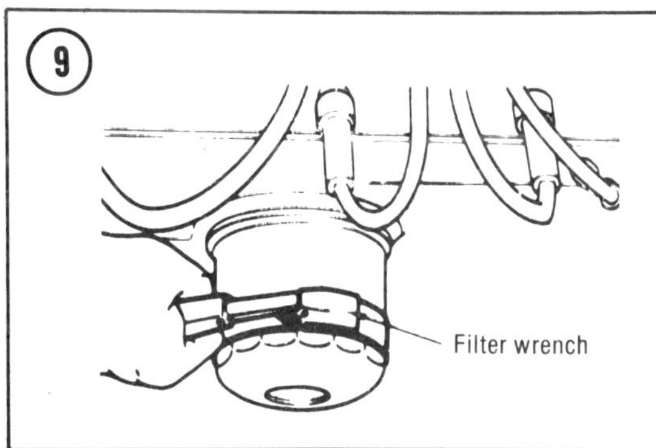

3. Unscrew the oil filter (**Figure 9**) counterclockwise. Use a filter wrench if the filter is too tight to remove by hand.
4. Wipe the gasket surface on the engine block clean with a lint-free cloth.
5. Coat the neoprene gasket on the new filter with clean engine oil. See **Figure 10**.
6. Screw the filter onto the engine *by hand* until the gasket just touches the engine block. At this point, there will be a very slight resistance when turning the filter.

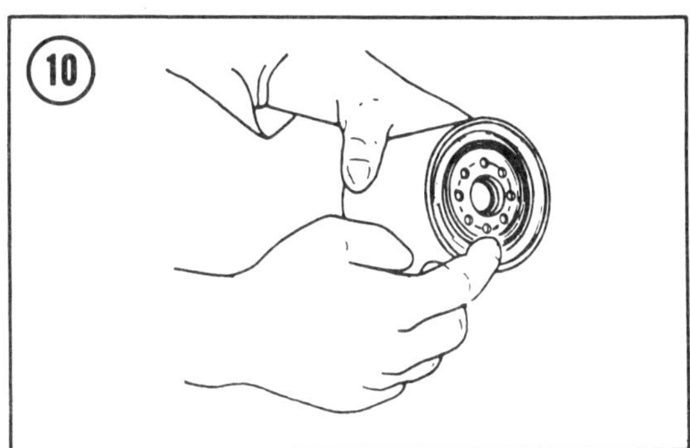

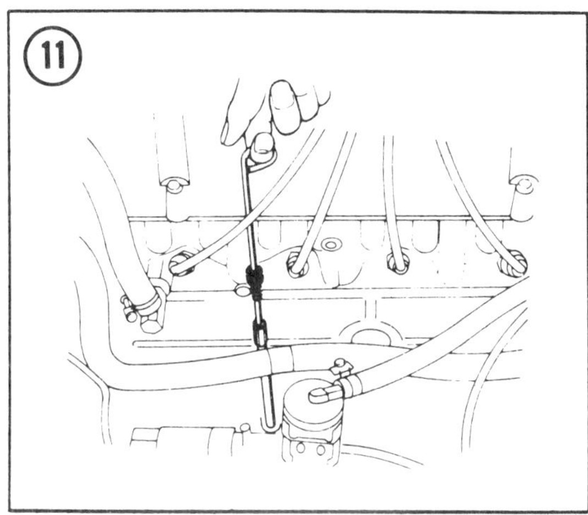

7. Tighten the filter 2/3 turn more *by hand*. If the filter wrench is used, the filter will probably be overtightened. This will cause an oil leak.
8. Install the oil pan drain plug. Tighten it securely.
9. Remove the oil filler cap (**Figure 8**).
10. Pour oil into the engine. Capacity is listed in **Table 11**.
11. Start the engine and let it idle. The instrument panel oil pressure light will remain on for 15-30 seconds, then go out.

CAUTION

Do not rev the engine to make the oil pressure light go out. It takes time for the oil to reach all areas of the engine and revving it could damage dry parts.

12. While the engine is running, check the drain plug and oil filter for leaks.
13. Turn the engine off. Let the oil settle for several minutes, then check level on the dipstick. See **Figure 11** (1970-1980) or **Figure**

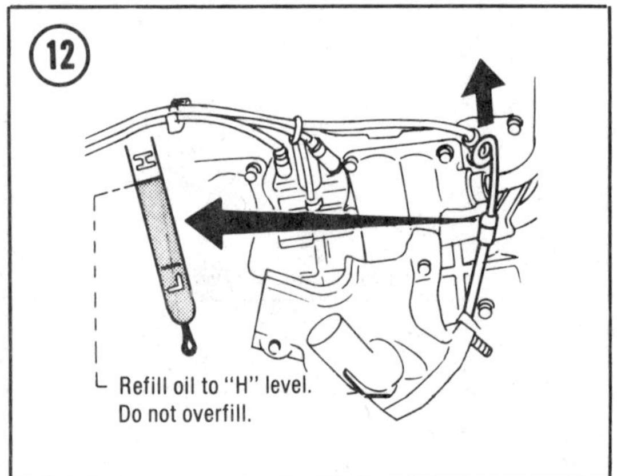

12 (1981). Add oil if necessary to bring the level up to the "H" mark, but *do not* overfill.

PERIODIC CHECKS AND MAINTENANCE

The following procedures are done at specified intervals of miles or time.

These service intervals are intended for trucks given normal use. More frequent service is required under the following conditions:

a. Stop-and-go driving
b. Constant high-speed driving
c. Severe dust
d. Rough or salted roads
e. Very hot, very cold, or rainy weather

Some maintenance procedures are included in the tune-up section at the end of the chapter, and detailed instructions will be found there. Other steps are explained in various chapters. Chapter references are included with these steps.

Manual Transmission Oil Level

To check, remove the filler plug (**Figure 13**) from the side of the transmission. Make sure the oil level is within 1/4 in. of the bottom of the filler plug threads. Top up with an oil recommended in **Table 8** and **Table 9** if it is low.

Automatic Transmission Fluid Level

Check the fluid level as described in *Automatic Transmission, Fluid Level Check*, Chapter Ten.

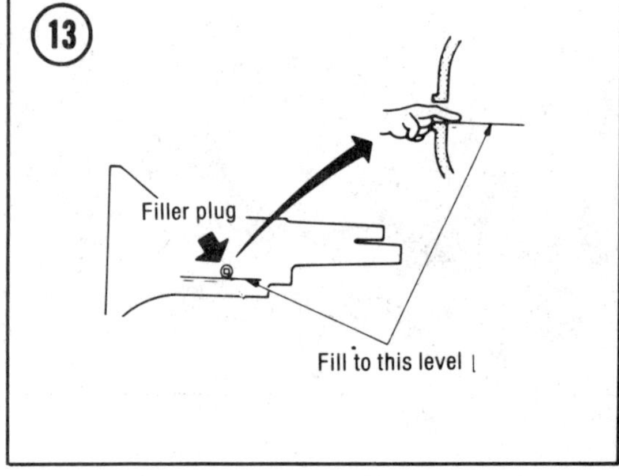

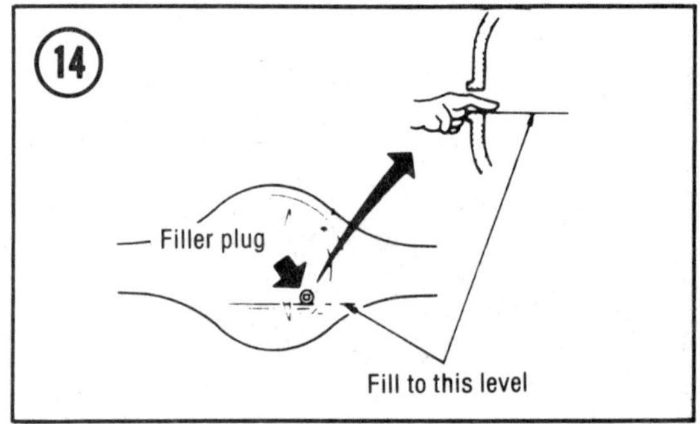

Differential Oil Level

To check, remove the filler plug (**Figure 14**) from the axle housing. Oil level should be within 1/4 in. of the bottom of the filler plug threads. If necessary, top up with an oil recommended in **Table 8** and **Table 9**.

Hydraulic Systems

Check for leaks. Inspect the brake master cylinder, calipers (disc brakes), and wheel cylinders for wetness. Do the same for the clutch master and operating cylinders, and for all hydraulic line connections.

Fuel Lines

Inspect the fuel lines. Start at the gas tank and work forward, checking all connections for wetness. Make sure the lines are securely in their clips.

Engine Leak Inspection

The engine should be checked visually for leaks. Check the oil pan drain plug, oil pan gasket, oil filter, front cover and check the oil

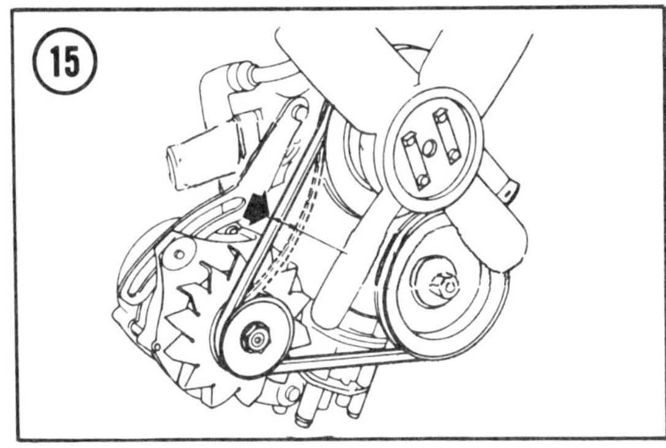

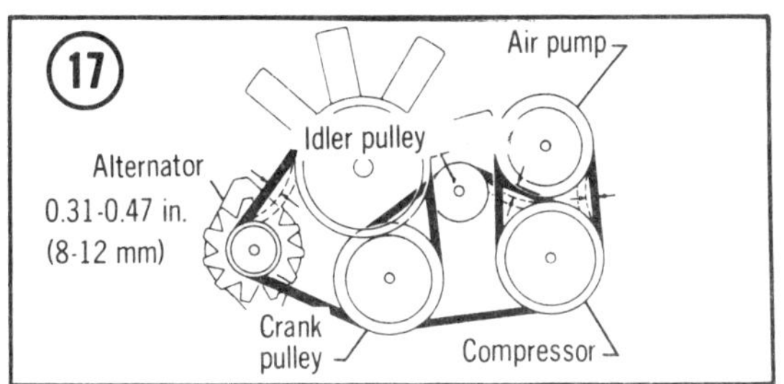

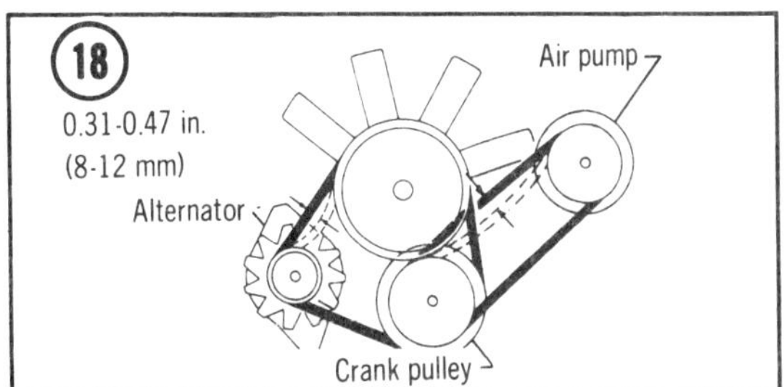

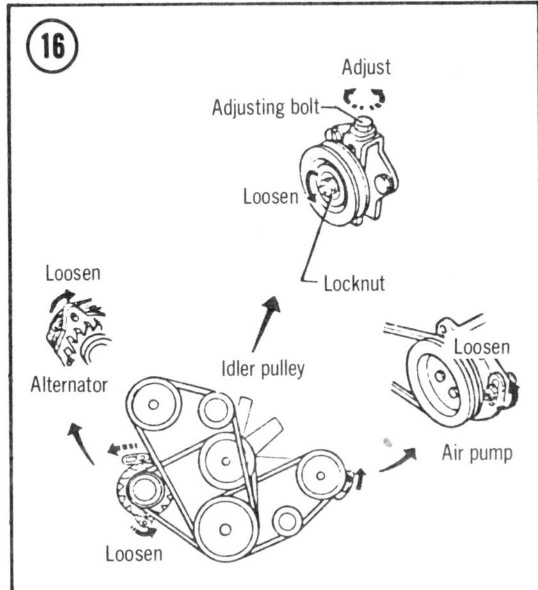
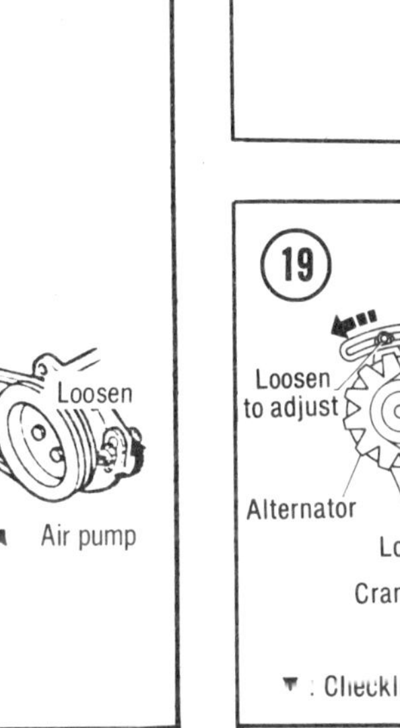

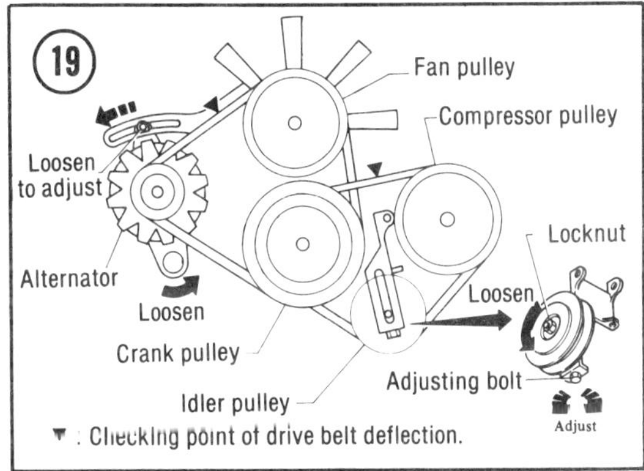

pump. Greasy looking dirt at these points may indicate an oil leak. Inspect the radiator and hose connections for coolant residue or rust. Check the fuel connections (fuel filter, fuel pump, carburetor) for wetness that may indicate gasoline leakage.

Drive Belts

Refer to the following illustrations:

Figure 15—1970-1979, without air pump or air conditioning

Figure 16—1970-1979, with air pump and air conditioning

Figure 17—1980, with air conditioning

Figure 18—1980, without air conditioning

Figure 19—1981 (all)

To check drive belt tension, press on the belt halfway between pulleys. Play should be as follows:

Alternator—1/3-1/2 in. (8-12mm)

Air pump—1/3-1/2 in. (8-12mm)

1970-1979 air conditioning compressor (between idler pulley and compressor)—1/4-1/3 in. (6-8mm)

1980 and later air conditioning compressor (between idler pulley and compressor)— 1/3-1/2 in. (8-12mm)

To adjust an alternator belt, loosen the alternator mounting and adjusting bolts. Pull or pry the alternator away from the engine to tighten the belt, then tighten the bolts.

To adjust an air pump or air conditioning compressor belt, loosen the idler pulley locknut. Turn the adjusting bolt to set belt tension, then tighten the locknut.

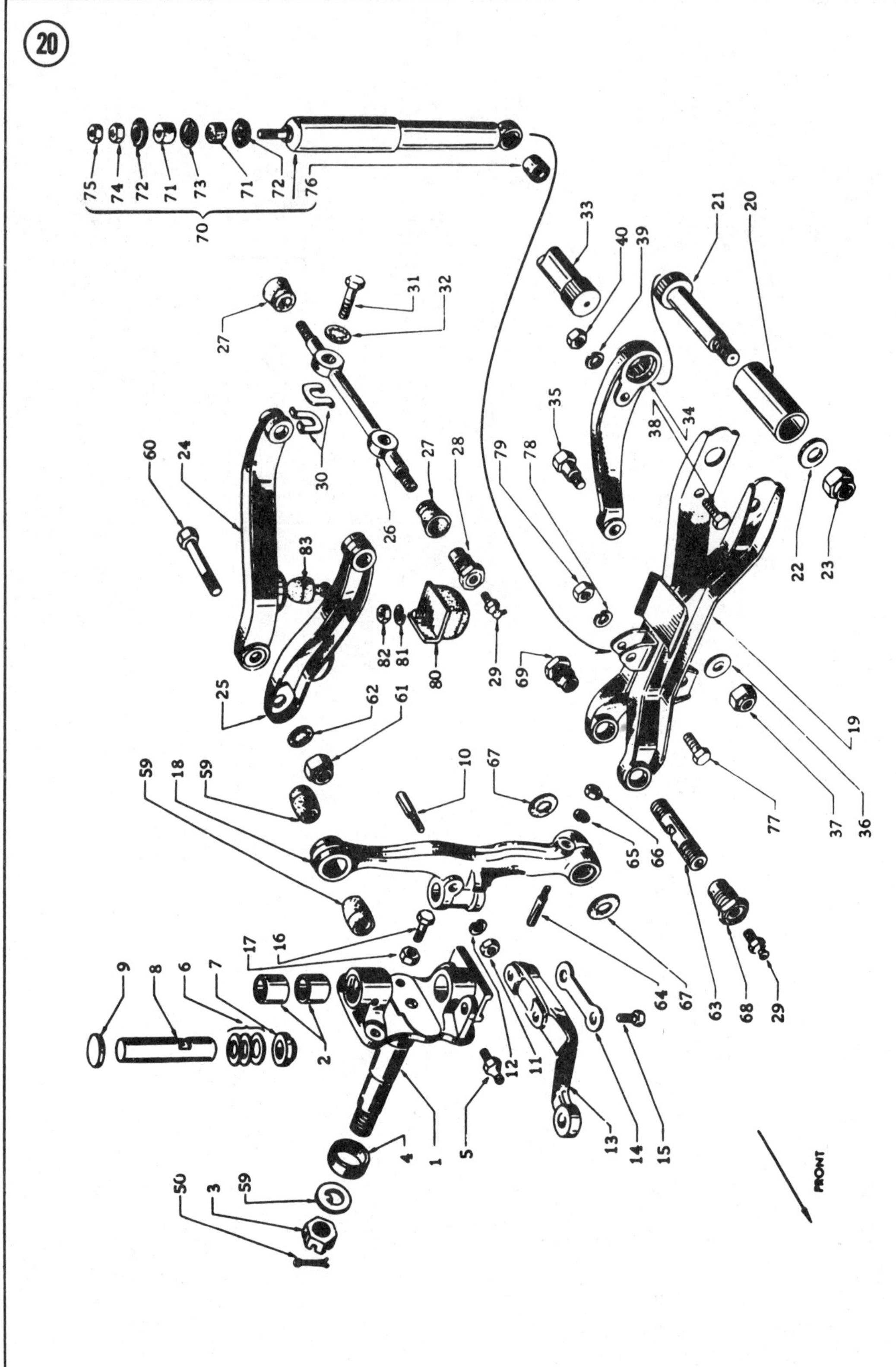
20
FRONT

KINGPINS AND KNUCKLE SPINDLE—1970-1977

1. Knuckle spindle assembly with nut
2. Front spindle bushing
3. Knuckle spindle nut
4. Front spindle collar
5. Grease plug or nipple
6. Front spindle shims
7. Front spindle thrust washer assembly
8. King pin
9. Front spindle plug
10. Bolt
11. Nut
12. Lockwasher
13. Knuckle arm
14. Lock plate
15. Knuckle arm bolt
16. Bolt
17. Nut
18. Knuckle spindle support
19. Front suspension lower link assembly
20. Front suspension lower link bushing assembly
21. Front suspension lower link spindle
22. Special lower link washer
23. Self-locking nut
24. Front suspension upper link assembly (rear)
25. Front suspension upper link assembly (front)
26. Front suspension upper link spindle
27. Upper link bushing dust seal
28. Front suspension upper link bushing assembly
29. Grease plug or nipple
30. Camber shim A
31. Upper link spindle bolt
32. Lockwasher
33. Front spring
34. Front spring torque arm
35. Front suspension torque arm bolt
36. Plain washer
37. Self-locking nut
38. Bolt
39. Lockwasher
40. Nut
59. Upper link bushing assembly
60. Upper link fulcrum bolt
61. Self-locking nut
62. Lockwasher
63. Front suspension lower link fulcrum pin
64. Taper pin
65. Lockwasher
66. Nut
67. Lower link fulcrum pin ring
68. Front suspension lower link bushing assembly (front)
69. Front suspension lower link bushing assembly (rear)
70. Front shock absorber kit
71. Shock absorber rubber bushing
72. Shock absorber special washer
73. Special washer
74. Nut
75. Locknut
76. Front shock absorber bushing assembly
77. Front shock absorber clamp bolt
78. Lockwasher
79. Nut
80. Front suspension rebound bumper assembly
81. Lockwasher
82. Nut
83. Front suspension rebound bumper

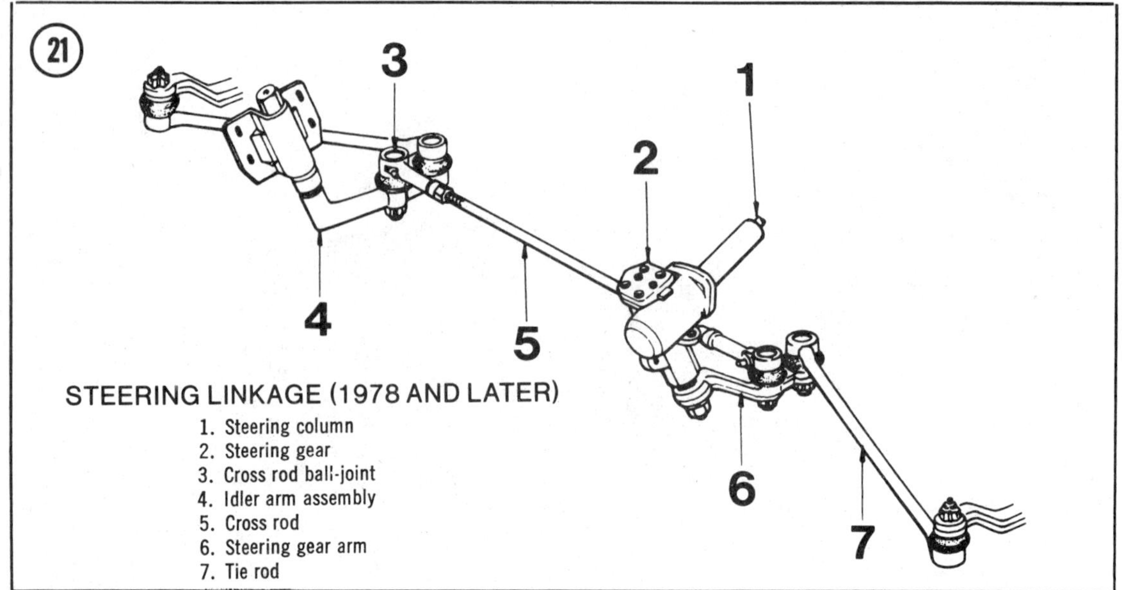

STEERING LINKAGE (1978 AND LATER)

1. Steering column
2. Steering gear
3. Cross rod ball-joint
4. Idler arm assembly
5. Cross rod
6. Steering gear arm
7. Tie rod

Throttle Cable

Check the cable for sticking or binding. Correct if necessary with a lubricant such as Cable Ease.

Choke Mechanism

On 1970-1971 trucks, check the choke cable for sticking or binding. Lubricate as needed. On 1972 and later models, check the automatic choke mechanism for sticking. Lubricate if necessary with a spray lube such as WD-40.

Steering Linkage, Suspension

Lubricate the suspension with multipurpose grease. Early pickups have suspension grease nipples; later models have plugs. The plugs must be removed and replaced with grease nipples to lubricate the suspension.

On 1970-1977 models, inject grease into the screw bushings at the inner end of the upper link, the upper and lower knuckle spindle bushings, and the screw bushings at the outer end of the lower link. See **Figure 20**.

On 1978 and later models, the suspension has ball-joints at the upper and lower end of the knuckle spindle. Remove the plugs from these, install grease fittings, and inject multipurpose grease. Grease the cross rod ball-joints. See **Figure 21**. While greasing the steering linkage, check all fasteners in the front suspension for looseness.

Hinges, Latches, Locks

Lightly grease the hood latch and trunk or tailgate lock with molybdenum disulphide grease. Apply 1-2 drops of oil to hinges on doors, hood, and tailgate or trunk. Lubricate striker plates with a non-staining stick lube such as Door Ease. Lubricate lock tumblers by applying a thin coat of Lubriplate, lock oil, or graphite to the key. Insert and work the lock several times. Wipe the key clean.

PCV System

The positive crankcase ventilation (PCV) system is designed to route crankcase emissions into the combustion chambers for burning.

1. On 1970-1979 models and 1980 Canadian trucks, replace the PCV valve and filter at intervals specified in the maintenance schedules. On 1980 U.S. trucks, and all later models, the PCV valve does not require periodic replacement. The PCV filter needs to be replaced only if it becomes clogged.

To replace the PCV valve, disconnect its hose and unscrew the valve. See **Figure 22** (1970-1980) or **Figure 23** (1981).

To replace the PCV filter, remove the air

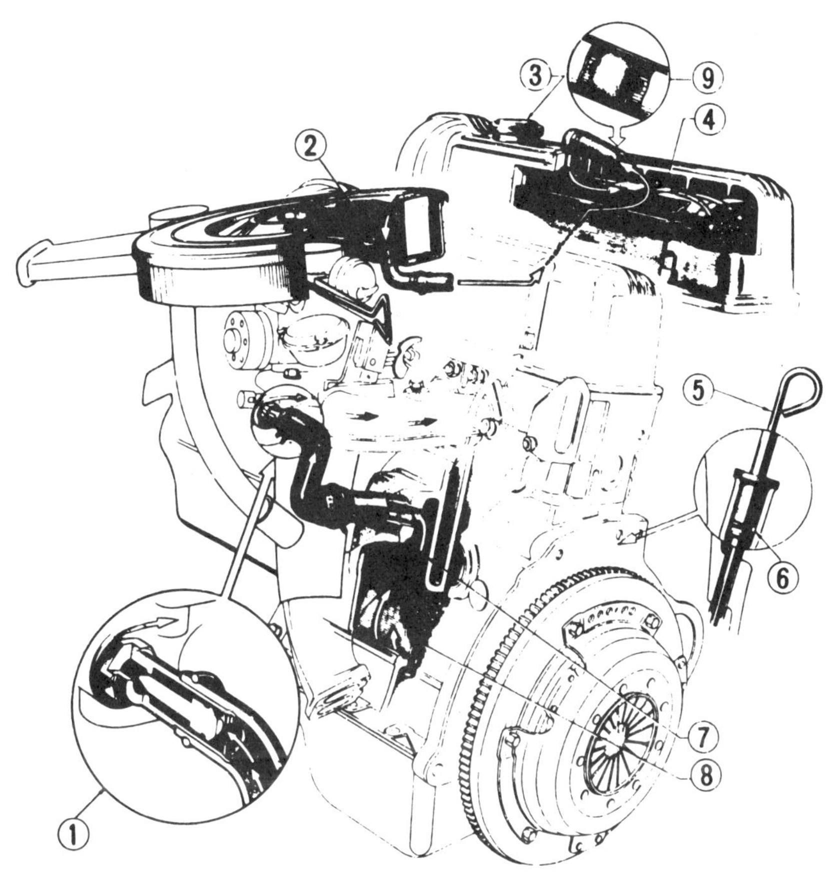

CRANKCASE EMISSION CONTROL

1. PCV valve
2. Flame arrester
3. Sealed filler cap
4. Baffle plate
5. Oil level gauge
6. O-ring
7. Oil separator
8. Baffle plate
9. Flame arrester

3

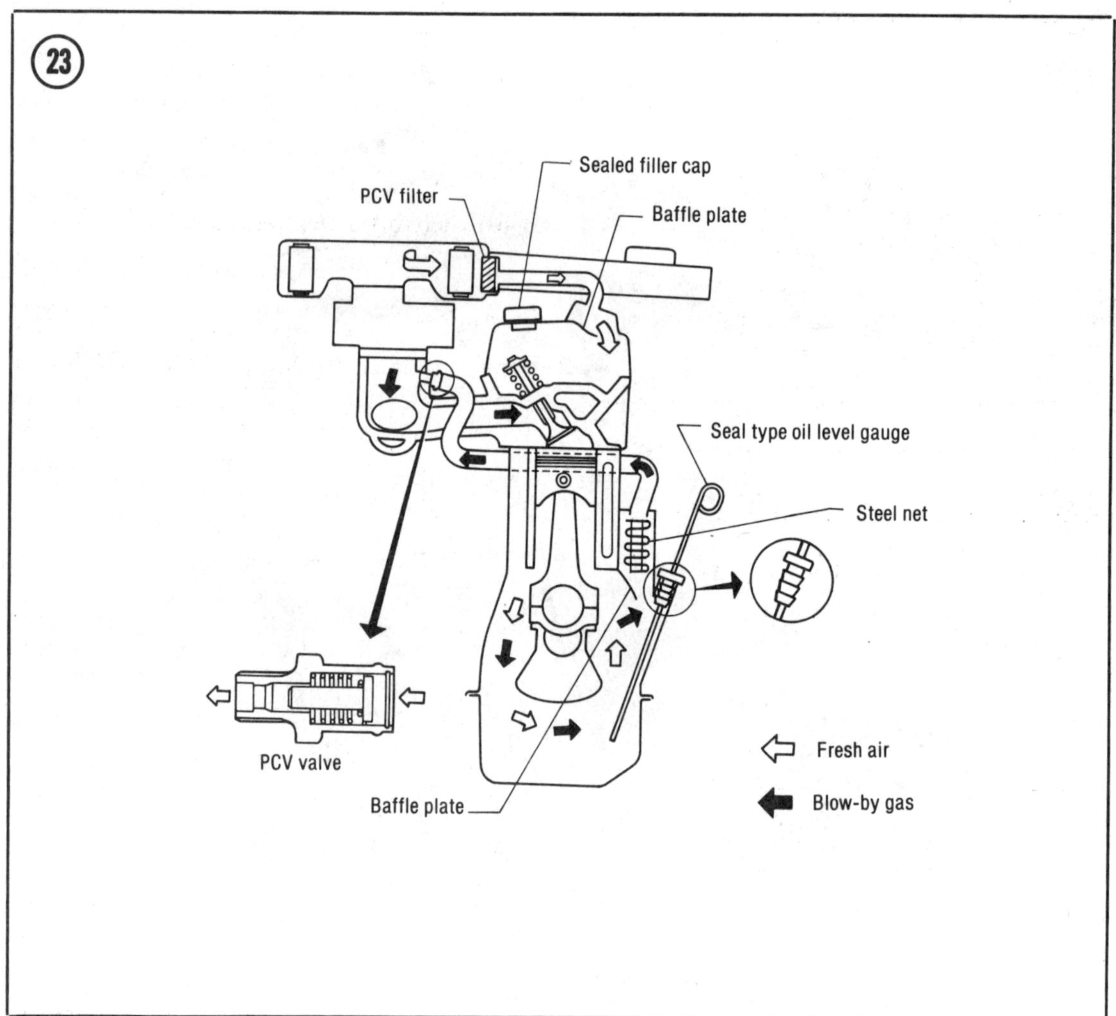

cleaner cover. Pull the filter out of its holder (**Figure 24**) and install a new one.

2. Check PCV hoses for leaks and loose connections. See **Figure 22** or **Figure 23**. On models which require periodic PCV valve replacement, disconnect the hoses and blow them out with compressed air at alternate inspections. On models which do not require periodic service, blow out the hoses whenever the PCV filter is replaced.

Vacuum Lines (L-Series Engines)

Check vacuum lines for cracks or deterioration at intervals specified in the maintenance schedules. Refer to *Vacuum Lines*, Chapter Six.

ATC Air Cleaner

The automatic temperature control air cleaner is used on 1972 and later models. It should be tested as described in Chapter Six.

Fuel Filter Replacement

Figure 25 shows a typical Datsun fuel filter. To replace, disconnect the inlet line and plug it. Then disconnect the outlet line and pull the filter out of its clip. Install a new filter in the reverse order.

EGR System

Test the exhaust gas recirculation system as decribed under *Exhaust Gas Recirculation System*, Chapter Six.

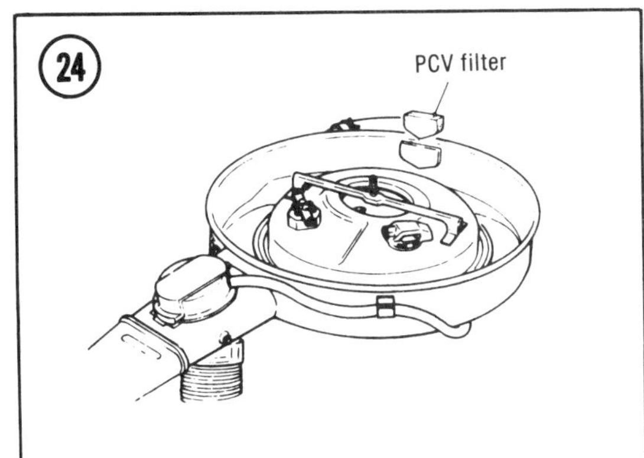

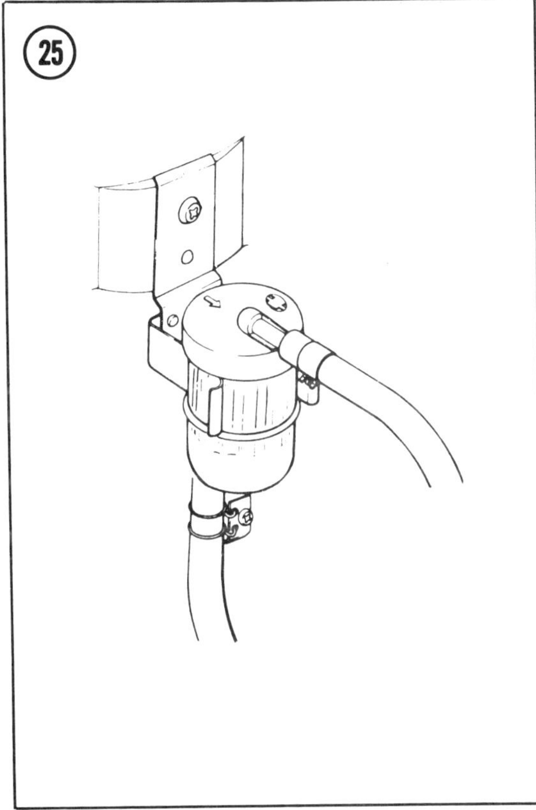

Evaporative Emission Control System

Inspect the system as described under *Evaporative Emission Control System*, Chapter Six.

Cooling System

Inspect all coolant hoses and connections. Replace hoses that are cracked, deteriorated, or extremely soft. Make sure all clamps are tight.

Spark Timing Control System

On 1970-1973 and 1979 trucks, test the system as described in Chapter Six. On 1976-1977 models (non-California only), replace the spark delay valve.

Boost Controlled Deceleration Device

Although the boost controlled deceleration device does not usually require adjustment, it should be checked regularly. With the transmission in neutral, hold engine speed at 3,000-3,500 rpm, then release the throttle quickly. The engine should slow to specified idle speed within a few seconds. If it does not, have the BCDD tested by a Datsun dealer.

Brake Fluid

Pump out the old brake fluid and replace it with new fluid. See *Brake Bleeding*, Chapter Eleven.

Brake Booster (Power Brakes)

Test the brake booster, check valve, and vacuum hose as described in Chapter Eleven.

Battery

Inspect the battery and test specific gravity as described under *Battery* in Chapter Eight.

Brake Inspection

Check brake drums and shoes for wear. Check wheel cylinders for fluid leaks. See Chapter Eleven for details.

Shock Absorbers

Check the shock absorbers for fluid leaks. To check for wear, press each corner of the truck down firmly, then let it up quickly. If it bounces more than once, the shock absorber is probably worn. Replace it.

Drive Shaft

Check the drive shaft for wear. The easiest way to do this is to shake the drive shaft while watching the universal joints. If play can be detected in the U-joints, disassemble and repair them as described in Chapter Thirteen. After checking for U-joint wear, tighten the bolts attaching the drive shaft to the differential flange (and to the transmission flange on early pickups).

Wheel Alignment

Have wheel alignment checked by a Datsun dealer or front end shop.

Pedals

Using multipurpose grease, lubricate brake and clutch pedals at their pivot points. Also lubricate the pivot points (in the pedals) of the brake and clutch master cylinder pushrods.

Coolant

Flush, drain, and refill the cooling system as described in Chapter Seven.

Air Filters

Replace the air cleaner element at specified intervals. To replace, detach the cover clips and wing nut. Lift off the cover and take out the element (**Figure 26**). Install a new element and reposition the cover. Align the arrows on cover and air intake nozzle (**Figure 27**).

On 1975 and later models equipped with air injection, replace the air pump air filter. To do this, disconnect the air filter hose, then remove the filter from the engine compartment sidewall. Remove the air filter and lower air cleaner body from the upper air cleaner body (**Figure 28**). Replace the air filter and lower body as an assembly, then reinstall the air pump air filter on the engine compartment sidewall.

On 1980 and later models equipped with air induction, replace the air induction filter. To do this, detach the filter case from the side of the air cleaner. See **Figure 29**. Take out the filter, install a new one, and reattach the filter case.

NOTE

If the valve is removed from the filter case, be sure it faces in the direction shown in ***Figure 30*** *when it is reinstalled.*

Load Sensing Valve

This valve is used on 1976 and later models

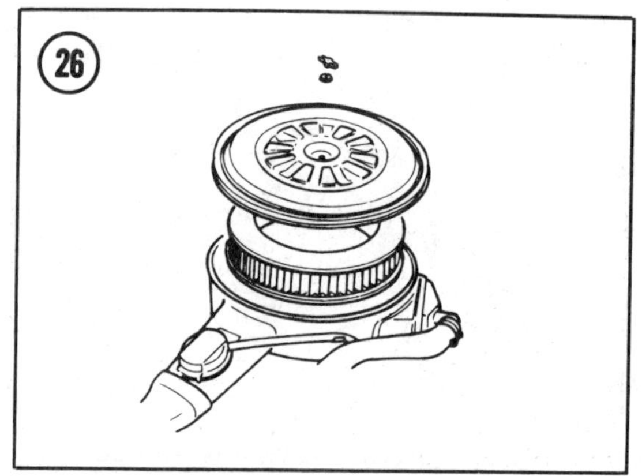

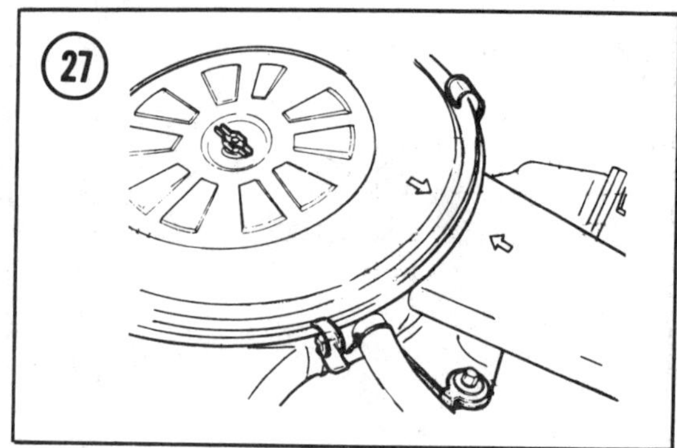

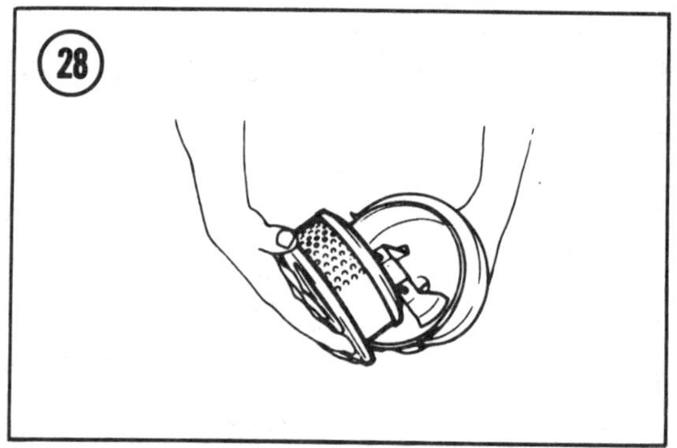

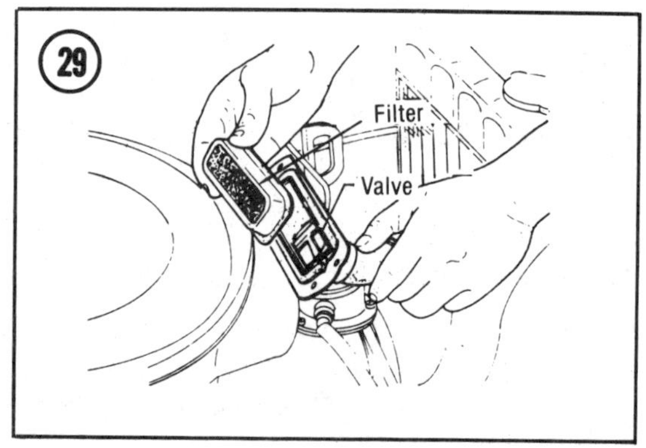

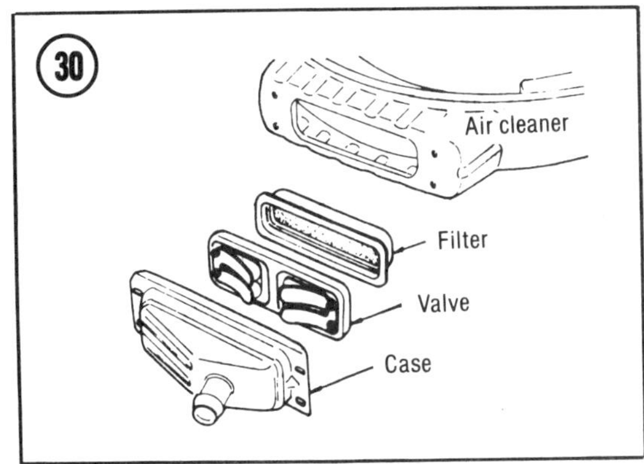

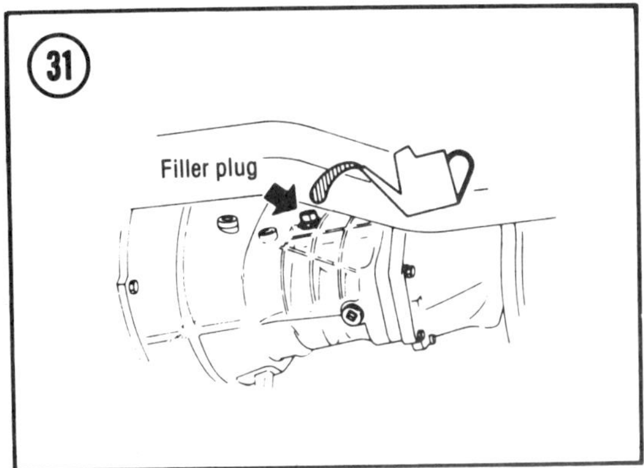

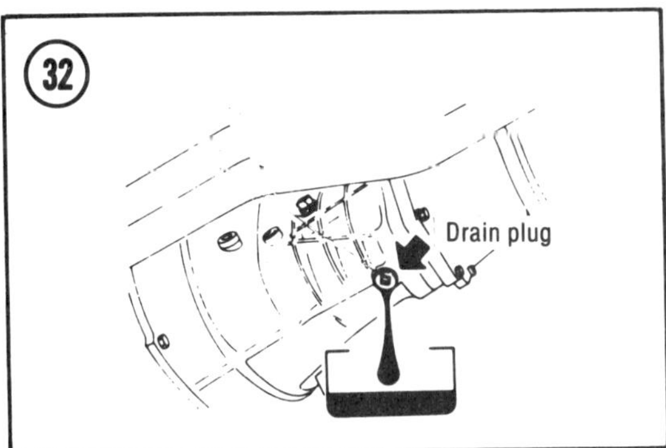

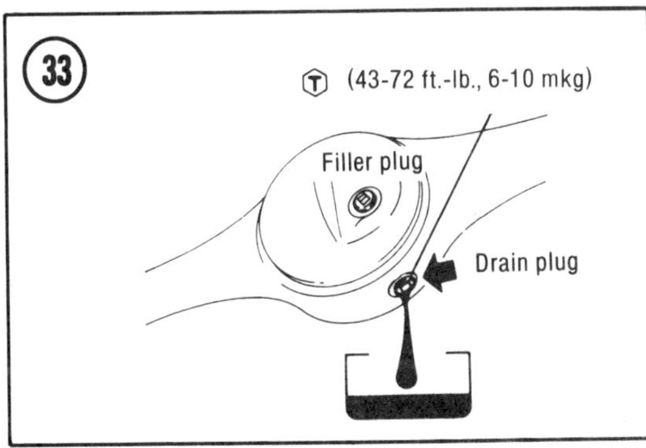

to prevent rear wheel lockup under varying loads. Test as described in Chapter Eleven.

Handbrake Linkage

Check all handbrake linkage friction points for wear or corrosion. Lubricate as needed with multipurpose grease.

Wheel Bearings

Clean, repack, and adjust wheel bearings as described in Chapter Thirteen.

Manual Transmission Oil Change

Warm up the oil by driving a short distance. Then remove the filler and drain plugs (**Figure 31** and **Figure 32**) and drain the oil. Reinstall the drain plug and fill with an oil recommended in **Table 8** and **Table 9**. The easiest way to fill the transmission is to run a long tube from the engine compartment along the right-hand side of the engine and transmission and into the filler hole.

Capacity is listed in **Table 11**. When the transmission is full, reinstall the filler plug.

NOTE

Check the old transmission oil for such signs of damage as gear teeth and pieces of brass from synchronizers.

Differential Oil Change

This procedure is much like that used to change the transmission oil. First drive the truck a short distance for warm the oil. Then remove the filler and drain plugs from the axle housing. See **Figure 33**. When the oil has drained, reinstall the drain plug and fill with gear oil recommended in **Table 8** and **Table 9**. Capacity is given **Table 11**. Reinstall the filler plug after filling.

Headlights

Have the aim of the headlights checked by a Datsun dealer or certified lamp adjusting station.

Drive Shaft

Check the universal joints for stiff movement, indicating lack of lubrication. If

3

necessary, disassemble, clean, and grease the U-joints. See Chapter Eleven.

MINOR TUNE-UP

On 1970-1973 trucks, perform a minor tune-up every 3,000 miles/3 months. This consists of:

a. Cleaning and regapping spark plugs
b. Cleaning and regapping breaker points
c. Checking and adjusting ignition timing
d. Checking carburetor adjustment

Spark Plugs

Inspect, clean and regap spark plugs.

CAUTION
*Refer to **Major Tune-up** in this chapter for correct removal and installation procedures.*

Distributor Points

Clean the points using fine emery paper or a file made for the purpose. Do not attempt to remove all roughness while cleaning. Check the point gap as described under *Major Tune-up* and adjust if needed.

Ignition Timing

Check the timing and adjust if needed, following the procedure outlined under *Major Tune-up*.

Carburetor

Check idle speed and fuel mixture as described under *Major Tune-up*.

MAJOR TUNE-UP

Under normal conditions, a complete tune-up should be done at intervals specified in the maintenance schedules. More frequent tune-ups may be required if the truck is used under the severe conditions described earlier in this chapter.

Since different engine systems interact, procedures should be done in the following order:

a. Test compression
b. Tighten cylinder head bolts
c. Adjust valve clearances

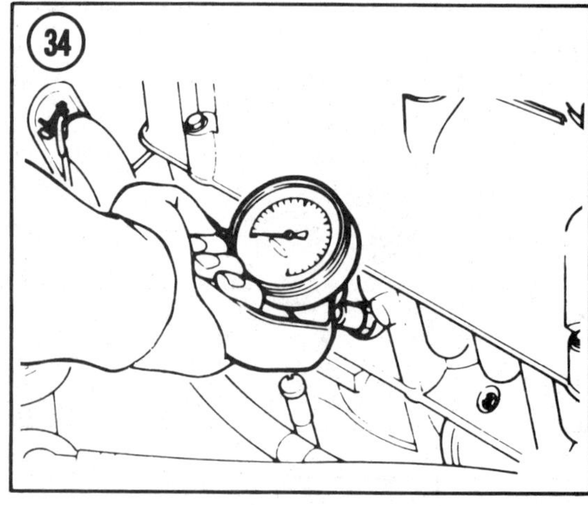
34

d. Work on ignition system
e. Adjust carburetor

COMPRESSION TEST

There are 2 types of compression test: "wet" and "dry." These tests are interpreted together to isolate problems in cylinders and valves. The dry compression test is done first. Test as follows.

1. Warm the engine to normal operating temperature.
2. Remove the air cleaner as described under *Air Cleaner*, Chapter Six. Make sure the choke is completely open. If it isn't, inspect the choke linkage and electrical circuit. See *Carburetor* and *Automatic Choke Circuit*, Chapter Six.
3. Remove the spark plugs. See *Spark Plugs* in this chapter for correct procedures.
4. Connect the compression tester to one cylinder following manufacturer's instructions. **Figure 34** shows a hand-held compression tester in use. You can also use the screw-in type described in Chapter One.

NOTE
Hand-held compression testers require 2 people, one to hold the compression tester and one to crank the engine. Screw-in compression testers only require one person.

5. Crank the engine over until there is no further increase in compression reading.
6. Remove the tester and write down the reading.

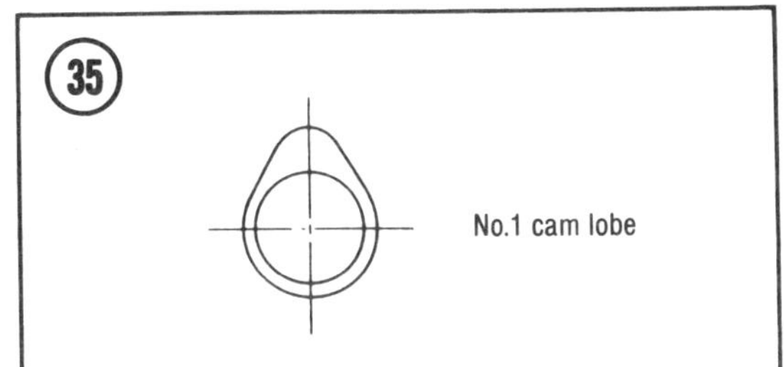

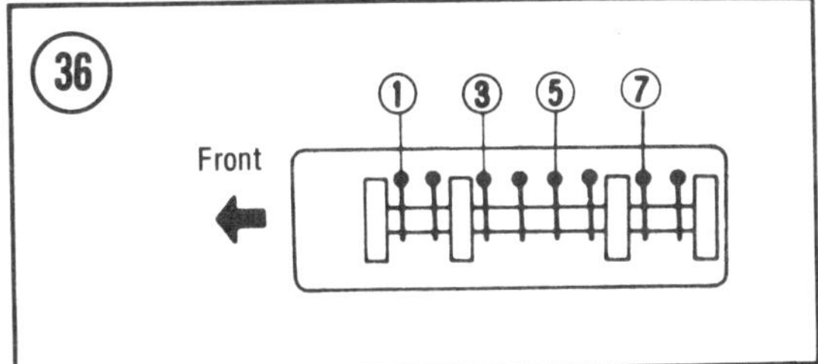

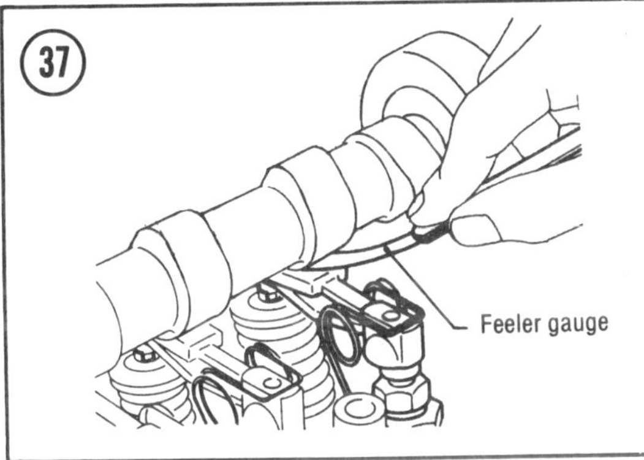

7. Repeat Steps 4-6 for each cylinder. Compare results with **Table 12** in this chapter.

When interpreting the results, actual readings are not as important as the differences in readings. Low readings, although they may be even, are a sign of wear. Low readings in 2 adjacent cylinders may indicate a defective head gasket. No cylinder should test at less than 80 per cent of the highest cylinder. A greater difference indicates worn or broken rings, leaky or sticking valves, a defective head gasket, or a combination of all.

If the dry compression test indicates a problem, isolate the cause with a wet compression test. This is done in the same way as the dry compression test, except that about one tablespoon of oil is poured down the spark plug holes before performing Steps

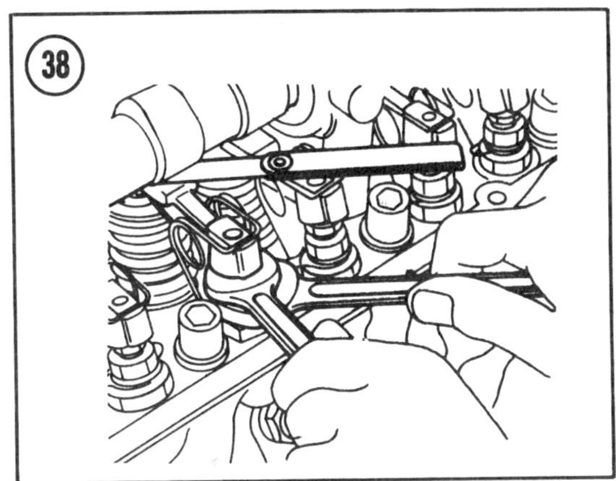

4-6. If the wet compression readings are much geater than the dry readings, the trouble is probably due to worn or broken rings. If there is little difference between wet and dry readings, the trouble is probably due to leaky or sticking valves. If 2 adjacent cylinders are low and the wet and dry readings are close, the head gasket may be damaged.

CYLINDER HEAD BOLTS

Check tightness of cylinder head bolts. Refer to tightening instructions under *Cylinder Head*, Chapter Four or Chapter Five.

VALVE ADJUSTMENT

L-Series Engines (1970-1980)

1. Warm the engine to normal operating temperature.
2. Remove the valve cover.
3. Find valve clearance specifications in **Table 12**.
4. Remove the spark plugs. This makes it easier to turn the engine.

CAUTION

Refer to ***Spark Plugs*** *in this chapter for proper removal procedures.*

5. Turn the engine so No. 1 cam lobe points straight up. See **Figure 35**.
6. Check clearance of valves 1, 3, 5, and 7 (**Figure 36**). Measure with a feeler gauge as shown in **Figure 37**.

NOTE

Valves 1 and 5 are exhaust valves; valves 3 and 7 are intake valves.

3

7. If valve clearance is incorrect, loosen the pivot locknut as shown in **Figure 38**. Turn the pivot to change clearance, then tighten the locknut. If available, use a 17mm crow's foot socket like the Datsun special tool shown in **Figure 39**. An open-end wrench can be used if the special tool isn't available, but the tool is necessary to torque the locknut accurately.
8. Turn the engine until No. 1 cam lobe points straight down. See **Figure 40**.
9. Check the clearances of valves 2, 4, 6, and 8 (**Figure 41**). Adjust if necessary as described in Step 7.

NOTE
Valves 2 and 6 are intake valves; valves 4 and 8 are exhaust valves.

NAPS-Z Engine (1981)

1. Find valve clearance specifications in **Table 12**.
2. Warm the engine to normal operating temperature.
3. Remove the spark plugs. This makes it easier to turn the engine.

CAUTION
*See **Spark Plugs** in this chapter for correct removal procedures.*

4. Remove the rocker arm cover.
5. Turn the engine until No. 1 cam lobe points straight down. See **Figure 42**.
6. Counting from the front of the engine, measure the clearances on valves 1, 4, 6, and 7. See **Figure 43**. Insert a feeler gauge of the specified clearance between valve stem and rocker arm (**Figure 44**). The feeler gauge should move with a very slight drag. If it is too loose or too tight, clearance must be adjusted.
8. To adjust, loosen the rocker pivot locknut (**Figure 45**). Turn the rocker pivot to change clearance, then tighten the nut securely.

NOTE
Valves 1 and 4 are intake valves; valves 6 and 7 are exhaust valves.

9. Turn the engine until No. 1 cam lobe points straight up (**Figure 46**). Check valves 2, 3, 5, and 8 (**Figure 47**).
10. If clearance is incorrect, adjust in the same manner as the first 4 valves.

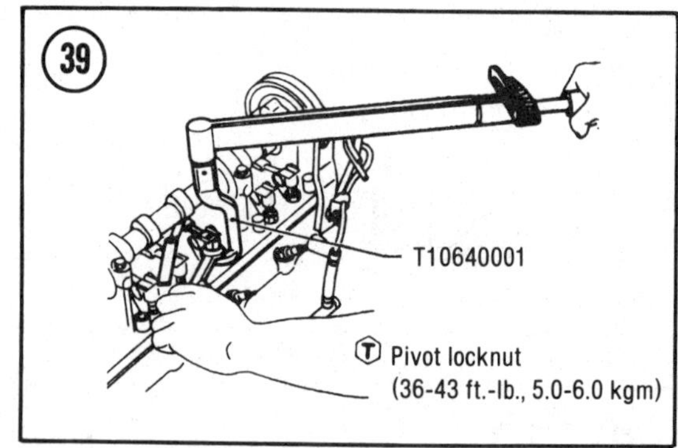

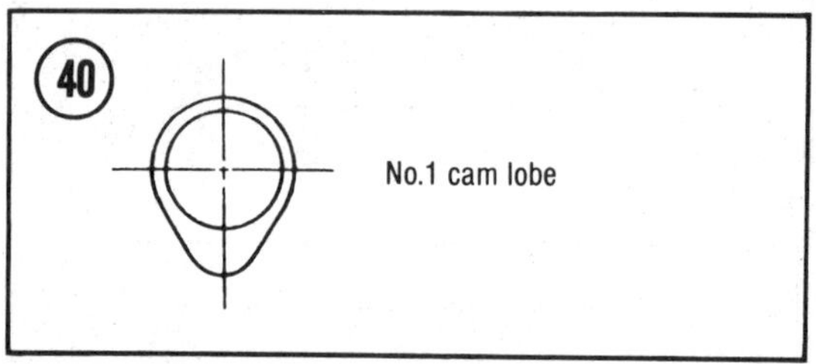

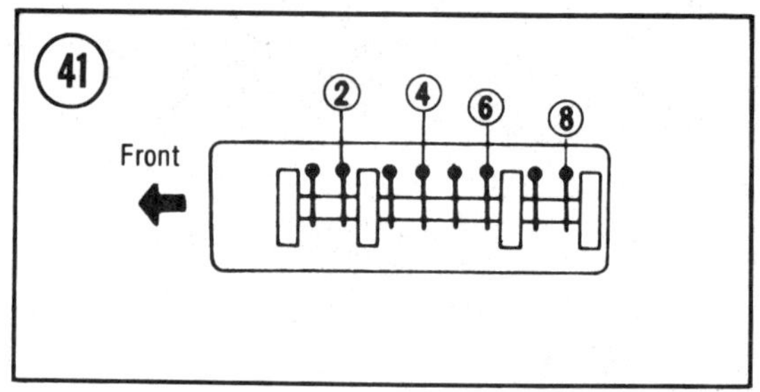

NOTE
Valves 5 and 8 are intake valves; valves 2 and 3 are exhaust valves.

11. Install the rocker arm cover.

SPARK PLUGS

On 1970-1979 trucks and 1980 Canadian models, spark plugs should be replaced at each tune-up. On all other models, spark plugs should be replaced at alternate tune-ups (every 30,000 miles or 2 years).

Removal

1. Blow out any foreign matter from around spark plugs with compressed air. Use a compressor if you have one. If not, most household vacuum cleaners can be set up to blow air. When most of the outlet is blocked with fingers, enough pressure is created to

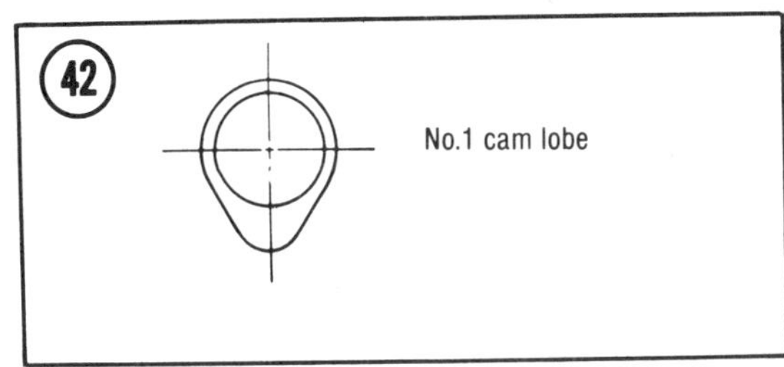

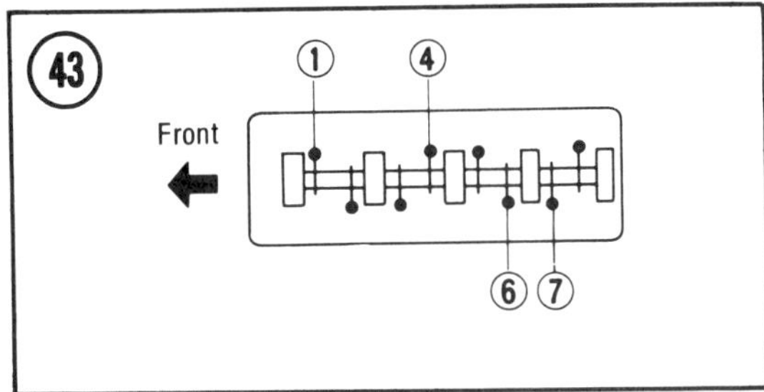

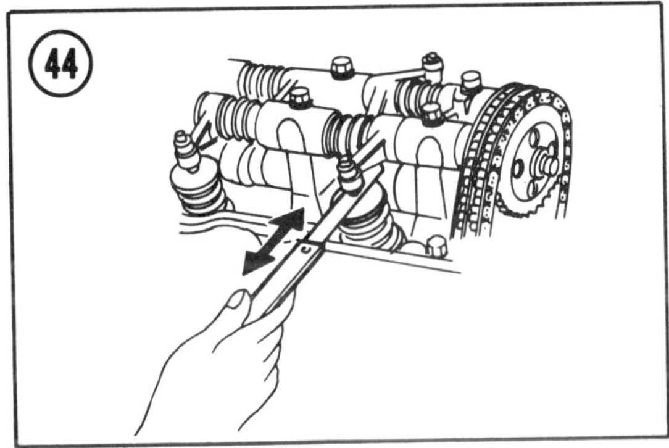

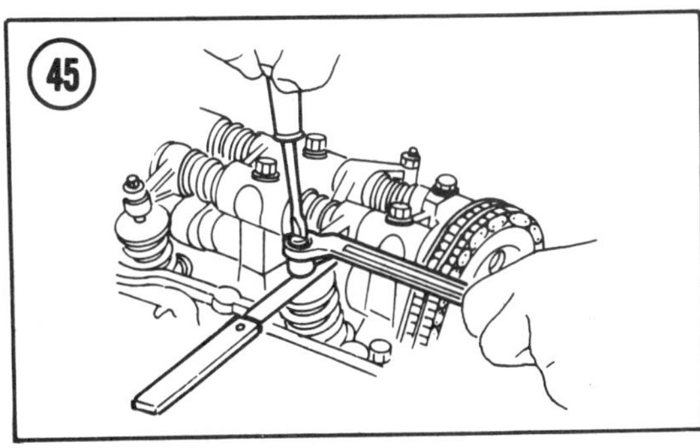

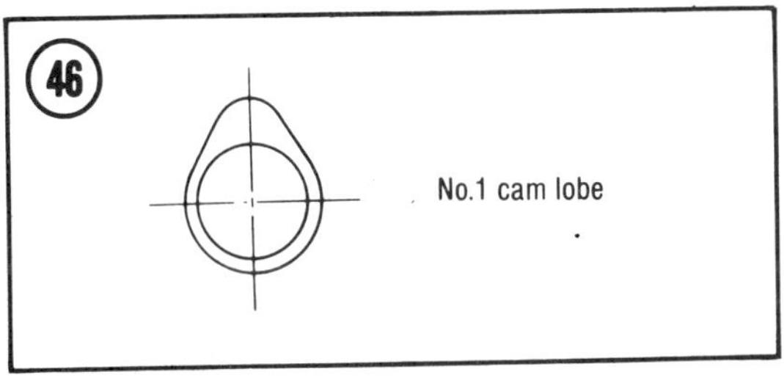

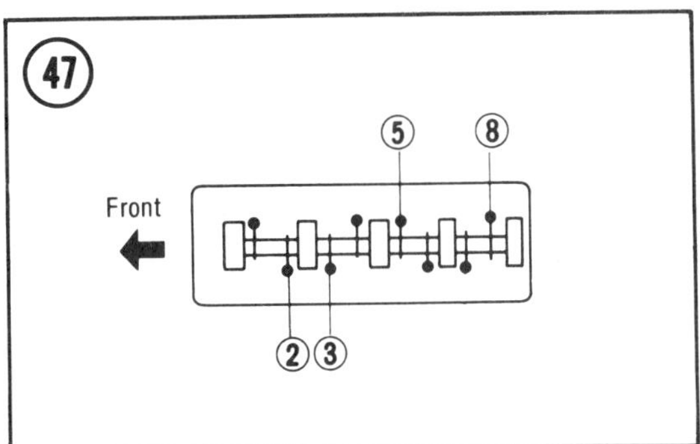

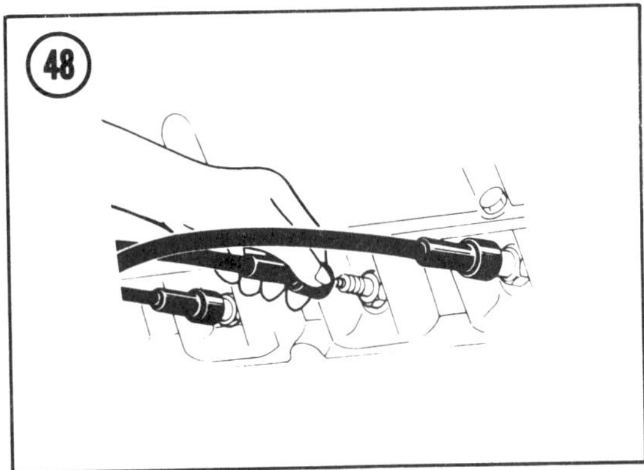

blow dirt away. Another method is to use a can of compressed inert gas, available from photo stores.

CAUTION

When spark plugs are removed, dirt from around the plugs can fall into the spark plug holes. This can cause expensive engine damage.

2. Mark spark plug wires with the cylinder numbers so you can reconnect them properly. Cylinders are numbered from front to rear of the engine.

NOTE

To make labels, wrap a small strip of masking tape around each wire.

3. Disconnect spark plug wires. Pull off by grasping the connector, *not* the wire. See **Figure 48**. Pulling on the wire may break it.

NOTE

If the boots seem to be stuck, twist them 1/2 turn to break the seal. Do not pull on boots with pliers. The pliers could cut the insulation, causing an electrical short.

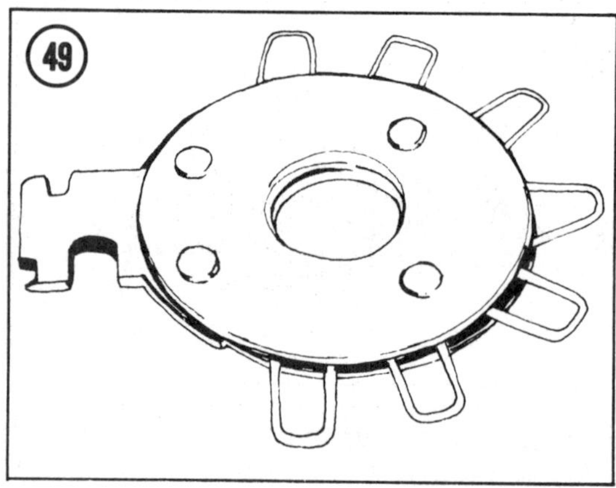

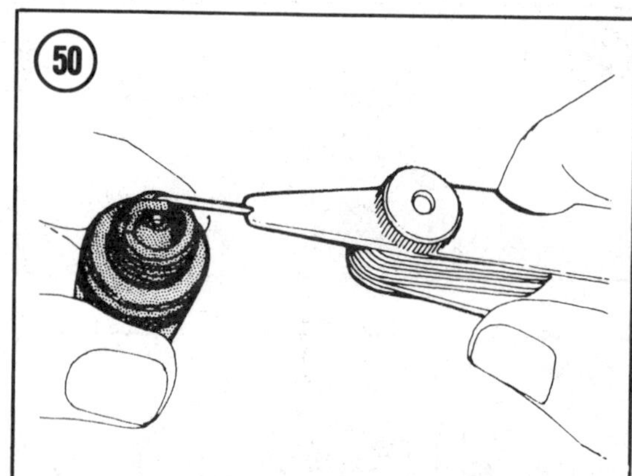

4. Remove the plugs with a 13/16 in. spark plug socket. Keep the plugs in order so you know which cylinder they came from.
5. Examine each spark plug. Compare its condition with the illustrations in Chapter Two. Spark plug condition indicates engine condition, and can warn of developing trouble.
6. Discard the plugs. Although they could be cleaned, regapped, and reused if in good condition, they seldom last very long; new plugs are inexpensive and far more reliable.

Gapping and Installing the Plugs

New plugs should be carefully gapped to ensure a reliable, consistent spark. Use a special spark plug tool with a wire gauge. See **Figure 49** or **Figure 50**.

1. Remove the plugs from the boxes. See if the small end pieces (**Figure 51**) are screwed on. If not, install them.
2. Find the correct spark plug gap for your truck in **Table 12**. Insert the correct diameter wire gauge between the spark plug electrodes. See **Figure 50**. If the gap is correct, there will be a slight drag as the wire is pulled through. If there is no drag, or if the wire won't pull through, bend the side electrode with the gapping tool (**Figure 52**) to change the gap.
3. Put a small drop of oil on the threads of each spark plug.
4. Crank the starter for about 5 seconds to blow away any dirt around the spark plug holes.
5. Screw each plug in by hand until it seats. Very little effort is required. If force is necessary, the plug is cross-threaded. Unscrew it and try again.

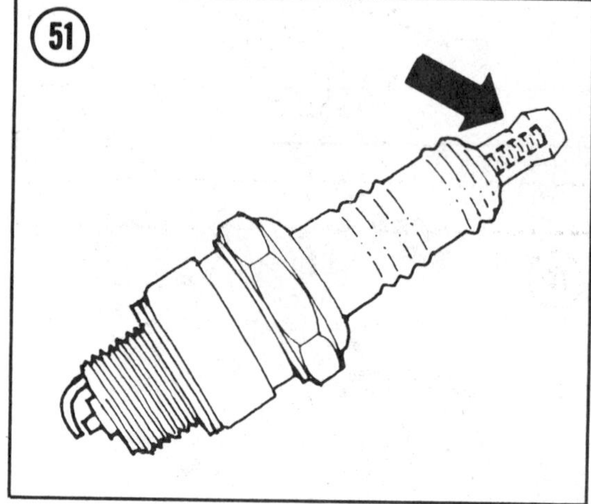

6. Tighten the spark plugs. If you have a torque wrench, tighten to 1.5-2.0 mkg (11-14 ft.-lb.). If not, tighten the plug with fingers, then tighten an additional 1/4-1/2 turn with the plug wrench.

CAUTION

Do not overtighten. This prevents the plugs from seating.

DISTRIBUTOR CAP, WIRES, AND ROTOR

On 1970-1980 models, the cap, wires, and rotor should be inspected at each tune-up. On 1981 models, the inspection should be done at alternate tune-ups (every 30,000 miles or 2 years).

1. Pry back the distributor cap clips and remove the cap.

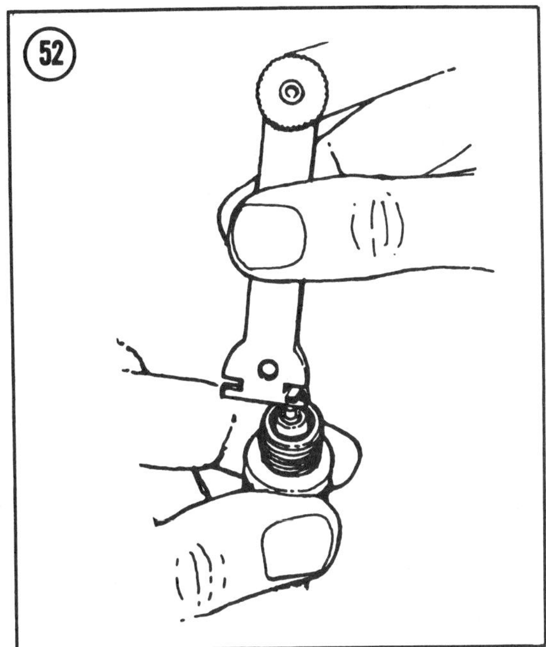

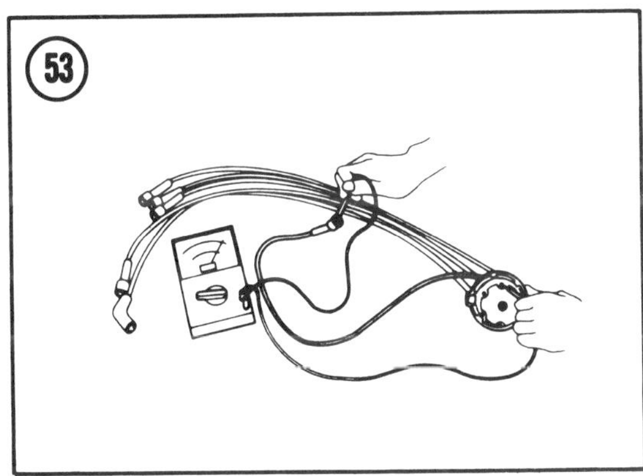

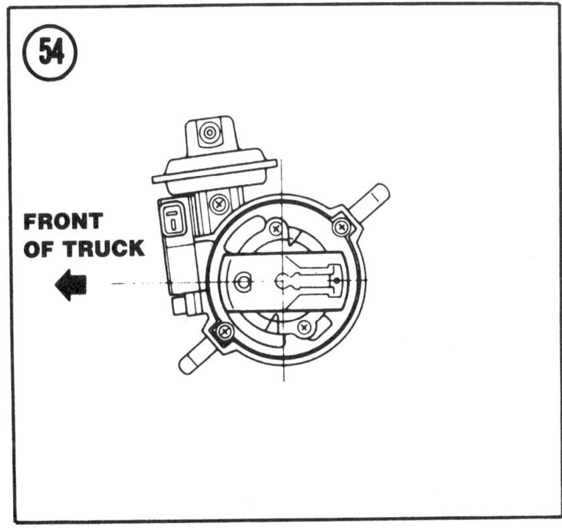

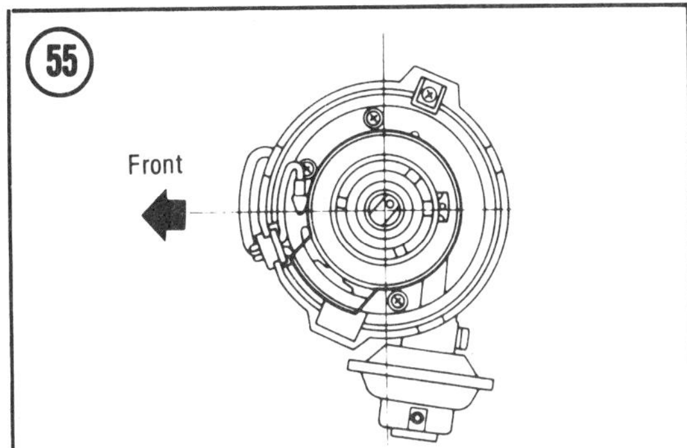

2. If you have an ohmmeter, connect it between each wire end and distributor cap terminal (**Figure 53**). Resistance should be less than 30,000 ohms. If it is higher, remove the wire and test it separately. If resistance is still too high, replace the wire. If not, replace the distributor cap.

If you don't have an ohmmeter, check the distributor cap terminals for dirt or corrosion. Clean or replace as needed.

Replace the wires if the insulation is melted, brittle, or cracked.

3. Check the rotor for burns, cracks, or wear. Replace it if these conditions can be seen.

4. Install the rotor. Install the distributor cap and reconnect the wires. Be sure they are connected to the right terminals. Terminals are numbered counterclockwise, in the following order: 1, 3, 4, 2. **Figure 54** shows the rotor pointing to No. 1 terminal on 1970-1980 models; **Figure 55** shows the rotor pointing to No. 1 terminals on 1981 trucks.

BREAKER POINTS AND CONDENSER

Breaker point ignition is used on 1970-1977 non-California models and 1970-1975 California trucks.

1. Loosen the screw on the primary lead terminal(s). See **Figure 56** (single-point distributors) or **Figure 57** (dual-point distributors). Slide the points lead wire(s) off the terminal(s).

2. Remove 2 screws securing the points (2 screws from each point set on dual-point distributors). Carefully note how the points are positioned, then lift them out of the distributor. Install new points exactly as the old ones were.

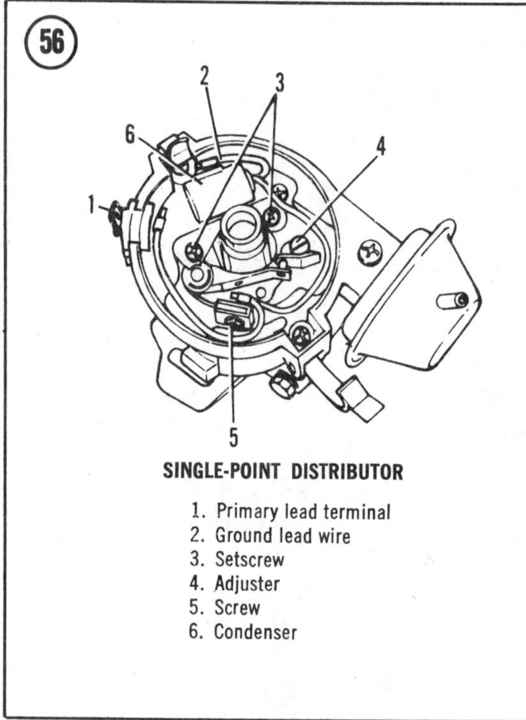

SINGLE-POINT DISTRIBUTOR

1. Primary lead terminal
2. Ground lead wire
3. Setscrew
4. Adjuster
5. Screw
6. Condenser

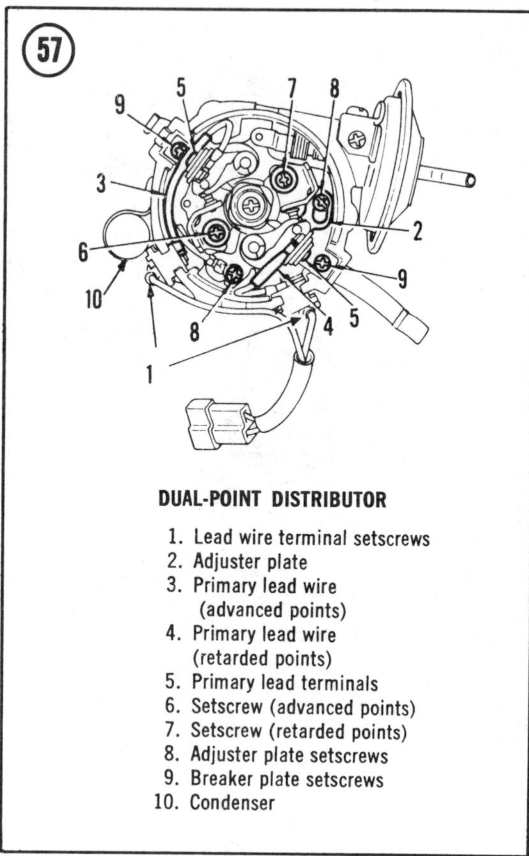

DUAL-POINT DISTRIBUTOR

1. Lead wire terminal setscrews
2. Adjuster plate
3. Primary lead wire (advanced points)
4. Primary lead wire (retarded points)
5. Primary lead terminals
6. Setscrew (advanced points)
7. Setscrew (retarded points)
8. Adjuster plate setscrews
9. Breaker plate setscrews
10. Condenser

3. Apply a *small* amount of distributor cam lubricant to the distributor cam lobes.
4. Remove the condenser and install a new one.
5. Using a crayon or felt pen, make alignment marks on the distributor body and engine. Then loosen the distributor fixing bolt and carefully turn the distributor by hand until a cam lobe opens the points to the maximum gap. Insert a feeler gauge in the gap (**Figure 58**) and adjust by turning the eccentric adjusting screw. On dual-point distributors, adjust both point sets in this manner.
6. After setting point gap, rotate the distributor back to its original position and tighten the fixing bolt.
7. Install the distributor rotor and cap. Be sure the spark plug and coil wires are connected properly.

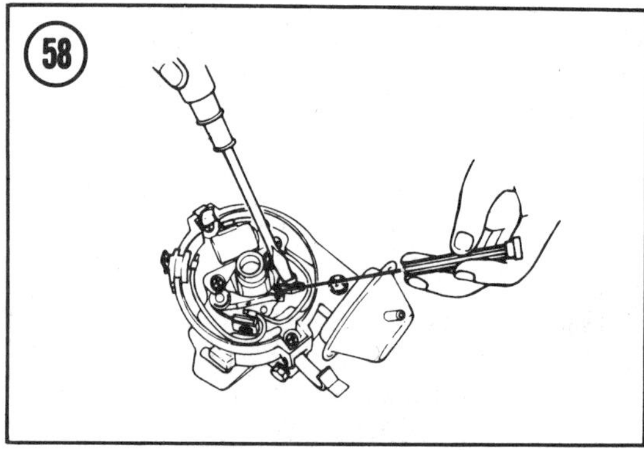

IGNITION TIMING

Single-Point and Breakerless Distributors

Ignition timing shuld be checked at each tune-up on 1970-1979 models, as well as on 1980 non-California trucks. Periodic ignition timing inspection is not required on 1980 California trucks or any 1981 models.

Ignition timing requires a stroboscopic timing light of the type described in Chapter One. Connect the light according to manufacturer's instructions.

1. Clean the crankshaft pulley and timing marks. Early L-series engines have timing marks on the crankshaft pulley and a pointer on the engine front cover (**Figure 59**).

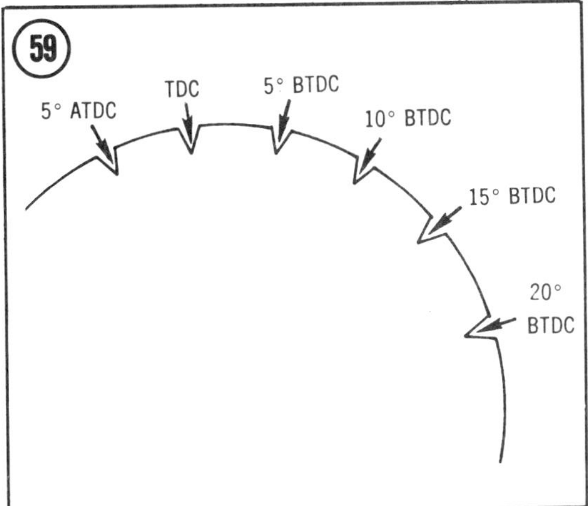

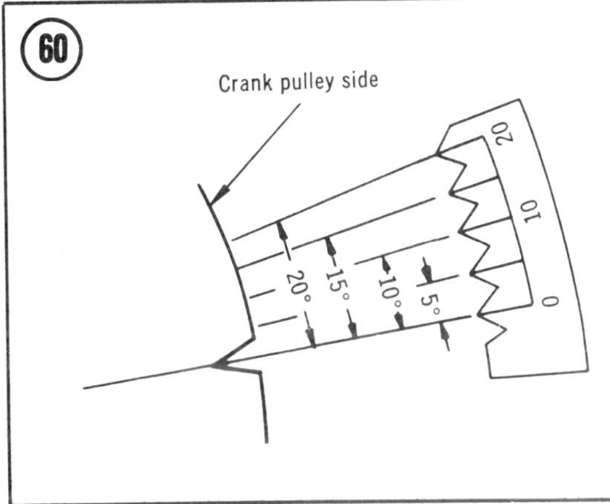

NOTE
Some early L-series engines do not have a 20° mark.

Late L-series engines have timing marks on the front cover and an indicator notch in the front pulley (**Figure 60** or **Figure 61**).

2. Find the correct timing setting in **Table 12**. Apply white paint to the mark and to the pointer or crankshaft pulley notch.

3. Disconnect the vacuum line from the distributor. Plug the line with tape.

4. Start the engine. If necessary, adjust idle speed to specifications (**Table 12**). Loosen the distributor fixing bolt (**Figure 62**) and turn the distributor until the correct timing mark aligns with the timing pointer. Tighten the fixing bolt, shut the engine off, and reconnect the vacuum line.

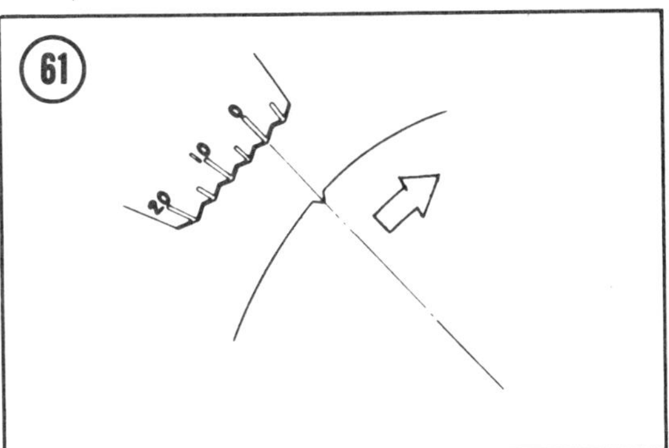

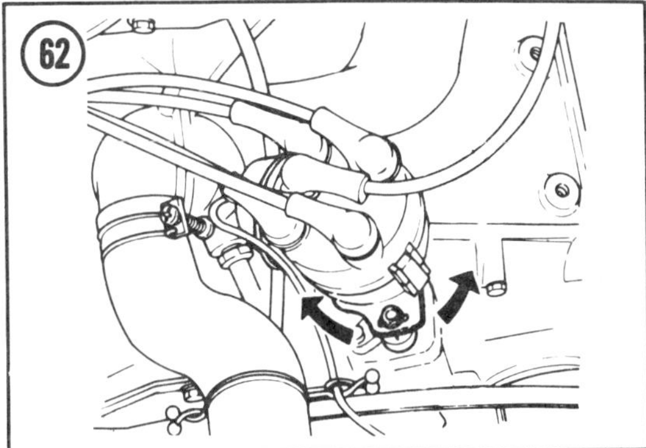

Ignition Timing (Dual-point Distributors)

1. Clean the crankshaft pulley and timing marks. Early engines have timing marks on the crankshaft pulley and a timing pointer on the front cover (**Figure 59**). Late L-series engines have timing marks on the front cover and an indicator notch in the crankshaft pulley (**Figure 60** or **Figure 61**).

2. Find the correct advanced and retarded timing settings in **Table 12**. Apply chalk or paint to the corresponding timing marks. Use different colors so the marks can be told apart under the timing light.

3. Disconnect the vacuum line from the distributor. Plug the line with tape.

4. Start the engine. Compare idle speed with **Table 12** and adjust if necessary.

5. On 1970-1972 models, advanced points should function when engine is warm and idling. To check this, detach wire from retarded points terminal. The terminal, on the side of the distributor, is farther from the vertically mounted condenser than the advanced points terminal.

If the engine keeps running, the advanced points are functioning. If it dies, test the spark timing control system (Chapter Eight).

6. On 1973 models, the retarded points normally function with the engine warm and idling. To set timing, however, the advanced points must be made to function. To do this, disconnect the wiring connector from the distributor harness. Connect a jumper wire as shown in **Figure 63**.

7. Point the timing light at the crankshaft pulley and check the advanced timing setting. If necessary, loosen the distributor fixing bolt and rotate the distributor to change timing. Then tighten the setscrew.

8. On 1970-1972 models, disconnect the wire from the advanced points terminal on the side of the distributor. This is the terminal closest to the vertically mounted condenser. Connect a jumper wire from the disconnected wire to the retarded points terminal (farthest from the condenser). This will cause retarded points to function. Engine speed should drop 100-150 rpm.

9. On 1973 models, disconnect the jumper wire (**Figure 63**) from the *distributor* side of the wiring connector. Connect the jumper wire to the other terminal in distributor side of connector. This causes the retarded points to function.

10. Point the timing light at the crankshaft pulley. Timing should be at the retarded setting specified in **Table 12**. If it is, no further steps are necessary.

11. If retarded timing is incorrect, adjust the position of the retarded breaker points.

NOTE

Adjust the point position, not point gap.

To adjust, loosen the adjuster plate setscrews. **Figure 63** shows the screws on a 1973 distributor; earlier models are the same. Insert a screwdriver in the adjusting slot (**Figure 64**) and twist it to change phase difference (the difference between advanced and retarded settings). Twisting the screwdriver clockwise increases phase difference (retards retarded timing). Twisting it counterclockwise decreases phase difference (advances retarded timing).

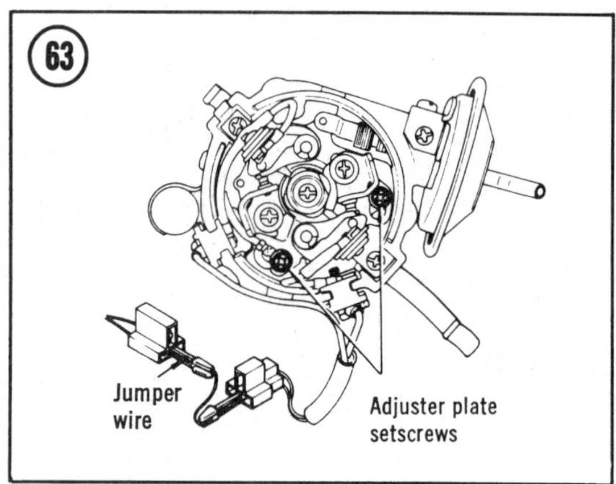

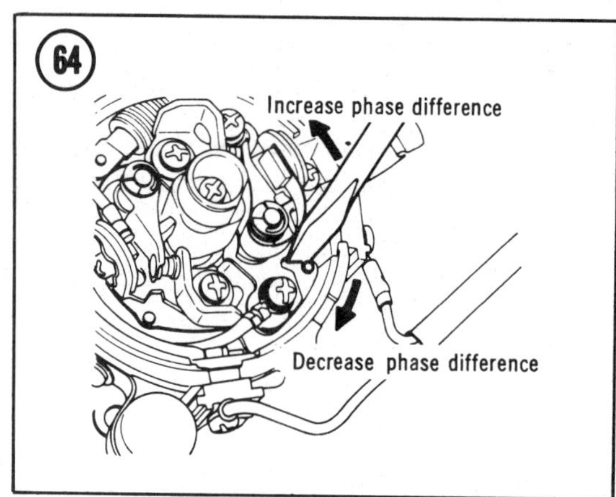

To gauge the adjustment, refer to the graduations on the breaker plate (**Figure 65**). Each graduation represents a 4° change in ignition timing (measured at the crankshaft pulley).

12. Once the retarded timing is set properly, recheck advanced timing as described in Steps 4-7. If it is incorrect, repeat Steps 8-11.

CARBURETOR ADJUSTMENT

1970-1972 L-Series Engines

1. Remove the air cleaner. Connect an accurate tune-up tachometer to the engine.

2. Warm the engine to normal operating temperature. Run it at 2,000 rpm for 15 seconds, then let it idle for one minute.

3. Set idle speed at 750 rpm. **Figure 66** shows the idle speed and mixture screws on an automatic choke carburetor. The screws are the same on manual choke carburetors.

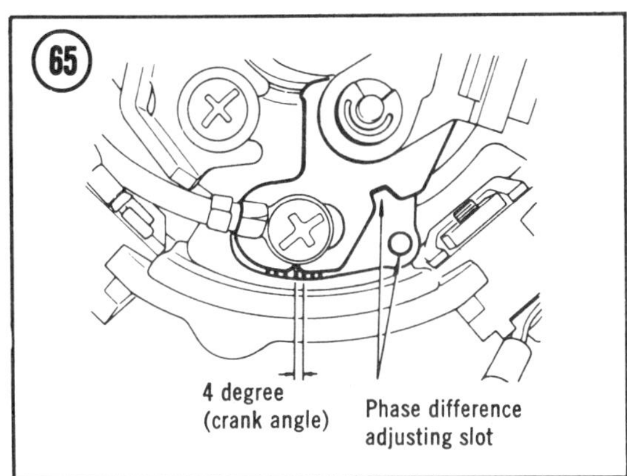

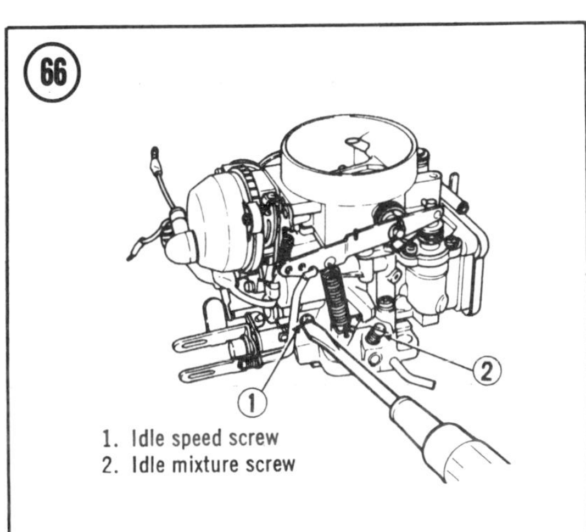

4. Adjust the idle mixture screw to obtain the smoothest possible idle. If necessary, rest idle speed to 750 rpm.
5. Turn the idle mixture screw clockwise (for a leaner mixture) until idle speed drops to 700 rpm.

1973-1974 L-Series Engines

Datsun recommends using a CO meter to adjust the idle on 1973-1974 engines. Although it is possible to adjust the carburetor without the CO meter, the instrument is necessary to ensure that exhaust emissions are within legal limits.

1. Remove the air cleaner and connect an accurate tune-up tachometer to the engine.
2. Warm the engine to normal operating temperature, then let it idle for one minute.
3. Set engine speed at 800 rpm. **Figure 66** shows the idle speed and mixture screws.

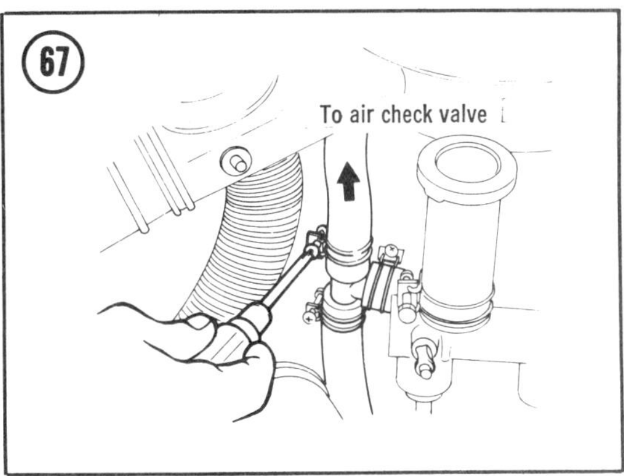

4. Place automatic transmission in DRIVE.
5. Using the idle mixture screw, set CO percentage at 1.5 percent. If a CO meter is not available, turn the mixture screw as far clockwise (lean) as possible without roughening the idle. This method should not be used unless absolutely necessary and results should be checked on a CO meter as soon as possible.
6. Check engine speed. It should be 800 rpm in NEUTRAL. Adjust if necessary.
7. On automatic transmissions, shift to DRIVE. Engine speed should drop to 650 rpm.

1975-1977 L-Series Engines

Datsun recommends the use of a CO meter to set idle mixture. While mixture can be set without a CO meter, the instrument is necessary to ensure that exhaust emissions are within legal limits.

1. Disconnect the air hose from the check valve (**Figure 67**).
2. Warm the engine to normal operating temperature, then connect a tune-up tachometer.
3. Race the engine 2 or 3 times at 1,500-2,000 rpm.
4. On automatic transmissions, block the wheels so the car can't roll forward, then shift to DRIVE.
5. Set idle speed at 750 rpm (manual transmission) or 650 rpm (automatic). **Figure 66** shows the idle speed and mixture screws.
6. If a CO meter is available, set CO percentage at 1-3 per cent. Do this by turning the idle mixture screw. If this adjustment

changes idle speed, reset it with the idle speed screw. Then race the engine 2 or 3 times at 1,500-2,000 rpm and check CO percentage.

7. If a CO meter is not available, set idle speed at 815 rpm (manual transmission) or 670 rpm (automatic). Adjust with the idle speed screw. Then turn the idle mixture screw to obtain the fastest smooth idle. Reset idle speed to 815 rpm (manual) or 670 rpm (automatic) with the idle speed screw. Then turn the idle *mixture* screw clockwise until engine speed drops by 60-70 rpm (manual) or 15-25 rpm (automatic).

8. Reconnect the air hose to the check valve. If engine speed increases, reset it with the idle speed screw.

1978-1979 L-Series Engines

On California models, a CO meter is required. On non-California models, the carburetor can be adjusted without a CO meter in the same manner as 1975-1977 models. In Step 7, set idle speed at 650 in NEUTRAL for manual transmissions; 650 rpm in DRIVE for 1978 automatics; and 630 rpm in DRIVE for 1979 automatics. Then turn the mixture screw clockwise until engine speed drops to 595-605 rpm.

1980 L-Series Engines

1. Warm the engine until the instrument panel temperature needle points to the middle of the gauge.
2. Open the hood. Run the engine at approximately 2,000 rpm for about 5 minutes.
3. Let the engine idle for 10 minutes. During this time, disconnect and plug the air injection or air induction hose. On 49-state standard models, disconnect and plug the distributor vacuum hose (**Figure 68**).

NOTE

Standard models include all trucks without the letter "E" in their vehicle identification number. Refer to the number plate in the engine compartment.

4. Race the engine 2 or 3 times, then let it idle for one minute.
5. Check idle speed. It should be 600+/-100 rpm (manual transmissions in NEUTRAL; automatics in DRIVE). Adjust if necessary by turning the idle speed screw (**Figure 69**).
6. Check ignition timing on the timing scale (**Figure 70**). It should be 12+/-2° on before top dead center on all except U.S. heavy duty models. On U.S. heavy duty models, it should be 10+/-2° BTDC.

NOTE

Heavy duty models are designated by the letter "E" in their vehicle identification number. Refer to the number plate in the engine compartment.

7. If ignition timing is incorrect, shut off the engine. Loosen the distributor lockbolt (**Figure 71**) and turn the distributor to change timing. Tighten the lockbolt, start the engine, and recheck the adjustment. Readjust if necessary.

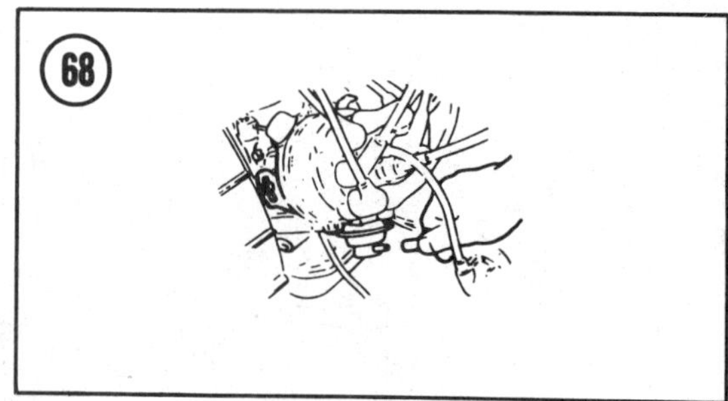

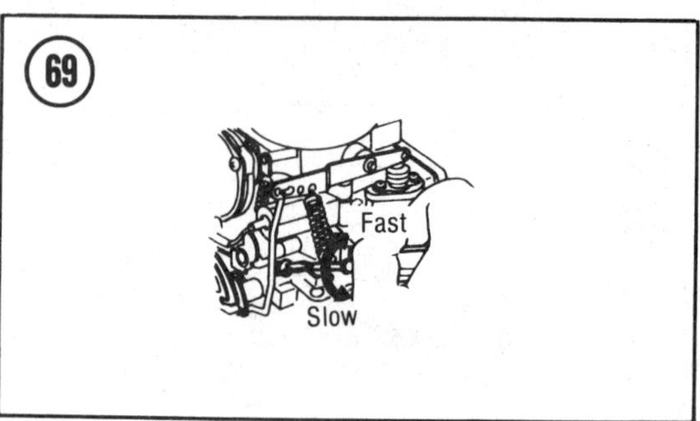

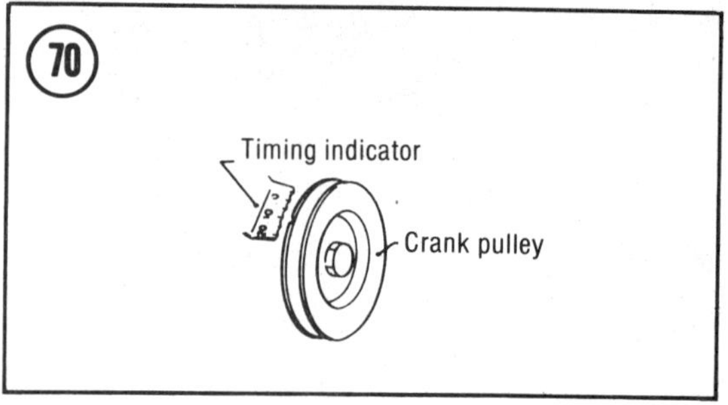

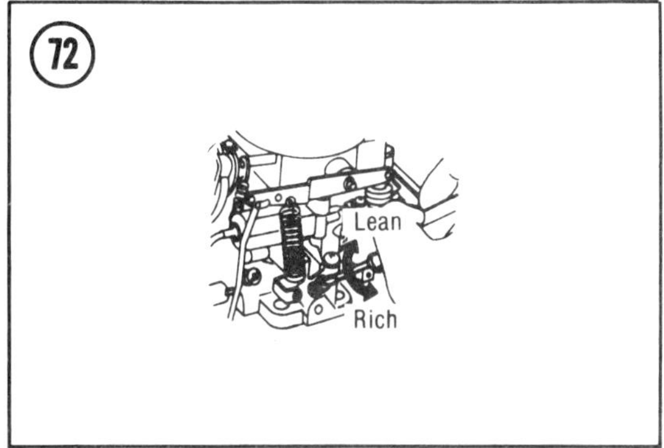

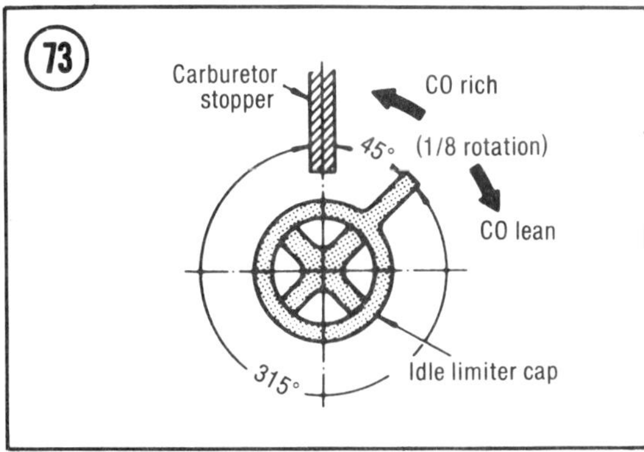

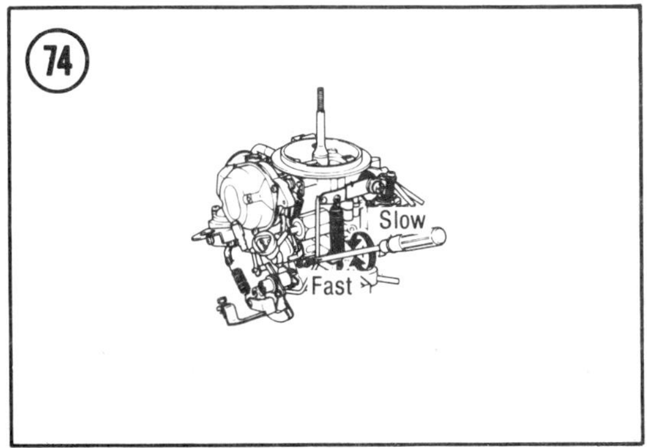

WARNING

Never touch the distributor's thick wires with the engine running. This can cause a painful shock, even if the insulation is in perfect condition.

8. Race the engine 2 or 3 times, then let it idle.
9. Check CO percentage with the CO meter. It should range from 0.3 to 2.0 per cent, with 1.0 per cent preferred. Adjust if necessary by turning the idle mixture screw (**Figure 72**). The mixture screw has a stopper and limiter cap (**Figure 73**) to prevent overrich settings.

NOTE

If you don't have a CO meter, turn the mixture screws as far clockwise as possible without causing a rough idle. Have CO percentage checked on a CO meter as soon as possible.

10. Reconnect the air injection or induction hose. On 49-state standard models, reconnect the distributor vacuum advance line.

1981 NAPS-Z Engines

Idle speed should be adjusted at each tune-up on non-California models. Periodic idle speed adjustment is not required on California models. Idle mixture is not adjustable on any 1981 truck.

1. Warm the engine to normal operating temperature.
2. After the engine is warm, run the engine at 2,000 rpm for 2 minutes with the hood open.
3. Check idle speed. Compare with **Table 12**.
4. If necessary, adjust idle speed with the idle speed screw (**Figure 74**).

Table 1 ROUTINE CHECKS

Interval	Item	Procedure
Fuel stop	Engine oil	Check level
	Coolant	Check level
	Battery electrolyte	Check level
	Windshield washers	Check container level
	Brake fluid	Check level
	Clutch fluid	Check level
	Tire pressures	Check

Table 2 SCHEDULED MAINTENANCE, 1970-1973

Service	Months or Thousands of Miles 3	6	12	24	30	36
Engine oil	X					
Manual transmission oil	X					
Automatic transmission fluid	X					
Differential oil	X					
Hydraulic systems	X					
Fuel lines			X			
Carburetor	X					
Engine leak inspection		X				
Drive belts		X				
Throttle cables		X				
Choke mechanism		X				
Steering linkage, suspension	X					
Hinges, latches, locks		X				
PCV system			X			
Evaporative emission control system			X			
Cooling system			X			
Vacuum lines			X			
ATC air cleaner			X			
Fuel filter*			X			
Spark timing control system*			X			
Boost controlled deceleration device			X			
Brake fluid				X		
Brake booster (power brakes)			X			
Battery			X			
Brake inspection			X			
Shock absorbers			X			
Drive shaft			X			
Wheel alignment			X			
Pedals			X			
Engine compression			X			
Coolant				X		
Air cleaner element				X		
Air injection system				X		
Handbrake linkage			X			
Wheel bearings			X			
Manual transmission					X	
Differential					X	
Headlights					X	
Drive shaft					X	
Minor Tune-up	X					
Major Tune-up			X			

*24,000 miles on 1973 models.

Table 3 SCHEDULED MAINTENANCE, 1974

Service	Months or Thousands of Miles 4	8	12	24	36
Engine oil	X				
Manual transmission oil	X				
Automatic transmission fluid	X				
Differential oil	X				
Hydraulic systems	X				
Fuel lines	X				
Engine leak inspection	X				
Drive belts			X		
Throttle cable		X			
Choke mechanism			X		
Steering linkage, suspension	X				
Hinges, latches, locks		X			
PCV system			X		
EGR system			X		
Evaporative emission control system			X		
Cooling system			X		
Vacuum lines			X		
ATC air cleaner			X		
Fuel filter				X	
*Boost controlled deceleration device					
Brake fluid			X		
Brake booster			X		
Battery		X			
Brake inspection			X		
Shock absorbers			X		
Drive shaft				X	
Wheel alignment		X			
Engine compression			X		
Coolant				X	
Air cleaner element				X	
Handbrake linkage		X			
Wheel bearings			X		
Manual transmission					X
Differential					X
Headlights					X
Major tune-up			X		

*See text for checking procedure

Table 4 SCHEDULED MAINTENANCE,1975-1977

Service	Thousands of Miles (Months) 6.25 (6)	12.5 (12)	25 (24)
Engine oil	X		
Manual transmission oil	X		
Automatic transmission fluid	X		
Differential oil	X		
Hydraulic systems	X		
Fuel lines	X		
Drive belts		X	
Choke mechanism		X	
Steering linkage, suspension	X		
Hinges, latches, locks	X		
PCV system		X	
EGR system		X	
Evaporative emission control system		X	
Cooling system		X	
Vacuum lines		X	
ATC air cleaner		X	
Fuel filter			X
Spark timing control system			X
Boost controlled deceleration device			
Brake fluid		X	
Brake booster(power brakes)		X	
Brake inspection		X	
Wheel alignment		X	
Coolant		X	
Air cleaner element			X
Load sensing valve	X		
Wheel bearings			X
Manual transmission			X
Differential			X
Major tune-up		X	

Table 5 SCHEDULED MAINTENANCE 1978-1979

Interval	Service
Every 7,500 miles (6 months)	• Engine oil and filter • Manual transmission oil • Automatic transmission fluid • Differential oil • Steering gear oil • Brakes • Hinges, latches, locks • Leak inspection
Every 15,000 miles (12 months)	• Drive belts • Coolant hoses and connections • Vacuum lines • Air cleaner • Choke plate and linkage • Brake fluid • Steering, suspension, and drive shaft • Wheels and tires • Tune-up
Every 30,000 miles (24 months)	• Coolant • Brakes and brake booster • Air filters • Fuel filter • Evaporative emission control system • PCV valve and filter • Ball-joints • Front wheel bearings • Manual transmission oil • Differential oil

Table 6 SCHEDULED MAINTENANCE 1980

Interval	Service
Every 7,500 miles (6 months)	• Engine oil and filter
Every 15,000 miles (24 months)	• Manual transmission oil • Differential oil • Automatic transmission fluid • Steering gear oil • Hinges, latches, locks • Leak inspection • Drive belts • Cooling system hoses and connections* • Vacuum lines* • Choke plate and linkage* • Brake fluid • Steering, suspension, and drive shaft • Wheels and tires • ATC air cleaner* • Tune-up
Every 30,000 miles (24 months)	• Coolant • Brake booster • Air filters • Fuel filter** • Evaporative emission control system • ATC air cleaner • Air induction valve filter • PCV system* • Front wheel bearings

*Canadian standard models only.

**Periodic replacement is required only on Canadian standard models. On U.S. models, and Canadian heavy duty trucks, replace the filter if it becomes clogged.

***All U.S. models and Canadian heavy duty trucks.

Table 7 SCHEDULED MAINTENANCE, 1981

Interval	Service
Every 7,500 miles (6 months)	Engine oil and filter
Every 15,000 miles (12 months)	Transmission oil level check Differential oil level check Brakes Leak inspection Drive belts Brake fluid Steering, suspension, and drive shaft Wheels and tires Hinges, latches, locks Tune-up
Every 30,000 miles (24 months)	Coolant Air cleaner element Air induction valve filter Evaporative emission control system Front wheel bearings

Table 8 LUBRICANT VISCOSITY

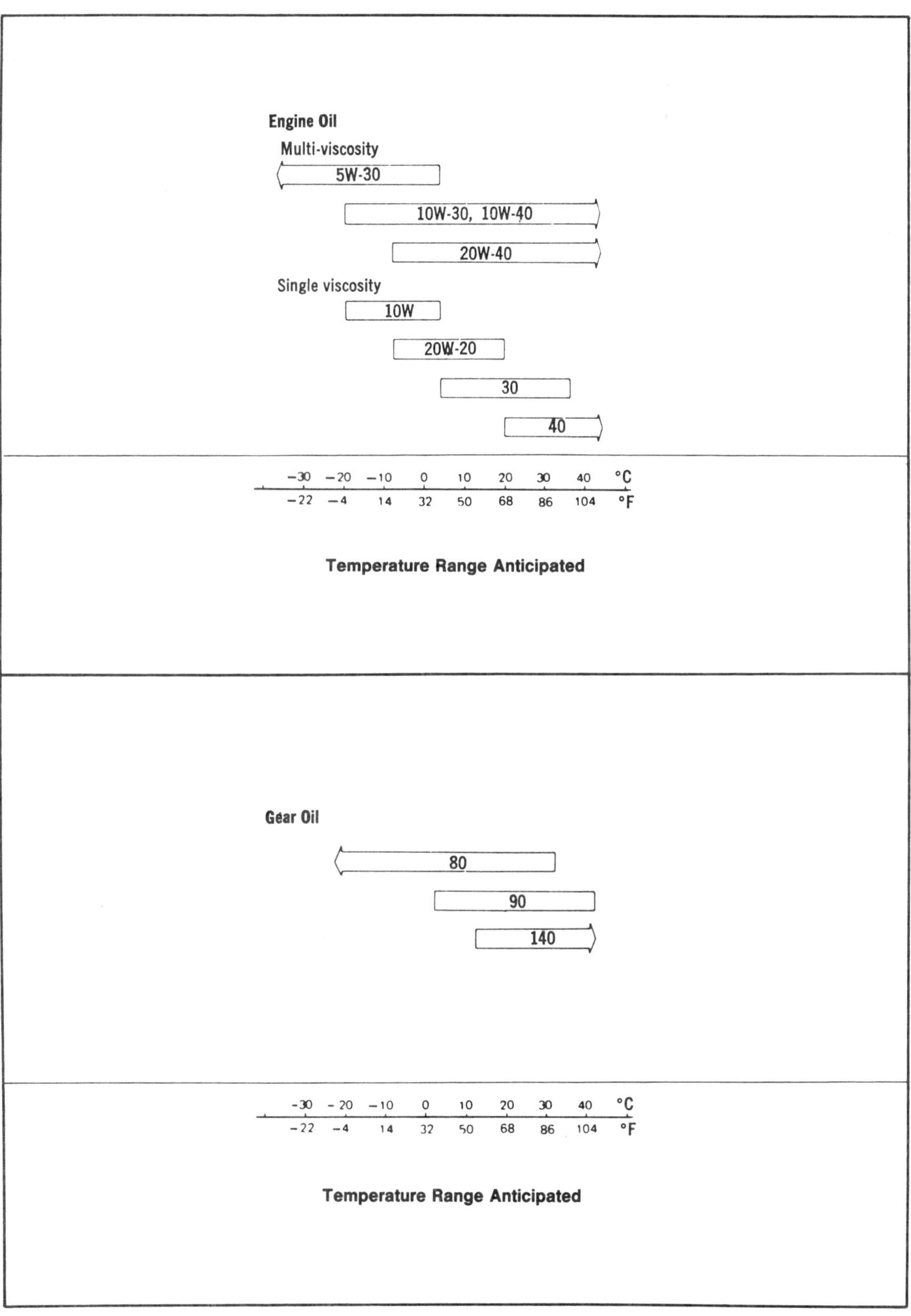

Table 9 RECOMMENDED LUBRICANTS

Engine	API Service SE OR SF		
Manual transmission	API GL-4	Differential	API GL-5
Automatic transmission	Dexron	Brake and clutch fluid	DOT 3

Table 10 TIRE PRESSURES

	Front	Rear
521 pickups		
Moderate load, under 60 mph	21	25
Heavy load, under 60 mph	21	42 (1)
Moderate load, more than 60 mph	26	29
Heavy load, more than 60 mph	26	46 (1)
620 pickups (1972-1978)		
Moderate load, under 60 mph	21	25 (2)
Heavy load, under 60 mph	21	42 (1, 2)
Moderate load, more than 60 mph	26	32 (2)
Heavy load, more than 60 mph	26	49 (1, 2, 3)
620 pickups (1979)		
6.00-14 6-ply rating		
Moderate load, under 60 mph	21	25
Heavy load, under 60 mph	21	42 (1)
Moderate load, over 60 mph	26	32
Heavy load, over 60 mph	26	45 (1)
185SR-14		
Moderate load	24	24
Heavy load	24	31
E78-14 8-ply rating		
Moderate load	26	39
Heavy load	26	60 (1)
720 pickups		
7.00-14		
Moderate load	22	22
Heavy load	22	32
185SR-14		
Moderate load	24	24
Heavy load	24	32
195SR-14		
Moderate load	24	24
Heavy load	24	28
E78-14LT		
Moderate load	26	40
Heavy load	26	60 (1)

1. Do not exceed the maximum pressure molded in the tire sidewall.
2. On 1975 trucks with 8-ply rating tires, increase rear pressures 14 psi for moderate loads and 18 psi for heavy loads.
3. 45 psi on 1976-1978 models.

Table 11 APPROXIMATE REFILL CAPACITIES

Engine oil		Cooling system	
1970-1973 and 1975-1980		521 pickup	7 qt. (6.6 liters)
With filter change	4 1/2 qt. (4.3 liters)		
Without filter change	4 qt. (3.8 liters)	620 pickup	
1974			
With filter change	5 1/8 qt. (4.8 liters)	1972-1974	6 3/8 qt. (6.0 liters)
Without filter change	4 3/8 qt. (4.1 liters)	1975-1977 (manual)	8 1/2 qt. (8 liters)
1981		1975-1977 (automatic)	8 1/4 qt. (7.8 liters)
With filter change	4 5/8 qt. (4.4 liters)	1978-1979 manual (including	
Without filter change	4 1/8 qt. (3.9 liters)	reservoir tank)	9 3/8 qt. (8.9 liters)
		1978-1979 automatic (including	
Manual transmission oil		reservoir tank)	9 1/8 qt. (8.7 liters)
1970-1973	2 1/8 qt. (2.0 liters)		
1974 and later 4-speed	3 5/8 pt. (1.7 liters)	720 pickup	
1977 and later 5-speed	4 1/4 pt. (2 liters)		
		1980 manual (including	
Automatic transmission fluid	5 7/8 qt. (5.5 liters)	reservoir tank)	9 3/8 qt. (8.9 liters)
		1980 automatic (including	
		reservoir tank)	9 1/8 qt. (8.9 liters)
Differential oil		1981 manual (including	
521 pickup	1 3/4 pt. (0.8 liter)	reservoir tank)	10 3/4 qt. (10.2 liters)
620 pickup	2 1/8 pt. (1.0 liter)	1981 automatic (including	
720 pickup	2 5/8 pt. (1.25 liters)	reservoir tank)	10 5/8 qt. (10.1 liters)

Table 12 TUNE-UP SPECIFICATIONS

Compression pressure	
Standard	**171 psi (12 kg/cm^2)**
Minimum	**128 psi (9 kg/cm^2)**
Valve clearance	
L-series engines	
Intake, hot	**0.010 in. (0.25 mm)**
Exhaust, hot	**0.012 in. (0.30 mm)**
Intake, cold	**0.008 in. (0.20 mm)**
Exhaust, cold	**0.010 in. (0.25 mm)**
NAPS-Z engine	
Intake, hot	**0.012 in. (0.30 mm)**
Exhaust, hot	**0.012 in. (0.30 mm)**
Intake, cold	**0.008 in. (0.21 mm)**
Exhaust, cold	**0.009 in. (0.23 mm)**
Firing order	**1-3-4-2**
Distributor rotation	**Counterclockwise**
Spark plug type (NGK brand)	
1970-1971	**BP6E**
1972	**BP5ES**
1973-1974	**B6ES**
1975-1976	**BP6ES**
1977 California, all 1978	
Standard type	**BP6ES-11**
Hot type	**BP4E-11, BP5ES-11**
Cold type	**BP7ES-11**

(continued)

Table 12 TUNE-UP SPECIFICATIONS (continued)

1977 non-California	
Standard type	BP6ES-11
Hot type	BP4E, BP5ES
Cold type	BP7ES
1979	
Standard type	BP6ES-11, BPR63S-11*
Hot type	BP4E-11, BP5ES-11, BPR4E-11*, BPR5ES-11*
Cold type	BP7ES-11, BPR7ES-11*
1980 U.S.	
Standard type	BP6ES-11, BPR6ES-11*
Hot type	BP4ES-11, BP5ES-11, BPR4ES-11,* BPR5ES-11*
Cold type	BP7ES-11, BPR7ES-11*
1980 Canada	
Standard type	BPR6ES
Hot type	BPR4ES, BPR5ES
Cold type	BPR7ES
1981 U.S.	
Standard type	BP6ES, BPR6ES*
Hot type	BP5ES, BPR5ES*
Cold type	BP7ES, BPR7ES*
1981 Canada	
Standard type	BPR6ES
Hot type	BPR5ES
Cold type	BPR7ES
Spark plug gap	
1970-1972	0.031-0.035 in. (0.8-0.9 mm)
1973-1974	0.028-0.031 in. (0.7-0.8 mm)
1975 California, 1975-1977 non-California	0.031-0.035 in. (0.8-0.9 mm)
1976-1977 California	0.039-0.043 in. (1.0-1.1 mm)
1978-1979	0.039-0.043 in. (1.0-1.1 mm)
1980	
U.S.	0.039-0.043 in. (1.0-1.1 mm)
Canada	0.031-0.035 in. (0.8-0.9 mm)
1981	0.031-0.035 in. (0.8-0.9 mm)
Points gap (breaker point ignition)	0.018-0.022 in. (0.45-0.55 mm)
Dwell angle (breaker point ignition)	49-55°
Ignition timing (at idle speed,° BTDC)	
1970-1971 (advanced)	10
1970-1971 (retarded)	0 (top dead center)
1972 (advanced)	7
1972 (retarded)	0 (top dead center)
1973 (advanced)	12
1973 (retarded)	
Through chassis No. PL620-141296	5
From chassis No. PL620-141297	8
1974	12
1975-1977	
California	10
Non-California	12
1978-1979	12

(continued)

Table 12 TUNE-UP SPECIFICATIONS (continued)

1980	
California	
Standard**	12 ±2
Heavy duty**	10 ±2
49-state	12 ±2
Canada	
Standard**	12
Heavy duty**	12 ±2
1981	5 ±2
Idle speed	
1970-1972	700 rpm
1973-1974	
Manual	800 rpm
Automatic	650 rpm in DRIVE
1975-1979	See text
1980	
All except Canadian standard models**	600 ±100 rpm (automatics in DRIVE)
Canadian standard models**	600 rpm (automatics in DRIVE)
1981-on	650 ±100 rpm (automatics in DRIVE)

* Optional resistor type.
** Heavy duty models include the letter "E" in the vehicle identification number. Standard models do not. King Cabs and long beds are standard models.

3

CHAPTER FOUR

L-SERIES ENGINE

All 1970-1980 models use versions of the Datsun L-series engine.

The L-series engine is an inline four with overhead cam. The camshaft, mounted in 4 brackets on top of the cylinder head, operates the valves through finger rockers. The crankshaft, supported by 5 main bearings, drives the camshaft through a double-row chain and 2 sprockets. The lubrication system consists of an external oil pump and full-flow filter.

The L16 engine, used through 1973, displaces 97.3 cu. in. (1595 cc). The L18, used in 1974, was bored to a displacement of 108.1 cu. in. (1770 cc). The L20B, used in 1975 and later, was stroked to 119.1 cu. in. (1952 cc). The specifications and tightening torques (**Table 1** and **Table 2**) are at the end of the chapter.

A few special tools are used in this chapter. All are available through your dealer. A few are manufactured by Kent-Moore Tool Division, 29784 Little Mack, Roseville, Michigan, 48066, and may be ordered directly from them.

ENGINE REMOVAL

Although it is possible to remove the engine separately from the transmission, it is much easier to remove engine and transmission as a single unit and separate them. Remove as follows.

1. Using a soft lead pencil, scribe alignment marks around the hood hinges onto the hood. Remove the hood. The marks will ease hood installation.
2. Disconnect negative cable from battery.
3. Completely drain the cooling system, then remove the radiator (Chapter Seven).
4. Remove the air cleaner (Chapter Six).
5. On 1970-1974 evaporative emission control systems, disconnect the hoses running from flow guide valve to intake manifold and air cleaner. See **Figure 1**.
6. On 1975 and later evaporative emission control systems, disconnect 2 hoses running from carbon canister to engine.
7. On 1975 and later models, disconnect hose running from air pump to air pump cleaner.
8. Disconnect the engine ground cable from the cylinder head. See **Figure 2**.

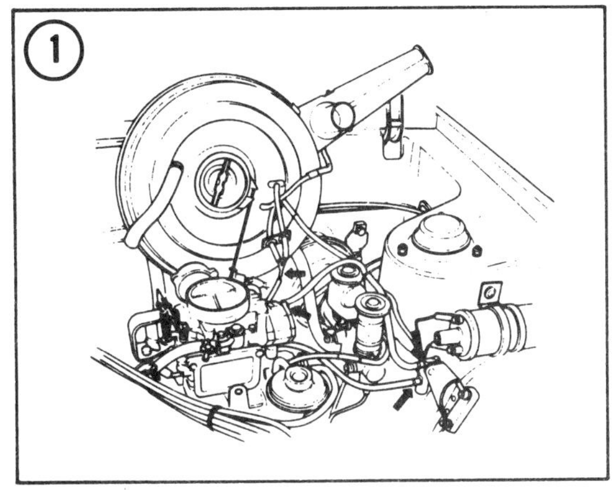

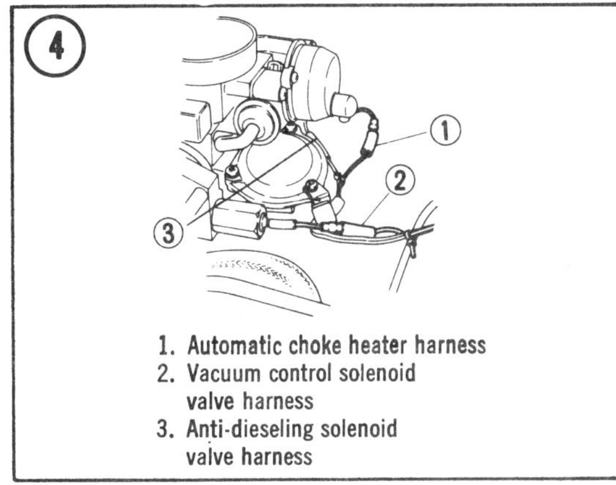

1. Automatic choke heater harness
2. Vacuum control solenoid valve harness
3. Anti-dieseling solenoid valve harness

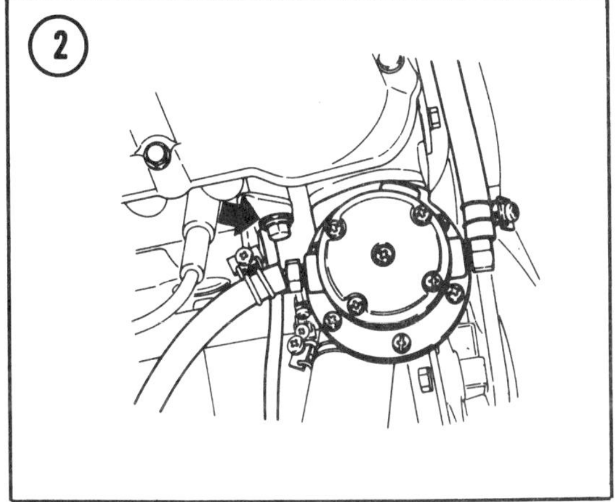

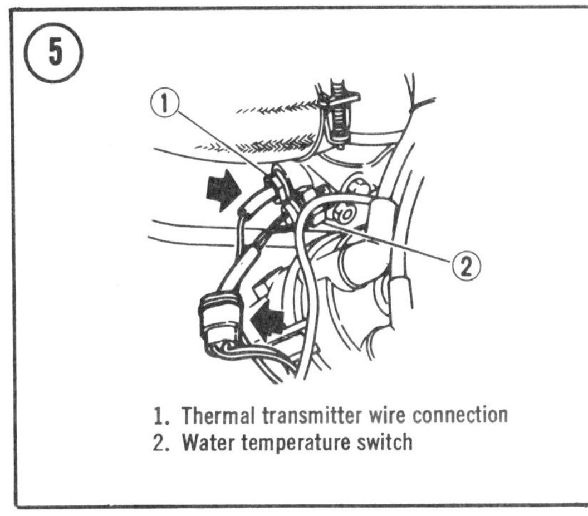

1. Thermal transmitter wire connection
2. Water temperature switch

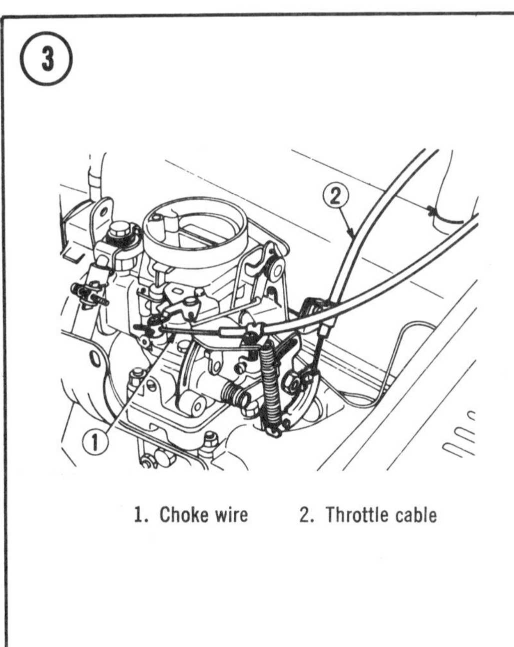

1. Choke wire 2. Throttle cable

9. Disconnect the heater hoses from the engine.

10. Disconnect the inlet line from the fuel pump. Plug the line so it won't siphon fuel from the tank.

11. Disconnect the throttle cable from the carburetor (**Figure 3**). On 1970-1971 trucks, disconnect the manual choke cable.

12. Disconnect the following wires (if so equipped): automatic choke heater, vacuum cutoff solenoid, and anti-dieseling solenoid. See **Figure 4**.

13. Disconnect the temperature switch wire(s) from the thermostat housing. See **Figure 5**. Disconnect the oil pressure sender wire from the right-hand side of the cylinder block, next to the oil filter.

14. On 1974 and later models, disconnect the EGR solenoid wire (**Figure 6**).

4

15. If equipped with power brakes, disconnect the brake booster vacuum hose (**Figure 7**).
16. Disconnect the wires (thick and thin) running from ignition coil to distributor.
17. Label and disconnect the alternator and starter wires.
18. Working in the passenger compartment, remove the console (if so equipped).
19. On manual transmissions, remove the shift lever. To do this on 1970-1973 models, unscrew the bottom nut (**Figure 8**) and lift the lever out. On 1974 and later models, remove the snap ring and pivot pin (**Figure 9**) and lift the lever out.
20. On automatic transmissions, disconnect the selector range lever from the manual shaft on the right-hand side of the transmission. See **Figure 10**.
21. Working beneath the truck, detach the speedometer cable from the transmission rear extension. Disconnect the wires from the electrical switch(es) on the right side of the transmission.
22. Remove the drive shaft (Chapter Twelve).
23. Drain the transmission oil or fluid. Otherwise it will run onto the floor during engine removal. On automatic transmissions, the transmission oil pan must be removed to drain the fluid.
24. On manual transmission models, unbolt the clutch operating cylinder from the transmission, then remove the cylinder and flexible hose as a unit. See Chapter Nine for details.
25. Unbolt the front exhaust pipe from the manifold.
26. On 1976 and later models, unbolt the idler arm bracket from the frame, then push the cross rod down. See Chapter Thirteen.
27. Remove 2 bolts (1, **Figure 11**) securing the transmission mounting bracket to the transmission.
28. Place a jack beneath the center of the transmission mounting bracket. Remove the 4 bolts (2, **Figure 11**) securing the bracket to the truck's frame.

NOTE
At this point, there should be no wires, hoses, or linkages attaching the engine or transmission to the vehicle. Recheck this

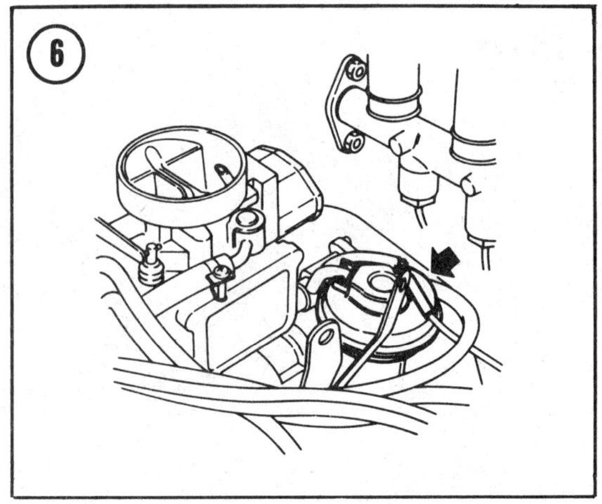

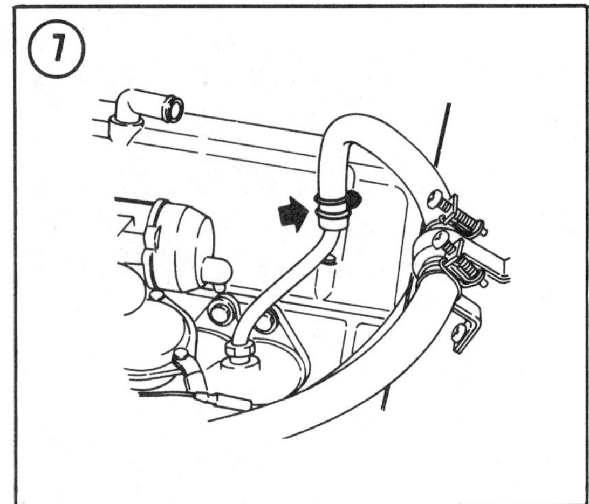

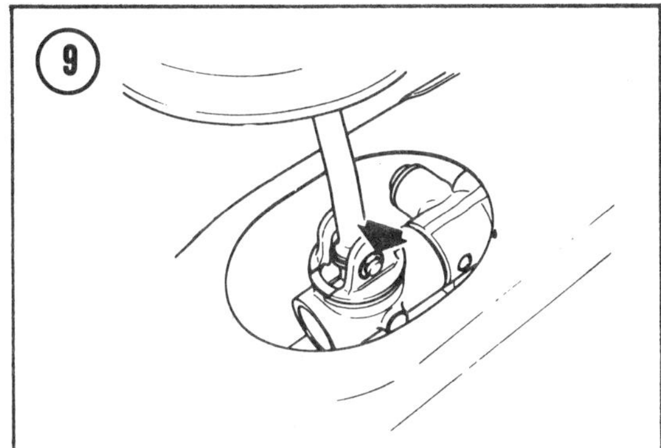

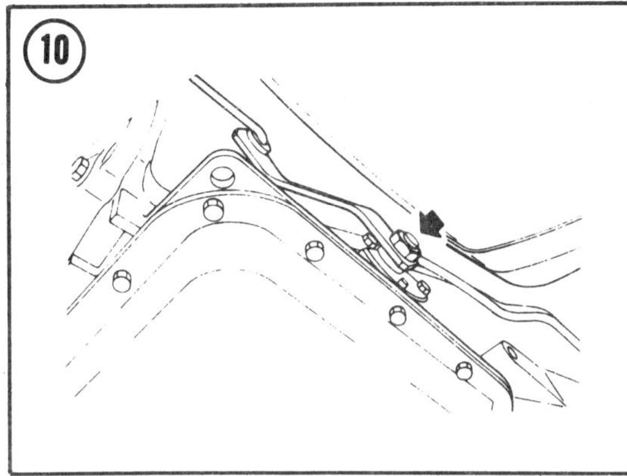

to be sure nothing will hamper engine removal.

29. Attach a hoist to the engine slinger brackets at front and rear ends of the engine. Gradually lower the jack beneath the transmission while raising the engine. Remove the jack from beneath the transmission. Continue raising the engine, tilting as necessary, until it is clear of the vehicle.

CAUTION

Do not let the engine strike equipment installed on the engine compartment walls during removal.

30. Once the engine and transmission are clear of the car, lower them to a suitable support or stand and disconnect the hoist.
31. Remove the bolts attaching the transmission to the engine.
32. Check the rubber mounting insulators for wear or damage. Replace as needed.

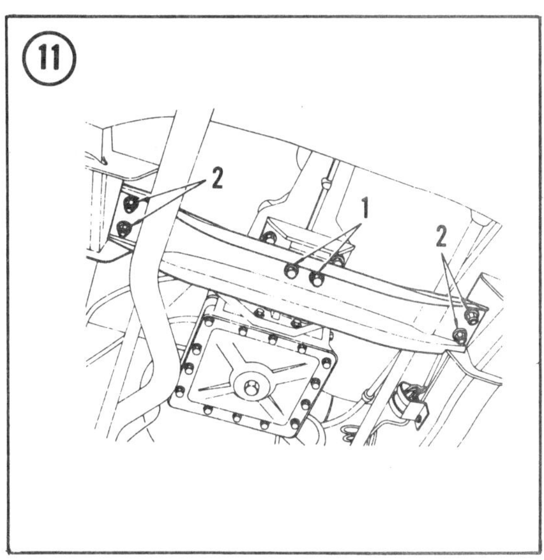

ENGINE INSTALLATION

Engine installation is simply the reverse of removal. Fasten the engine securely to its mounts before tightening anything else. Bleed and adjust the clutch as described in Chapter Nine. Fill the engine and transmission with oils recommended in Chapter Three. Fill the cooling system with a 50/50 mixture of antifreeze and water.

DISASSEMBLY SEQUENCES

The following three sequences are basic outlines that tell how much of the engine to remove and disassemble to perform a specific type of service. They are designed to keep engine disassembly to a minimum, thus avoiding unnecessary work. The major assemblies mentioned in these sequences are covered in detail under their own headings in this chapter, unless otherwise noted.

To use these sequences, first determine what type of service you plan to do (a valve job, for example). Then turn to the sequence for that type of service. To perform a step within a sequence, turn to the section covering the major assembly mentioned in that step, and perform the removal and inspection procedures. Do the same for each step until all necessary disassembly has been completed. To reassemble, reverse the sequences, performing the installation procedure for each major assembly mentioned.

Decarbonizing or Valve Service

1. Remove the exhaust and intake manifolds.
2. Remove the rocker arms and camshaft.
3. Remove the cylinder head.
4. Remove and inspect valves. Inspect valve guides and seats, repairing or replacing as necessary.
5. Assemble by reversing Steps 1-4.

Valve and Ring Service

1. Perform Steps 1-4 for valve service.
2. Remove the oil pan.
3. Remove the pistons together with the connecting rods.
4. Remove the piston rings. It is not necessary to separate the pistons from the connecting rods unless a piston, connecting rod or piston pin needs repair or replacement.
5. Assemble by reversing Steps 1-4.

General Overhaul

1. Remove the engine and transmission and separate them. Remove the clutch (Chapter Nine) from manual transmission vehicles.
2. Remove the oil filter, dipstick, and oil pressure sender from the right-hand side of the cylinder block.
3. Remove the motor mounts.
4. Remove the fuel pump, carburetor, and manifolds. If equipped with an air pump, remove it also. See Chapter Six.
5. Remove the fan, water pump, and thermostat (Chapter Seven). Remove the thermostat housing from the cylinder head.
6. Remove the alternator and the distributor (Chapter Eight).
7. Remove the rocker arms and camshaft.
8. Remove the cylinder head.
9. Remove the flywheel.
10. Remove the oil pan, strainer, oil pump, and pump driving spindle.
11. Remove the engine front cover. Remove the timing chain and related parts.
12. Remove the piston/connecting rod assemblies.
13. Remove crankshaft.
14. Remove cylinder block.
15. Assembly is the reverse of these steps.

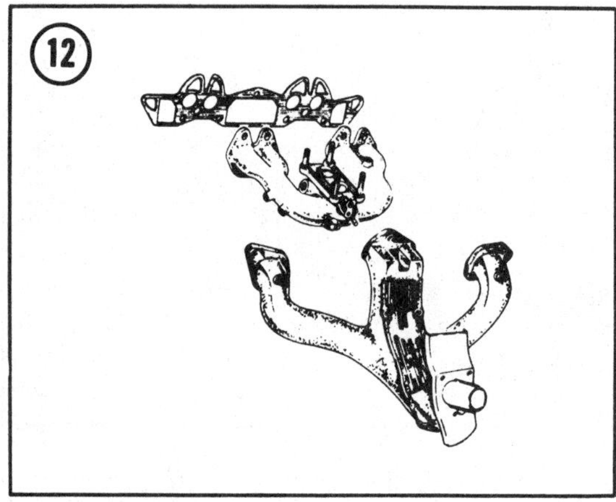

INTAKE AND EXHAUST MANIFOLDS

Figure 12 shows the 1973 intake and exhaust manifolds. Other years are similar.

Removal/Installation

1. Perform Steps 1-8, *Carburetor Removal/ Installation*, Chapter Six.
2. Drain the cooling system by opening the radiator drain tap. If the antifreeze is good, drain it into a clean container and reuse it.
3. Detach the PCV hose from the intake manifold.
4. On 1974 models, detach the vacuum tube from the exhaust gas recirculation solenoid. On 1974 and later models, detach the exhaust gas tube running from the exhaust manifold to the exhaust gas recirculation valve.
5. Detach the manifolds from the engine, then lift them off.
6. Installation is the reverse of removal. Use a new gasket. Tighten manifold fasteners to 9-12 ft.-lb. (1.2-1.6 mkg).

CAMSHAFT AND ROCKER ARMS

Figure 13 shows the camshaft. **Figure 14** shows the rocker arm and valve parts.

Rocker Arm Removal

1. Remove the rocker arm cover.
2. Remove the springs looped over the tops of the rocker arms.
3. Loosen the locknut on the rocker arm pivot. Compress the valve spring by using a

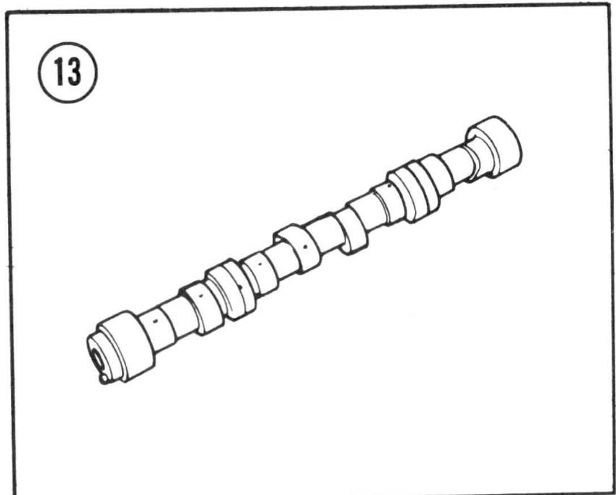

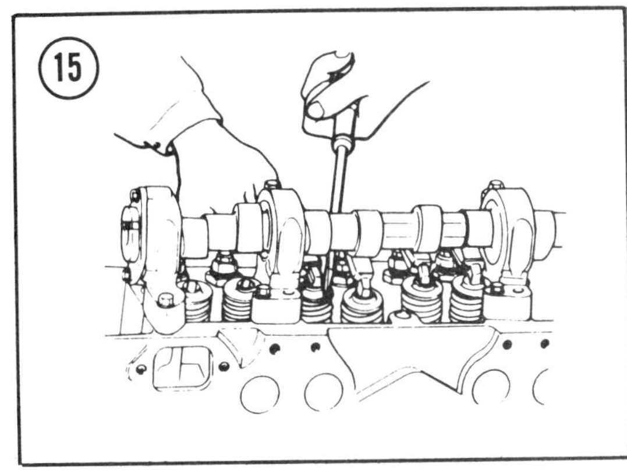

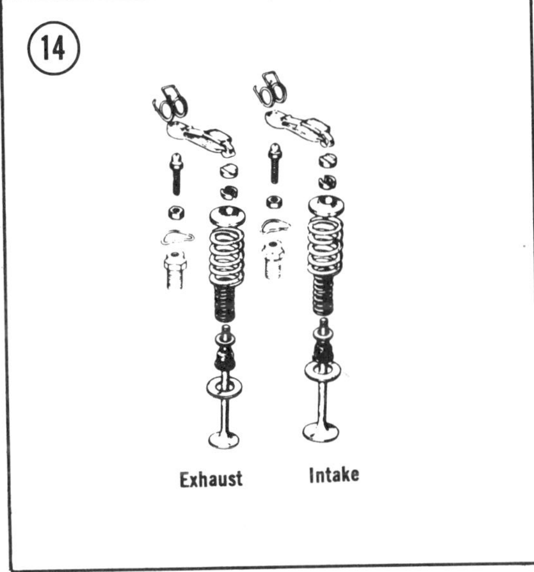

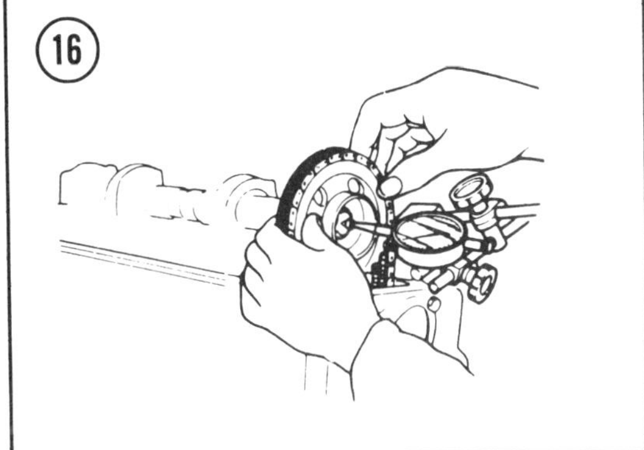

heavy-bladed screwdriver as a lever and the camshaft as a fulcrum. See **Figure 15**.

4. Withdraw the rocker arm while holding the valve springs down with the screwdriver. Be careful not to lose the rocker arm guide located between the rocker arm and the top of the valve stem.
5. If the rocker pivot is visibly worn, unscrew it from the cylinder head, together with its locknut.
6. Install by reversing Steps 1-5.

Rocker Arm Inspection

Examine the rocker arm for visible wear on its cam contact surface, pivot contact surface, and valve contact surface. If wear or any defects can be seen, replace the rocker arm.If the rocker arm pivot is visibly worn, both the pivot and its corresponding rocker arm must be replaced.

Camshaft Removal

1. Remove the rocker arm cover.
2. Remove the fuel pump (Chapter Six).
3. Check camshaft end play. Position a dial gauge as shown in **Figure 16**. Slide the camshaft back and forth against the dial gauge pointer. The reading on the gauge is camshaft end play. It should range from 0.003-0.015 in. (0.08-0.38mm). Replace the camshaft locate plate if end play is not within specifications.
4. Turn the engine over by hand until the timing marks on camshaft and timing chain are aligned. See **Figure 17**. This will enable you to position the camshaft correctly during installation.
5. Remove all rocker arms as described earlier.

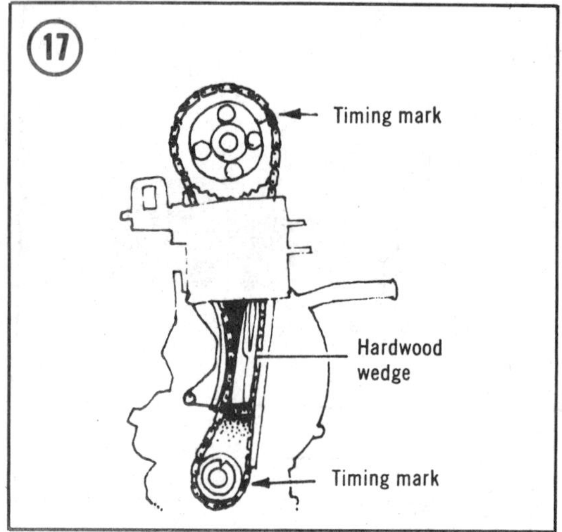

6. Insert a hardwood wedge such as Datsun tool ST 17420001 (Kent-Moore J-25660-01) between the sides of the chain (**Figure 17**). If the special tool is not available, make your own according to dimensions in **Figure 18**. This tool keeps the timing marks on crankshaft sprocket and chain aligned. It also prevents the chain tensioner piston from popping out. If the chain slips off the sprocket, or the piston falls out, the front cover and oil pan must be removed to reinstall them.

NOTE

If you make your own tool, use a piece of hardwood about 5/8 inch thick. Do not use plywood, since this may leave fragments in the engine. Drill a hole in the top of the tool so it can be pulled out. Insert the tool firmly. Make sure it blocks the tensioner piston before removing the camshaft sprocket.

7. Remove the bolt from the front end of the camshaft. Remove the fuel pump cam and camshaft sprocket. Take the sprocket out of the chain and drape chain over the tool (**Figure 19**).

NOTE

There are 3 locating holes in the camshaft sprocket, all of which will fit the dowel on the front end of the camshaft. Carefully note which locating hole is over the pin.

8. Remove 2 bolts and take the camshaft locate plate off the front camshaft bracket.

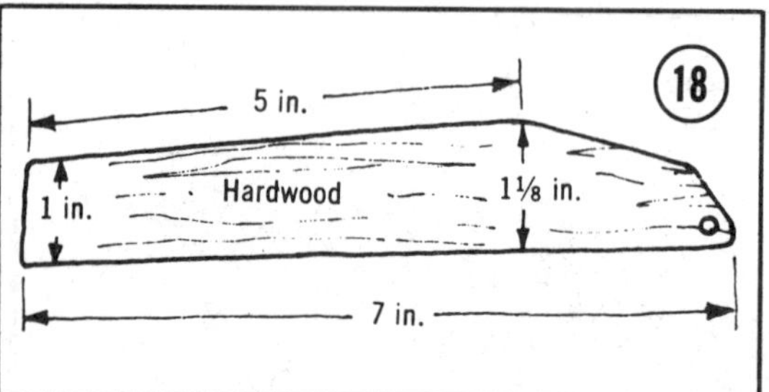

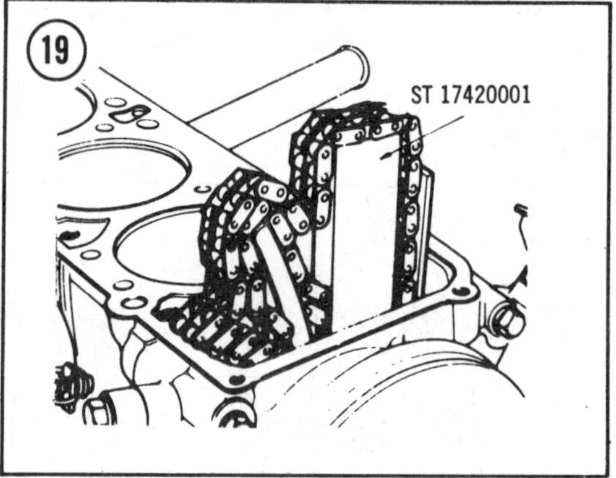

9. Carefully withdraw the camshaft toward the front of the engine. Rotate the camshaft slowly while removing. Be careful not to scratch the camshaft bearing surfaces.

CAUTION

Never remove camshaft brackets from the cylinder head, even though removal looks easy. If the brackets are removed, it will be extremely difficult if not impossible to realign the bearing centers.

Camshaft Inspection

1. Measure the inner diameter of the camshaft bearings (**Figure 20**). This figure must be between 1.8898-1.8904 in. (48.000-48.016mm). If any bearings are worn beyond the maximum, replace the entire cylinder head.

2. Measure outer diameter of the camshaft journals. Subtract these figures from the bearing inner diameters to determine oil clearance. Normal oil clearance is 0.0015-0.0026 in. (0.038-0.076mm). If the bearings were within specifications in Step 1,

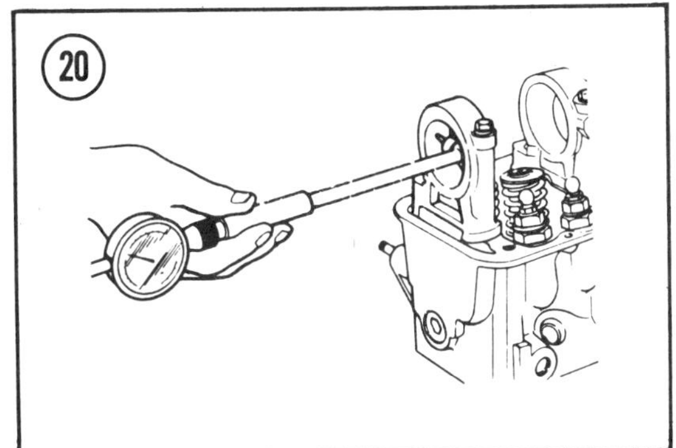

20

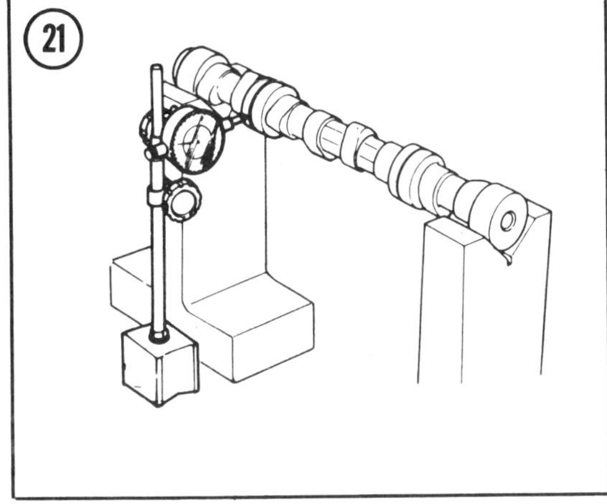

21

and oil clearance exceeds 0.004 in. (0.1mm), camshaft must be replaced.

3. Measure camshaft bend. Rotate the camshaft between accurate centers (such as V-blocks or a lathe) with a dial indicator contacting the second and third journals. See **Figure 21**. Actual bend is half the reading shown on the gauge when the camshaft is rotated one full turn. Normal bend is 0.008 in. (0.02mm) or less. Replace the camshaft if bend exceeds 0.002 in. (0.05mm).

4. Check the camshaft sprocket for runout. Measure with the sprocket installed on the camshaft, as shown in **Figure 22**. Replace sprocket if runout exceeds 0.004 in. (0.1mm).

Camshaft Installation

1. Coat the camshaft journals and bearing surfaces with clean engine oil.

2. Carefully install the camshaft in the brackets. Rotate the camshaft slowly while inserting to ease installation.

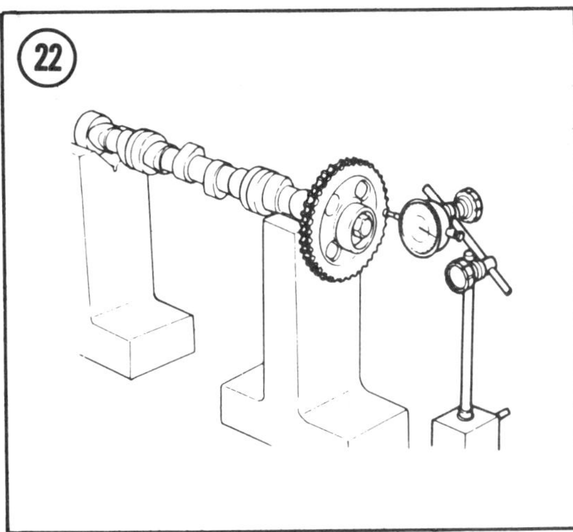

22

3. Install the camshaft locate plate and secure it with 2 bolts. The small groove in the locate plate goes on top and faces the front.

4. Install the rocker arms as described earlier.

5. Lift up the timing chain and remove the support tool. Place the camshaft sprocket in the chain, making sure the timing marks on sprocket and chain are aligned.

6. Slide the sprocket onto the camshaft. Use the sprocket locating hole that was used before removal. Install the fuel pump cam, then the sprocket bolt and lockwasher. Tighten to 87 116 ft. lb. (12-16 mkg)

7. Install the fuel pump (Chapter Six) and rocker arm cover.

OIL PAN

Removal/Installation

1. Set the handbrake and place the transmission in gear. Jack up the front end of the vehicle and place it on jackstands.

2. Remove the splash pan from under the front end (if so equipped).

3. Remove the front frame member. Remove the lower bolts from the clutch or torque converter housing.

4. Unbolt the oil pan from the engine. Lower it until it is clear of the engine and take it out from under the vehicle.

5. Clean the oil pan thoroughly. If it is difficult to clean, have the pan boiled out by a machine shop. Check for cracks, dents, bent gasket surfaces, and damaged drain hole

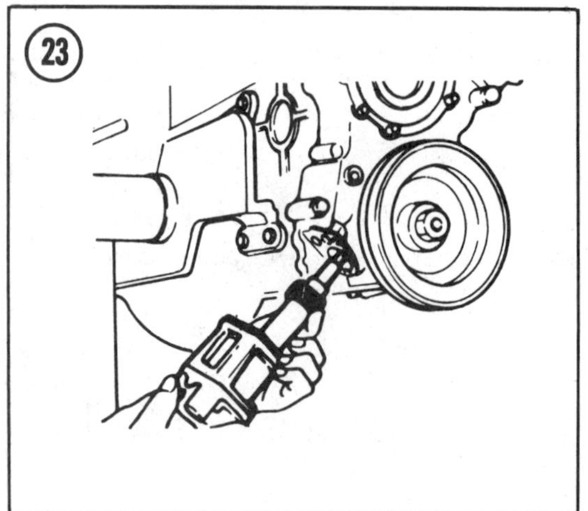

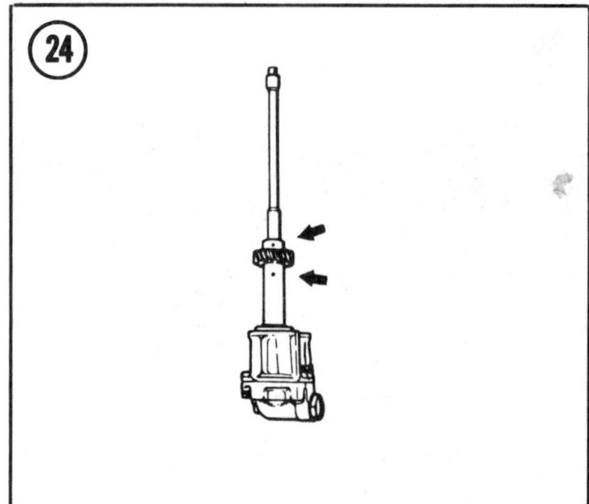

threads. Replace the oil pan if damage is severe.

6. Check for a clogged oil strainer. Remove the strainer and clean it if necessary.

7. Installation is the reverse of these steps. Remove all traces of old gasket and sealer from the oil pan and cylinder block. Use new gaskets, coated on both sides with gasket sealer. Tighten the oil pan bolts evenly, a little at a time, to prevent warping the oil pan.

OIL PUMP

Removal/Installation

1. Turn the engine over until No.1 piston is at top dead center (TDC) on the compression stroke. When this occurs, the timing pointer will point to the 0 degree mark on the crankshaft pulley and the distributor rotor will point to No. 1 spark plug's wire terminal in the distributor cap.

2. Remove the distributor (Chapter Eight).

3. Drain the engine oil.

4. Remove the splash pan from under the front of the car (if so equipped).

5. Remove 4 pump mounting bolts. Take out the pump and its driving spindle. See **Figure 23**.

6. Installation is the reverse of these steps. Make sure the punched mark on the distributor driving spindle lines up with the hole in the oil pump (**Figure 24**). Install the distributor as described in Chapter Eight. Fill the engine with an oil recommended in Chapter Three.

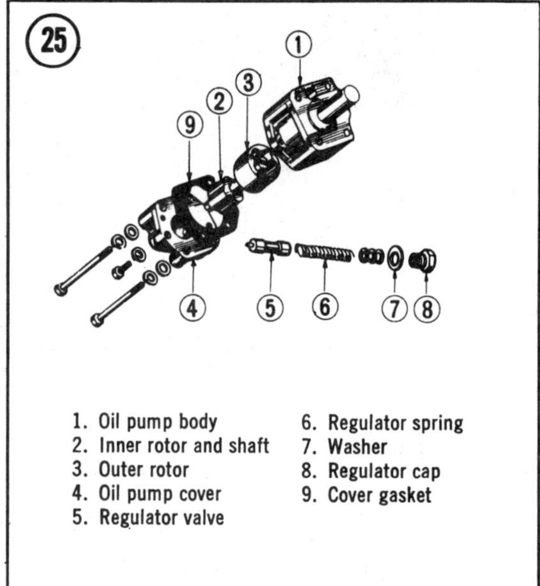

1. Oil pump body
2. Inner rotor and shaft
3. Outer rotor
4. Oil pump cover
5. Regulator valve
6. Regulator spring
7. Washer
8. Regulator cap
9. Cover gasket

Disassembly, Inspection, and Assembly

1. Remove the oil pump cover and gasket. See **Figure 25**.

2. Lift out the inner and outer pump rotors. Remove the regulator valve parts.

3. Clean all parts in solvent. Check the distributor driving spindle and pump rotors for wear, scoring, or visible damage. Check oil pump clearances (**Figure 26**) and compare with specifications at the end of the chapter. Replace the pump if any clearances are excessive.

4. Measure the regulator valve spring free length. Compare with specifications (end of

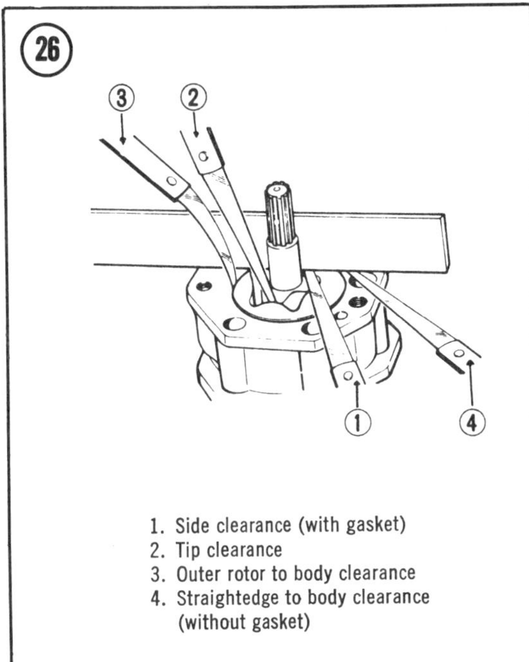

1. Side clearance (with gasket)
2. Tip clearance
3. Outer rotor to body clearance
4. Straightedge to body clearance (without gasket)

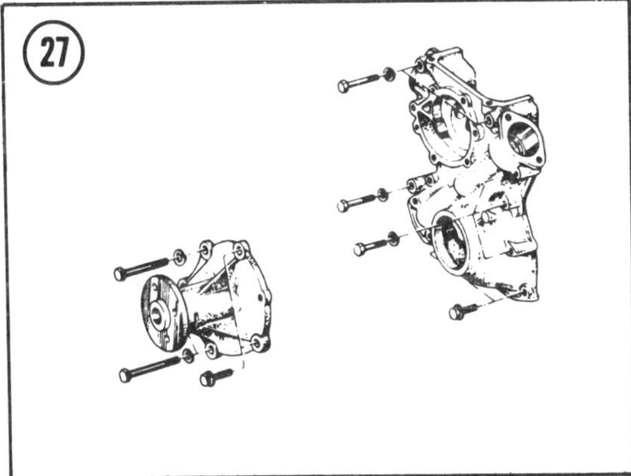

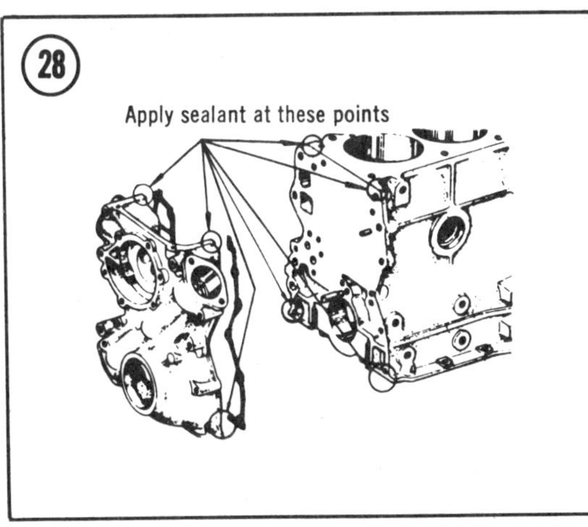

chapter). Replace the spring if it is too long or too short.

5. Install the regular valve parts. Tighten the valve cap to 29-36 ft.-lb. (4-5 mkg).

6. Install the inner rotor in the pump. Place the outer rotor over it. Install a new cover gasket, coated lightly on both sides with gasket sealer. Install the pump cover. Take care not to fold the cover gasket.

4

FRONT COVER, TIMING CHAIN, AND SPROCKETS

Front Cover Removal

1. Remove the radiator and fan (Chapter Seven). Remove the air pump belt (if so equipped).
2. Remove the distributor (Chapter Eight).
3. Remove the oil pan, oil pump, and pump driving spindle as described earlier in this chapter.
4. Remove the crankshaft pulley.
5. Remove bolts attaching the front cover to cylinder head and block. See **Figure 27**.
6. Withdraw the front cover forward and down, together with the water pump.

Front Cover Installation

Front cover installation is the reverse of removal plus the following.

1. Use new left and right cover gaskets, coated on both sides with gasket sealer. Apply small amounts of sealer to the corners of the front cover. See **Figure 28**.
2. Install a new front cover oil seal as described in the next procedure. This should be done whenever the front cover is removed.
3. Take care not to bend the front portion of the head gasket when installing the cover. Be sure to install the cylinder head-to-cover bolts.
4. Fill the engine with oil and the radiator with coolant.

Front Oil Seal Replacement

1. Remove the front cover as described earlier.
2. Carefully pry out the old oil seal. Do not gouge the aluminum front cover.
3. Tap in a new oil seal. Coat the seal lip with multipurpose grease.
4. Install the front cover as described earlier.

Sprocket and Chain Removal

1. Remove the valve rocker cover.
2. Remove the fuel pump (Chapter Six).
3. Remove the oil pan, oil pump, and pump driving spindle as described earlier in this chapter.
4. Remove the front cover as described earlier.
5. Install the crankshaft pulley bolt in the crankshaft. Put a wrench on the bolt and turn the engine over by hand until the timing marks in chain and sprockets are aligned (**Figure 17**).
6. Referring to **Figure 29**, remove 2 bolts and lockwashers that attach the chain tensioner to the block.
7. Remove 4 bolts and lockwashers holding the left and right chain guides to the block. Remove the guides.
8. Remove the camshaft sprocket and fuel pump from the front of the camshaft.
9. Remove the timing chain from the crankshaft sprocket.
10. Remove the crankshaft sprocket, distributor drive gear, and oil thrower with a puller as shown in **Figure 30**.

CAUTION
Do not rotate the crankshaft and camshaft separately, or the valves may strike the piston tops.

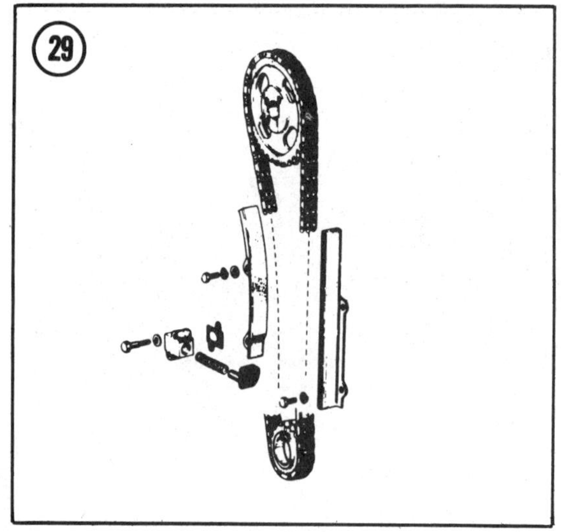

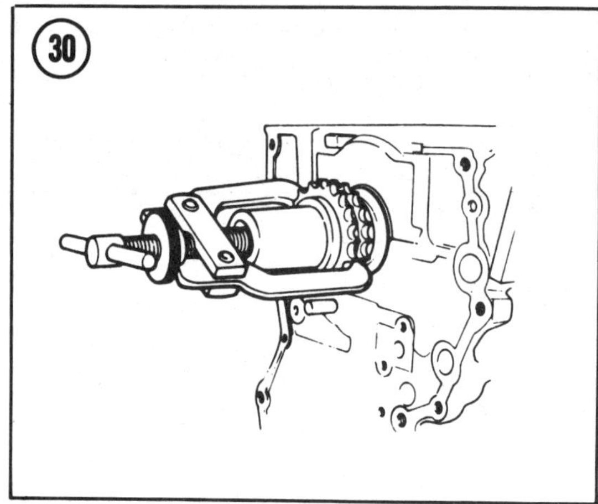

Inspection

1. Thoroughly clean all parts in solvent before inspection.
2. Check the chain tensioner assembly and chain guides for wear or damage. Replace if excessive wear or damage is evident.
3. Inspect the sprockets, distributor drive gear, and oil thrower for wear or damage. Replace as needed.
4. Check the chain for wear, damage, or stretching of the roller links. Replace the chain if visibly defective. Check again for stretching as described in the next procedure.

Sprocket and Chain Installation

1. Install the Woodruff keys in the crankshaft keyways if they have been removed.
2. Install the crankshaft sprocket, distributor drive gear, and oil thrower. See **Figure 31**.
3. Install the timing chain over the crankshaft and camshaft sprockets. Make sure the timing marks on the chain are aligned with the timing marks on the sprockets. See **Figure 17**.
4. Slide the camshaft sprocket onto the camshaft. Make sure the Woodruff keys on the crankshaft point straight up.
5. Bolt the chain guides to the cylinder block.
6. Install the chain tensioner. Push the tensioner spindle as far into the tensioner body as it will go.
7. Make sure that No. 1 piston is still at top dead center on its compression stroke.
8. Refer to **Figure 32** and **Figure 33** for this step. **Figure 32** shows the camshaft locate plate; **Figure 33** shows the camshaft sprocket.

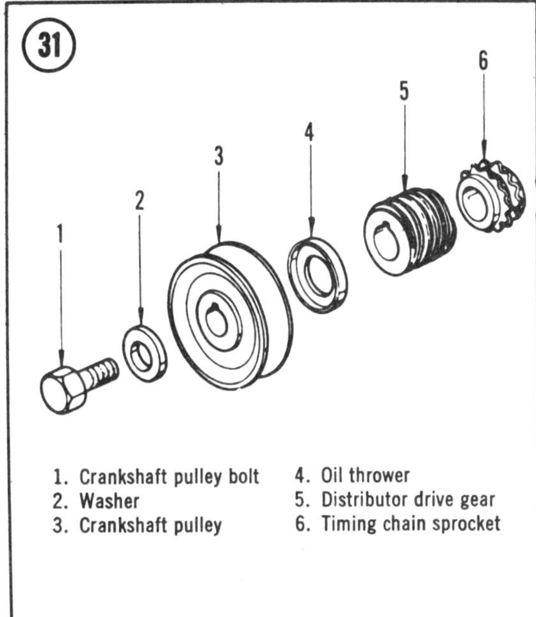

1. Crankshaft pulley bolt
2. Washer
3. Crankshaft pulley
4. Oil thrower
5. Distributor drive gear
6. Timing chain sprocket

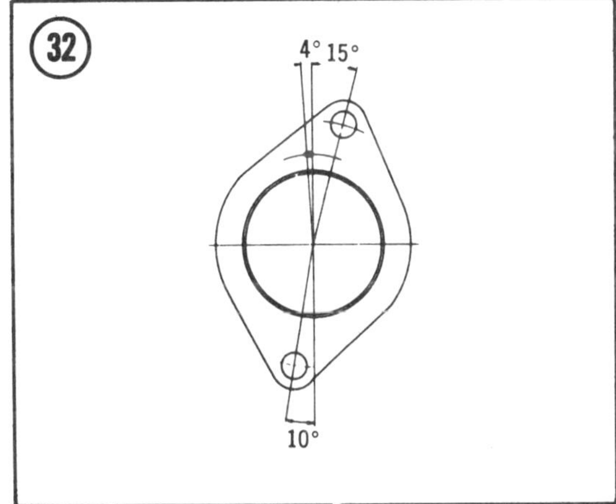

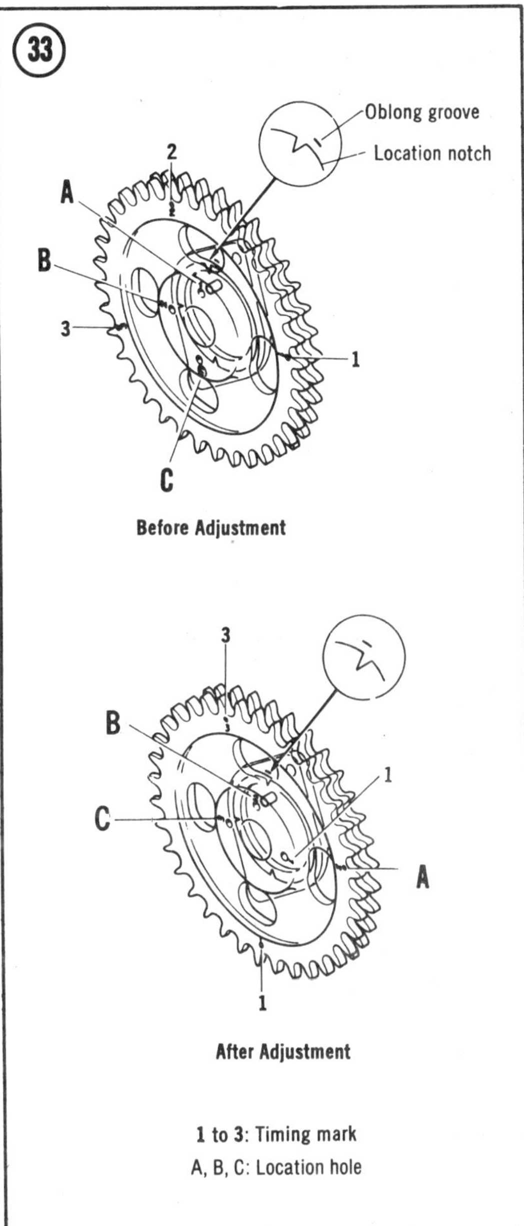

Before Adjustment

After Adjustment

1 to 3: Timing mark
A, B, C: Location hole

Note that there are 3 location holes in the sprocket each with its own location notch and timing mark. Face the engine from the front. Note the relative positions of the location notch in the sprocket and the oblong groove in the camshaft locate plate. If the notch is completely to the left of the groove (as shown in top drawing, **Figure 33**), the timing chain is stretched excessively. Perform Steps 9-11 to adjust it. If the notch is not completely to the left (couterclockwise) of the groove, the timing chain is satisfactory and Steps 9-11 may be skipped.

9. Remove the camshaft sprocket and reinstall it, using No. 2 location hole. No. 2 notch should now be at the right (clockwise) end of the oblong groove.
10. If the location notch position still is not correct, remove the camshaft sprocket again and reinstall it, this time using No. 3 location hole. No. 3 notch should now be at the right end of the oblong groove.
11. If the hole still is not in the correct position, the timing chain is stretched beyond

use and must be replaced. Install the new chain as described in Steps 3 and 4, using No. 1 location hole in the camshaft sprocket.

12. Install the front cover as described earlier.
13. Install the oil pan and pump as described earlier in this chapter.
14. Install the distributor (Chapter Eight).
15. Install the fuel pump (Chapter Six).
16. Install the rocker arm cover.
17. Install the fan and radiator (Chapter Seven).
18. Fill the engine with oil and the radiator with coolant.

CYLINDER HEAD

Some of the following procedures must be done by a dealer or machine shop, since they require special knowledge and expensive machine tools. Others, while possible for the home mechanic, are difficult or time-consuming. A general practice among those who do their own service is to remove the cylinder head, perform all disassembly except valve removal, and take the head to a machine shop for inspection and service. Since the cost is low in relation to the required effort and equipment, this is usually the best approach, even for more experienced owners.

Removal

1. Completely drain the cooling system.
2. Remove all spark plugs.
3. Remove the air cleaner (Chapter Six).
4. Remove the rocker arm cover.
5. Remove the intake manifold, exhaust manifold, and fuel pump (Chapter Six).
6. Detach heater hoses from cylinder head.
7. Remove the thermostat housing and water outlet elbow from the left front of cylinder head.
8. Turn the camshaft so its sprocket locating pin is straight up. This provides a reference point for later installation.
9. Remove the camshaft sprocket as described under *Camshaft Removal* in this chapter.
10. Remove 2 bolts attaching the cylinder head to the engine front cover.
11. Remove the 10 cylinder head bolts with a 10mm Allen socket (**Figure 34**). To prevent

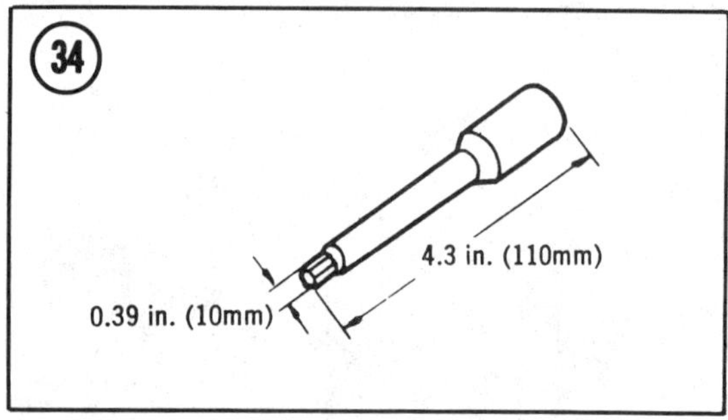

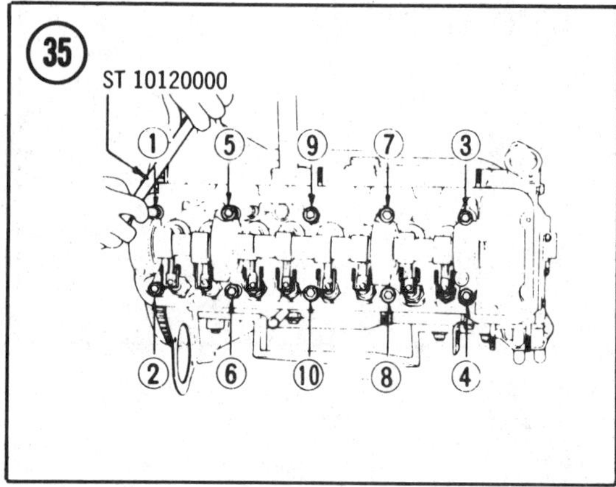

warping the cylinder head, loosen the bolts in several stages, following the order given in **Figure 35**.

NOTE

There are different lengths of cylinder head bolts. Tag them as they are removed so they can be reinstalled in the same holes later.

12. Once the head bolts are removed, lift the cylinder head off the engine. If the head is difficult to remove, tap it gently with a rubber mallet.

CAUTION

Never remove the camshaft brackets from the cylinder head, even though removal appears easy. If the brackets are removed, it will be extremely difficult, if not impossible, to realign the bearing centers.

Inspection

1. Check head for water leaks before cleaning.
2. Clean the cylinder head thoroughly in solvent. While cleaning, check for cracks or other visible damage. Look for corrosion or

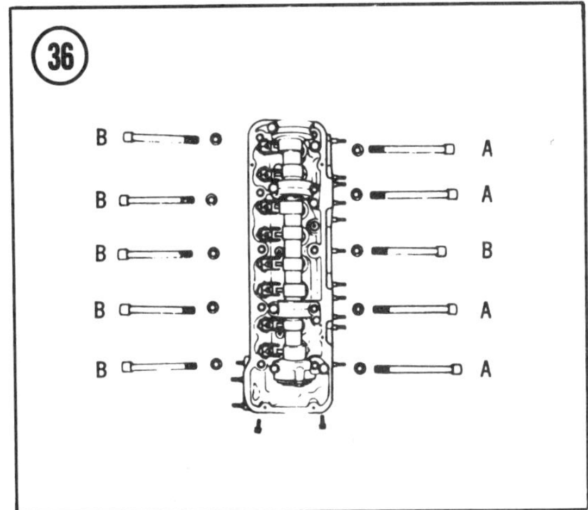

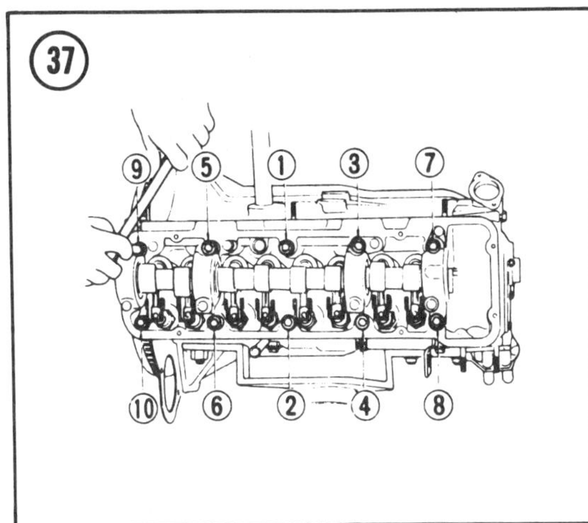

foreign material in oil or water passages. Clean the passages with a stiff spiral wire brush, then blow them out with compressed air.

3. Check the cylinder head bottom (block mating) surface for flatness. Place an accurate straightedge along the surface. If there is any gap between the straightedge and cylinder head surface, measure it with a feeler gauge. Have the cylinder head resurfaced by a machine shop if the gap exceeds 0.004 in. (0.1mm).

4. Check studs in cylinder head for general condition. Replace damaged studs.

Decarbonizing

1. Without removing valves, remove all deposits from the combustion chambers, intake ports, and exhaust ports. Use a wire brush dipped in solvent, or make a scraper out of hardwood. Be careful not to scratch or gouge the combustion chambers.

2. After all carbon is removed from the combustion chambers and ports, clean the entire head in solvent.

3. Clean away all carbon on the piston tops. Do not remove the carbon ridge at the top of the cylinder bore.

Installation

1. Be sure the cylinder head, block, and cylinder bores are clean. Check all visible oil passages for cleanliness.

2. Install the camshaft and rocker arms in the cylinder head. Turn the camshaft so its sprocket locating pin is straight up. This must be done before the cylinder head is installed to prevent the valves from striking the piston tops.

3. Install a new cylinder head gasket. Never re-use an old head gasket. Do *not* use gasket sealer on the head gasket.

4. Position cylinder head on block. On early engines, install bolts according to labels made during disassembly. On late engines, install the 4 long bolts in the "A" holes (**Figure 36**). Install the 6 short bolts in the "B" holes.

NOTE

When positioning the cylinder head, look at the valves and make sure none are open far enough to strike the piston tops.

5. With engine cool, tighten head bolts in order given in **Figure 37**. Tighten in 3 stages, referring to **Table 2** (end of chapter).

NOTE

Retorque the head after driving 600 miles.

6. Install the timing chain, camshaft sprocket, and fuel pump cam as described under *Camshaft Installation* in this chapter.

7. Install the thermostat housing and water outlet elbow on the left front of the cylinder head.

8. Install the manifolds, carburetor, and fuel pump (Chapter Six).

9. Attach the heater hoses to the right rear of the cylinder head.

10. Install spark plugs and rocker arm cover.

4

11. Install the air cleaner (Chapter Six).
12. Fill the cooling system with a 50/50 mixture of anti-freeze and water. Check the oil level and top up if necessary with a grade recommended in Chapter Three.
13. Run the engine for several minutes, let it cool, then recheck head bolt tightness.

VALVE AND VALVE SEATS

Valve Removal

1. Remove the cylinder head as described earlier. Remove the camshaft from the head.
2. Compress each valve spring with a compressor like the one shown in **Figure 38**. Remove the valve locking collets (valve keepers) and release the spring tension. Remove the spring washer, oil seal(s), inner and outer valve springs, and spring seat. **Figure 39** shows the valves and related parts.

CAUTION
Remove any burrs from valve stem grooves before removing valves. Otherwise the valve guides will be damaged.

Valve and Valve Guide Inspection

1. Clean the valves with a wire brush and solvent. Discard cracked, warped, or burned valves.
2. Measure the valve stems at the bottom, center and top for wear, using a micrometer. A machine shop can do this when the valves are ground. Also measure the length of each valve and the diameter of each valve head.
3. The valve faces and stem ends should be refaced when the valves are ground. No more than 0.020 in. (0.5mm) may be removed from valve stem ends. Valve faces may not be ground thinner than 0.020 in. (0.5mm).
4. Remove all carbon and varnish from valve guides with a stiff spiral wire brush.

NOTE
The next step assumes that all valve stems have been measured and are within specifications. Replace any valves with worn stems before performing this step.

5. Insert each valve into the guide from which it was removed. Hold the valve just slightly off

38

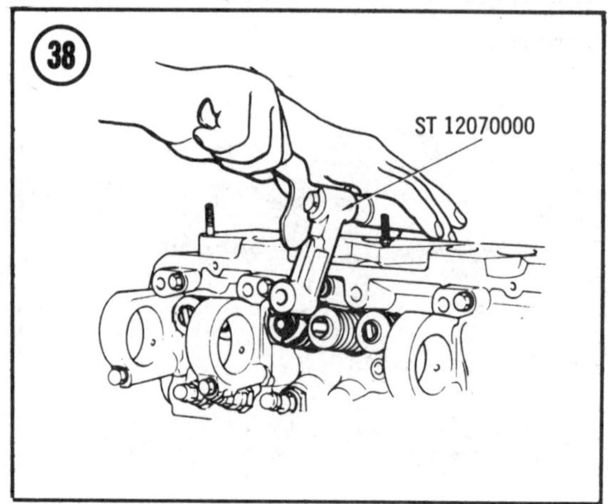

39

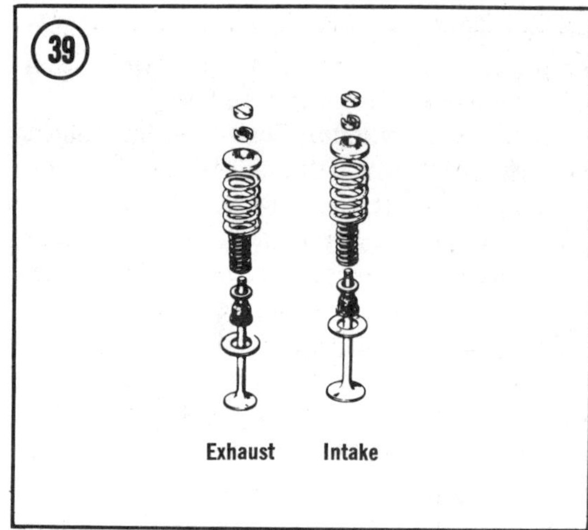

its seat and rock it back and forth in a direction parallel with the rocker arms. This is the direction in which the greatest wear normally occurs. If the valve stem rocks more than approximately 0.008 in. (0.2mm), the valve guide is probably worn.
6. If there is any doubt about valve guide condition after performing Step 5, measure the valve guide at top, bottom, and center with bore gauge. Compare with specifications (end of chapter). Have worn guides replaced.
7. Measure valve spring free length and compare with specifications. Replace springs that are too long or too short. Measure spring bend with a square. Replace springs that are bent more than 0.063 in. (1.6mm).
8. Have the valve springs tested under load on a spring tester (**Figure 40**). Replace weak springs.

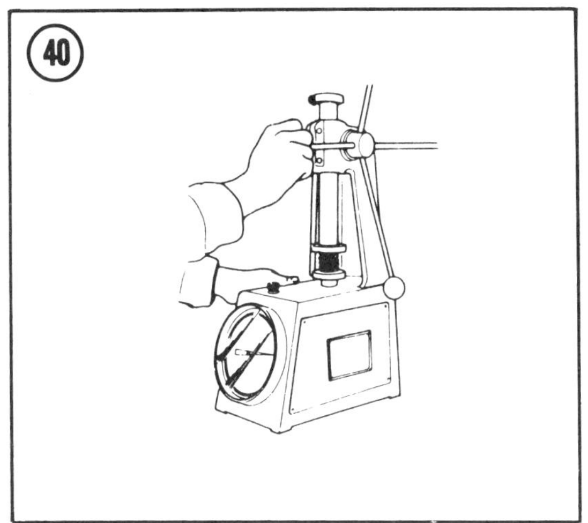

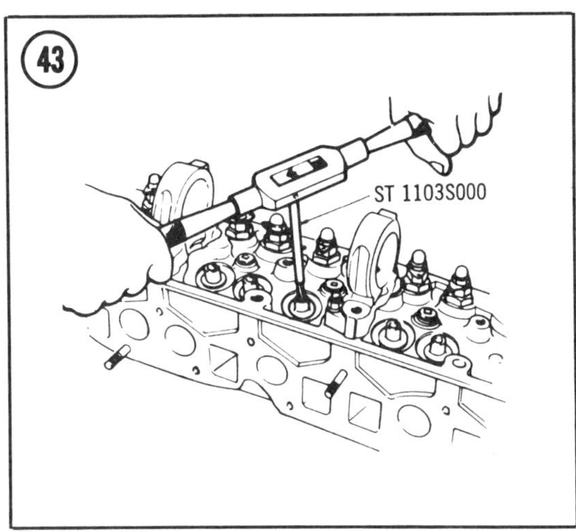

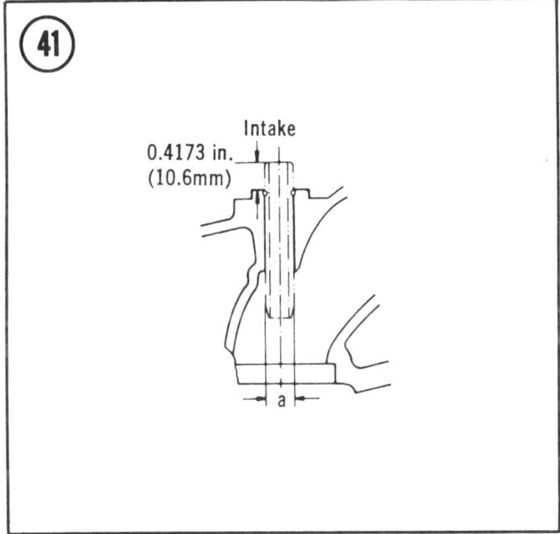

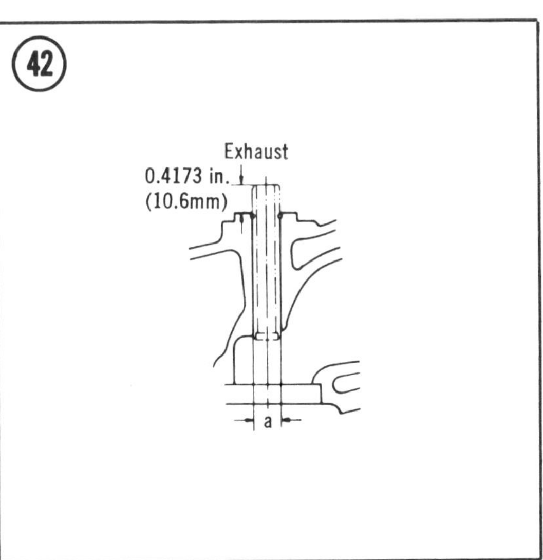

9. Inspect valve seat inserts. If worn or burned, they must be reconditioned. This should be done by a dealer or machine shop, although the procedure is described later in this section.

Valve Guide Replacement

This procedure requires a press and reaming tools. If you don't have the necessary equipment, take the job to a dealer or machine shop.

1. Remove worn guides with a press and suitable drift. This can be done at room temperature. Removal will be easier if the cylinder head is heated first.
2. Ream the guide holes in the cylinder head to specifications (end of chapter).
3. Heat the cylinder head to 302-392° F (149-200° C).
4. Press the guides into place from the top of the cylinder head. The guides should protrude 0.417 in. (10.6mm) from the top of the cylinder head. See **Figure 41** (intake) or **Figure 42** (exhaust).
5. Measure valve guide bores. Ream to specifications (**Figure 43**).

Valve Seat Inserts

L-series valve seats are cut into inserts. Intake valve seats are aluminum-bronze alloy; exhaust valve seats are heat-resistant steel. Replacement requires precision machine tools and special skills. Take the job to a Datsun dealer or machine shop.

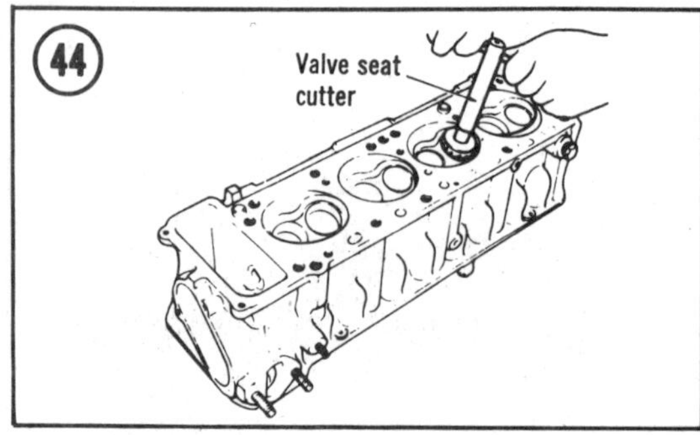

1. Remove the old valve seat by boring it out until it collapses. Be sure not to cut the cylinder head during boring.
2. Select a valve seat insert and check its outside diameter. Compare with specifications (end of chapter).
3. Machine the cylinder head recess diameter to fit the valve seat insert, using the valve guide as an axis.
4. Heat the cylinder head to 302-392° F (150-200° C).
5. Press the valve seat insert into place. Be sure it beds securely on the cylinder head. Stake the insert at 5 or more places.
6. Grind the valve seats as described in the following procedure.

Valve Seat Reconditioning

1. Cut the valve seats to specified dimensions, using a cutter (**Figure 44**) or a special stone. **Figure 45** shows valve seat dimensions for early L16 engines. **Figure 46** shows the intake valve seat for all 1972 and later L-series engines. **Figure 47** shows the 1972-1973 L16 exhaust valve seat. **Figure 48** shows the 1973 and later L18 and L20B exhaust valve seat.
2. Coat the corresponding valve face with Prussian blue.
3. Insert the valve into the valve guide.
4. Lift the valve out. If it seats properly, the dye will transfer evenly to the valve face.

Valve Installation

1. Coat the valves with oil and insert them in the cylinder head.
2. Install the valve spring seats, oil seals, springs, and spring washers. Compress the valve springs and install the keepers.

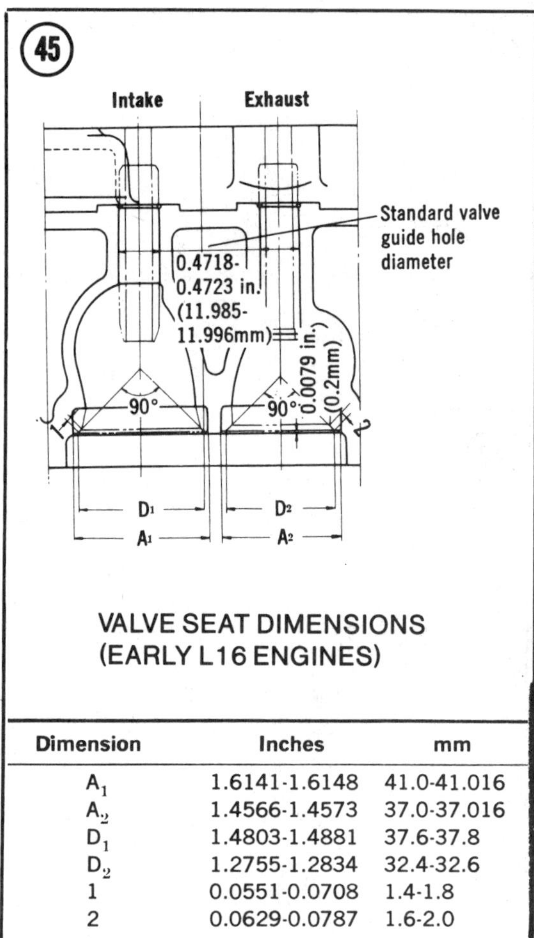

VALVE SEAT DIMENSIONS (EARLY L16 ENGINES)

Dimension	Inches	mm
A_1	1.6141-1.6148	41.0-41.016
A_2	1.4566-1.4573	37.0-37.016
D_1	1.4803-1.4881	37.6-37.8
D_2	1.2755-1.2834	32.4-32.6
1	0.0551-0.0708	1.4-1.8
2	0.0629-0.0787	1.6-2.0

PISTON AND CONNECTING ROD ASSEMBLIES

Figure 49 shows the late L-series piston and connecting rod components. The early design was the same, but used a one-piece oil ring.

Piston Removal

1. Remove the cylinder head and oil pan as described earlier.
2. Remove the carbon ridge at the top of the cylinder bores with a ridge reamer.
3. Rotate the crankshaft so the connecting rod is centered in the bore.
4. Remove the nuts securing the connecting rod cap. Lift off the cap, together with the lower bearing half.
5. Push the piston and connecting rod out of the bore with a wooden hammer handle (**Figure 50**).

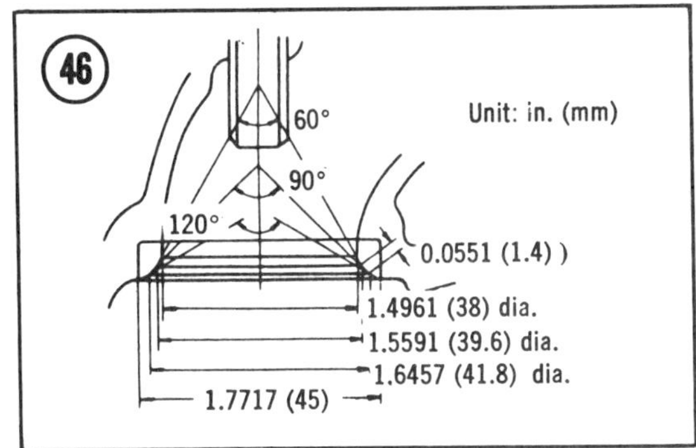

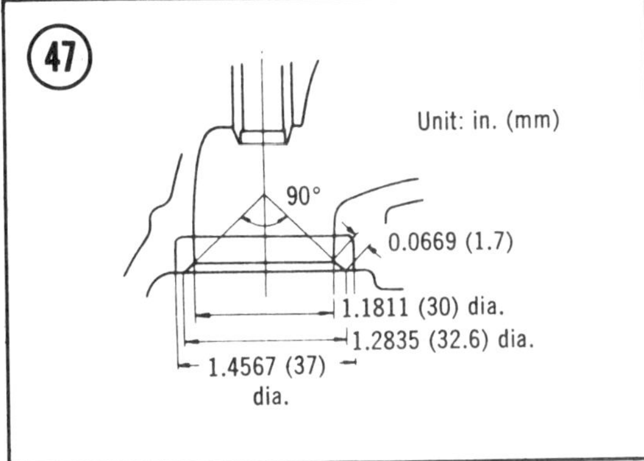

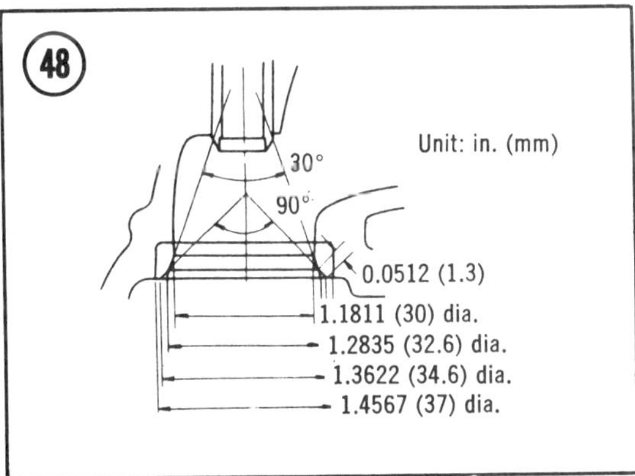

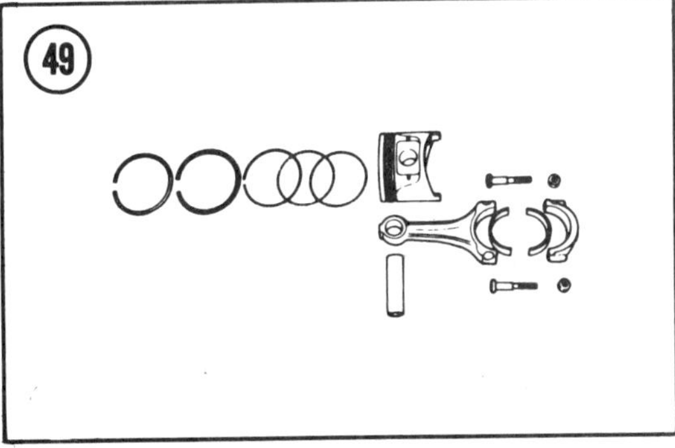

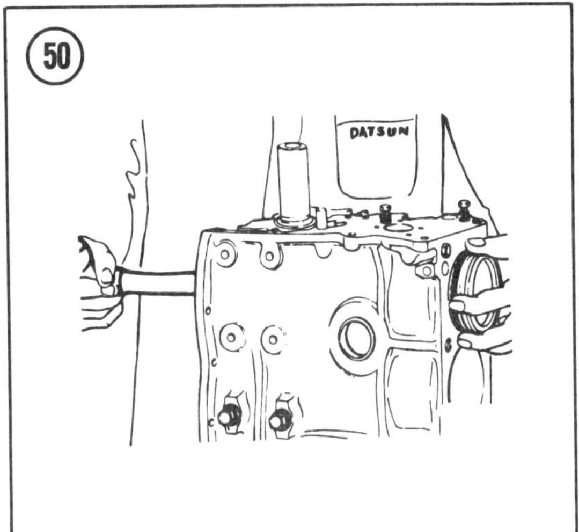

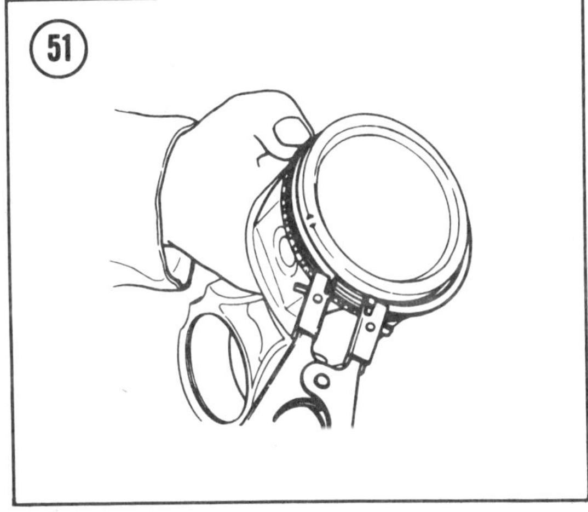

NOTE

Check for cylinder numbers stamped on connecting rod and cap. Make your own number marks if they are not present. Mark rods and caps on the right side.

6. Remove the rings with a ring remover (**Figure 51**).

Piston Pin Removal/Installation

The piston pins are press-fitted to the connecting rods and hand-fitted to the pistons. Removal requires a press and support stand. This is a job for a dealer or machine shop which is equipped to fit the pistons to the pins, ream the pin bushings to the correct diameter, and install the pistons on the connecting rods.

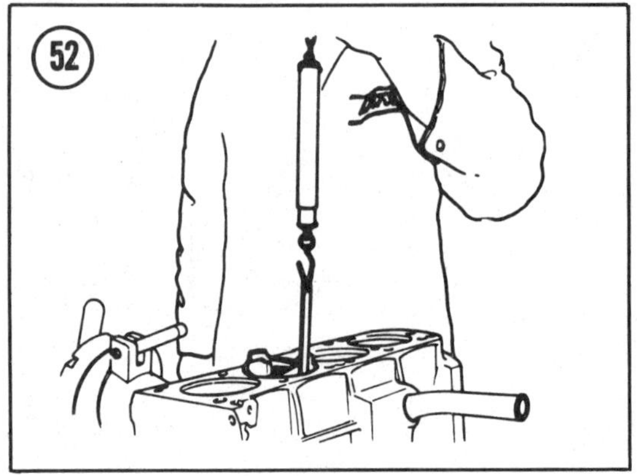

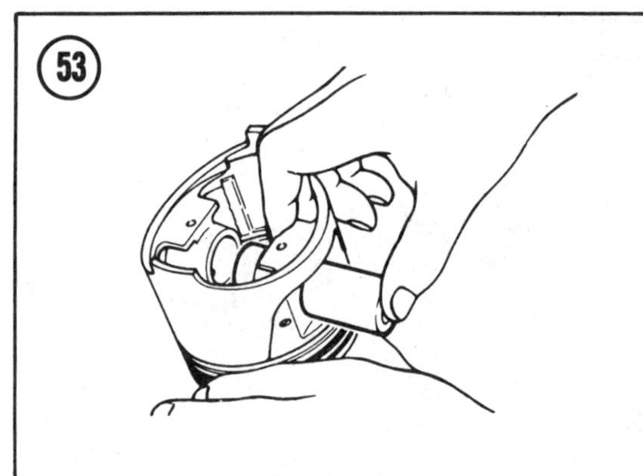

Piston Clearance Check

This procedure should be done at room temperature. Cylinder walls must be clean and dry.

1. Referring to **Figure 52**, insert the piston (without rings) upside down in the cylinder bore. Insert a 0.0016 in. (0.04mm) feeler gauge between piston and cylinder wall and attach a spring scale as shown.
2. Pull on the spring scale. Note the amount of force required to pull the feeler gauge out of the cylinder. The pull should range from 0.44-3.30 lb. (0.2-1.5 kg). If the required pull is greater than specified, piston clearance is less than it should be. If the pull is less, piston clearance is greater.
3. Repeat the procedure for all 4 cylinders and pistons.

Piston Pin Clearance Check

This procedure must be done at room temperature.

1. Push the piston pin into the piston by hand (**Figure 53**). The pin should be tight enough not to wobble, but not too tight to push in with a thumb.
2. Check piston pin diameter with a micrometer (**Figure 54**). Measure the pin hole on the piston and determine the difference between the 2 measurements. If it exceeds specifications (end of chapter), replace piston and pin.

Piston Ring Fit/Installation

1. Check the ring gap of each piston ring. To do this, position the ring at the top or bottom

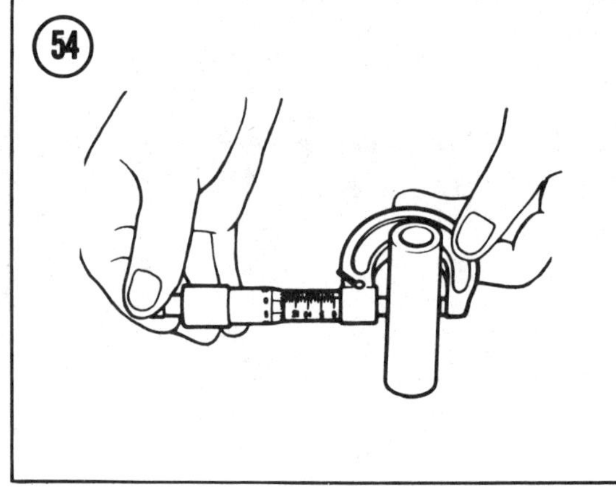

of the ring travel area and square it by tapping gently with an inverted piston.

NOTE

If the cylinders have not been rebored, check the gap at the bottom of the ring travel, where the cylinder is least worn.

2. Measure ring gap with a feeler gauge as shown in **Figure 55**. Compare with specifications at the end of the chapter.
3. Check side clearance of the rings as shown in **Figure 56**. Place the feeler gauge alongside the ring all the way into the groove. Specifications are given at the end of the chapter.
4. Using a ring expander tool, carefully install the oil control ring, then the compression rings. Late L-series engines use a 3-piece oil ring. The wavy segment goes between the 2 flat segments to act as a spacer. Top compression rings have a chrome plated friction surface (**Figure 57**). Second

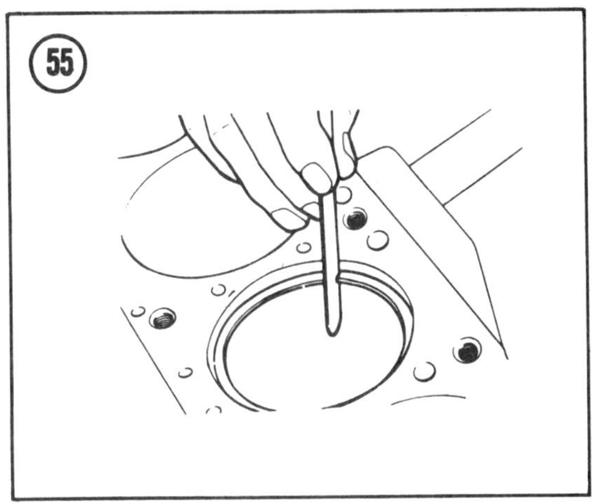

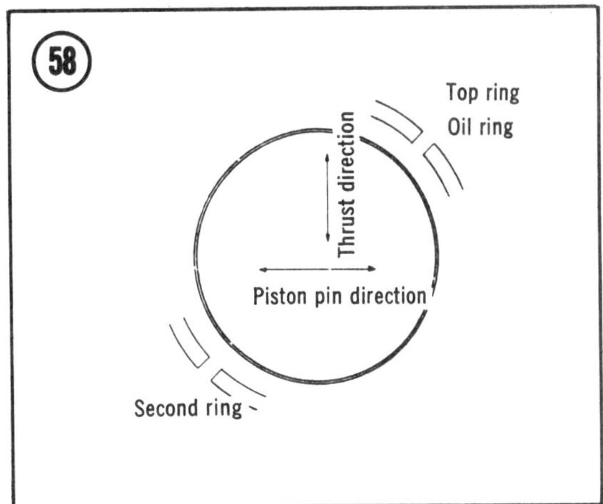

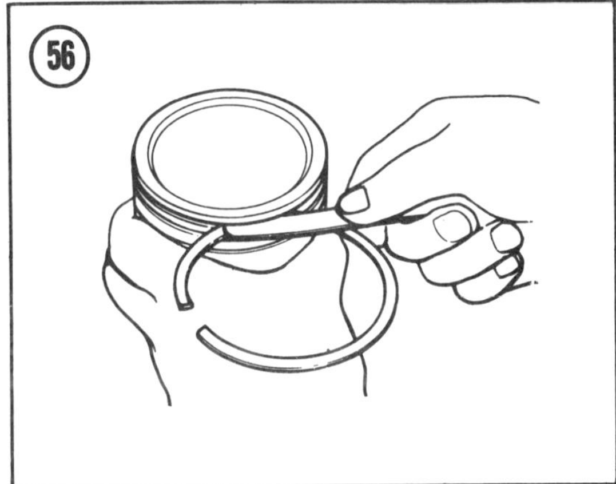

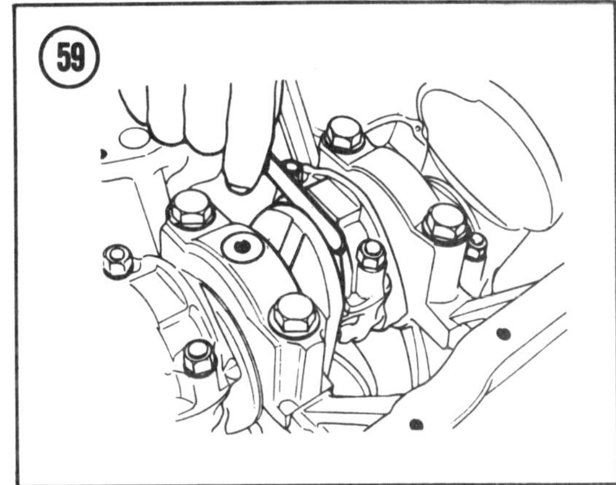

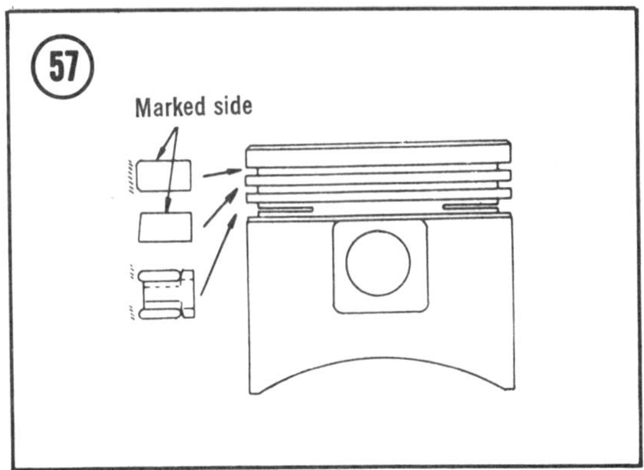

compression rings are tapered. The flat segments of 3-piece oil rings are interchangeable.

5. Turn the ring gaps 180° from each other. Turn the gaps so they are not in the front-rear or side-to-side directions of an installed piston. See **Figure 58**.

Connecting Rod Inspection

1. Have connecting rod straightness checked by a dealer or machine shop. Maximum permissible bend or twist is 0.002 in. (0.05mm) per 3.94 in. (100mm) of connecting rod length.
2. Install the connecting rods and bearings on the crankshaft. Insert a feeler gauge between the connecting rod big end and crankshaft and measure the clearance (**Figure 59**). Replace the connecting rod if clearance exceeds specifications (end of chapter).
3. If any connecting rods are replaced, make sure new ones are within 0.25 oz. (7 grams) of the old ones.

Measuring Bearing Clearance

1. Place connecting rods and upper bearing halves on the proper crankpins (connecting rod journals).

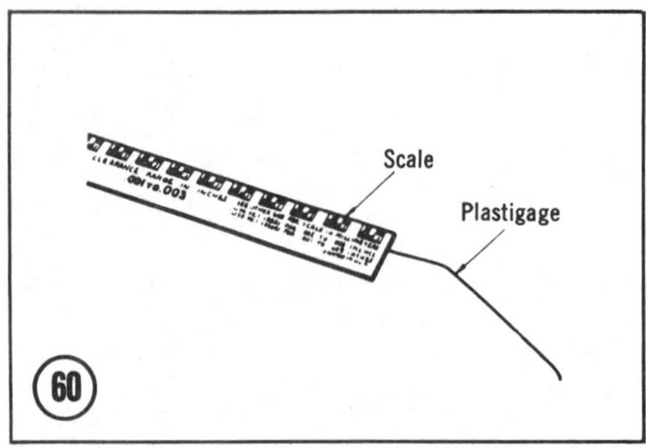

2. Cut a piece of Plastigage (**Figure 60**) the width of the bearing. Place the Plastigage on the crankpin, then install the lower bearing half and cap.

NOTE
Do not place Plastigage over the crankpin oil hole.

3. Tighten the connecting rod cap to specifications (end of chapter). Do not rotate the crankshaft while the Plastigage is in place.
4. Remove the connecting rod cap. Bearing clearance is determined by comparing the width of the flattened Plastigage to the markings on the envelope (**Figure 61**). If clearance is excessive, the crankshaft must be reground and undersized bearings installed.

Installing Piston/Connecting Rod Assembly

Refer to **Figure 49**.
1. Make sure the pistons are correctly installed on the connecting rods. The notch on the piston goes toward the front of the engine. The oil hole in the connecting rod big end goes toward the right-hand side of the engine.
2. Be sure the ring gaps are positioned correctly (**Figure 58**).
3. Immerse the entire piston in clean engine oil. Coat the cylinder wall with oil.
4. Slide a ring compressor over the rings. Compress the rings into the grooves.
5. Install the piston/connecting rod assembly in its cylinder as shown in **Figure 62**. Tap lightly with a wooden hammer handle to insert the piston. Be sure the connecting rod number (or punch mark) on the connecting rod corresponds with the cylinder number (counting from the front of the engine).

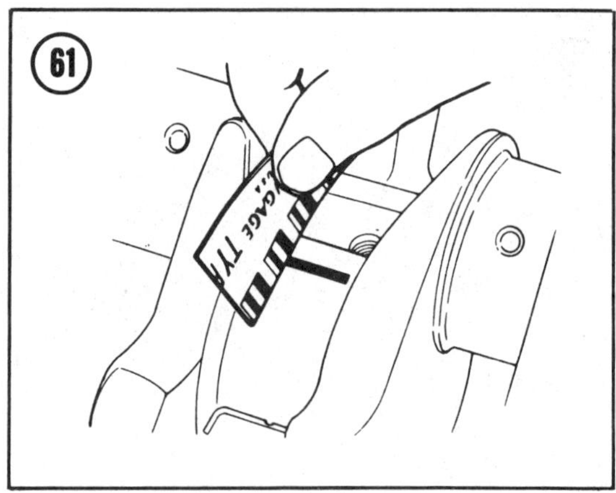

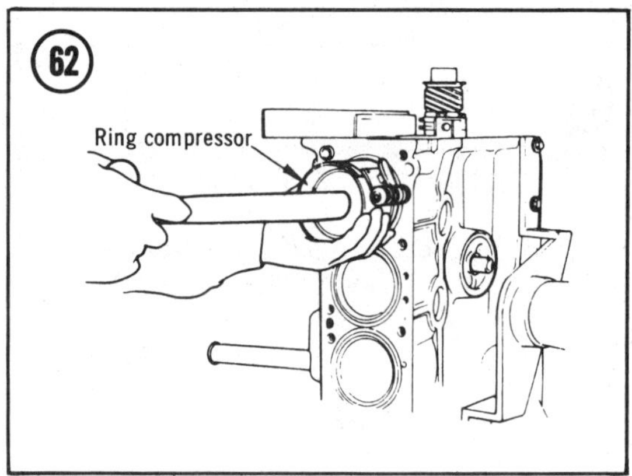

CAUTION
Use extreme care not to let connecting rod nick crankshaft journal.

6. Clean the connecting rod bearings carefully, including the back sides. Coat the crankpins and bearings with clean engine oil. Place the bearings in the connecting rod and cap.
7. Install the connecting rod cap. Make sure the cylinder number on the rod and cap are on the same side. Tighten the cam nuts to specifications (end of chapter).
8. Recheck connecting rod big end play as described under *Connecting Rod Inspection*, Step 2.

CRANKSHAFT

Removal

1. Unbolt the main bearing caps. Place the caps in order on a bench. A puller may be necessary to remove the center and rear caps.

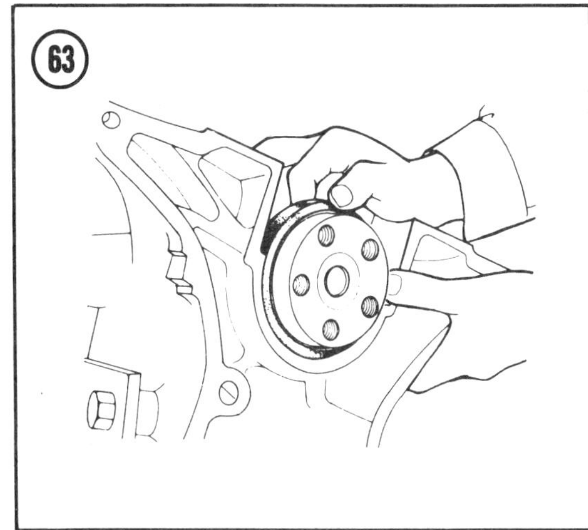

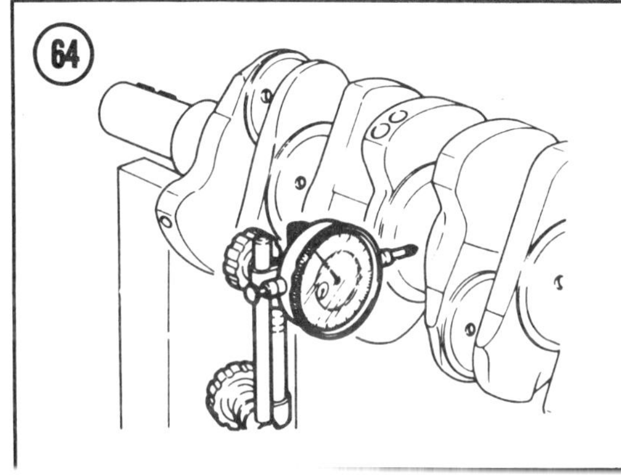

2. Remove 2 side oil seals, then take the rear oil seal off the crankshaft (**Figure 63**).
3. Lift the crankshaft out of the engine. Lay the crankshaft, main bearings, and bearing caps in order on a clean surface.

Inspection

1. Clean the crankshaft thoroughly in solvent. Blow out the oil passages with compressed air.

NOTE
If you don't have precision measuring equipment, have a machine shop perform Steps 2 and 3.

2. Examine crankpins and main bearing journals for wear, scoring, and cracks. Check all journals against specifications (end of chapter) for out-of-roundness, taper, and wear. If necessary, have the crankshaft reground.

3. Check the crankshaft for bending. Mount the crankshaft between accurate centers (such as V-blocks or a lathe) and rotate it one full turn with a dial gauge contacting the center journal. See **Figure 64**. Actual bend is half the reading shown on the gauge. The crankshaft must be reground if bent beyond specifications.
4. Measure crankshaft end play. Install the crankshaft in the block. Insert a feeler gauge between the crankshaft and the center bearing flange. See **Figure 65**. Replace center bearing if end play exceeds specifications.

Measuring Main Bearing Clearance

Main bearing clearance is measured in the same manner as connecting rod bearing clearance, described earlier in this chapter. Excessive clearance requires that the bearings be replaced, the crankshaft be reground, or both.

Installation

1. Thoroughly clean bearings, including the back sides.
2. Install the bearings in the cylinder block and bearing caps. The center bearing is flanged. No. 2 and 4 bearings are interchangeable. No. 1 and 5 bearings look alike, but No. 1 has an oil hole and No. 5 does not. On 1970-1973 models, all upper and lower bearing halves are interchangeable except No. 1. On 1974 and later engines, all upper and lower bearings are interchangeable.

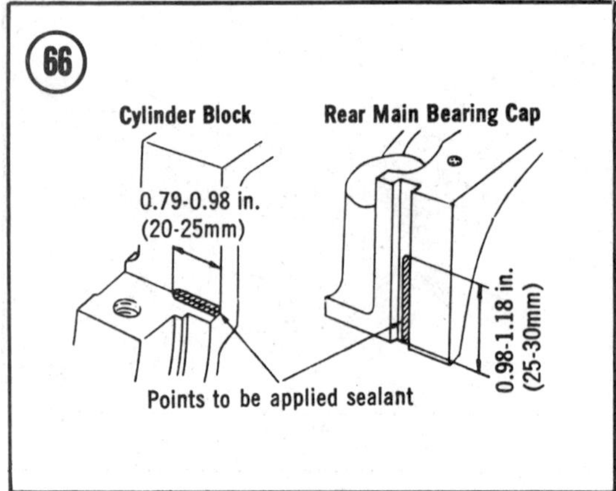

3. Make sure the bearing locating tangs are correctly positioned in the cylinder block and bearing cap grooves.
4. Coat the bearings freely with clean engine oil. Lay the crankshaft in the block. Coat the crankshaft journals with engine oil.
5. Install the bearing caps and tighten the cap bolts slightly. Make sure the arrow marks on the caps face the front of the engine.

NOTE

Apply small amounts of gasket sealer to the rear bearing cap and block as shown in ***Figure 66.***

6. Gently push the crankshaft toward the front and rear of the engine to verify that the bearings and caps are properly aligned and seated.
7. Tighten the cap bolts to specifications (end of chapter). Tighten gradually in 2 or 3 separate stages, starting with the center cap and working outward. Rotate the crankshaft during tightening to make sure it isn't binding. If the crankshaft is difficult to turn, stop and find out why before tightening further. Check for foreign material on bearings and journals. Make absolutely certain that bearings are the correct size, especially if the crankshaft has been reground. Never use undersize bearings if the crankshaft has not been reground.
8. Recheck crankshaft end play (**Figure 65**).
9. Tap the rear side seals into place (**Figure 67**). Install the rear seal with a drift such as Datsun ST 15310000 or Kent-Moore J-25640-01 (**Figure 68**). Use a piece of 2-inch pipe if the drift is not available.

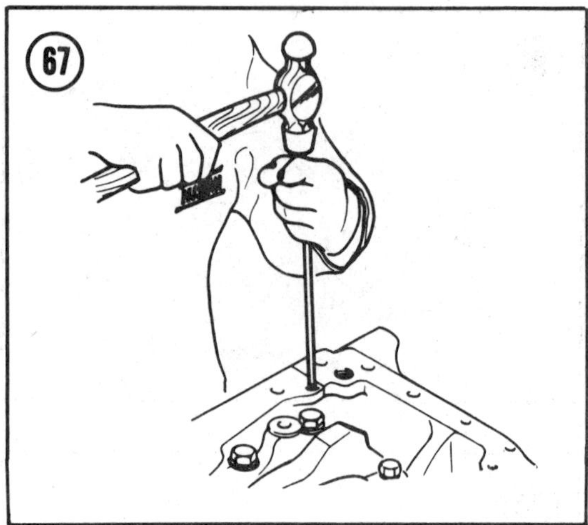

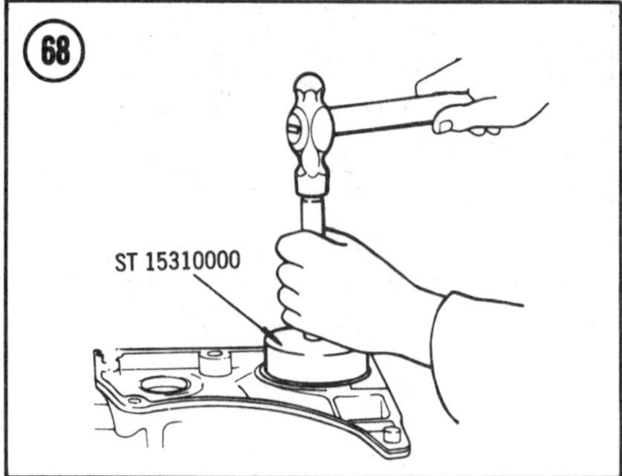

Pilot Bushing

The pilot bushing, located inside the rear end of the crankshaft, supports the transmission input on manual transmission vehicles. Inspect the bushing for visible wear and damage. Have it replaced by a Datsun dealer or machine shop if defects are apparent.

CYLINDER BLOCK INSPECTION

1. Remove the crankcase oil separator prior to inspection. See **Figure 69**.
2. Clean the block thoroughly with solvent and check all freeze plugs for leaks. Replace any freeze plugs that are suspect. It is a good idea to replace all of them. While cleaning, check oil and water passages for dirt, sludge, and corrosion. If the passages are very dirty, the block should be boiled out by a dealer or machine shop.

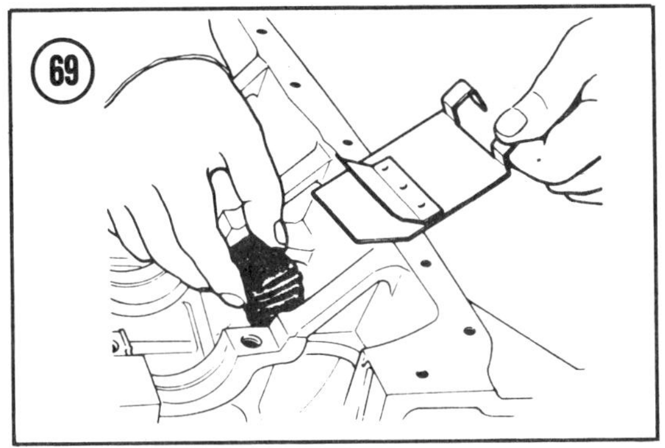

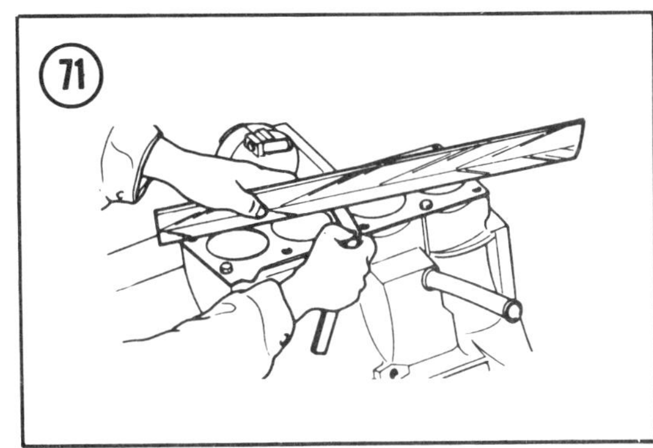

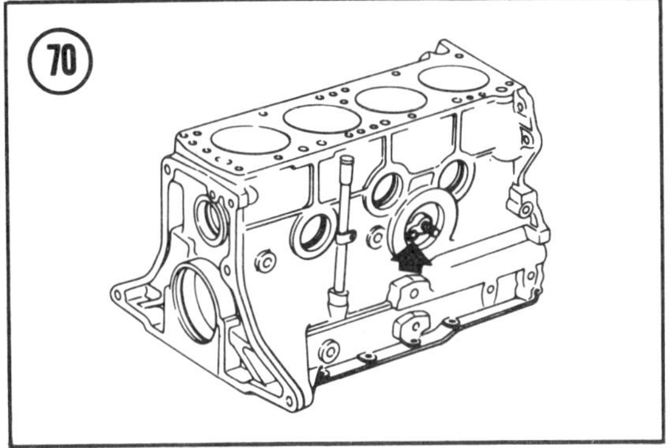

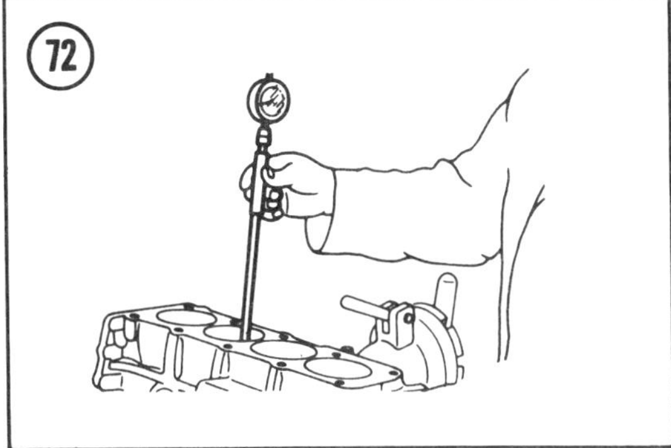

NOTE

Block boiling necessitates replacement of all freeze plugs. However, a block dirty enough to need boiling almost certainly needs to have these parts replaced anyway.

3. Check the oil pressure relief valve (**Figure 70**) for cracks or other damage. If damaged, pry the valve out with a screwdriver and tap in a new one.
4. Examine the block for cracks.
5. Check flatness of the cylinder block's top surface. Use an accurate straightedge as shown in **Figure 71**. Have the block resurfaced if it is warped more than 0.004 in. (0.1mm).
6. Measure the cylinder bores for out-of-roundness or excessive wear with a bore gauge (**Figure 72**). Measure the bores at top, center, and bottom, in front-rear and side-to-side directions. Compare the measurements to specifications at the end of the chapter. If the cylinders exceed maximum tolerances, they must be rebored. Reboring is also necessary if the cylinder walls are badly scuffed or scored.

NOTE

If one cylinder is bored out, all cylinders must be bored to the same diameter. Cylinders must be bored in the following order: 2 4 1 3.

FLYWHEEL

Removal/Installation

1. Remove the engine. Separate the engine and transmission.
2. Remove the clutch from the flywheel (see Chapter Nine).
3. Unbolt the flywheel from the crankshaft (**Figure 73**).
4. Install by reversing Steps 1-3. Tighten flywheel bolts to specifications (end of chapter). Tighten the bolts gradually in a diagonal pattern.

Inspection

1. Check the flywheel for scoring and wear. If the surface is glazed or slightly scratched, have it resurfaced by a machine shop. Replace the flywheel if damage is severe.

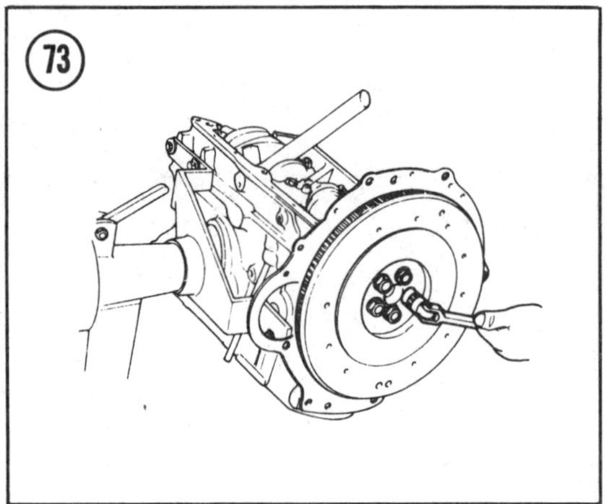

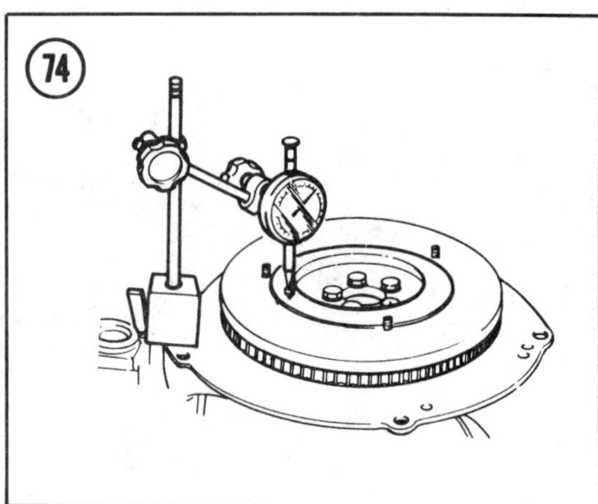

2. Measure flywheel runout with a dial gauge (**Figure 74**). If runout is excessive, check for foreign material between flywheel and crankshaft flange. If there is none, replace the flywheel or have it resurfaced by a machine shop.

3. Inspect the flywheel ring gear teeth. If the teeth are chipped, broken, or excessively worn, have a new starter ring shrunk onto the flywheel by a dealer or machine shop.

TORQUE CONVERTER DRIVE PLATE

The torque converter drive plate is bolted to the crankshaft in the same manner as the flywheel. The drive plate bolts are torqued to 101-116 ft.-lb. (14-16 mkg).

Drive plate runout is measured in the same manner as flywheel runout. Replace the drive plate if runout exceeds 0.020 in. (0.5mm). The drive plate must also be replaced if the ring gear is damaged or worn excessively.

Table 1 L-SERIES ENGINE SPECIFICATIONS

Cylinder head	
Maximum surface warp	0.1 mm (0.004 in.)
Valve face angle	45°
Valves	
Head diameter, intake	
Early L16	1.496 in. (38mm)
Late L16, L18	1.654 in. (42mm)
1975 L20B	1.650-1.657 in. (41.9-42.1mm)
1976 and later L20B	1.654-1.661 in. (42.0-42.2mm)
Head diameter, exhaust	
L16	1.299 in. (33mm)
L18	1.378 in. (35mm)
L20B	1.378-1.386 in. (35.0-35.2mm)
Stem diameter, intake	
Early L16	0.315 in. (8mm)
All others	0.3136-0.3142 in. (87.965-7.980mm)
Stem diameter, exhaust	
Early L16	0.315 in. (8mm)
All others	0.3128-0.3132 in. (7.945-7.960mm)
Valve length, intake	
Early L16	4.56 in. (115.9mm)
All others	4.524-4.535 in. (114.9-115.2mm)
Valve length, exhaust	
Early L16	4.567 in. (116mm)
All others	4.555-4.567 in. (115.7-116.0mm)
Valve face angle	45° 30'
Head edge thickness, minimum	0.5 mm (0.020 in.)
Valve springs	
Free length, inner	1.766 in. (44.85mm)
Free length, outer	
Early L-16	2.05 in. (52mm)
All others	1.968 in. (49.98mm)
Loaded length	
Inner	0.965 in. @ 56.2 lb. (24.5mm @ 25.5 kg)
Early L16 outer	1.21 in. @ 105 lb. (39.7mm @ 47.8 kg)
All other outer	1.161 in. @ 108 lb. (29.5mm @ 49.0 kg)
Bend, maximum	
1970-1977	0.063 in. (1.6mm)
1978-1980 inner	1.9 mm (0.075 in.)
1978-1980 outer	2.2 mm (0.087 in.)

(continued)

Table 1 L-SERIES ENGINE SPECIFICATIONS (continued)

Valve Guides	
Valve stem-to-guide clearance, standard	
Early L16 intake	0.0006-0.0018 in. (0.015-0.045mm)
All other intake	0.0008-0.0021 in. (0.020-0.053mm)
All exhaust	0.0016-0.0029 in. (0.040-0.073mm)
Valve stem-to-guide clearance, maximum	0.1 mm (0.004 in.)
Guide inner diameter	0.3150-0.3157 in. (8.000-8.018mm)
Guide hole diameter	
Standard	0.4718.0.4723 in. (11.985-11.996mm)
Oversize	0.4797-0.4802 in. (12.185-12.196mm)
Camshaft	
End play, 1970-1979	0.003-0.015 in. (0.08-0.38mm)
End play, 1980	Less than 0.008 in. (0.2mm)
Lobe height	
Early L16	1.5728-1.5748 in. (39.95-40.00mm)
All others	1.5866-1.5886 in. (40.30-40.35mm)
Maximum lobe wear	0.010 in. (0.25mm)
Journal diameter	1.8878-1.8883 in. (47.949-47.962mm)
Bend, maximum	0.002 in. (0.05mm)
Bearing inner diameter	1.8898-1.8904 in. (48.000-48.016mm)
Journal-to-bearing clearance, through 1979	
Standard (1970-1978)	0.0010-0.0022 in. (0.025-0.055mm)
Standard (1979)	0.0009-0.0026 in. (0.024-0.066mm)
Maximum	0.005 in. (0.012mm)
Journal-to-bearing clearance, 1980	
Standard	0.038-0.067 mm (0.0015-0.002 in.)
Maximum	0.1 mm (0.004 in.)
Oil pump	
Outer rotor to body clearance	
Standard	0.006-0.008 in. (0.15-0.21 mm)
Maximum	0.020 in. (0.05mm)
Rotor tip clearance	
Standard	0.005 in. (0.12mm) or less
Maximum	0.008 in. (0.20mm)
Rotor to straightedge clearance	0.002 in. (0.06mm) or less
Pump body to straightedge clearance	0.001 in. (0.03mm) or less
Connecting rods	
Big end play	
Standard	0.2-0.3 mm (0.008-0.012 mm)
Maximum	0.6 mm (0.024 in.)

(continued)

Table 1 L-SERIES ENGINE SPECIFICATIONS (continued)

Bearing clearance	
Standard	0.0010-0.0022 in. (0.025-0.055mm)
Maximum	0.005 in. (0.12mm)
Bend or twist per 100 mm (3.94 in.) of connecting rod length	
Standard	0.0012 in. (0.03mm)
Maximum	0.002 in. (0.05mm)
Pistons	
Ring gap, early L16 (1)	
Top ring	0.009-0.015 in. (0.23-0.38mm)
Second and oil rings	0.006-0.012 in. (0.15-0.30mm)
Ring gap, late L16 (2)	
Top ring	0.010-0.016 in. (0.25-0.50mm)
Second ring	0.006-0.012 in. (80.15-0.30mm)
Oil ring	0.012-0.036 in. (0.30-0.90mm)
Ring gap, L18	
Top ring	0.014-0.022 in. (0.35-0.55mm)
Second ring	0.012-0.020 in. (0.30-0.50mm)
Oil ring	0.012-0.036 in. (0.30-0.90mm)
Ring gap, L20B	
Top ring	0.010-0.016 in. (0.25-0.40mm)
Second ring (through 1979)	0.012-0.020 in. (0.30-0.50mm)
Second ring (1980)	0.006-0.012 in. (0.15-0.30mm)
Oil ring	0.30-0.90 mm (0.012-0.036 in.)
Maximum gap, all rings	1 mm (0.039 in.)
Ring side clearance, L16	
Top ring	0.0016-0.0031 in. (0.04-0.08mm)
Second ring	0.0012-0.0028 in. (0.03-0.07mm)
Oil ring (3)	0.0010-0.0025 in. (0.025-0.063mm)
Ring side clearance, L18	
Top ring	0.0018-0.0031 in. (0.045-0.080mm)
Second ring	0.0012-0.0028 in. (0.03-0.07mm)
Oil ring	None
Side clearance, L20B	
Top ring	0.0016-0.0029 in. (0.040-0.073mm)
Second ring (through 1979)	0.0012-0.0028 in. (0.030-0.070mm)
Second ring (1980)	0.0012-0.0025 in. (0.030-0.063mm)
Oil ring	None
Side clearance, maximum	
Top and second rings	0.004 in. (0.1mm)
One-piece oil rings	0.004 in. (0.1mm)
3-piece oil rings	None
Piston diameter, L16	
Standard	3.2671-3.2691 in. (82.985-83.035mm)
0.020 in. (0.5mm) oversize	3.2860-3.2880 in. (83.465-83.515mm)
0.039 in. (1mm) oversize	3.3057-3.3077 in. (83.965-84.015mm)
Piston diameter, L18 and L20B	
Standard	3.3459-3.3478 in. (84.985-85.035mm)
0.5 mm (0.020 in.) oversize	3.3648-3.3667 in. (84.465-85.515mm)
1.0 mm (0.039 in.) oversize	3.3844-3.3864 in. (95.965-86.015mm)

(continued)

Table 1 L-SERIES ENGINE SPECIFICATIONS (continued)

Crankshaft	
Main bearing clearance	
Standard	0.0008-0.0024 in. (0.020-0.062mm)
Maximum	0.005 in. (0.12mm)
Journal diameter	
L16 and L18	2.1631-2.1636 in. (54.942-54.955mm)
L20B (1975-1979)	2.3599-2.3604 in. (59.942-59.955mm)
L20B (1980)	2.1631-2.1636 in. (54.942-54.955mm)
Crankpin diameter (all)	1.9670-1.9675 in. (49.961-49.974mm)
Journal and crankpin out-of-round and taper	
Standard	Less than 0.01 mm (0.0004 in.)
Maximum	0.03 mm (0.0012 in.)
Crankshaft bend (total indicator reading)	
Standard	Less than 0.002 in. (0.05mm)
Maximum	0.004 in. (0.1mm)
Crankshaft end play	
Standard	0.002-0.007 in. (0.05-0.18 mm)
Maximum	0.012 in. (0.3mm)

1. One-piece oil ring.
2. Three-piece oil ring.
3. Side clearance is measured on one-piece oil rings only.

Table 2 TIGHTENING TORQUES, L-SERIES ENGINES

Fastener	Ft.-lb.	Mkg
A/C compressor bracket	33-40	4.5-5.5
Alternator bracket	29-43	4-6
Alternator to adjusting bar	14-22	2-3
Camshaft locate plate bolts	4.5-6.5	0.6-0.9
Camshaft sprocket bolt	87-116	2-16
Carburetor nuts	4-7	0.5-1.0
Chain guides	4.5-7	0.6-1.0
Chain tensioner	4.5-7	0.6-1.0
Connecting rod caps		
8mm bolt shaft diameter	23-27	3.2-3.8
9mm bolt shaft diameter	33-40	4.5-5.5
Crankshaft pulley bolt	87-116	12-16
Cylinder head to block		
First turn	29	4
Second turn	43	6
Third turn (early)*	43-51	6-7
Third turn (late)*	51-61	7.0-8.5
Cylinder head to front cover	3-6	0.4-0.8
Exhaust manifold	9-12	1.2-1.6
Flywheel to crankshaft		
Early (separate lockwashers)	69-76	9.5-10.5
Late (integral washers)	101-116	14-16
Front cover bolts		
M8 (large)	7-9	1.0-1.2
M6 (small)	3-4	0.4-0.6
Intake manifold	9-12	1.2-1.6
Main bearing caps	33-40	4.5-5.5
Motor mounts, 521 pickup		
Bracket to cylinder block	18-22	2.5-3.0
Bracket to rubber insulator	19-23	2.6-3.2
Insulator to frame	8-12	1.1-1.6
Motor mounts, 620 and 720 pickups		
Bracket to engine (1972-1974)	14-18	1.9-2.5
Bracket to engine (1975-on)	19-26	2.6-3.6
Bracket to insulator (1972-1974)	14-18	1.9-2.5
Bracket to insulator (1975-on)	19-26	2.6-3.6
Insulator to frame	10-13	1.4-1.8
Oil pan	4.5-7	0.6-0.9
Oil pan drain plug	14-22	2-3
Oil pump	8-11	1.1-1.5
Oil strainer	7-12	1.0-1.6
Rocker cover	7-12	1.0-1.6
Rocker pivot locknuts	36-43	5-6
Spark plugs	11-14	1.5-2.0
Water inlet and outlet	7-12	1.0-1.6
Water pump		
M8 (large)	7-12	1.0-1.6
M6 (small)	3-4	0.4-0.5

*Late type head bolts, used from engine no. L16-203416, have a circular groove in the top surface of the bolt head. Early type head bolts do not.

4

NOTE: If you own a 1982 or later model, first check the Supplement at the back of the book for any new service information.

CHAPTER FIVE

NAPS-Z ENGINE

The 1981 models use the NAPS-Z engine, model Z22. NAPS stands for Nissan Anti-pollution System. Z is the engine design code. 22 indicates piston displacement of 2.2 liters.

The engine uses a crossflow cylinder head with hemispherical combustion chambers. The ignition system uses 2 spark plugs per cylinder. This ensures that the fuel mixture will burn, even though a larger than normal percentage of exhaust gas is recirculated. Exhaust gas recirculation is used to control emissions.

The overhead camshaft, mounted in 4 brackets on top of the cylinder head, operates the valves through finger rockers. The crankshaft, supported by 5 main bearings, drives the camshaft through a double-row chain and 2 sprockets. The lubrication system consists of an external oil pump and full-flow filter.

Specifications and tightening torques are listed in **Table 1** and **Table 2** at the end of the chapter.

ENGINE REMOVAL

The engine and transmission are removed as a unit, then separated.

1. Disconnect the negative cable from the battery.
2. Remove the hood. See *Hood*, Chapter Fourteen.
3. Drain the oil from engine and transmission.
4. Remove the air cleaner. See *Air Cleaner Removal/Installation*, Chapter Six.
5. Disconnect the hoses and wires connecting the engine to the truck. See **Figure 1**.
6. If equipped with air conditioning, loosen the idler pulley locknut (**Figure 2**). Loosen the adjusting bolt, then remove the compressor drive belt. Unbolt the compressor from the engine, then tie it back out of the way. See **Figure 3**.

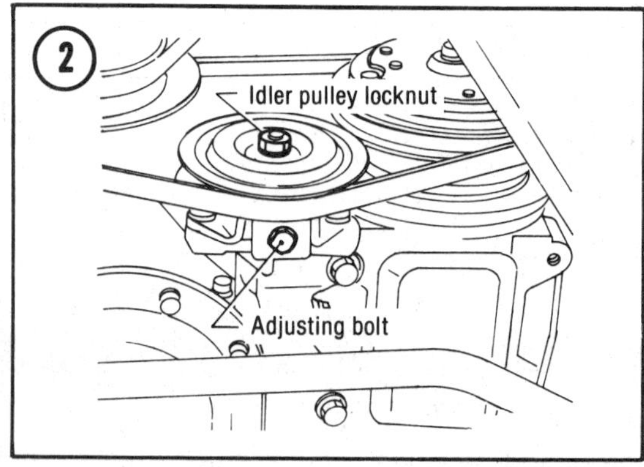

1

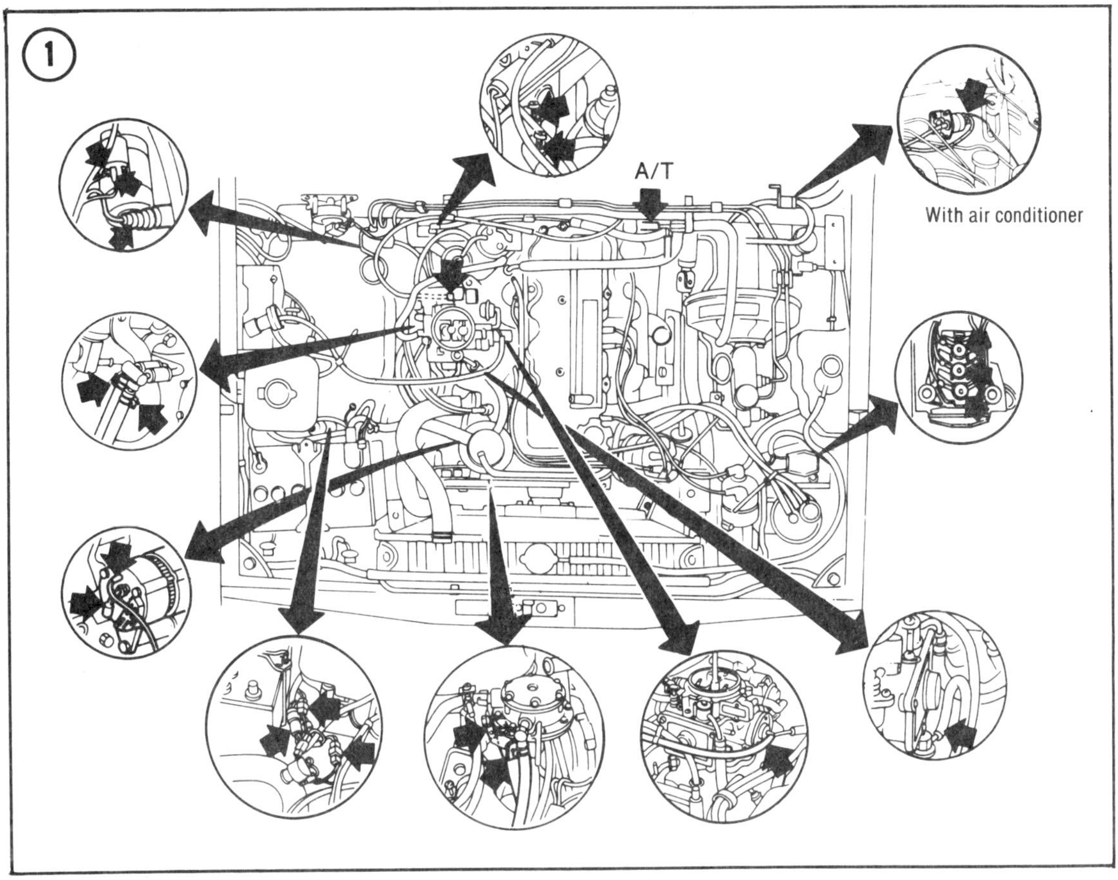

A/T

With air conditioner

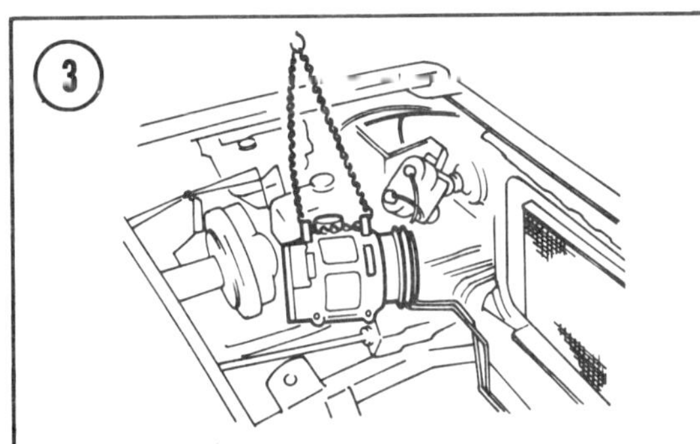

3

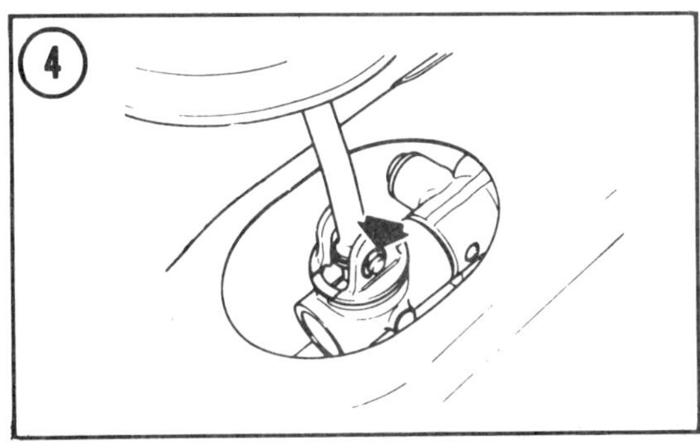

4

WARNING

Never disconnect the compressor hoses. The refrigerant can cause frostbite if it touches skin, and blindness if it touches the eyes. If discharged near an open flame, the refrigerant forms poisonous gas.

7. Remove the console. See *Console*, Chapter Fourteen.
8. If equipped with a manual transmission, remove the snap ring and shift lever pivot pin (**Figure 4**). Take the shift lever out.
9. If equipped with automatic transmission, disconnect the shift linkage. See **Figure 5**.
10. Drain the cooling system. See *Cooling System Flushing*, Chapter Seven.
11. Remove the upper and lower radiator hoses. Remove the radiator and shroud. See *Radiator*, Chapter Seven.
12. On manual transmissions, disconnect the reverse switch and neutral switch wires from the side of the transmission. See **Figure 6**.
13. On automatic transmissions, disconnect

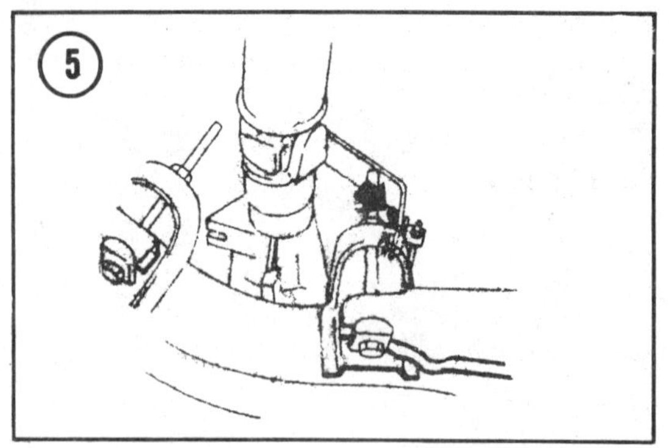
5

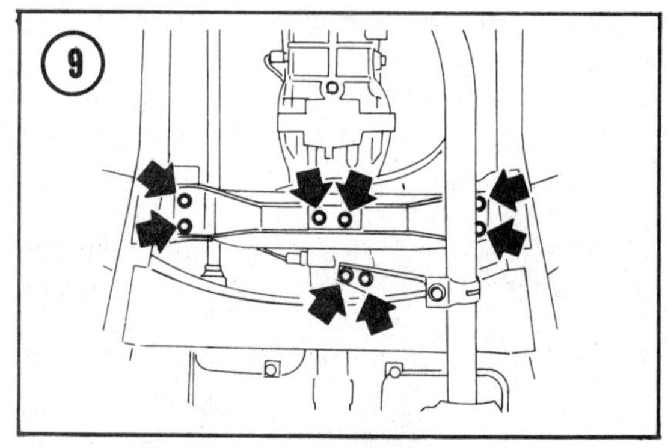
9

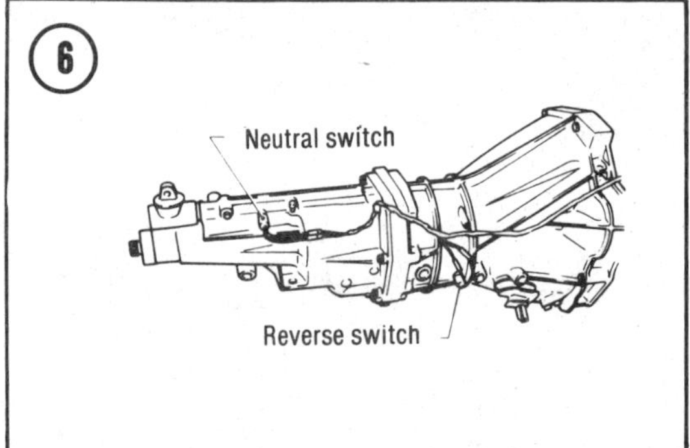
6
Neutral switch
Reverse switch

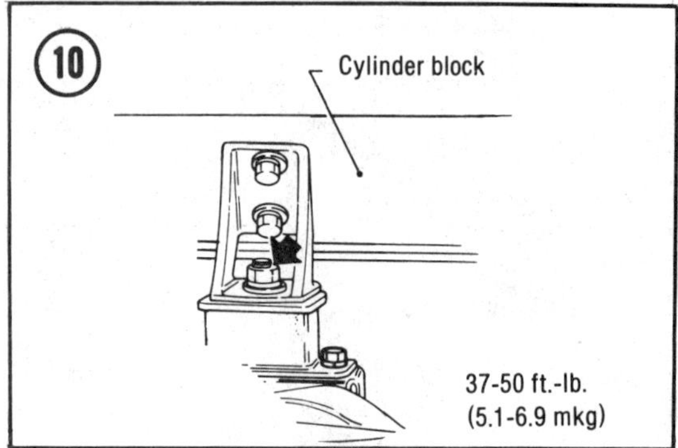
10
Cylinder block
37-50 ft.-lb.
(5.1-6.9 mkg)

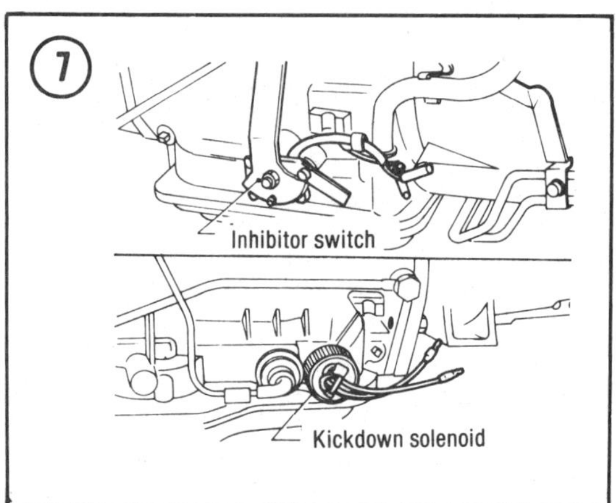
7
Inhibitor switch
Kickdown solenoid

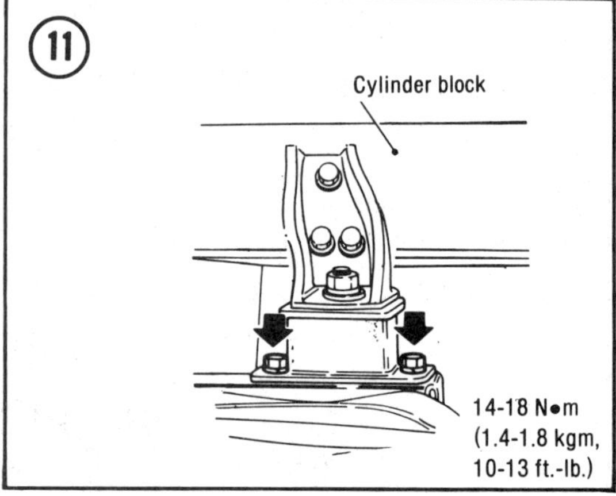
11
Cylinder block
14-18 N•m
(1.4-1.8 kgm,
10-13 ft.-lb.)

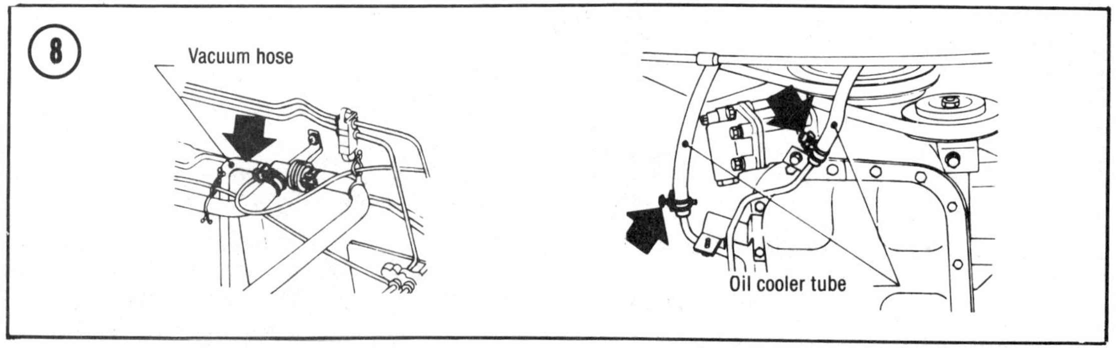
8
Vacuum hose
Oil cooler tube

the inhibitor switch and kickdown solenoid wires. See **Figure 7**.

14. Detach the handbrake cables from the balance lever. See *Handbrake*, Chapter Eleven.

15. Remove the drive shaft. See *Drive Shaft*, Chapter Twelve.

16. Remove the clutch operating cylinder. See *Operating Cylinder, Removal/Installation*, Chapter Nine.

17. Remove the front exhaust pipe. See *Exhaust System*, Chapter Five.

18. If equipped with automatic transmission, disconnect the vacuum hose and oil cooler tubes. See **Figure 8**. Plug the cooler tubes.

19. Attach a hoist to the engine. Hydraulic crane type hoists, available from rental dealers, are the easiest to use.

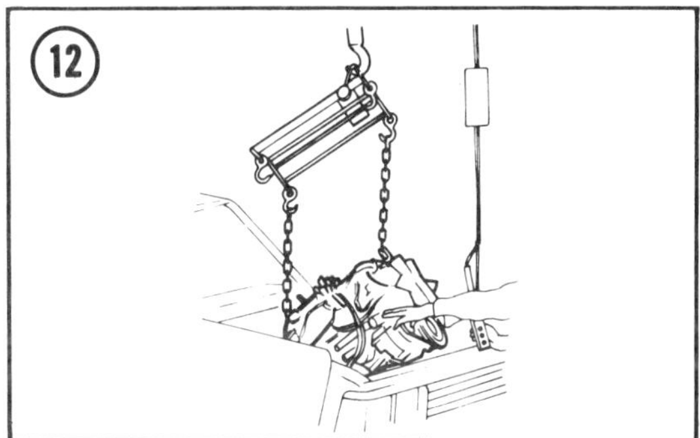

20. Detach the transmission mounting member from the transmission and body. See **Figure 9**.

21. Remove the motor mount nuts and bolts. See **Figure 10** and **Figure 11**.

CAUTION
At this point, there should not be any hoses, wires, or linkages connecting the engine and transmission to the truck. Recheck this to be sure nothing can hamper engine removal.

22. Lift the engine and transmission out of the engine compartment. See **Figure 12**.

CAUTION
Do not let the engine and transmission strike equipment on the engine compartment sidewalls.

ENGINE INSTALLATION

Engine installation is simply the reverse of removal. Fasten the engine and transmission securely to their mounts before tightening anything else. **Figure 13** shows the engine and transmission mounts. Fill the cooling system with a 50/50 mixture of antifreeze and water. Fill the engine and transmission with oils recommended in Chapter Three.

5

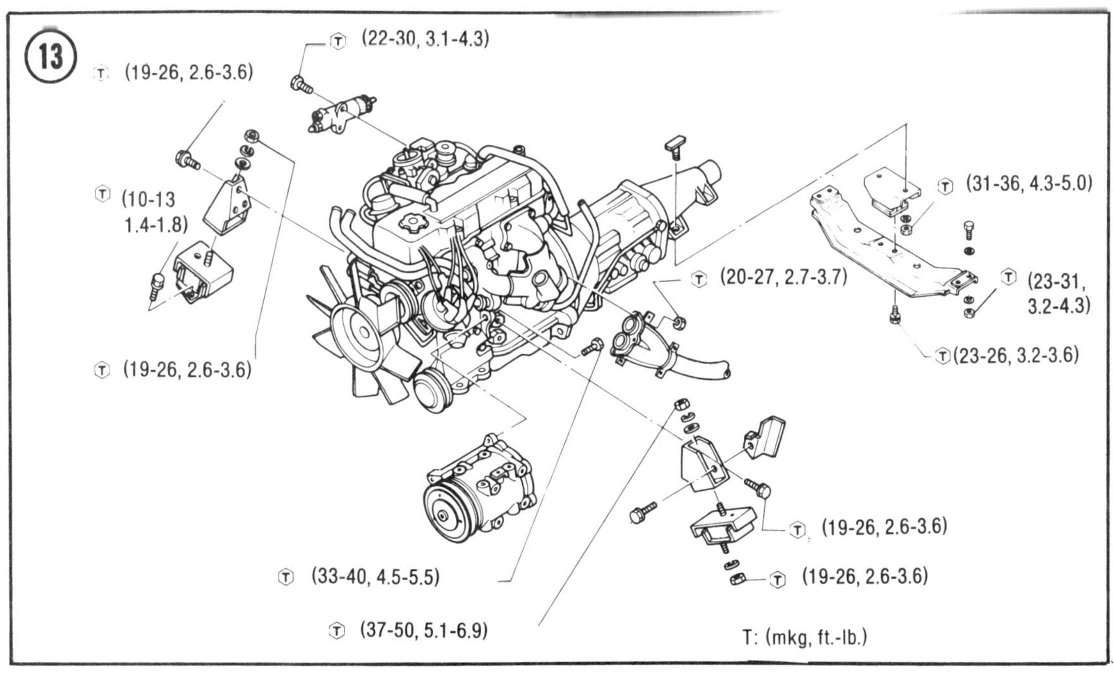

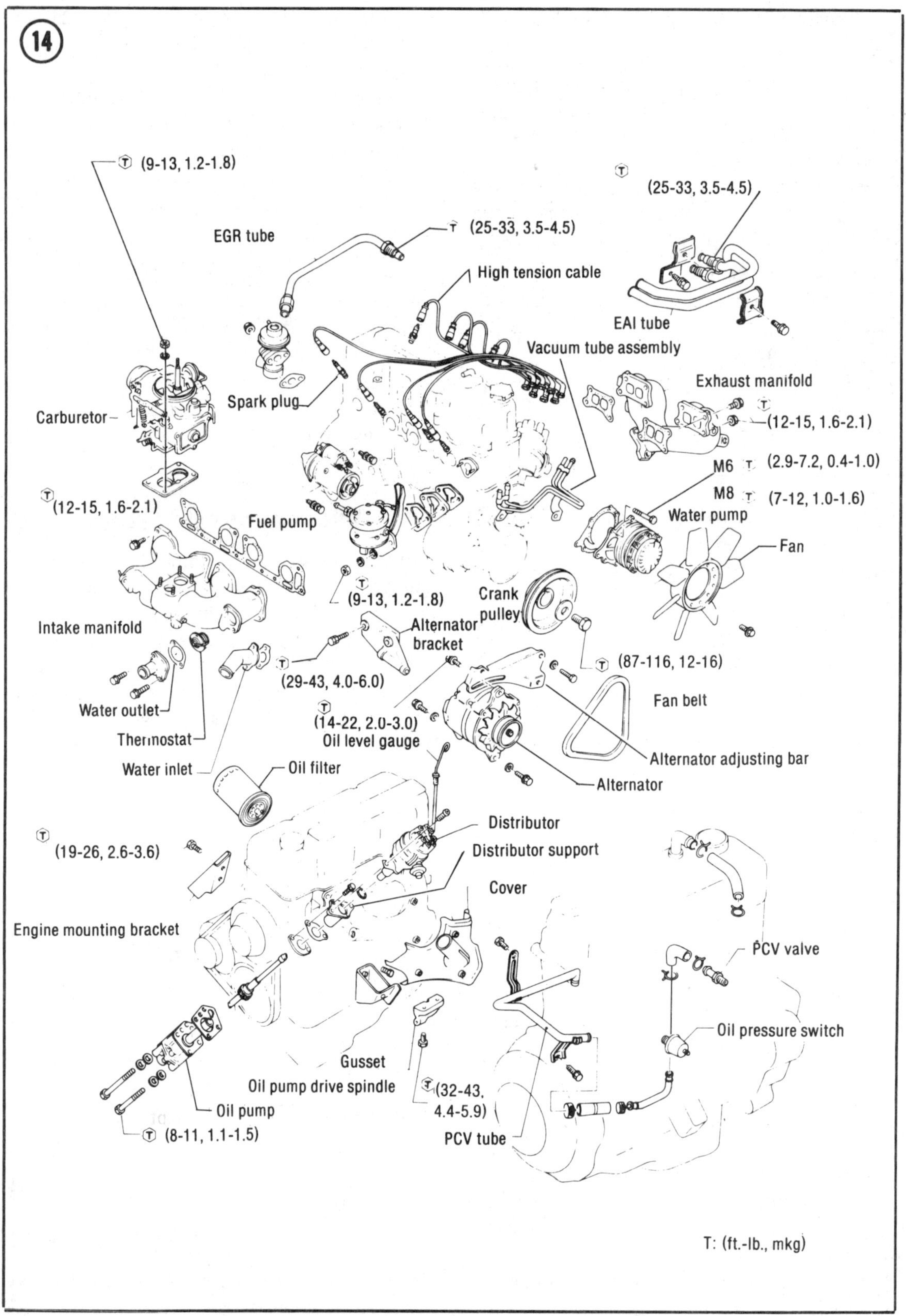
14
(9-13, 1.2-1.8)
(25-33, 3.5-4.5)
EGR tube
(25-33, 3.5-4.5)
High tension cable
EAI tube
Vacuum tube assembly
Exhaust manifold
Spark plug
Carburetor
(12-15, 1.6-2.1)
M6 (2.9-7.2, 0.4-1.0)
M8 (7-12, 1.0-1.6)
Water pump
(12-15, 1.6-2.1)
Fuel pump
Fan
(9-13, 1.2-1.8)
Crank pulley
Intake manifold
Alternator bracket
(87-116, 12-16)
(29-43, 4.0-6.0)
Fan belt
Water outlet
(14-22, 2.0-3.0)
Oil level gauge
Thermostat
Alternator adjusting bar
Water inlet
Oil filter
Alternator
Distributor
(19-26, 2.6-3.6)
Distributor support
Cover
Engine mounting bracket
PCV valve
Oil pressure switch
Gusset
Oil pump drive spindle
(32-43, 4.4-5.9)
Oil pump
(8-11, 1.1-1.5)
PCV tube
T: (ft.-lb., mkg)

DISASSEMBLY CHECKLISTS

These checklists tell how much of the engine to remove and disassemble to do a specific type of service (such as a valve job). They will prevent unnecessary work, and make sure nothing is left out.

To use the checklists, remove and inspect each part mentioned. Then go through the checklists backwards, installing the parts. Each major part is covered under its own heading in this chapter, unless otherwise noted.

Figure 14 shows the engine's external parts. **Figure 15** shows internal parts. Refer to them as needed for these procedures.

Decarbonizing or Valve Service

1. Remove the intake and exhaust manifolds.
2. Remove the rocker arms and camshaft.
3. Remove the cylinder head.
4. Remove and inspect valves. Inspect valve guides and seats, repairing or replacing as necessary.
5. Assemble by reversing Steps 1-4.

Valve and Ring Service

1. Perform Steps 1-4 for valve service.
2. Remove the oil pan.
3. Remove the pistons together with the connecting rods.
4. Remove the piston rings. It is not necessary to separate the pistons from the connecting rods unless a piston, connecting rod, or piston pin needs repair or replacement.
5. Assemble by reversing Steps 1-4.

General Overhaul

1. Remove the engine and transmission and separate them. Remove the clutch (Chapter Nine) from manual transmission cars.
2. Remove the motor mount bracket, oil filter, and oil pressure sender from the right-hand side of the engine.
3. If available, place the engine in a stand. **Figure 16** shows the Datsun stand and adapter. Similar stands are available from rental dealers. The stand isn't absolutely necessary, but will make the job much easier.
4. Check the engine for signs of coolant and oil leaks.
5. Clean the outside of the engine.
6. Remove the distributor. See *Ignition System*, Chapter Eight.
7. Remove the hoses and tubes connected to the engine.
8. Remove the fuel lines.
9. Remove the intake and exhaust manifolds.
10. Remove the water pump. See *Water Pump*, Chapter Seven.
11. Remove the oil pump.
12. Remove the rocker arms and camshaft.
13. Remove the front cover, timing chain, and sprockets.
14. Remove the cylinder head.
15. Remove the oil pan and pickup.
16. Remove the pistons and connecting rods.
17. Remove the flywheel or torque converter drive plate.
18. Remove the crankshaft.
19. Inspect the cylinder block.
20. Assemble by reversing Steps 1-19.

INTAKE AND EXHAUST MANIFOLDS

Intake Manifold Removal/Installation

1. If the engine is still in the truck, drain about one gallon of coolant from the radiator. If the coolant is clean, drain it into a clean container and save it for reuse.
2. Remove the air cleaner. See *Air Cleaner, Removal/Installation*, Chapter Six.
3. Disconnect the wires for automatic choke and carburetor solenoid.
4. Disconnect the throttle linkage from the carburetor. See *Throttle Linkage*, Chapter Six.
5. Disconnect the fuel inlet line. Plug the line so it won't leak gasoline.
6. If carburetor removal is planned, do it now. See *Carburetor, Removal/Installation*, Chapter Six.
7. Disconnect the emission control hoses connecting the manifold to engine and car body. See *Vacuum Lines*, Chapter Six.

CAUTION

The intake manifold should come off easily during the next step. If not, make sure all fasteners have been removed.

8. Disconnect the hose shown in **Figure 17** and detach the manifold from the engine.

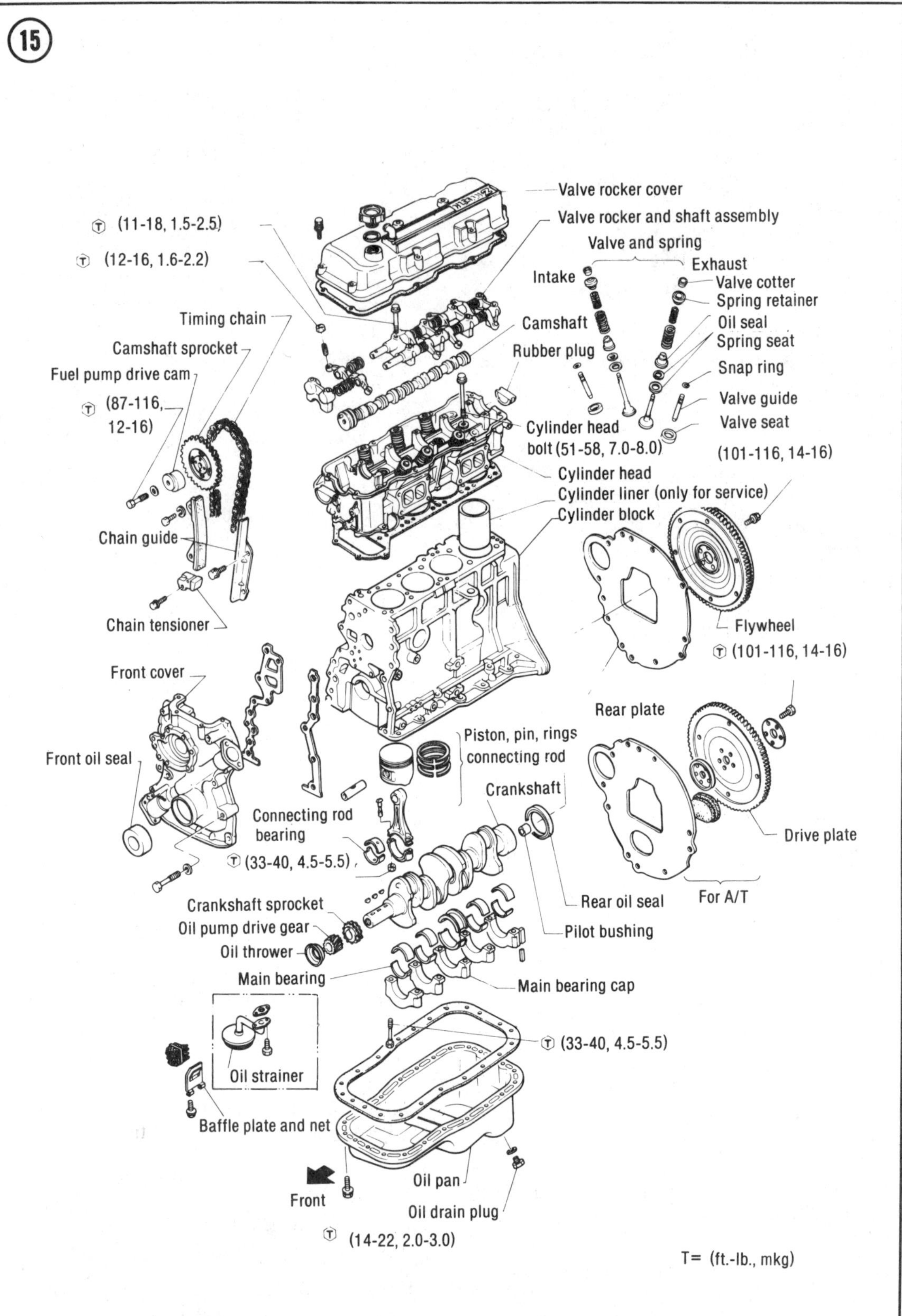
15
Valve rocker cover
(11-18, 1.5-2.5)
Valve rocker and shaft assembly
(12-16, 1.6-2.2)
Valve and spring
Exhaust
Intake
Valve cotter
Spring retainer
Timing chain
Camshaft
Oil seal
Camshaft sprocket
Rubber plug
Spring seat
Fuel pump drive cam
Snap ring
(87-116, 12-16)
Valve guide
Valve seat
Cylinder head bolt (51-58, 7.0-8.0)
(101-116, 14-16)
Cylinder head
Cylinder liner (only for service)
Cylinder block
Chain guide
Chain tensioner
Flywheel
(101-116, 14-16)
Front cover
Rear plate
Piston, pin, rings connecting rod
Front oil seal
Crankshaft
Connecting rod bearing
Drive plate
(33-40, 4.5-5.5)
Crankshaft sprocket
Rear oil seal
For A/T
Oil pump drive gear
Pilot bushing
Oil thrower
Main bearing
Main bearing cap
(33-40, 4.5-5.5)
Oil strainer
Baffle plate and net
Oil pan
Front
Oil drain plug
(14-22, 2.0-3.0)
T= (ft.-lb., mkg)

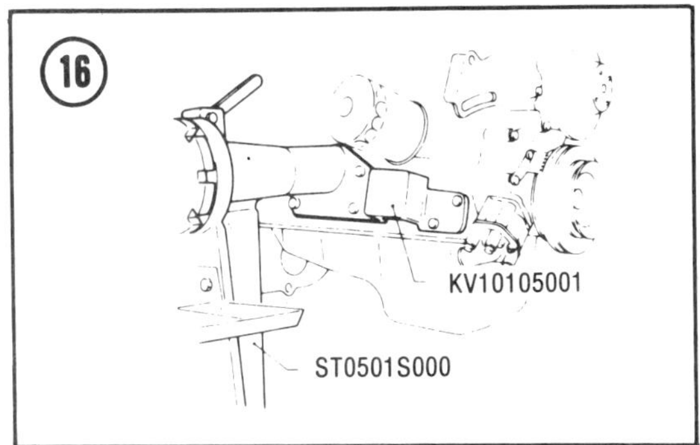

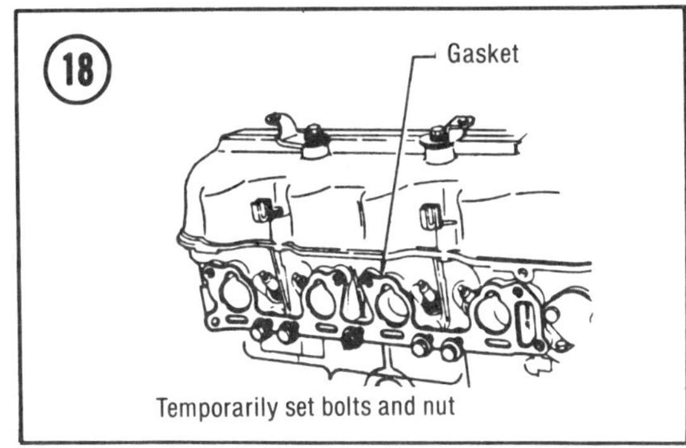

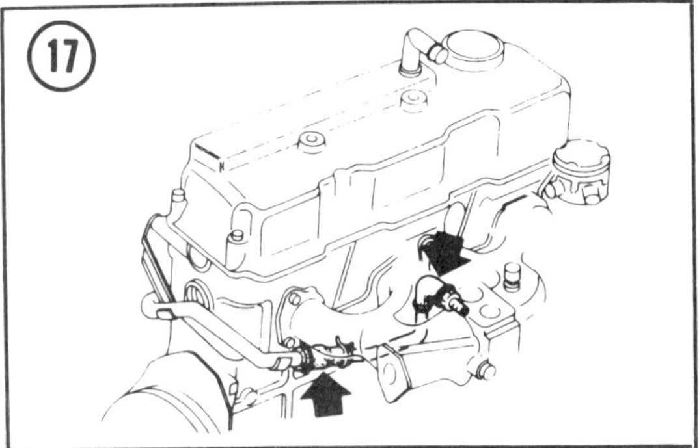

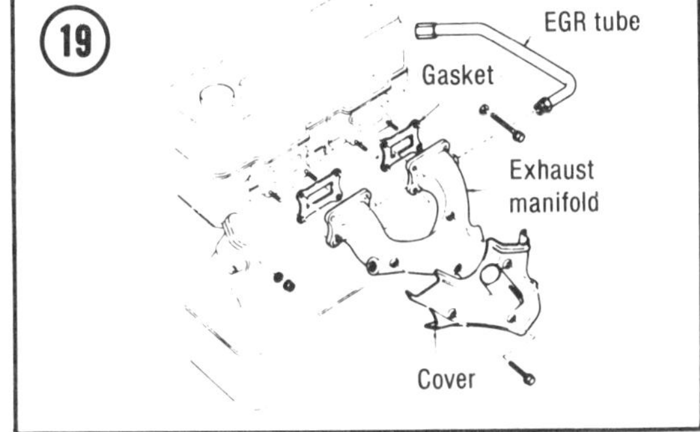

9. Installation is the reverse of removal. To ease installation, loosely install the lower center bolts and nut before installing the manifold. See **Figure 18**. Use a new gasket. Tighten the manifold fasteners to specifications (**Table 2**).

Exhaust Manifold Removal/Installation

1. Remove the air cleaner. See *Air Cleaner, Removal/Installation*, Chapter Six.
2. Disconnect the exhaust pipe from the manifold.
3. Detach the EGR tube from the manifold. See **Figure 19**.

CAUTION
The manifold should come off easily during the next step. If not, make sure all fasteners have been removed.

4. Detach the manifold from the engine. Remove it together with the cover.
5. If necessary, remove the cover from the manifold.
6. Installation is the reverse of removal. Use new gaskets. Tighten fasteners to specifications (**Table 2**).

ROCKER ARMS AND CAMSHAFT

Removal

1. Remove the rocker arm cover.
2. Turn the engine until No. 1 piston is at top center on its compression stroke. When this occurs, the 0° mark on the timing scale aligns with the notch in the crankshaft pulley (**Figure 20**). In addition, the distributor rotor will point to No. 1 terminal in the distributor cap. See **Figure 21**.

NOTE
Check rotor position as well as the timing marks. The timing marks also line when No. 4 cylinder is at TDC on its compression stroke.

3. Paint alignment marks on timing chain and sprocket.
4. Remove the camshaft sprocket bolt.
5. Take the sprocket off the camshaft (**Figure 22**). Let it rest on the engine front cover.
6. If the sprocket is to be removed from the timing chain, support the timing chain with a hardwood wedge. **Figure 23** shows the tool; **Figure 24** shows it in use. This tool keeps the

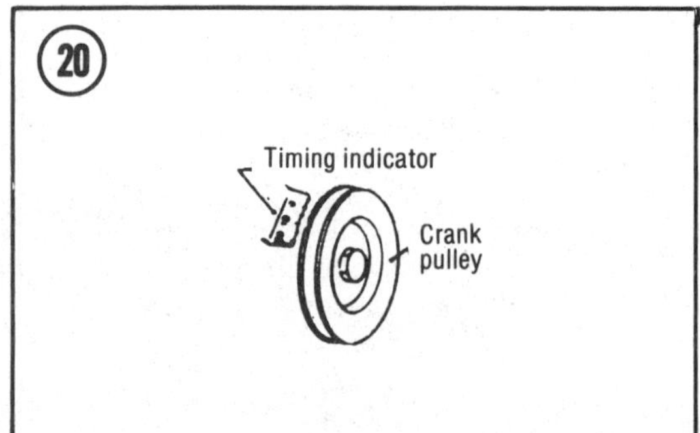

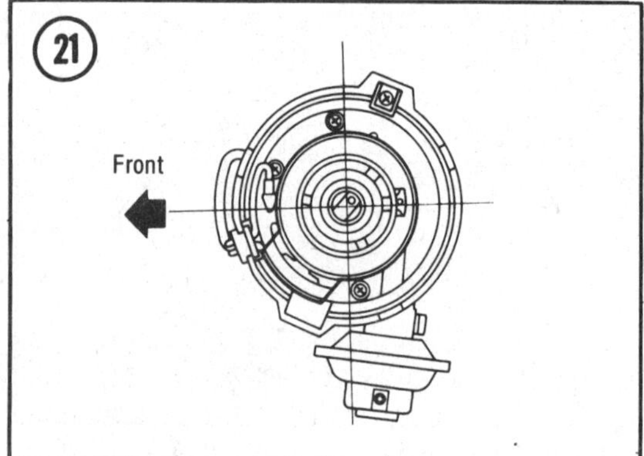

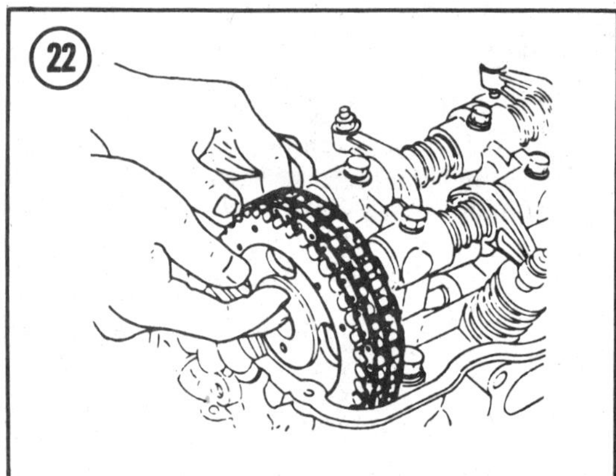

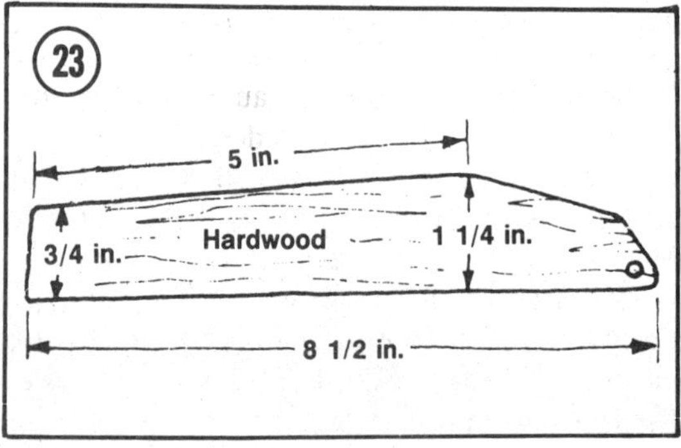

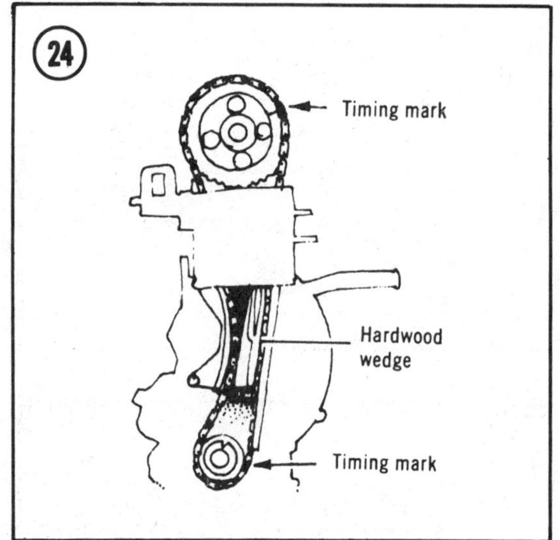

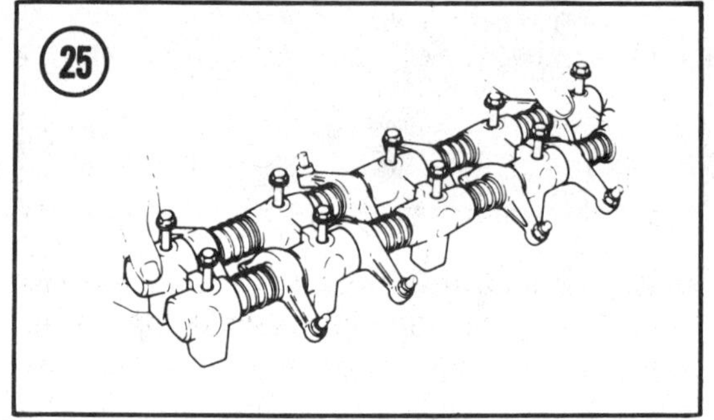

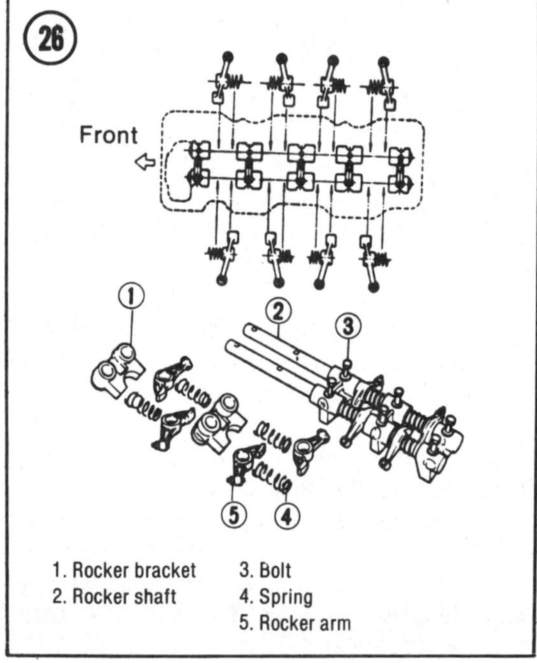

1. Rocker bracket
2. Rocker shaft
3. Bolt
4. Spring
5. Rocker arm

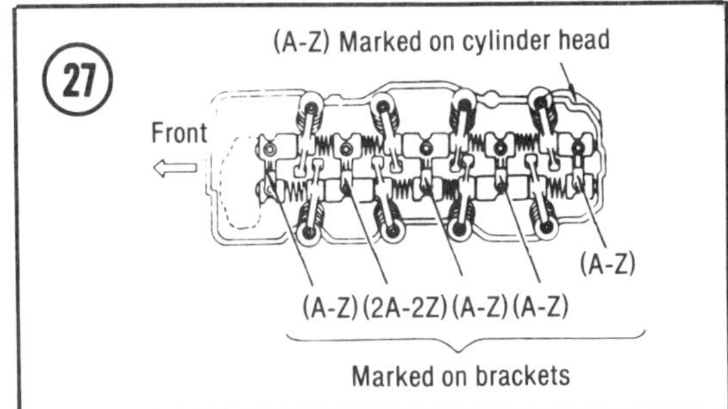

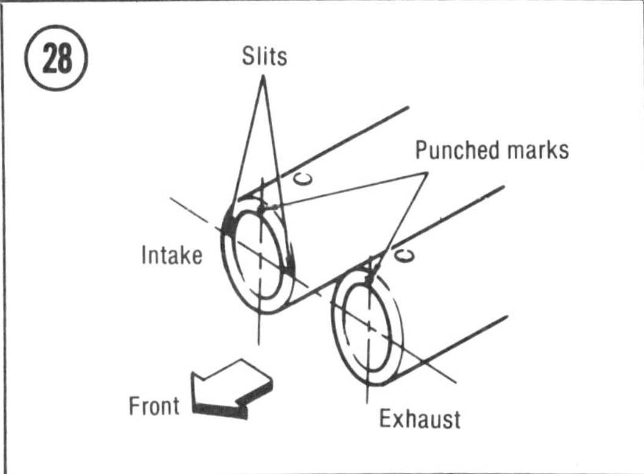

timing chain from falling off the crankshaft sprocket. It also keeps the timing chain tensioner from popping out. If the chain slips off the sprocket or the tensioner pops out, the front cover and oil pan will have to be removed to put them back.

NOTE

If you make your own tool, use a piece of hardwood about 5/8 inch thick. Do not use plywood, since this may leave fragments in the engine. Drill a hole in the top of the tool so it can be pulled out. Insert the tool firmly. Make sure it blocks the tensioner piston before removing the camshaft sprocket.

7. Remove the rocker assembly bolts. Loosen in several stages, starting with the center bolts and working outward.
8. Lift the rocker assembly off the cylinder head. See **Figure 25**.
9. Lift the camshaft out of the cylinder head.
10. Installation is the reverse of removal. Tighten the rocker bracket bolts to specifications (**Table 2**). Tighten in several stages, working inward from the front and rear rocker brackets.

Rocker Assembly Inspection

1. Remove the rocker arms, springs, and brackets. See **Figure 26**.

NOTE

The front and rear bolts hold the rocker brackets onto the shafts. When these bolts are removed, spring pressure will push the end rocker brackets off. Slide the brackets off slowly, so the springs don't fly off and get lost.

2. Check rocker arms for visible wear on the cam contact surface, pivot surface, and valve contact surface. Replace worn or damaged rocker arms.
3. Check rocker shafts for wear or damage. Replace as needed.
4. Make sure rocker bracket oil passages are clear.
5. Replace worn or deformed rocker springs.
6. Assemble the rocker assembly. Be sure rocker stand letter marks (**Figure 27**) correspond with the marks on the cylinder head. Be sure rocker shafts are positioned with their punch marks toward the front (**Figure 28**). The intake rocker shaft has slits as shown.

NOTE

Rocker arms for cylinders 1 and 3 (counting from the front of the engine) are interchangeable. These rocker arms are stamped with the number 1. Rocker arms for cylinders 2 and 4 are also interchangeable, and are stamped with the number 2.

Camshaft Inspection

If you don't have the necessary precision measuring equipment, the next steps can be done inexpensively by a machine shop.

1. Reinstall the rocker brackets. Measure inner diameter with a bore gauge (**Figure 29**). If excessive, replace the cylinder head.
2. Measure outer diameter of the camshaft journals with a micrometer. If worn to less than the minimum, replace the camshaft.
3. Measure camshaft lobe height. Compare with specifications (**Table 1**). If the lobes are worn to 0.25mm (0.010 in.) less than specified, replace the camshaft.

4. Place the camshaft between accurate centers, such as V-blocks or a lathe. Rotate the camshaft one full turn and measure bend with a dial indicator. See **Figure 30**. Maximum bend (total indicator reading) is 0.1mm (0.004 in.). If excessive, replace the camshaft.

5. Place the camshaft in the brackets. Measure end play with a dial indicator (**Figure 31**). If it exceeds 0.2 mm (0.008 in.), replace the camshaft or cylinder head, whichever is worn.

Installation

1. Liberally coat the camshaft bearing surfaces with clean engine oil.

CAUTION

The camshaft dowel must be up during the next step. Otherwise valves may strike the piston tops.

2. Lay the camshaft in the saddles with the dowel upward. See **Figure 32**.
3. Install the rocker assembly (**Figure 33**). Tighten to specifications (**Table 2**). Tighten in 2 or 3 stages, working outward from the center bolts.

CAUTION

*If the cylinder head is off the engine, place it on blocks so the valves aren't pushed into the workbench. See **Figure 33**.*

4. Install the camshaft sprocket in the timing chain (if it was removed). Be sure the chain and sprocket timing marks are aligned (**Figure 34**).
5. Bolt the sprocket to the camshaft. Be sure the camshaft dowel is in No. 2 sprocket dowel hole (**Figure 34**).
6. Apply gasket sealer to the end seal saddles (**Figure 35**), then install the rocker arm cover.

OIL PAN AND PUMP

Oil Pan Removal/Installation

1. Set the handbrake. Place the transmission in FIRST (manual) or PARK (automatic).
2. Jack up the front end of the truck and place it on jackstands.
3. Remove the transmission-to-engine stiffener braces.

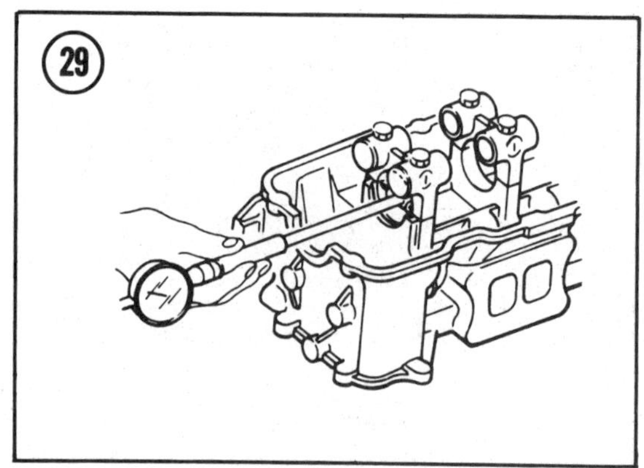

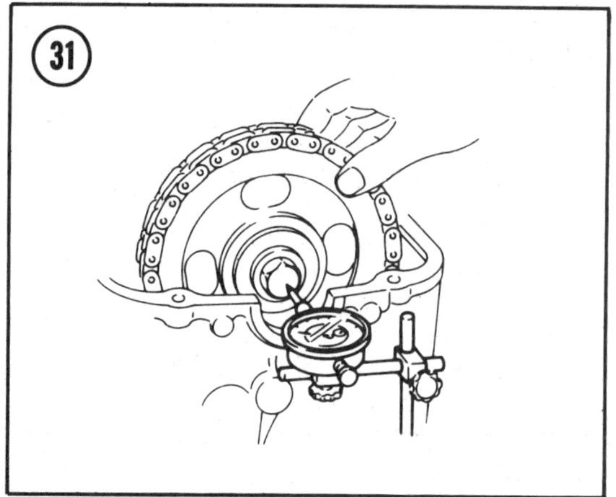

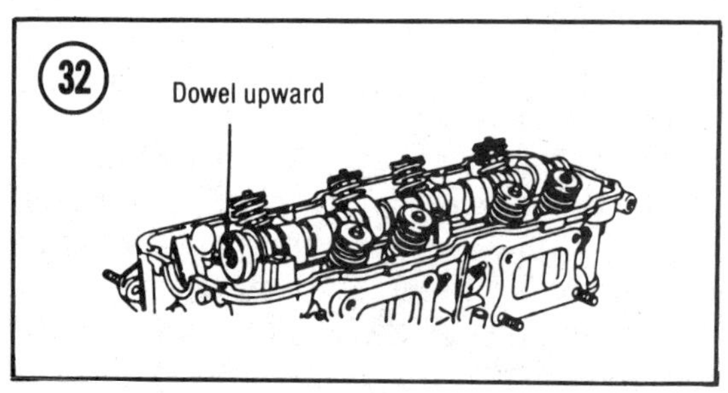

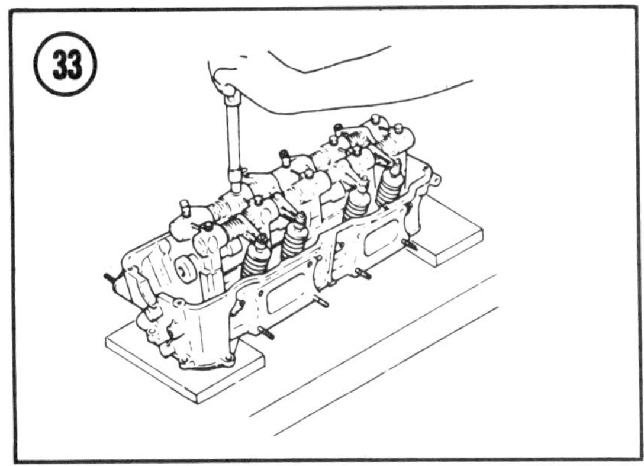

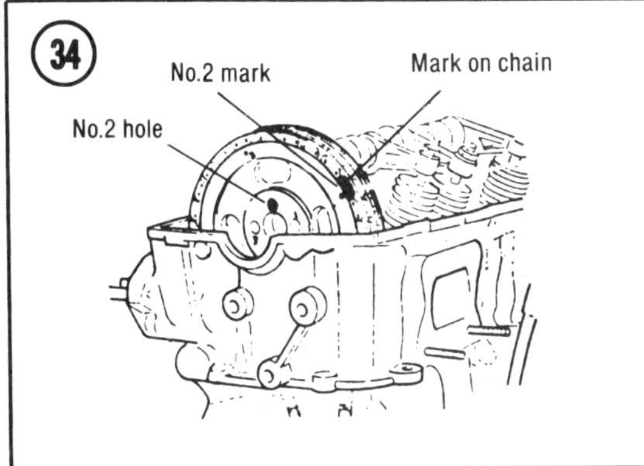

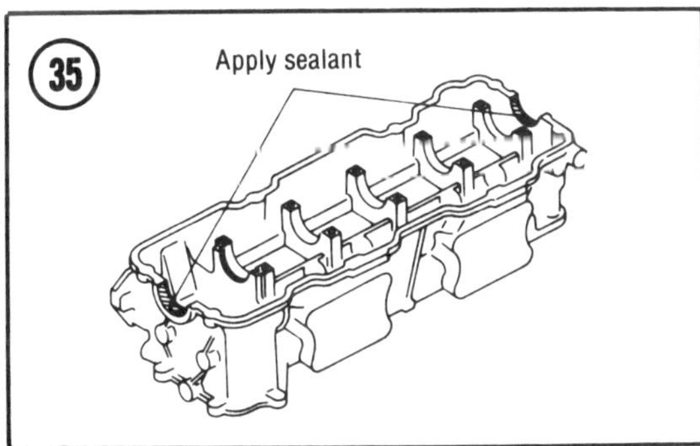

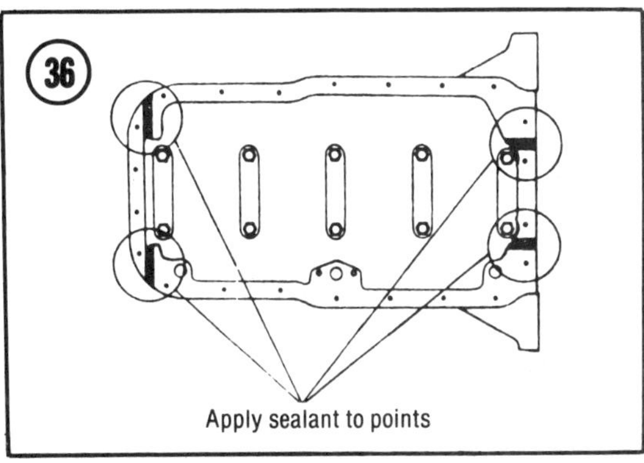

4. Remove the small frame crossmember from beneath the oil pan.
5. Unbolt the oil pan and take it off. Tap gently with a rubber mallet if necessary to break the gasket seal.
6. Unbolt the oil strainer and take it off.
7. Clean the oil pan and strainer thoroughly. If difficult to clean, have the pan and strainer boiled out by a machine shop.
8. Check for cracks, dents, bent gasket surfaces, and damaged drain hole threads. Replace the oil pan if damage is serious.
9. Install by reversing Steps 1-6. Remove all traces of old gasket and sealer fom the oil pan and cylinder block. Use a new gasket, coated on the bottom side with gasket sealer. Apply sealer to the cylinder block at the 4 points shown in **Figure 36**. Tighten the oil pan bolts evenly, a little at a time, to prevent warping the oil pan.

Oil Pump Removal/Installation

1. Remove the distributor cap. Turn the engine so No. 1 piston is at top dead center on its compression stroke. When this occurs, the 0° mark on the timing scale will align with the crankshaft pulley notch (**Figure 37**). In addition, the rotor will point to No. 1 terminal in the distributor cap. See **Figure 38**.

NOTE
Be sure to check rotor position as well as the timing marks. The timing marks also line up when No. 1 piston is at TDC on its exhaust stroke.

2. Drain the engine oil.

NOTE
It is possible to remove the oil pump without draining the oil. However, if an oil pump problem is suspected, the oil should be changed as a matter of good practice.

3. Remove the pump mounting bolts, then take the pump off. See **Figure 39**.
4. Installation is the reverse of removal. Make sure the punch mark on the distributor driving spindle lines up with the oil hole in the oil pump drive shaft (**Figure 40**). Make sure the drive spindle fits securely in the base of the distributor. Tighten the oil pump mounting bolts to specifications (**Table 2**).

Disassembly/Inspection/Assembly

1. Remove the oil pump cover and gasket. See **Figure 41**.
2. Lift out the inner and outer pump rotors. Remove the regulator valve parts.
3. Clean all parts in solvent. Check the distributor drive spindle and pump rotors for wear, scoring, or damage. Replace parts that show these conditions.
4. Reinstall the rotors. Check oil pump clearances (**Figure 42**) and compare with specifications at the end of the chapter. Replace the pump if any clearances are excessive.
5. Lay a straightedge across the pump body and rotors (**Figure 43**). Measure the gap between rotors and straightedge, or pump body and straightedge, with a feeler gauge. If the gap exceeds specifications (end of chapter), replace the oil pump.
6. Check the regulator valve and spring for wear or damage. Replace the valve assembly if any parts are defective.
7. Reassemble the pump, using a new gasket. The chamfered side of the outer rotor (**Figure 44**) faces into the oil pump.

FRONT COVER, TIMING CHAIN, AND SPROCKETS

Front Cover Removal

1. Remove the radiator and fan. See *Radiator Removal/Installation*, Chapter Seven.
2. Remove the drive belts. See *Drive Belts*, Chapter Three.
3. Remove the distributor. See *Ignition System*, Chapter Eight.
4. Remove the oil pan, oil pump, and oil pump driving spindle as described under *Oil Pan and Pump* in this chapter.
5. Remove the crankshaft pulley.
6. Unbolt the front cover from the engine block and cylinder head. Remove it forward and down, together with the water pump.

Front Oil Seal Replacement

1. Remove the front cover as described in the preceding section.
2. Carefully pry out the old oil seal. Do not gouge the aluminum front cover.

37

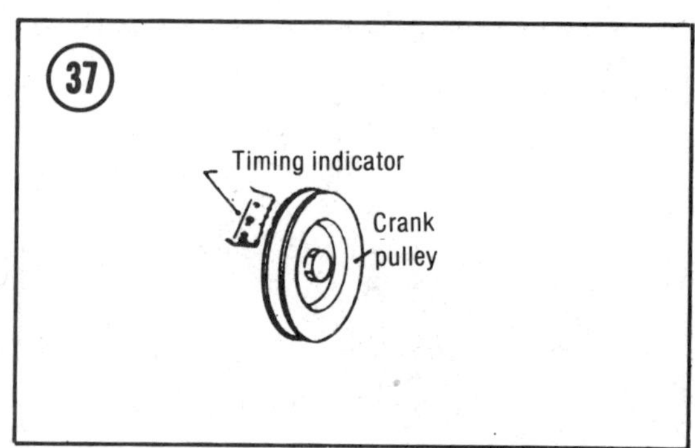

38

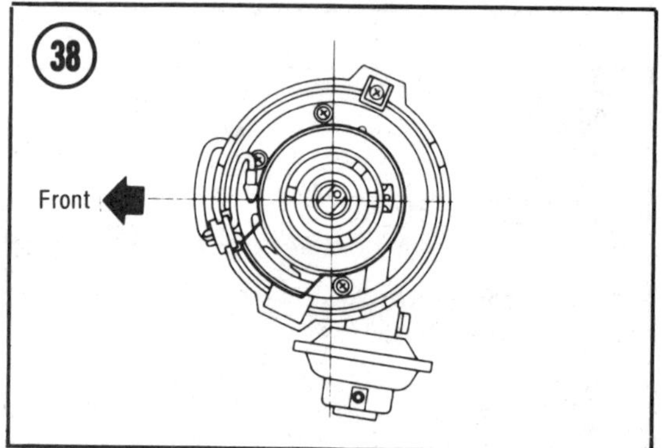

39

40

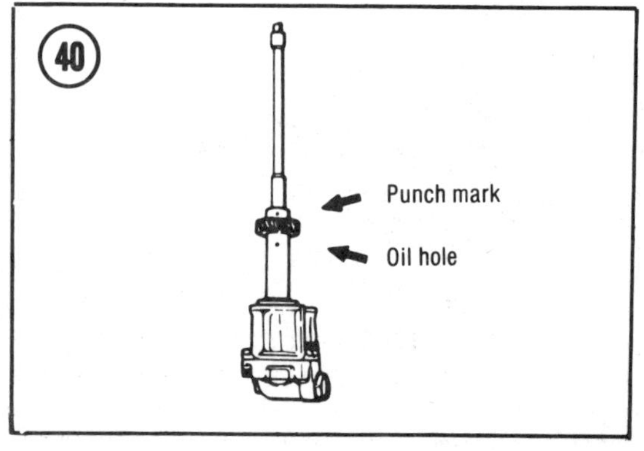

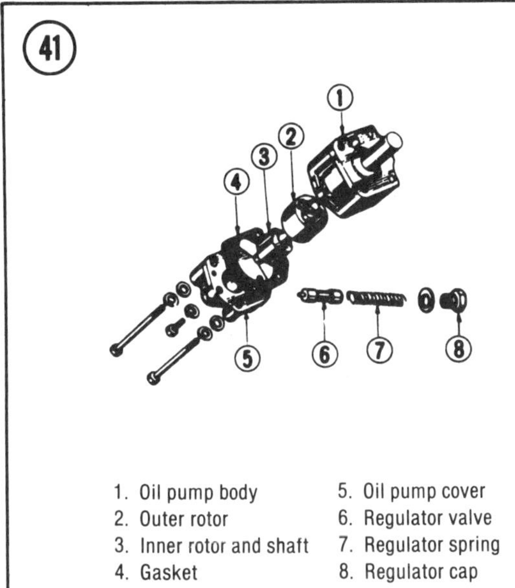

1. Oil pump body
2. Outer rotor
3. Inner rotor and shaft
4. Gasket
5. Oil pump cover
6. Regulator valve
7. Regulator spring
8. Regulator cap

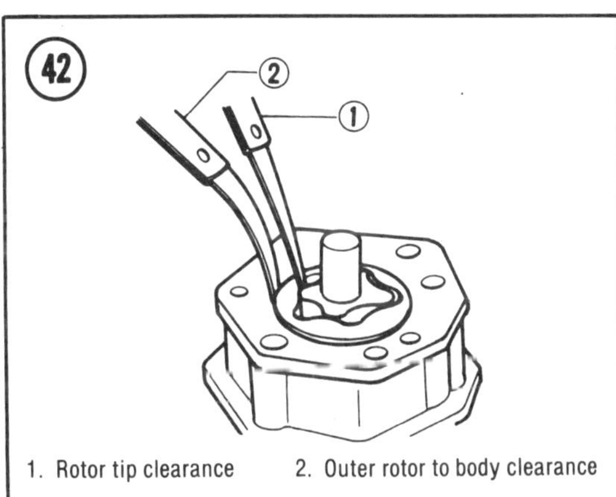

1. Rotor tip clearance 2. Outer rotor to body clearance

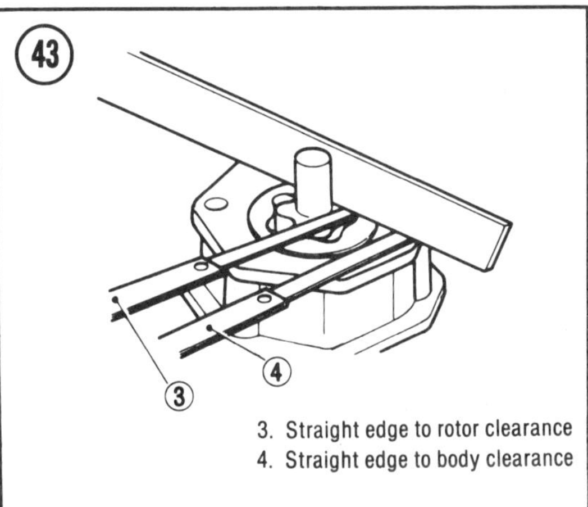

3. Straight edge to rotor clearance
4. Straight edge to body clearance

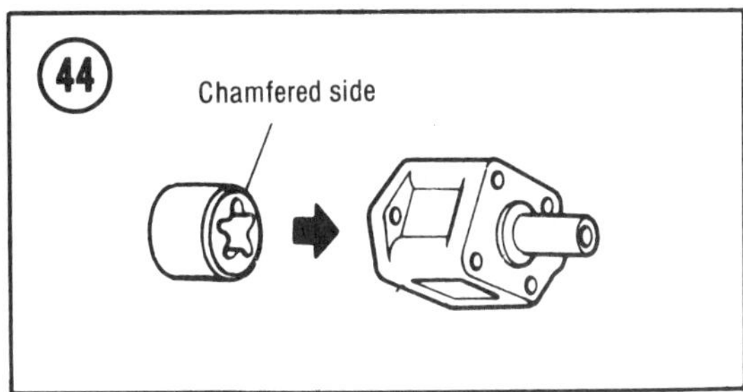

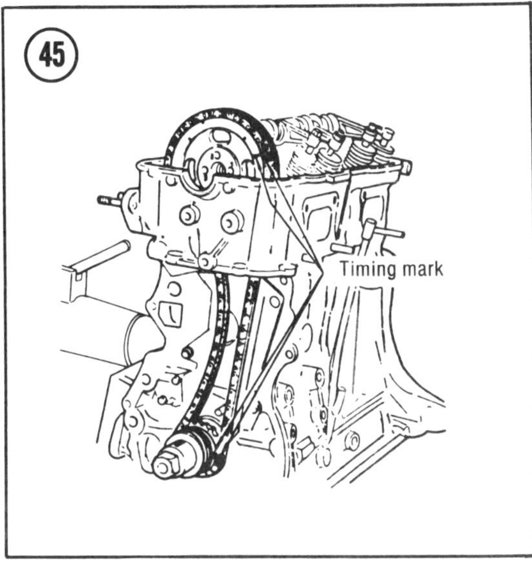

3. Tap in a new oil seal. Coat the lip of the seal with multipurpose grease.

Sprocket and Chain Removal

1. Remove the front cover as described earlier.
2. Remove the valve rocker cover.
3. Install the crankshaft pulley bolt in the crankshaft. Put a wrench on the bolt and turn the engine over until the timing marks on chain and sprockets are aligned. See **Figure 45**.
4. Unbolt the chain tensioner and guides from the block. See **Figure 46**.
5. Unbolt the camshaft sprocket from the camshaft.
6. Remove the timing chain from the crankshaft sprocket.
7. Remove the oil thrower, oil pump drive gear, and crankshaft sprocket from the front of the crankshaft. If the sprocket is difficult to remove, use a puller as shown in **Figure 47**. These are available from rental dealers.

5

CAUTION
Do not rotate the crankshaft and camshaft separately, or the valves will be forced against the piston tops.

Inspection

1. Thoroughly clean all parts in solvent before inspection.
2. Check the chain tensioner assembly and chain guides for wear or damage. Replace if these are evident.
3. Check the sprockets, oil pump drive gear, and oil thrower for wear or damage. Replace as needed.
4. Check the chain for wear, damage, or stretching of the roller links. Replace if these can be seen.

Chain and Sprocket Installation

1. Install the Woodruff keys in the crankshaft keyways if they have been removed.
2. Install the crankshaft sprocket, oil pump drive gear, and oil thrower.

NOTE
The crankshaft sprocket timing mark faces forward. The side of the oil pump drive gear with the large inner chamfer faces rearward.

3. Install the chain guides on the cylinder block.
4. Install the timing chain on the crankshaft sprocket. Be sure the timing mark on the chain is aligned with the mark on the sprocket. See **Figure 45**.
5. Install the camshaft sprocket in the chain. Be sure the chain and sprocket timing marks align (**Figure 45**).
6. Slide the camshaft sprocket onto the camshaft. Be sure the camshaft dowel is straight up. Align No. 2 dowel hole (center hole of the 3) with the camshaft dowel. See **Figure 48**.
7. Install the camshaft sprocket bolt. Tighten to specifications (**Table 1**).
8. Push the chain tensioner piston all the way into the tensioner. Install the tensioner on the engine.
9. Position the slack side chain guide so the tensioner piston is held all the way in. See **Figure 49**.

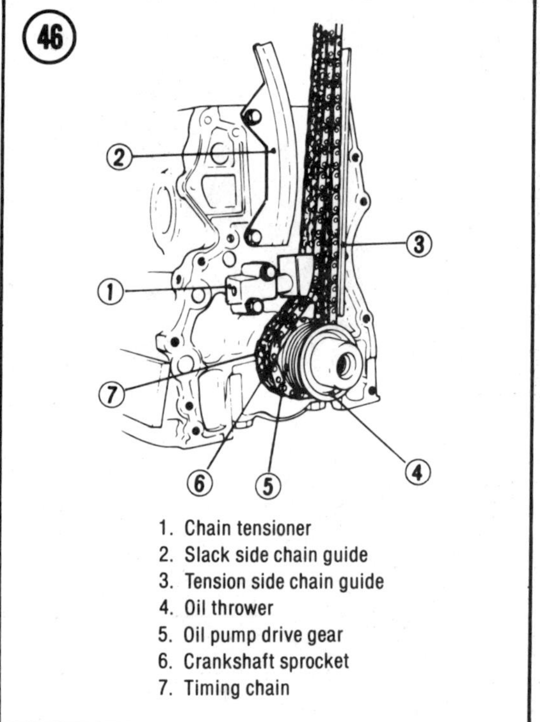

1. Chain tensioner
2. Slack side chain guide
3. Tension side chain guide
4. Oil thrower
5. Oil pump drive gear
6. Crankshaft sprocket
7. Timing chain

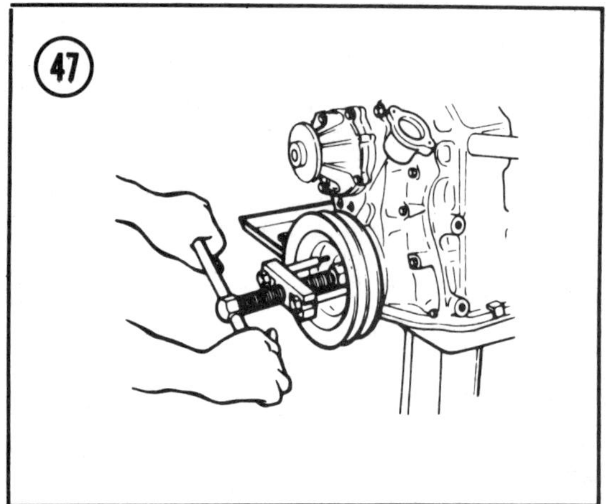

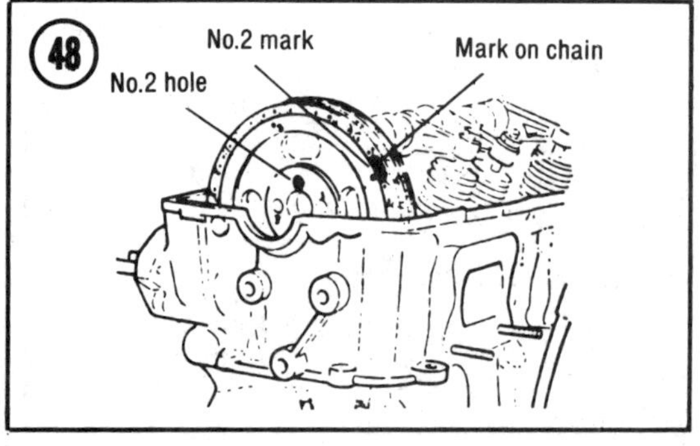

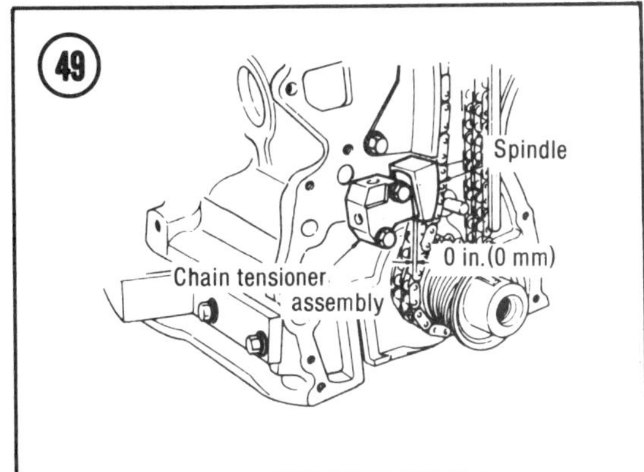

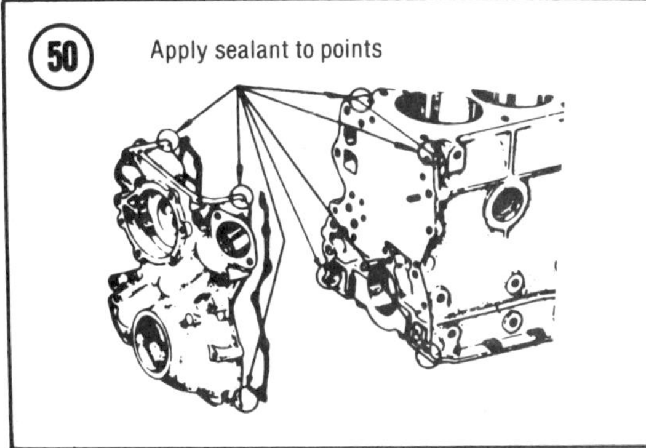

10. Make sure the chain and sprocket timing marks are aligned.

Front Cover Installation

Installation is the reverse of removal, plus the following.

1. Use new left and right cover gaskets, coated on both sides with gasket sealer. Apply small amounts of sealer to the corners of the front cover. See **Figure 50**.
2. Take care not to bend the front portion of the head gasket when installing the cover. Be sure to install the cylinder head-to-cover bolts.
3. Tighten all nuts and bolts to specifications (end of chapter).
4. Fill the engine with oil and the radiator with coolant.

CYLINDER HEAD

Cylinder Head Removal

1. Completely drain the cooling system. See *Cooling System Flushing*, Chapter Seven.
2. Remove all spark plugs.

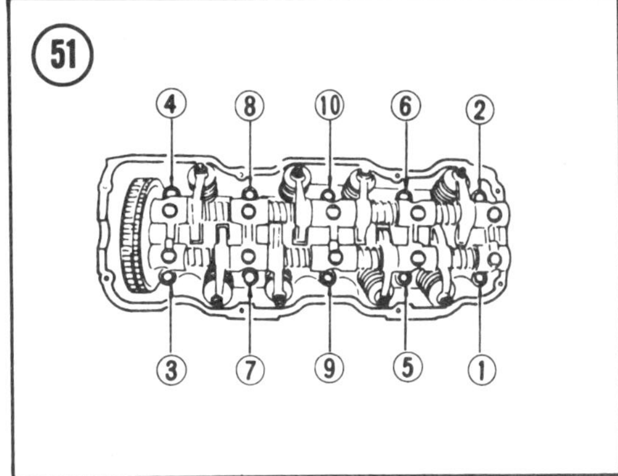

3. Remove the air cleaner. See *Air Cleaner*, Chapter Six.
4. Remove the valve rocker cover.
5. Remove the intake and exhaust manifolds. See *Intake and Exhaust Manifolds* in this chapter.
6. Turn the camshaft so its sprocket locating pin is straight up. This provides a reference point for later installation.
7. Remove the camshaft sprocket as described under *Camshaft and Rocker Arms* in this chapter.
8. Remove the small bolts attaching the cylinder head to the engine front cover.
9. Remove the cylinder head bolts. To prevent warping the head, loosen the bolts in several stages. Follow the order shown in **Figure 51**.
10. Once the head bolts are removed, lift the cylinder head off the engine. If the head is difficult to remove, tap it gently with a rubber mallet. Under no circumtances pry the head off.

Cylinder Head Inspection

1. Check the cylinder head for water leaks before cleaning.
2. Clean the cylinder head thoroughly in solvent. While cleaning, check for cracks or other visible damage. Look for corrosion or foreign material in oil or water passages. Clean the passages with a stiff spiral wire brush, then blow them out with compressed air.
3. Check the cylinder head bottom (block mating) surface for flatness. Place an accurate straightedge along its surface (**Figure 52**). If

5

there is any gap, measure it with a feeler gauge. Measure along the 6 lines shown. If the gap exceeds specifications, have the head resurfaced by a machine shop.

NOTE

Total material milled from head and block must not be more than 0.2 mm (0.008 in).

4. Check studs in the cylinder head for damage. Replace damaged studs.

Decarbonizing

1. Without removing valves, remove all deposits from the combustion chambers, intake ports, and exhaust ports. Use a wire brush dipped in solvent, or make a scraper out of hardwood. Be careful not to scratch or gouge the combustion chambers.
2. After all carbon is removed from the combustion chambers and ports, clean the entire head in solvent.
3. Clean away all carbon on the piston tops. Do not remove the carbon ridge at the top of the cylinder bore.

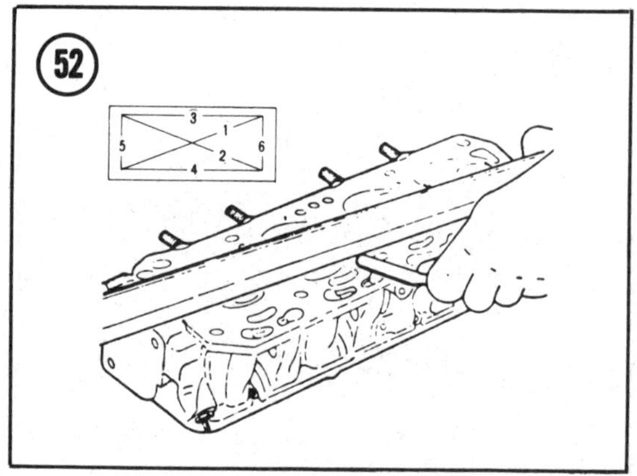

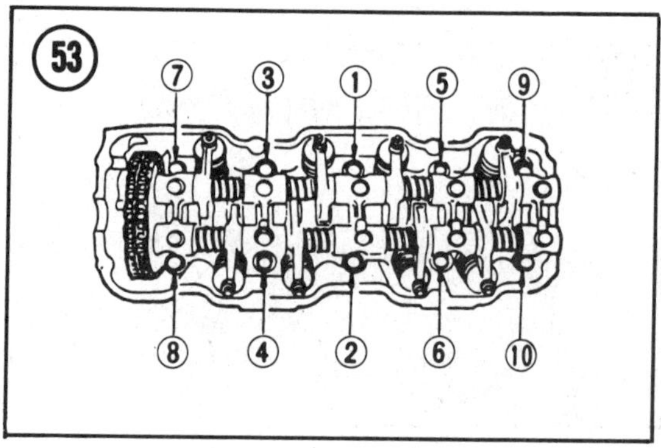

Cylinder Head Installation

1. Be sure the cylinder head, block, and cylinder bores are clean. Check all visible oil passages for cleanliness.
2. Install the camshaft and rocker arms in the cylinder head. Turn the camshaft so its sprocket locating dowel is straight up. This must be done before the cylinder head is installed to prevent the valves from striking the piston tops.
3. Install a new cylinder head gasket. Never reuse an old head gasket. Do *not* use gasket sealer on the head gasket.

CAUTION

During the next step, look at the valves and make sure none of them are open far enough to strike the piston tops.

4. Position the cylinder head on the block. Install the cylinder head bolts.
5. With the engine cool, tighten the head bolts. Follow the sequence in **Figure 53**. Tighten the bolts a little at a time, in several stages, to prevent warping the cylinder head. Correct final torque is 51-58 ft.-lb. (7-8 mkg).
6. Install the timing chain and camshaft sprocket as described in this chapter.
7. Install the intake and exhaust manifolds as described in this chapter.
8. Install the spark plugs and rocker arm cover.
9. Fill the cooling system with a 50/50 mixture of ethylene glycol-based antifreeze and water.
10. Change the oil. See *Engine Oil and Filter*, Chapter Three.
11. Run the engine for several minutes, let it cool, then recheck head bolt tightness.

VALVES AND VALVE SEATS

Some of the following procedures must be done by a dealer or machine shop, since they require special knowledge and expensive machine tools. Others, while possible for the home mechanic, are difficult or time-consuming. A general practice among those who do their own service is to remove the cylinder head, perform all disassembly except valve removal, and take the head to a

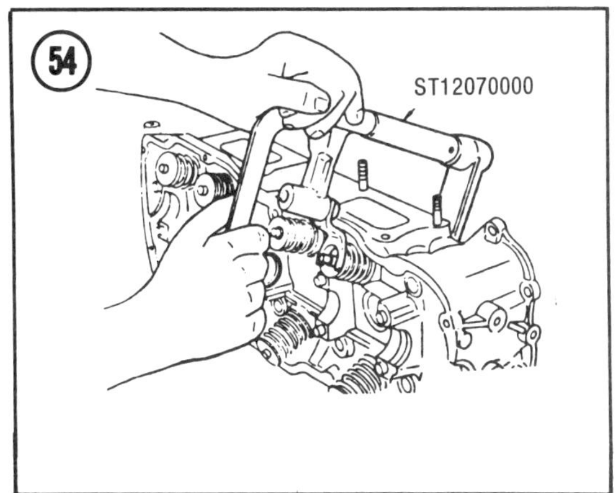

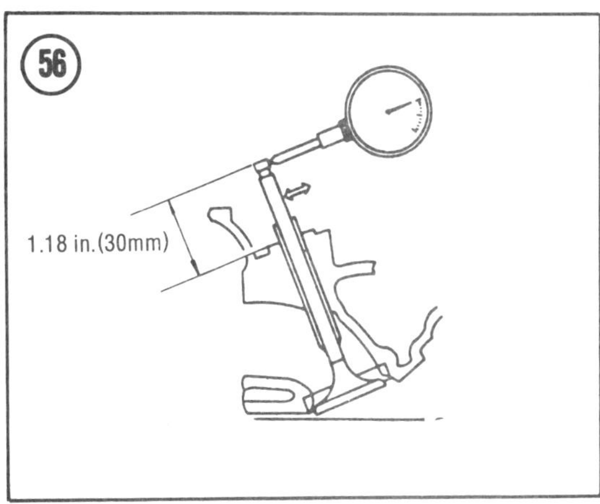

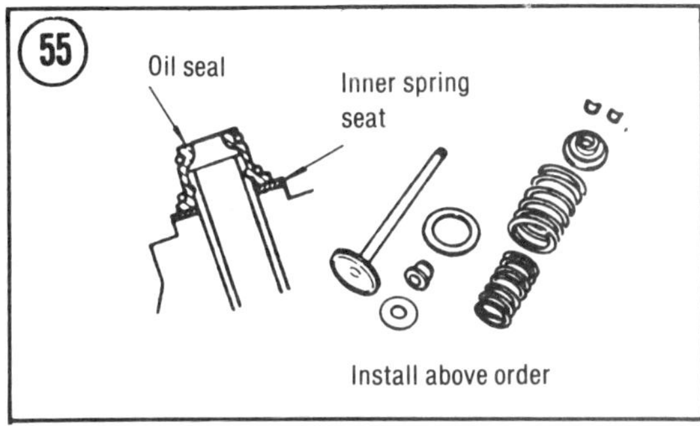

machine shop for inspection and service. Since the cost is low in relation to the required effort and equipment, this is usually the best approach, even for experienced mechanics.

Valve Removal

1. Remove the cylinder head as described in this chapter.
2. If you haven't already done so, remove the camshaft and rocker arms from the head.
3. Compress each valve spring with a compressor like the one shown in **Figure 54**. Remove the valve keepers and release the spring tension. Remove the spring washer, oil seal, inner and outer valve springs, and inner and outer spring seats. See **Figure 55**.

CAUTION

Remove any burrs from valve stem grooves before removing the valves. Otherwise the valve guides will be damaged.

Valve and Valve Guide Inspection

1. Clean the valves with a wire brush and solvent. Discard cracked, warped, or burned valves.
2. Measure valve stems at top, center, and bottom for wear. A machine shop can do this when the valves are ground. Also measure the length of each valve and the diameter of each valve head.
3. The valve faces and stem ends should be resurfaced when the valves are ground. No more than 0.5mm (0.020 in.) may be removed from valve stem ends. Valve faces may not be ground thinner than 0.5mm (0.020 in.).
4. Remove all carbon and varnish from valve guides with a stiff spiral wire brush.

NOTE

The next step assumes that all valve stems have been measured and are within specifications. Replace valves with worn stems before performing this step.

5. Insert each valve into the guide from which it was removed. Hold the valve just slightly off its seat and rock it back and forth in a direction parallel with the rocker arms (**Figure 56**). This is the direction in which the greatest wear normally occurs. If the valve stem rocks more than approximately 0.2 mm (0.008 in.), the valve guide is probably worn.
6. If there is any doubt about valve guide condition after performing Step 5, measure the valve guide at top, center, and bottom with a bore gauge. See **Figure 57**.
7. Measure valve spring free length and compare with specifications. Replace springs that are too long or too short. Measure spring

bend with a square. Replace springs bent beyond specifications.

8. Test the valve springs under load on a spring tester. Replace weak springs.

9. Inspect valve seat inserts. If worn or burned, they must be reconditioned. This is a job for a dealer or machine shop, although the procedure is described later in this section.

Valve Guide Replacement

This procedure requires a press and reaming tools. If you do not have the necessary equipment, take the job to a dealer or machine shop.

1. Remove worn guides with a press and suitable drift. This can be done at room temperature, but will be easier if the head is heated first.
2. Ream the guide holes in the cylinder head to specifications (end of chapter).
3. Heat the cylinder head to 150-200° C (302-392° F).
4. Press the guides in from the top of the cylinder head until their snap rings contact the head.
5. Measure valve guide bores. Ream to specifications. See **Figure 58**.

Valve Seat Inserts

The valve seats are cut into inserts. Replacement requires precision machine tools and special skills. Take the job to a Datsun dealer or machine shop.

1. Remove the old valve seat by boring it out until it collapses. Be sure not to cut the cylinder head during boring.
2. Select a valve seat insert and check its outside diameter. Compare with specifications (end of chapter).
3. Machine the cylinder head recess diameter to fit the valve seat insert, using the valve guide as an axis.
4. Heat the cylinder head to 150-200° C (302-392° F).
5. Press the valve seat insert into place. Be sure it beds securely on the cylinder head. Stake the insert at 4 or more places.
6. Grind the valve seats as described in the following procedure.

57

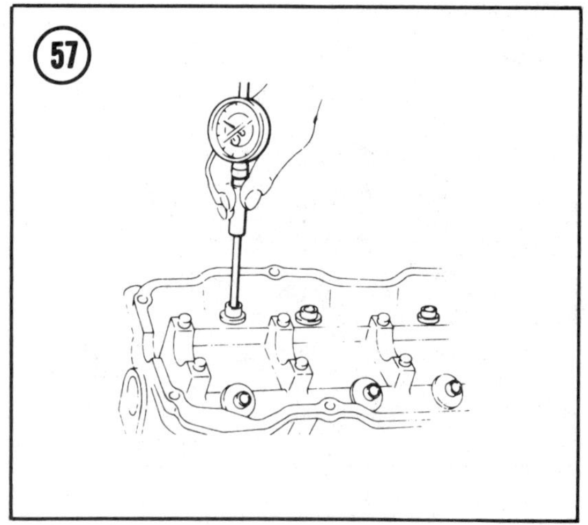

58

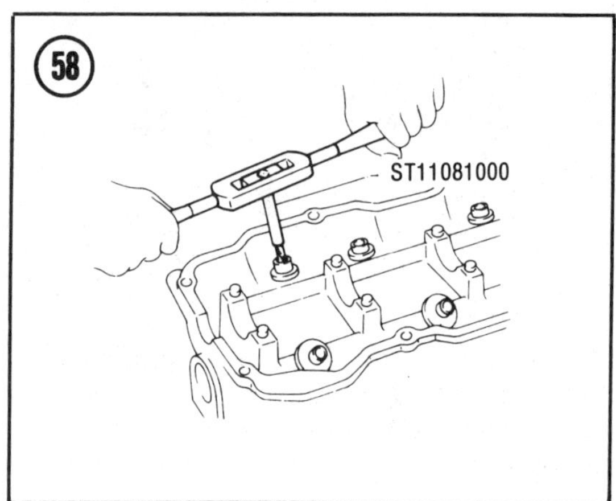

Valve Seat Reconditioning

1. Cut the valve seats to specified dimensions, using a cutter or special stone. See **Figure 59** (intake) or **Figure 60** (exhaust).
2. Coat the corresponding valve face with Prussian blue dye.
3. Insert the valve into the valve guide.
4. Rotate the valve under light pressure approximately 1/4 turn.
5. Lift the valve out. If it seats properly, the dye will transfer evenly to the valve face.

Valve Installation

1. Coat the valves with oil and install them in the cylinder head.
2. Install the valve spring seats, oil seals, springs, and spring washers. Compress the valve springs and install the keepers.

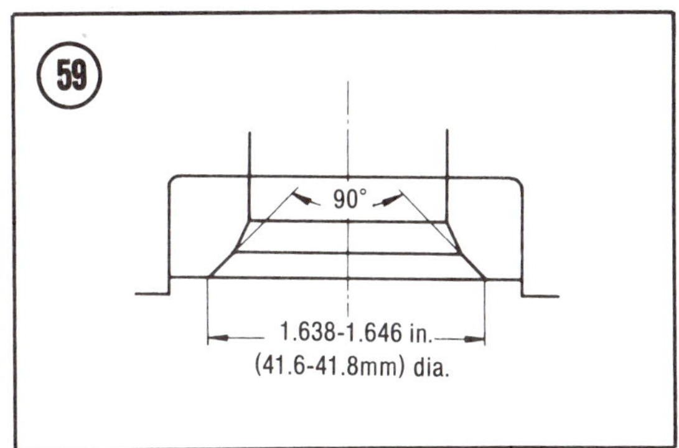

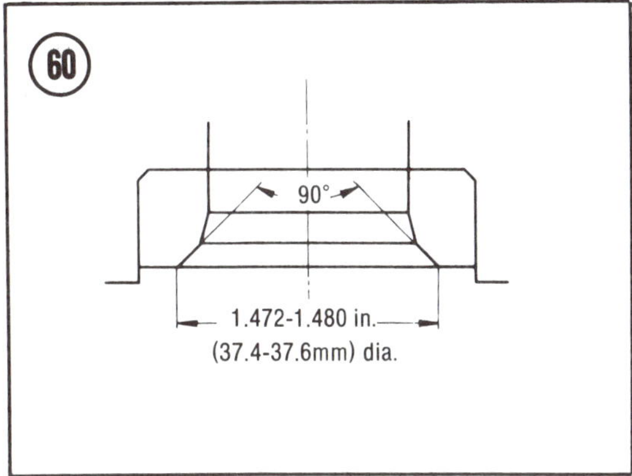

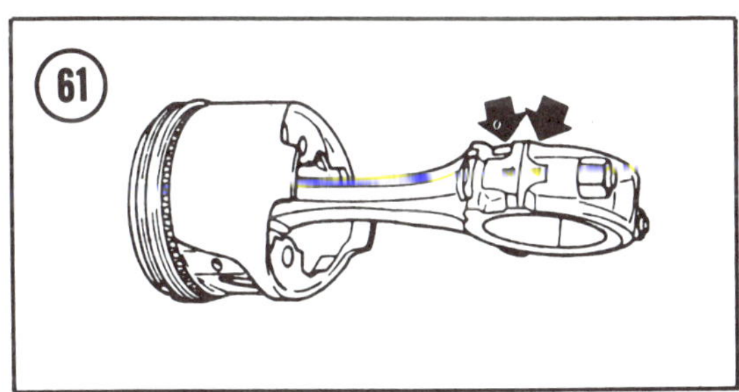

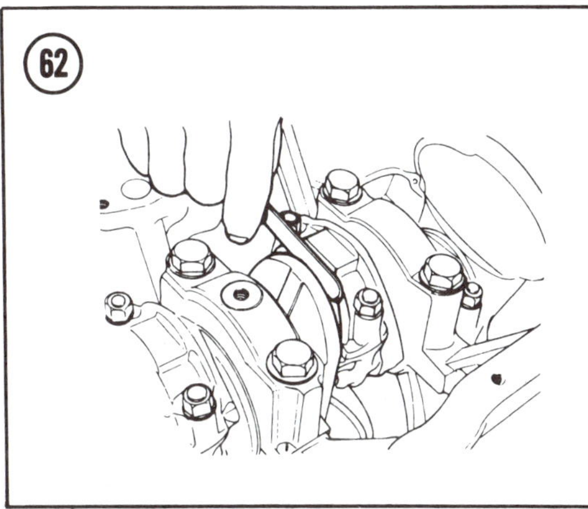

PISTON/CONNECTING ROD ASSEMBLY

Piston Removal

1. Remove the cylinder head and oil pan as described in this chapter.
2. Remove the carbon ridge at the top of the cylinder bores with a ridge reamer. These are available from rental dealers.
3. Rotate the crankshaft so the connecting rod is centered in the bore.

NOTE
*Check for cylinder numbers stamped on connecting rod and cap (**Figure 61**). If they aren't visible, make your own.*

4. Insert a feeler gauge between the connecting rod big end and crankshaft and measure the clearance (**Figure 62**). Replace the connecting rod if clearance exceeds specifications (end of chapter).
5. Remove the nuts securing the connecting rod cap. Lift off the cap, together with the lower bearing half.
6. Push the piston and connecting rod out of the bore with a wooden hammer handle (**Figure 63**).
7. Remove the piston rings with a ring remover (**Figure 64**).

Piston Pin Removal/Installation

The piston pins are press-fitted to the connecting rods and hand-fitted to the pistons. Removal requires a press and support stand. This is a job for a dealer or machine shop, which is equipped to fit the pistons to the pins, ream the pin bushings to the correct diameter, and install the pistons on the connecting rods.

Piston Clearance Check

This procedure should be done at room temperature. The cylinder walls must be clean and dry.

1. Referring to **Figure 65**, insert the piston without rings upside down into the cylinder bore. Insert a 0.04mm (0.0016 in.) feeler gauge between piston and cylinder wall and attach a spring scale as shown.

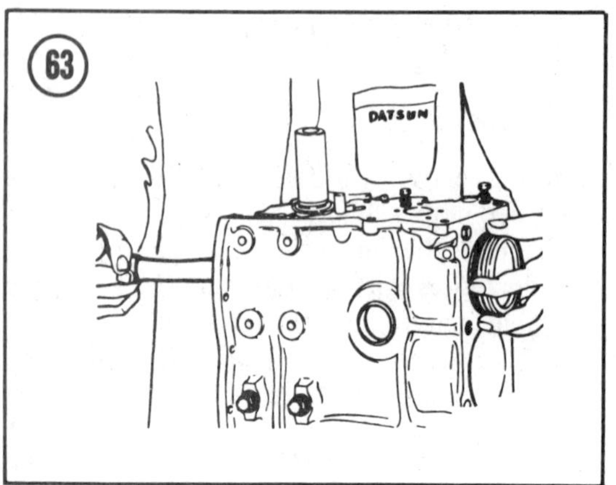

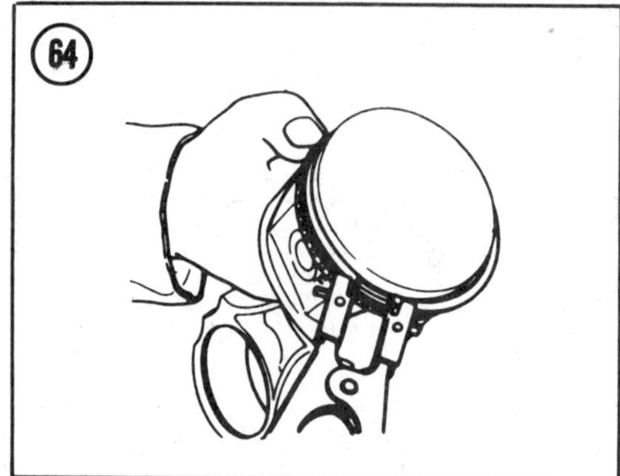

2. Pull on the spring scale. Note the amount of force required to pull the feeler gauge out of the cylinder. This should range from 0.2-1.5 kg (0.4-3.3 lb.). If the required pull is greater than specified, piston clearance is less than it should be. If the pull is less, piston clearance is greater.
3. Repeat the procedure for all 4 cylinders and pistons.

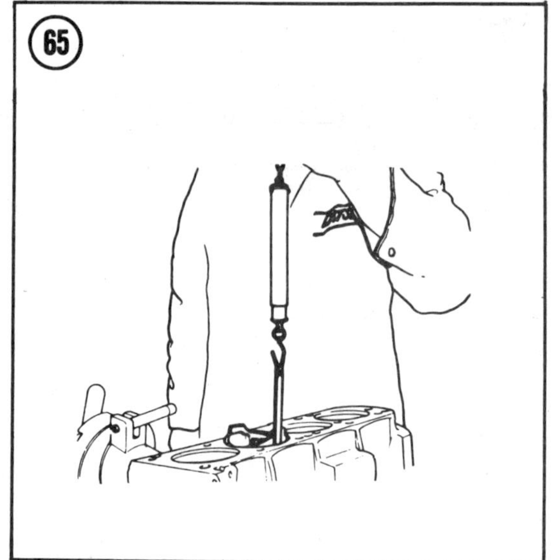

Piston Ring Fit/Installation

1. Check the ring gap of each piston ring. To do this, position the ring at the top or bottom of the ring travel area and square it by tapping gently with an inverted piston.

NOTE
If the cylinders have not been rebored, check the gap at the bottom of the ring travel, where the cylinder is least worn.

2. Measure ring gap with a feeler gauge as shown in **Figure 66**. Compare with specifications at the end of the chapter.
3. Check side clearance of the rings as shown in **Figure 67**. Place the feeler gauge alongside the ring all the way into the groove. Specifications are listed in **Table 1**.
4. Using a ring expander tool, carefully install the oil control ring, then the compression rings. Oil rings consist of 3 segments. The wavy segment goes between the flat segments to act as a spacer. Upper and lower flat segments are interchangeable. The second compression ring is undercut and tapered (**Figure 68**). The top compression ring has a chrome plated friction surface. The top sides

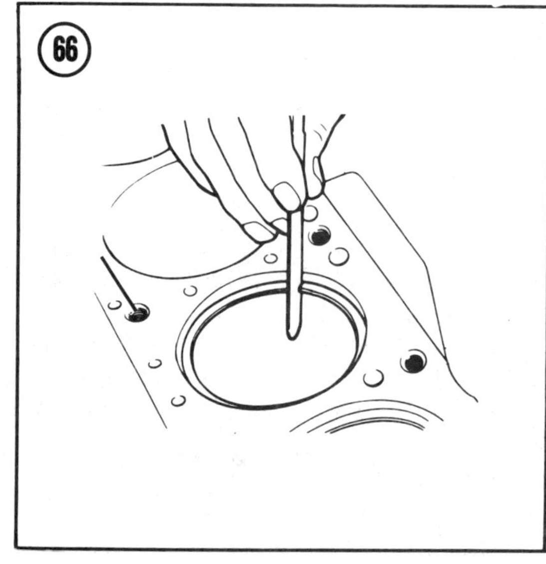

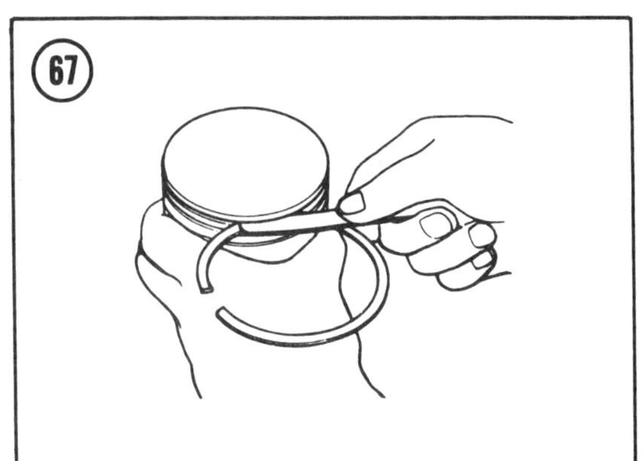

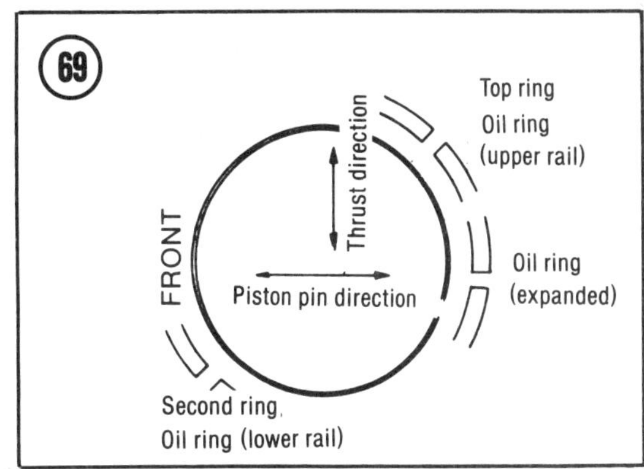

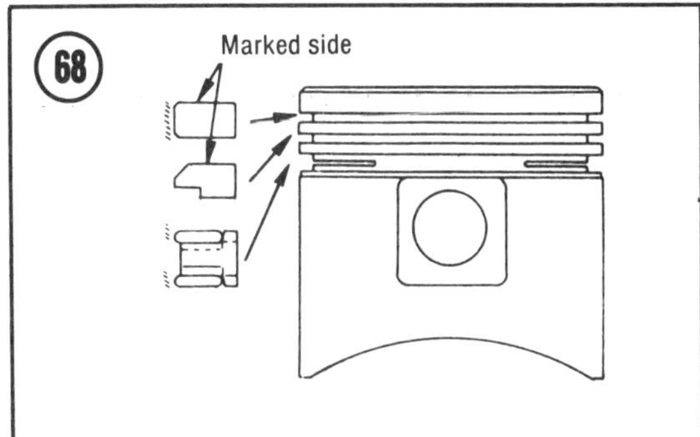

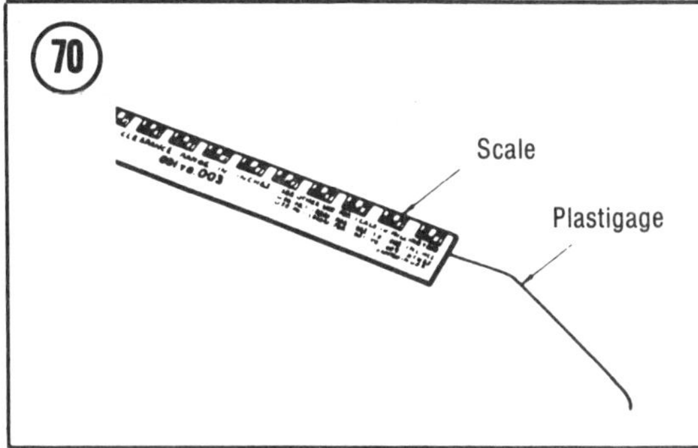

5

of both compression rings are marked and must be up.

5. Position the ring gaps as shown in **Figure 69**.

Connecting Rod Inspection

1. Have connecting rod straightness checked by a dealer or machine shop. Compare with specifications for bend and twist (**Table 1**).
2. If any connecting rods are replaced, make sure new ones are within 7 grams (0.25 oz.) of the old ones.

Measuring Bearing Clearance

1. Place connecting rods and upper bearing halves on the proper crankpins (connecting rod journals).
2. Cut a piece of Plastigage (**Figure 70**) the width of the bearing. Place the Plastigage on the crankpin, then install the lower bearing half and cap.

NOTE

Do not place Plastigage over the crankpin oil hole.

3. Tighten the connecting rod cap to specifications (end of chapter). Do not rotate the crankshaft while the Plastigage is in place.
4. Remove the connecting rod cap. Bearing clearance is determined by comparing the width of the flattened Plastigage to the markings on the envelope (**Figure 71**). If clearance is excessive, the crankshaft must be reground and undersize bearings installed.

Installing Piston/Connecting Rod Assembly

1. Make sure the pistons are correctly installed on the connecting rods. The notch in the piston goes toward the front of the engine. The oil hole in the connecting rod big end goes toward the right-hand side of the engine. See **Figure 72**.
2. Be sure ring gaps are positioned correctly.
3. Immerse the entire piston in clean engine oil. Coat the cylinder wall with oil.
4. Slide a ring compressor over the rings. Compress the rings into the grooves.
5. Install the piston/connecting rod assembly in its cylinder as shown in **Figure 73**. Tap

lightly with a wooden hammer handle to insert the piston. Be sure the connecting rod number corresponds to the cylinder number (counting from the front of the engine).

CAUTION
Use extreme care not to let the connecting rod nick the crankshaft journal.

6. Clean the connecting rod bearings carefully, including the back sides. Coat the crankpins and bearings with clean engine oil. Place the bearings in the connecting rod and cap.
7. Install the connecting rod cap. Make sure the cylinder numbers on the rod and cap are on the same side. Tighten the cap nuts to specifications (end of chapter).
8. Check connecting rod big end play as described under *Connecting Rod Inspection*, Step 2.

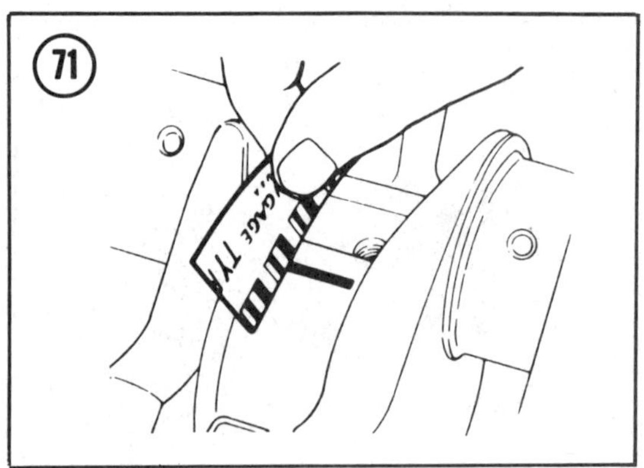

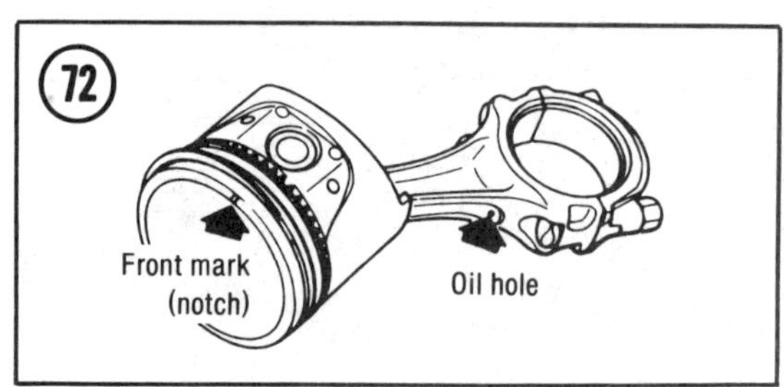

CRANKSHAFT

Removal

1. Pry the crankshaft to front or rear with a wooden hammer handle (**Figure 74**). Measure the clearance between center bearing and crankshaft with a feeler gauge as shown. If the clearance exceeds specifications (end of chapter), replace the bearings.
2. Unbolt the main bearing caps. Loosen the caps in 2 or 3 stages, in the order shown in **Figure 75**.
3. Place the caps in order on a clean workbench (**Figure 76**). A puller (Datsun part no. KV101041S0; Kent-Moore no. J25647) may be necessary to remove the center and rear caps. See **Figure 77**. If you do not have such a tool, take the engine to a Datsun dealer for cap removal.
3. Remove 2 side oil seals, then take the rear oil seal off the crankshaft (**Figure 78**).
4. Lift the crankshaft out of the engine. Lay the crankshaft, main bearings, and bearing caps in order on a clean workbench.

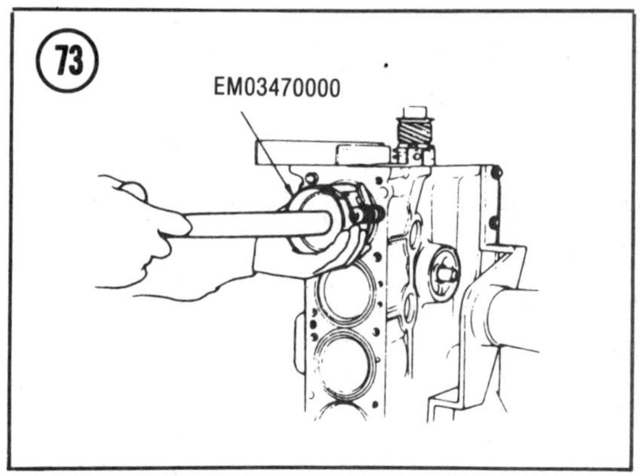

Inspection

1. Clean the crankshaft thoroughly with solvent. Blow out the oil passages with compressed air.

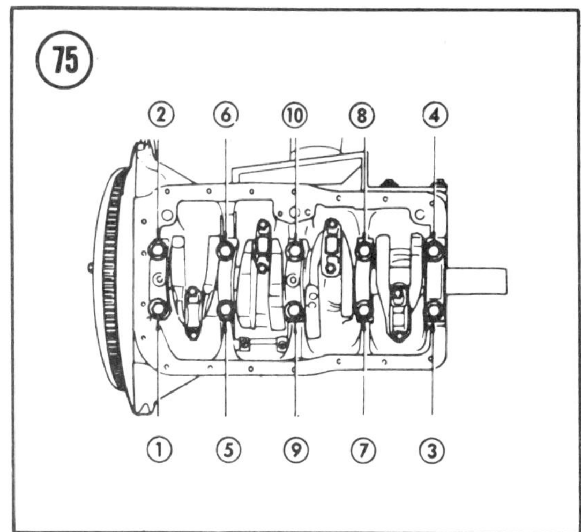

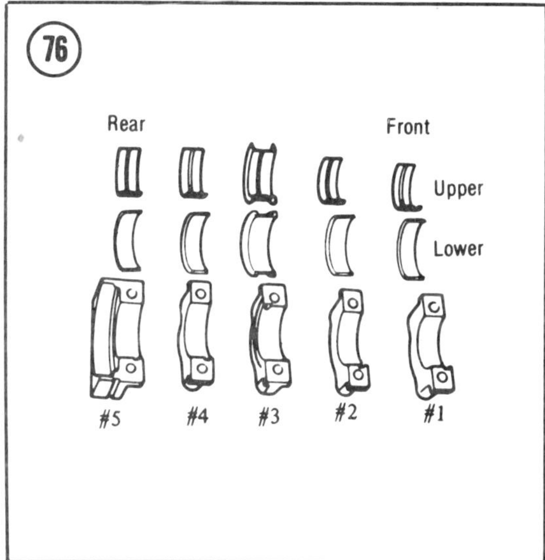

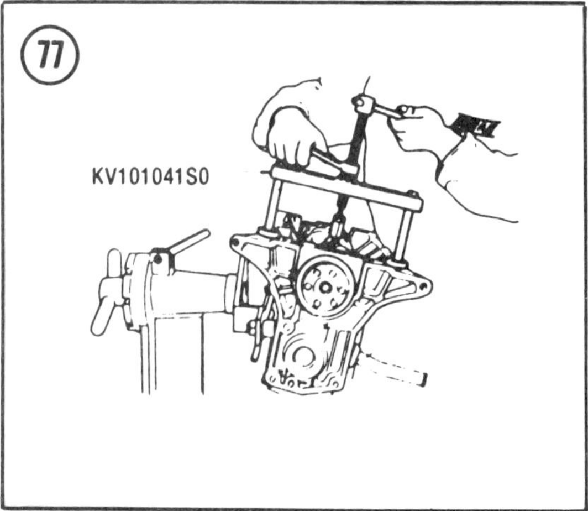

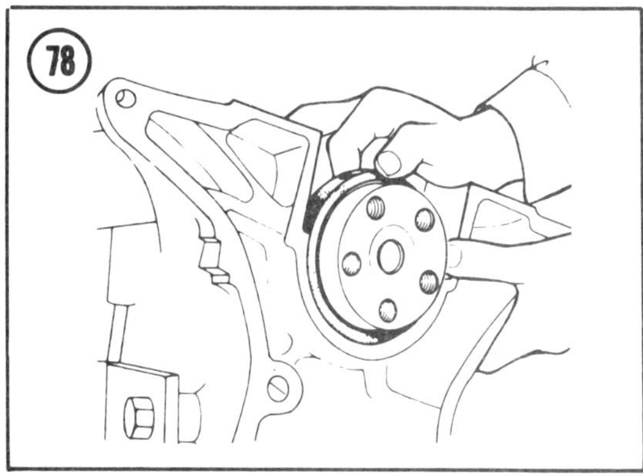

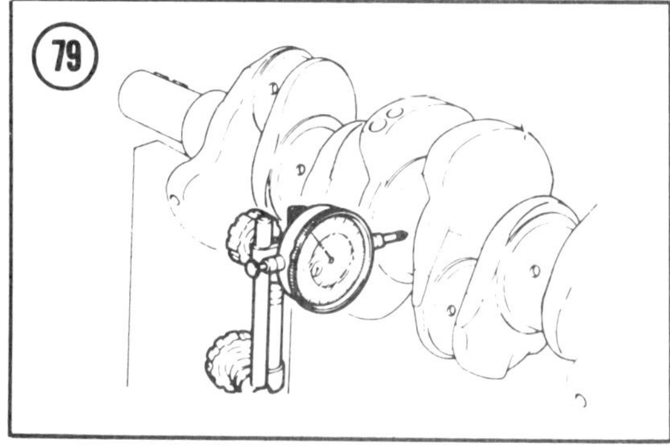

NOTE
If you do not have precision measuring equipment, have a machine shop perform Steps 2 and 3.

2. Check crankpins and main bearing journals for wear, scoring, and cracks. Check all journals against specifications (end of chapter) for out-of-roundness, taper, and wear. If necessary, have the crankshaft reground.

3. Check the crankshaft for bending. Mount the crankshaft between accurate centers (such as V-blocks or a lathe) and rotate it one full turn with a dial indicator contacting the center journal. See **Figure 79**. The crankshaft must be reground if bent beyond specifications.

Measuring Main Bearing Clearance

Main bearing clearance is measured in the same manner as connecting rod bearing clearance, described earlier in this chapter. Excessive clearance requires that the bearings be replaced, the crankshaft be reground, or both.

5

Installation

1. Thoroughly clean bearings, including the back sides.
2. Install the bearings in the cylinder block and bearing caps. Bearings 1 and 5 (counting from the front of the engine) are interchangeable. Bearings 2 and 4 are interchangeable. Bearing No. 3 is flanged.

NOTE
Upper bearing halves have oil grooves; lower bearing halves do not.

3. Make sure the bearing locating tangs are correctly positioned in the cylinder block and bearing cap grooves.
4. Coat the bearings freely with clean engine oil. Lay the crankshaft in the block. Coat the crankshaft journals with engine oil.
5. Install the bearing caps and tighten the cap bolts slightly. Make sure the arrow marks on the caps face the front of the engine.

NOTE
*Apply small amounts of gasket sealer to the rear bearing cap and block(**Figure 80**).*

6. Gently push the crankshaft toward front and rear of the engine to verify that the bearings and caps are properly aligned and seated.
7. Tighten the cap bolts to specifications (end of chapter). Tighten gradually in 2 or 3 stages, in the order shown in **Figure 81**. Rotate the crankshaft during tightening to make sure it isn't binding. If the crankshaft becomes hard to turn, stop and find out why before continuing. Check for foreign material on bearings and journals. Make absolutely certain that bearings are the correct size, especially if the crankshaft has been reground. Never use undersize bearings if the crankshaft has not been reground.
8. Recheck crankshaft end play (**Figure 74**).
9. Apply small amounts of gasket sealer to the rear side oil seals, then tap them into place (**Figure 82**). Install the rear seal with a drift such as Datsun tool KV10105500 (Kent-Moore no. J25640-01). See **Figure 83**. If the tool is not available, use a piece of pipe the same diameter as the seal.

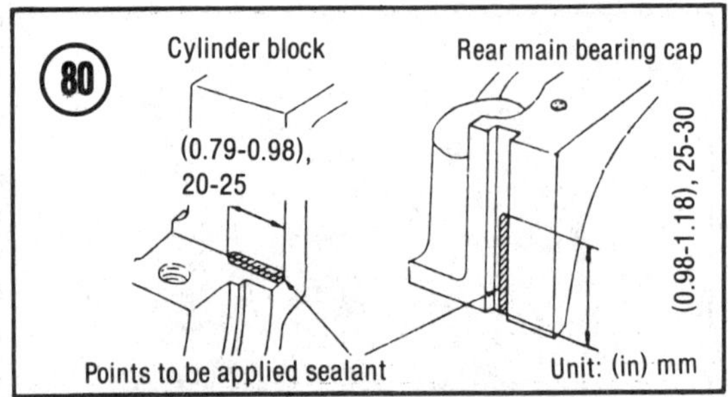

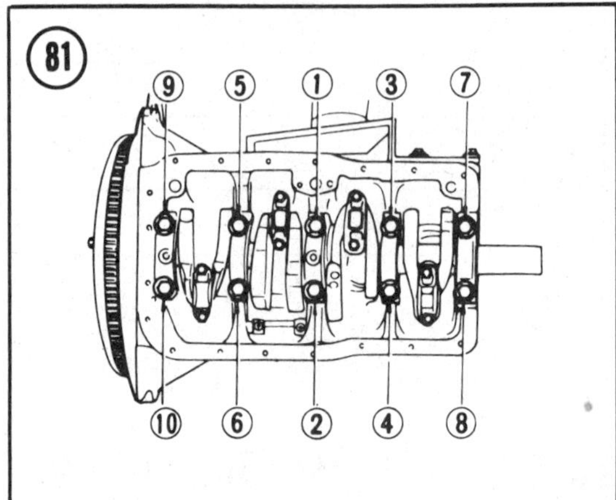

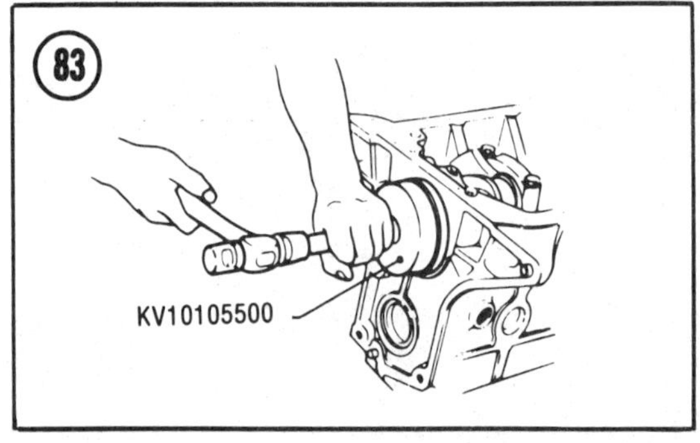

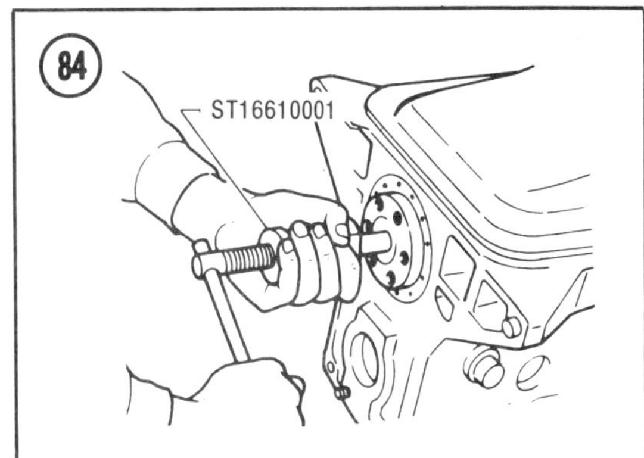

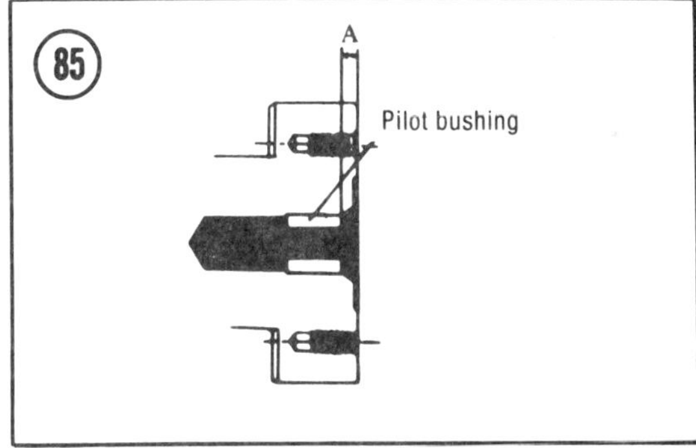

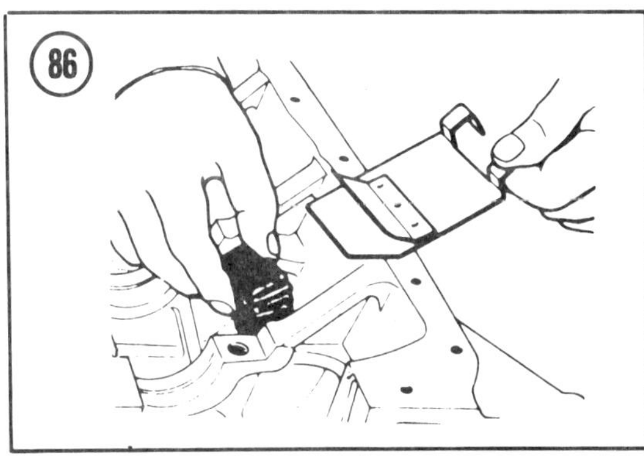

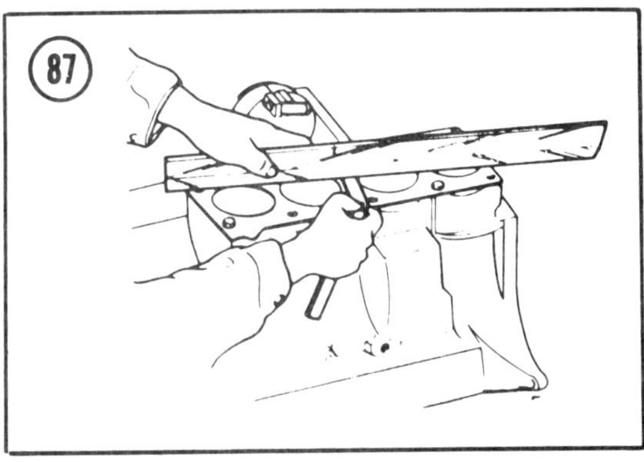

Pilot Bushing

The pilot bushing, located inside the rear end of the crankshaft, supports the transmission input shaft on manual transmission cars.

1. Check the bushing for visible wear and damage. If wear or damage can be seen, remove the bushing with a puller such as Datsun tool ST16610001 (Kent-Moore no. J23907). See **Figure 84**.

NOTE

Pilot bushing pullers are usually available from rental dealers. If you can't find one, another method is to fill the bushing with grease, then tap a clutch pilot tool into the bushing hole. The hydraulic force should push the bushing out.

2. Tap a new bushing in to a depth of 4 mm (0.157 in.). This is indicated by dimension "A," **Figure 85**.

CAUTION

Do not tap hard enough to damage the bushing. Do not drive the bushing in too far.

CYLINDER BLOCK INSPECTION

1. Remove the crankcase oil separator prior to inspection. See **Figure 86**.

2. Clean the block thoroughly with solvent and check all freeze plugs for leaks. Replace any freeze plugs that are suspect. It is a good idea to replace all of them. While cleaning, check oil and water passages for sludge, dirt, and corrosion. If the passages are very dirty, the block should be boiled out by a machine shop.

NOTE

Block boiling necessitates replacement of all freeze plugs. However, a block dirty enough to need boiling almost certainly needs these parts replaced anyway.

3. Examine the block for cracks.

4. Check flatness of the cylinder block's top surface. Use an accurate straightedge as shown in **Figure 87**. Have the block resurfaced if it is warped more than 0.1mm (0.004 in.).

5

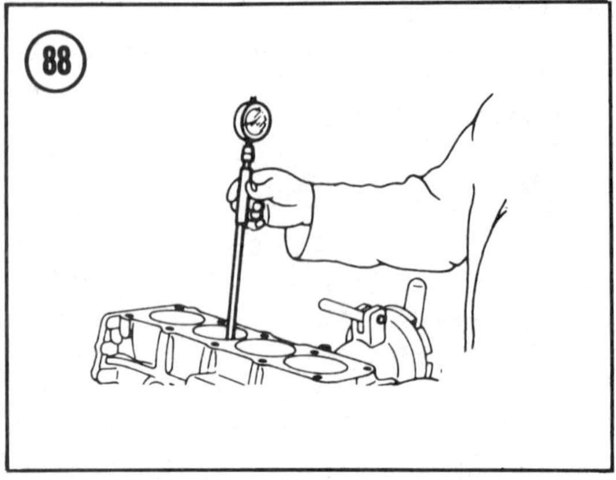

NOTE
Total material removed from block and cylinder head must not be more than 0.2 mm (0.008 in.).

5. Measure the cylinder bores for out-of-roundness or excessive wear with a bore gauge (**Figure 88**). Measure the bores at top, center, and bottom, in front-to-rear and side-to-side directions. Compare measurements to specifications at the end of the chapter. If the cylinders exceed maximum tolerances, they must be rebored. Reboring is also necessary if the cylinder walls are badly scuffed or scored.

NOTE
Before boring, install all main bearing caps and tighten to specifications. Bore in the following order: 2-4-1-3.

FLYWHEEL

Removal/Installation

1. Remove the engine. Separate the engine and transmission.
2. Remove the clutch from the flywheel. See *Clutch Removal*, Chapter Nine.
3. Unbolt the flywheel from the crankshaft (**Figure 89**).
4. Installation is the reverse of removal. Tighten flywheel bolts to specifications (end of chapter). Tighten gradually in a diagonal pattern.

Inspection

1. Check the flywheel for scoring and wear. If the surface is glazed or slightly scratched, have it resurfaced by a machine shop. Replace the flywheel if damage is severe.
2. Measure flywheel runout with a dial indicator (**Figure 90**). Replace or resurface the flywheel if runout is excessive.
3. Inspect the flywheel ring gear teeth. If the teeth are chipped, broken, or excessively worn, have a new ring gear shrunk onto the flywheel by a machine shop.

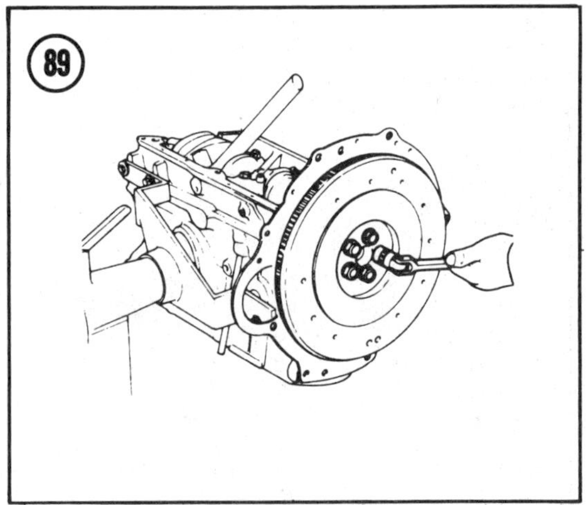

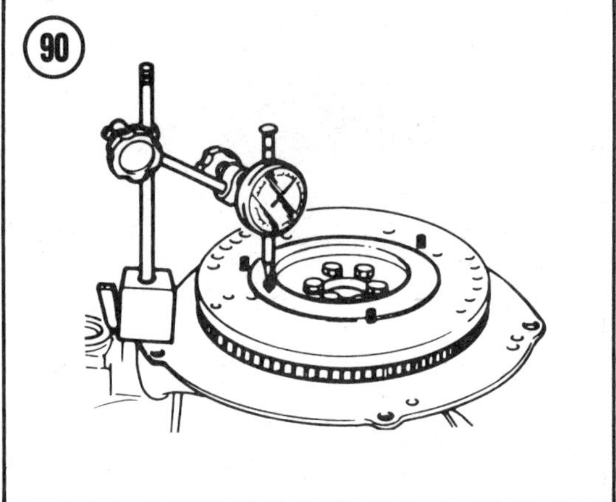

TORQUE CONVERTER DRIVE PLATE

The torque converter drive plate, used with automatic transmissions, is bolted to the crankshaft in the same manner as the flywheel.

Drive plate runout is measured in the same manner as flywheel runout. Replace the drive plate if runout exceeds 0.5mm (0.020 in.). The drive plate must also be replaced if the ring gear is damaged or worn excessively.

Table 1 NAPS-Z ENGINE SPECIFICATIONS

Cylinder head	
Maximum surface warp	0.1 mm (0.004 in.)
Valve face angle	45°
Valves	
Head diameter	
Intake	1.654-1.661 in. (42.0-42.2 mm)
Exhaust	1.496-1.504 in. (38.0-38.2mm)
Stem diameter	
Intake	0.3136-0.3142 in. (7.965-7.980mm)
Exhaust	0.3128-0.3134 in. (7.945-7.960mm)
Valve length	
Intake	4.835-4.846 in. (122.8-123.1mm)
Exhaust	4.866-4.878 in. (123.6-123.9mm)
Valve face angle	45° 30'
Head edge thickness, standard	
Intake	0.051 in. (1.3mm)
Exhaust	0.059 in. (1.5mm)
Head edge thickness, minimum	0.020 in. (0.5mm)
Valve springs	
Free length	
Inner	1.7362 in. (44.1 mm)
Outer	1.9594 in. (49.77mm)
Loaded length, standard	
Inner	1.3783 in. @ 24.3 lb. (35 mm @ 11 kg)
Outer	1.575 in. @ 50.7 lb. (40 mm @ 23 kg)
Loaded length, minimum	
Inner	1.3783 in. @ 10.6 lb. (35 mm @ 9.8 kg)
Outer	1.575 in. @ 42.6 lb. (40 mm @ 19.3 kg)
Bend, maximum	
Inner	0.075 in. (1.9mm)
Outer	0.087 in. (2.2mm)
Valve Guides	
Valve stem-to-guide clearance, standard	
Intake	0.0008-0.0021 in. (0.020-0.053mm)
Exhaust	0.0016-0.0029 in. (0.040-0.073mm)
Valve stem-to-guide clearance, maximum	0.004 in. (0.1mm)
Guide inner diameter	0.3150-0.3157 in. (8.000-8.018mm)
Guide hole diameter	
Standard	0.4718-0.4723 in. (11.985-11.996mm)
Oversize	0.4797-0.4802 in. (12.185-12.196mm)
Rocker arm to shaft clearance	0.0003-0.00019 in. (0.007-0.049mm)

(continued)

5

Table 1 NAPS-Z ENGINE SPECIFICATIONS (continued)

Camshaft	
End play, maximum	0.008 in. (0.2mm)
Lobe height	1.5148-1.5168 in. (38.477-38.527mm)
Lobe wear, maximum	0.010 in. (0.25mm)
Journal diameter	1.2967-1.2974 in. (32.935-32.955mm)
Bend, maximum (total indicator reading)	0.008 in. (0.2mm)
Bearing inner diameter	1.2992-1.3002 in. (33.000-33.025mm)
Journal-to-bearing clearance	
Standard	0.0018-0.0028 in. (0.045-0.090mm)
Maximum	0.004 in. (0.1mm)
Oil pump	
Outer rotor to body clearance	
Standard	0.006-0.008 in. (0.15-0.21mm)
Maximum	0.020 in. (0.5mm)
Rotor tip clearance	
Standard	0.005 in. (0.12mm) or less
Maximum	0.008 in. (0.2mm)
Rotor to straightedge clearance	0.002 in.(0.06mm) or less
Pump body to straightedge clearance	0.001 in. (0.03mm) or less
Connecting rods	
Big end play	
Standard	0.008-0.012 in. (0.2-0.3mm)
Maximum	0.024 in. (0.6mm)
Bearing clearance	
Standard	0.0010-0.0022 in. (0.025-0.055mm)
Maximum	0.005 in. (0.2mm)
Bend or twist per 100 mm (3.94 in.) of connecting rod length	
Standard	0.0012 in. (0.03mm)
Maximum	0.002 in. (0.05mm)
Pistons	
Ring gap, standard	
Top ring	0.010-0.016 in. (0.25-0.40mm)
Second ring	0.006-0.012 in. (0.15-0.30mm)
Oil ring	0.012-0.036 in. (0.30-0.90mm)
Maximum gap, all rings	0.039 in. (1mm)
Side clearance, standard	
Top ring	0.0016-0.0029 in. (0.040-0.073mm)
Second ring	0.0012-0.0025 in. (0.030-0.063mm)
Oil ring	None
Side clearance, maximum	
Top and second rings	0.004 in. (0.1mm)
Oil ring	None
Piston diameter	
Standard	3.3459-3.3478 in. (84.985-85.035mm)
0.5 mm (0.020 in.) oversize	3.3648-3.3667 in. (84.465-85.515mm)
1.0 mm (0.039 in. oversize	3.3844-3.3864 in. (95.965-86.015mm)

(continued)

Table 1 NAPS-Z ENGINE SPECIFICATIONS (continued)

Crankshaft	
Main bearing clearance	
Standard	0.0008-0.0024 in. (0.020-0.062mm)
Maximum	0.005 in. (0.12mm)
Journal diameter	2.1631-2.1636 in. (54.942-54.955mm)
Crankpin diameter	1.9670-1.9675 in. (49.961-49.974mm)
Journal and crankpin out-of-round and taper	
Standard	Less than 0.0004 in. (0.01mm)
Maximum	0.0012 in. (0.03mm)
Crankshaft bend (total indicator reading)	
Standard	Less than 0.001 in. (0.025mm)
Maximum	0.002 in. (0.05mm)
Crankshaft end play	
Standard	0.002-0.007 in. (0.05-0.18mm)
Maximum	0.012 in. (0.03mm)

5

Table 2 TIGHTENING TORQUES, NAPS-Z ENGINE

Fastener	Ft.-lb.	mkg
A/C compressor bracket	33-40	4.5-5.5
Alternator bracket	29-43	4-6
Alternator to adjusting bar	14-22	2-3
Camshaft sprocket bolt	87-116	12-16
Chain guides	4.5-7	0.6-1.0
Chain tensioner	4.5-7	0.6-1.0
Connecting rod caps	33-40	4.5-5.5
Crankshaft pulley bolt	87-116	12-16
Cylinder head to block	51-58	7.0-8.0
Cylinder head to front cover	3-6	0.4-0.8
Exhaust manifold	12-15	1.6-2.1
Flywheel to crankshaft	101-116	14-16
Front cover bolts		
M8 (large)	7-12	1.0-1.6
M6 (small)	3-7	0.4-1.0
Intake manifold	12-15	1.6-2.1
Main bearing caps	33-40	4.5-5.5
Motor mounts		
Brackets to engine	19-26	2.6-3.6
Brackets to insulator	37-50	5.1-6.9
Left insulator to body	19-26	2.6-3.6
Right insulator to body	10-13	1.4-1.8
Insulator to transmission	31-36	4.3-5.0
Transmission member to insulator	23-26	3.2-3.6
Transmission member to body	23-31	3.2-4.3
Oil pan	3.5-5	0.5-0.7
Oil pan drain plug	14-22	2-3
Oil pump	8-11	1.1-1.5
Oil strainer	7-12	1.0-1.6
Rocker arm locknuts	12-16	1.6-2.2
Rocker cover	6-7	0.8-1.0
Rocker shaft brackets	11-18	1.5-2.5
Spark plugs	11-14	1.5-2.0
Water inlet and outlet	7-12	1.0-1.6
Water pump		
M8 (large)	7-12	1.0-1.6
M6 (small)	3-7	0.4-1.0

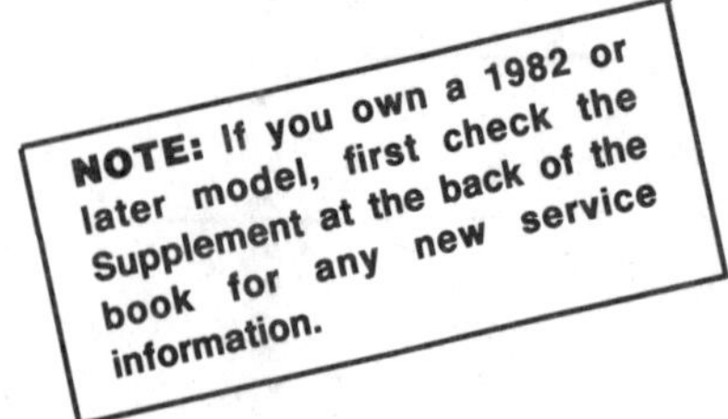
NOTE: If you own a 1982 or later model, first check the Supplement at the back of the book for any new service information.

CHAPTER SIX

FUEL AND EXHAUST SYSTEMS

This chapter includes service procedures for the air cleaner, carburetor, fuel pump, fuel tank, emission controls, exhaust system, and throttle linkage. **Tables 1-3** are at the end of the chapter.

AIR CLEANER

The ATC air cleaner is designed to regulate the temperature of incoming air. When the engine is cold, the air cleaner closes its inlet valve and draws heated air from around the exhaust manifold. When the engine is warm, the inlet valve opens and inducts air through the air cleaner in the normal manner. **Figure 1** shows a typical L-series ATC air cleaner. **Figure 2** shows the air cleaner used on NAPS-Z engines.

Automatic Temperature Control System

This system regulates the temperature of air entering the engine. When the engine is cold, the vacuum motor closes the air control valve. Hot air is then drawn from around the exhaust manifold. As the engine warms up, the valve

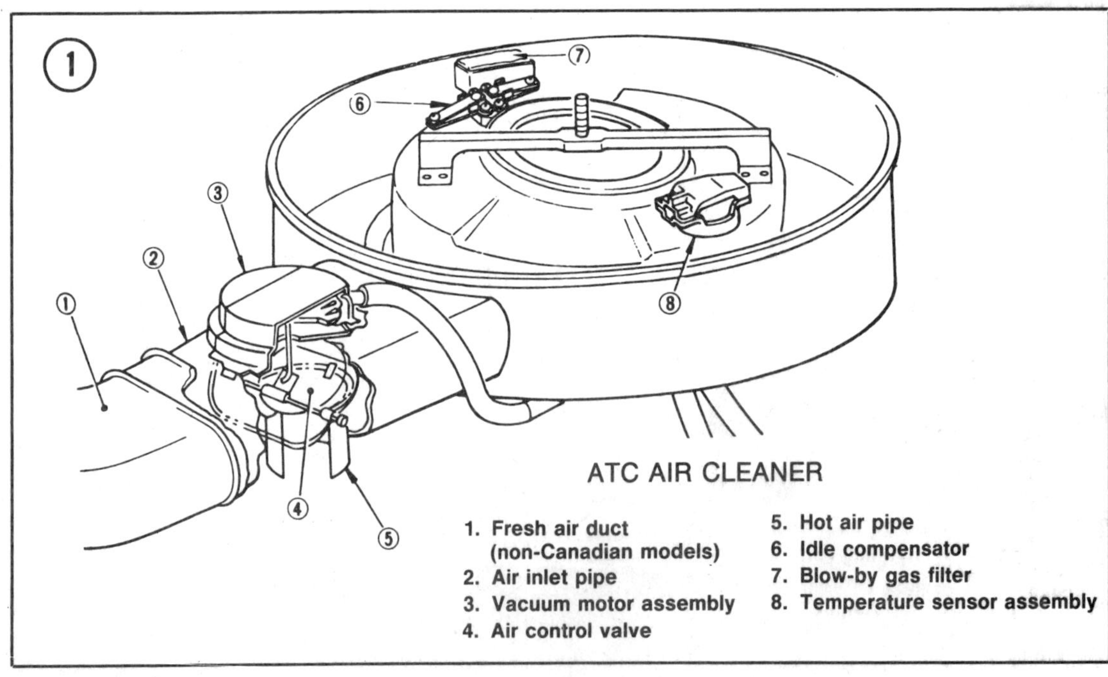

ATC AIR CLEANER

1. Fresh air duct (non-Canadian models)
2. Air inlet pipe
3. Vacuum motor assembly
4. Air control valve
5. Hot air pipe
6. Idle compensator
7. Blow-by gas filter
8. Temperature sensor assembly

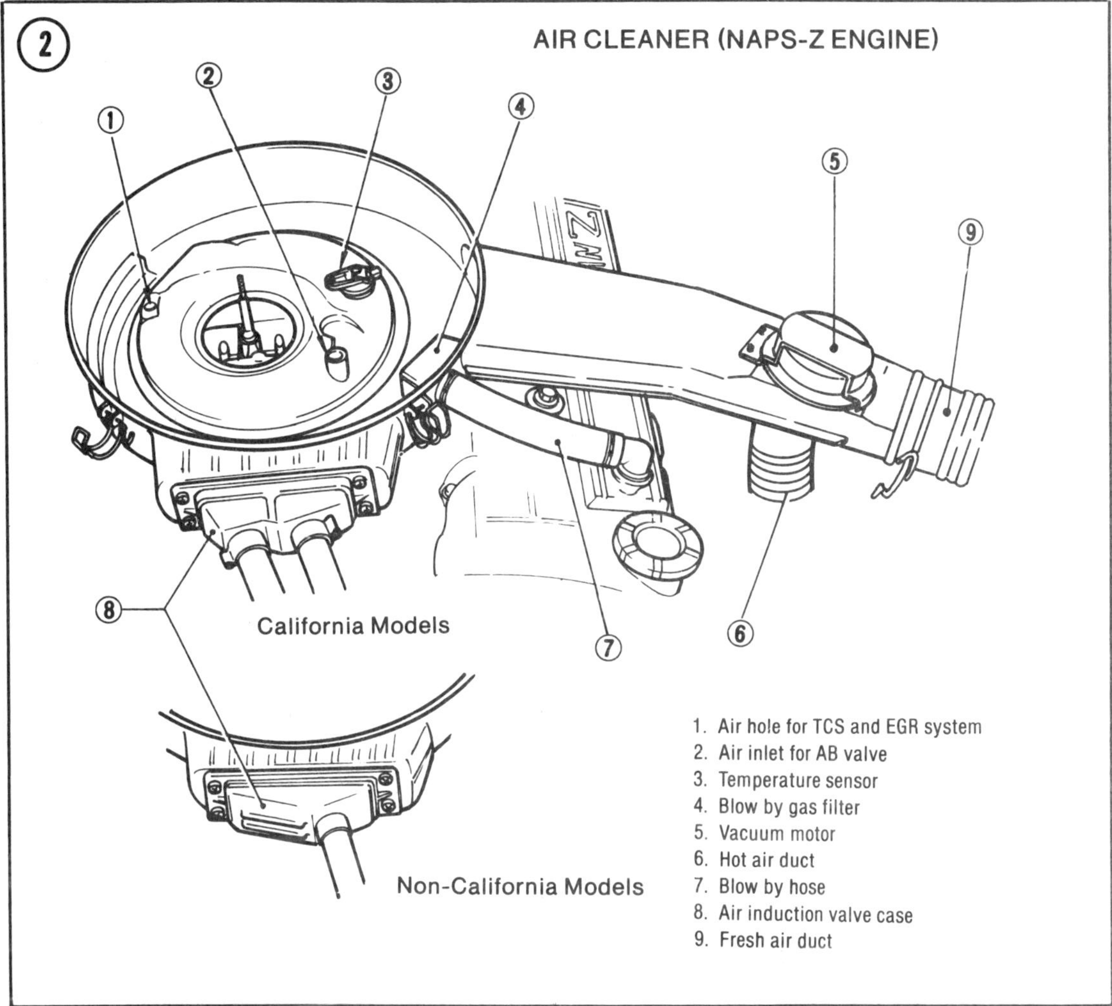

opens, and the air cleaner draws air through the fresh air duct. Inspect as follows.

1. Make sure vacuum hoses are properly connected and in good condition. Refer to *Vacuum Lines* in this chapter.
2. With the engine cold, disconnect the fresh air duct from the air cleaner.
3. Look down the air cleaner inlet with a mirror (**Figure 3**). The valve should be blocking the hot air duct. When the engine is started, the valve should move to block the fresh air duct.
4. Warm the engine to normal operating temperature. The valve should move to block the hot air duct. In very cold weather, the valve may take a long time to do this.
5. If the valve doesn't work properly, disconnect the hose from the vacuum motor. See **Figure 4**. Start the engine. There should be vacuum at the end of the hose. If not, check for damaged or disconnected hoses. Replace or connect as needed.
6. If the hoses are good, connect a length of hose to the vacuum motor and suck on it. The valve should move to block the fresh air intake. If it doesn't, check the vacuum motor linkage for binding. If the linkage isn't binding, replace the vacuum motor.
7. If the flap valve does move to close the fresh air intake, and the hoses are good, replace the temperature sensor.

Idle Compensator (L-Series Engines)

The idle compensator (6, **Figure 1**) is a thermostatic valve operated by underhood temperature. It prevents overrich fuel mixture

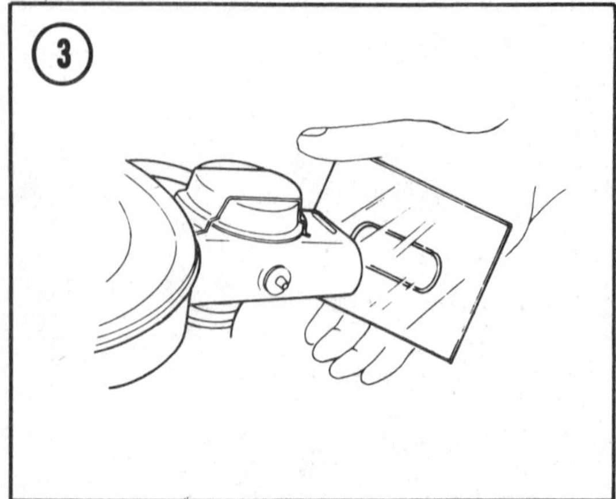

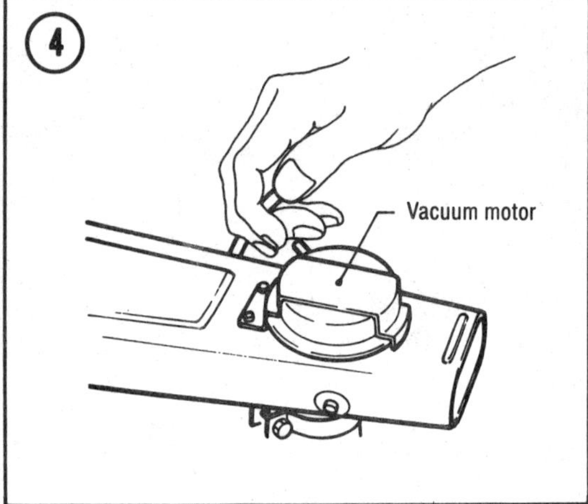

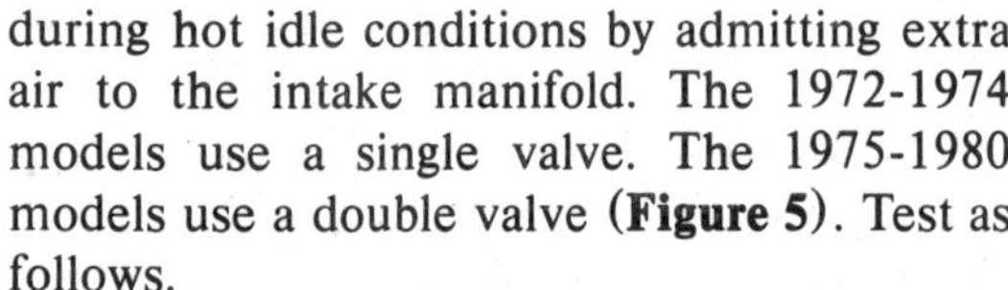

during hot idle conditions by admitting extra air to the intake manifold. The 1972-1974 models use a single valve. The 1975-1980 models use a double valve (**Figure 5**). Test as follows.

1. Remove the air cleaner cover.

2. Remove the idle compensator securing screws. Detach the air hose and take the idle compensator out.

3. Connect a tube to the bottom of the idle compensator. On double-valve compensators, block one side with a finger (**Figure 6**). Suck on the tube. It should be extremely difficult or impossible to suck air through the tube at temperatures below those specified in **Table 1**.

4. Place the idle compensator in water with a thermometer (**Figure 7**). Heat the water and watch the valve(s). They should open at temperatures specified in **Table 1**.

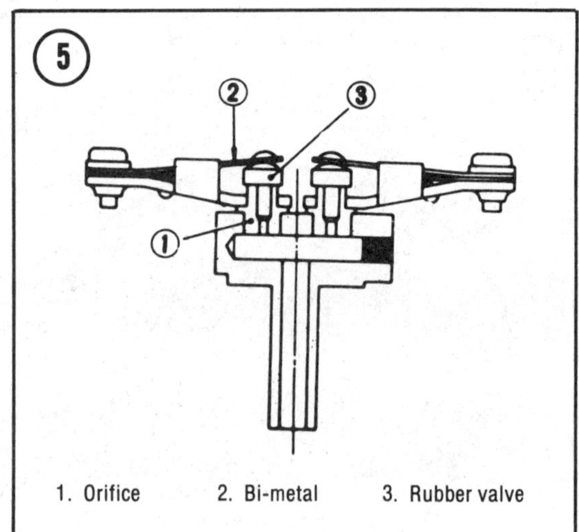

1. Orifice 2. Bi-metal 3. Rubber valve

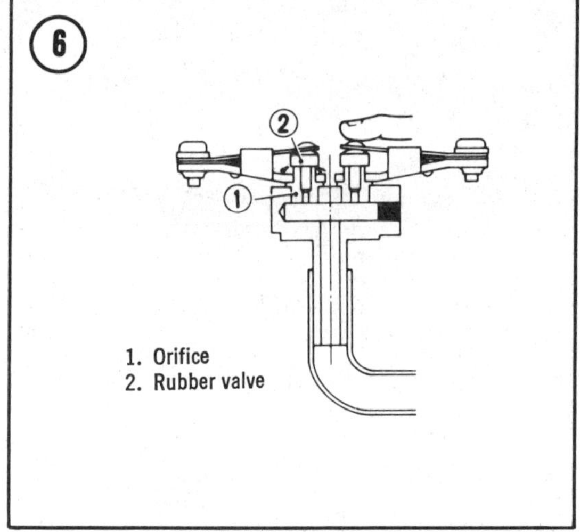

1. Orifice
2. Rubber valve

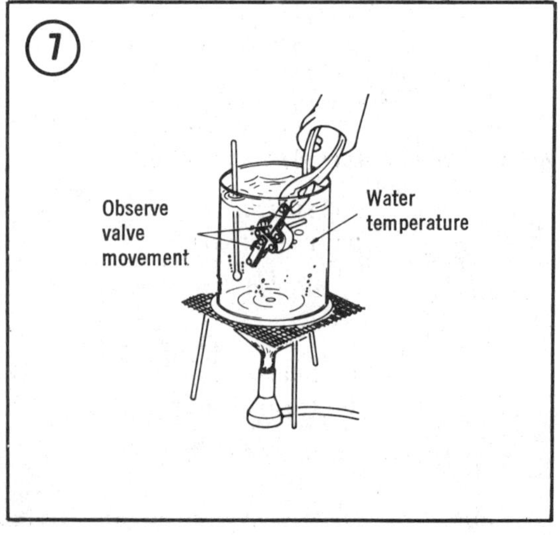

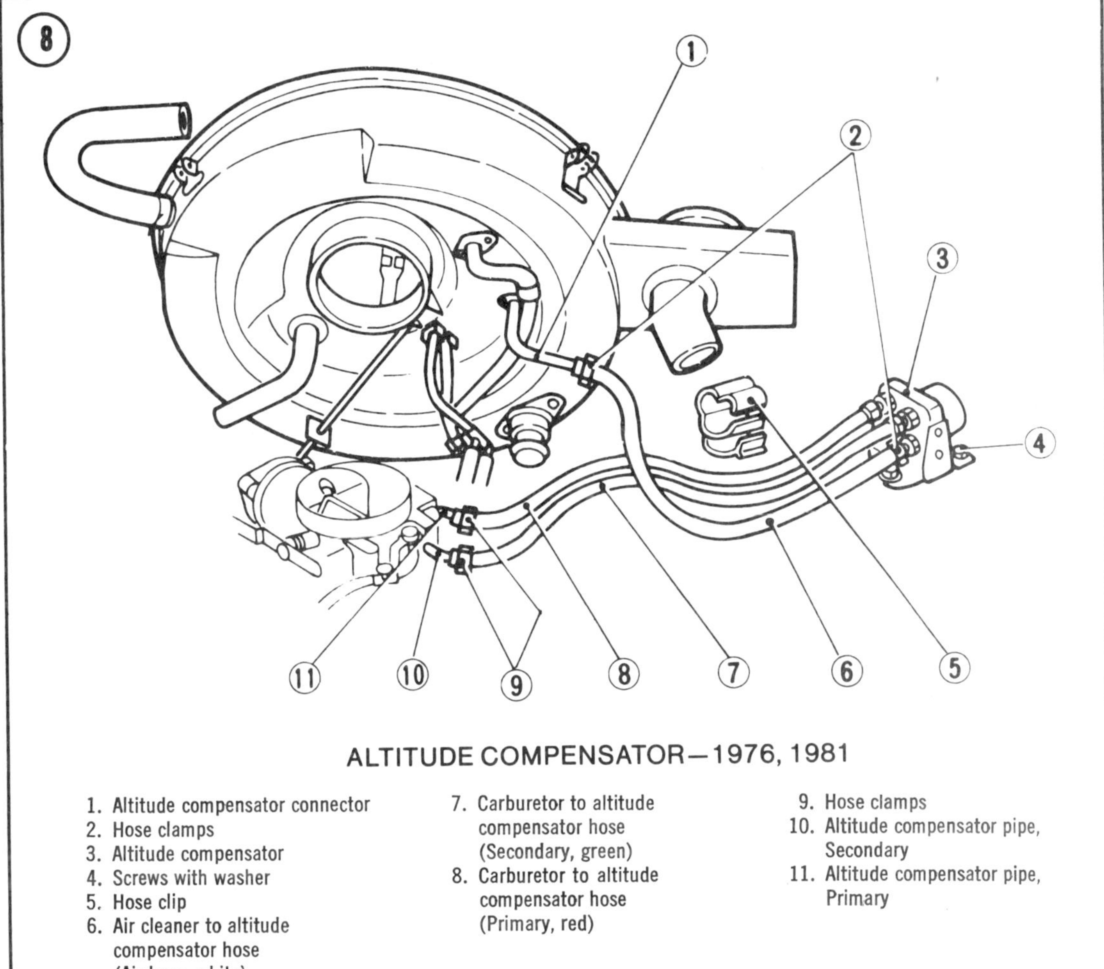

ALTITUDE COMPENSATOR—1976, 1981

1. Altitude compensator connector
2. Hose clamps
3. Altitude compensator
4. Screws with washer
5. Hose clip
6. Air cleaner to altitude compensator hose (Air hose, white)
7. Carburetor to altitude compensator hose (Secondary, green)
8. Carburetor to altitude compensator hose (Primary, red)
9. Hose clamps
10. Altitude compensator pipe, Secondary
11. Altitude compensator pipe, Primary

NOTE

On double-valve compensators, the valve marked "9" should open first; the valve marked "10" should open second. Replace the compensator if a valve fails to open or opens at the wrong temperature.

Air Cleaner Removal/Installation

1. Unbolt the air cleaner from its bracket.
2. If equipped with air induction, detach the air induction valve case from the side of the air cleaner.
3. Loosen the air cleaner base bolt.
4. Remove the air cleaner cover nut.
5. Disconnect the fresh air duct, hot air duct, and hoses.
6. Lift the air cleaner off.
7. Installation is the reverse of removal.

ALTITUDE COMPENSATOR

This device is optional on 1976-1978 California models, and mandatory for those years in some high altitude counties of the West. It is also used on all 1981 California models.

The altitude compensator admits additional air to the carburetor at high altitudes. This compensates for the overrich mixture caused by the thin ambient air.

The 1976 and 1981 device is automatic. The 1977-1978 version is set by hand.

Testing (1976 and 1981)

To test, disconnect the carburetor end of each carburetor-to-compensator line. See **Figure 8**. Try to blow air through each line

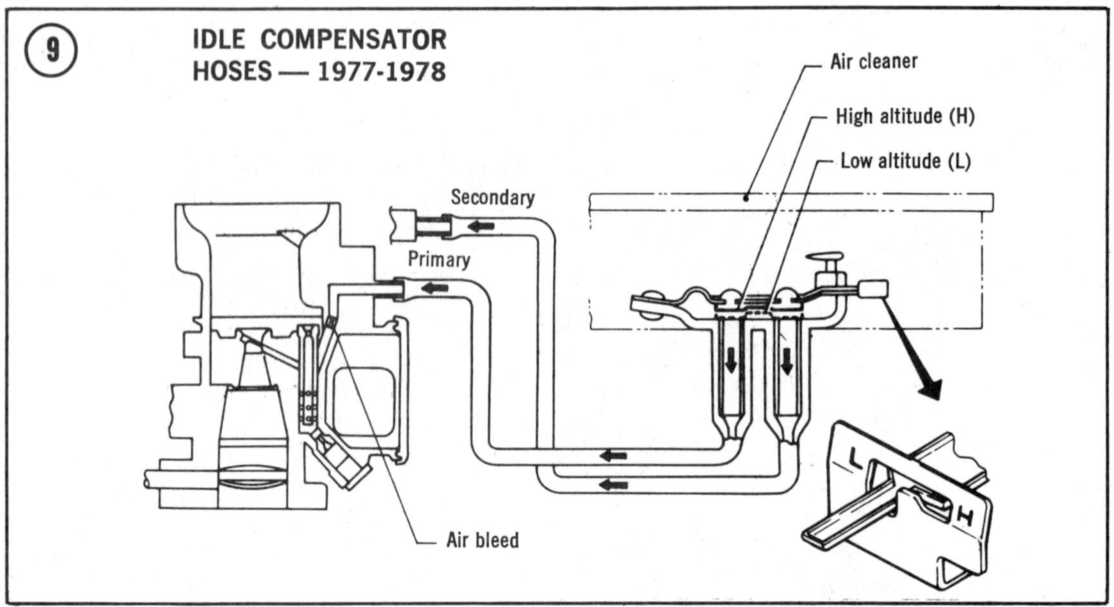

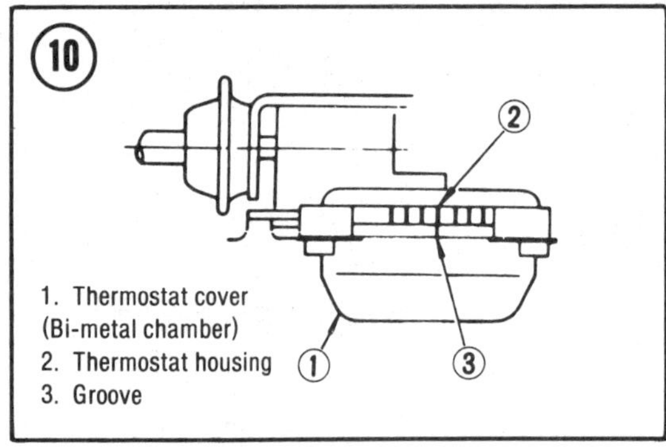

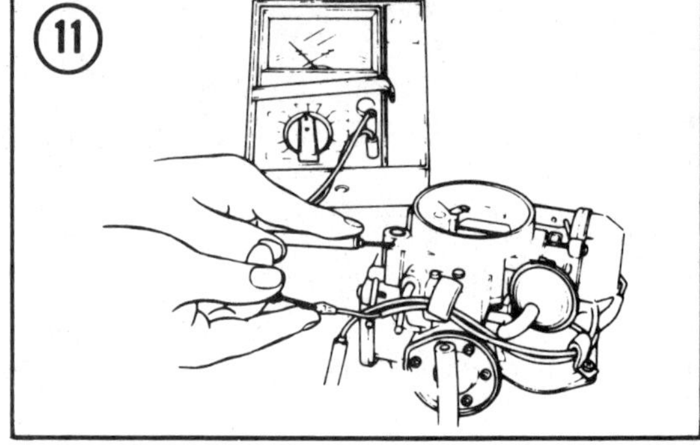

into the compensator. This should be impossible below 2,000 ft. (600 m). If it is possible, replace the compensator.

Testing (1977-1978)

Disconnect the altitude compensator hoses from the carburetor. See **Figure 9**. With the lever in the "L" position, it should be impossible to blow air through the hoses. In the "H" position, it should be possible to blow air through. If the idle compensator doesn't perform properly, replace it.

CARBURETOR

All models use a 2-barrel downdraft carburetor. The 1970-1971 models use a manual choke. The 1972 and later trucks use an electrically heated automatic choke. The choke heater causes the choke to open quickly and at a precise rate.

Automatic Choke Inspection

1. Remove the air cleaner as described in this chapter.
2. Move the choke plate by hand and check for binding. If the plate does not move smoothly, clean or repair the linkage as needed.
3. On 1972-1980 models, make sure the choke cover groove aligns with the center mark on the thermostat housing. See **Figure 10**.
4. Connect an ohmmeter between the choke heater terminal and carburetor body. See **Figure 11**. Resistance should be 3.7-8.9 ohms. If not, replace the choke cover.

Carburetor Removal/Installation

1. Remove the air cleaner as described in this chapter.
2. Label and disconnect the fuel and vacuum lines. Plug the fuel lines so they won't leak gasoline.
3. On 1972 and later models, disconnect the wires for choke heater and anti-dieseling solenoid.
4. Disconnect the throttle linkage.
5. Remove the carburetor mounting nuts. Lift the carburetor off the intake manifold.
6. Installation is the reverse of removal. Use a new gasket. Tighten the mounting nuts to 12-18 N•m (9-13 ft.-lb.).

Carburetor Disassembly

Refer to the following illustrations:
Figure 12—1970-1971
Figure 13—1972-1977
Figure 14—1978-1979 California
Figure 15—1978-1979 49 states, 1980 Canada

Figure 16—1980 U.S
Figure 17—1981

1. When removing jets, note their locations and the number stamped in each jet.
2. Make sure wrenches and screwdrivers fit exactly.
3. Lay all parts in order to ease reassembly.
4. Do not remove parts marked with an asterisk in the illustrations.
5. Do not remove linkage parts from the throttle shafts unless they are bent or otherwise damaged. Be sure replacement parts are available before removing.
6. On 1970-1980 models, remove the limiter cap from the idle mixture screw (if so equipped). Count the number of turns required to remove the screw to the nearest 1/8 turn and write this number down for use during installation.
7. On 1981 models, drill out the idle mixture screw seal (**Figure 18**). Pry the seal out, then remove the screw. Write down the number of turns required to remove the screw (to the nearest 1/8 turn).

Carburetor Inspection

1. Thoroughly clean all metal parts (except BCDD and solenoid) in solvent or carburetor cleaner. The secondary throttle diaphragm should be replaced if it is included in the repair kit. If not, clean it with a lint-free cloth.

CAUTION
Do not insert objects such as drill bits or pieces of wire into jets and passages while cleaning them. These openings are carefully calibrated, and scratching them may seriously affect carburetor performance.

2. If jets and passages are difficult to clean, blow them out with compressed air. If a compressor is not available, use a spray carburetor cleaner. These usually come with plastic tubes which fit into the can's nozzle, making it easy to spray the cleaner into jets and passages.
3. Check the needle valve and seat for wear. Replace as needed. If a new needle valve and seat are included in the repair kit, install them no matter what the old parts look like.
4. Check all castings for cracks. Replace cracked castings.
5. Check the idle mixture screw for wear at the tip. Replace if wear is detected.
6. Check the accelerator pump piston seal and cover for wear, damage, or deterioration. Replace as needed.
7. If equipped with an automatic choke, inspect the vacuum break diaphragm. To do this, disconnect the vacuum break hose from the carburetor body. Hold the choke valve shut and suck on the hose. There should be a strong pull on the choke valve. If not, replace the choke chamber assembly.
8. Test the solenoid(s). Connect a 12-volt battery between the solenoid body and solenoid wire. The solenoid should click each time current is applied. If not, replace it.

Carburetor Assembly

Assembly is the reverse of disassembly, plus the following.
1. Use new gaskets and seals.
2. When assembling the center body and throttle chamber, note that the center bottom

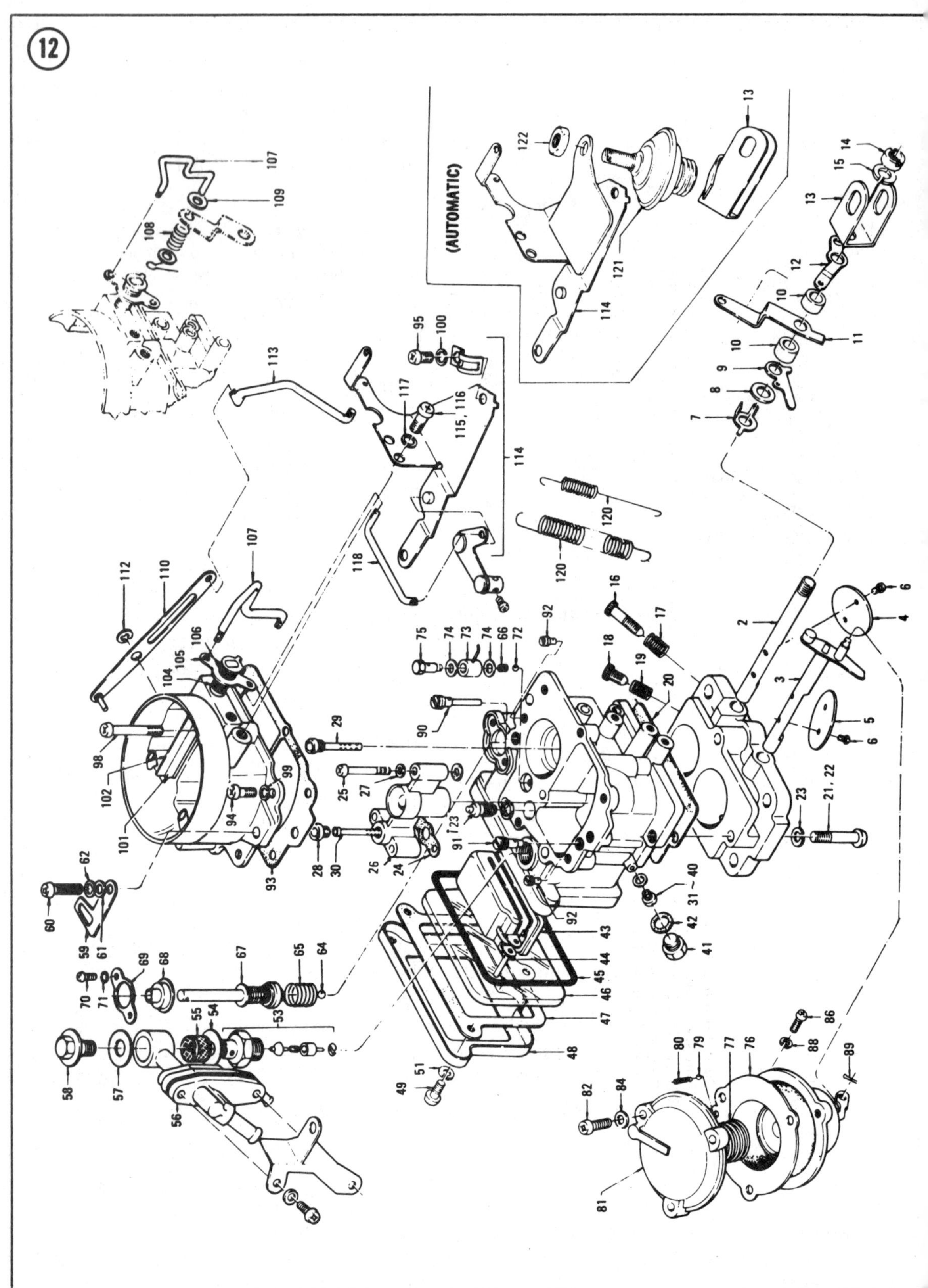
12
(AUTOMATIC)

MANUAL CHOKE CARBURETOR — EARLY MODELS

1. Carburetor assembly
2. Primary throttle shaft
3. Secondary throttle shaft
4. Primary throttle valve
5. Secondary throttle valve
6. Screw
7. Throttle adjustment lever
8. Washer
9. Return plate
10. Sleeve
11. Connecting lever
12. Throttle lever
13. Throttle lever
14. Nut
15. Spring washer
16. Throttle adjustment screw
17. Throttle adjustment spring
18. Idle adjustment screw
19. Adjustment screw spring
20. Throttle chamber gasket
21. Screw
22. Screw
23. Spring washer
24. Venturi gasket
25. Screw
26. Secondary venturi
27. Spring washer
28. Main air bleed
29. Main air bleed
30. Secondary emulsion tube
31. Primary main jet

32-40. Secondary main jet

41. Drain plug
42. Packing
43. Float assembly
44. Collar
45. Rubber seal
46. Float chamber glass
47. Float cover gasket
48. Glass frame
49. Screw
51. Spring washer
53. Needle valve assembly
54. Washer
55. Filter
56. Fuel vapor discharge connector
57. Washer
58. Inlet bolt
59. Fuel return clamp
60. Screw
61. Plain washer
62. Lockwasher
64. Ball
65. Piston return spring
66. Pump injector spring
67. Piston
68. Pump cover
69. Cylinder plate
70. Screw
71. Spring washer
72. Ball
73. Pump nozzle
74. Washer
75. Nozzle setscrew
76. Diaphragm assembly
77. Diaphragm spring
79. Ball
80. Valve spring
81. Diaphragm cover
82. Screw
84. Spring washer
86. Screw
88. Spring washer
89. Stopper pin
90. Slow jet
91. Slow jet
92. Slow air bleed
94. Screw
95. Screw
98. Screw
99. Spring washer
100. Spring washer
101. Choke shaft
102. Choke valve
104. Choke lever spring
105. Choke lever
106. Choke valve spring
107. Fast idle rod
108. Pump spring rod
109. Choke rod washer
110. Pump lever
112. Ring
113. Pump rod
114. Throttle return spring bracket
115. Screw
116. Screw
117. Spring washer
118. Choke rod
120. Throttle return spring
121. Dash pot assembly
122. Nut
123. Power valve

6

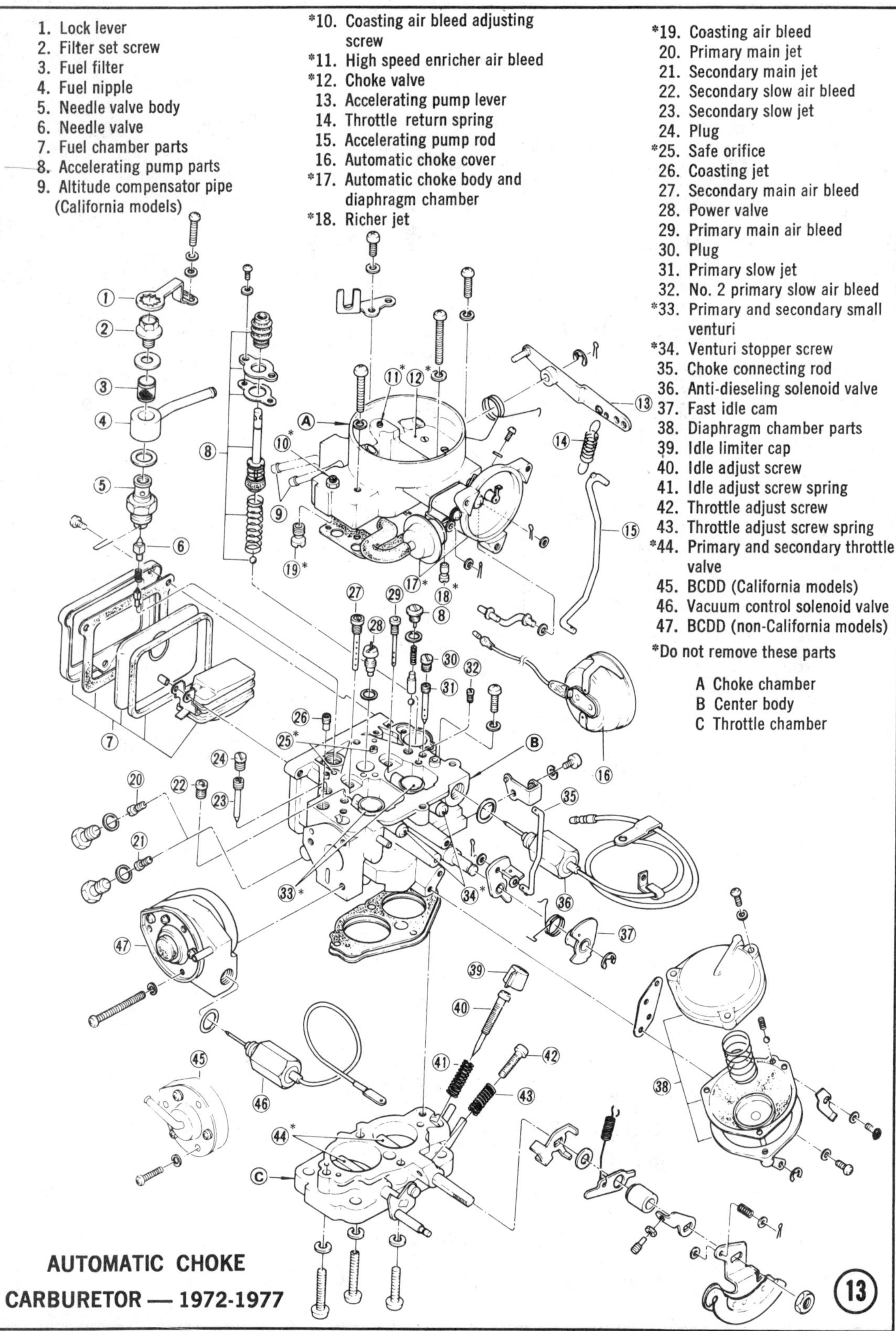
1. Lock lever
2. Filter set screw
3. Fuel filter
4. Fuel nipple
5. Needle valve body
6. Needle valve
7. Fuel chamber parts
8. Accelerating pump parts
9. Altitude compensator pipe (California models)
*10. Coasting air bleed adjusting screw
*11. High speed enricher air bleed
*12. Choke valve
13. Accelerating pump lever
14. Throttle return spring
15. Accelerating pump rod
16. Automatic choke cover
*17. Automatic choke body and diaphragm chamber
*18. Richer jet
*19. Coasting air bleed
20. Primary main jet
21. Secondary main jet
22. Secondary slow air bleed
23. Secondary slow jet
24. Plug
*25. Safe orifice
26. Coasting jet
27. Secondary main air bleed
28. Power valve
29. Primary main air bleed
30. Plug
31. Primary slow jet
32. No. 2 primary slow air bleed
*33. Primary and secondary small venturi
*34. Venturi stopper screw
35. Choke connecting rod
36. Anti-dieseling solenoid valve
37. Fast idle cam
38. Diaphragm chamber parts
39. Idle limiter cap
40. Idle adjust screw
41. Idle adjust screw spring
42. Throttle adjust screw
43. Throttle adjust screw spring
*44. Primary and secondary throttle valve
45. BCDD (California models)
46. Vacuum control solenoid valve
47. BCDD (non-California models)
*Do not remove these parts
A Choke chamber
B Center body
C Throttle chamber
AUTOMATIC CHOKE
CARBURETOR — 1972-1977
13

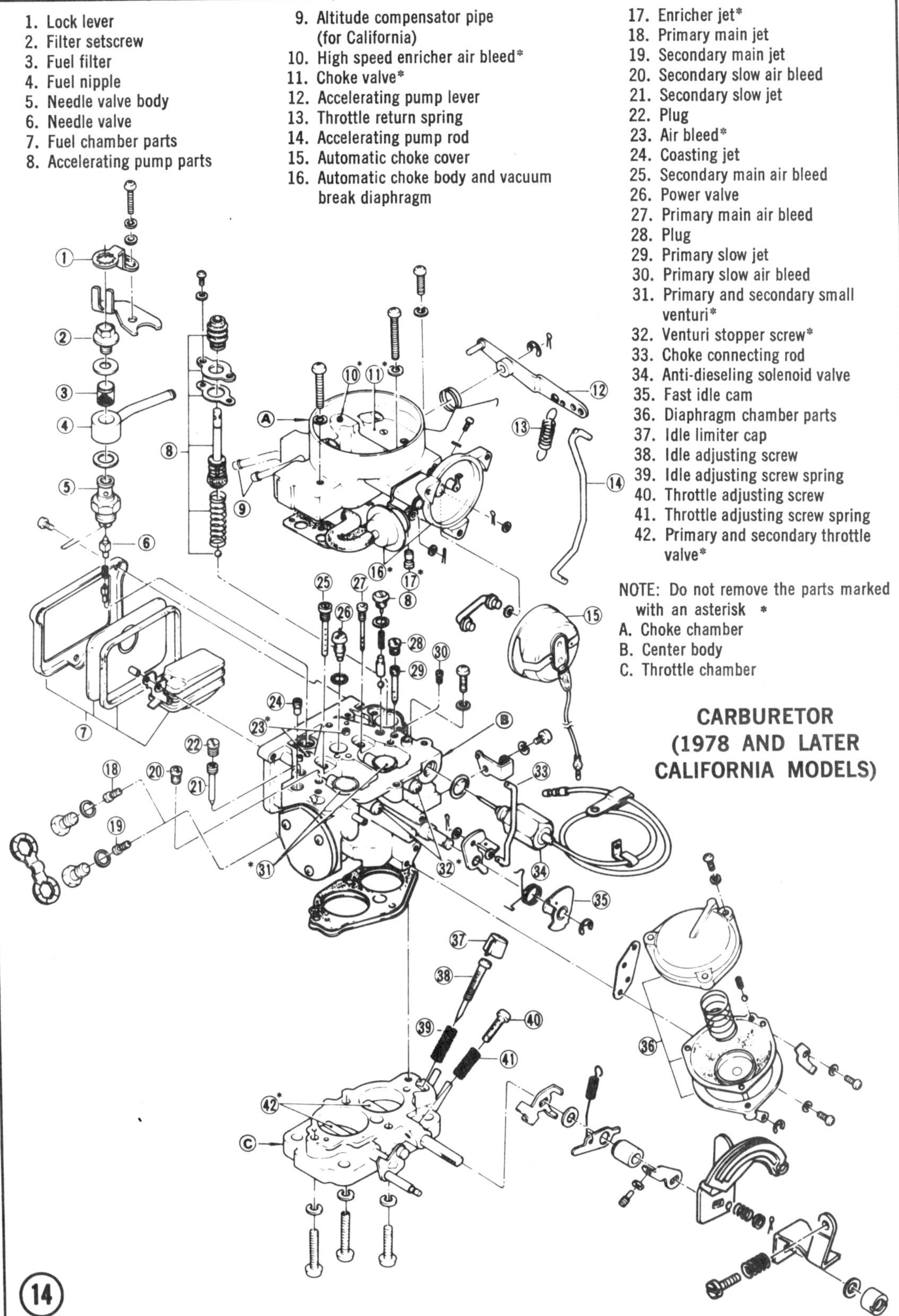

CARBURETOR (1978 AND LATER CALIFORNIA MODELS)

15

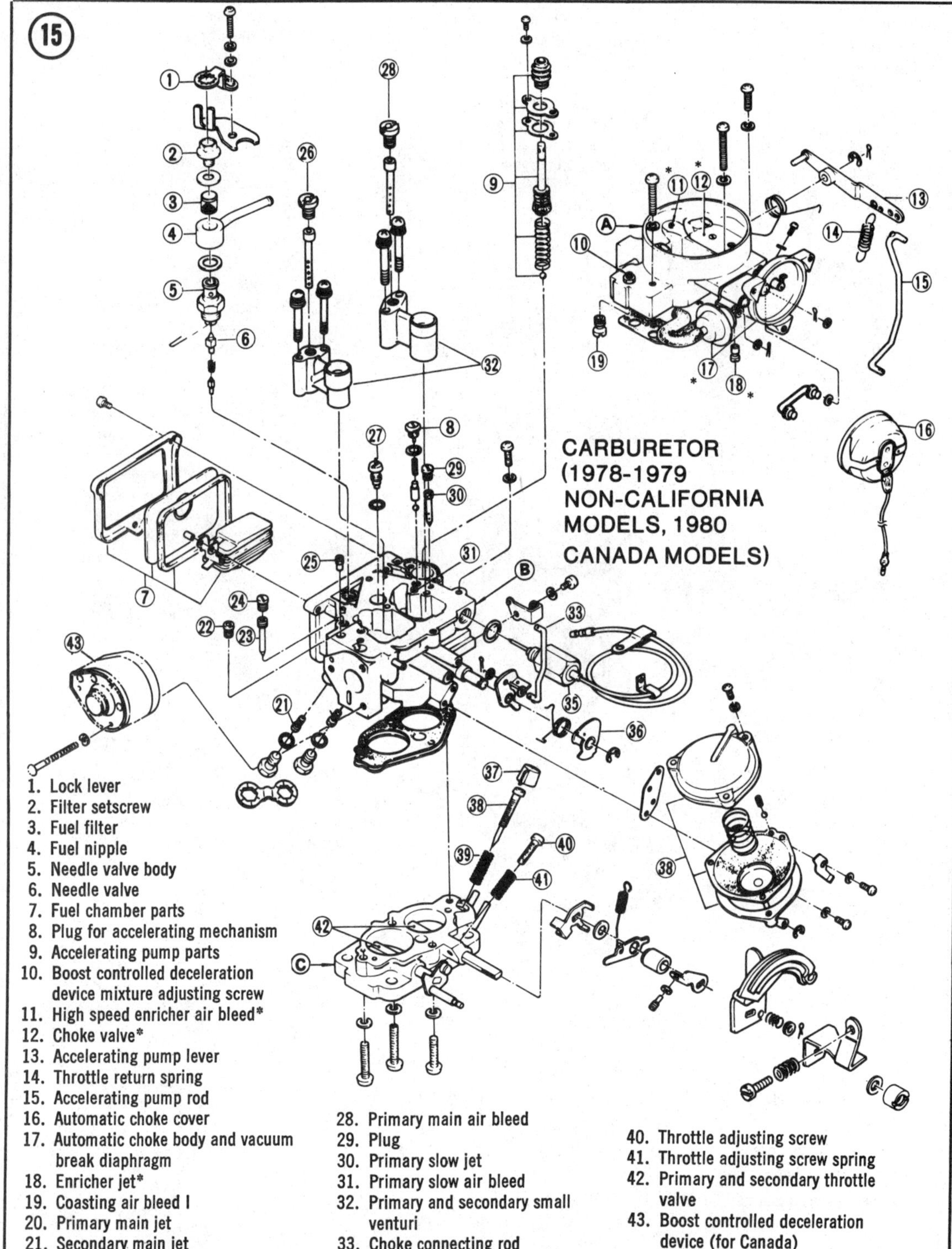

1. Lock lever
2. Filter setscrew
3. Fuel filter
4. Fuel nipple
5. Needle valve body
6. Needle valve
7. Fuel chamber parts
8. Plug for accelerating mechanism
9. Accelerating pump parts
10. Boost controlled deceleration device mixture adjusting screw
11. High speed enricher air bleed*
12. Choke valve*
13. Accelerating pump lever
14. Throttle return spring
15. Accelerating pump rod
16. Automatic choke cover
17. Automatic choke body and vacuum break diaphragm
18. Enricher jet*
19. Coasting air bleed I
20. Primary main jet
21. Secondary main jet
22. Secondary slow air bleed
23. Secondary slow jet
24. Plug
25. Coasting jet
26. Secondary main air bleed
27. Power valve
28. Primary main air bleed
29. Plug
30. Primary slow jet
31. Primary slow air bleed
32. Primary and secondary small venturi
33. Choke connecting rod
34. Anti-dieseling solenoid valve
35. Fast idle cam
36. Diaphragm chamber parts
37. Idle limiter cap
38. Idle adjusting screw
39. Idle adjusting screw spring
40. Throttle adjusting screw
41. Throttle adjusting screw spring
42. Primary and secondary throttle valve
43. Boost controlled deceleration device (for Canada)

A. Choke chamber
B. Center body
C. Throttle chamber

NOTE: Do not remove the parts marked with an asterisk *

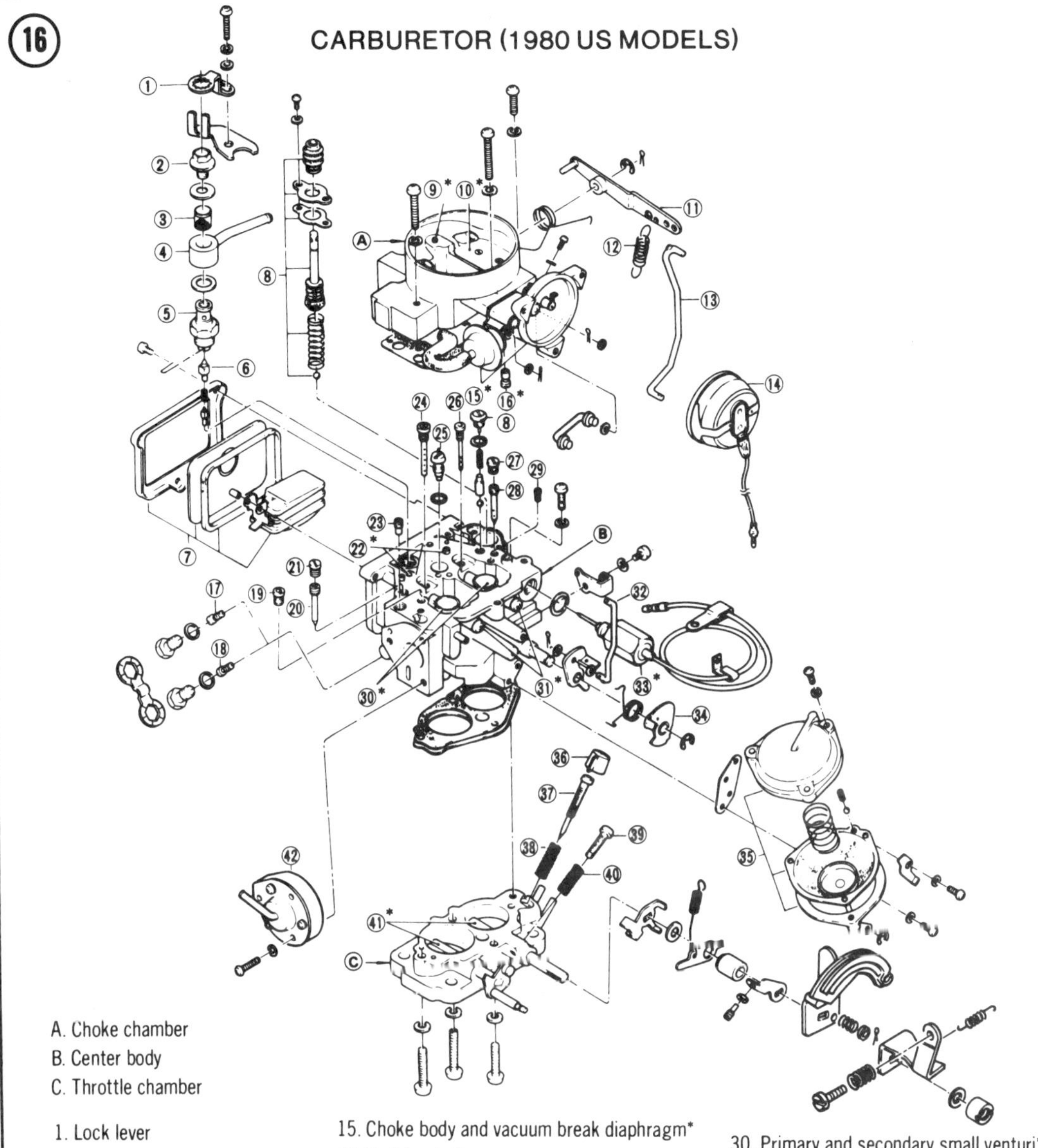

16 CARBURETOR (1980 US MODELS)

A. Choke chamber
B. Center body
C. Throttle chamber

1. Lock lever
2. Filter setscrew
3. Fuel filter
4. Fuel nipple
5. Needle valve body
6. Needle valve
7. Float chamber cover
8. Accelerator pump
9. High speed enricher air bleed*
10. Choke valve
11. Accelerator pump lever
12. Throttle return spring
13. Accelerator pump lever
14. Choke cover
15. Choke body and vacuum break diaphragm*
16. Enricher jet*
17. Primary main jet
18. Secondary main jet
19. Secondary slow air bleed
20. Secondary slow jet
21. Plug
22. Air bleed*
23. Coasting jet
24. Secondary main air bleed
25. Power valve
26. Primary main air bleed
27. Plug
28. Primary slow jet
29. Primary slow air bleed
30. Primary and secondary small venturi*
31. Venturi stopper screw*
32. Choke connecting rod
33. Anti-dieseling solenoid
34. Fast idle cam
35. Diaphragm chamber parts
36. Idle limiter cap
37. Idle mixture screw
38. Idle mixture screw spring
39. Idle speed screw
40. Idle speed screw spring
41. Primary and secondary throttle valves*
42. Bypass air control unit

*Do not remove these parts.

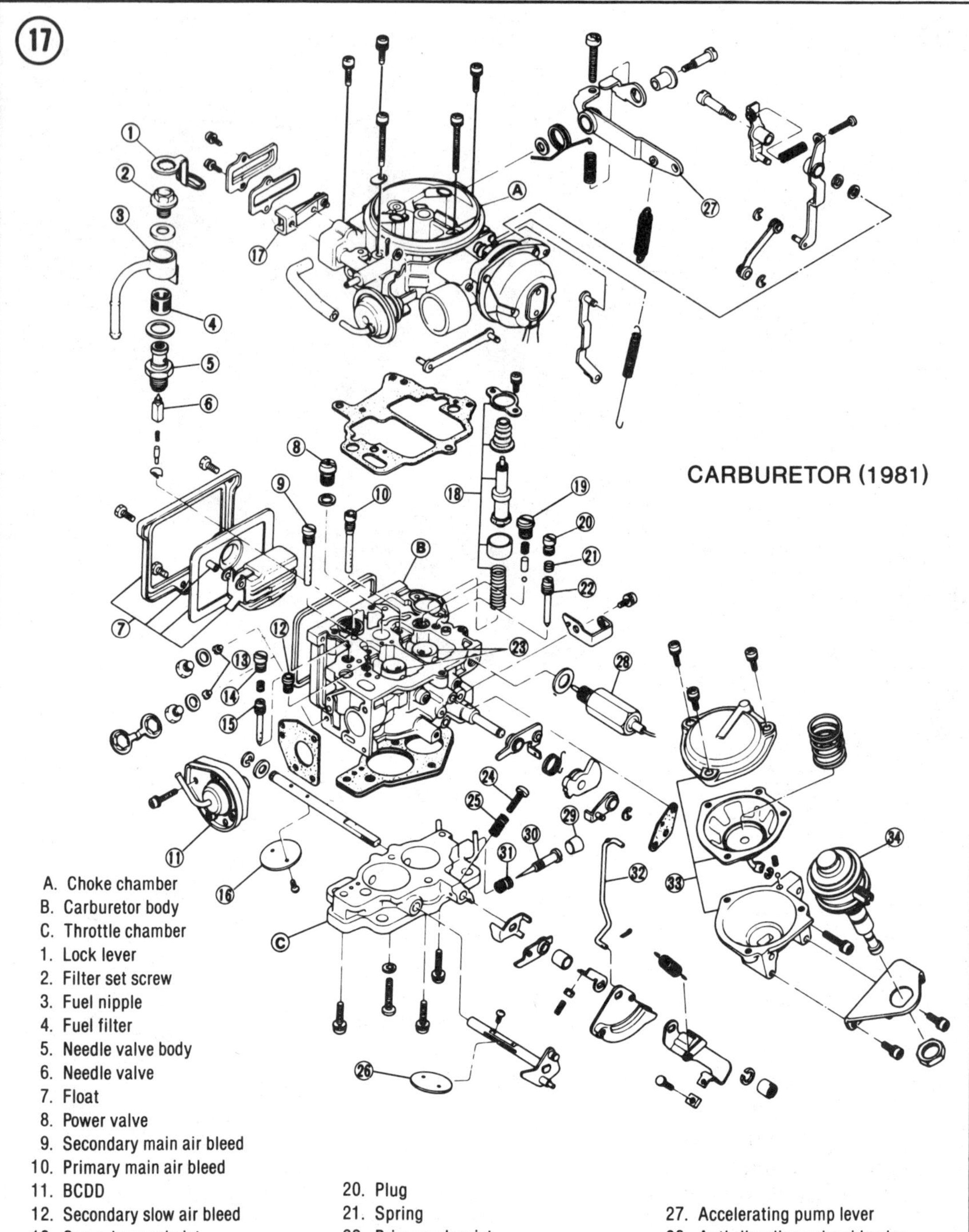

A. Choke chamber
B. Carburetor body
C. Throttle chamber
1. Lock lever
2. Filter set screw
3. Fuel nipple
4. Fuel filter
5. Needle valve body
6. Needle valve
7. Float
8. Power valve
9. Secondary main air bleed
10. Primary main air bleed
11. BCDD
12. Secondary slow air bleed
13. Secondary main jet
14. Plug
15. Secondary slow jet
16. Primary throttle valve
17. Idle compensator
18. Accelerating pump parts
19. Plug for accelerating mechanism
20. Plug
21. Spring
22. Primary slow jet
23. Primary and secondary small venturi
24. Throttle adjusting screw
25. Throttle adjusting screw spring
26. Secondary throttle valve
27. Accelerating pump lever
28. Anti-dieseling solenoid valve
29. Blind plug
30. Idle adjusting screw
31. Idle adjusting screw spring
32. Choke connecting rod
33. Diaphragm chamber parts
34. Dash pot

18

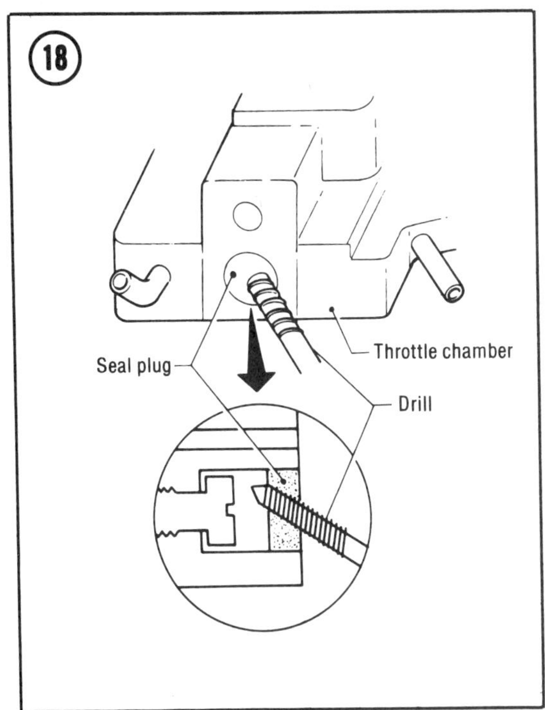

20

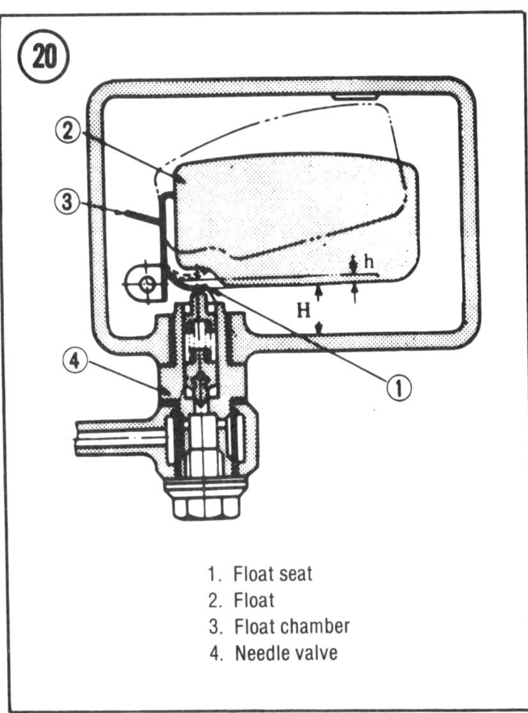

1. Float seat
2. Float
3. Float chamber
4. Needle valve

19

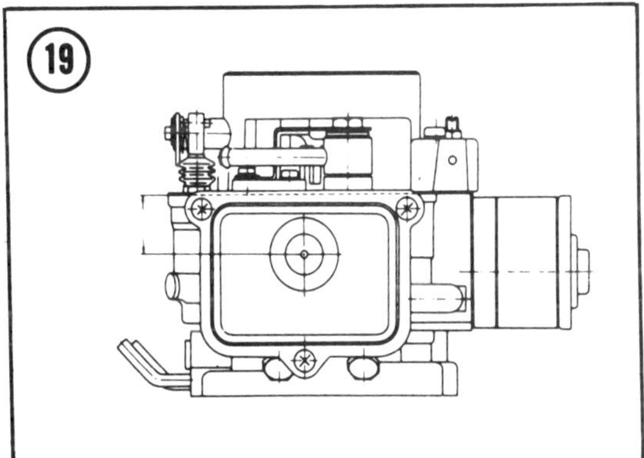

screw has a hole in it for the power valve. Be sure this screw goes in the center hole.

3. Be sure the main jets and air bleeds are installed in the correct holes. Refer to the numbers written down during disassembly. If you didn't write the numbers down, refer to **Table 2**.

4. Screw in the idle mixture screw the same number of turns required for removal.

5. After assembly, adjust float level, fast idle (1972-1981 only), and choke cover (1972-1980 only) as described in this chapter. If you have a CO meter, check idle mixture. If not, have this done by a dealer.

Float Level Adjustment

This adjustment can be made with the carburetor on or off the engine.

1. If the carburetor is on the engine, check fuel level at idle speed. It should be approximately halfway up the sight glass (**Figure 19**). If not, adjust float level.

WARNING

Let the engine cool before the next step. It may be impossible to avoid spilling gasoline. Place a fire extinguisher nearby.

2. If the carburetor is on the engine, place a container beneath it to catch dripping fuel, then remove the float chamber cover.

3. Raise the float all the way. Measure the gap between float and float chamber (dimension "H", **Figure 20**). Compare with specifications in **Table 2**. If incorrect, slide the float off its pivot and bend float seat to change dimension "H."

4. Let the float hang down. Raise the needle valve with a knife blade or similar tool. Measure the gap between needle valve and float seat (dimension "h", **Figure 20**) with a gauge rod or drill bit. Compare with **Table 2**. Adjust if necessary by bending the float stopper.

6

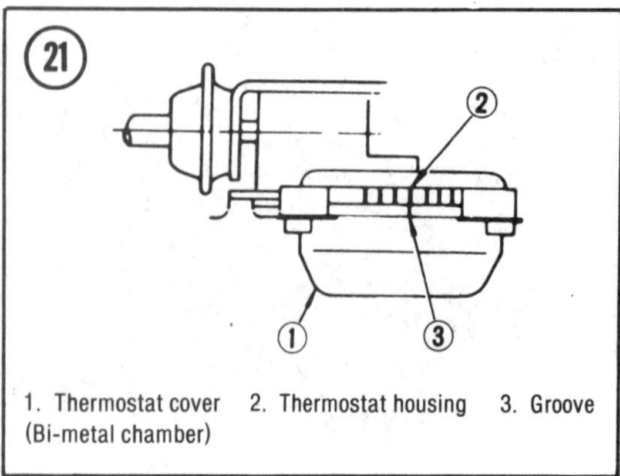

1. Thermostat cover (Bi-metal chamber) 2. Thermostat housing 3. Groove

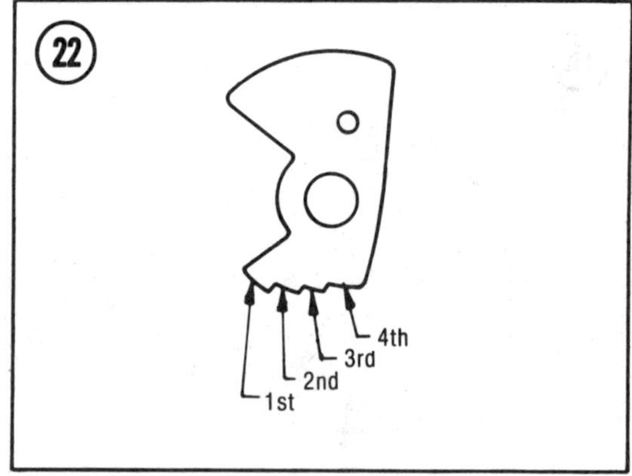

Choke Cover Adjustment (1970-1980 Only)

1. Have an assistant floor the accelerator. The choke valve should close. It should open without binding when pushed with a finger. If not, check the choke linkage for worn, damaged, disconnected, or missing parts. Replace or reconnect as needed.
2. Align the groove on the choke cover with the center mark on the choke housing. See **Figure 21**. Then tighten the choke cover screws.

Fast Idle Adjustment (1972-1981)

Fast idle is the speed at which the engine idles when it is cold and the choke is operating. As the engine warms, idle speed gradually returns to normal.

The adjustment is made with the carburetor off the engine.

1. Place the fast idle screw on the specified step of the fast idle cam. See **Figure 22** and **Figure 23**. **Table 2** lists specified steps.
2. Check clearance between the primary throttle bore and venturi (A, **Figure 24**). Compare with **Table 2**. To adjust, loosen the nut (2, **Figure 23**) and turn the fast idle screw (3). When clearance is correct, tighten the nut.

Anti-stall Dashpot Adjustment

An anti-stall dashpot is used on the following models:

1973-1974—with automatic transmission

1975-1979—all

1980—U.S. trucks with automatic transmission, Canadian trucks with manual transmission

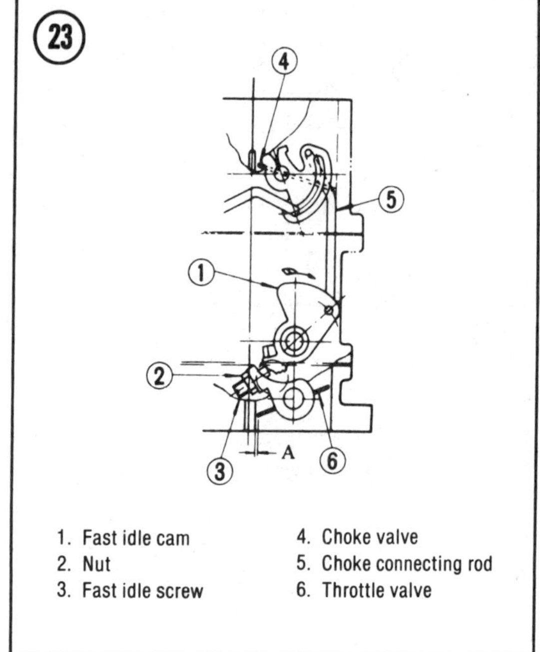

1. Fast idle cam
2. Nut
3. Fast idle screw
4. Choke valve
5. Choke connecting rod
6. Throttle valve

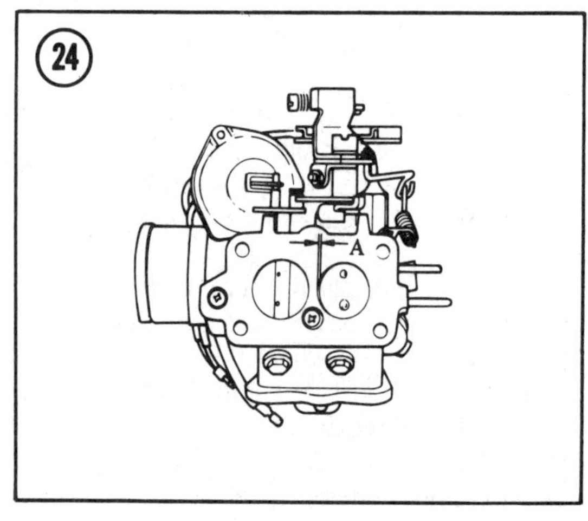

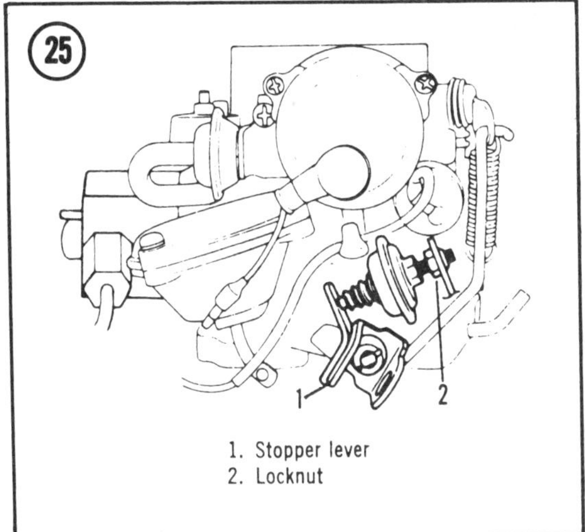

1. Stopper lever
2. Locknut

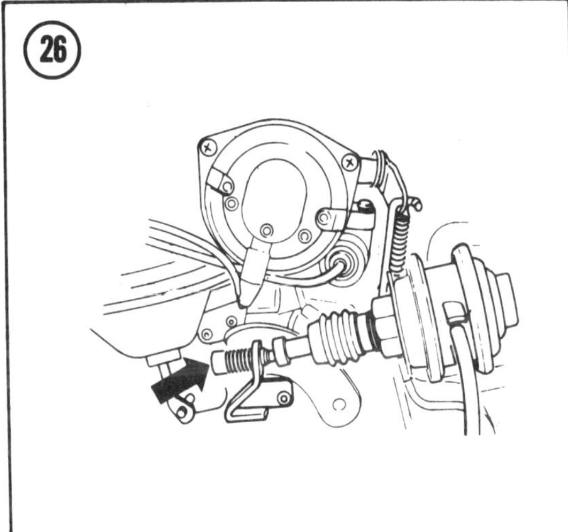

1981—with automatic transmission

Adjust as follows.

1. Warm the engine to normal operating temperature. Check idle speed (and mixture on 1979-1980 models). Refer to *Tune-up*, Chapter Three.
2. Move the throttle by hand until the dashpot just touches the stopper lever. Compare engine speed with **Table 2**. On 1973-1980 models without air conditioning, loosen the locknut and turn the dashpot to adjust. See **Figure 25**. On 1973-1980 models with air conditioning, turn the adjusting screw. See **Figure 26**. On 1981 models, turn the adjusting screw. See **Figure 27**.

FUEL PUMP

All 1970-1976 models, as well as 1977-1979 models without air conditioning, use a mechanical fuel pump mounted on the engine. Air-conditioned 1977-1979 models use an electric fuel pump mounted near the fuel tank. All 1980 models use a mechanical fuel pump. For 1981, trucks with automatic transmission or sold originally without beds use an electric fuel pump. All others use a mechanical fuel pump.

Fuel pump testing is covered in Chapter Two, under *Fuel System Troubleshooting*. Refer to **Table 3** for performance specifications.

Removal/Installation (Mechanical Pump)

1. Disconnect the fuel inlet and outlet lines from the pump.
2. Remove the fuel pump nuts and take the pump off. See **Figure 28**.

(29) ELECTRIC FUEL PUMP (1977-1979)

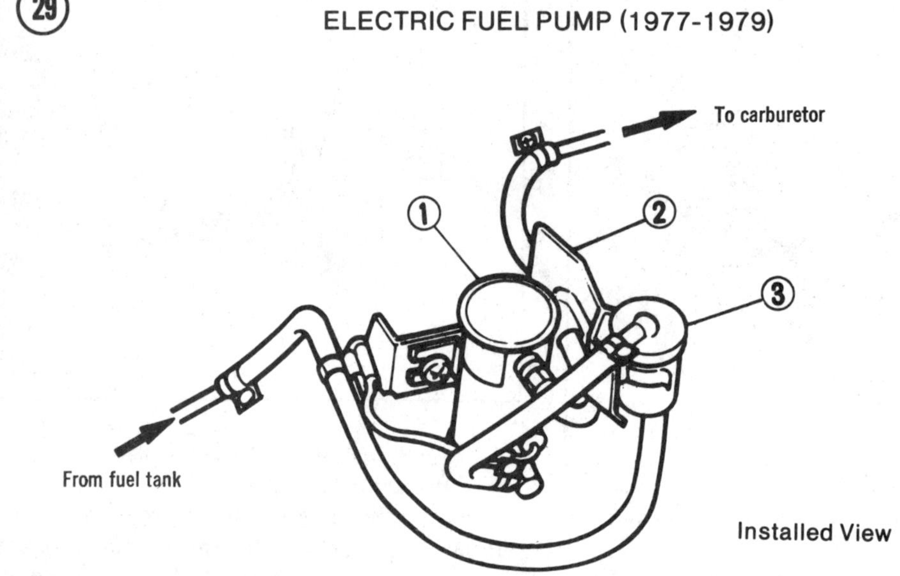

1. Electric fuel pump
2. Mounting bracket
3. Fuel filter

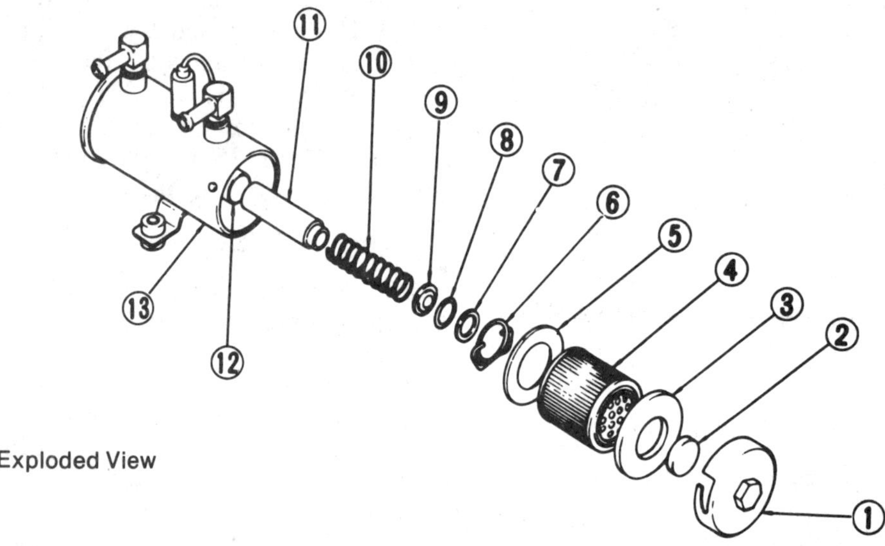

1. Cover
2. Magnet
3. Cover gasket
4. Filter
5. Gasket
6. Spring retainer
7. Washer
8. O-ring
9. Inlet valve
10. Return spring
11. Plunger
12. Plunger cylinder
13. Body

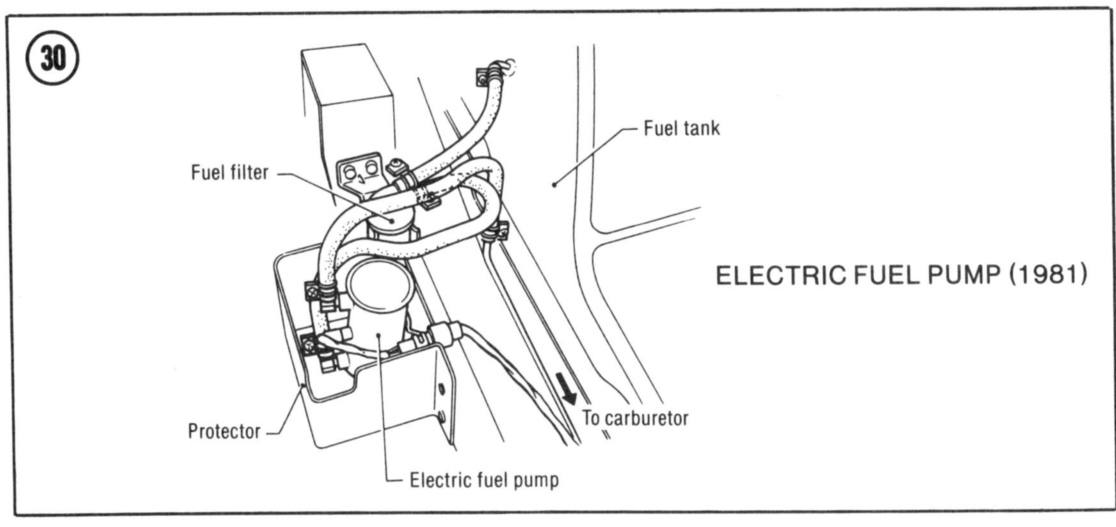

ELECTRIC FUEL PUMP (1981)

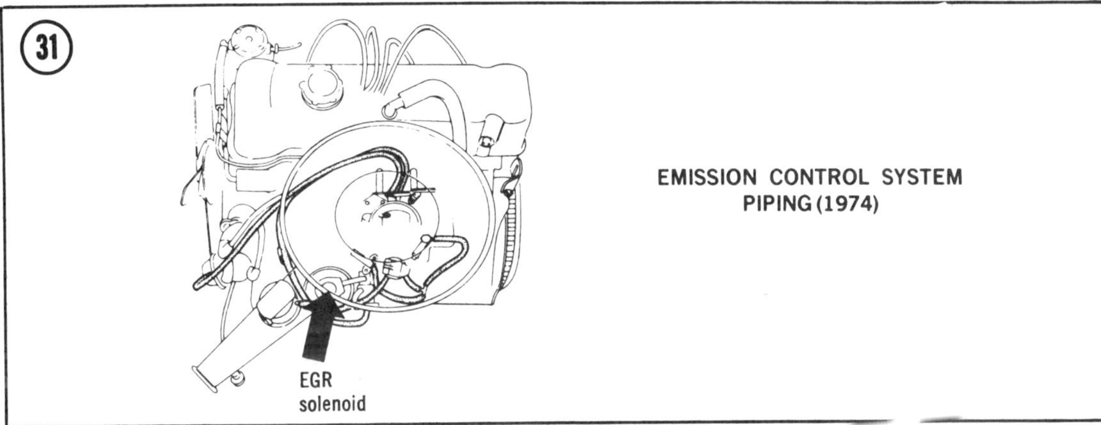

EMISSION CONTROL SYSTEM PIPING (1974)

3. Installation is the reverse of removal. Use new gaskets, coated on both sides with gasket sealer. After installation, run the engine and check for leaks.

Removal/Installation (Electric Pump)

1. Disconnect the negative cable from the battery.
2. Place a container below the pump to catch dripping gasoline.
3. Disconnect the inlet and outlet lines from the pump. See **Figure 29** (1977-1979) or **Figure 30** (1981).
4. Unplug the pump wiring connector.
5. Unbolt the pump from the bracket and take it out.
6. Installation is the reverse of removal. After installation, run the engine and check for leaks.

VACUUM LINES

The following illustrations show vacuum lines:

Figure 31—1974 (earlier models similar)
Figure 32—1975
Figure 33—1976-1977 California
Figure 34—1976-1977 non-California
Figure 35—1978-1979 California
Figure 36—1978-1979 non-California
Figure 37—1980 California standard
Figure 38—1980 California heavy duty (letter "E" in vehicle identification number)
Figure 39—All 1980 49-state models, 1980 Canadian heavy duty
Figure 40—1980 Canadian standard
Figure 41—1981 California
Figure 42—1981 non-California

1. Vacuum tube to distributor (yellow)
2. Vacuum tube to carbon canister (yellow)
3. Vacuum tube to thermal vacuum valve (white)
4. Vacuum tube
5. Thermal vacuum valve to EGR control valve (white)
6. AB valve to intake manifold (green)
7. Vacuum tube to carburetor (yellow)
8. Vacuum tube to carburetor (white)

EMISSION CONTROL SYSTEM PIPING (1976-1977 CALIFORNIA MODELS)

1. Vacuum tube to distributor (yellow)
2. Vacuum tube to carbon canister (yellow)
3. Thermal vacuum valve to EGR control valve (white)
4. Vacuum tube to thermal vacuum valve (white)
5. Vacuum tube
6. Vacuum hose connector to intake manifold (green)
7. Air control valve to vacuum hose connector (green)
8. Carburetor to altitude compensator (Secondary, green) (Optional)
9. Air cleaner to altitude compensator (Air hose, white) (Optional)
10. Carburetor to altitude compensator (Primary, red) (Optional)
11. AB valve to intake manifold (green)
12. BCDD to control valve (white)
13. Vacuum hose connector to EAR control valve (green)
14. BCDD control valve to intake manifold (green)
15. Control valve to air pump air cleaner
16. Vacuum tube to carburetor (yellow)
17. Vacuum tube to carburetor (white)

6

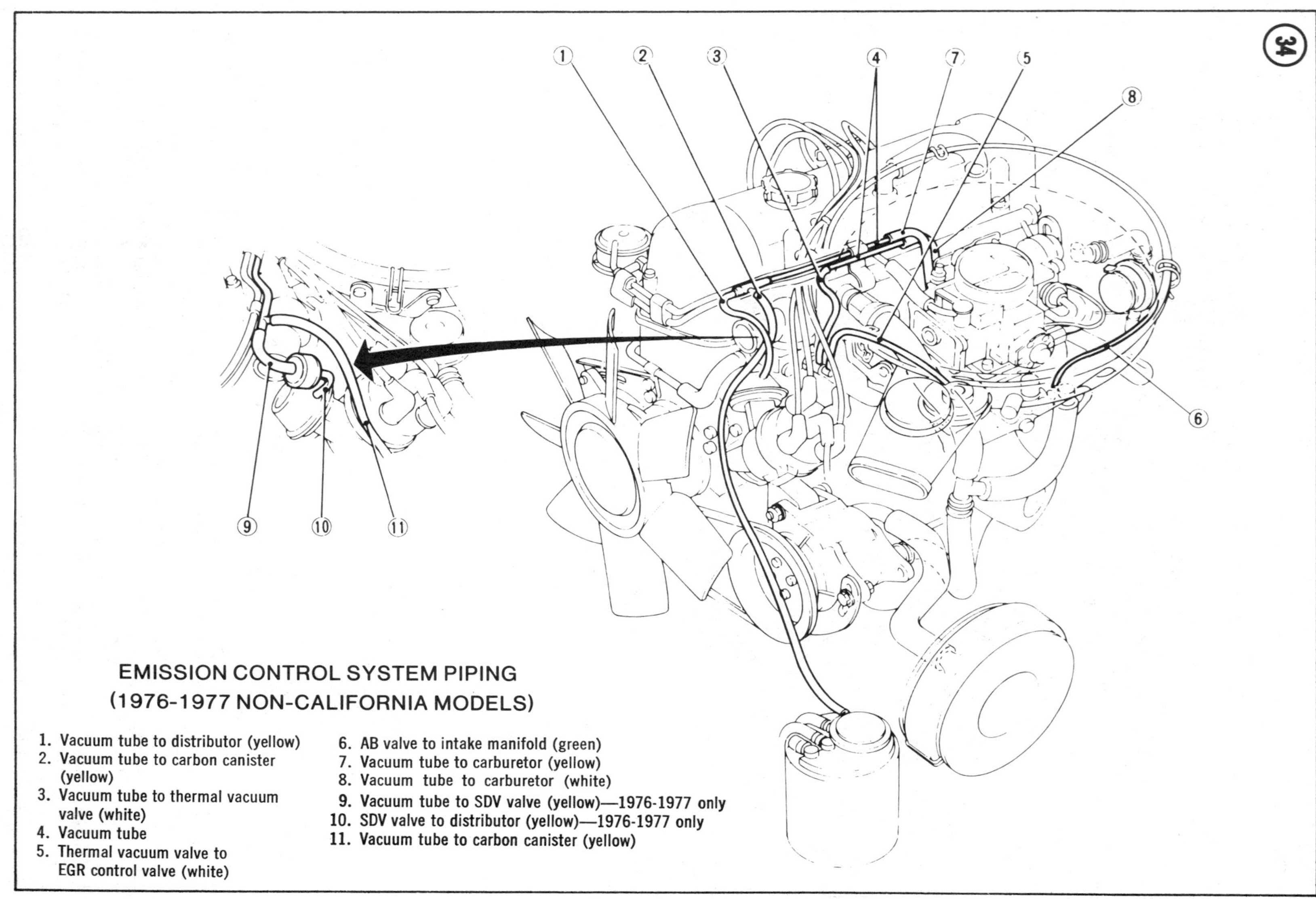

EMISSION CONTROL SYSTEM PIPING (1976-1977 NON-CALIFORNIA MODELS)

1. Vacuum tube to distributor (yellow)
2. Vacuum tube to carbon canister (yellow)
3. Vacuum tube to thermal vacuum valve (white)
4. Vacuum tube
5. Thermal vacuum valve to EGR control valve (white)
6. AB valve to intake manifold (green)
7. Vacuum tube to carburetor (yellow)
8. Vacuum tube to carburetor (white)
9. Vacuum tube to SDV valve (yellow)—1976-1977 only
10. SDV valve to distributor (yellow)—1976-1977 only
11. Vacuum tube to carbon canister (yellow)

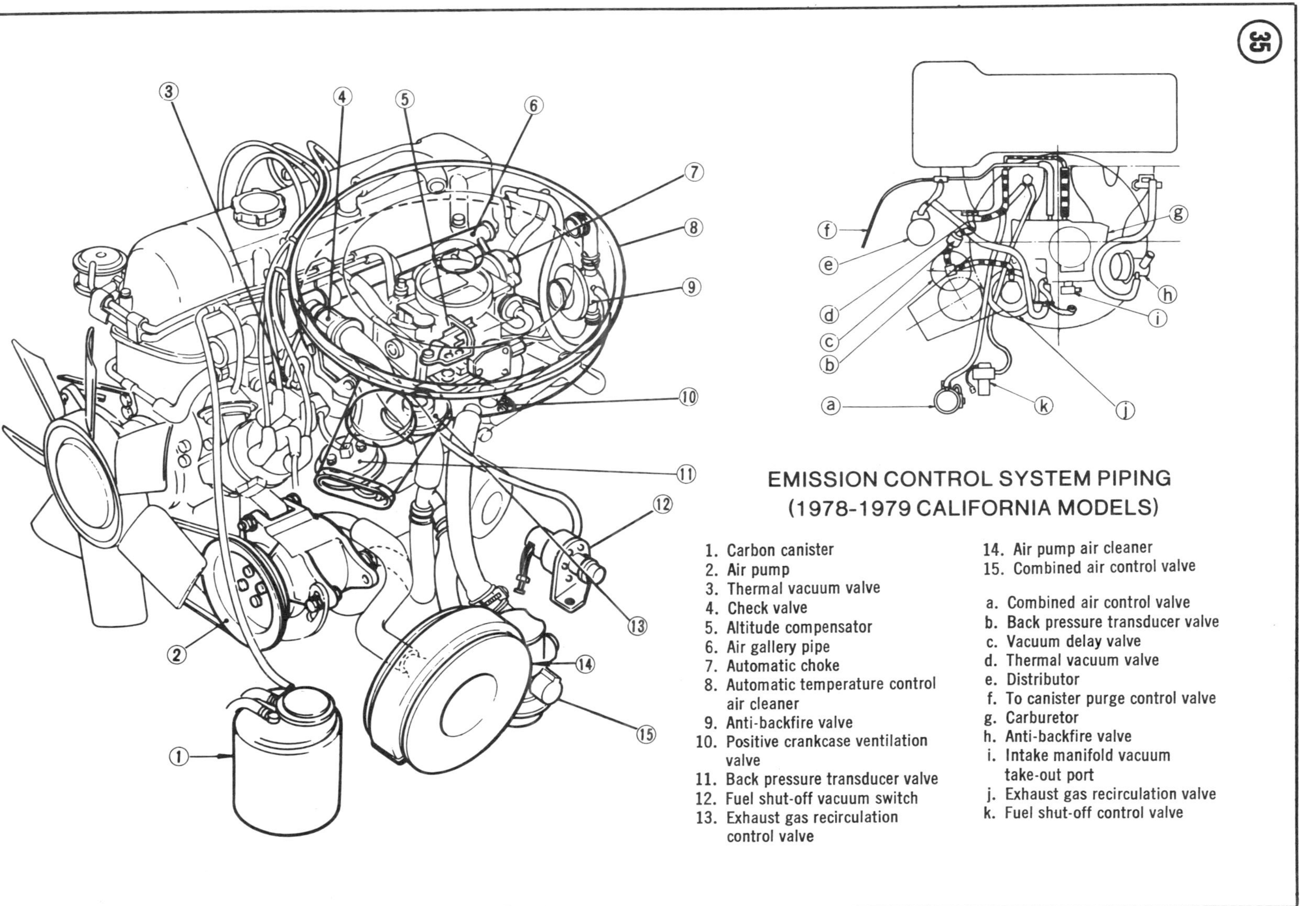

EMISSION CONTROL SYSTEM PIPING (1978-1979 CALIFORNIA MODELS)

1. Carbon canister
2. Air pump
3. Thermal vacuum valve
4. Check valve
5. Altitude compensator
6. Air gallery pipe
7. Automatic choke
8. Automatic temperature control air cleaner
9. Anti-backfire valve
10. Positive crankcase ventilation valve
11. Back pressure transducer valve
12. Fuel shut-off vacuum switch
13. Exhaust gas recirculation control valve
14. Air pump air cleaner
15. Combined air control valve

a. Combined air control valve
b. Back pressure transducer valve
c. Vacuum delay valve
d. Thermal vacuum valve
e. Distributor
f. To canister purge control valve
g. Carburetor
h. Anti-backfire valve
i. Intake manifold vacuum take-out port
j. Exhaust gas recirculation valve
k. Fuel shut-off control valve

6

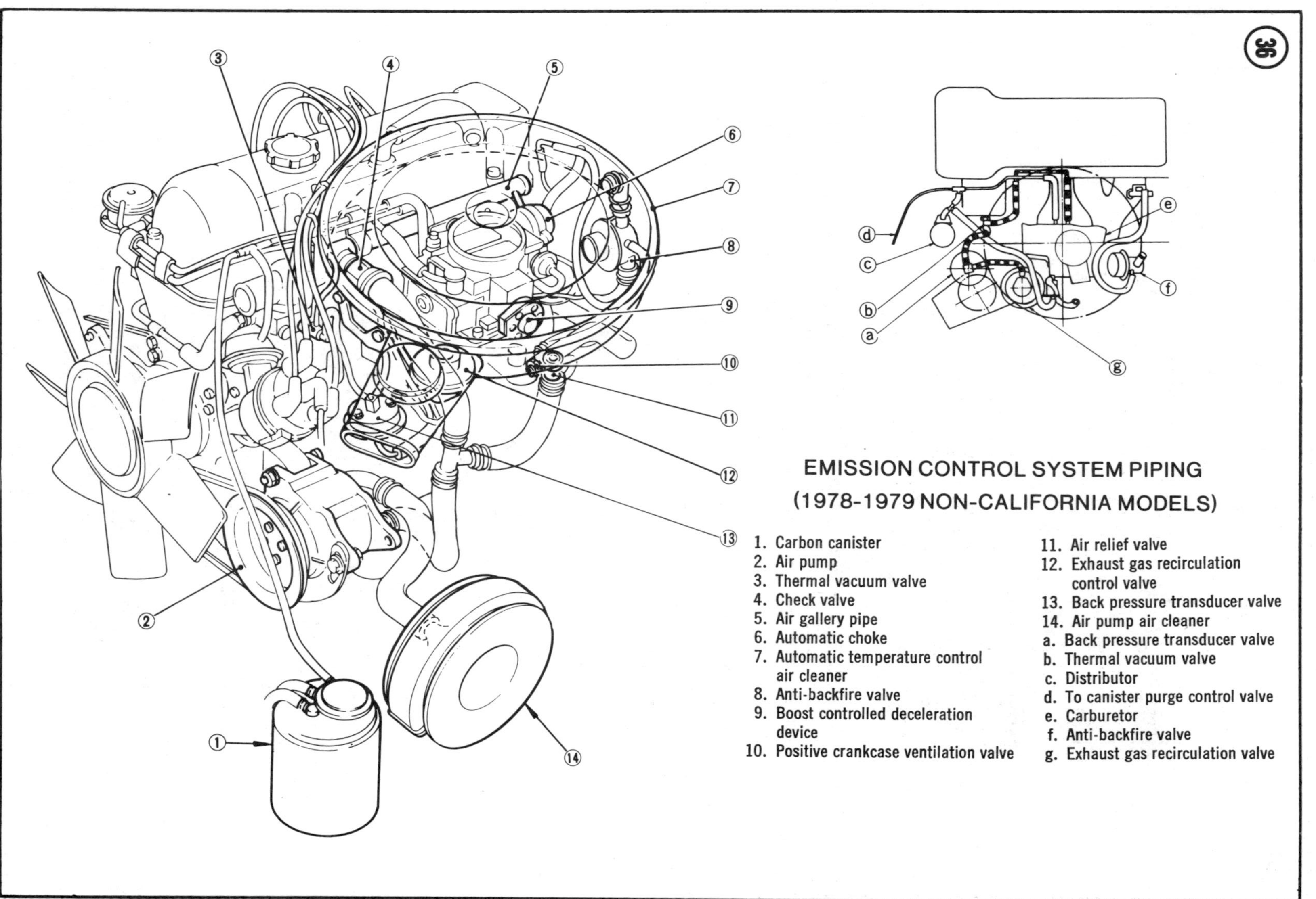
36
EMISSION CONTROL SYSTEM PIPING
(1978-1979 NON-CALIFORNIA MODELS)
1. Carbon canister
2. Air pump
3. Thermal vacuum valve
4. Check valve
5. Air gallery pipe
6. Automatic choke
7. Automatic temperature control air cleaner
8. Anti-backfire valve
9. Boost controlled deceleration device
10. Positive crankcase ventilation valve
11. Air relief valve
12. Exhaust gas recirculation control valve
13. Back pressure transducer valve
14. Air pump air cleaner
a. Back pressure transducer valve
b. Thermal vacuum valve
c. Distributor
d. To canister purge control valve
e. Carburetor
f. Anti-backfire valve
g. Exhaust gas recirculation valve

37

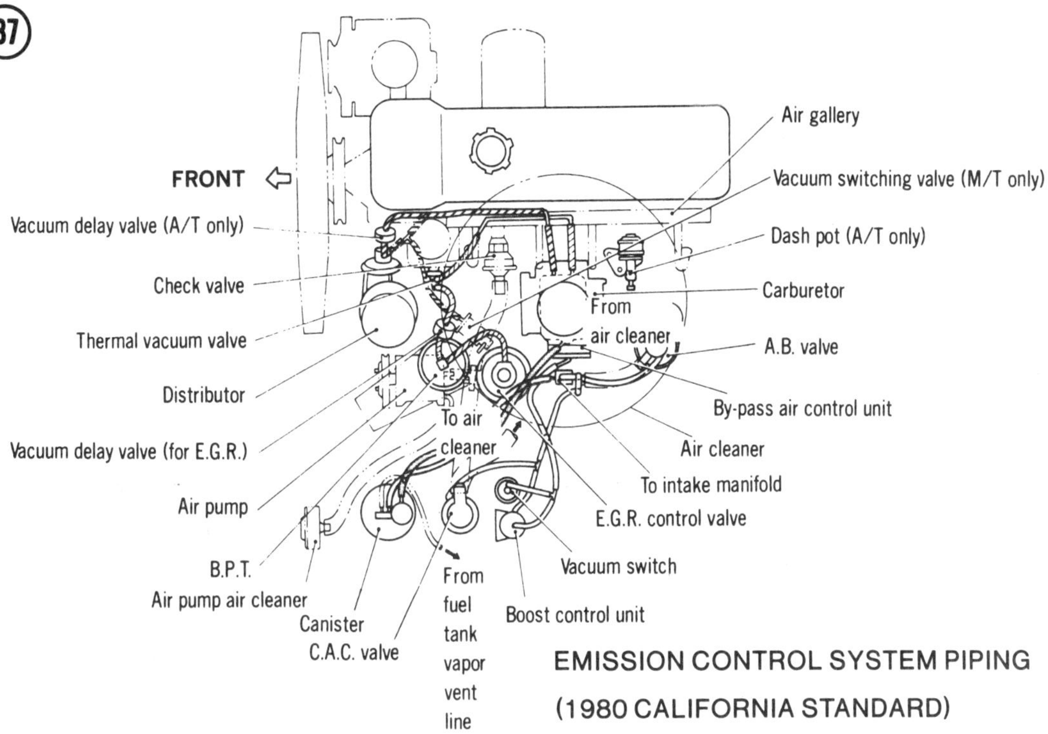

FRONT

Vacuum delay valve (A/T only)

Check valve

Thermal vacuum valve

Distributor

Vacuum delay valve (for E.G.R.)

Air pump

B.P.T.

Air pump air cleaner

Canister

C.A.C. valve

From fuel tank vapor vent line

To air cleaner

From air cleaner

Air gallery

Vacuum switching valve (M/T only)

Dash pot (A/T only)

Carburetor

A.B. valve

By-pass air control unit

Air cleaner

To intake manifold

E.G.R. control valve

Vacuum switch

Boost control unit

EMISSION CONTROL SYSTEM PIPING (1980 CALIFORNIA STANDARD)

6

38

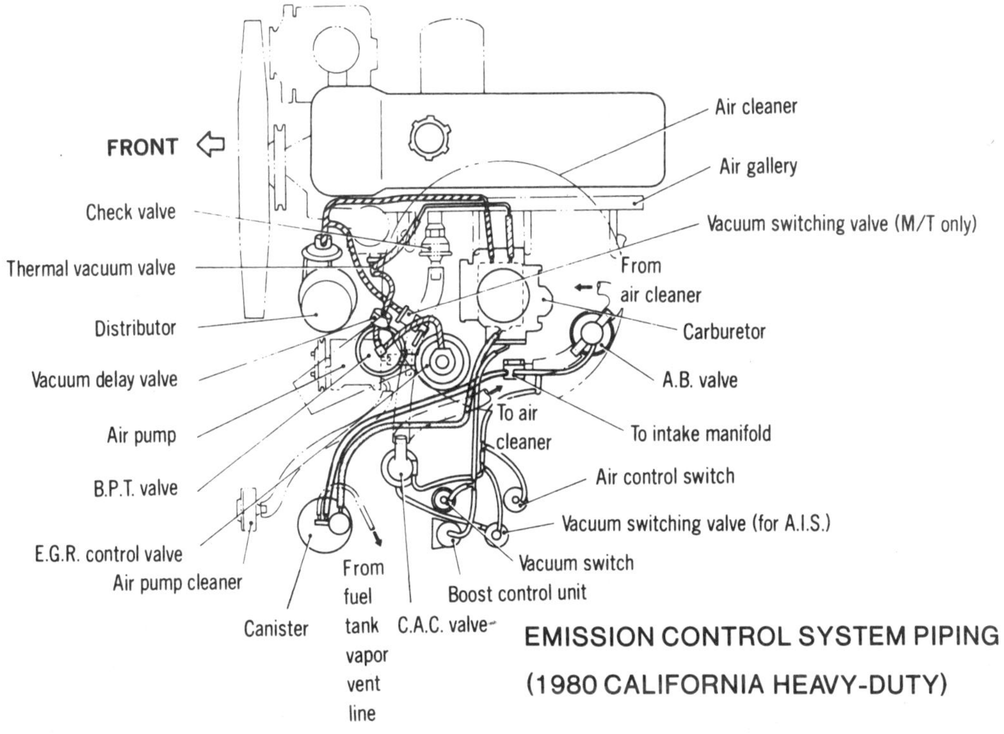

FRONT

Check valve

Thermal vacuum valve

Distributor

Vacuum delay valve

Air pump

B.P.T. valve

E.G.R. control valve

Air pump cleaner

Canister

From fuel tank vapor vent line

C.A.C. valve

Air cleaner

Air gallery

Vacuum switching valve (M/T only)

From air cleaner

Carburetor

A.B. valve

To air cleaner

To intake manifold

Air control switch

Vacuum switching valve (for A.I.S.)

Vacuum switch

Boost control unit

EMISSION CONTROL SYSTEM PIPING (1980 CALIFORNIA HEAVY-DUTY)

39

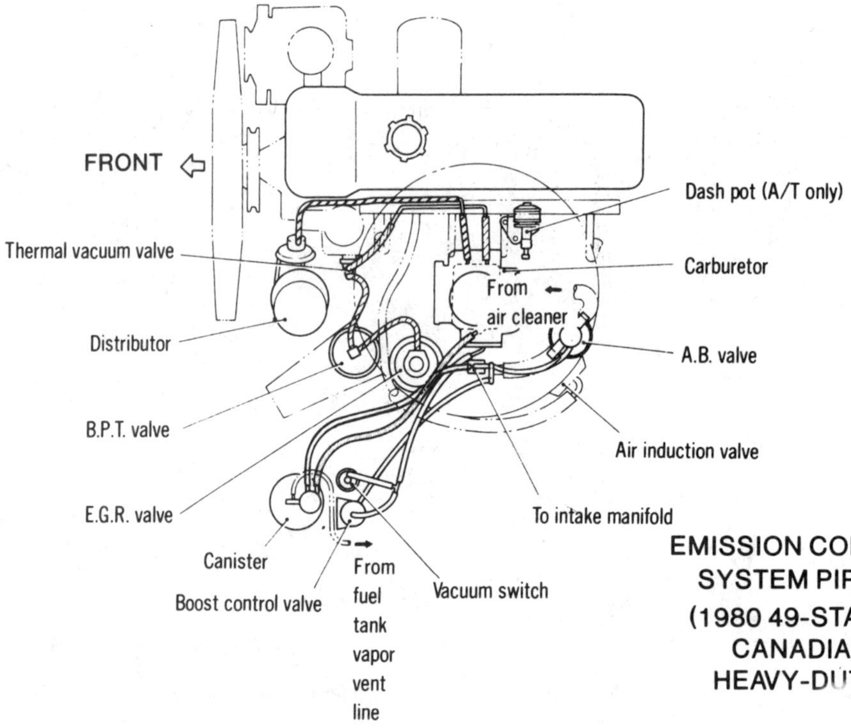

FRONT
Dash pot (A/T only)
Thermal vacuum valve
Carburetor
From air cleaner
Distributor
A.B. valve
B.P.T. valve
Air induction valve
E.G.R. valve
To intake manifold
Canister
Boost control valve
From fuel tank vapor vent line
Vacuum switch

EMISSION CONTROL SYSTEM PIPING (1980 49-STATES CANADIAN HEAVY-DUTY)

40

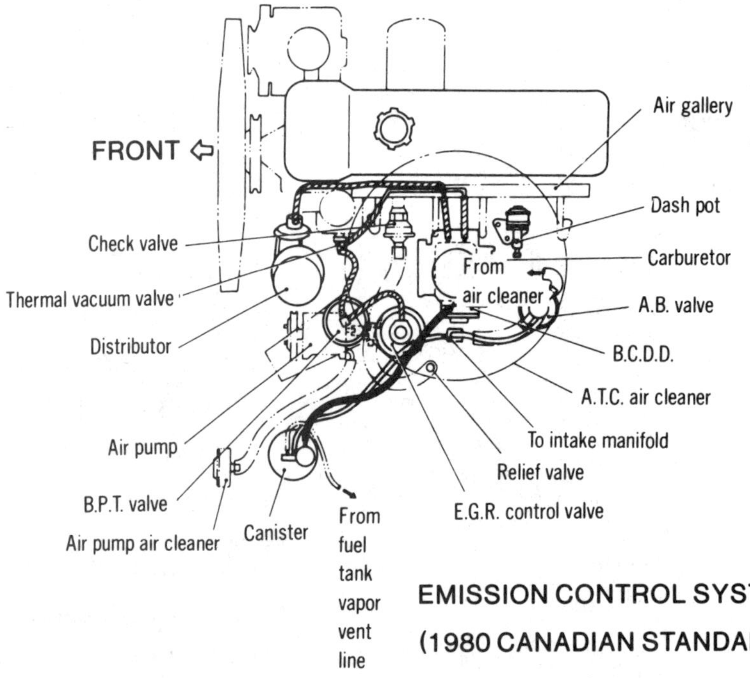

Air gallery
FRONT
Dash pot
Check valve
Carburetor
From air cleaner
Thermal vacuum valve
A.B. valve
Distributor
B.C.D.D.
A.T.C. air cleaner
To intake manifold
Air pump
Relief valve
B.P.T. valve
E.G.R. control valve
Air pump air cleaner
Canister
From fuel tank vapor vent line

EMISSION CONTROL SYSTEM PIPING (1980 CANADIAN STANDARD)

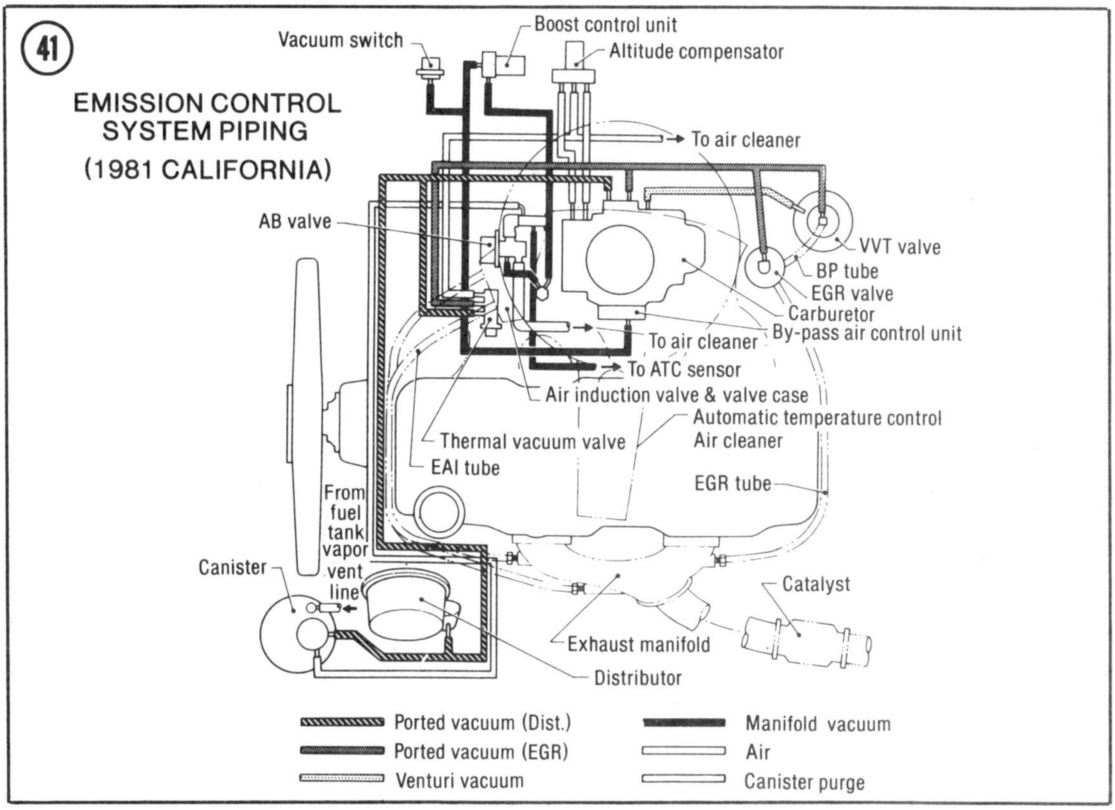

(41)

EMISSION CONTROL SYSTEM PIPING (1981 CALIFORNIA)

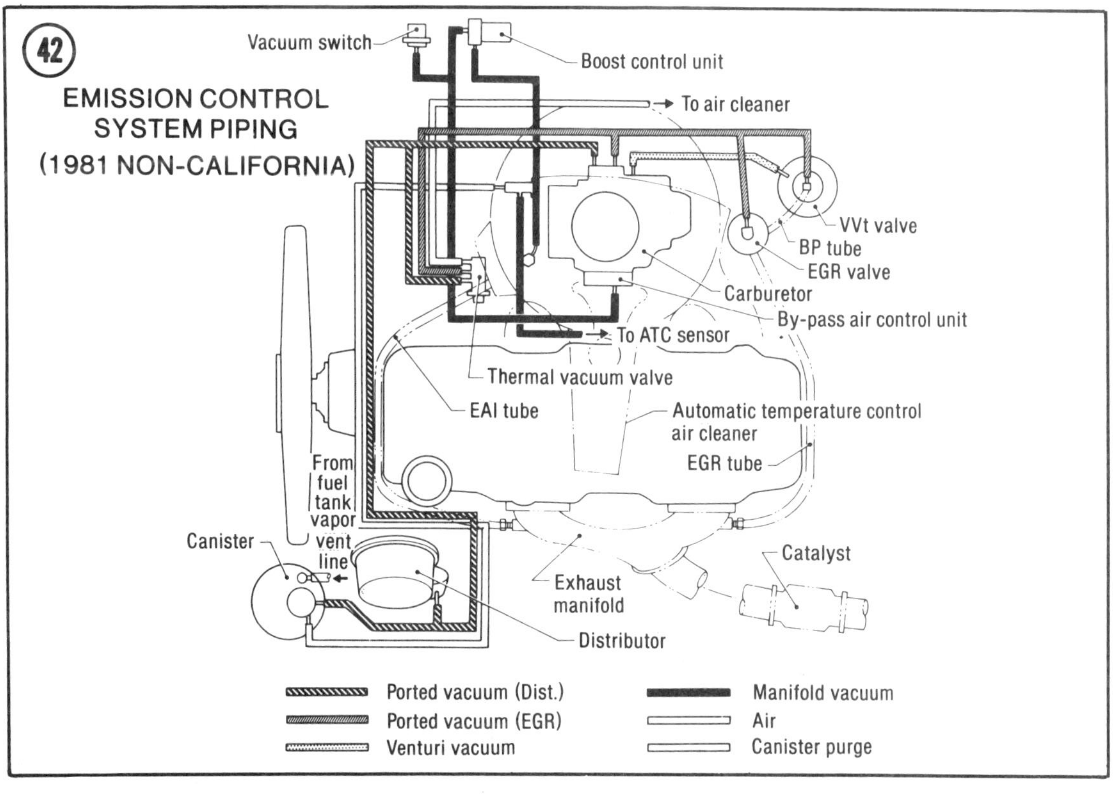

Vacuum switch
Boost control unit
Altitude compensator
To air cleaner
AB valve
VVT valve
BP tube
EGR valve
Carburetor
To air cleaner
By-pass air control unit
To ATC sensor
Air induction valve & valve case
Automatic temperature control Air cleaner
Thermal vacuum valve
EAI tube
EGR tube
From fuel tank vapor vent line
Canister
Catalyst
Exhaust manifold
Distributor

Ported vacuum (Dist.)
Ported vacuum (EGR)
Venturi vacuum
Manifold vacuum
Air
Canister purge

(42)

EMISSION CONTROL SYSTEM PIPING (1981 NON-CALIFORNIA)

Vacuum switch
Boost control unit
To air cleaner
VVt valve
BP tube
EGR valve
Carburetor
By-pass air control unit
To ATC sensor
Thermal vacuum valve
EAI tube
Automatic temperature control air cleaner
EGR tube
From fuel tank vapor vent line
Canister
Catalyst
Exhaust manifold
Distributor

Ported vacuum (Dist.)
Ported vacuum (EGR)
Venturi vacuum
Manifold vacuum
Air
Canister purge

6

AIR INJECTION SYSTEM

An air injection system is used on 1970-1971 models, 1975-1979 models, and some 1980 trucks. The system uses a pump to force air under pressure into the exhaust ports. This allows combustion to continue for a longer time to reduce carbon monoxide and unburned hydrocarbons in the exhaust.

Air pump repair requires special tools and should be left to a Datsun dealer or other competent shop. None of the other components is repairable.

Refer to the following illustrations:

Figure 43—1970-1971

Figure 44—early 1975 California, 1975-1979 non-California

Figure 45—late 1975 through 1977 California

Figure 46—1978-1979 California

Figure 47—1980 non-California

Figure 48—1981 California standard (all models without the letter "E" in vehicle identification number)

Figure 49—1981 California heavy duty (identified by letter "E" in vehicle identification number)

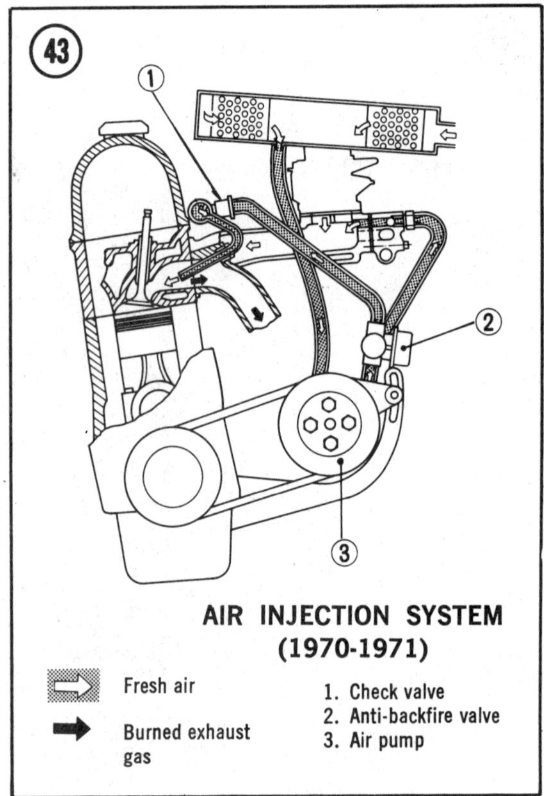

AIR INJECTION SYSTEM (1970-1971)

Fresh air

Burned exhaust gas

1. Check valve
2. Anti-backfire valve
3. Air pump

Air Pump Removal/Installation

1. Disconnect the hoses from the air pump.
2. Remove the nut attaching the air pump to its adjusting bracket.
3. Remove the bolt attaching the air pump to its mounting bracket. Remove the air pump belt, then lift the air pump off.
4. Install in the reverse order.

Anti-backfire Valve Test (1970-1971)

1. Warm the engine to normal operating temperature.
2. Check all air injection hoses for leaks. Replace as needed.
3. Disconnect the hose running from the anti-backfire valve to intake manifold (**Figure 43**). Plug the hose so it is airtight.
4. Working the throttle linkage by hand, open and close the throttle rapidly. Air should flow from the valve for 1-2 seconds. No air flow or continuous air flow indicates a defective valve. Replace it.

Anti-backfire Valve Test (1975 and Later)

1. Disconnect the anti-backfire valve hose from the air cleaner.
2. Run the engine at 3,000 rpm, then release the throttle quickly. Suction should be felt at the disconnected hose end. If not, replace the anti-backfire valve.

Check Valve Test

1. Warm the engine to normal operating temperature.
2. Check air injection hoses for leaks. Replace as needed.
3. Disconnect the long hose from the check valve. Look inside the valve. The valve plate should be against its seat (toward you, away from the engine). Push the valve plate in. It should return to its seat without binding.
4. With the hose disconnected, start the engine and watch the valve plate. Plate vibration at idle is permissible. Raise engine speed to 1,500 rpm. There should be no exhaust gas leakage past the plate. If there is, replace check valve.

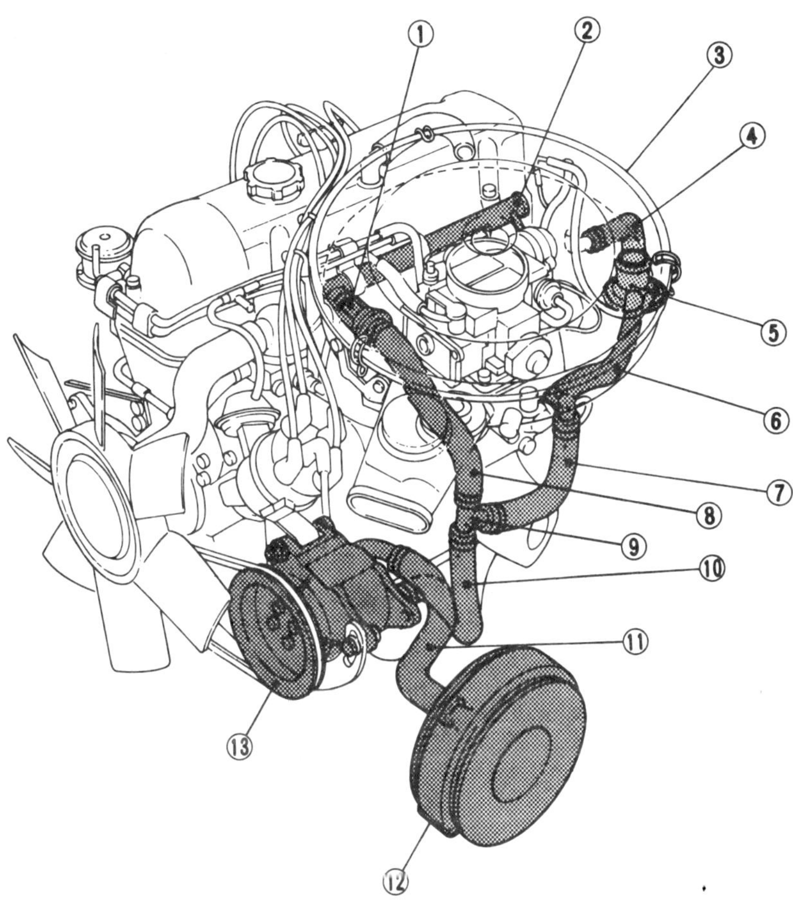

AIR INJECTION SYSTEM
(EARLY 1975 CALIFORNIA AND 1975-1979 NON-CALIFORNIA)

1. Check valve
2. Air gallery pipe
3. Automatic temperature control air cleaner
4. Air hose (carburetor air cleaner to anti-backfire valve)
5. Anti-backfire valve
6. Air hose (anti-backfire valve to intake manifold)
7. Air hose (carburetor air cleaner to air hose connector)
8. Air hose (check valve to air hose connector)
9. 3-way connector
10. Air hose (air hose connector to air pump)
11. Air hose (air pump to air pump air cleaner)
12. Air pump air cleaner
13. Air pump

6

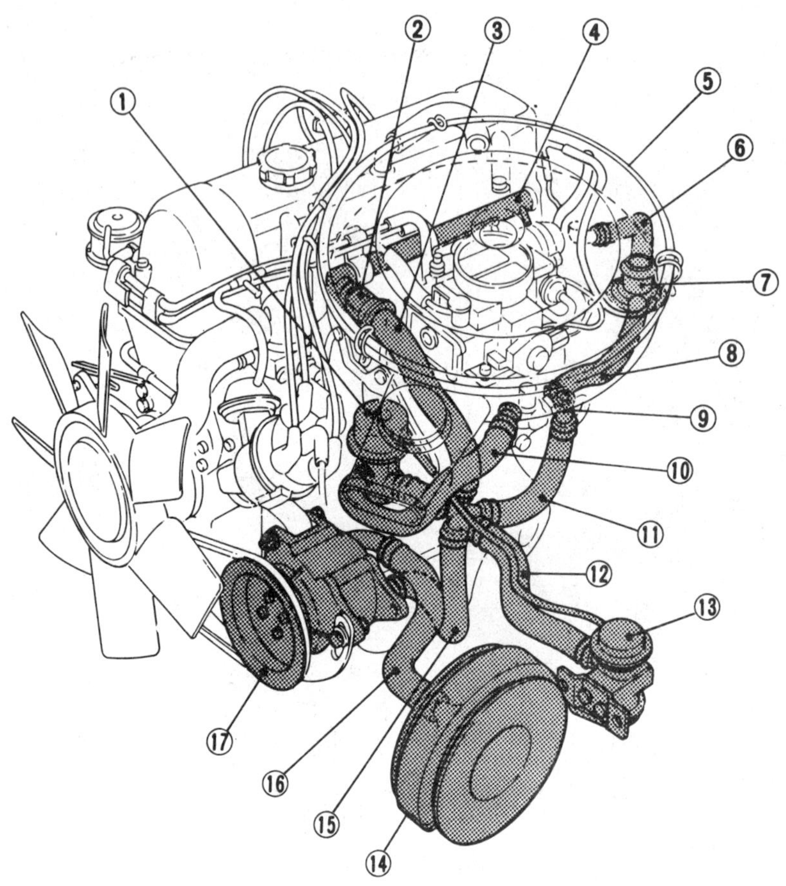

AIR INJECTION SYSTEM (MID-1975 TO 1977 CALIFORNIA)

1. Air control valve
2. Check valve
3. Air hose (check valve to air hose connector)
4. Air gallery pipe
5. Automatic temperature control air cleaner
6. Air hose (carburetor air cleaner to anti-backfire valve)
7. Anti-backfire valve
8. Air hose (anti-backfire valve to intake manifold)
9. Air relief valve
10. Air hose (carburetor air cleaner to air control valve)
11. Air hose (air relief valve to air hose connector)
12. Air hose (air hose connector to emergency air relief valve)
13. Emergency air relief valve
14. Air pump air cleaner
15. Air hose (air hose connector to air pump
16. Air hose (air pump to air pump air cleaner)
17. Air pump

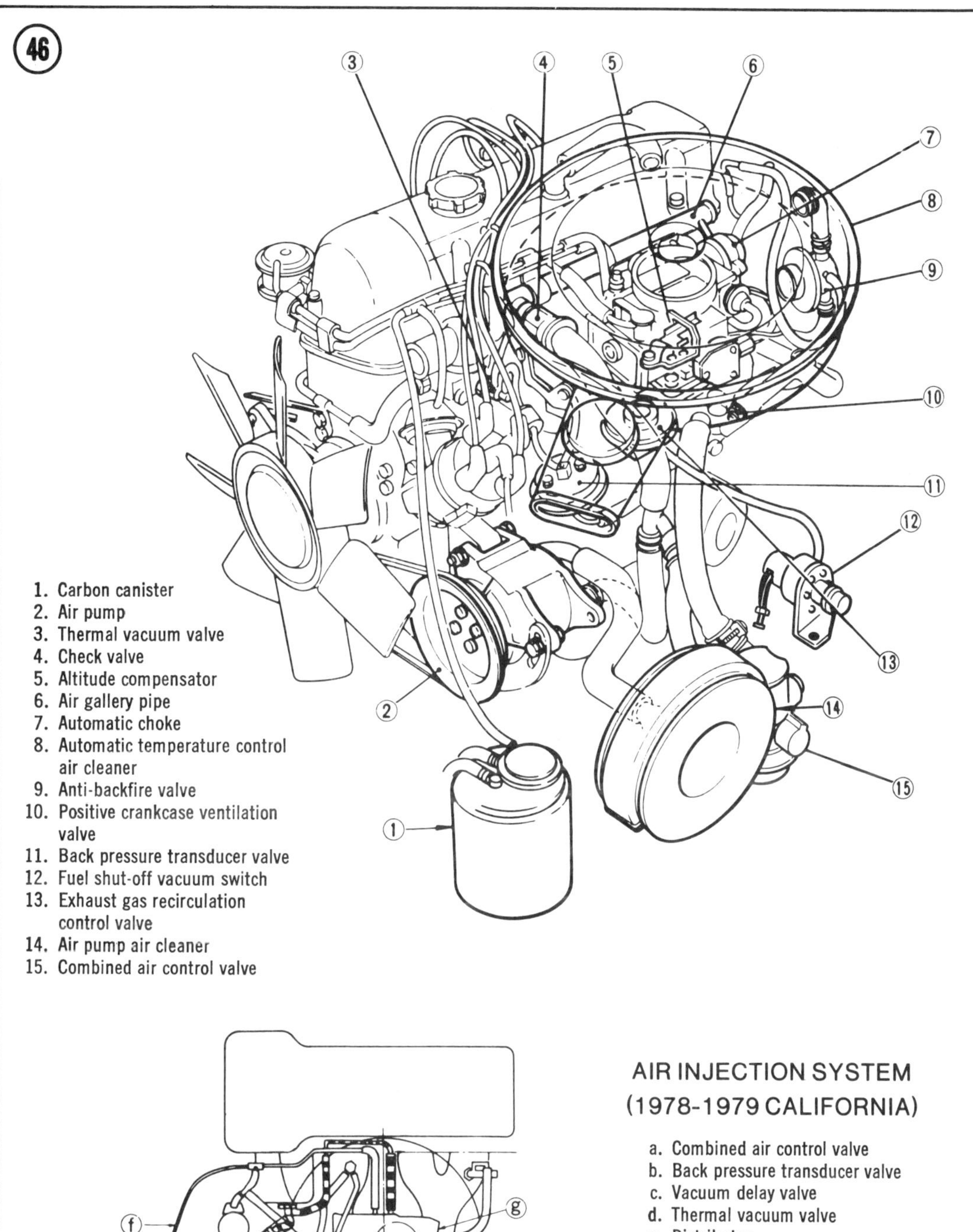

1. Carbon canister
2. Air pump
3. Thermal vacuum valve
4. Check valve
5. Altitude compensator
6. Air gallery pipe
7. Automatic choke
8. Automatic temperature control air cleaner
9. Anti-backfire valve
10. Positive crankcase ventilation valve
11. Back pressure transducer valve
12. Fuel shut-off vacuum switch
13. Exhaust gas recirculation control valve
14. Air pump air cleaner
15. Combined air control valve

AIR INJECTION SYSTEM (1978-1979 CALIFORNIA)

a. Combined air control valve
b. Back pressure transducer valve
c. Vacuum delay valve
d. Thermal vacuum valve
e. Distributor
f. To canister purge control valve
g. Carburetor
h. Anti-backfire valve
i. Intake manifold vacuum take-out port
j. Exhaust gas recirculation valve
k. Fuel shut-off control valve

47

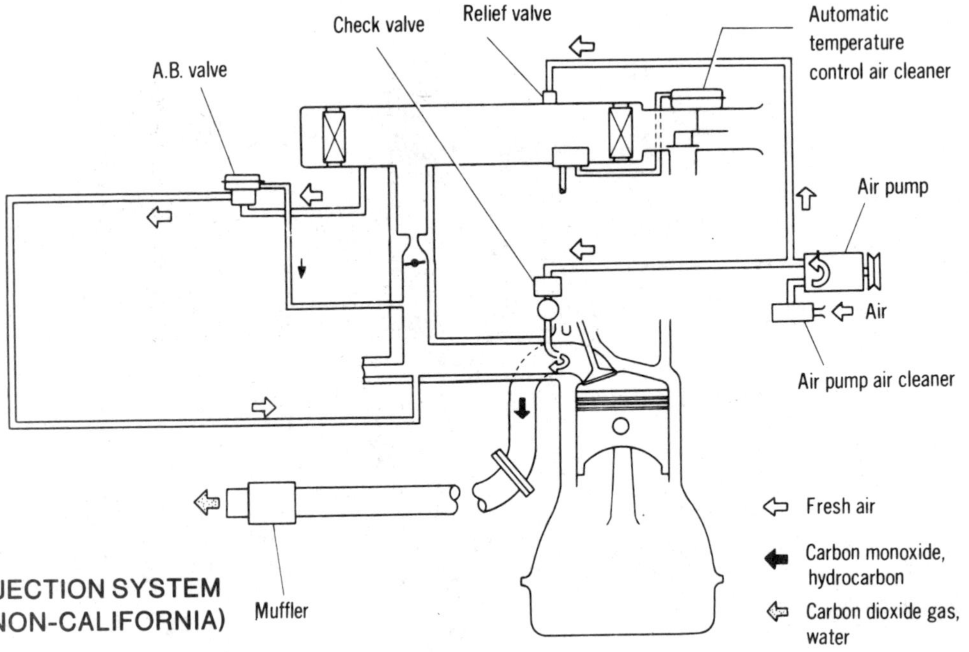

Check valve
Relief valve
Automatic temperature control air cleaner
A.B. valve
Air pump
Air
Air pump air cleaner
Fresh air
Carbon monoxide, hydrocarbon
Carbon dioxide gas, water
Muffler

AIR INJECTION SYSTEM
(1980 NON-CALIFORNIA)

48

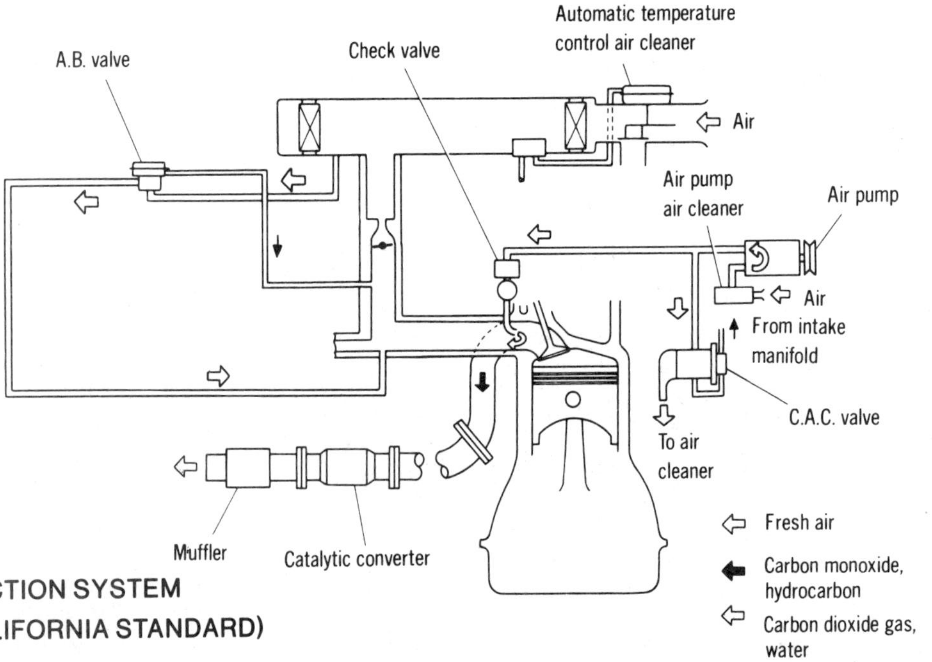

Automatic temperature control air cleaner
A.B. valve
Check valve
Air
Air pump air cleaner
Air pump
Air
From intake manifold
C.A.C. valve
To air cleaner
Fresh air
Carbon monoxide, hydrocarbon
Carbon dioxide gas, water
Muffler
Catalytic converter

AIR INJECTION SYSTEM
(1980 CALIFORNIA STANDARD)

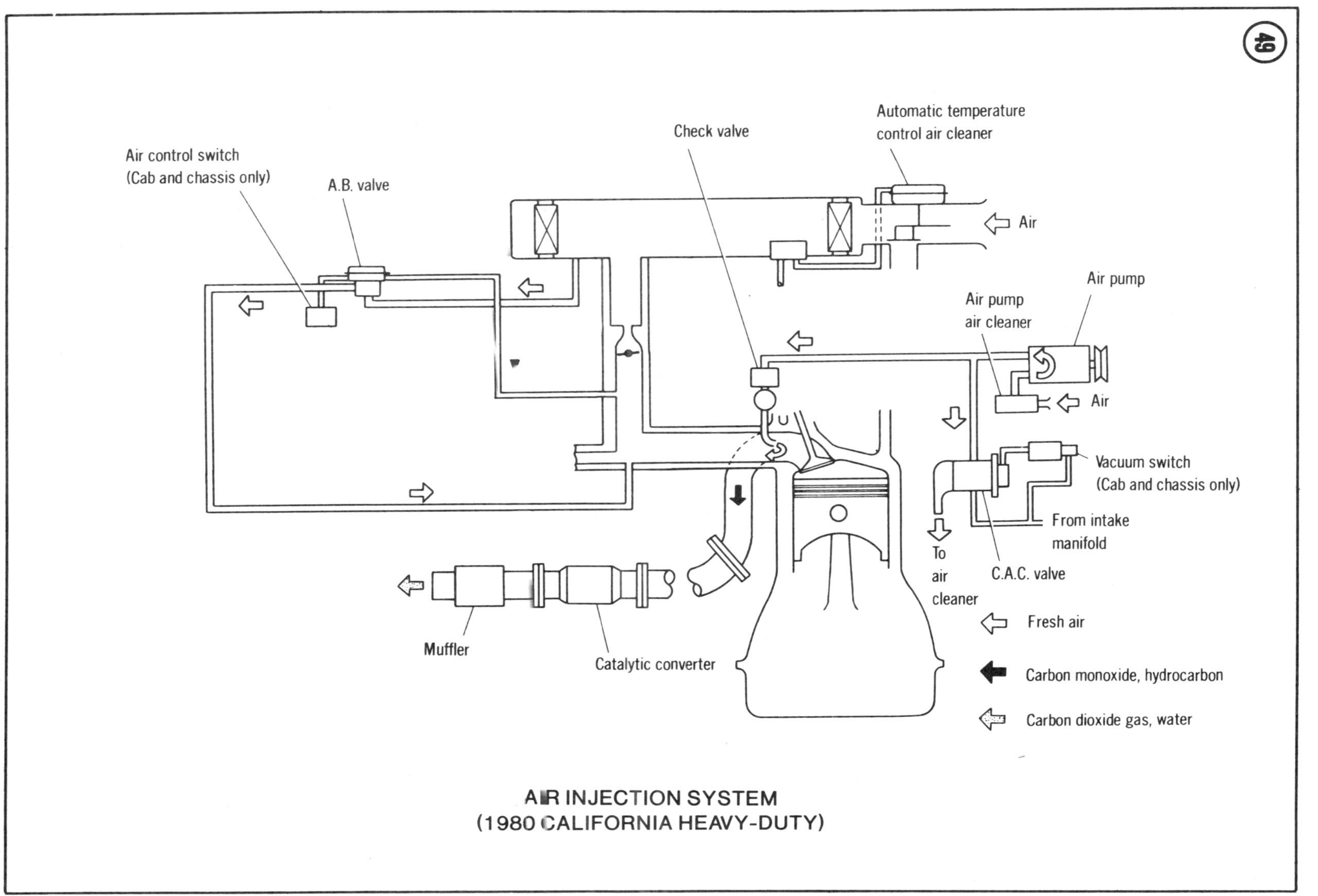

AIR INJECTION SYSTEM
(1980 CALIFORNIA HEAVY-DUTY)

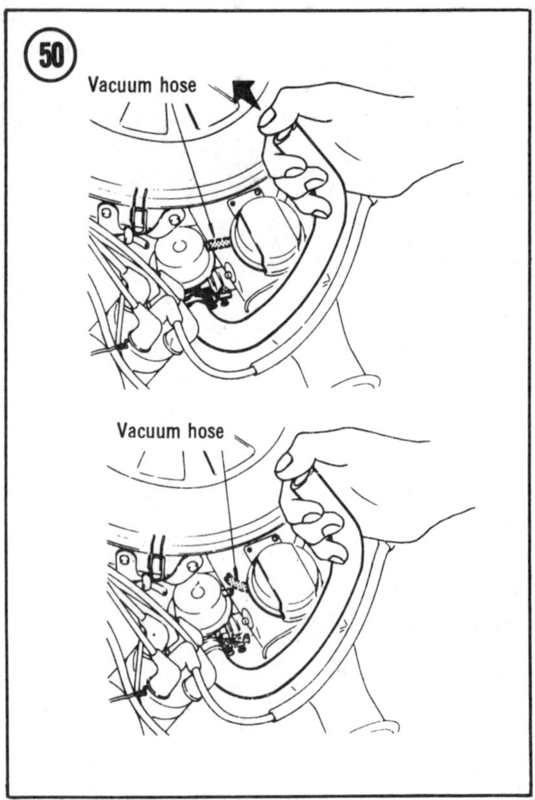

Emergency Air Relief Valve (1976-1977 California Models)

1. Warm the engine to normal operating temperature.
2. Check all hoses for leaks or damage. Tighten or replace as needed.
3. Run the engine at 2,000 rpm. Place a hand over the air outlet at the top of the EAR valve. No air should be felt.
4. Disconnect the vacuum (thin) hose from the EAR valve. There should now be air flow from the valve outlet at 2,000 rpm. If not, replace the valve.

Air Control Valve (1976-1977 California Models)

1. Warm the engine to normal operating temperature.
2. Check all hoses for leaks or damage. Tighten or replace as needed.
3. With the engine idling, disconnect the valve's outlet hose (**Figure 50**). If there is no air flow from the hose, replace the valve.
4. Disconnect the vacuum (thin) hose from

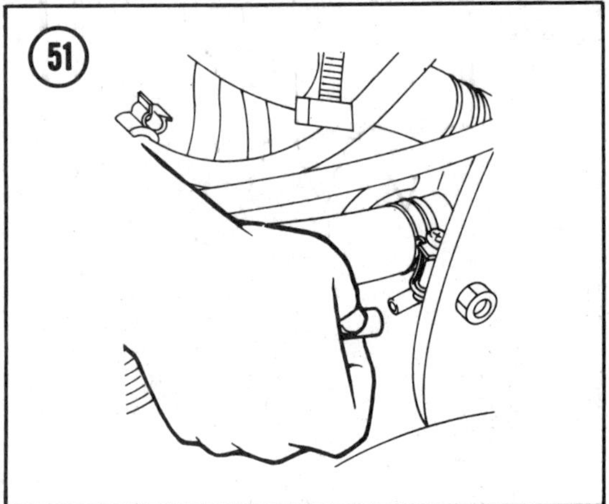

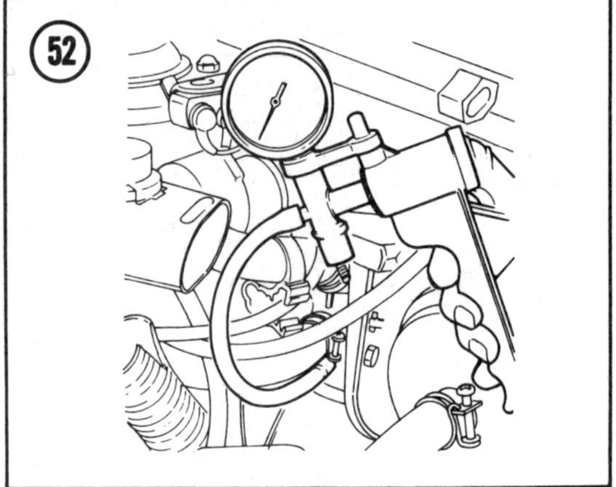

the valve. Air flow at idle should stop. If not, replace the valve.

Combined Air Control Valve (1978 and Later California Models)

1. Warm the engine to normal operating temperature. Check the CAC valve hoses for cracks or other damage.
2. Remove the air cleaner cover and filter element. Let the engine idle. Air should flow from the CAC valve outlet. This is in the air cleaner wall next to the main air intake nozzle.
3. Disconnect and plug the CAC valve vacuum hose (**Figure 51**). The CAC valve should discharge air into the atmosphere.
4. Connect a vacuum pump to the CAC valve vacuum hose (**Figure 52**). Raise vacuum to 8-10 in. Hg (200-250mm Hg). With the engine at 3,000 rpm, no air should flow from the CAC valve.

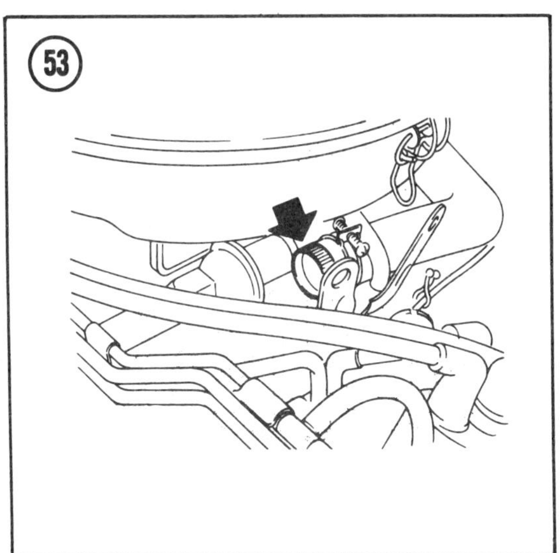
53

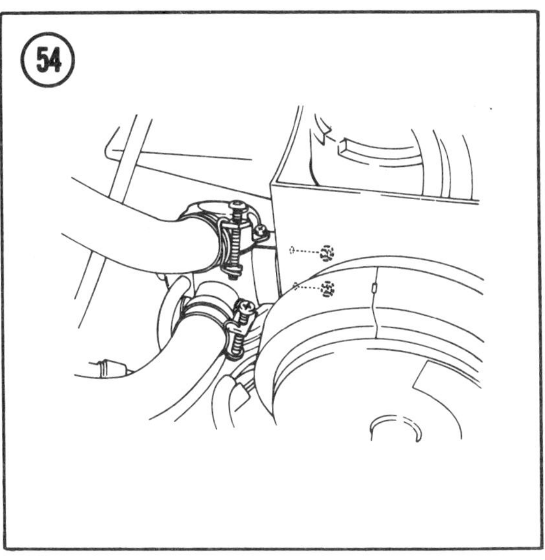
54

5. Disconnect the air hose from the check valve (**Figure 53**). Plug the hose and repeat Step 4. Air should now flow from the CAC valve.

CAC Valve Replacement

The CAC valve is mounted behind the carbon canister and air pump air cleaner. To replace, disconnect the valve hoses and remove their securing nuts. See **Figure 54**. Installation is the reverse of removal.

Air Injection Tubing

Removal of the air injection tubing is very difficult without bending the tubes. Removal should not be attempted unless the tubes are damaged. To remove, disconnect the short air hose from the check valve. Apply penetrating oil to the 4 nuts attaching the tubes to the exhaust manifold. Remove the nuts and lift the tubing off. Install in the reverse order.

AIR INDUCTION SYSTEM

This system uses exhaust gas pulses to draw air into the exhaust ports. The extra air allows combustion to continue for a longer time, reducing carbon monoxide and unburned hydrocarbons in the exhaust.

Refer to the following illustrations:

a. **Figure 55**—1980 non-California
b. **Figure 56**—1981 California
c. **Figure 57**—1981 non-California

System Inspection

1. Check the system for visible damage. Check the hoses for cracks or loose connections. Replace or tighten as needed.
2. At specified intervals, replace the air induction valve filter. Refer to *Air Induction System*, Chapter Three.

EXHAUST GAS RECIRCULATION SYSTEM

This system, used on 1974 and later models, recirculates part of the exhaust gas into the combustion chambers. This lowers combustion temperature, reducing the emission of oxides of nitrogen.

On trucks that use leaded gas, the system should be inspected at intervals specified in Chapter Three. On trucks that use unleaded, the system doesn't require periodic service. If it develops a problem, however, it may cause a rough idle. If a problem is suspected, test as described in the following section.

Refer to the following illustrations:

Figure 58—1974
Figure 59—1975-1977
Figure 60—1978-1980
Figure 61—1981

6

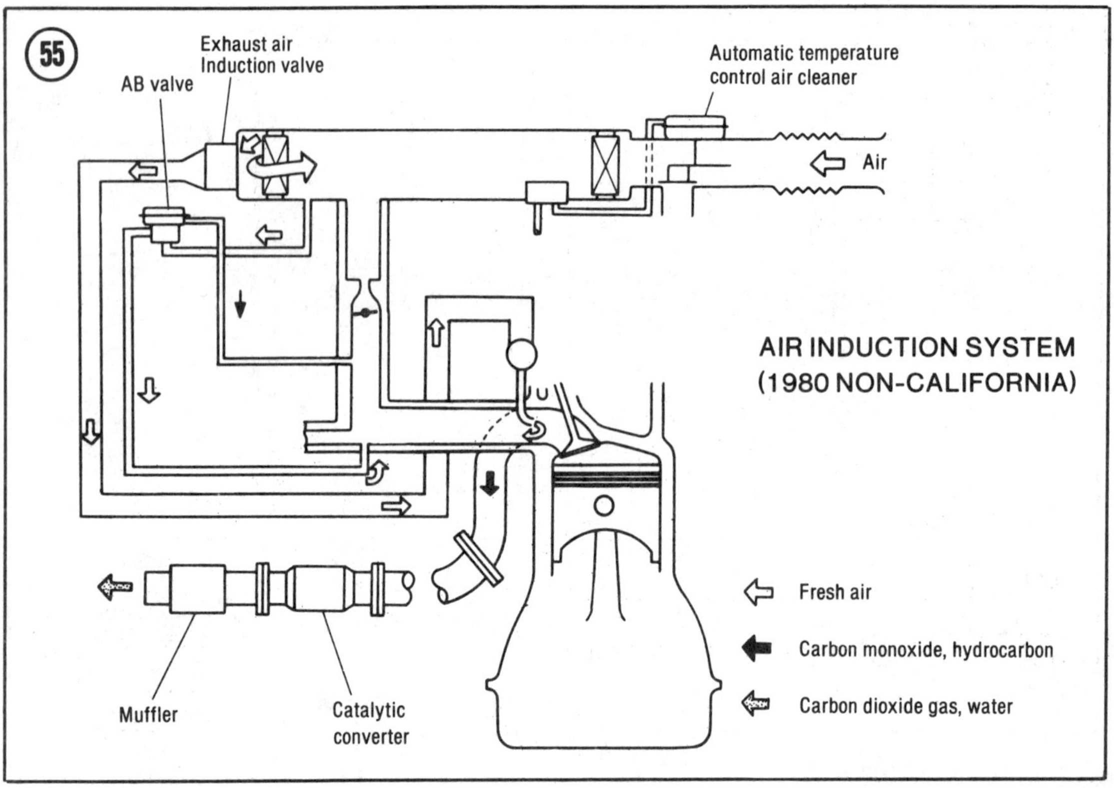

(55)

Exhaust air
Induction valve
AB valve
Automatic temperature
control air cleaner
Air

AIR INDUCTION SYSTEM
(1980 NON-CALIFORNIA)

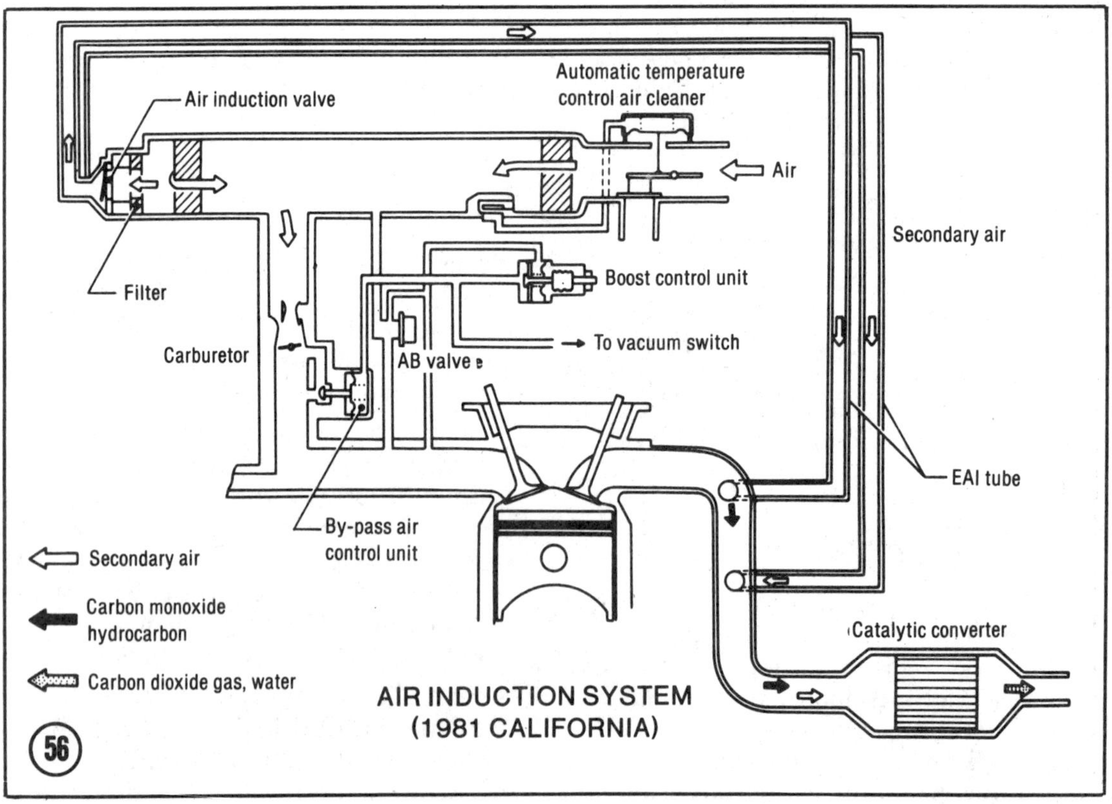

Muffler
Catalytic
converter

Fresh air
Carbon monoxide, hydrocarbon
Carbon dioxide gas, water

Air induction valve
Automatic temperature
control air cleaner
Air
Secondary air
Filter
Boost control unit
Carburetor
To vacuum switch
AB valve
EAI tube
By-pass air
control unit
Secondary air
Carbon monoxide
hydrocarbon
Carbon dioxide gas, water
Catalytic converter

AIR INDUCTION SYSTEM
(1981 CALIFORNIA)

(56)

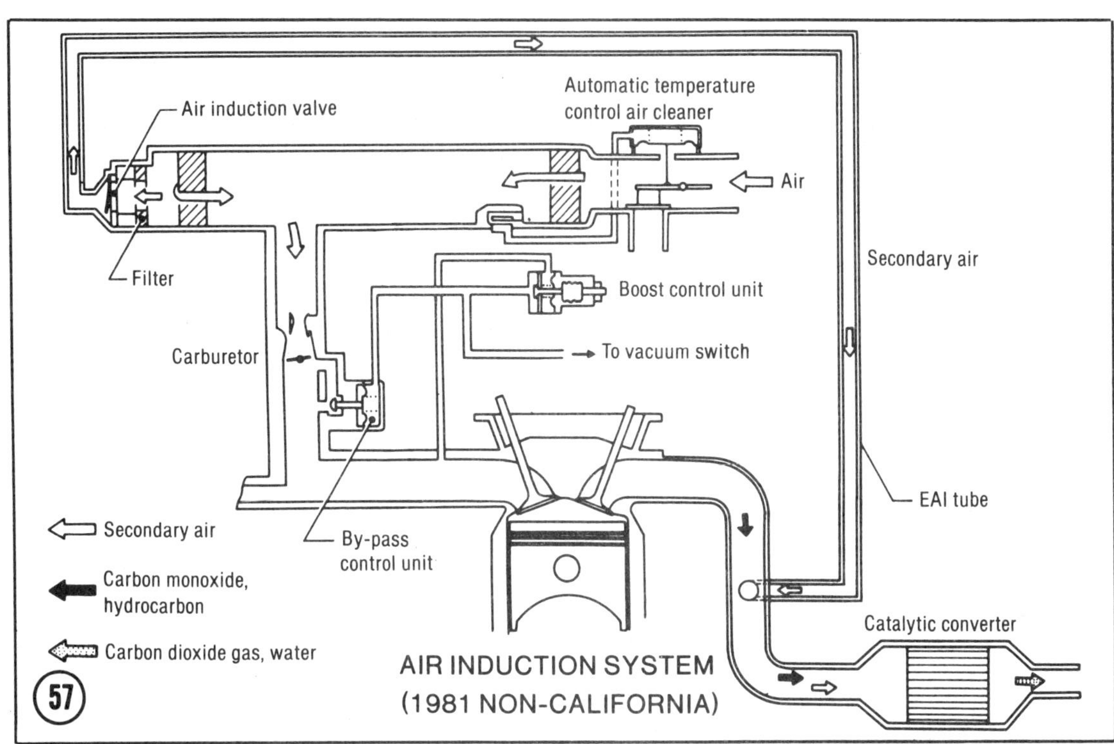

57

AIR INDUCTION SYSTEM
(1981 NON-CALIFORNIA)

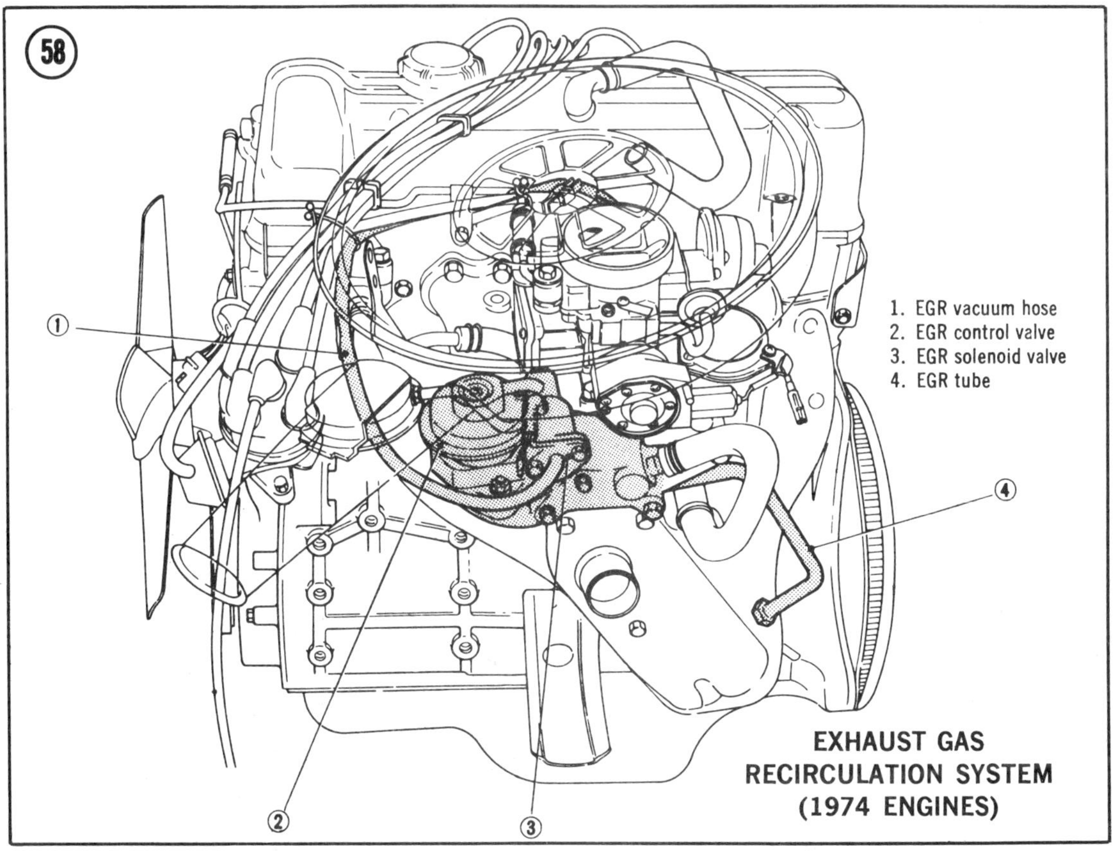

58

1. EGR vacuum hose
2. EGR control valve
3. EGR solenoid valve
4. EGR tube

EXHAUST GAS
RECIRCULATION SYSTEM
(1974 ENGINES)

59

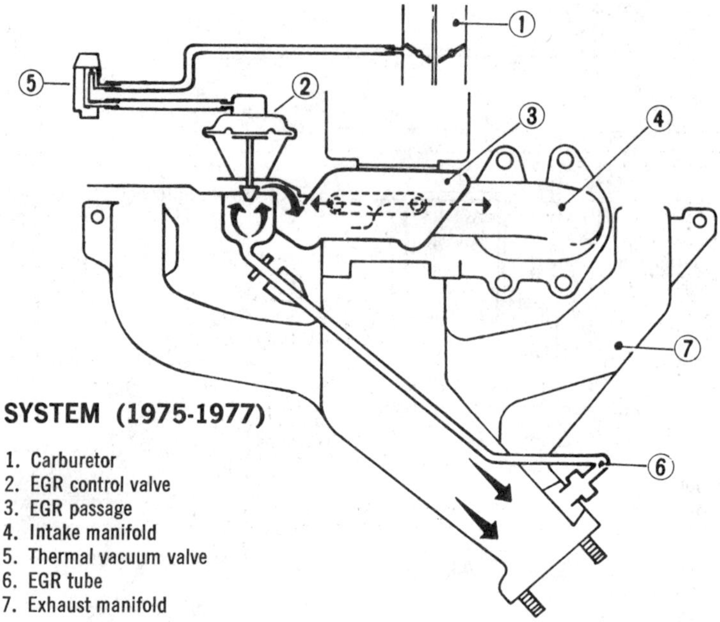

EGR SYSTEM (1975-1977)

1. Carburetor
2. EGR control valve
3. EGR passage
4. Intake manifold
5. Thermal vacuum valve
6. EGR tube
7. Exhaust manifold

60

EGR SYSTEM
(1978-1980)

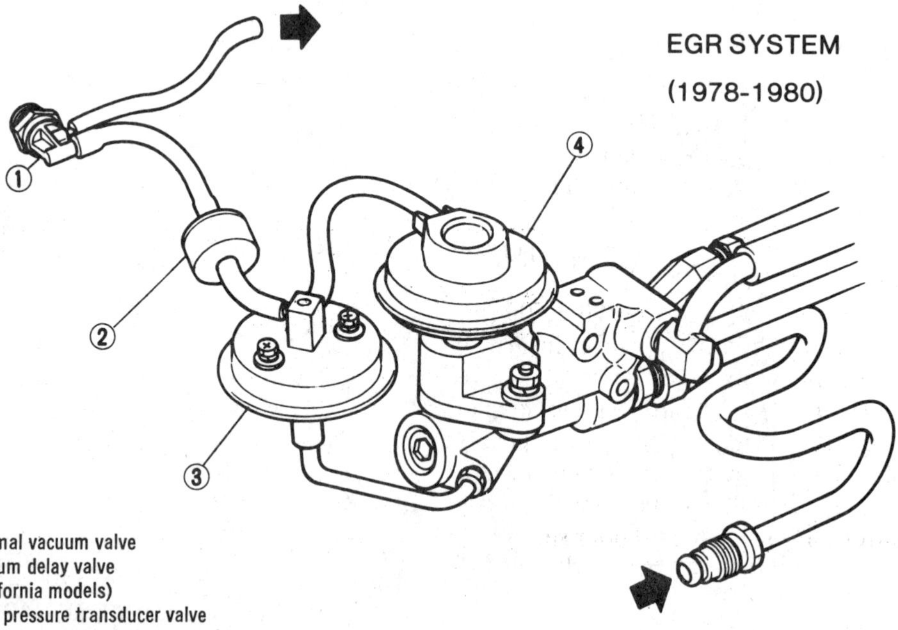

1. Thermal vacuum valve
2. Vacuum delay valve (California models)
3. Back pressure transducer valve
4. Exhaust gas recirculation control valve

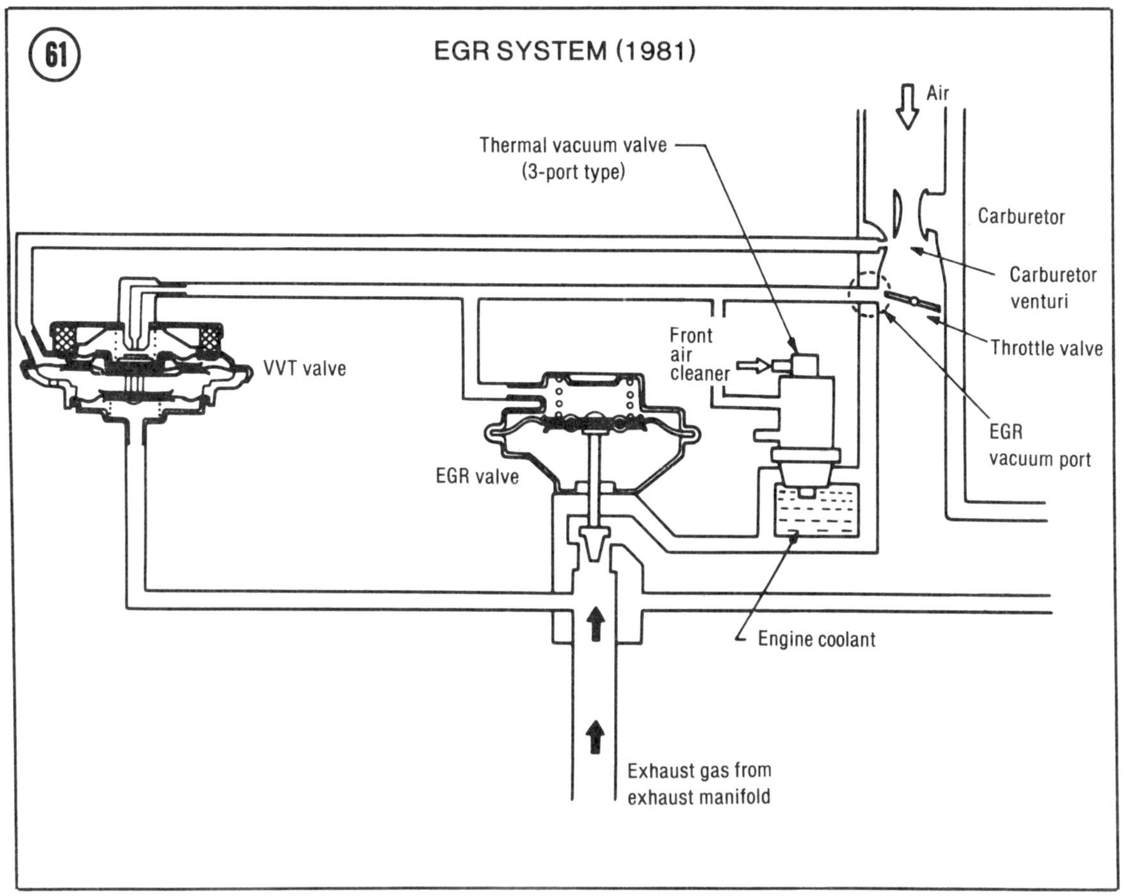

Inspection (Through 1977)

1. Examine the EGR system. Replace cracked or worn hoses and tubes. Replace any parts showing obvious mechanical damage.
2. On 1974 models, make sure the solenoid valve wire is securely connected.
3. Warm the engine to normal operating temperature.
4. Increase engine speed to 3,000-3,500 rpm. The control valve shaft (visible inside the lower part of the valve) should rise.
5. On 1974 models, disconnect the solenoid valve wire. Connect it to the battery positive terminal with a jumper wire. Again, increase engine speed to 3,000-3,500 rpm. This time the control valve shaft should not rise.
6. With the engine idling, reach into the control valve and push the diaphragm up. The idle should become unstable.

WARNING
The control valve and surrounding area will be hot. Use a screwdriver or similar tool to raise the diaphragm.

7. On all except 1975-1977 California trucks, disconnect the control valve vacuum hose, remove 2 attaching nuts, and lift the control valve off the intake manifold (**Figure 62**).
8. Check the control valve for visible wear or damage. On all except 1975 California trucks, clean the base of the valve with a wire brush and compressed air. Check the intake manifold passage for excessive carbon buildup. If necessary, remove the manifold and clean it.

Inspection (1978-on)

1. Check the EGR system for loose or damaged hoses. Tighten or replace as needed.
2. With the engine off, reach beneath the EGR control valve and lift the diaphragm. It should move smoothly, without sticking or binding.

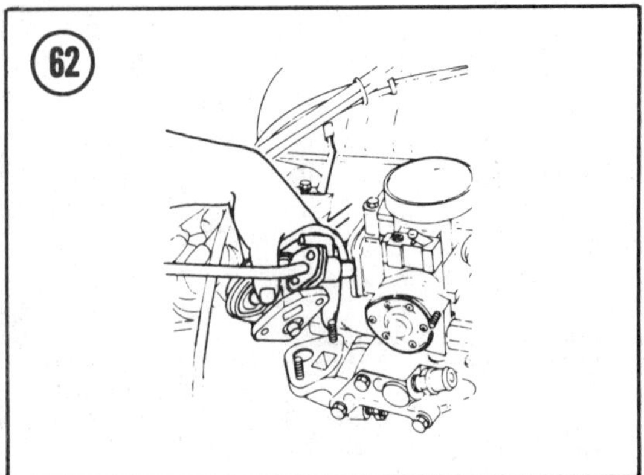

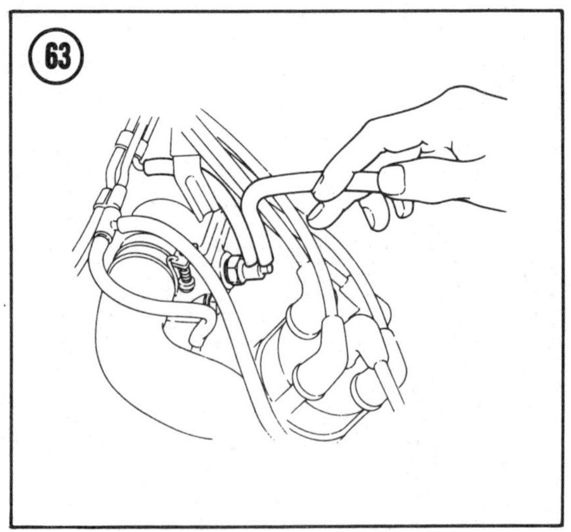

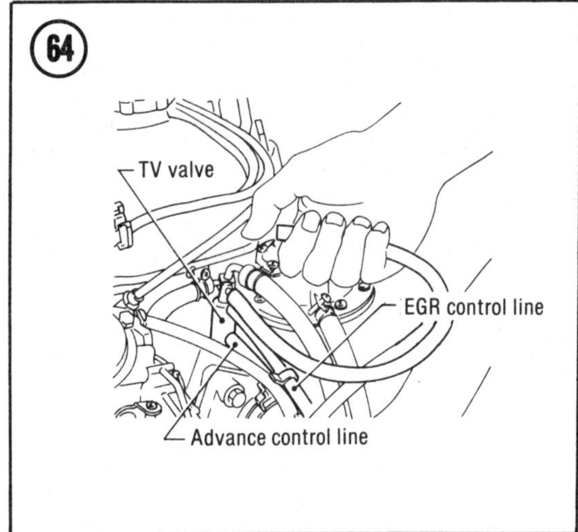

3. Start the engine. With the engine cold, the EGR valve should not operate when engine speed is raised to 3,000-3,500 rpm (1978-1980) or 2,000-2,500 rpm (1981).

4. Warm the engine to normal operating temperature. The EGR valve's diaphragm should rise when engine speed is raised to 3,000-3,500 rpm (1978-1980) or 2,000-2,500 rpm (1981).

5. If the valve doesn't rise, disconnect the EGR valve vacuum line. See **Figure 63** (1878-1980) or **Figure 64** (1981). There should be vacuum at the end of the line when engine speed is raised. If there is, replace the EGR valve. If not, replace the thermal vacuum valve. If there is any doubt, have the system tested further by a Datsun dealer or a mechanic familiar with Datsun emission controls.

EVAPORATIVE EMISSION CONTROL SYSTEM

This system is used on all California models and on all non-California models manufactured since May, 1970. The system is designed to prevent gasoline vapor from escaping into the atmosphere. The system should be inspected, and the carbon canister filter replaced, at intervals specified in Chapter Three.

Inspection

Refer to the following illustrations:

Figure 65—1970-1972
Figure 66—1973-1974
Figure 67—1975-1979
Figure 68—1980-on

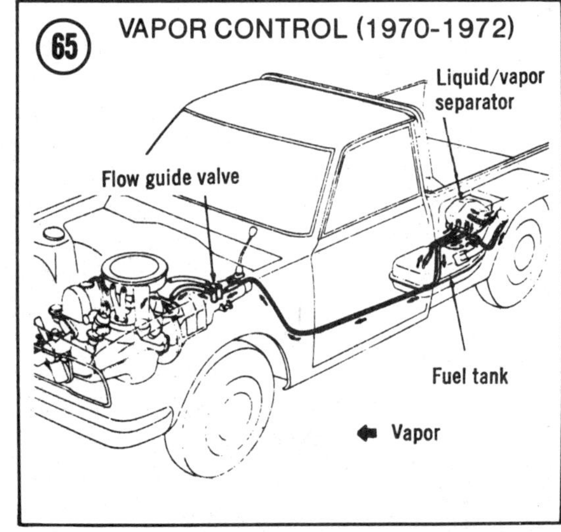

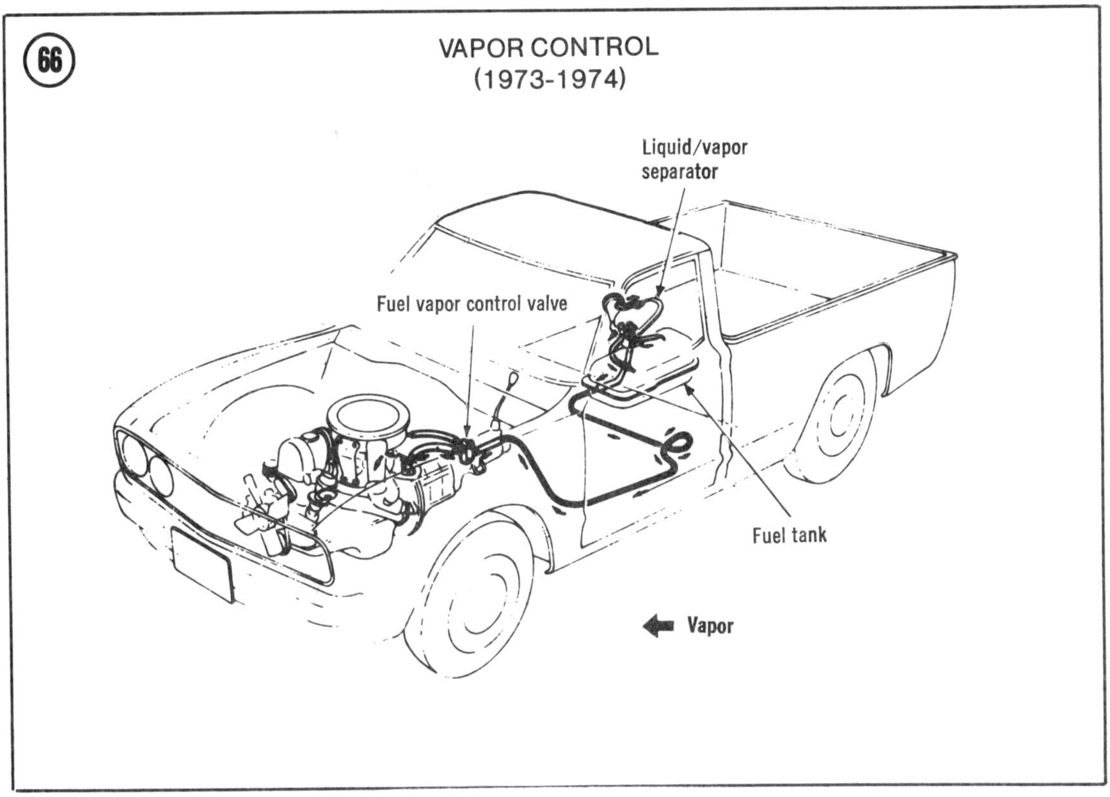

66

VAPOR CONTROL
(1973-1974)

Liquid/vapor separator

Fuel vapor control valve

Fuel tank

Vapor

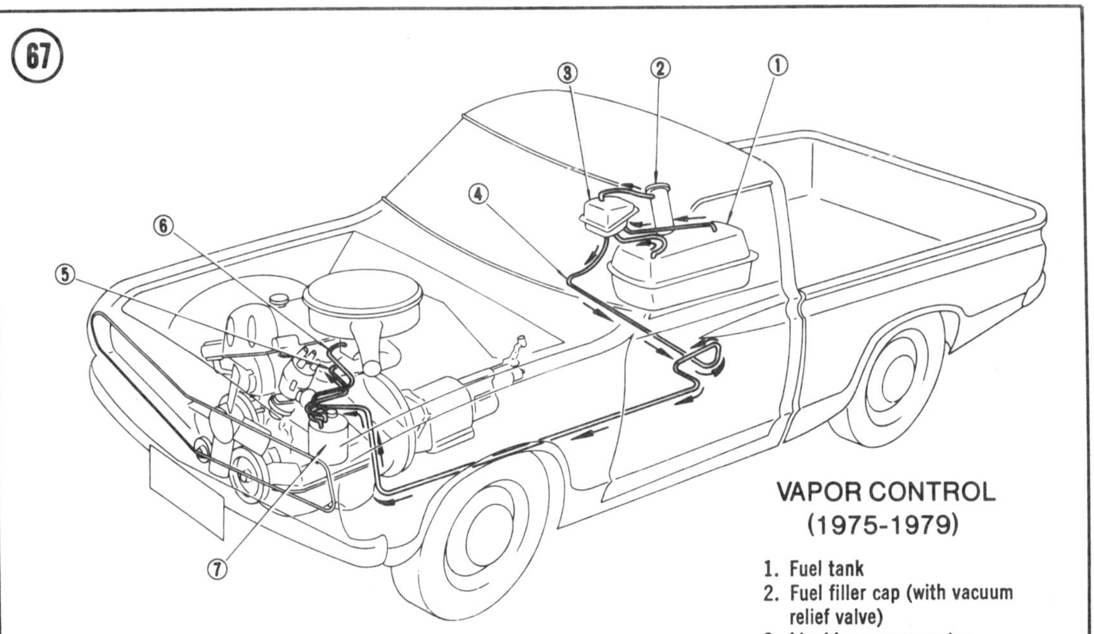

67

VAPOR CONTROL
(1975-1979)

1. Fuel tank
2. Fuel filler cap (with vacuum relief valve)
3. Liquid vapor separator
4. Vapor vent line
5. Canister purge line
6. Vacuum signal line
7. Carbon canister

6

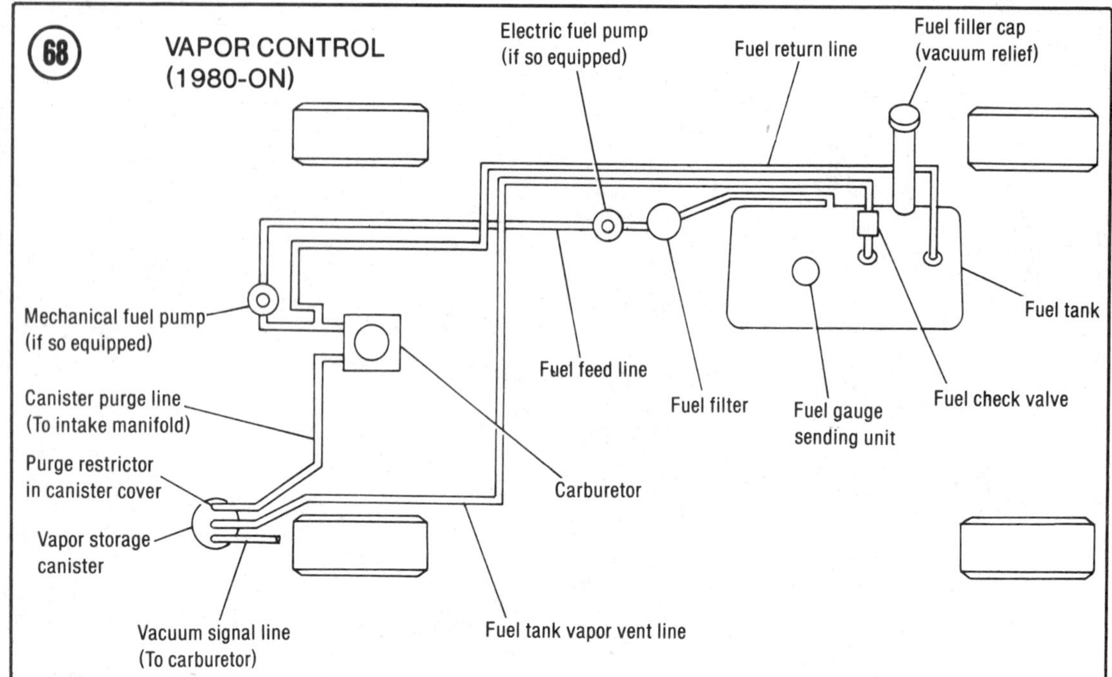

1. Check the vapor lines for loose connections or damage. Tighten or replace as needed.
2. Remove the filter from the bottom of the carbon canister (**Figure 69**). Install a new one.
3. Remove the fuel filler cap and wipe the inside of it clean. Suck on the cap's valve (**Figure 70**). There should be resistance, then the valve should click and air should flow into the valve. If there is no resistance, or if air can't be sucked through the valve, replace the fuel filler cap.

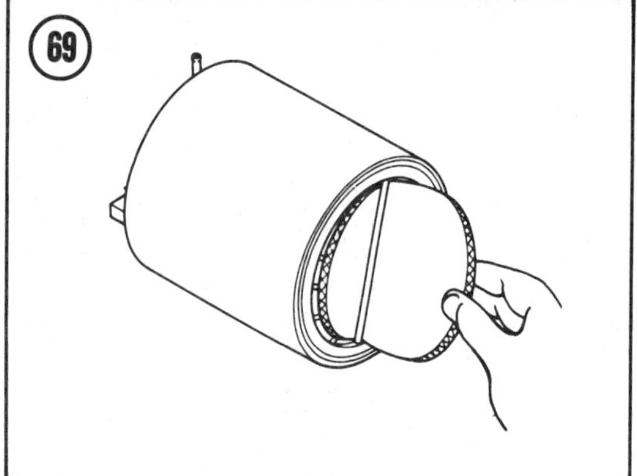

SPARK TIMING CONTROL SYSTEM

This system is used on 1970-1973 and some 1976 and later trucks to control ignition timing under specified driving conditions.

The 1970-1973 system uses a dual-point distributor. One set of points has a more advanced timing setting than the other. Various switches and relays determine which set of points is in use.

The 1976-1977 system is used only on 49-state models with automatic transmission. The only component is a delay valve in the distributor vacuum line. This arrangement is also used on 1979 models with automatic transmission.

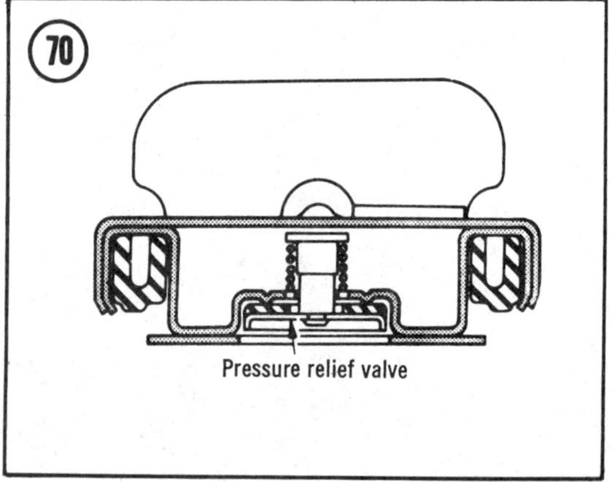

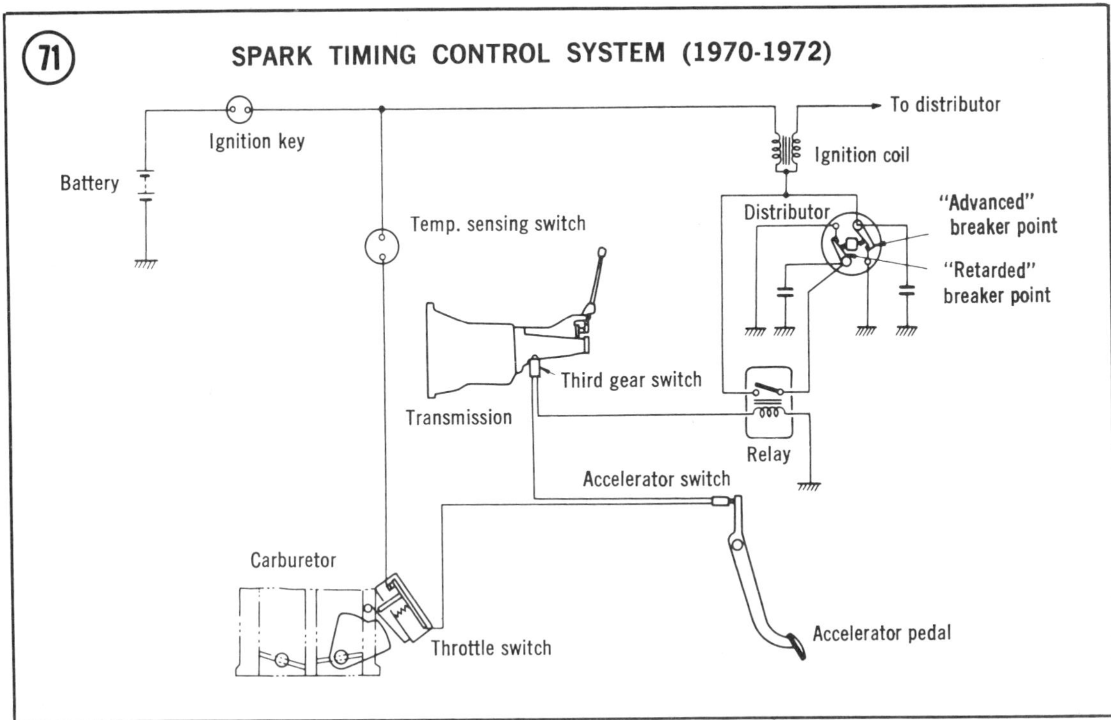

On 1979 models with manual transmission, and 1980 California models with manual transmission, the system consists of a vacuum switching valve and top gear detecting switch. In any gear but fourth (or fifth, if so equipped), the vacuum switching valve opens the distributor vacuum line to atmosphere. This weakens the vacuum signal to the distributor and retards ignition timing. In fourth or fifth gear, the vacuum switching valve closes. The full vacuum signal then reaches the distributor, and ignition timing is advanced.

On 1981 models, the system consists of a thermal vacuum valve and related hoses. With the engine cold, the thermal vacuum valve closes to allow full vacuum to the distributor. As the engine warms up, the valve opens to expose the distributor vacuum line to air. This blocks the vacuum signal and retards ignition timing.

System Test (1970-1972)

1. Warm the passenger compartment above 55° F. Use the truck's heater if necessary.
2. Disconnect the thin wires from the side of the distributor.
3. Connect an ammeter between the retarded wire (not the retarded terminal) and ground (bare metal in the engine compartment). See **Figure 71**.
4. Turn the ignition on, but do not start the engine.
5. Place the shift lever in third gear and press the accelerator. The ammeter should show approximately 3 amps when the pedal is partway down. The ammeter should indicate zero when the pedal is on the floor or nearly all the way up, and also when the shift lever is taken out of the third gear position.
6. If the system performed properly in the preceding steps, it is OK. If it didn't, have it tested further by a Datsun dealer or a mechanic familiar with Datsun emission controls.

System Test (1973)

The 1973 system is tested as part of ignition timing adjustment. This is described in the *Tune-up* section of Chapter Three. If a system defect becomes apparent during a tune-up, have the system tested further by a Datsun dealer or a mechanic familiar with Datsun emission controls.

6

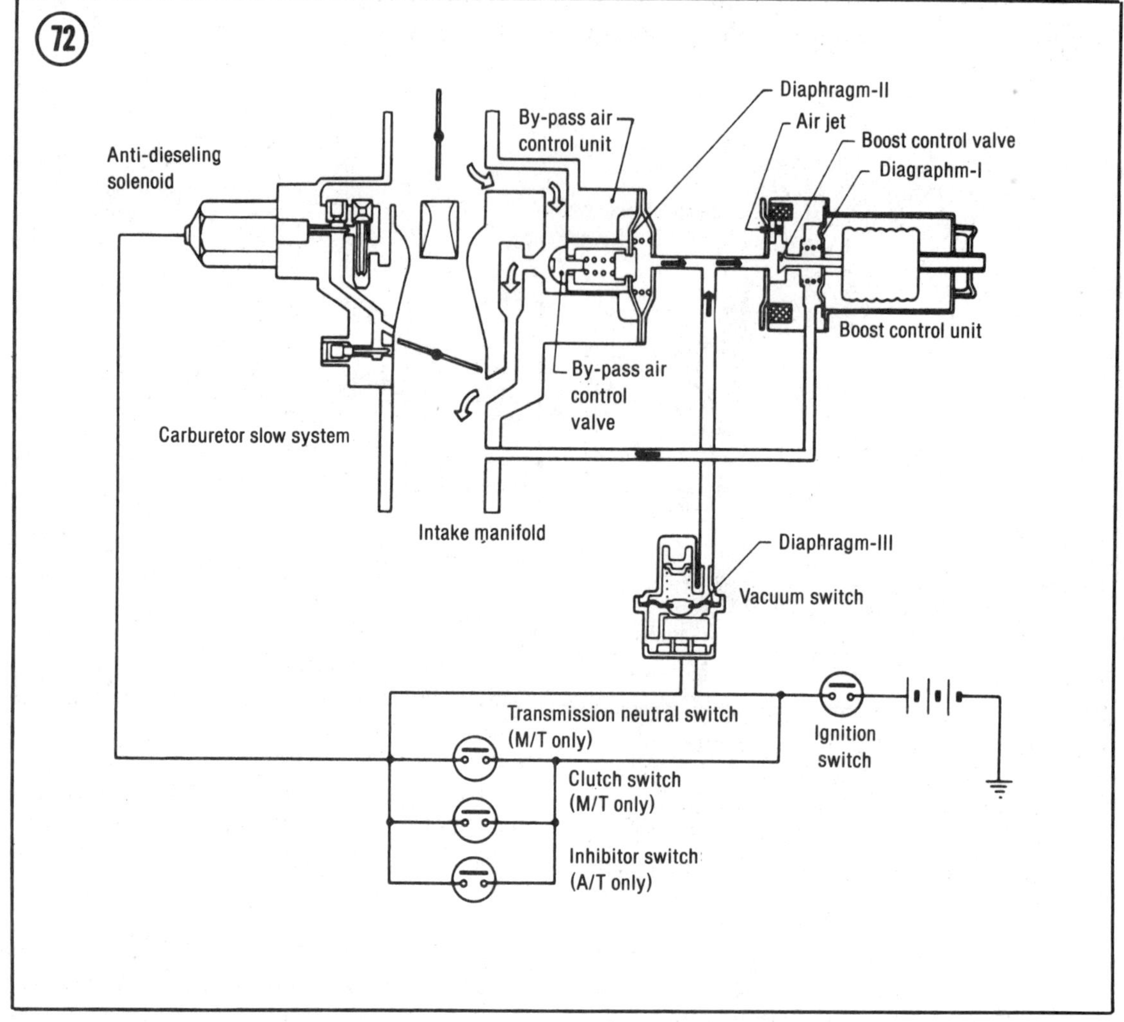

System Test (Spark Delay Valve)

To test the valve, disconnect it from the vacuum line and try to blow air through it. It should be easy to blow air into the distributor side of the valve, and hard to blow air into the carburetor side. If this isn't the case, replace the valve. On 1976-1977 models, replace the valve every 25,000 miles or 24 months. On 1979 models, periodic replacement is not required.

System Test (1979 Manual Transmission; 1980 California Manual Transmission)

This procedure requires 2 people.

1. Make sure all wires and hoses are properly connected and in good condition. Tighten or replace as needed.
2. Connect a timing light to the engine.
3. Run the engine at approximately 2,000 rpm. Have an assistant move the shift lever to all gear positions and note ignition timing. It should be more advanced in fourth gear (and fifth, if so equipped) than in the other gears. If not, have the system tested further by a Datsun dealer or a mechanic familiar with Datsun emission controls.

System Test (1981)

This procedure requires 2 people.

1. Connect a timing light to the engine.

NOTE

If air temperature is above 59° F (15° C), cool the thermal vacuum valve (mounted on the water outlet elbow) with ice.

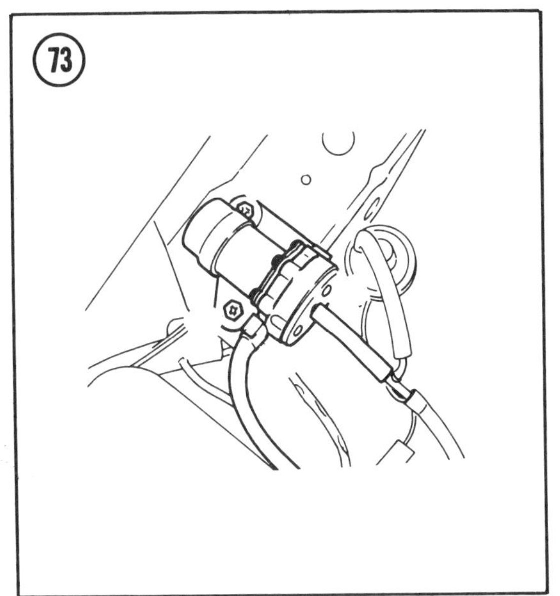

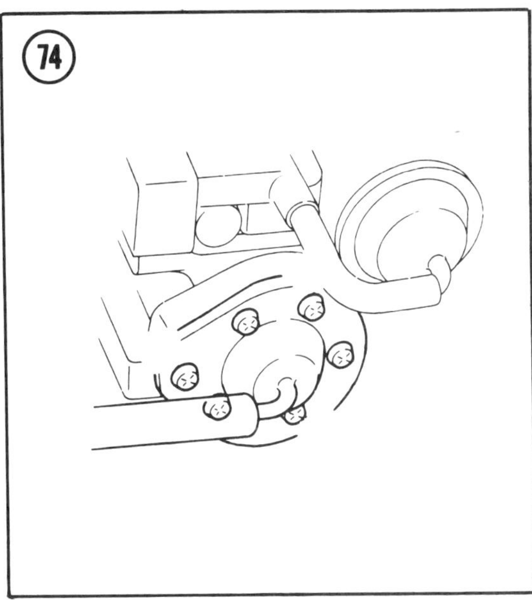

2. Start the engine and let it idle. Note ignition timing.

3. Warm the engine until the coolant temperature needle is in the center of the gauge, then recheck ignition timing. It should be more advanced than it was with the engine cold. If not, have the system tested further by a Datsun dealer or mechanic familiar with Datsun emission controls.

FUEL SHUTOFF SYSTEM

This system (**Figure 72**) is used on all 1980 models except Canadian standard trucks (those without the letter "E" in their vehicle identification number). The system shuts off fuel flow to the carburetor slow circuit during deceleration. The system does not need periodic inspection. System testing should be left to a Datsun dealer or mechanic familiar with Datsun emission controls.

INTAKE MANIFOLD VACUUM CONTROL SYSTEM

This system, used on 1981 models, reduces engine oil consumption by reducing intake manifold vacuum during hard deceleration. It consists of a boost control unit (**Figure 73**) and bypass air control valve (**Figure 74**). When intake manifold vacuum reaches high levels, the boost control valve signals the bypass air control valve to admit additional air to the intake manifold.

The system doesn't need periodic inspection. Testing and adjustment should be left to a Datsun dealer or a mechanic familiar with Datsun emission controls.

CATALYTIC CONVERTER

A catalytic converter is used on 1976-1979 California models, all 1980 models except Canadian standard trucks (those without the letter "E" in their vehicle identification number), and all 1981 trucks. The converter is mounted in the exhaust line and resembles a muffler. It uses a platinum or palladium catalyst to convert unburned hydrocarbons and carbon monoxide into carbon dioxide and water. No periodic service is needed.

EXHAUST PIPE AND MUFFLER

Refer to the following illustrations:

Figure 75—1970 to mid-1972
Figure 76—mid-1972 to 1974
Figure 77—1975
Figure 78—1976-1979 California
Figure 79—1976-1979 non-California
Figure 80—1980 U.S. standard models (no letter "E" in vehicle identification number)

(75)

EXHAUST SYSTEM
(1970-mid 1972)

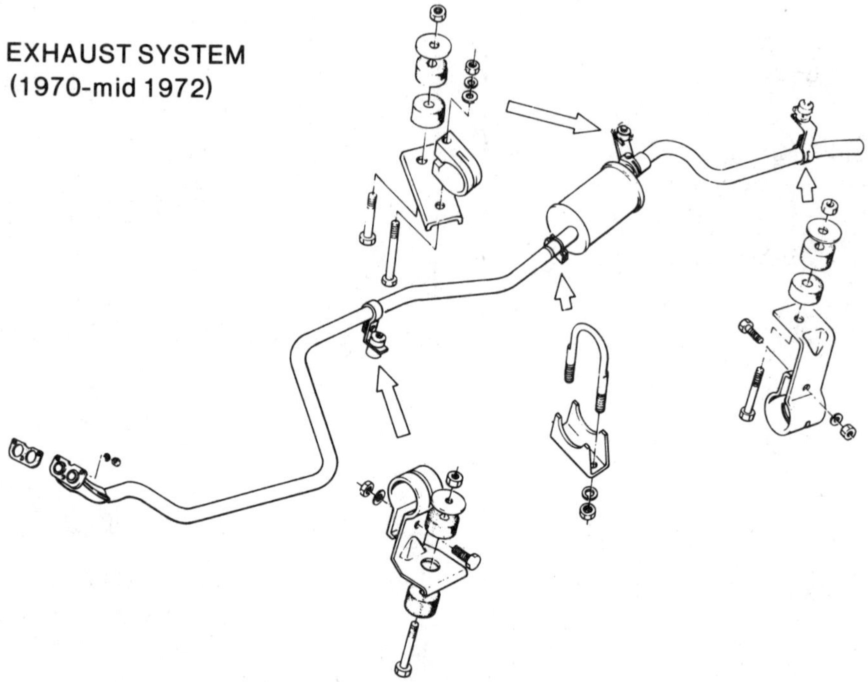

(76)

EXHAUST SYSTEM
(MID 1972-1974)

1. Front tube
2. Exhaust tube clip
3. Rear tube assembly
4. Muffler assembly
5. Rear tube mounting bolt

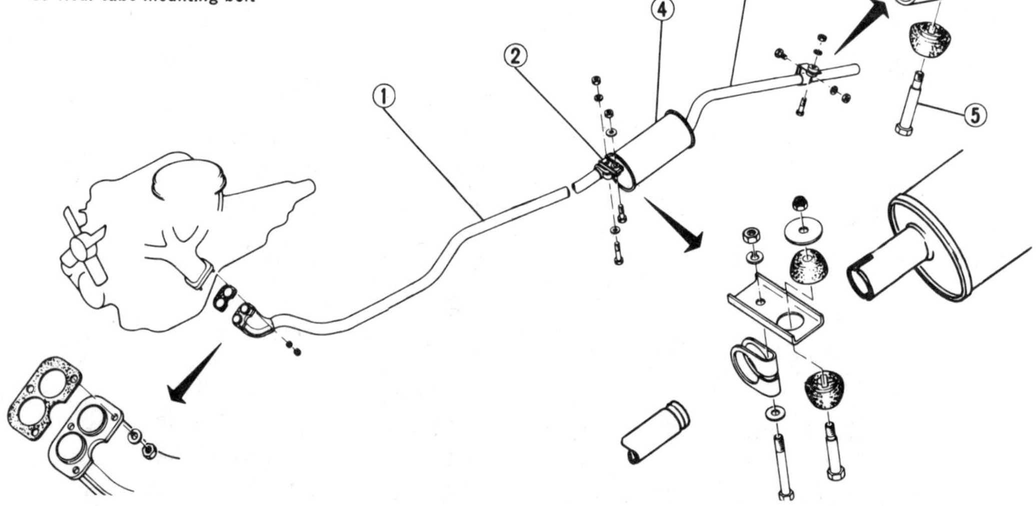

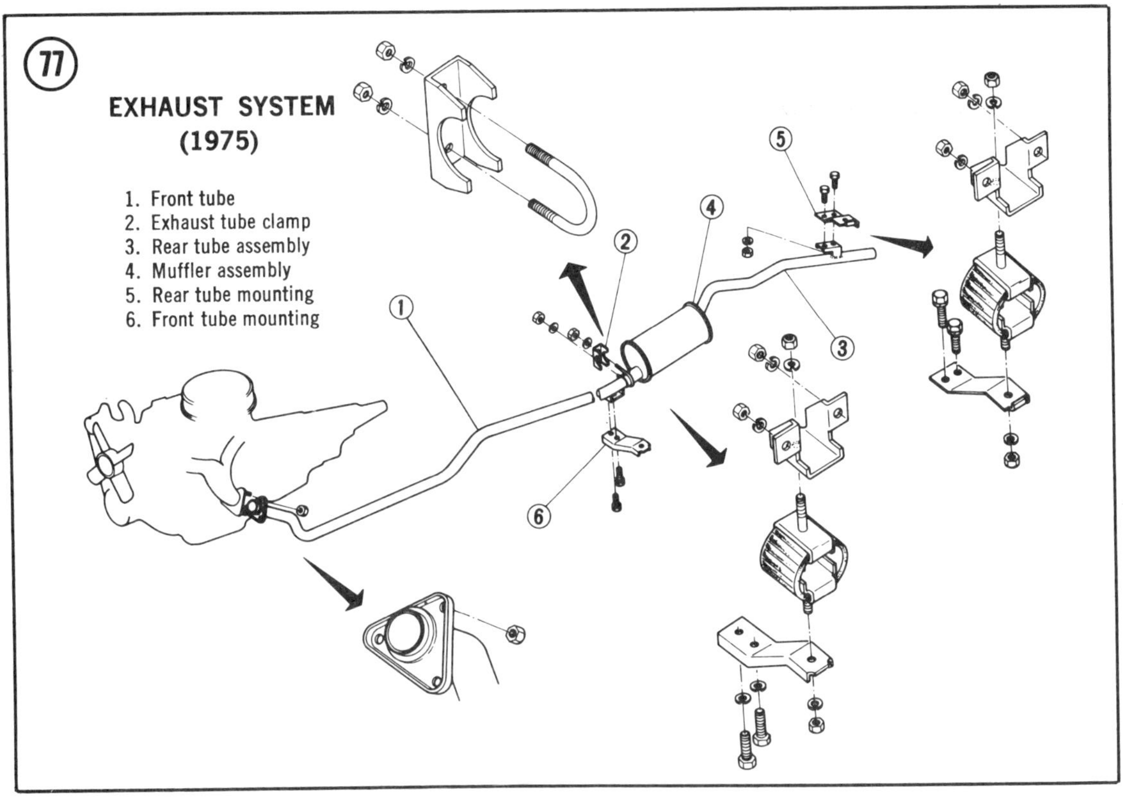

77

EXHAUST SYSTEM (1975)

1. Front tube
2. Exhaust tube clamp
3. Rear tube assembly
4. Muffler assembly
5. Rear tube mounting
6. Front tube mounting

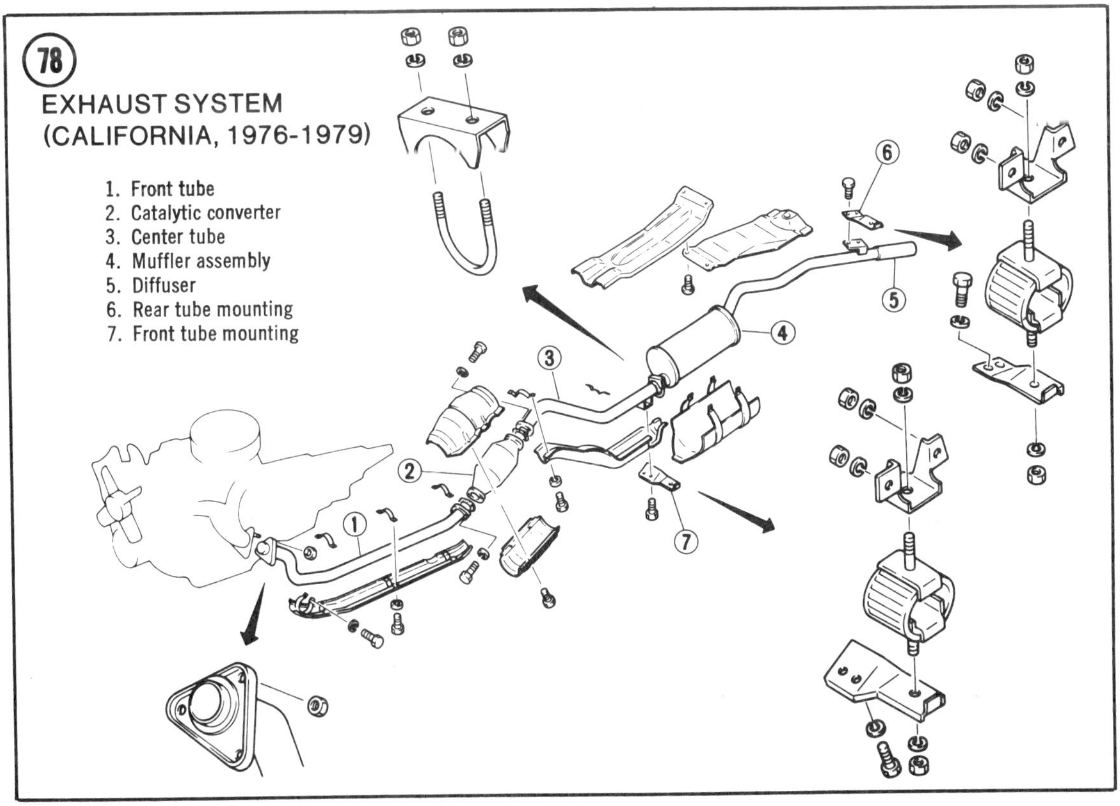

78

EXHAUST SYSTEM (CALIFORNIA, 1976-1979)

1. Front tube
2. Catalytic converter
3. Center tube
4. Muffler assembly
5. Diffuser
6. Rear tube mounting
7. Front tube mounting

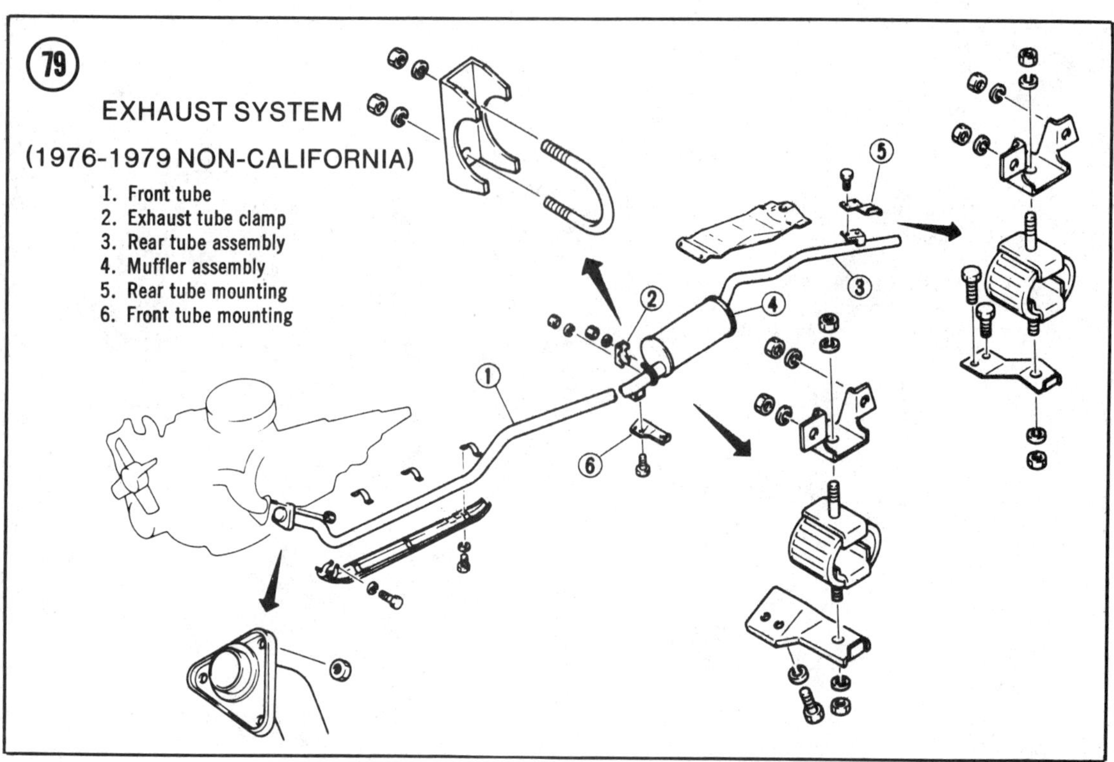

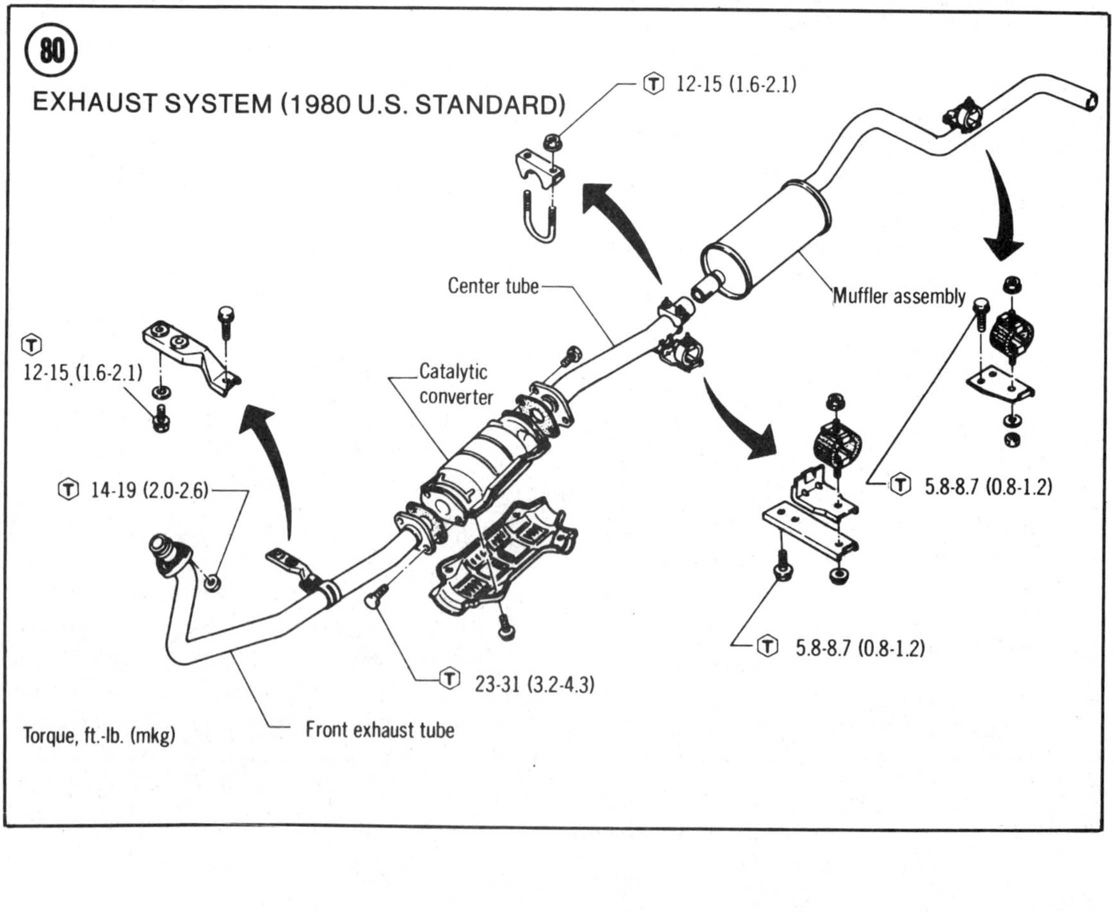

80

EXHAUST SYSTEM (1980 U.S. STANDARD)

T 12-15 (1.6-2.1)

Center tube

Muffler assembly

T 12-15 (1.6-2.1)

Catalytic converter

T 14-19 (2.0-2.6)

T 5.8-8.7 (0.8-1.2)

T 5.8-8.7 (0.8-1.2)

T 23-31 (3.2-4.3)

Torque, ft.-lb. (mkg)

Front exhaust tube

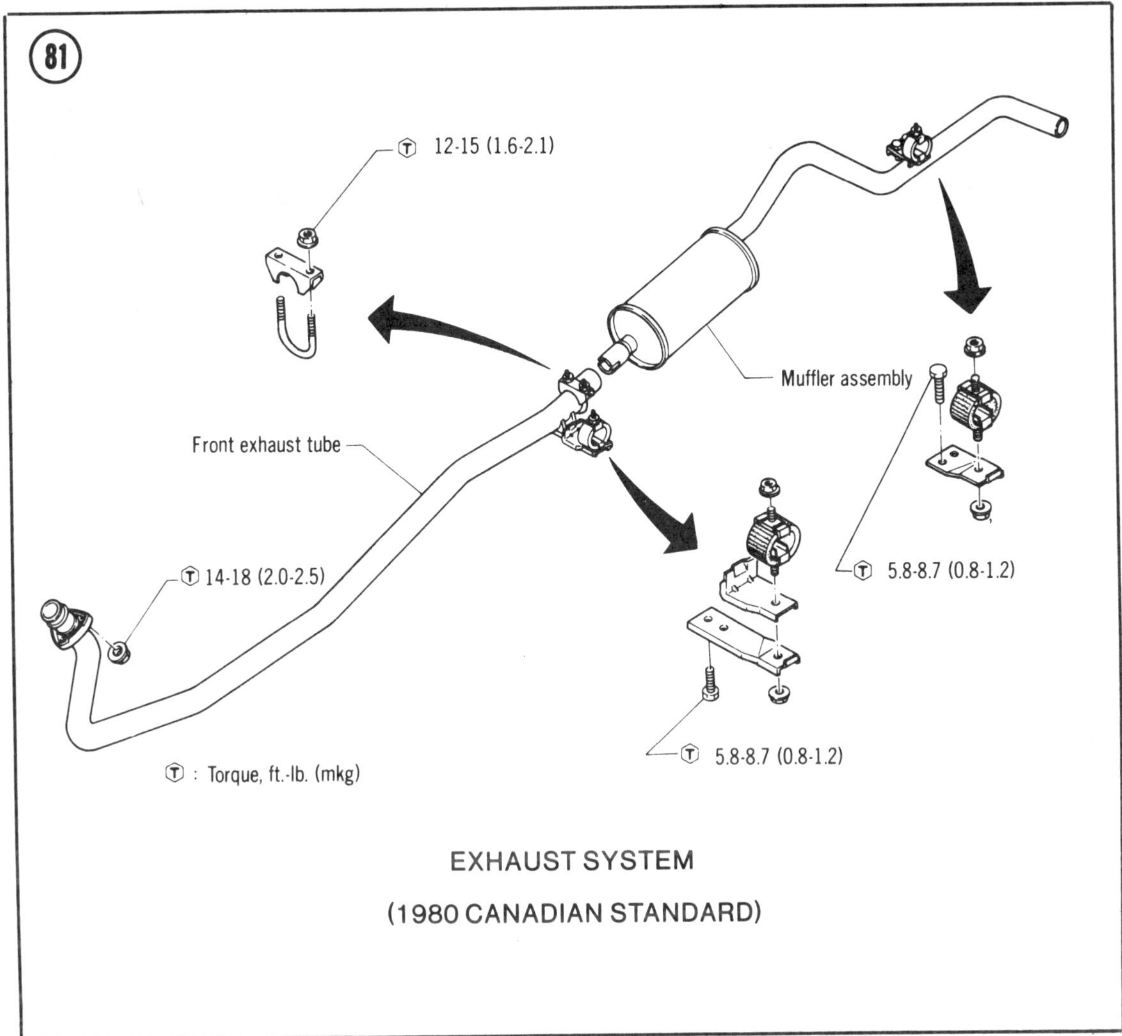

Figure 81—1980 Canadian standard models (no letter "E" in vehicle identification number)

Figure 82—1980 heavy duty models (letter "E" in vehicle identification number)

Figure 83—1981 standard models (no letter "E" in vehicle identification number)

Figure 84—1981 heavy duty models (letter "E" in vehicle identification number).

Removal/Installation

1. Prior to removal, soak all bolts, nuts, and pipe joints with penetrating oil such as WD-40.
2. Undo the necessary clamps and hanger brackets referring to the appropriate illustration.

NOTE

*1974 and later models use an injected sealer at the front end of the muffler (**Figure 85**). To remove, break the seal by tapping the joint with a metal hammer. Twist the muffler back and forth, then tap it off with rubber mallet.*

3. Check removed parts for excessive rust and for damage caused by bottoming the vehicle. Check rubber mounts for melting, cracks or deterioration. Replace as needed.
4. Install in the reverse order. On 1974 and later models, inject sealer into the muffler front connection. Use a Datsun sealer kit as shown in **Figure 85**. Let the engine idle for 10 minutes to cure the sealer. Do not accelerate sharply for 20-30 minutes.

82

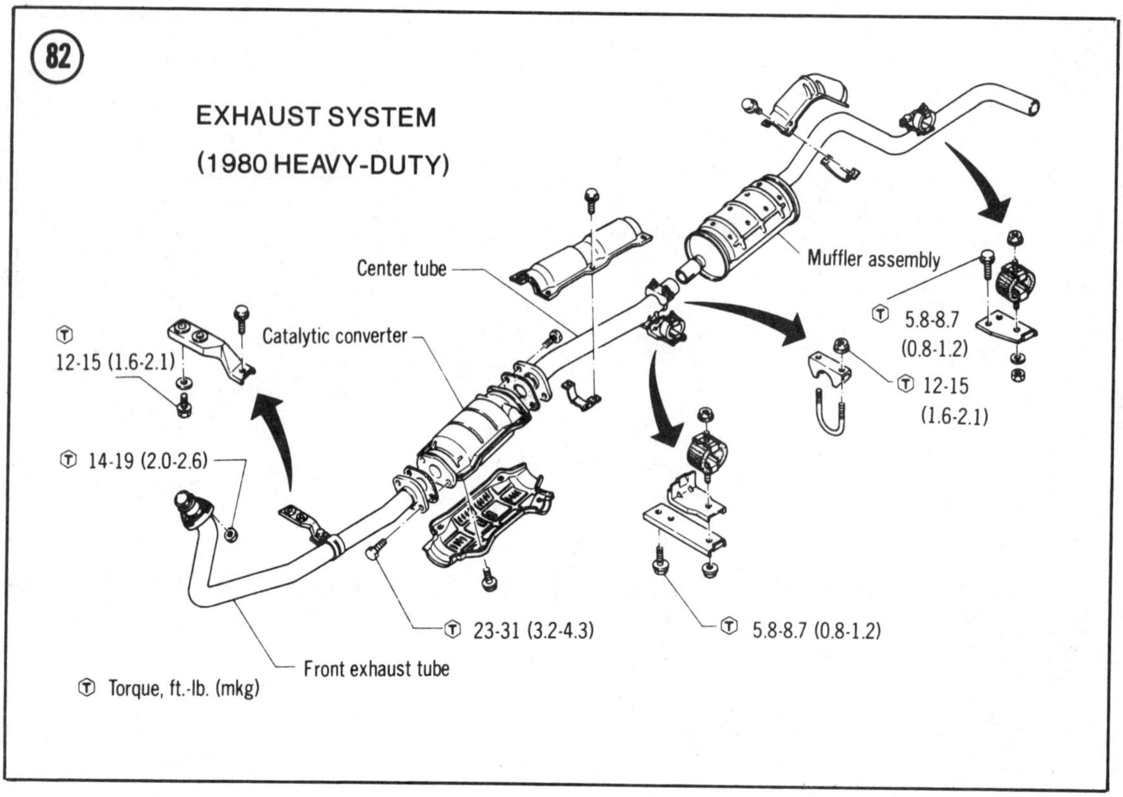

EXHAUST SYSTEM
(1980 HEAVY-DUTY)

Center tube
Muffler assembly
Catalytic converter
12-15 (1.6-2.1)
5.8-8.7
(0.8-1.2)
12-15
(1.6-2.1)
14-19 (2.0-2.6)
23-31 (3.2-4.3)
5.8-8.7 (0.8-1.2)
Front exhaust tube
Torque, ft.-lb. (mkg)

83

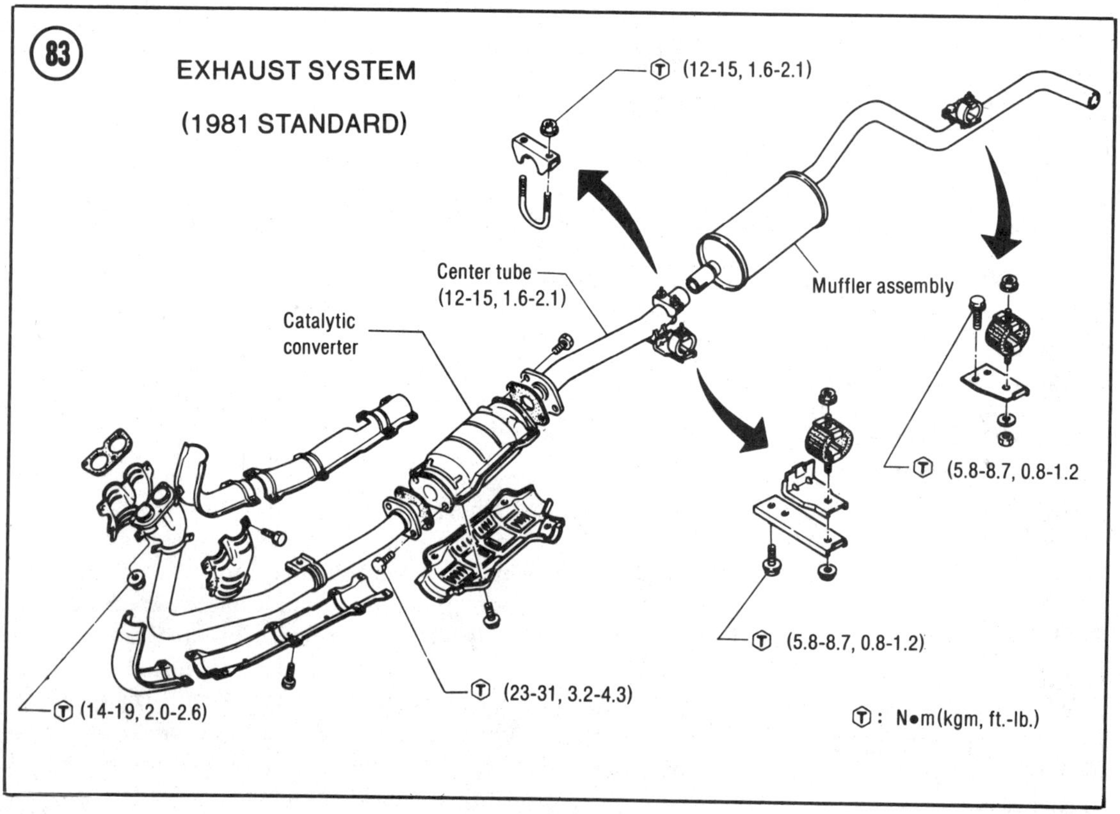

EXHAUST SYSTEM
(1981 STANDARD)

(12-15, 1.6-2.1)
Center tube
(12-15, 1.6-2.1)
Muffler assembly
Catalytic
converter
(5.8-8.7, 0.8-1.2
(5.8-8.7, 0.8-1.2)
(14-19, 2.0-2.6)
(23-31, 3.2-4.3)
: N•m(kgm, ft.-lb.)

84

EXHAUST SYSTEM
(1981 HEAVY-DUTY)

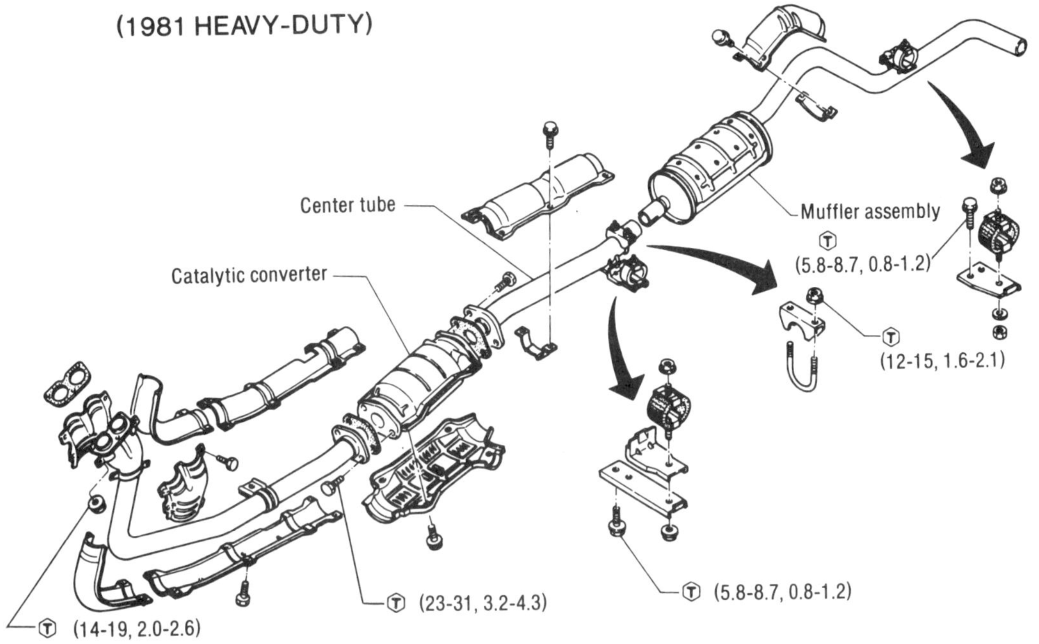

Center tube
Catalytic converter
Muffler assembly
Ⓣ (5.8-8.7, 0.8-1.2)
Ⓣ (12-15, 1.6-2.1)
Ⓣ (5.8-8.7, 0.8-1.2)
Ⓣ (23-31, 3.2-4.3)
Ⓣ (14-19, 2.0-2.6)

Ⓣ : N•m (mkg, ft.-lb.)

85

Sealant
Bead
Injector
Guide
Injector

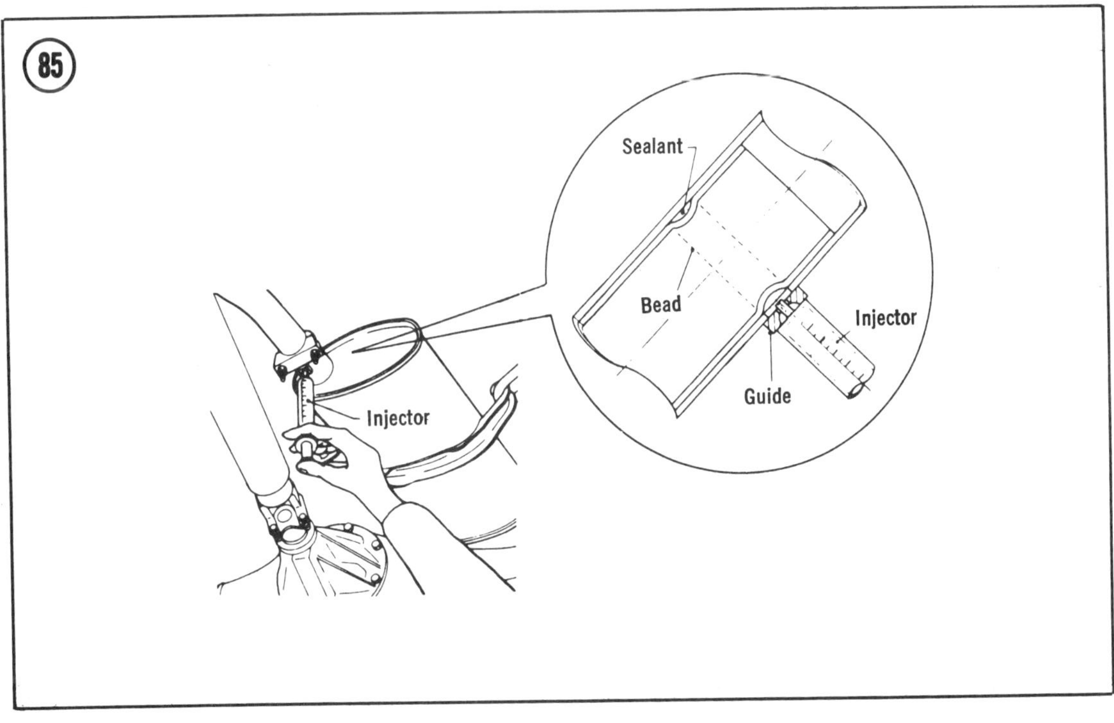

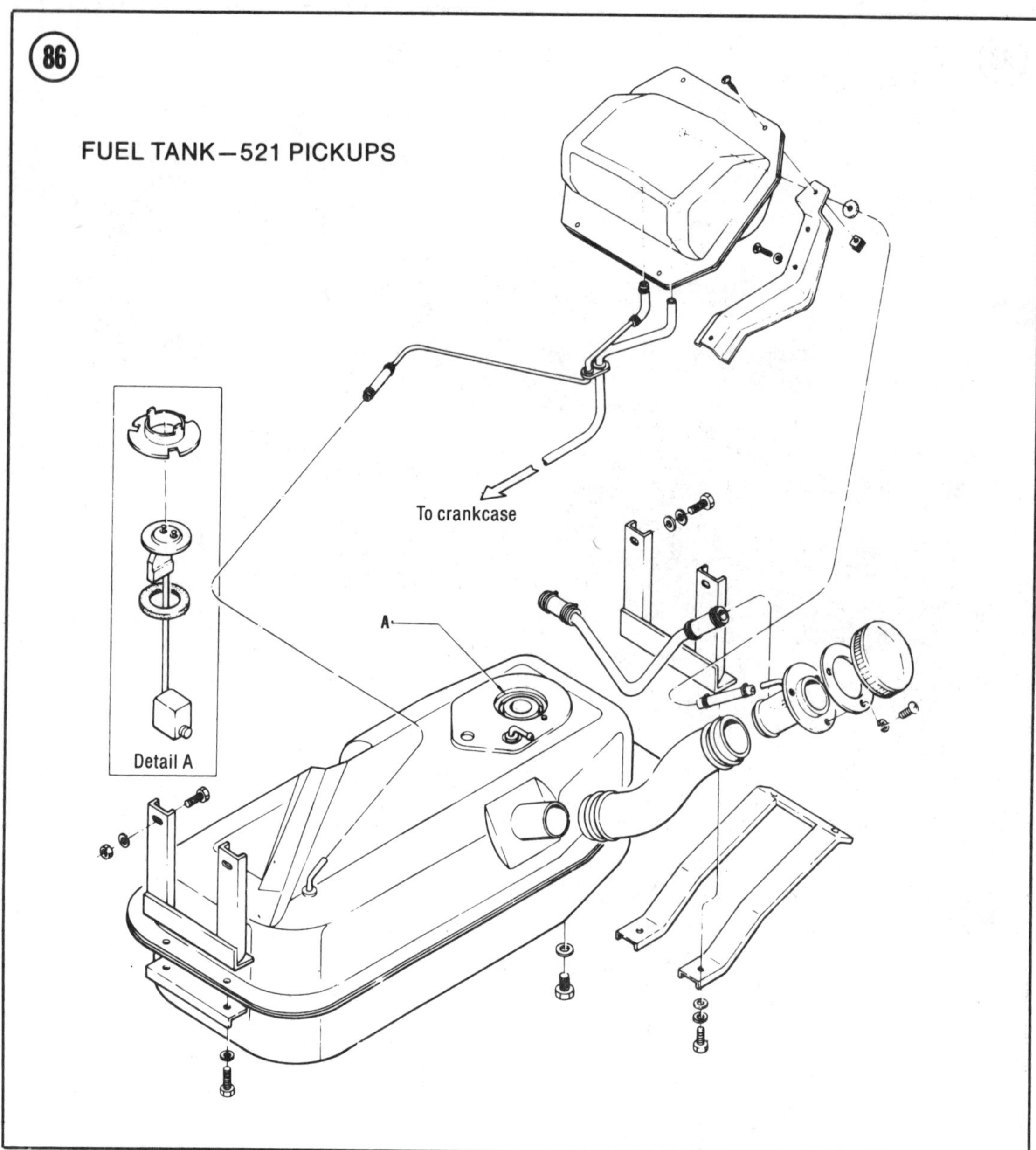

FUEL TANK

Removal/Installation

Refer to the following illustrations:
Figure 86—521 pickups

NOTE
The reservoir tank and associated tubing are not used on non-California trucks built before May, 1970.

Figure 87—early 620 pickups
Figure 88—late 620 pickups
Figure 89—720 pickups

1. Disconnect the negative cable from the battery.
2. Drain the fuel from the tank.

WARNING
Do not store the fuel in an open container, since it represents an extreme fire hazard. Store it in a sealed metal container, away from heat, flames, or sparks.

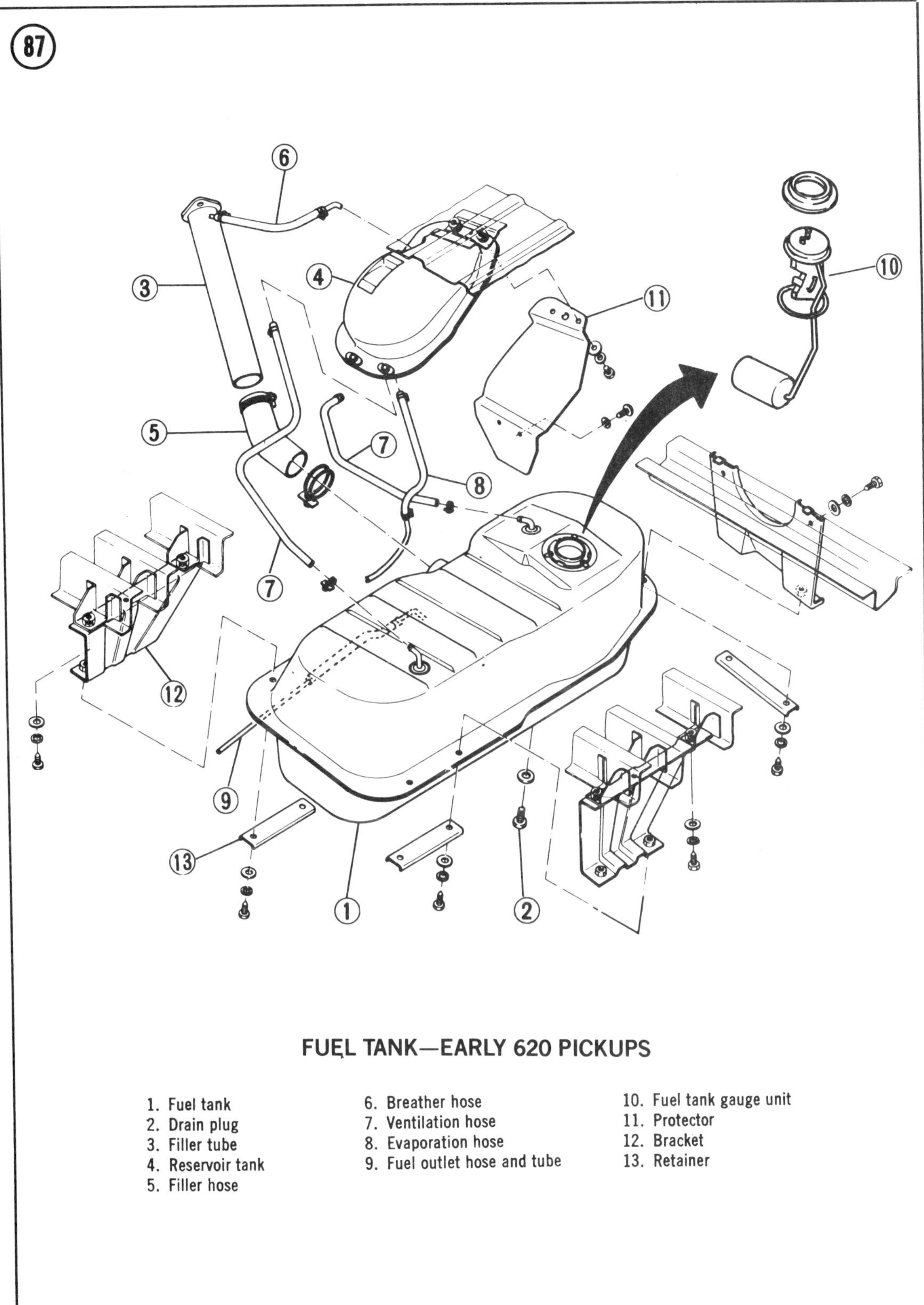

FUEL TANK—EARLY 620 PICKUPS

1. Fuel tank
2. Drain plug
3. Filler tube
4. Reservoir tank
5. Filler hose
6. Breather hose
7. Ventilation hose
8. Evaporation hose
9. Fuel outlet hose and tube
10. Fuel tank gauge unit
11. Protector
12. Bracket
13. Retainer

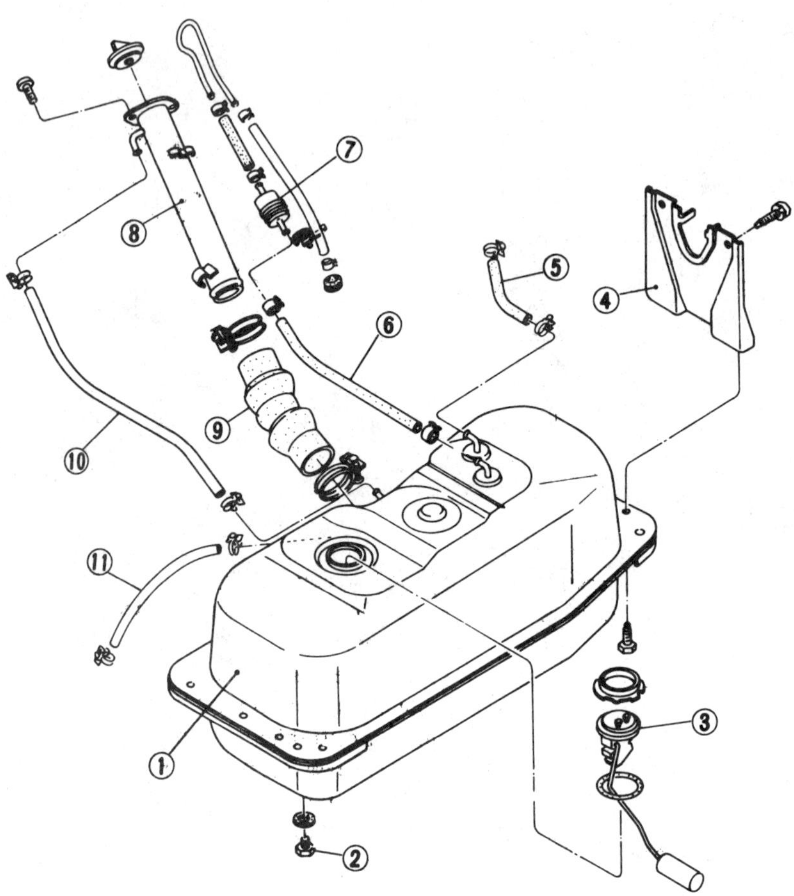

FUEL TANK—LATE 620 PICKUPS

1. Fuel tank
2. Drain plug
3. Fuel tank gauge unit
4. Fuel tank rear bracket
5. Fuel return hose
6. Breather hose
7. Check valve
8. Filler tube
9. Filler hose
10. Ventilation hose
11. Fuel outlet hose

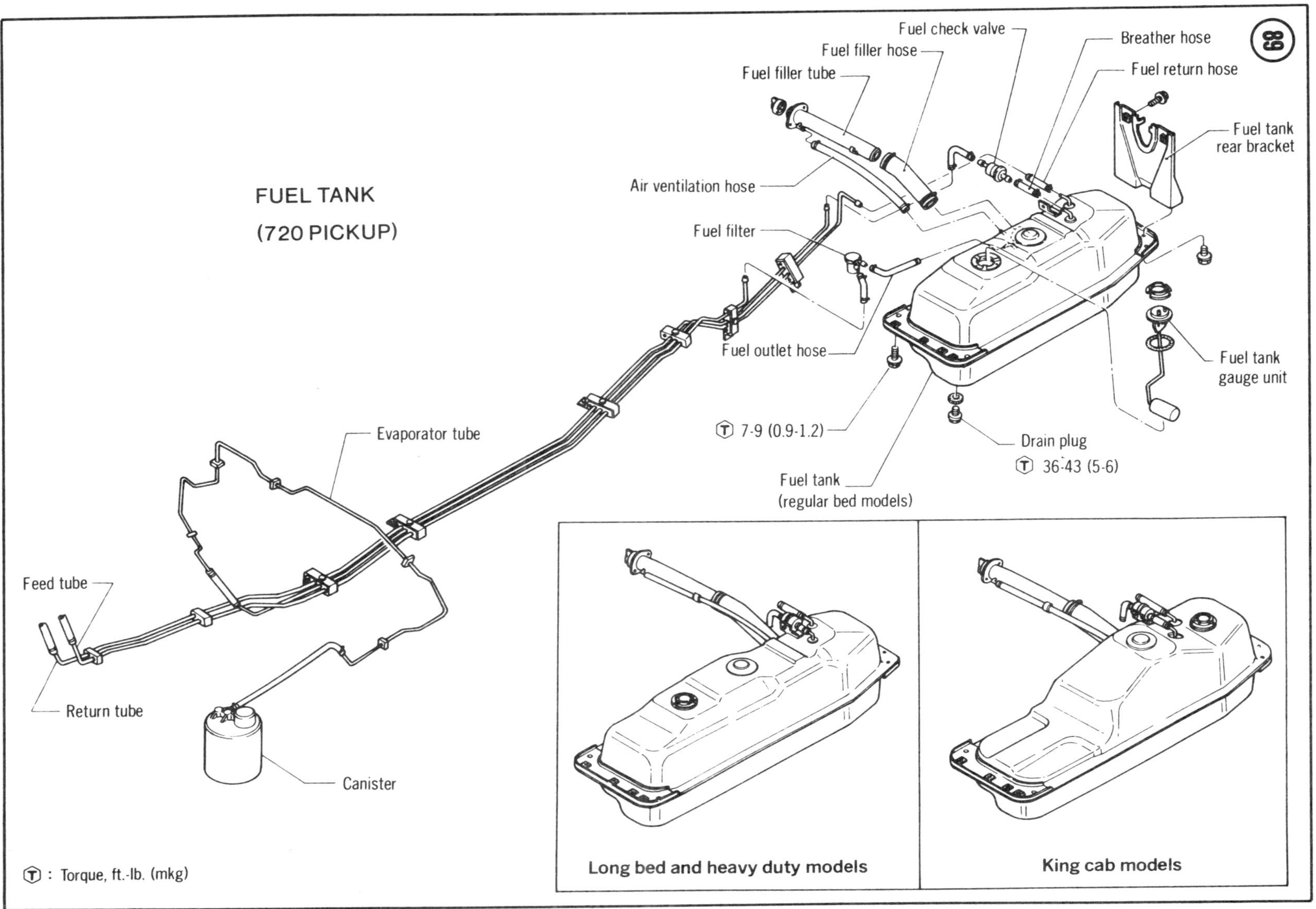
89
FUEL TANK
(720 PICKUP)
Fuel check valve
Fuel filler hose
Fuel filler tube
Breather hose
Fuel return hose
Fuel tank rear bracket
Air ventilation hose
Fuel filter
Fuel outlet hose
Fuel tank gauge unit
T 7-9 (0.9-1.2)
Drain plug
T 36-43 (5-6)
Fuel tank (regular bed models)
Evaporator tube
Feed tube
Return tube
Canister
Long bed and heavy duty models
King cab models
T : Torque, ft.-lb. (mkg)

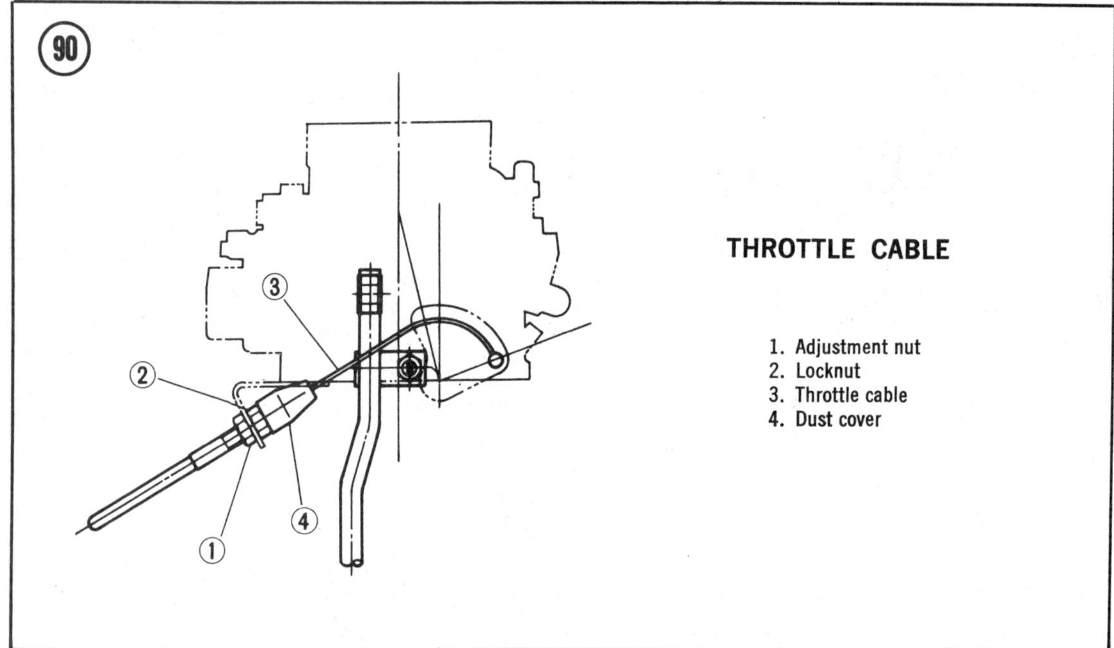

3. On 521 pickups, release the handbrake. Remove the inspection cover from the cargo area floor. Disconnect the wires from the fuel level sending unit. Disconnect the outlet and vent lines from the tank.
4. Disconnect the fuel filler hose from the tank.
5. On 620 pickups, remove the tank installation bolts. Lower the tank away from the truck. Disconnect the outlet line, 2 vent lines, and the fuel level sending unit wires from the tank.
6. On 720 pickups, disconnect the hoses, vent lines, and fuel gauge sending unit wire. Remove the tank mounting bolts.
7. Lower tank clear of truck and take it out.
8. Install in the reverse order. Be sure all hoses and tubes are securely connected.

Repairing Leaks

Fuel tank leaks can be repaired by soldering.

WARNING
A fuel tank is capable of exploding and killing anyone nearby. Always observe the following precautions when repairing a tank.

1. Have tank steam cleaned *inside and outside.*
2. Fill the tank with inert gas such as carbon dioxide or nitrogen, or fill the tank *completely* with water.
3. Set a fire extinguisher nearby.

After the repair is made, pour the water out, put about a quart of gasoline in the tank, and slosh it around. Pour the gasoline out, blow the tank dry, and install it in the car.

THROTTLE CABLE ADJUSTMENTS 1970-1977

1. On 1970-1977 automatic chokes, hold the choke valve fully open and move the throttle lever by hand. This disengages automatic choke mechanism.
2. Loosen the locknut and the adjusting nut (**Figure 90**).
3. Make sure the throttle valve is fully closed. Tighten the adjusting nut until the throttle valve is just about to open. This reduces accelerator pedal play to zero.
4. Loosen the adjusting nut 1 1/2 turns (521 pickups); 4 turns (1972-1975 620 pickups); or 2 1/2 turns (1976-1977 620 pickups).
5. Check pedal play. It should be 0.04-0.08 in. (1-2 mm) on 521 pickups; 0.16-0.20 in. (4-5 mm) on 1972-1975 pickups; and 0.12 in. (3 mm) on 1976 models.
6. If accelerator pedal play is correct, tighten the locknut.

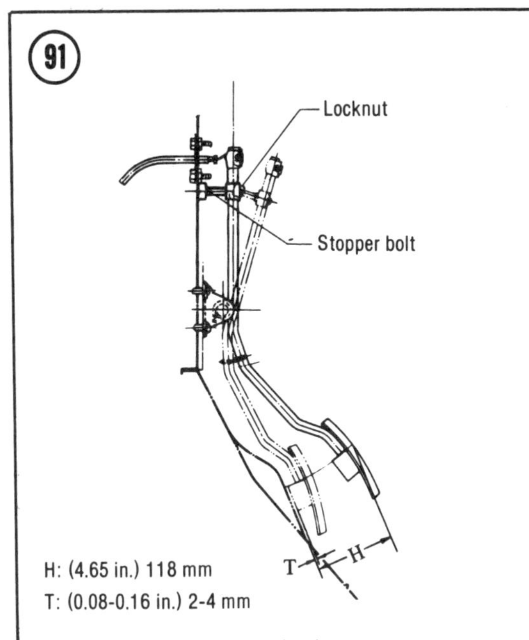

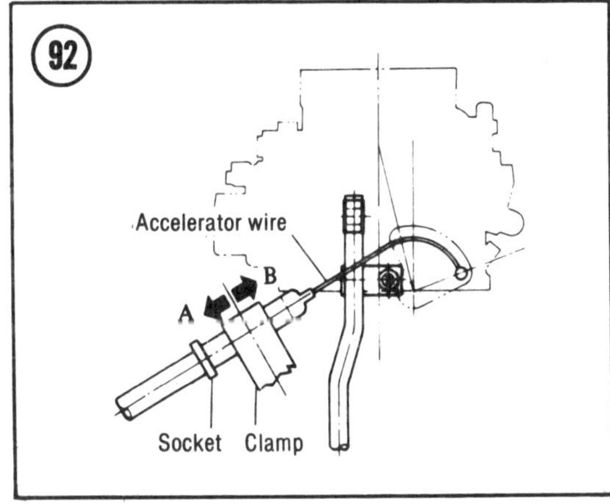

1978-1980

1. Check pedal height (dimension "H", **Figure 91**). It should be 4 5/8 in. (118mm). To adjust, loosen the locknut and turn the stopper bolt. Then tighten the locknut.
2. Disengage the fast idle cam. To do this, hold the choke valve fully open and move the throttle lever by hand.
3. Move the throttle lever to the completely closed position.
4. Loosen clamp (**Figure 92**). Pull the socket in direction "A" until the throttle lever is just about to move. Accelerator pedal play should be zero at this point.

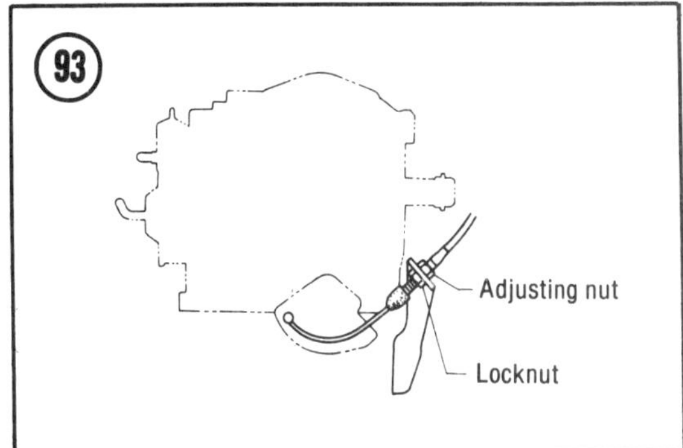

5. Pull the socket 0.039-0.059 in. (1.0-1.5mm) in direction "B." Then tighten the clamp.
6. Floor the accelerator and measure clearance "T" (**Figure 91**). This is the clearance between the back of the accelerator petal and the floor (not the floor mat or carpet). It should be 0.08-0.16 in. (2-4mm). To adjust, loosen the locknut and turn the pedal stopper. Then tighten the locknut.
7. Make sure the throttle closes completely when the accelerator pedal is released.

1981

1. Check pedal height (dimension "H", **Figure 91**). It should be 4 5/8 in. (118mm). To adjust, loosen the locknut and turn the stopper bolt. Then tighten the locknut.
2. Disengage the fast idle cam. To do this, hold the choke valve fully open and move the throttle lever by hand.
3. Move the throttle lever to the completely closed position.
4. Loosen the locknut (**Figure 93**). Tighten the adjusting nut until the throttle lever is just about to move.
5. Loosen the adjusting nut one or 2 turns to give throttle cable play of 0.039-0.098 in. (1.0-2.5mm). Then tighten the locknut.
6. Floor the accelerator and measure clearance "T" (**Figure 91**). This is the clearance between the back of the accelerator peal and the floor (not the floor mat or carpet). It should be 0.08-0.16 in. (2-4mm). To adjust, loosen the locknut and turn the pedal stopper. Then tighten the locknut.
7. Make sure the throttle closes completely when the accelerator pedal is released.

Table 1 IDLE COMPENSATOR OPENING TEMPERATURES

Model Year	Begin Open	Fully Open
1974	140F° (60°C)	167°F (75°C)
1975 on		
No. 1 valve	140°F (60°C)	158°F (70°C)
No. 2 valve	158°F (70°C)	194°F (90°C)

Table 2 CARBURETOR SPECIFICATIONS

Jets and air bleeds	
1970-1971	
Primary main jet	115
Secondary main jet	155
Primary main air bleed	240
Secondary main air bleed	120
Primary slow air bleed	180
Secondary slow air bleed	100
1972	
Primary main jet	112
Secondary main jet	155
Primary main air bleed	240
Secondary main air bleed	120
Primary slow jet	48
Secondary slow jet	180
Primary slow air bleed	150
Secondary slow air bleed	100
1973	
Primary main jet	97.5
Secondary main jet	170
Primary main air bleed	65
Secondary main air bleed	60
Primary slow jet	48
Secondary slow jet	90
Primary slow air bleed	145
Secondary slow air bleed	100
Power jet	53
1974	
Primary main jet	100
Secondary main jet	170
Primary main air bleed	60
Secondary main air bleed	60
Primary slow jet	45
Secondary slow jet	90
Primary slow air bleed	145
Secondary slow air bleed	100
Power jet	41
1975	
Primary main jet	99
Secondary main jet	160
Primary main air bleed	70
Secondary main air bleed	60
Primary slow jet	48
Secondary slow jet	80
Power valve	43

(continued)

Table 2 CARBURETOR SPECIFICATIONS (continued)

1976	
Primary main jet	
California automatic transmission	101
All others	99
Secondary main jet	160
Primary main air bleed	70
Secondary main air bleed	60
Primary slow jet	48
Secondary slow jet	100
Power valve	
California automatic transmission	40
All others	43
1977	
Primary main jet	
California	101
Non-California	99
Secondary main jet	160
Primary main air bleed	70
Secondary main air bleed	60
Primary slow jet	48
Secondary slow jet	100
Power valve	
California	40
Non-California	43
1978 California	
Primary main jet	101
Secondary main jet	158
Primary main air bleed	70
Secondary main air bleed	60
Primary slow jet	48
Secondary slow jet	70
Power valve	40
1978 non-California	
Primary main jet	103
Secondary main jet	100
Primary main air bleed	60
Secondary main air bleed	60
Primary slow jet	48
Secondary slow jet	70
Power valve	43
1979 (except cab and chassis)*	
Primary main jet	
U.S.	103
Canada	106
Secondary main jet	
U.S.	158
Canada	160
Primary main air bleed	
California	70
Non-California	60
Secondary main air bleed	60
Primary slow jet	48
Secondary slow jet	70
Power valve	
California	35
Non-California	43
1979 (cab and chassis)*	
Primary main jet	
California	101
Non-California	103

(continued)

Table 2 CARBURETOR SPECIFICATIONS (continued)

Secondary main jet	150
Primary main air bleed	
California	70
Non-California	60
Secondary main air bleed	60
Primary slow jet	48
Secondary slow jet	
California	60
Non-California	50
Power valve	35
1980	
Primary main jet	
California	104
49 states	105
Canada	106
Secondary main jet	
U.S. (except heavy duty)**	158
U.S. (heavy duty)**	140
Canada (except cab and chassis)*	160
Canada (cab and chassis)	140
Primary main air bleed	
California	70
Non-California	60
Secondary main air bleed	60
Primary slow jet	48
Secondary slow jet	
U.S. (except heavy duty)**	70
California (heavy duty)	60
49 states (heavy duty)	50
Canada (except cab and chassis)*	70
Canada (cab and chassis)	50
Power valve	
All U.S., Canada cab and chassis*	35
Canada (except cab and chassis)	43
1981	
Primary main jet	
California (except heavy duty)**	112
California (heavy duty)**	110
Non-California	105
Secondary main jet	
California (except heavy duty)**	155
California (heavy duty)**	145
Non-California	155
Primary main air bleed	
California	90
Non-California	80
Secondary main air bleed	60
Primary slow jet	47
Secondary slow jet	
California (except heavy duty)**	100
California (heavy duty)**	80
Non-California	100
Power valve	
California	35
Non-California	40

(continued)

Table 2 CARBURETOR SPECIFICATIONS (continued)

Float adjustment		
Dimension "h" (needle valve stroke)		
1970-1974		0.059 in. (1.5mm)
1975-on		0.051-0.067 in. (1.3-1.7mm)
Dimension "H" (float level)		
1970-1974		Not measured
1975-on		0.283 in. (7.2mm)
Fast idle cam adjustment	**Step**	**Clearance**
1972 (manual)	First	0.047 in. (1.19mm)
1972 (automatic)	First	0.055 in. (1.40mm)
1973-1974 (manual)	Second	0.035-0.039 in. (0.9-1.0mm)
1973-1974 (automatic)	Second	0.044-0.048 in. (1.12-1.22mm)
1975-1976 (manual)	Second	0.040-0.048 in. (1.01-1.21mm)
1975-1976 (automatic)	Second	0.048-0.052 in. (1.23-1.33mm)
1977-1979 (manual)	First	0.053-0.058 in. (1.33-1.47mm)
1977-1979 (auomatic)	First	0.062-0.068 in. (1.58-1.72mm)
1980 (manual)	Second	0.032-0.037 in. (0.81-0.95mm)
1980 (automatic)	Second	0.040-0.046 in. (1.02-1.16mm)
1981 (manual)	Second	0.032-0.037 in. (0.81-0.95mm)
1981 (automatic)	Second	
California		0.038-0.044 in. (0.98-1.12mm)
Non-California		0.039-0.043 in. (1.0-1.10mm)
Dashpot adjusting speed		
1972	2,400-2,500 rpm	
1973-1974	1,600-1,800 rpm	
1975-1980 (manual)	1,900-2,100 rpm	
1975-1980 (automatic)	1,650-1,850 rpm	
1981 (automatic only)	1,400-1,600 rpm	

*Cab and chassis models were sold originally without beds.
**Heavy duty models have a letter "E" in the vehicle identification number. Standard models do not.

Table 3 FUEL PUMP SPECIFICATIONS

Mechanical pump	
Capacity	
1970-1980	2 1/8 pt. (1,000cc) in one minute at 1,000 rpm
1981	1 3/4 qt. (1,700cc) in one minute at 1,000 rpm
Fuel pressure	
1970-1974	2.6-3.4 psi (0.18-0.24 kg/cm^2)
1975-on	3.0-3.8 psi (0.21-0.27 kg/cm^2)
Electric fuel pump	
Capacity	1 1/2 qt. (1,400cc) in one minute
Fuel pressure	
1977-1978	**4.6 psi (0.32 kg/cm^2) or less**
1979-on	**3.1-3.8 psi (0.22-0.27 kg/cm^2)**

6

NOTE: If you own a 1982 model, first check the Supplement at the back of the book for any new service information.

CHAPTER SEVEN

COOLING, HEATING, AND AIR CONDITIONING

This chapter includes service procedures for the thermostat, water pump, radiator, heater and air conditioner. Cooling system flushing procedures are also described. Cooling system specifications are listed in **Table 1** at the end of the chapter.

COOLING SYSTEM FLUSHING

Refer to **Figure 1** (L-series) or **Figure 2** (NAPS-Z). The recommended coolant is a 50/50 mixture of ethylene glycol-based antifreeze and water. This protects the system from freezing to approximately -36° C (-32°

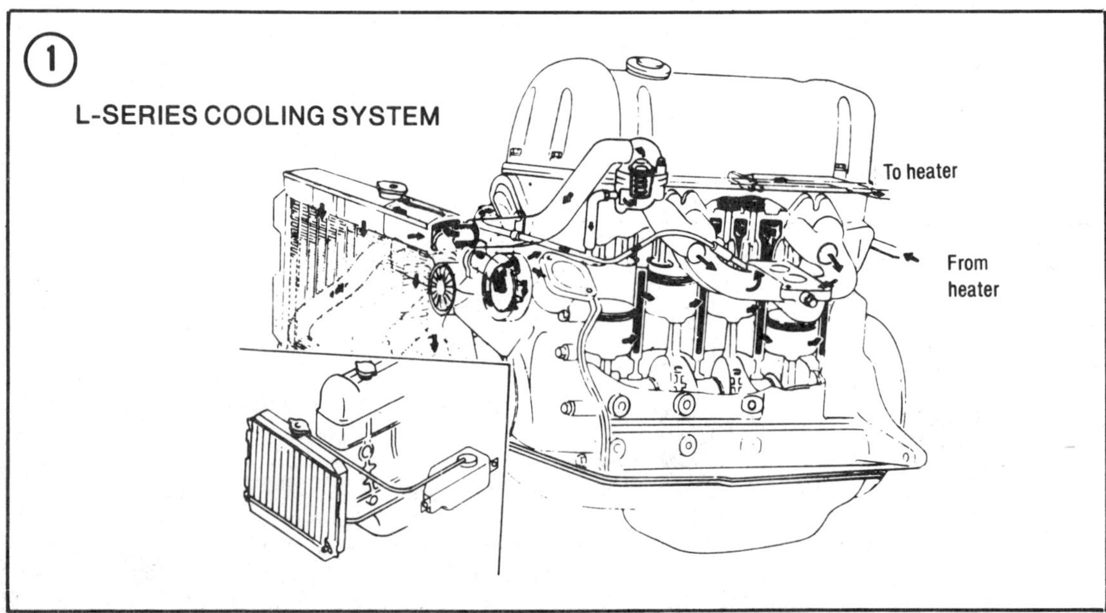

2

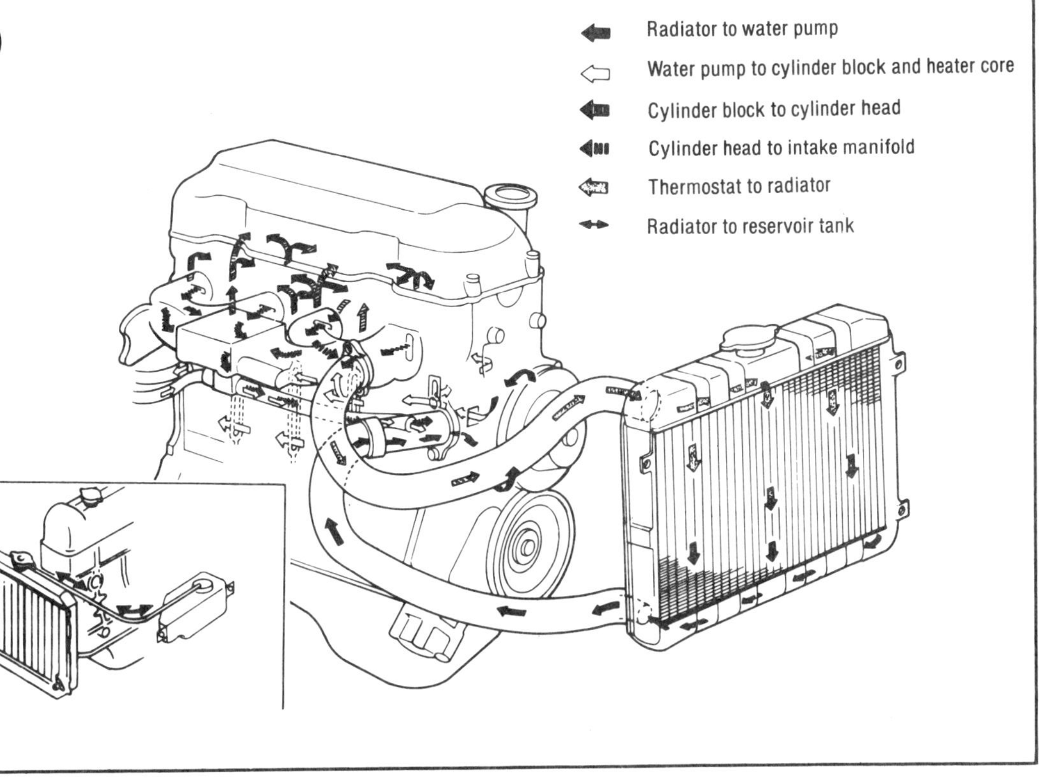

Radiator to water pump

Water pump to cylinder block and heater core

Cylinder block to cylinder head

Cylinder head to intake manifold

Thermostat to radiator

Radiator to reservoir tank

3

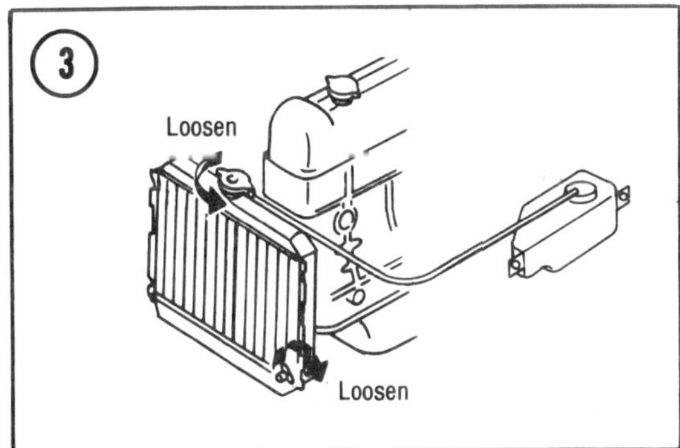

4

F). Higher antifreeze concentrations may be used in colder areas.

The system should be drained, flushed and refilled at intervals specified in Chapter Three. If desired, a chemical flushing agent may be used prior to the flushing method described here.

1. Coolant can stain concrete and harm plants. Park the truck over a gutter or similar area.
2. Place the heater temperature lever on the instrument panel in the HOT position.
3. Open the tap at the bottom of the radiator (**Figure 3**). Remove the engine drain plug. See **Figure 4** (L-series) or **Figure 5** (NAPS-Z).
4. After the engine has finished draining, install the plug and close the tap.
5. Remove the thermostat as described under *Thermostat* in this chapter. Temporarily reinstall the water outlet elbow.
6. Disconnect the top radiator hose from the radiator. Disconnect the bottom hose from the engine.
7. Disconnect the heater hoses from the engine.

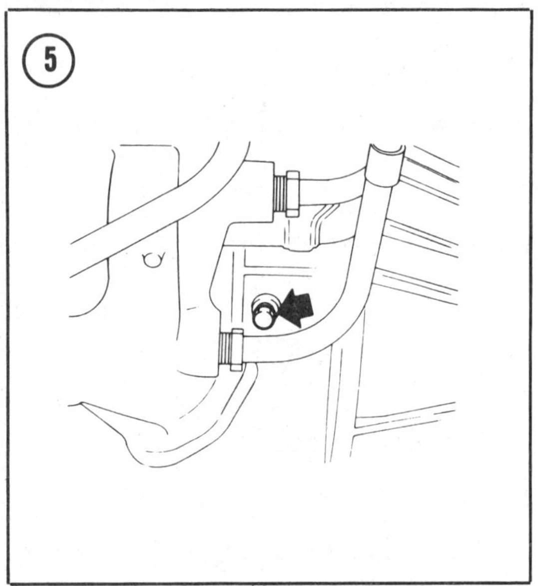

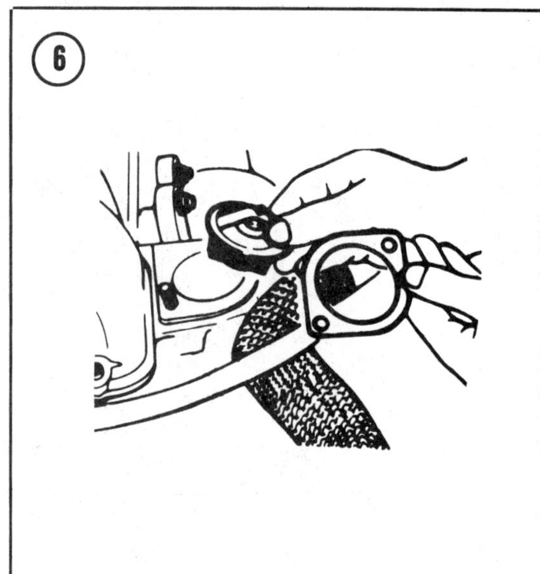

8. Connect a garden hose to one heater hose. This does not have to be a positive fit, as long as most of the water enters the heater hose. Run water into the heater hose until clear water flows from the other heater hose.
9. Insert the garden hose into the top radiator hose. Run water into the hose until clear water flows from the bottom hose.
10. Insert the garden hose into the hose fitting at the bottom of the radiator. Run water into the radiator until clear water flows from the top fitting.
11. Turn off the water.
12. Remove the engine drain plug and let out any remaining water. Reinstall the drain plug.
13. Connect the hoses to the engine and radiator.
14. Fill the cooling system with a 50/50 mixture of ethylene glycol-based antifreeze and water, even if you live in an area that doesn't require this degree of freeze protection. The antifreeze makes a good corrosion inhibitor. Cooling system capacity is listed in **Table 1**.
15. Run the engine for several minutes and check for leaks. Recheck coolant level and top off as needed.

THERMOSTAT

The thermostat blocks water flow to the radiator when the engine is cold. As the engine warms up, the thermostat gradually opens, allowing water to circulate through the radiator.

Removal and Testing

1. Make sure the engine is cool.
2. Drain about one gallon of coolant from the radiator. If the coolant is clean, save it for reuse.
3. Detach the hose from the water outlet elbow.
4. Unbolt the outlet elbow from the engine and lift it off. Lift out the thermostat. See **Figure 6** (L-series) or **Figure 7** (NAPS-Z).
5. Submerge the thermostat in water with a thermometer (**Figure 8**).

NOTE
Support the thermostat with wire so it doesn't touch the sides or bottom of the pan.

6. Heat the water until the thermostat just begins to open, then check the water temperature (**Table 1**). If the valve opens at the wrong temperature or fails to open, replace the thermostat.

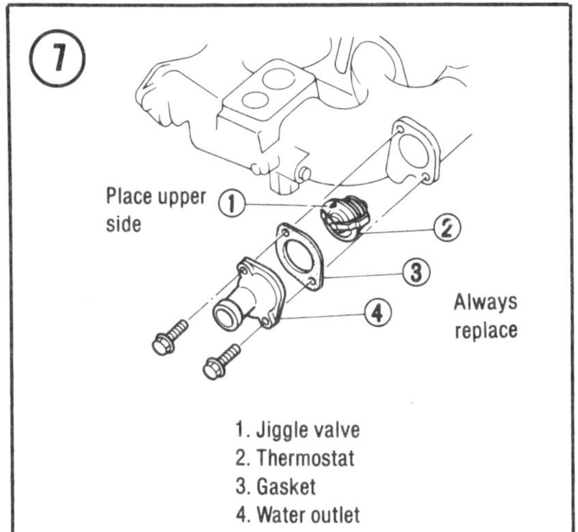

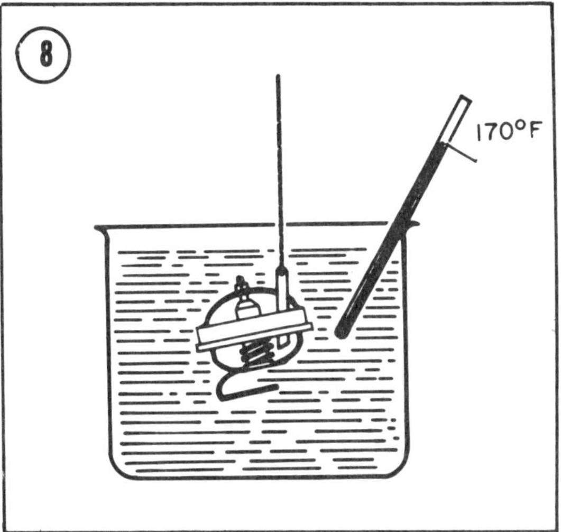

7. Measure the maximum lift of the thermostat valve. To do this, mark a screwdriver at a point 8 mm (0.31 in.) from the tip. The screwdriver is used as a measuring device. Heat the water to specified opening temperature and measure the lift of the valve with the marked screwdriver. If valve lift is less than 8 mm (0.31 in.), replace the thermostat.
8. Let the water cool. Make sure the thermostat closes.

Installation

1. If a new thermostat is being installed, test as described in the preceding section. The new thermostat might be bad and testing will prevent the need to do the job over.
2. Install the thermostat in the engine. On NAPS-Z engines, make sure the jiggle valve (**Figure 7**) is toward the top when the thermostat is installed.
3. Install the water outlet elbow. Use a new gasket, coated on both sides with gasket sealer.
4. Tighten the outlet elbow, then reconnect the hose.

RADIATOR

Removal/Installation

1. Make sure the engine is cool enough to touch.
2. Coolant can stain concrete and harm plants. Park the car over a gutter or similar area.
3. Open the drain tap at the bottom of the radiator (**Figure 3**). Let the coolant drain.
4. Disconnect the radiator hoses (and reservoir tank hoses if so equipped).
5. Detach the fan shroud from the radiator. Lay it back over the fan.
6. Remove the radiator mounting bolts and lift the radiator out.
7. Installation is the reverse of removal. Fill the engine with a 50/50 mixture of ethylene glycol-based antifreeze and water. Run the engine and check for leaks.

FAN

Removal/Installation

1. Remove the radiator and shroud as described in the preceding section.
2. Loosen the alternator mounting and adjusting bolts. Push the alternator toward the engine to loosen the fan belt, then take the belt off.
3. Detach the fan from the water pump and take it out. **Figure 9** shows the fluid-drive fan used on late L-series and NAPS-Z engines. The fixed-blade fan used on early L-series engines is basically the same.
4. Installation is the reverse of removal. Fill the cooling system with a 50/50 mixture of ethylene glycol-based antifreeze and water. Run the engine and check for leaks.

9
FAN (LATE L-SERIES)
M6: (2.9-7.2, 0.4-1.0)
M8: (7-12, 1.0-1.6)
(0.31-0.47)8-12/(22, 10)
Fan
Pump gasket
(Always replace)
Water pump with fan
coupling
Fan belt
T: (ft.-lb., mkg)
Belt deflection (in.)mm/(lb.,kg)

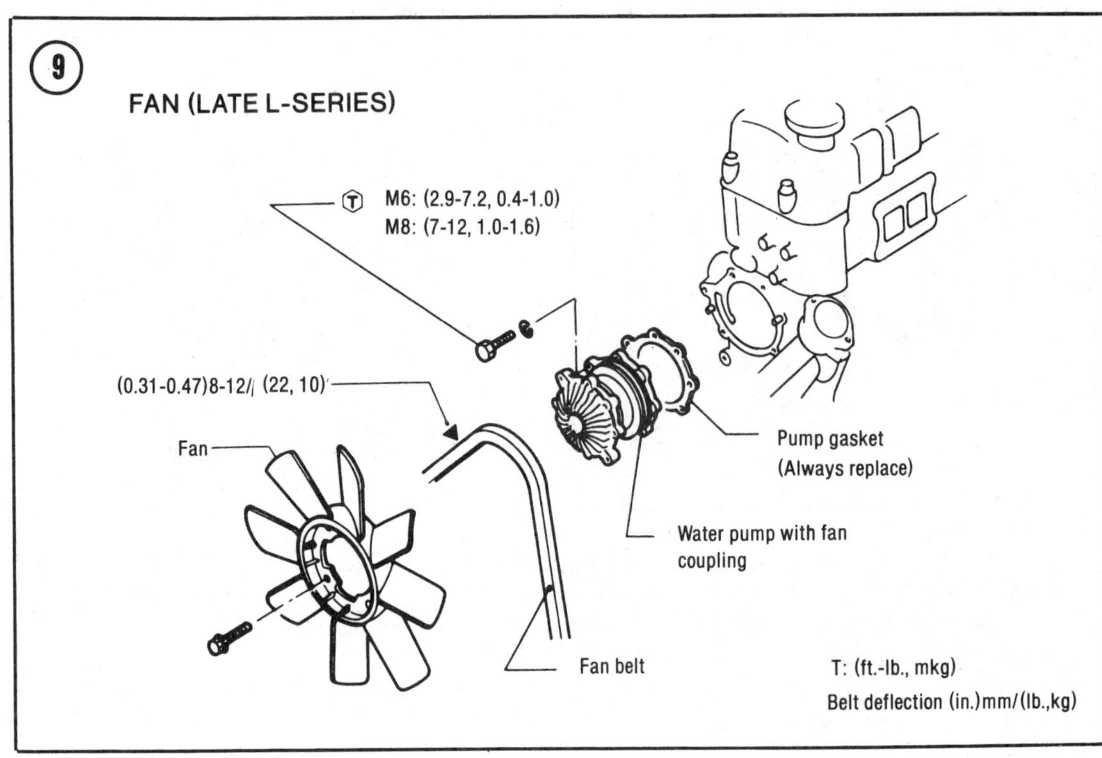

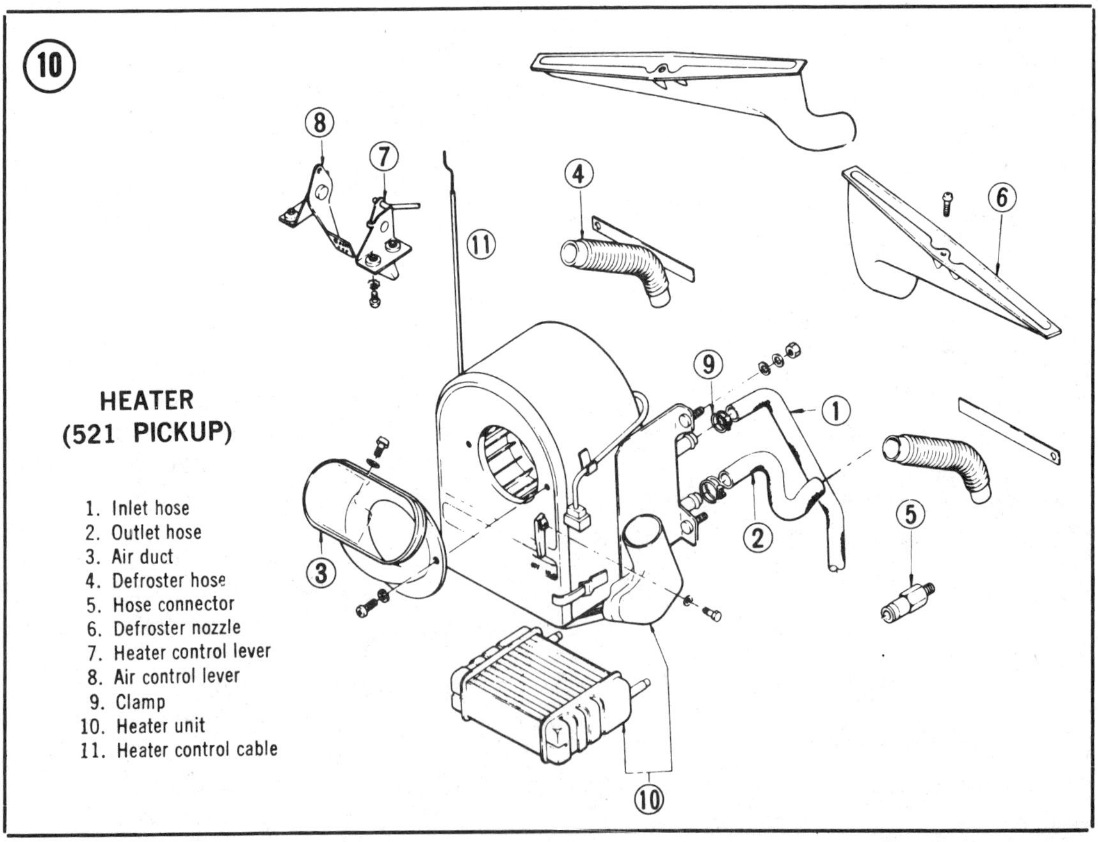

10
HEATER
(521 PICKUP)
1. Inlet hose
2. Outlet hose
3. Air duct
4. Defroster hose
5. Hose connector
6. Defroster nozzle
7. Heater control lever
8. Air control lever
9. Clamp
10. Heater unit
11. Heater control cable

Inspection

1. Check the fan for obvious damage such as broken blades. Replace as needed.
2. On fluid-drive fans, check the fan coupling for damage or oil leaks. Replace if these are found. Since the fan coupling and water pump are a single unit, the water pump must be replaced if the fan coupling is defective.

WATER PUMP

On fluid-drive fans, the water pump and fan coupling are combined into a single unit. If one or the other is defective, both must be replaced.

A water pump may warn of impending failure by making noise. If the seal is defective, coolant may leak from behind the fan.

Removal/Installation

1. Remove the fan as described in the preceding section.
2. Remove the water pump bolts. See **Figure 9**. Take the water pump off the engine.
3. Installation is the reverse of removal. Use a new gasket, coated on both sides with gasket sealer. Tighten the thin bolts to 3.9-9.8 N•m (3-7 ft.-lb.) Tighten the thick bolts to 10-16 N•m (7-12 ft.-lb.).

HEATER

Removal/Installation (521 Pickup)

Refer to **Figure 10** for this procedure.

1. Disconnect negative cable from battery.
2. Drain the cooling system by opening the tap on the bottom of the radiator. Remove the plug from the right side of the cylinder block.
3. Place a plastic sheet (such as a painting dropcloth) on the floor to catch any coolant remaining in the heater core.
4. Disconnect the heater hoses at the firewall.
5. Label and disconnect the heater wires and control cables.
6. Working in the engine compartment, remove 4 nuts securing the heater to the firewall. Withdraw heater into passenger compartment.
7. Installation is the reverse of these steps. Fill the cooling system with a 50/50 mixture of ethylene glycol-based antifreeze and water.

Removal/Installation (620 Pickup)

Figure 11 shows the 620 pickup heater.

1. Disconnect negative cable from battery.
2. Drain the cooling system by opening the tap at the bottom of the radiator and removing the plug from the left side of the engine block.
3. Place a plastic sheet (such as a painting dropcloth) on the floor to catch any coolant remaining in the heater core.
4. Detach the heater hoses from the heater core and water cock.
5. Remove the console (if so equipped).
6. Remove the defroster hoses.
7. Disconnect the cables from the air intake valve (**Figure 12**), room valve (**Figure 13**), and water cock (**Figure 14**).
8. Disconnect 2 fan motor wires and 2 resistor wires from the heater.
9. Remove 3 heater securing bolts. Take the heater out.
10. Install in the reverse order. Turn the air lever on the instrument panel to HOT. Take the truck for a short drive, then top up the cooling system as needed.

Removal/Installation (720 Pickup)

Refer to **Figure 15** for this procedure.

1. Disconnect the negative cable from the battery.
2. Drain the cooling system. See *Cooling System Flushing* in this chapter.
3. Place a plastic sheet, such as a painting dropcloth, on the floor of the truck.
4. On 1980 trucks without air conditioning, remove the heater duct, then disconnect the heater hoses. See **Figure 16**.

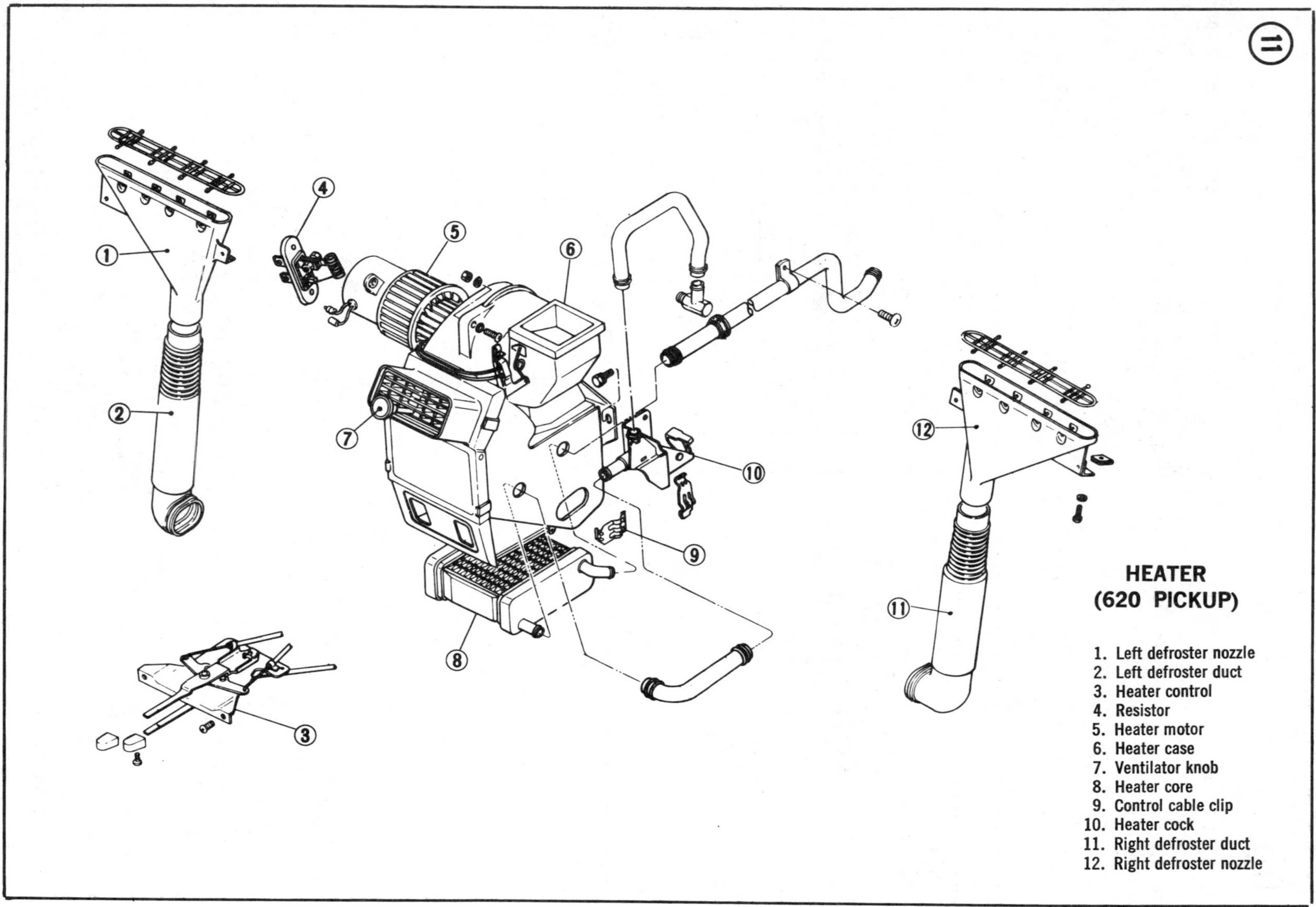
11
1
2
3
4
5
6
7
8
9
10
11
12
HEATER
(620 PICKUP)
1. Left defroster nozzle
2. Left defroster duct
3. Heater control
4. Resistor
5. Heater motor
6. Heater case
7. Ventilator knob
8. Heater core
9. Control cable clip
10. Heater cock
11. Right defroster duct
12. Right defroster nozzle

(12)

(13)

(14)

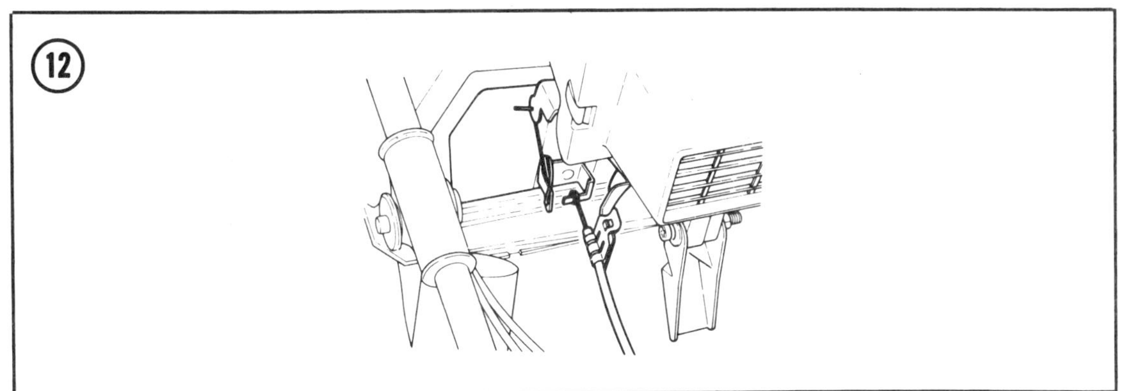

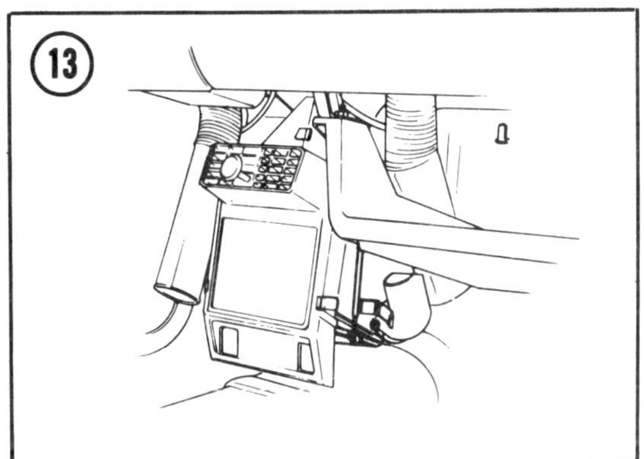

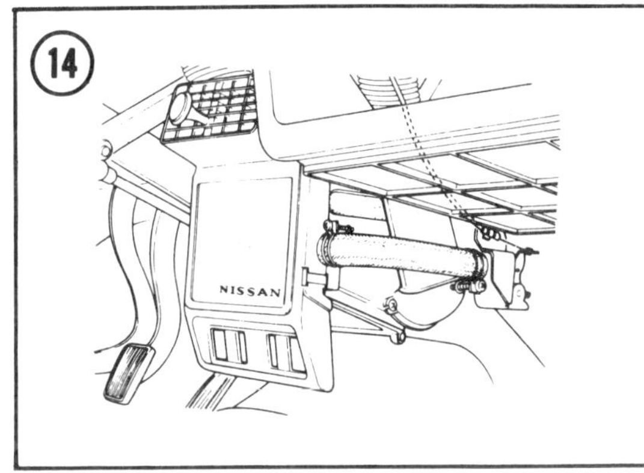

(15)

Side defroster nozzle
Defroster nozzle
Center defroster duct
Defroster nozzle
Center ventilator duct
Side defroster nozzle
Blower unit
Heater duct
Heater unit

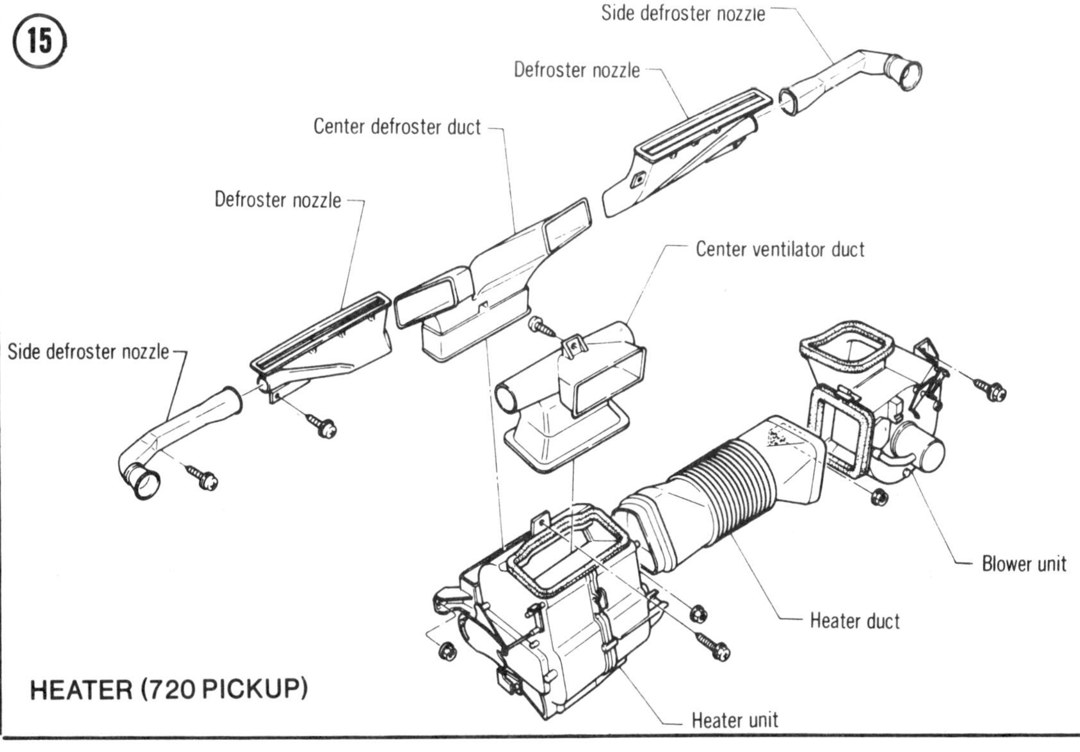

HEATER (720 PICKUP)

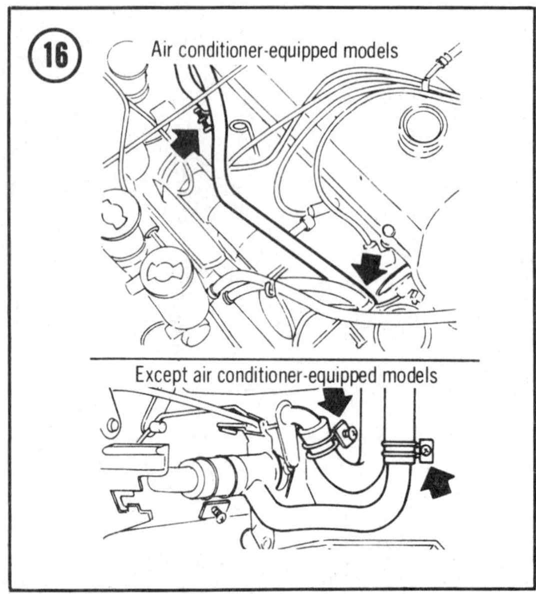

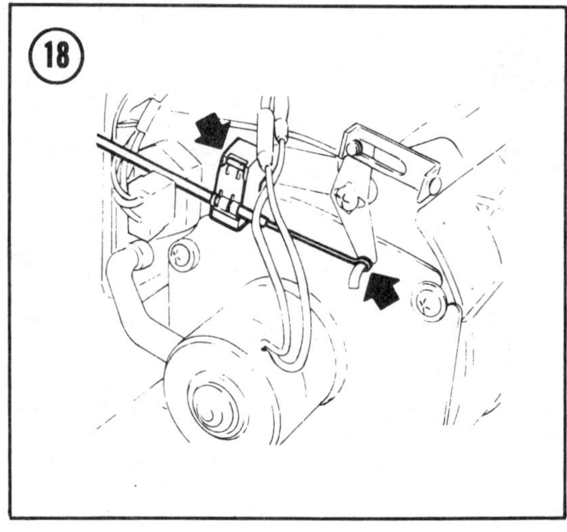

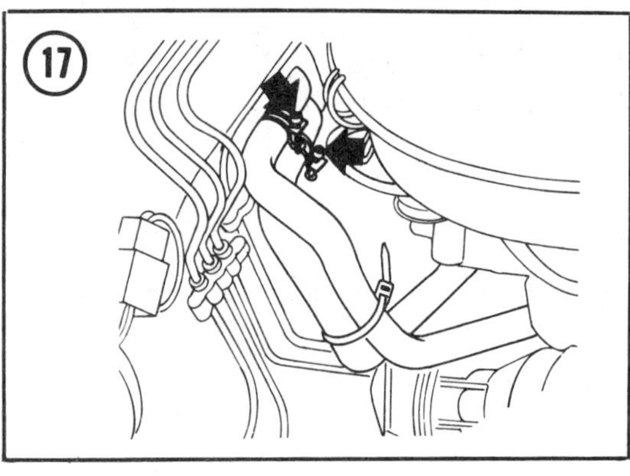

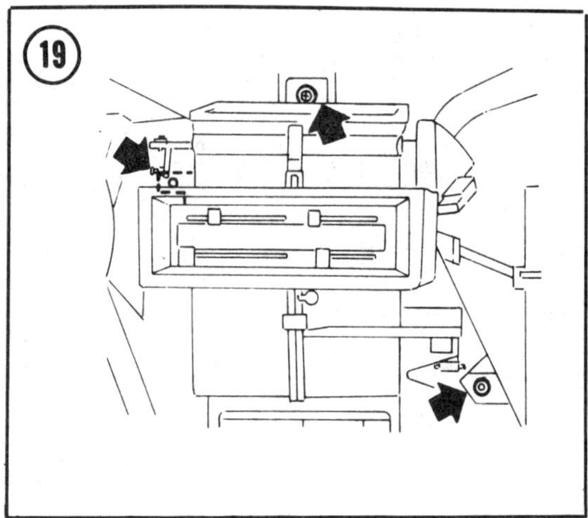

5. On 1980 trucks with air conditioning, disconnect the heater hoses from the engine. See **Figure 16**.

6. On 1981 trucks, disconnect the heater hoses at the firewall. See **Figure 17**.

7. Remove the console and instrument panel as described in Chapter Fourteen.

8. Disconnect the air intake cable from the heater blower unit. See **Figure 18**.

9. If equipped with air conditioning, remove the heater blower unit (**Figure 15**). Remove the air conditioner mounting nuts and bolts, but do not take the air conditioner out.

10. Remove the heater fasteners (**Figure 19**), then take the heater out.

11. Installation is the reverse of removal. Fill the cooling system as described under *Cooling System Flushing*. Turn the temperature control lever to HOT and run the engine for several minutes. Recheck coolant level and top up as needed.

AIR CONDITIONING

This section covers the maintenance and minor repairs that can prevent or correct most air conditioning problems. Major repairs require special training and tools, and should be left to a Datsun dealer or air conditioning shop.

SYSTEM OPERATION

A schematic of the air conditioning system is shown in **Figure 20**. These 5 basic components are common to all air conditioning systems:

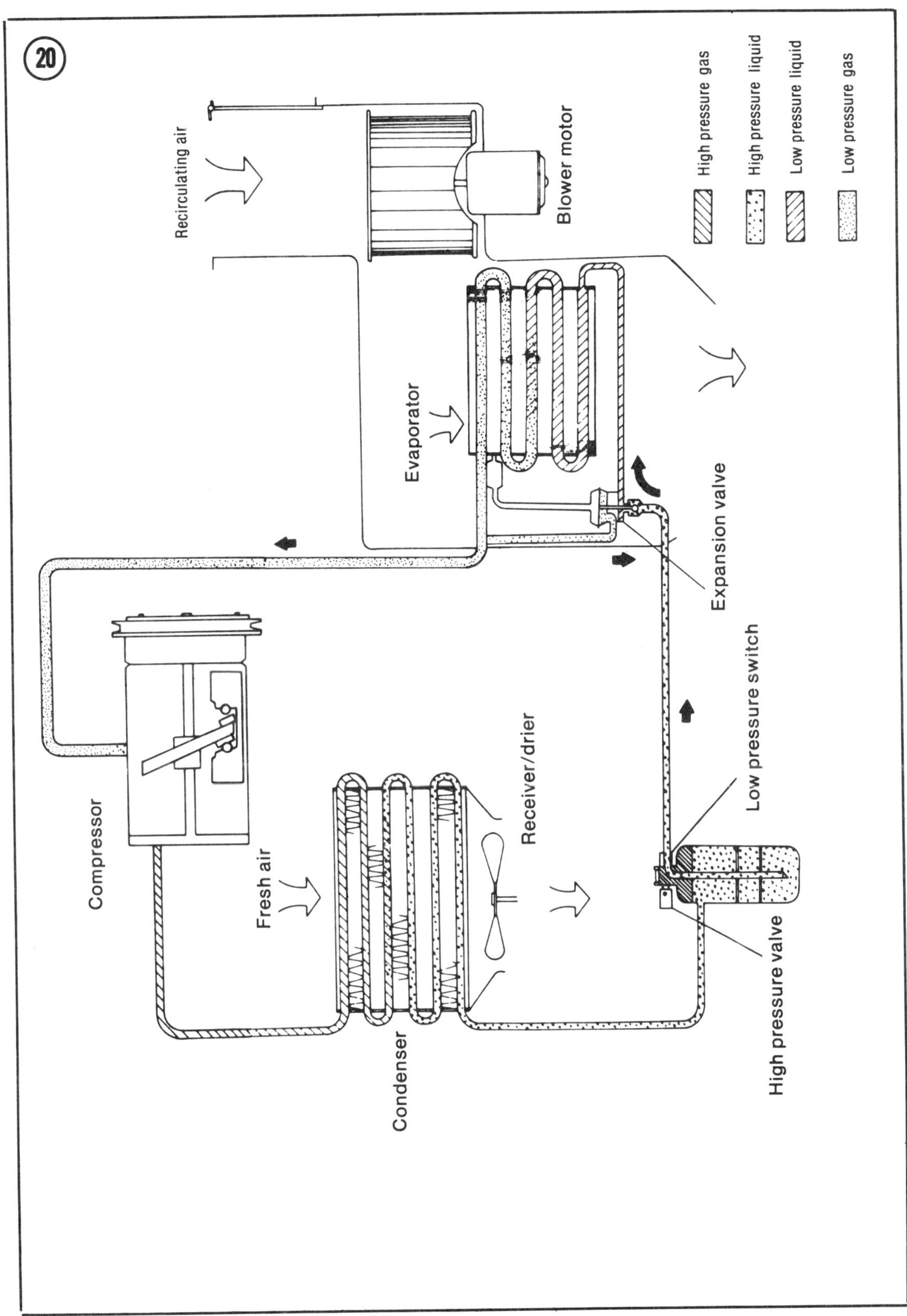
20
Recirculating air
Blower motor
High pressure gas
High pressure liquid
Low pressure liquid
Low pressure gas
Evaporator
Expansion valve
Low pressure switch
Receiver/drier
Compressor
Fresh air
Condenser
High pressure valve

a. Compressor
b. Condenser
c. Receiver/drier
d. Expansion valve
e. Evaporator

CAUTION
The components, connected with high-pressure hoses and tubes, form a closed loop. The refrigerant in the system is under very high pressure. It can cause frostbite if it touches skin, and blindness if it touches the eyes. If discharged near a flame, the refrigerant creates poisonous gas. If the refrigerant can is hooked up wrong, it can explode. For these reasons, ***read this entire section*** *before working on the system.*

For practical purposes, the cycle begins at the compressor. The refrigerant, in a warm, low-pressure vapor state, enters the low-pressure side of the compressor. It is compressed to a high-pressure hot vapor and pumped out of the high-pressure side to the condenser.

Air flow through the condenser removes heat from the refrigerant and transfers the heat to the outside air. As the heat is removed, the refrigerant condenses to a warm, high-pressure liquid.

The refrigerant then flows to the receiver/drier where moisture is removed and impurities are filtered out. The refrigerant is stored in the receiver/drier until it is needed. The receiver/drier incorporates a sight glass that permits visual monitoring of the condition of the refrigerant as it flows. From the receiver/drier, the refrigerant then flows to the expansion valve. The expansion valve is thermostatically controlled and meters refrigerant to the evaporator. As the refrigerant leaves the expansion valve it changes from a warm, high-pressure liquid to a cold, low-pressure liquid.

In the evaporator, the refrigerant removes heat from the passenger compartment air that is blown across the evaporator's fins and tubes. In the process, the refrigerant changes from a cold, low-pressure liquid to a warm, high-pressure vapor. The vapor flows back to the compressor, where the cycle begins again.

GET TO KNOW YOUR VEHICLE'S SYSTEM

Locate each of the following components in turn:

a. Compressor
b. Condenser
c. Receiver/drier
d. Expansion valve
e. Evaporator

Compressor

The compressor (**Figure 21**) is located on the front of the engine, like the alternator, and is driven by a V-belt. The large pulley on the front of the compressor contains an electromagnetic clutch. This activates and operates the compressor when the air conditioning is switched on.

Condenser

The condenser is mounted in front of the radiator (**Figure 21**). Air passing through the fins and tubes removes heat from the refrigerant in the same manner it removes heat from the engine coolant as it passes through the radiator.

Receiver/Drier

The receiver/drier (**Figure 21**) is a small tank-like unit, usually mounted to one of the wheel wells. It incorporates a sight glass through which refrigerant flow can be seen. The refrigerant's appearance is used to troubleshoot the system.

Expansion Valve

The expansion valve (**Figure 22**) is located between the receiver/drier and the evaporator. It is mounted on the evaporator housing.

Evaporator

The evaporator (**Figure 22**) is located in the passenger compartment cooling unit, beneath the instrument panel. Warm air is blown across the fins and tubes, where it is cooled and dried and then ducted into the passenger compartment.

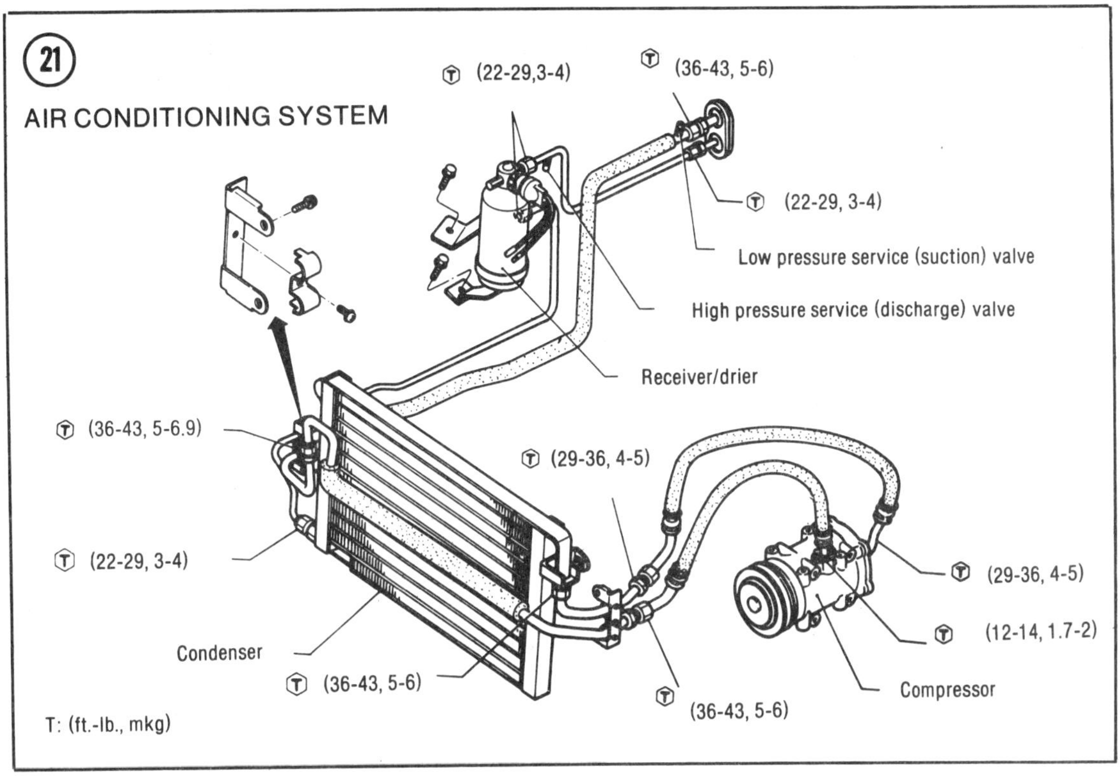

21

AIR CONDITIONING SYSTEM

T (22-29,3-4)
T (36-43, 5-6)
T (22-29, 3-4)
Low pressure service (suction) valve
High pressure service (discharge) valve
Receiver/drier
T (36-43, 5-6.9)
T (29-36, 4-5)
T (22-29, 3-4)
T (29-36, 4-5)
T (12-14, 1.7-2)
Condenser
T (36-43, 5-6)
T (36-43, 5-6)
Compressor
T: (ft.-lb., mkg)

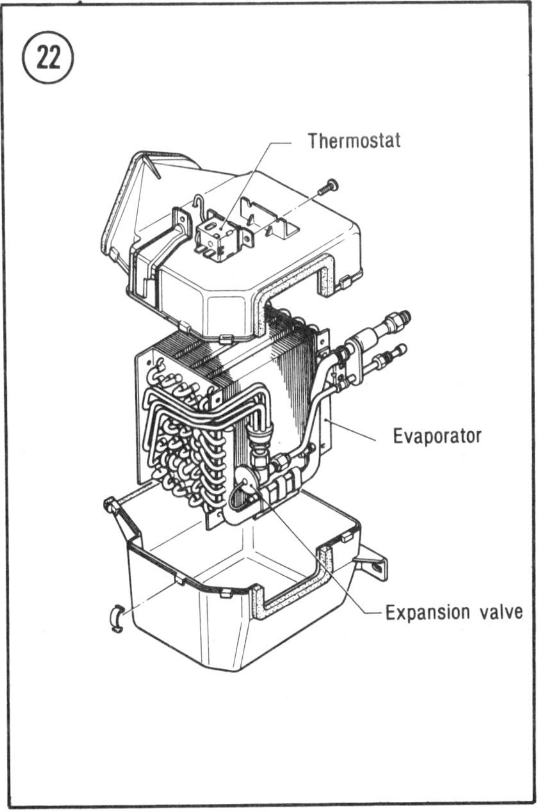

ROUTINE MAINTENANCE

Basic maintenance of the air conditioning system is easy; at least once a month, even in cold weather, start your engine, turn on the air conditioner, and operate it at each of the control settings. Operate the air conditioner for about 10 minutes, with the engine running at 1,500 rpm. This will ensure that the compressor seal does not deform from sitting in the same position for a long period of time. If this occurs, the seal is likely to leak.

The efficiency of the air conditioning system also depends in great part on the efficiency of the cooling system. This is because the heat from the condenser passes through the radiator. If the cooling system is dirty or low on coolant, it may be impossible to operate the air conditioner without overheating. Inspect the coolant. If necessary, flush and refill the cooling system as described under *Cooling System Flushing* in this chapter.

With an air hose and a soft brush, clean the radiator and condenser fins and tubes to remove bugs, leaves, and other imbedded debris.

Check drive belt tension as described under *Drive Belts*, Chapter Three.

If the condition of the cooling system thermostat is in doubt, test it as described under *Thermostat* in this chapter.

Once you are sure the cooling system is in good condition, the air conditioning system can be inspected.

Inspection

1. Clean all lines, fittings, and system components with solvent and a clean rag. Pay particular attention to the fittings; oily dirt around connections almost certainly indicates a leak. Oil from the compressor will migrate through the system to the leak. Carefully tighten the connection, but don't overtighten and strip the threads. If the leak persists, it will soon be apparent once again as oily dirt accumulates. Clean the sight glass with a clean, dry cloth.
2. Clean the condenser fins and tubes with a soft brush and an air hose, or with a high-pressure stream of water from a garden hose. Remove bugs, leaves, and other imbedded debris. Carefully straighten any bent fins with a screwdriver, taking care not to puncture or dent the tubes.
3. Start the engine and check the operation of the blower motor and the compressor clutch by turning the controls on and off. If either the blower or the clutch fails to operate, shut off the engine and check the fuses and fusible links. If they are burned out, replace them. If the fuses are good, remove them and clean the fuse holder contacts. Then check the clutch and blower operation again.

Testing

1. Place the transmission in neutral. Set the parking brake.
2. Start the engine and run it at a fast idle.
3. Set the temperature control to its coldest setting and the blower to high. Allow the system to operate for 10 minutes with the doors and windows open. Then shut them and set the blower on its lowest setting.
4. Check air temperature at the outlet. It should be noticeably colder than the surrounding air. If not, the refrigerant level is probably low. Check the sight glass as described in the following step.
5. Run the engine at a fast idle and switch on the air conditioning. Look at the sight glass (**Figure 23**) and check for the following:
   a. Bubbles—the refrigerant level is low.
   b. Oily or cloudy—the system is contaminated. Have it serviced by a dealer or air conditioning shop.
   c. Clear glass—either there is enough refrigerant, too much, or the system is so close to empty it can't make bubbles. If there is no difference between the inlet and outlet air temperatures, the system is probably near empty. If the system does blow cold air, it either has the right amount of refrigerant, or too much. To tell which, turn off the air conditioner while watching the sight glass. If the refrigerant foams, then clears up, the amount is correct. If it doesn't foam, but stays clear, there is too much.

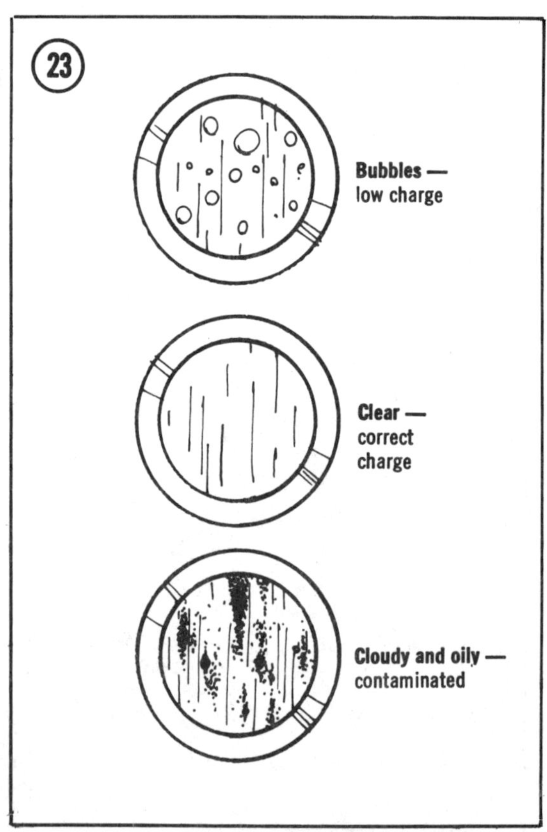

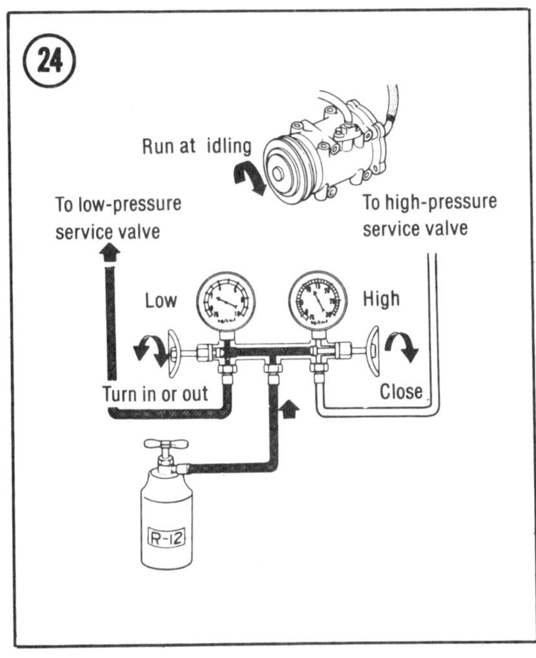

REFRIGERANT

The air conditioning system uses a refrigerant called dichlorodifluoromethane, or R-12.

WARNING
R-12 creates freezing temperatures when it evaporates. This can cause frostbite if it touches skin, and blindness if it touches the eyes. If discharged near an open flame, R-12 creates poisonous gas. If the refrigerant can is hooked up to the pressure side of the compressor, it may explode. Always wear safety goggles when working with R-12.

Charging

This section applies to partially discharged or empty air conditioning systems. If a hose has been disconnected, or any internal part of the system exposed to air, the system should be evacuated and recharged by a dealer or air conditioning shop. Recharge kits are available from auto parts stores. Be sure the kit includes a gauge set.

1. Carefully read and understand the gauge manufacturer's instructions before charging the system.
2. Place the refrigerant can in a pan of ***warm not hot*** water.

WARNING
Water temperature must not exceed 40° C (104° F). If it does, the can may explode.

4. Turn the handle of the refrigerant can tap valve all the way counterclockwise to retract the needle.
5. Turn the disc on the can tap valve all the way counterclockwise. Install the valve on the can.
6. Connect the center hose to the can tap valve.
7. Make sure the gauge valves are closed.
8. Turn the can tap valve clockwise to make a hole in the can.
9. Turn the handle all the way counterclockwise to fill the center hose with air.
10. Slowly loosen the nut connecting the center hose to the gauge set, until hissing can be heard. Let this continue for a few seconds to purge air from the hose, then tighten the nut.

CAUTION
During the next steps, the refrigerant can must remain upright. If it is turned upside down, refrigerant will enter the system as a liquid, which may damage the compressor.

11. Open the low pressure valve (**Figure 24**). Adjust the valve so the gauge reads no more than 2.8 kg/cm^2 (40 psi).

CAUTION
Leave the high pressure valve closed at all times.

12. Run the engine at idle (below 1,500 rpm) and turn on the air conditioner. Let the system charge until the sight glass is free of air bubbles. See **Figure 23**.

NOTE
If the system is nearly empty, another can of refrigerant will be needed. Attach it as described in the following steps.

13. Close the low pressure valve.
14. Remove the can tap valve, and attach a new can. Don't make a hole in the new can yet.

7

15. Slightly loosen the can tap valve disc. Barely open the low pressure valve for a few seconds to purge air from the hose. Close the low pressure valve, then tighten the can tap valve disc.
16. Turn the can tap valve handle clockwise to make a hole in the can. Let the system charge until the sight glass is free of air bubbles.
17. Once the system is fully charged, close the low pressure valve.
18. Close the can tap valve. Very slowly loosen the charge line to allow any remaining refrigerant to escape.

WARNING

Wear gloves and safety goggles to prevent frostbite and blindness. Do not allow any open flame near the refrigerant, or poisonous gas may be formed.

19. Turn off the engine. Cover the compressor service valve fittings with a shop rag, then quickly disconnect them.
20. Install the caps on the service valves.

TROUBLESHOOTING

If the air conditioner fails to blow cold air, the following steps will help locate the problem.

1. First, stop the truck and look at the control settings. One of the most common air conditioning problems occurs when the temperature is set for maxumum cold and the blower is set on low. This promotes ice buildup on the evaporator fins and tubes, particularly in humid weather. Eventually, the evaporator will ice over completely and restrict air flow. Turn the blower on high and place a hand over an air outlet. If the blower is running but there is little or no air flowing through the outlet, the evaporator is probably iced up. Leave the blower on high and turn the temperature control off or to its warmest setting, and wait. It will take 10-15 minutes for the ice to start melting.
2. If the blower is not running, the fuse or fusible link may be blown, there may be a loose wiring connection, or the motor may be burned out. First, check the fuse block for a blown or incorrectly seated fuse. Check for a burned out fusible link. Then check the wiring for loose connections.
3. Shut off the engine and inspect the compressor drive belt. If loose or worn, tighten or replace. See *Drive Belts*, Chapter Three.
4. Start the engine. Check the compressor clutch by turning the air conditioner on and off. If the clutch does not activate, its fuse or fusible link may be blown, or the evaporator temperature-limiting switches may be defective. If the fuse or fusible link is defective, replace it. If not, have the system checked by a Datsun dealer or air conditioning shop.
5. If the system checks out okay to this point, start the engine, turn on the air conditioner, and watch the refrigerant through the sight glass. If it fills with bubbles after a few seconds, the refrigerant level is low. If the sight glass is oily or cloudy, the system is contaminated and should be serviced by a shop as soon as possible. Corrosion and deterioration occur very quickly, and if not taken care of at once will result in a very expensive repair job.
6. If the system still appears to be operating as it should but air flow into the passenger compartment is not cold, check the condenser and cooling system radiator for debris that could block air flow. Recheck the cooling system as described under *Inspection.*
7. If the preceding steps have not solved the problem, take the car to a dealer or air conditioning shop for service.

Table 1 COOLING SYSTEM SPECIFICATIONS

Capacity	
521 pickup	7 qt. (6.6 liters)
620 pickup	
1972-1974	6 3/8 qt. (6.0 liters)
1975-1977 (manual)	8 1/2 qt. (8 liters)
1975-1977 (automatic)	8 1/4 qt. (7.8 liters)
1978-1979 manual (including reservoir tank)	9 3/8 qt. (8.9 liters)
1978-1979 automatic (including reservoir tank)	9 1/8 qt. (8.7 liters)
720 pickup	
1980 manual (including reservoir tank)	9 3/8 qt. (8.9 liters)
1980 automatic (including reservoir tank)	9 1/8 qt. (8.9 liters)
1981 manual (including reservoir tank)	10 3/4 qt. (10.2 liters)
1981 automatic (including reservoir tank)	10 5/8 qt. (10.1 liters)
Thermostat opening temperature*	
Standard type	180° F (82° C)
For cold areas	190° F (88° C)
For hot areas	170° F (76.5° C)

*Actual opening temperature may vary slightly from specified temperature. This does not indicate a defective thermostat.

7

NOTE: If you own a 1982 or later model, first check the Supplement at the back of the book for any new service information.

CHAPTER EIGHT

ELECTRICAL SYSTEM

All models use a 12-volt negative ground battery and a 3-phase alternator. This chapter includes service procedures for the battery, starter, charging system, lighting system, ignition system, fuses, instruments, and windshield wipers. **Table 1** and **Table 2** are at the end of the chapter.

BATTERY

Care and Inspection

1. Disconnect both battery cables and remove the battery.
2. Clean the top of the battery with a baking soda and water solution. Scrub with a stiff bristle brush. Wipe battery clean with a cloth moistened in ammonia or baking soda solution.

CAUTION
Keep cleaning solution out of battery cells or the electrolyte will be seriously weakened.

3. Clean battery terminals with a stiff wire brush or one of the many tools made for this purpose.
4. Check entire battery case for cracks.
5. Install the battery and reconnect the battery cables, positive first then ground.

CAUTION
Be sure the battery cables are connected to the proper terminals. Connecting the battery backwards can damage the alternator.

6. Coat the battery connections with Vaseline or light mineral grease after tightening.
7. If the battery has removable filler caps, check electrolyte level. Top up with distilled water if necessary.

Testing

This procedure applies to batteries with removable filler caps. Testing sealed maintenance-free batteries requires special equipment, but a service station can make the test for a nominal fee.

Hydrometer testing is the best way to check battery condition. Use a hydrometer with numbered graduations from 1.100-1.300 rather than one with just color-coded bands. To use the hydrometer, squeeze the rubber ball, insert the tip in the cell, and release the ball (**Figure 1**).

Draw enough electrolyte to float the weighted float inside the hydrometer. Note the number in line with the surface of the electrolyte. This is the specific gravity for the cell. Return the electrolyte to the cell from which it came.

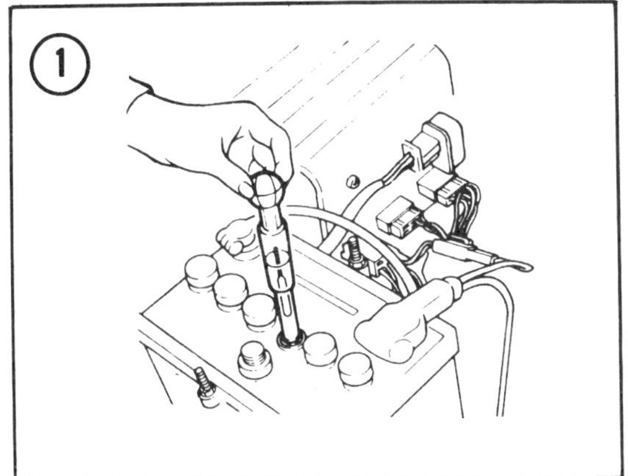

The specific gravity of the electrolyte in each battery cell is an excellent indicator of that cell's condition. A fully charged cell will read 1.260 or more at 20° C (68° F). If the cells test below 1.200, the battery must be recharged. Charging is also necessary if the specific gravity of the cell varies more than 0.025 from cell to cell.

NOTE

For every 10° F above 80° F (25° C) electrolyte temperature, add 0.004 to specific gravity reading. For every 10° below 80° F (25° C), subtract 0.004.

Charging

The battery need not be removed from the car for charging. Just make certain that the area is well ventilated, and that there is no chance of sparks or flames occurring near the battery.

WARNING

Charging batteries give off highly explosive hydrogen gas. If this explodes, it may spray battery acid over a wide area.

Disconnect the cables from the battery. On fillable batteries, make sure the electrolyte is fully topped up.

Connect the charger to the battery—negative to negative, positive to positive. If the charger output is variable, select a low setting (5-10 amps), set the voltage selector to 12 volts, and plug the charger in. If the battery is severely discharged, allow it to charge for at least 8 hours. Batteries that aren't as badly discharged require less charging time. **Table 1** gives approximate charge rates. On fillable batteries, check charging progress with the hydrometer.

ALTERNATOR

The alternator generates 3-phase alternating current in the armature coils. Silicon diodes act as one-way valves for the alternating current, letting only charging current through. In this manner, the AC is converted to DC.

The 1970-1977 models use an external regulator, mounted on the engine compartment sidewall. The 1978 and later models use an integrated circuit regulator, mounted inside the alternator.

Alternator Output Test (Through 1977)

This test requires a 30-volt voltmeter and a fully charged battery.

1. Disconnect the alternator wires.
2. Connect the voltmeter positive lead to the alternator "N" terminal. Connect the negative lead to ground. The voltmeter must indicate battery voltage.
3. Set up the test circuit shown in **Figure 2**.
4. Start the engine. Gradually increase engine speed to 1,100 rpm, then note the voltmeter reading.

CAUTION

Do not run the engine at speeds above 1,100 rpm. Do not race the engine.

The voltmeter should indicate 12.5 volts or more. If the reading is low, the alternator is defective. Replace it with a new or rebuilt unit.

Regulator Testing (Through 1977)

This is a complicated procedure, and requires equipment not usually possessed by the home mechanic. Take the job to a Datsun dealer or other competent garage. Some regulator problems can be corrected by adjustment, but the cost should be compared to that of a new regulator before choosing a course of action.

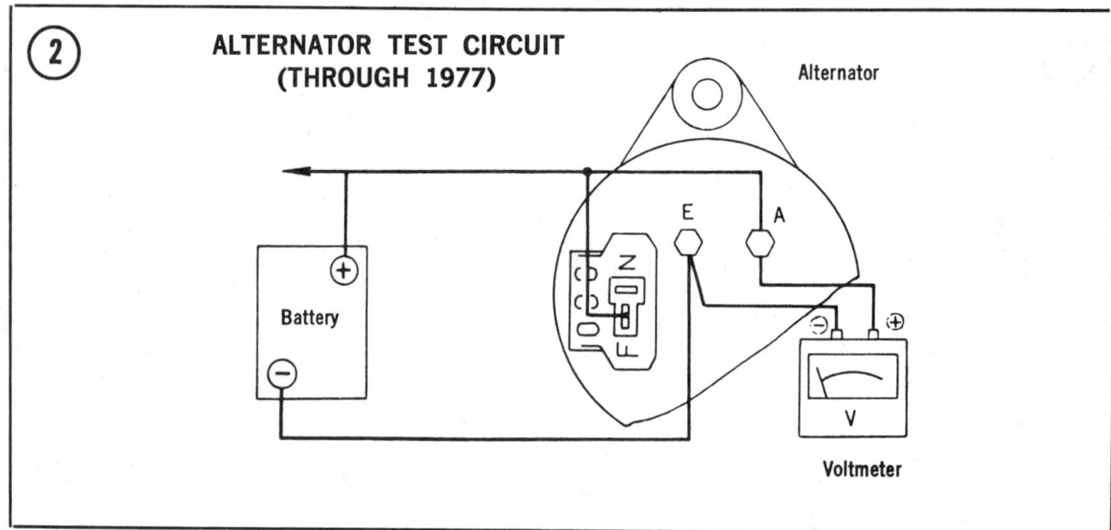

Alternator Output Test (1978 and Later)

Refer to **Figure 3** and **Figure 4** for this procedure.

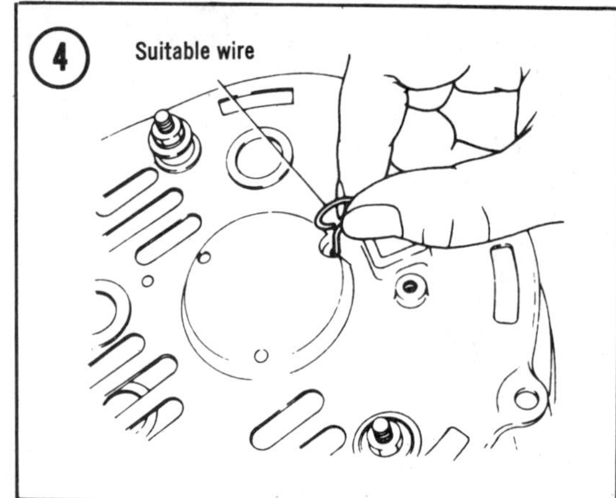

Alternator Removal/Installation

1. Disconnect the negative battery cable.
2. Detach the electrical connector from the alternator. Label and detach the single wires.
3. Loosen the alternator mounting bolts and remove the fan belt from the alternator pulley.
4. Remove the alternator mounting bolts and take the alternator out.
5. Installation is the reverse of these steps. After installation, adjust drive belt tension as described in Chapter Three.

STARTER

Three starter designs have been used. **Figure 5** shows the 1970-1974 design; **Figure 6** the 1975 and later standard starter; and **Figure 7** the reduction gear starter optional on 1978 and later models.

Removal/Installation

1. Disconnect negative cable from the battery.
2. Disconnect the wires from solenoid terminal S and B. **Figure 5** shows the 1970-1974 terminals. The 1975 and later design is the same.
3. Remove 2 starter securing bolts. Pull the starter forward until it is clear, then lift it out.
4. Install in the reverse order.

Solenoid Replacement (Standard Starter)

1. Remove the starter as described earlier.
2. Disconnect the wire running from the solenoid to the starter.
3. Remove 3 solenoid attaching bolts.
4. Unhook the solenoid plunger from the shift lever inside the starter. Lift the solenoid off.
5. Installation is the reverse of these steps.

Solenoid Replacement (Reduction Gear Starter)

1. Remove the starter as described earlier.
2. Disconnect the wire running from solenoid to starter.

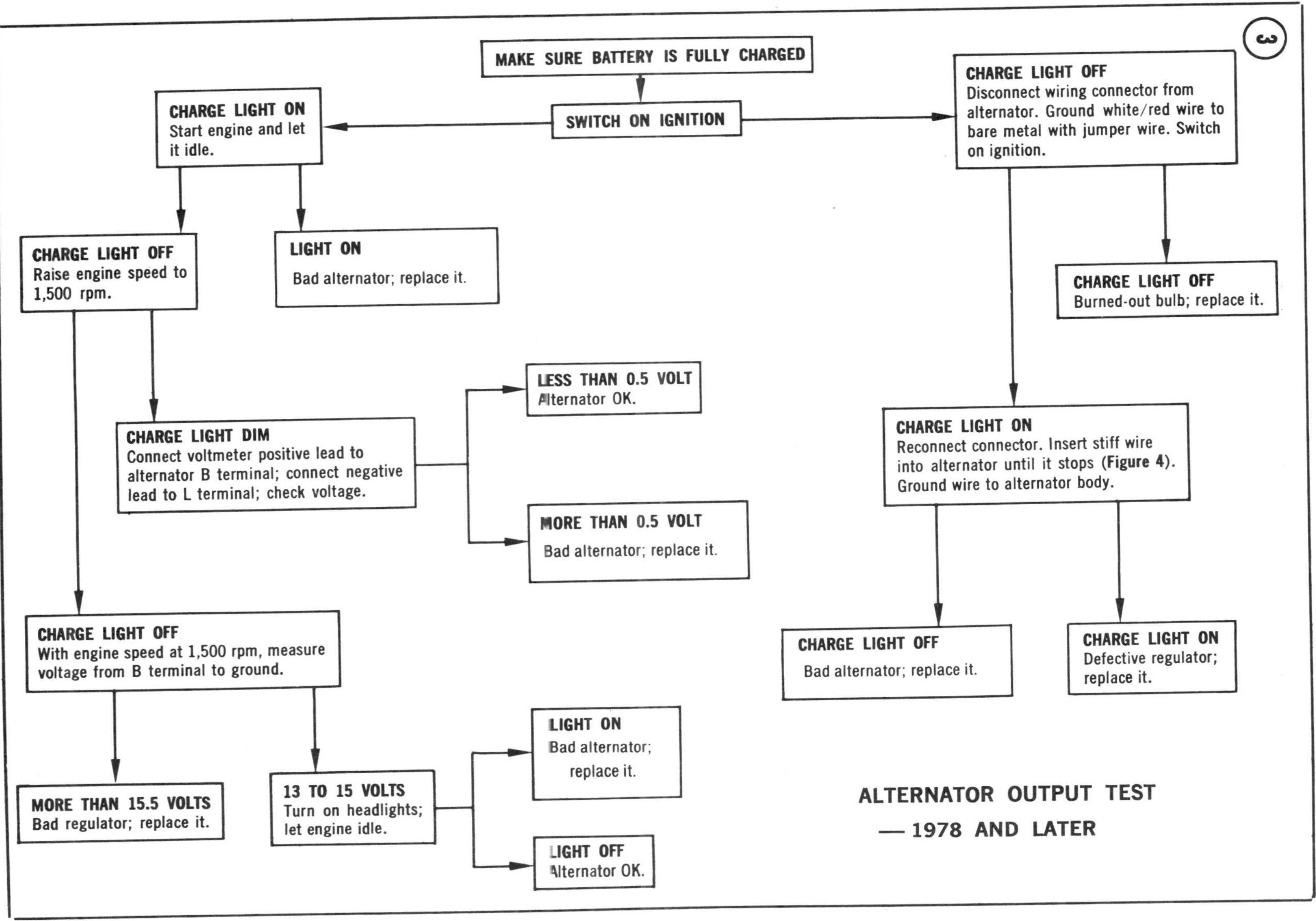
3
MAKE SURE BATTERY IS FULLY CHARGED
SWITCH ON IGNITION
CHARGE LIGHT ON Start engine and let it idle.
CHARGE LIGHT OFF Disconnect wiring connector from alternator. Ground white/red wire to bare metal with jumper wire. Switch on ignition.
CHARGE LIGHT OFF Raise engine speed to 1,500 rpm.
LIGHT ON Bad alternator; replace it.
CHARGE LIGHT OFF Burned-out bulb; replace it.
LESS THAN 0.5 VOLT Alternator OK.
CHARGE LIGHT DIM Connect voltmeter positive lead to alternator B terminal; connect negative lead to L terminal; check voltage.
CHARGE LIGHT ON Reconnect connector. Insert stiff wire into alternator until it stops (Figure 4). Ground wire to alternator body.
MORE THAN 0.5 VOLT Bad alternator; replace it.
CHARGE LIGHT OFF With engine speed at 1,500 rpm, measure voltage from B terminal to ground.
CHARGE LIGHT OFF Bad alternator; replace it.
CHARGE LIGHT ON Defective regulator; replace it.
LIGHT ON Bad alternator; replace it.
MORE THAN 15.5 VOLTS Bad regulator; replace it.
13 TO 15 VOLTS Turn on headlights; let engine idle.
LIGHT OFF Alternator OK.
ALTERNATOR OUTPUT TEST
—1978 AND LATER

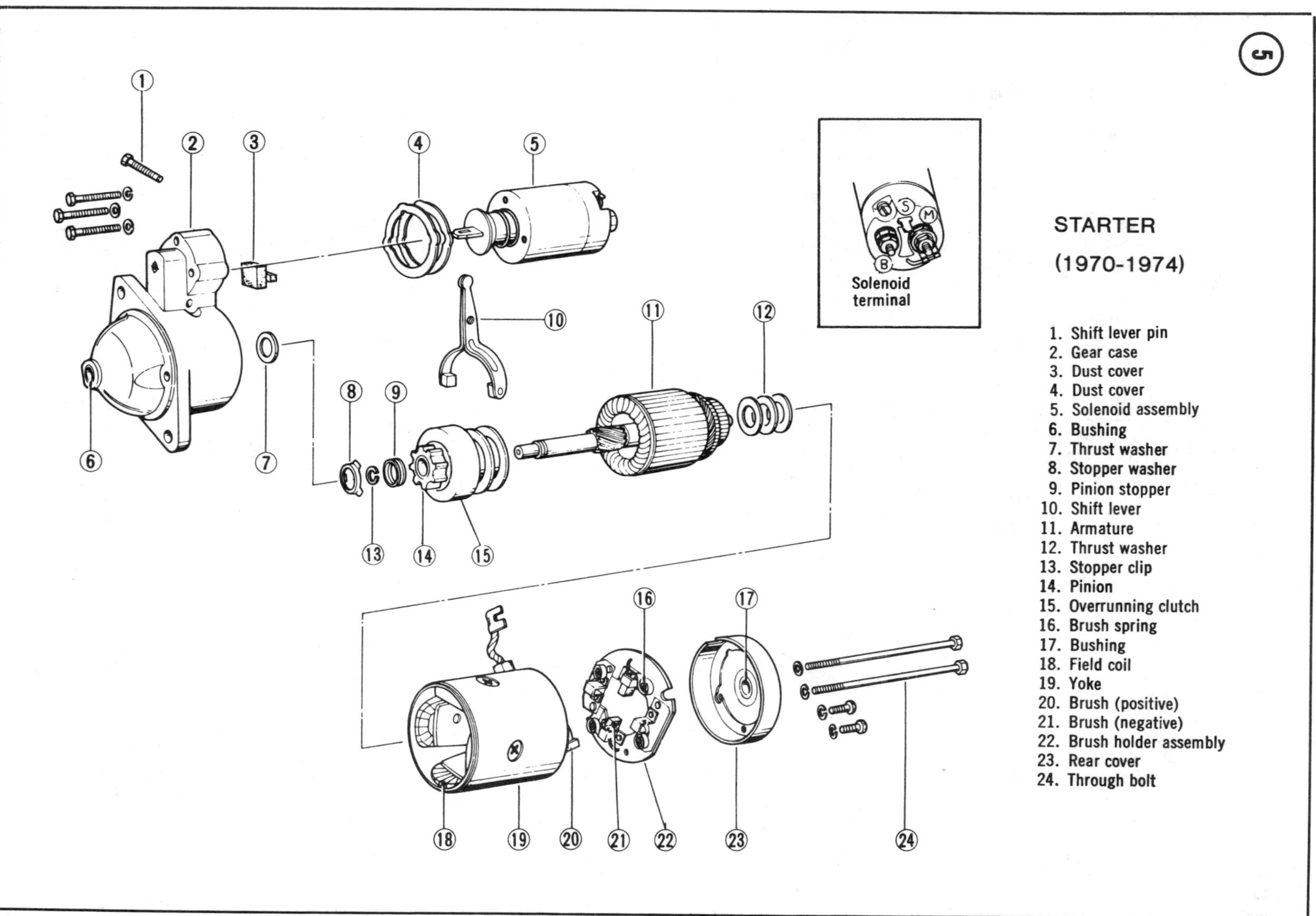
5
Solenoid terminal
S
M
B
STARTER
(1970-1974)
1. Shift lever pin
2. Gear case
3. Dust cover
4. Dust cover
5. Solenoid assembly
6. Bushing
7. Thrust washer
8. Stopper washer
9. Pinion stopper
10. Shift lever
11. Armature
12. Thrust washer
13. Stopper clip
14. Pinion
15. Overrunning clutch
16. Brush spring
17. Bushing
18. Field coil
19. Yoke
20. Brush (positive)
21. Brush (negative)
22. Brush holder assembly
23. Rear cover
24. Through bolt

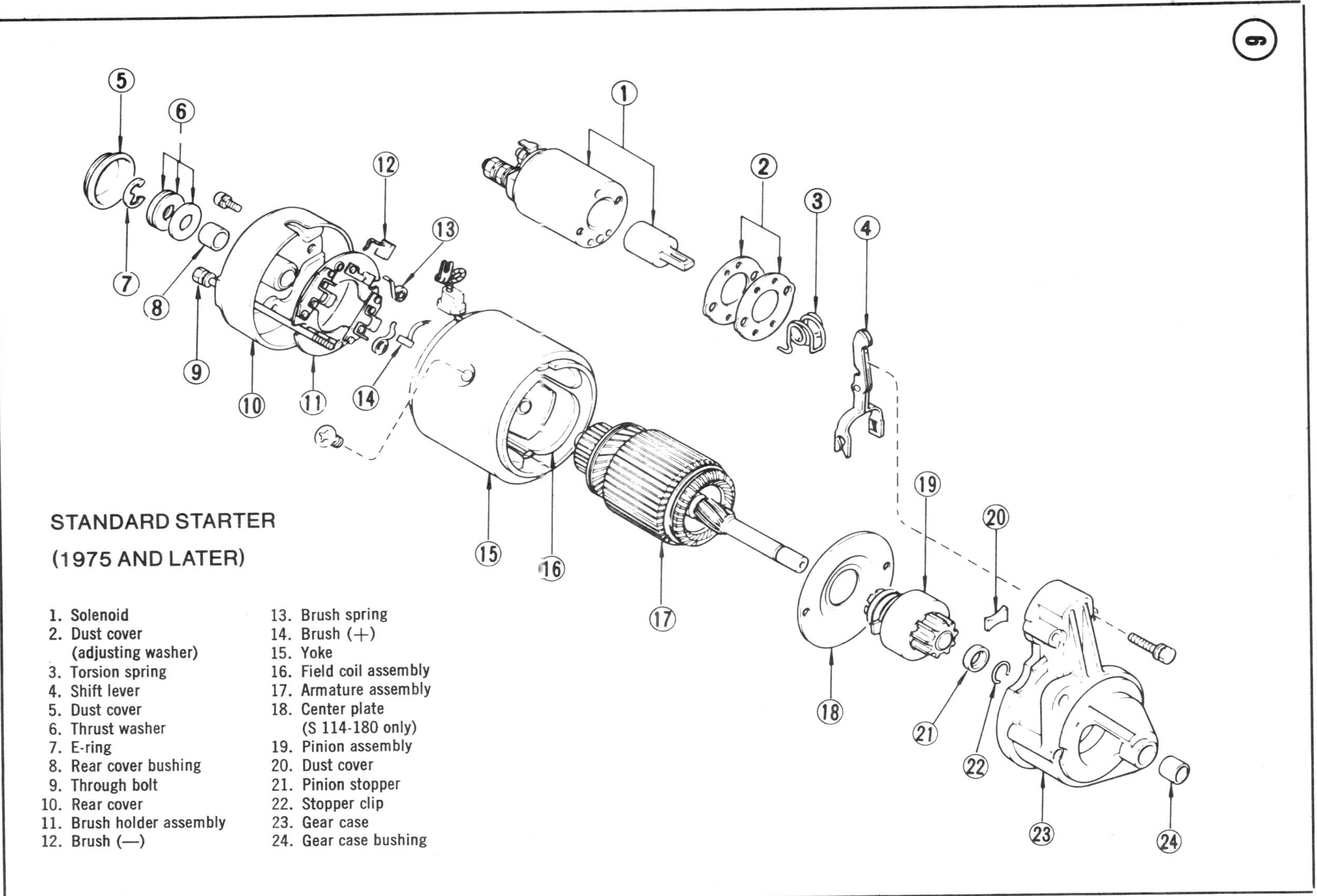
6
STANDARD STARTER
(1975 AND LATER)
1. Solenoid
2. Dust cover (adjusting washer)
3. Torsion spring
4. Shift lever
5. Dust cover
6. Thrust washer
7. E-ring
8. Rear cover bushing
9. Through bolt
10. Rear cover
11. Brush holder assembly
12. Brush (—)
13. Brush spring
14. Brush (+)
15. Yoke
16. Field coil assembly
17. Armature assembly
18. Center plate (S 114-180 only)
19. Pinion assembly
20. Dust cover
21. Pinion stopper
22. Stopper clip
23. Gear case
24. Gear case bushing
8

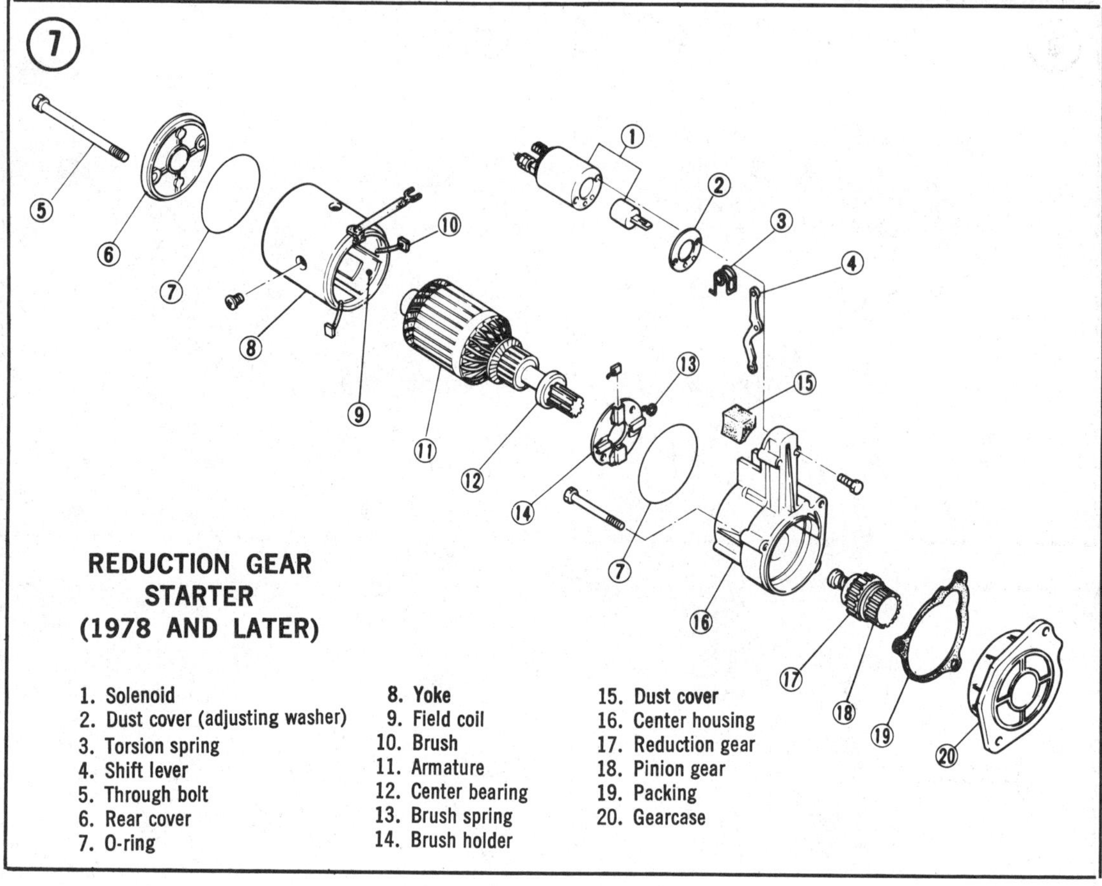

REDUCTION GEAR STARTER (1978 AND LATER)

3. Remove 2 screws, disconnect the solenoid from the shift lever, and take the solenoid off.
4. Installation is the reverse of removal.

Brush Replacement (Standard Starter)

1. Remove the starter as described earlier.
2. On 1975 and later starters, remove the dust cover, snap ring, and thrust washers from the starter's front end. See **Figure 8**.
3. Remove 2 through bolts and 2 setscrews (**Figure 9**). Take the end cover off the starter.
4. Make a wire hook and pull back the brush springs (**Figure 10**). Slide the brushes out of their slots.
5. Measure brush length. Minimum length is 0.49 in. (12.5mm) on 1970-1974 starters; 0.47 in. (12.0mm) on 1975 and later. Replace brushes if any are shorter than minimum.
6. Check brush movement in the slots. Clean the slots and brushes if the movement is not smooth. Examine brush springs. Replace if weak or damaged.
7. Check the brush holder for shorts to ground. Use an ohmmeter or self-powered test lamp. Touch one tester lead to the brush holder and the other to the positive brush slots. If the ohmmeter shows continuity (test lamp lights), a short circuit exists. Replace insulator or brush holder (**Figure 11**).
8. Install brushes by reversing Steps 1-4.

CAUTION

Use resin core solder when resoldering brush leads. Do not use acid core solder.

Brush Replacement (Reduction Gear Starter)

1. Remove the through bolts and front cover from the starter.
2. Separate the yoke from the center housing. See **Figure 12**.
3. Make a wire hook and pull back the positive brush springs. See **Figure 13**. Pull the positive brushes out of the slots.

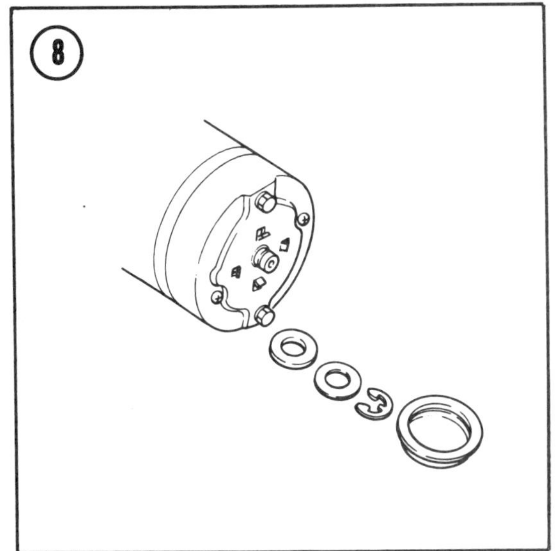
8

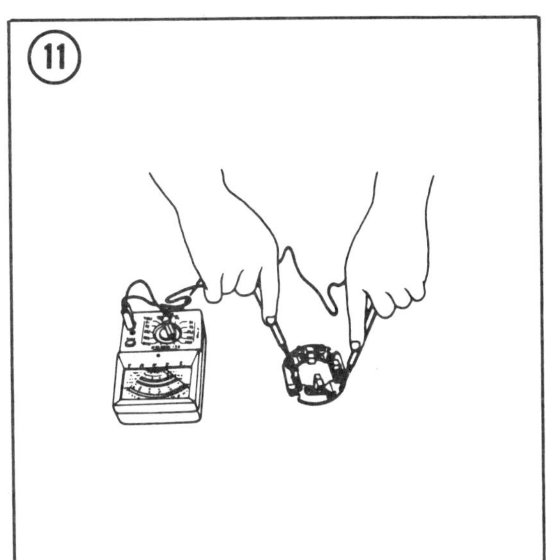
11

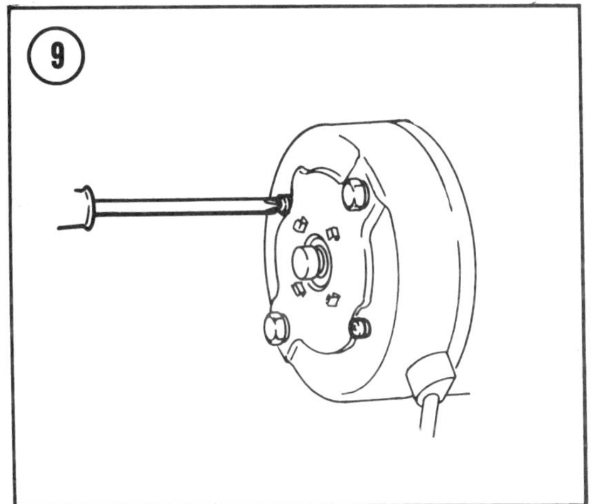
9

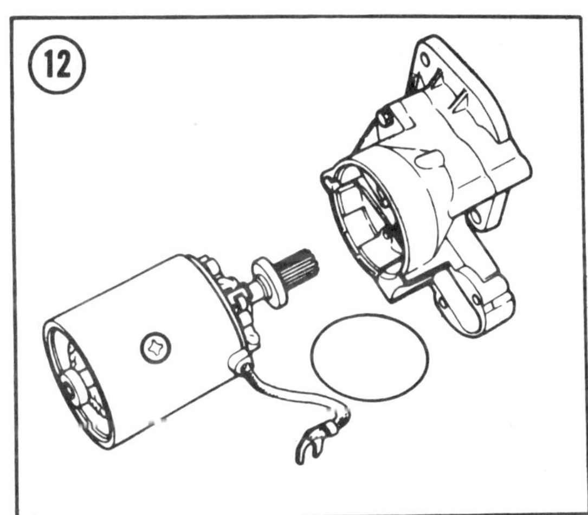
12

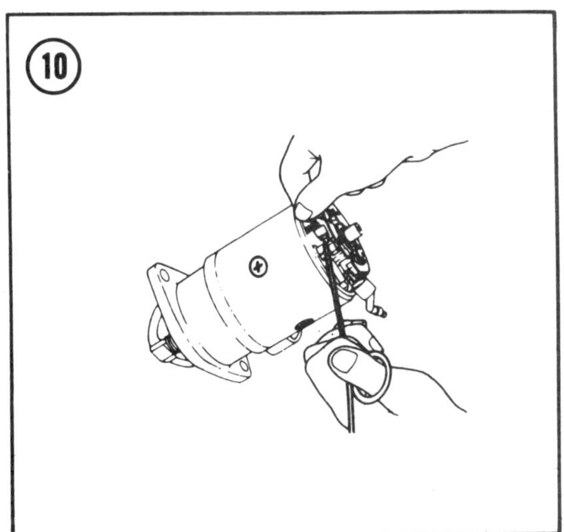
10

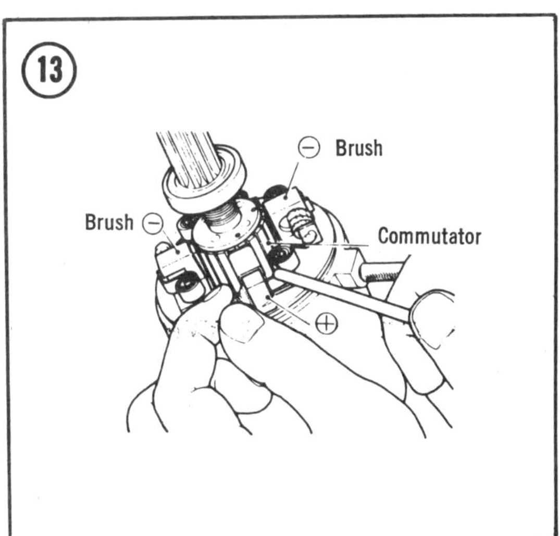
13
⊖ Brush
Brush ⊖
Commutator
⊕

NOTE
The positive brushes are attached to the field coils, not to the brush holder.

4. Slide the brush holder off of the commutator. Remove the negative brushes from their slots.
5. Measure the brush length. Minimum length is 0.43 in. (11mm). Replace the brushes if any are shorter than the minimum.
6. Check brush movement in the slots. Clean the slots and brushes if movement is not smooth. Examine brush springs. Replace if weak or damaged.
7. Check the brush holder for shorts to ground. Use an ohmmeter or a self-powered test lamp like the one shown in **Figure 14**. Touch one probe to the brush holder, and the other to the positive (insulated) brush slots. If the ohmmeter shows continuity (or test lamp lights), replace the brush holder.
8. Install by reversing Steps 1-4.

LIGHTING SYSTEM (521 AND 620)

Table 2 at the end of the chapter lists bulb specifications.

Headlight Replacement

Figure 15 shows a typical headlight assembly.

1. On 521 pickups, remove the headlight trim piece (**Figure 16**). On 620 pickups, remove the radiator grille as described in Chapter Fourteen.
2. On 521 pickups, reach inside the fender and disconnect the headlight wires.
3. Loosen 3 screws securing the headlight retaining ring. Rotate the ring clockwise and take it off.
4. Take the bulb out of its socket. On 620 pickups, disconnect the wires.

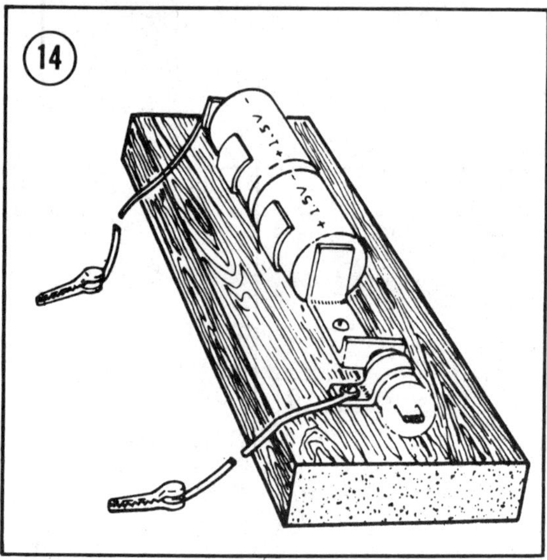

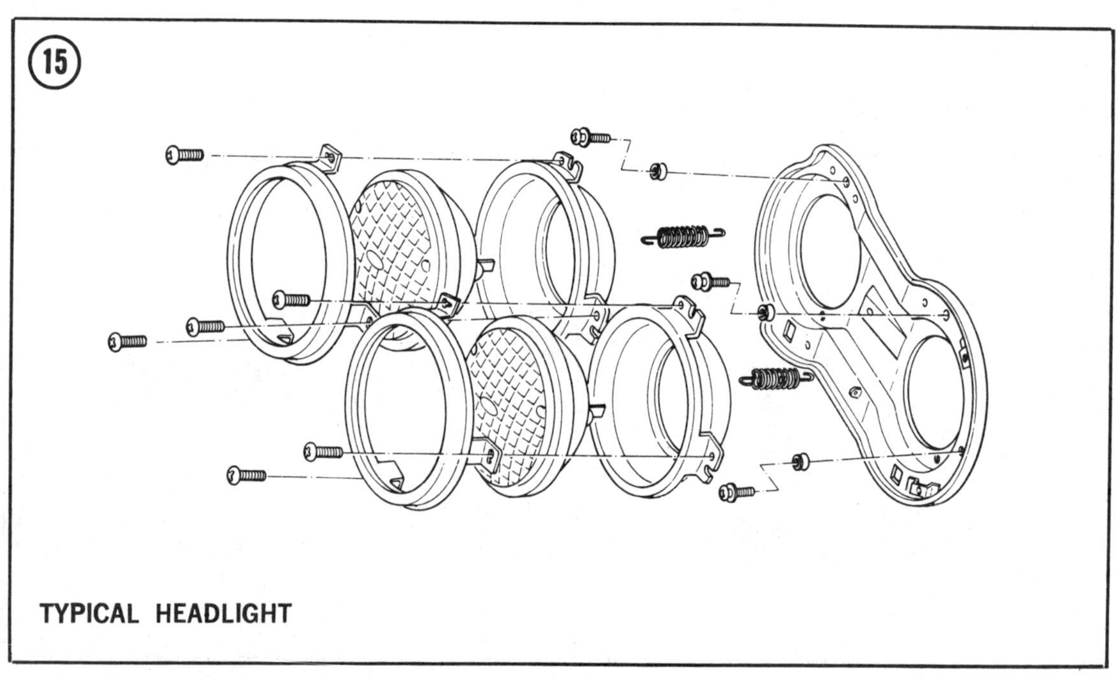

TYPICAL HEADLIGHT

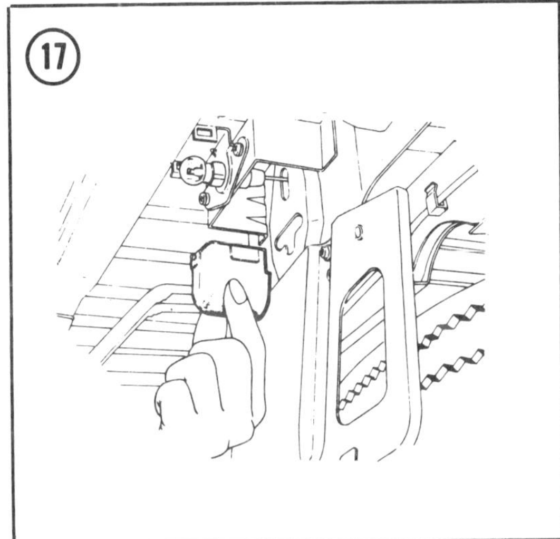

5. Installation is the reverse of these steps. The 3 locating tabs in the bulb fit into the indentations in the mounting ring. Be sure the word TOP (molded in the lens) is up.

Rear Combination Lights

1. Remove the lens securing screws and take off the lens.
2. Press bulb into the socket, turn counterclockwise, and pull out.
3. Install in the reverse order.

Side Marker Lights

To replace a bulb (all models), remove the lens securing screws and take off the lens. Push the bulb into the socket and turn counterclockwise to remove. Install in the reverse order.

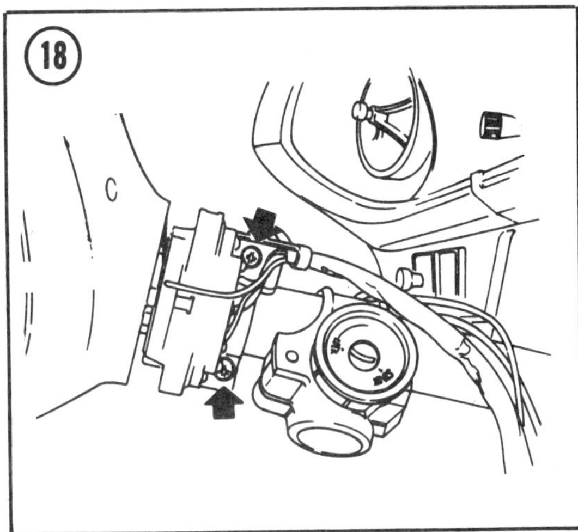

License Plate Light

To replace a bulb, reach beneath the rear bumper and pull the cover off the light (**Figure 17**). Push the bulb into the socket, turn counterclockwise, and remove. Install a new bulb in the reverse order.

8

Headlight Switch Removal/Installation

1. Press the switch knob in, turn it counterclockwise, and pull it off.
2. Reach behind the instrument panel and disconnect the switch wires.
3. Remove the switch securing nut and take the switch out.
4. Installation is the reverse of these steps.

Turn Signal/Dimmer Switch Removal/Installation

1. Disconnect negative cable from battery.
2. Remove the steering wheel and steering column shell. See Chapter Twelve.
3. Disconnect the turn signal/dimmer switch wiring connectors.
4. Loosen 2 screws clamping the switch to the steering column (**Figure 18**). Slide the switch off.
5. Installation is the reverse of these steps.

LIGHTING SYSTEM (720 PICKUP)

Table 2 at the end of the chapter lists bulb specifications.

Headlight Replacement

1. Turn the grille fasteners to release them (**Figure 19**), then lift the grille out.
2. Remove the bulb mounting screws (**Figure 20**), then take the bulb out.

NOTE

Do not turn the other screws. They control bulb aim.

3. Installation is the reverse of removal. If necessary, have headlight aim adjusted by a Datsun dealer or certified lamp adjusting station.

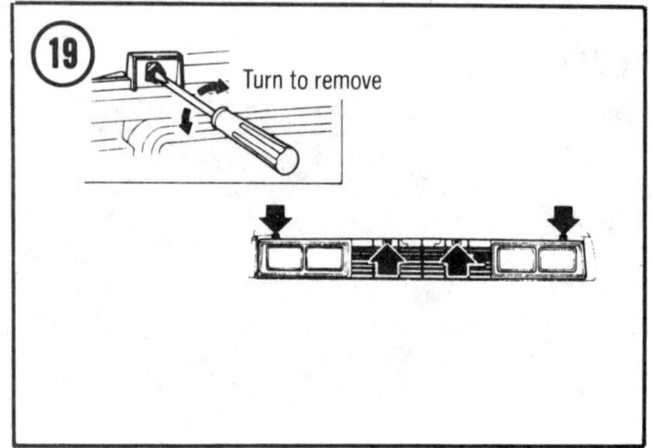

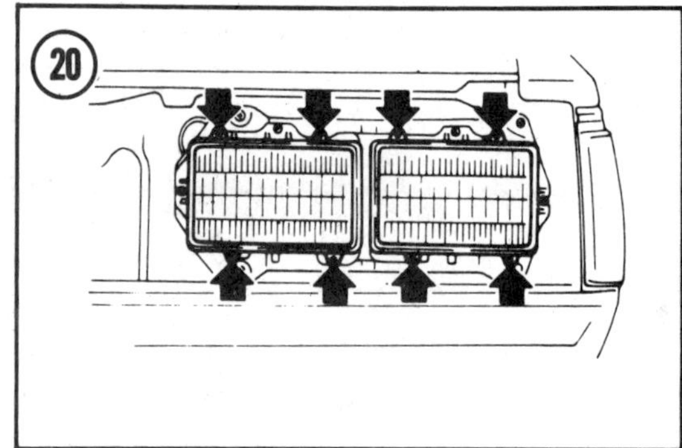

Other Bulbs

All bulbs except the headlight and instrument panel bulbs are type A, B, or C (**Figure 21**). To replace a type A bulb, press it into its socket and turn counterclockwise to remove. To replace type B or C bulbs, pull the bulb out.

Refer to the following illustrations:

Figure 22—front parking/turn signal lights

Figure 23—front side marker lights

Figure 24—rear side marker, brake, tail, and back-up lights

Figure 25—license plate lights

Figure 26—interior light

To replace instrument panel bulbs, remove the instrument cluster. Refer to *Instruments* in this chapter.

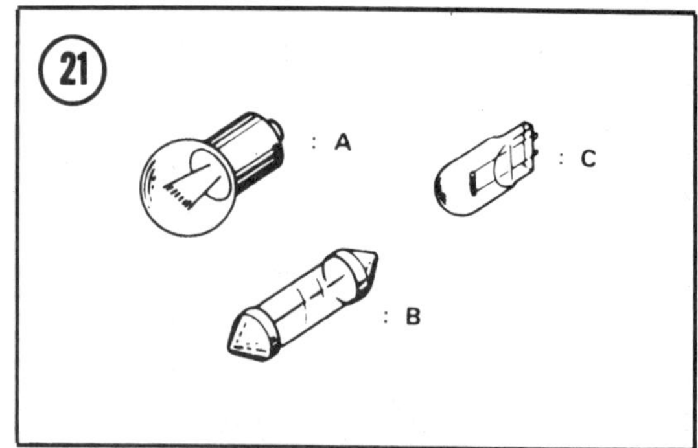

INSTRUMENTS

Cluster Removal/Installation (521 Pickup)

1. Disconnect negative cable from battery.
2. Remove 2 screws from the lower edge of the instrument cluster (one on each side of the steering column).
3. Disconnect the speedometer and multi-pole wiring connector from the back of the instrument cluster. Take the cluster out.
4. To remove gauges, remove the cover from the back of the cluster. Remove 2 gauge attaching screws, then take the gauge out.
5. Installation is the reverse of these steps.

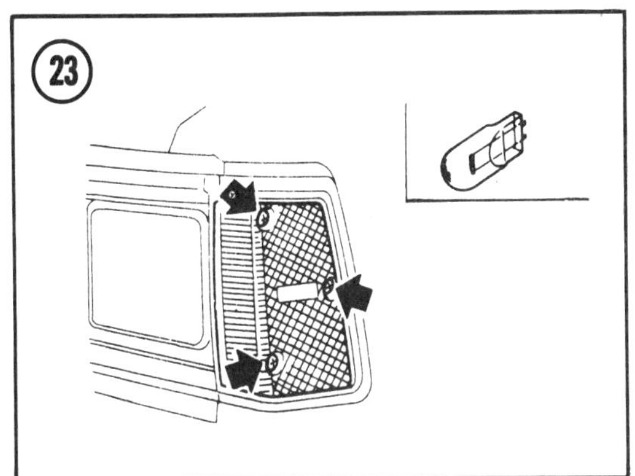

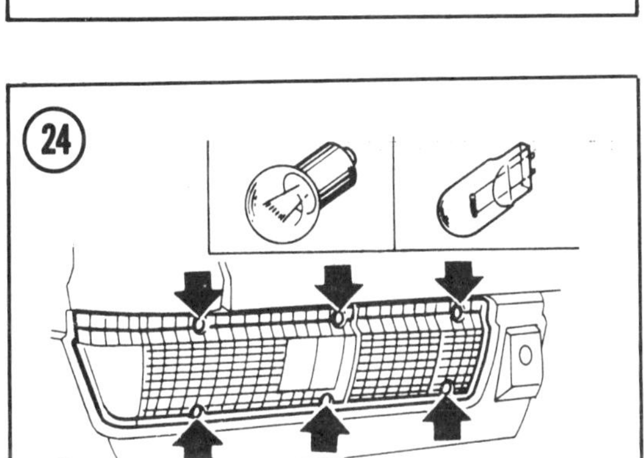

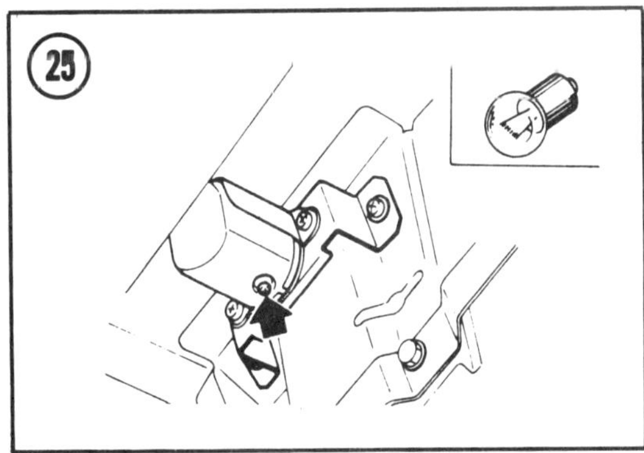

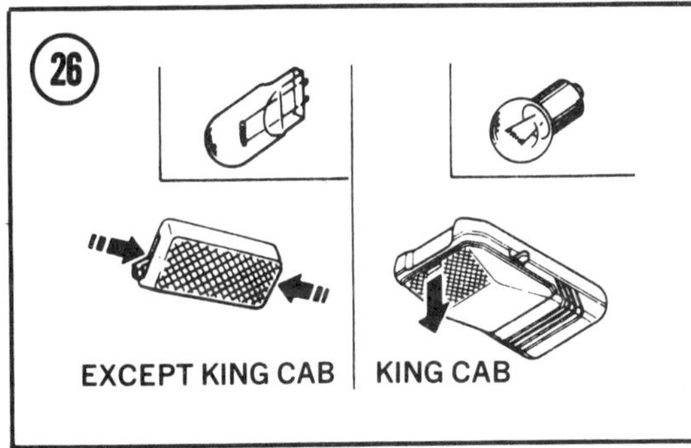

Cluster Removal/Installation (620 Pickup)

1. Disconnect negative cable from battery.
2. Remove the cluster attaching screw from the top of each of the 3 gauge openings.
3. Remove one screw securing the bottom of the instrument cluster.
4. Pull the cluster out slightly (**Figure 27**). Working behind it, disconnect the speedometer cable and multi-pole wiring connector.
5. If equipped with a clock, disconnect its wires from the instrument cluster printed circuit board.
6. Remove 4 screws securing the gauge assembly to the panel. Take the gauge assembly out.
7. To remove gauges, remove the front cover and shadow plate from the gauge assembly. Remove the gauge securing screws and take it out.
8. Installation is the reverse of these steps.

Cluster Removal/Installation (720 Pickup)

1. Disconnect the negative cable from the battery.
2. Remove the cluster lid screws (**Figure 28**) and take off the cluster lid.
3. Remove the cluster screws (**Figure 29**) and take off the cluster.
4. To replace individual gauges, refer to **Figure 30**.
5. To replace a bulb, twist its socket and take it out of the cluster. See **Figure 31**. Pull the bulb out of the socket, install a new one, and install the socket in the cluster.

8

28

29

DATSUN

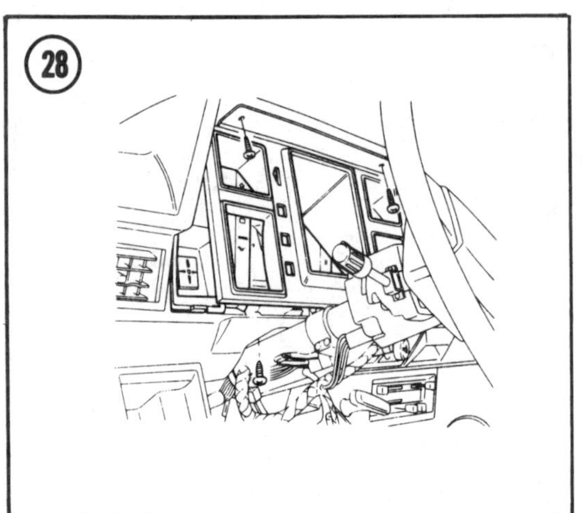

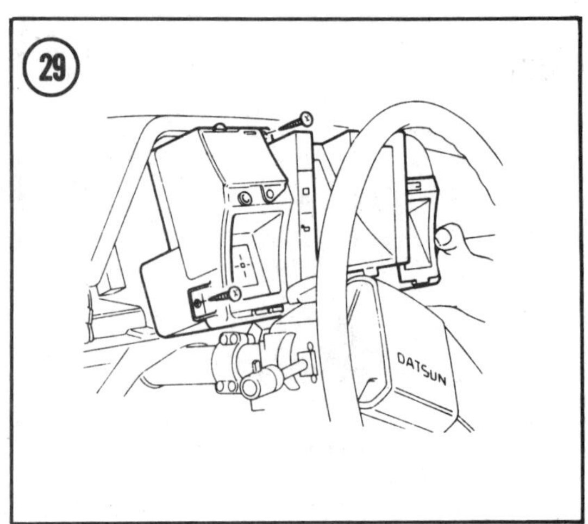

30

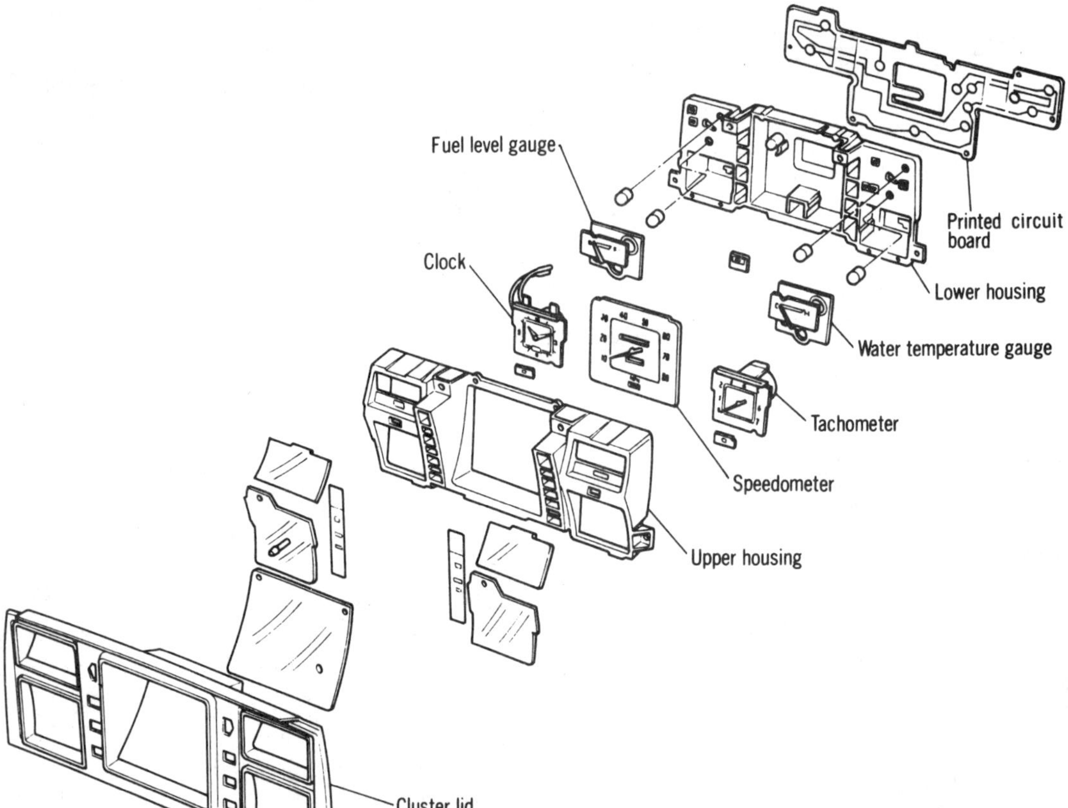

Fuel level gauge
Printed circuit board
Clock
Lower housing
Water temperature gauge
Tachometer
Speedometer
Upper housing
Cluster lid

31

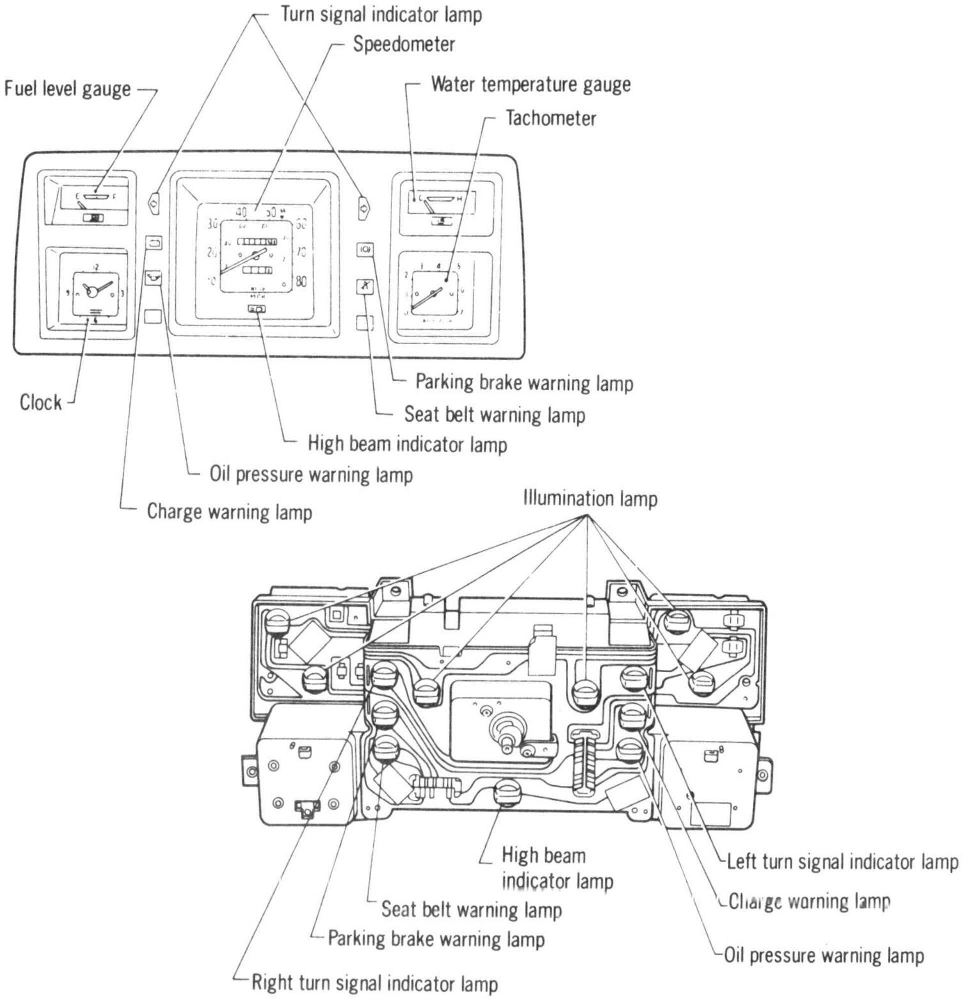

Turn signal indicator lamp
Speedometer
Fuel level gauge
Water temperature gauge
Tachometer
Parking brake warning lamp
Clock
Seat belt warning lamp
High beam indicator lamp
Oil pressure warning lamp
Charge warning lamp
Illumination lamp
High beam indicator lamp
Left turn signal indicator lamp
Charge warning lamp
Seat belt warning lamp
Parking brake warning lamp
Oil pressure warning lamp
Right turn signal indicator lamp

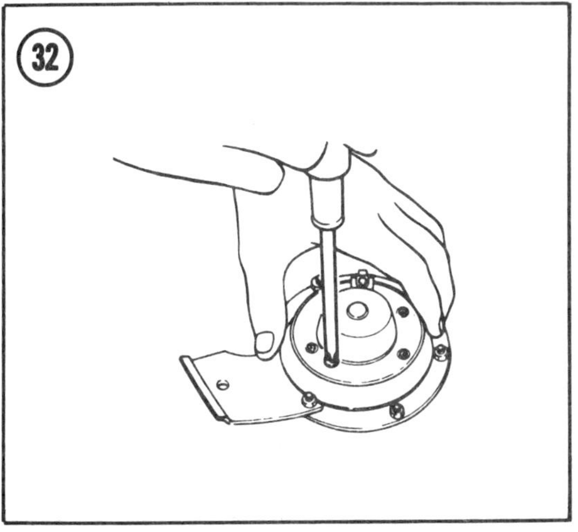

HORN

All models use two horns, mounted at the front of the engine compartment. If the horns work, but are not loud enough, make sure the wires are making good contact and the horns are properly grounded to the body. Horn volume can be adjusted by turning the screw at the back of the horn (**Figure 32**).

If only one horn works, check the wiring to the non-working horn. If the horn is receiving current and is grounded properly, it is probably defective.

If neither horn works, check the horn fuse, then the battery. If these are good, test the horn relay as described in this chapter.

33

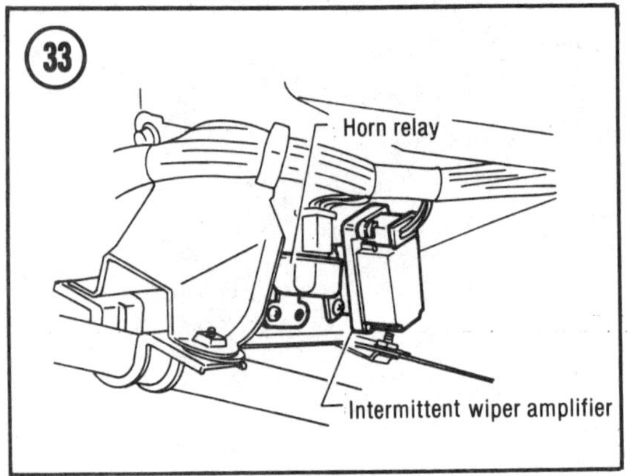

34

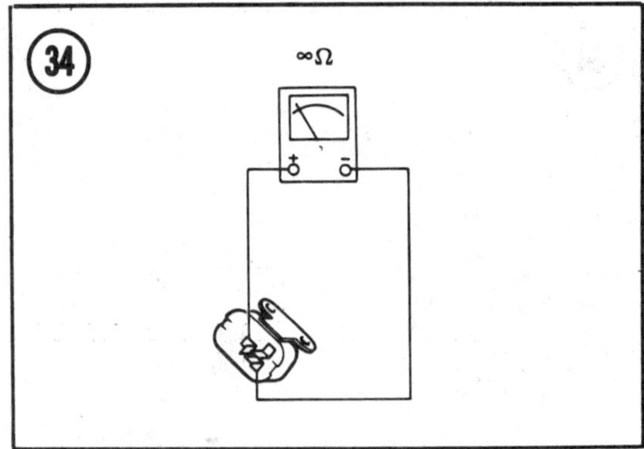

35

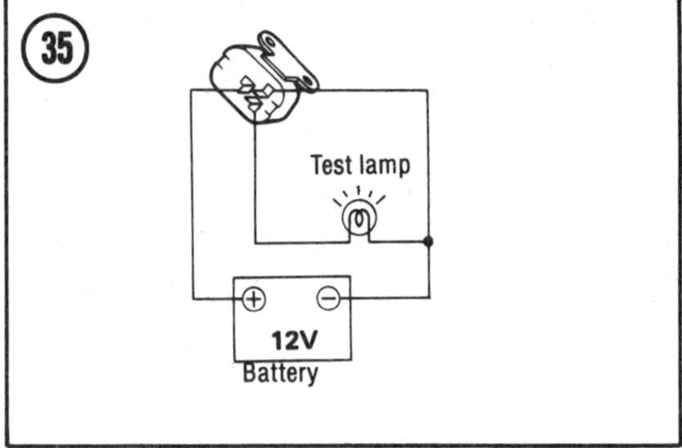

Horn Relay Testing/Replacement (521 and 620 Pickups)

On 521 pickups, the horn relay is mounted on the right-hand side of the engine compartment. It can be identified by its wires; green, green/blue, and light green/black.

On 620 pickups, the horn relay is mounted on the radiator support or on the relay bracket at the right side of the engine compartment. Its wires are colored green, green/white, and light green.

To test the relay, connect a jumper wire between the relay H and B terminals. If the horn sounds, the relay is probably defective. Replace it as described in this section.

If the horn still does not work, ground the relay S terminal with a jumper wire. If the horn sounds, the horn button is probably defective. Have it tested by a dealer or automotive electrical shop.

To replace the horn relay on early models, disconnect one wire at a time and connect it to the new relay. On late models with a one-piece wiring connector, simply remove the old relay, install the new one, and attach the wiring connector.

Horn Relay Testing/Replacement (720 Pickup)

1. Remove the horn relay. This is mounted near the steering column (**Figure 33**).
2. Connect an ohmmeter or battery powered test lamp between the relay terminals shown in **Figure 34**. The ohmmeter should indicate infinite resistance (test lamp should stay out). If not, replace the relay.

NOTE
For the next step, use a non-powered test lamp. Do not use a battery powered test lamp or ohmmeter.

6. Set up the test circuit shown in **Figure 35**. The test lamp should light. If not, replace the relay.
7. To replace the relay, detach the old relay, install a new one, and connect the wiring connector.

WINDSHIELD WIPERS AND WASHERS

Wiper Motor Replacement (521 Pickup)

1. Disconnect the wiper motor wiring connector. See **Figure 36**.
2. Separate the motor drive arm from the wiper linkage.
3. Remove 3 motor attaching bolts to take the motor out.
4. Installation is the reverse of these steps.

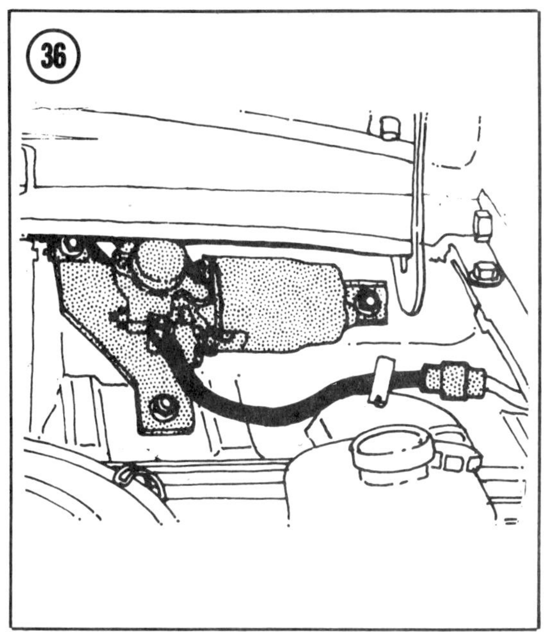

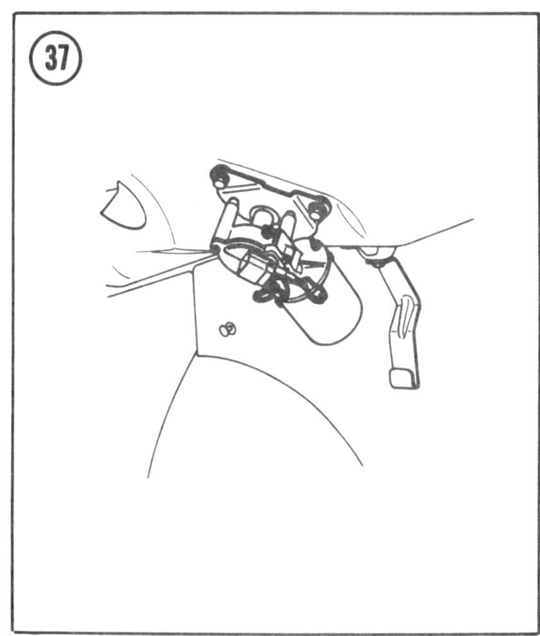

Wiper Motor Replacement (620 Pickup)

1. Remove the grille on top of the cowl.
2. Remove the stop ring connecting the wiper motor arm to the wiper linkage.
3. Working beneath the instrument panel, disconnect the wiper motor wiring connector.
4. Remove 3 bolts and take the motor out. See **Figure 37**.
5. Installation is the reverse of these steps.

Wiper Motor Replacement (720 Pickup)

1. Working in the engine compartment, disconnect the wiring connector from the wiper motor (**Figure 38**).
2. Detach the motor from the firewall.
3. Pull the motor partway out and disconnect it from the wiper linkage. Take the motor out.
4. Installation is the reverse of removal.

Washer Motor and Tank Replacement

The 521 washer motor and fluid bag are located on the left side of the engine compartment (**Figure 39**). The 620 washer motor and tank are located at the right rear corner of the engine compartment (**Figure 40**).

The 720 washer motor and tank are basically the same as the 620, but mounted closer to the front of the truck.

The motor and tank are replaced as a unit. Before replacing, check for a blown fuse, clogged fluid lines, and defective wiring.

To replace the motor and tank assembly, simply disconnect the motor wires and fluid line. Then remove the assembly, install a new one, and reconnect the wires and line.

FUSES AND FUSIBLE LINKS

Fuse Replacement

The 521 pickup fuse block is located at the right rear corner of the engine compartment (**Figure 41**). The 620 pickup fuse block is located beneath the instrument panel (**Figure 42**).

The 720 pickup fuse block is mounted near the hood release handle (**Figure 43**).

Fuse specifications are printed on the inside or outside of the fuse block cover.

Whenever a fuse blows, find out the cause before replacing. Usually the trouble is a short circuit in the wiring. This may be caused by worn-through insulation or by a wire that works its way loose and shorts to ground. Carry several spare fuses in the glove compartment.

38

Windshield wiper blade
Pivot
(R.H.)
Packing (Driver's side)
Pivot
(L.H.)
Windshield wiper motor

39

Window
washer bag
(optional)
Air cleaner
Ignition
coil

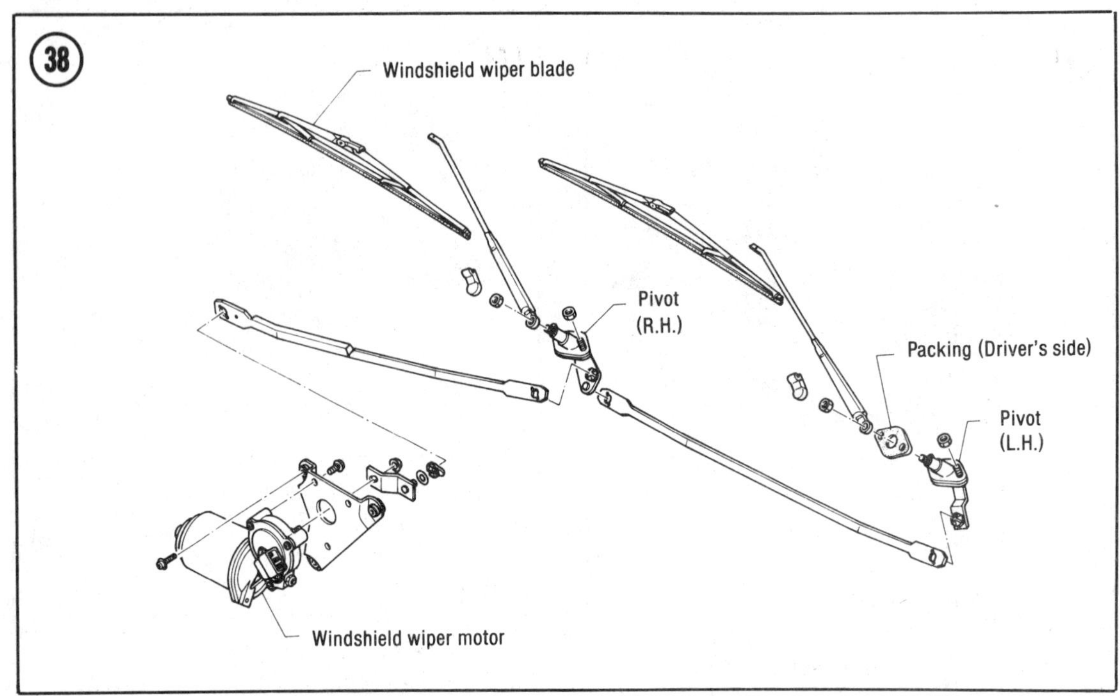

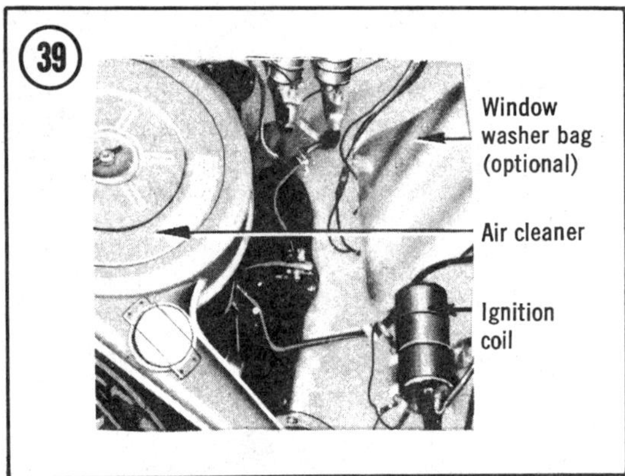

41

40

42

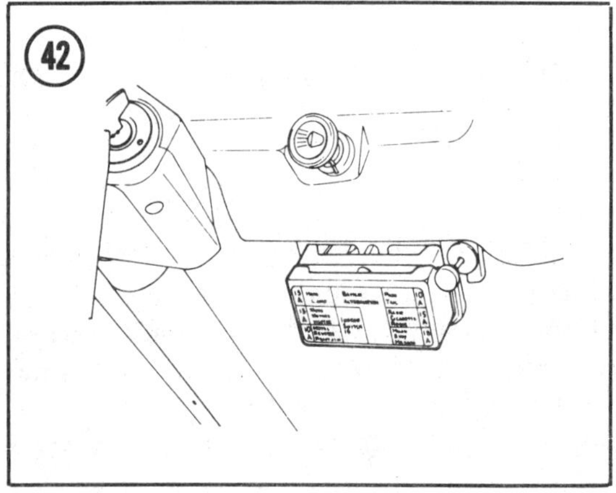

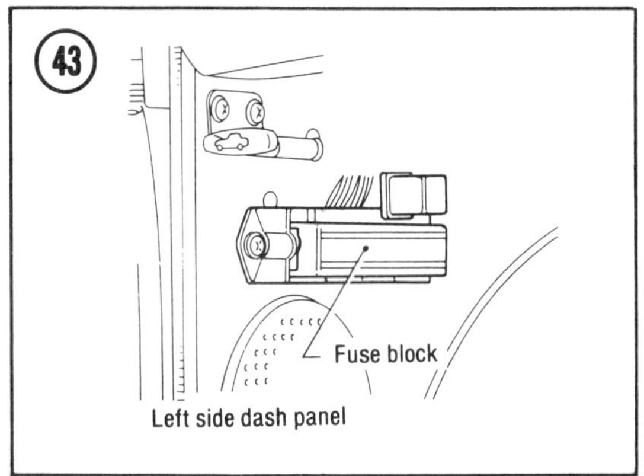

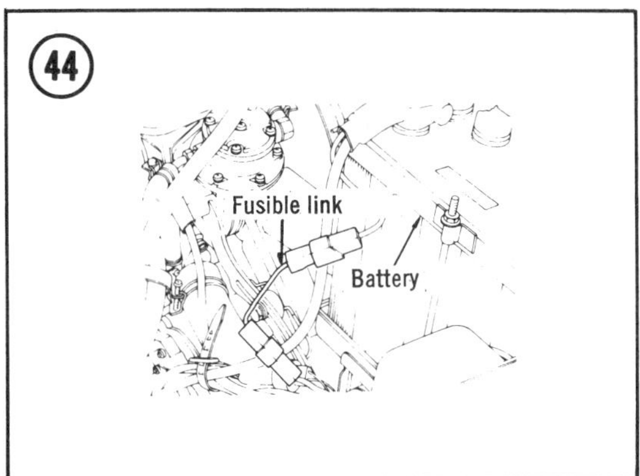

CAUTION
Never substitute tinfoil or wire for a fuse. An overload could cause a fire and complete loss of the vehicle.

Fusible Link Replacement

Fusible links are short sections of thin wire in a larger wire. They are intended to burn out if an overload occurs, thus protecting the wiring harnesses.

Fusible links are connected to the battery positive terminal. The number and amperage rating vary depending on model year and optional equipment. **Figure 44** shows a typical fusible link.

Burned-out fusible links can usually be detected by melted or burned insulation. Suspect links with no apparent damage can be tested for continuity with an ohmmeter or self-powered test lamp. If a link burns out, unplug it and plug in a new one.

CAUTION
Never replace a fusible link with a link of larger capacity. Never wrap fusible links with tape.

IGNITION SYSTEM

Breaker point ignition is used on all 1970-1975 models, as well as on 1976-1977 non-California trucks. The 1970-1973 system has two sets of points; all others have one set. **Figure 45** shows a dual-point system; **Figure 46** shows a single-point system. The system is made up of the battery, ignition switch, ignition coil, distributor, spark plugs and associated wiring.

Magnetic pulse-controlled electronic ignition is used on 1976-1977 California models and all 1978 and later models. A reluctor (rotor) is used in place of the distributor cam, and a pick-up coil (stator) replaces the breaker points. The reluctor has four protrusions, one for each cylinder. As each protrusion faces the pick-up coil, it causes the coil to send an electrical signal to the transistor unit (1976-1978) or integrated circuit unit (1979-on). The unit then triggers production of high-voltage current in the ignition coil. This current runs through the coil wire to the distributor, which routes it to the appropriate spark plug.

L-series engines (1970-1980) use one spark plug per cylinder. The NAPS-Z engine (1981) uses 2 plugs per cylinder. **Figure 47** shows the 1976-1978 system. **Figure 48** shows the 1979-1980 system. **Figure 49** shows the 1981 system.

The following section describes replacement procedures. No ignition components except the distributor are repairable. Distributor overhaul requires a very expensive special testing machine, and should be left to a dealer or automotive electrical shop.

Ignition Switch and Steering Lock Replacement

1. Disconnect the negative cable from the battery.
2. Disconnect the switch wiring connector.
3. On trucks equipped with steering locks, remove the switch mounting screw (**Figure 50**). Take the switch off the steering lock.

45

DUAL-POINT IGNITION SYSTEM

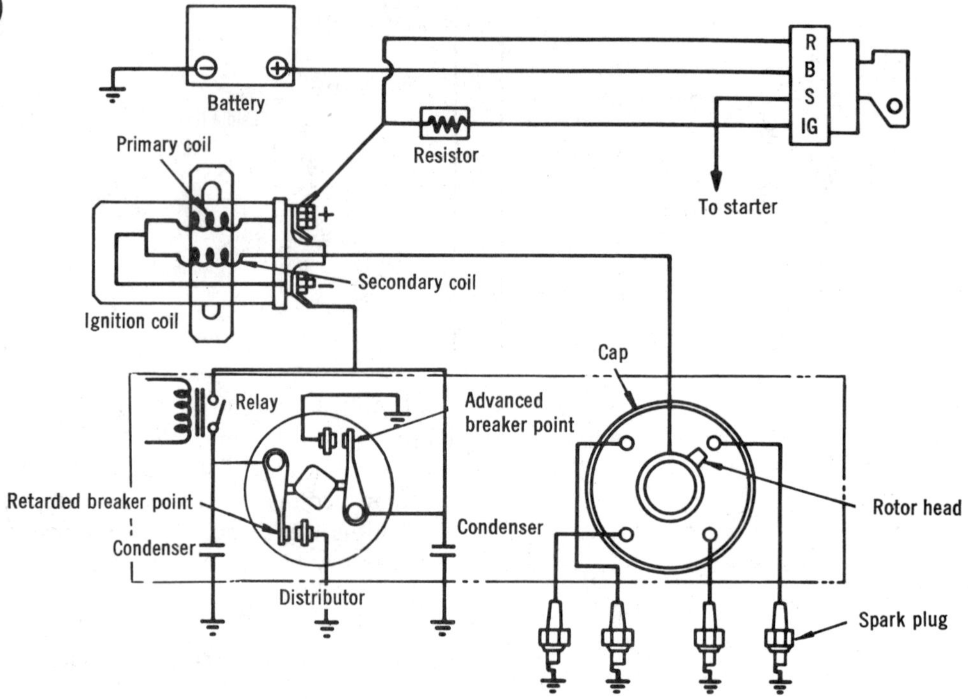

Battery
R
B
S
IG
Resistor
Primary coil
To starter
Secondary coil
Ignition coil
Cap
Relay
Advanced breaker point
Retarded breaker point
Condenser
Condenser
Rotor head
Distributor
Spark plug

46

SINGLE-POINT IGNITION SYSTEM

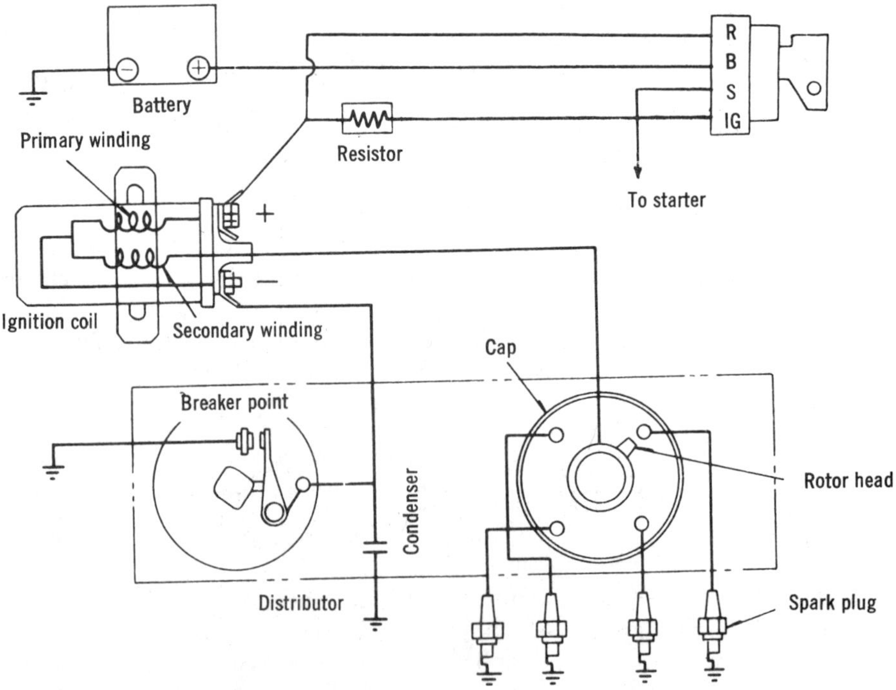

Battery
R
B
S
IG
Primary winding
Resistor
To starter
Ignition coil
Secondary winding
Cap
Breaker point
Rotor head
Condenser
Distributor
Spark plug

47

PULSE CONTROLLED TRANSISTOR IGNITION SYSTEM
(1976-1978 MODELS)

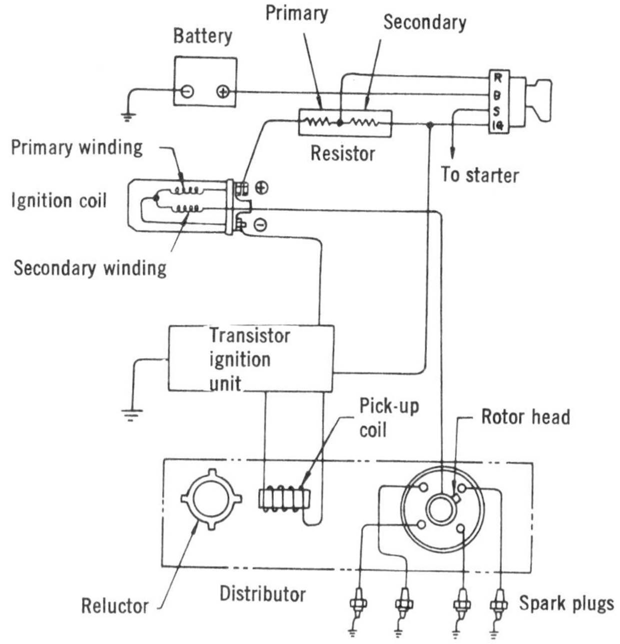

48

PULSE CONTROLLED IC IGNITION SYSTEM
(1979-1980 MODELS)

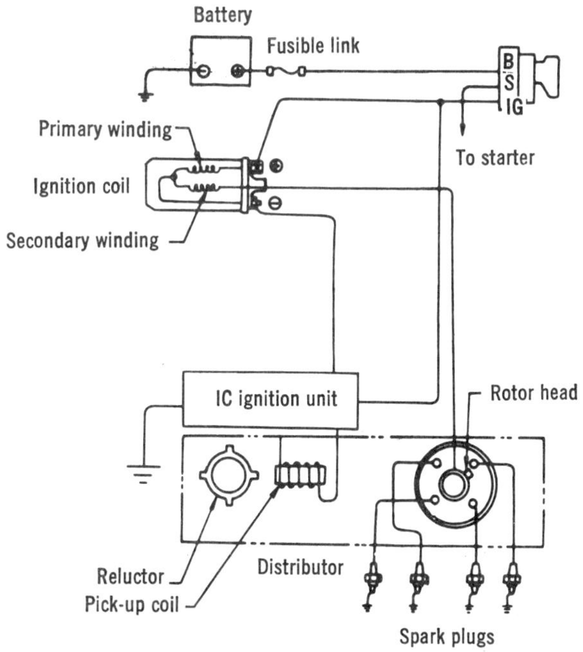

49

PULSE CONTROLLED IC IGNITION SYSTEM (1981 MODELS)

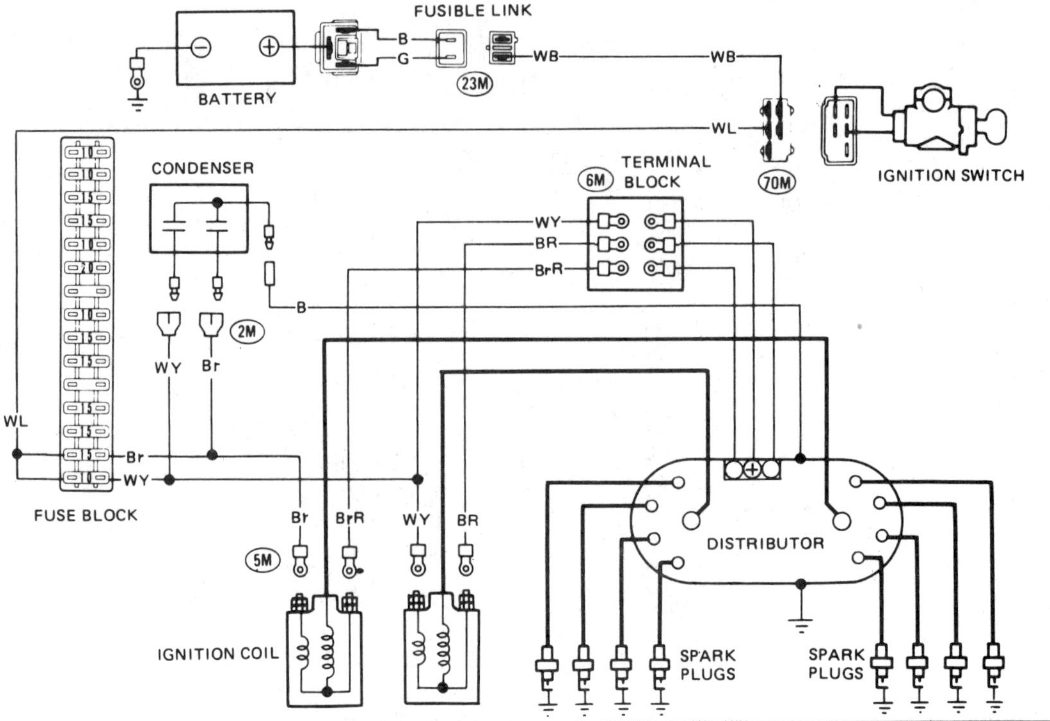

FUSIBLE LINK
B
G
WB
WB
23M
BATTERY
WL
WL
70M
IGNITION SWITCH
CONDENSER
TERMINAL
6M BLOCK
WY
BR
BrR
B
2M
WY Br
WL
Br
WY
FUSE BLOCK
Br BrR WY BR
5M
DISTRIBUTOR
IGNITION COIL
SPARK PLUGS
SPARK PLUGS

50

OFF
ACC
ON
START
LOCK
Ignition switch screw
R terminal
IG terminal
S terminal
A terminal
B terminal
Self-shear type screw

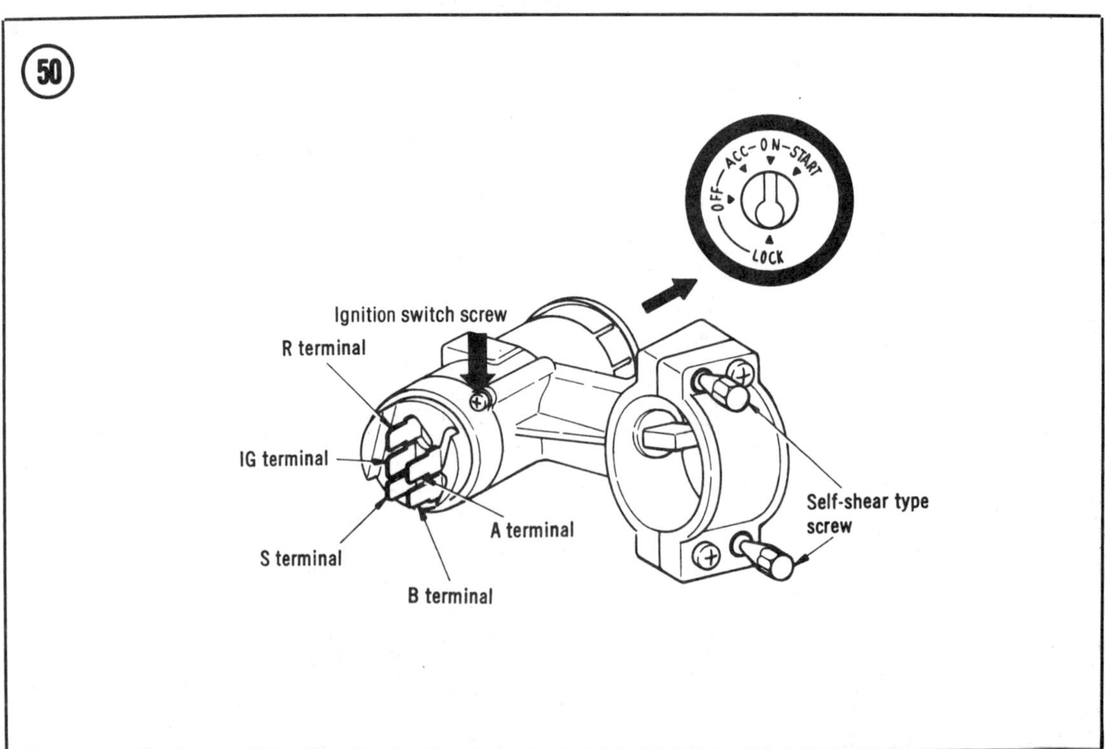

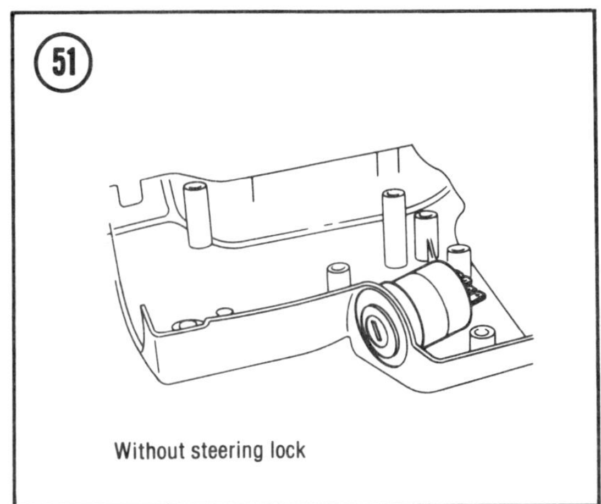
Without steering lock

4. On trucks without steering locks, remove the steering column cover, then detach the switch. See **Figure 51**.
5. To detach the steering lock, drill out the self-shearing screws, then remove them with a screw extractor. Remove the 2 plain screws and take the steering lock off.
6. Installation is the reverse of removal. If installing a steering lock, tighten new self-shearing screws until the heads snap off.

Ignition Coil Replacement

The coil (2 coils on NAPS-Z engines) is mounted on the left side of the engine compartment. On models equipped with resistors, the coil and resistor should be replaced as a matched set. To replace, disconnect the coil wires (and resistor wire, if so equipped). Remove the coil (and resistor, if so equipped), install the new one, and reconnect the wires.

DISTRIBUTOR

Proper engine operation depends very heavily on distributor advance characteristics. Advance is controlled by centrifugal and vacuum mechanisms, as well as by the spark timing control system on dual-point distributors. Adjustment of the advance mechanisms is critical and requires special test fixtures. Take the job to a Datsun dealer or automotive electrical specialist.

Distributor Removal

1. Remove the distributor cap.

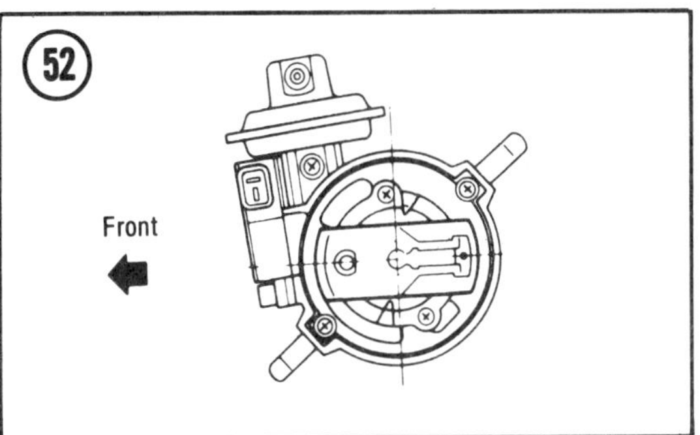

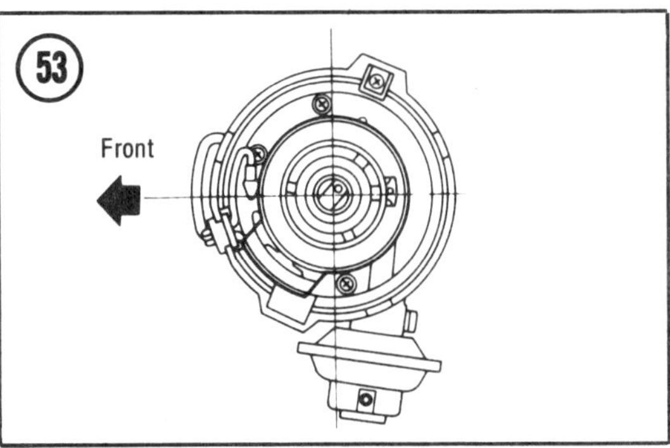

2. Disconnect the thin wires from the side of the distributor.
3. Disconnect the distributor vacuum line from the vacuum advance unit on the distributor.
4. Turn the engine over until No. 1 piston is at top dead center on its compression stroke. When this occurs, the timing notch in the crankshaft pulley will align with the pointer on the engine front cover (early L-series) or the 0 degree mark on the timing indicator (late L-series and NAPS-Z). Refer to *Ignition Timing*, Chapter Three.

In addition, the distributor rotor will point to No. 1 plug wire terminal(s) in the distributor cap. See **Figure 52** (L-series) or **Figure 53** (NAPS-Z).

NOTE
Check rotor position as well as the timing marks. The timing marks also line up when No. 1 piston is at TDC on its exhaust stroke.

5. To simplify installation, make alignment marks on the distributor body and engine.
6. Remove the distributor body setscrews. Lift the distributor out of the engine.

Distributor Installation

1. If the engine was turned with the distributor out, place No. 1 piston at top dead center on its compression stroke. See *Distributor Removal*, Step 4. The driving spindle should be positioned as shown in **Figure 54**.
2. Insert the distributor so it engages the driving spindle. Make sure the rotor points to No. 1 terminal in the distributor cap. Align the marks on engine and distributor body.
3. Install the body setscrews and distributor cap. Connect the thin wires and vacuum line to the distributor.
4. Adjust ignition timing as described in the *Tune-Up* section of Chapter Three.

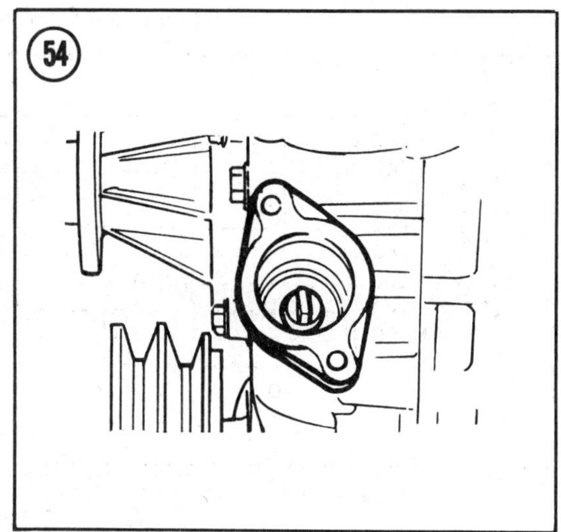

Table 1 BATTERY CHARGE PERCENTAGE

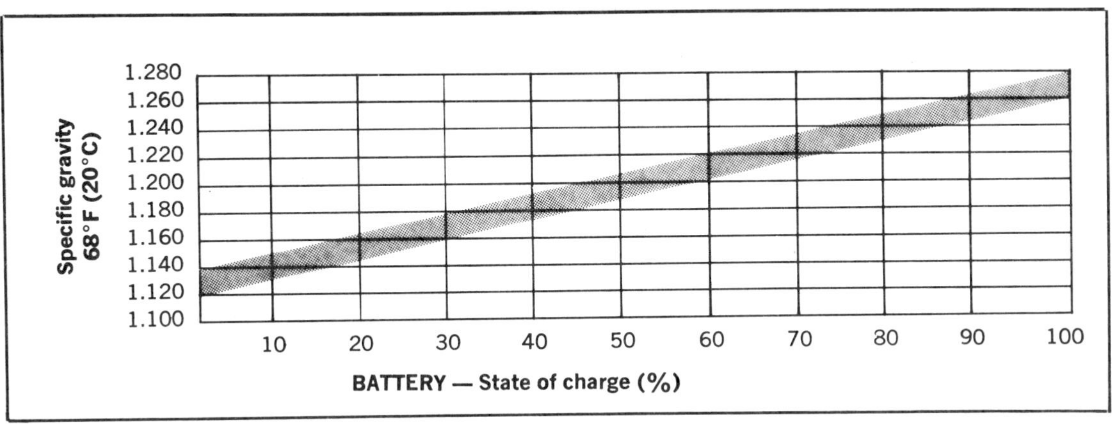

Table 2 BULB SPECIFICATIONS

Application	Wattage	Trade number
1970-1979		
Headlights		
High beams	37.5	4001
Low beams	37.5/50	4002
Front parking/turn signal lights	23/8	1034
Side marker lights	8	67
Rear combination lights (521 pickup)		
Stop/tail lights	23/8	1034
Rear turn signals	23	1073
Backup lights	23	1073
Rear combination lights (620 pickup)		
Turn/stop lights	23	1073
Tail, stop, and turn lights	23/8	1034
Tail lights	8	67
Backup lights	23	1073
License plate light	7.5	89
Interior light		
521 pickup	6	—
620 pickup	5	—
Engine compartment	6	—
Gauge illumination lights		
521 pickup	3.4	158
620 pickup	1.7	161
Indicator and warning lights		161
Knob and control illumination	3.4	158

(continued)

Table 2 BULB SPECIFICATIONS (continued)

Application	Wattage	Trade number
1980-on		
Headlights		
Inner	50	4651
Outer	40/60	4652
Front turn signals	27	1156
Front parking lights	5	—
Front side marker lights	5	—
Rear side marker lights	3.8	—
Stop/tail lights	27/8	1157
Rear turn signals	27	1156
Back-up lights	27	1156
License plate lights	10	—
Interior light		
Standard cab	5	—
King Cab	10	—
Oil pressure gauge illumination	3.4	158
Voltmeter illumination	3.4	158
Other gauge illumination	1.7	—
Warning lamps	3.4	158
Cigarette lighter illumination	1.4	—
Heater A/C illumination	3.4	158
Radio illumination	3.4	158
Rear defogger indicator lamp	1.4	—
Rear defogger switch illumination	3	158

NOTE: If you own a 1982 or later model, first check the Supplement at the back of the book for any new service information.

CHAPTER NINE

CLUTCH

All models use a single, dry-plate clutch with diaphragm spring. Major components are the pressure plate, disc, release mechanism, and hydraulic linkage. **Figure 1** shows clutch parts.

The release mechanism, which controls engagement and disengagement, consists of a bearing, sleeve, and withdrawal lever. The release mechanism is in turn controlled by the hydraulic linkage, which transmits pedal pressure through the clutch master cylinder, hydraulic line, and operating cylinder. The operating cylinder pushrod moves the withdrawal lever.

This chapter includes all service procedures practical for home mechanics. Specifications (**Table 1**) and tightening torques (**Table 2**) are found at the end of the chapter.

CLUTCH PART NAMES

Many clutch parts have two or more names. To prevent confusion, the following list gives part names used in this chapter and common synonyms:

Withdrawal lever—release lever, throwout arm

Release bearing—throw-out bearing

Operating cylinder—slave cylinder

Pressure plate—pressure plate assembly, clutch cover assembly

Disc—driven plate

9

CLUTCH PEDAL

Adjustment (521 Pickup)

1. Back off the pedal stopper until it is clear of the pedal. See **Figure 2**.
2. Measure pedal pad height from the floor. It should be 6.02 in. (153mm). If necessary, correct by inserting adjusting shims between the master cylinder and firewall. Be sure upper and lower shims are of the same thickness.
3. Lower the pedal to 5.91 in. (150 mm) by turning the pedal stopper. Tighten the pedal stopper locknut.

Adjustment (620 and 720 Pickups)

1. Loosen pedal stopper locknut. See **Figure 3**.
2. Turn the pedal stopper in or out to change pedal height. Compare with **Table 1**.
3. Tighten the pedal stopper locknut.
4. Loosen the locknut on the master cylinder pushrod. Rotate the pushrod in or out to adjust play at clevis pin. After adjustment, you should be able to move the pedal 0.04-0.12 in. (1-3 mm) without moving the master cylinder pushrod.

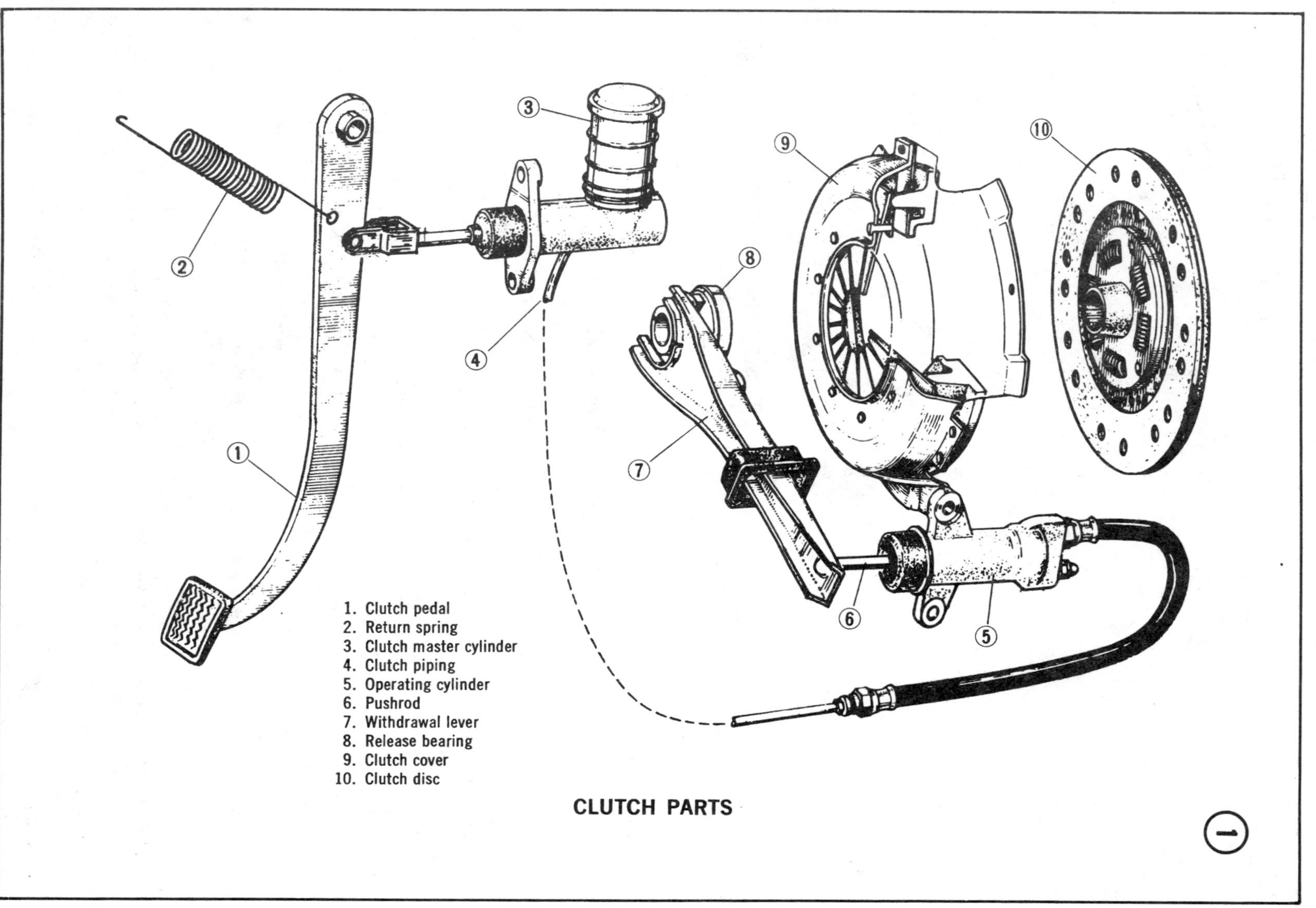

CLUTCH PARTS

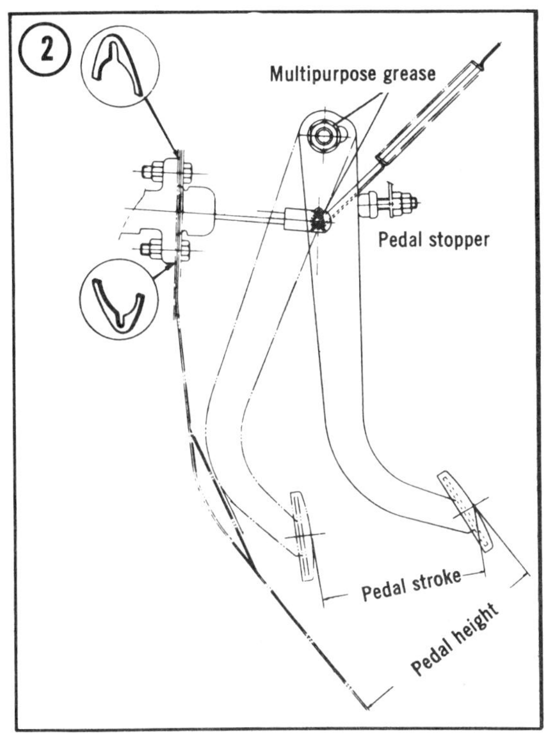

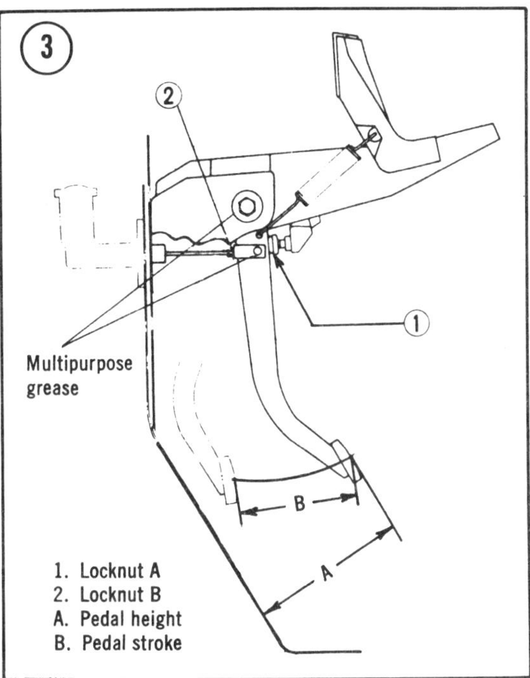

MASTER CYLINDER

Figure 4 shows typical master cylinders. Refer to it for the following procedure.

NOTE
Nabco and Tokico brand master cylinders are used in production. Although they are very similar, repair parts are not interchangeable between the 2 brands. Be sure to get the right brand when buying a repair kit.

Removal/Installation

1. Remove the clevis pin attaching the master cylinder pushrod to the clutch pedal.
2. With a container handy to catch dripping hydraulic fluid, disconnect the hydraulic line from the master cylinder.

CAUTION
Hydraulic fluid will damage paint. Wipe up any spilled fluid immediately, then wash area of the spill with soap and water.

3. Remove both master cylinder installation nuts and lift the cylinder out.
4. Installation is the reverse of these steps. Adjust pedal height. Bleed air out of the hydraulic system as described later in this chapter.

Disassembly

Refer to **Figure 4**.

1. Remove the filler cap from the fluid reservoir. Pour the fluid from the cylinder.
2. Pull back the dust cover and remove the stopper ring.
3. Take the stopper out of the cylinder. Remove the pushrod, then the piston assembly.
4. Take the piston cup off the piston and discard it.

NOTE
Do not remove the fluid reservoir unless absolutely necessary.

Inspection

1. Thoroughly clean all parts in brake fluid before inspection. Never use gasoline or kerosene for cleaning.
2. Check the piston for excessive or uneven wear, scoring, cracks or corrosion. Replace the piston if any of these defects are found.
3. Check the cylinder bore for wear, cracks, scoring, or corrosion. Replace the cylinder if defects are visible.

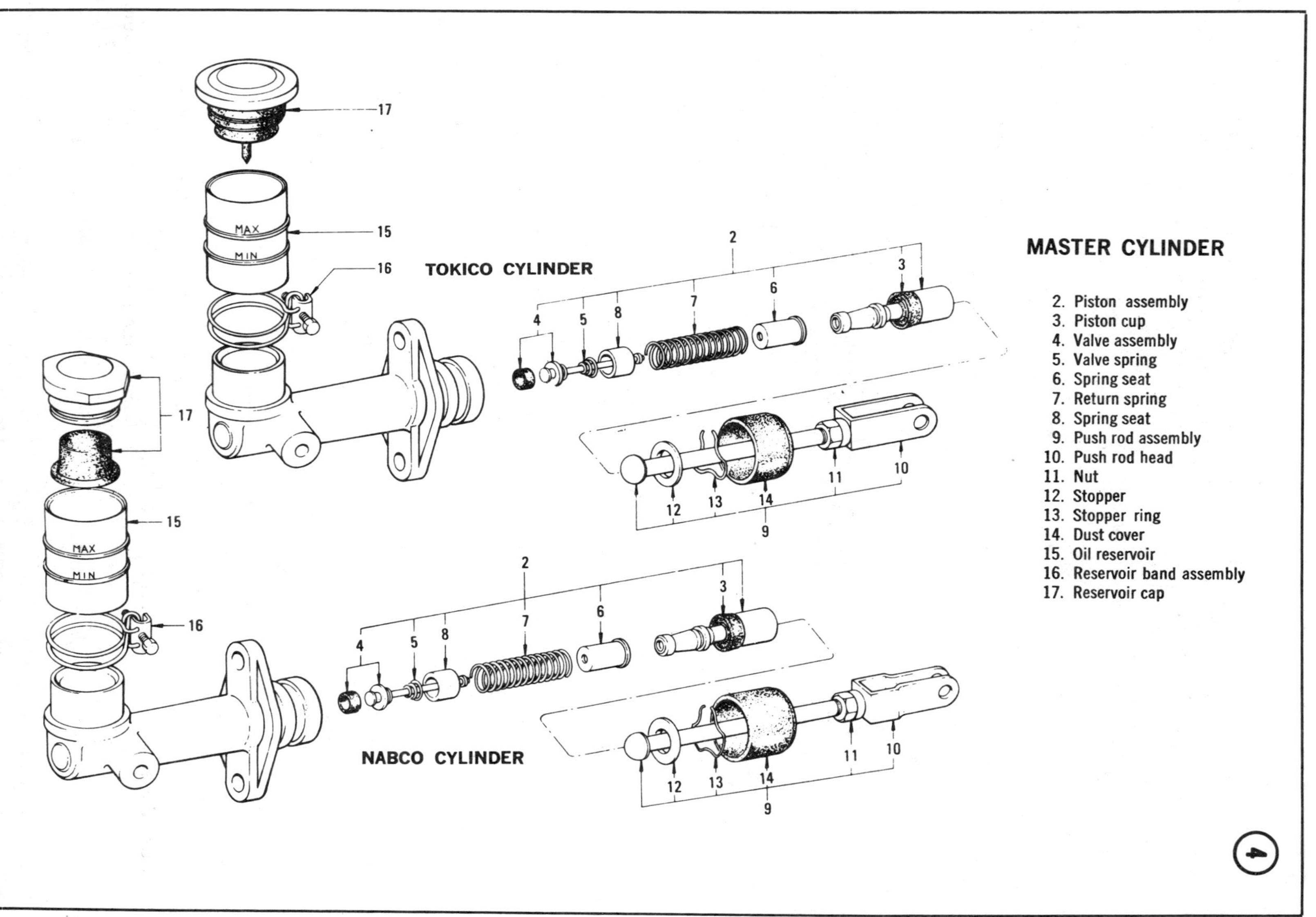
MASTER CYLINDER
2. Piston assembly
3. Piston cup
4. Valve assembly
5. Valve spring
6. Spring seat
7. Return spring
8. Spring seat
9. Push rod assembly
10. Push rod head
11. Nut
12. Stopper
13. Stopper ring
14. Dust cover
15. Oil reservoir
16. Reservoir band assembly
17. Reservoir cap
TOKICO CYLINDER
NABCO CYLINDER
MAX
MIN
MAX
MIN
4

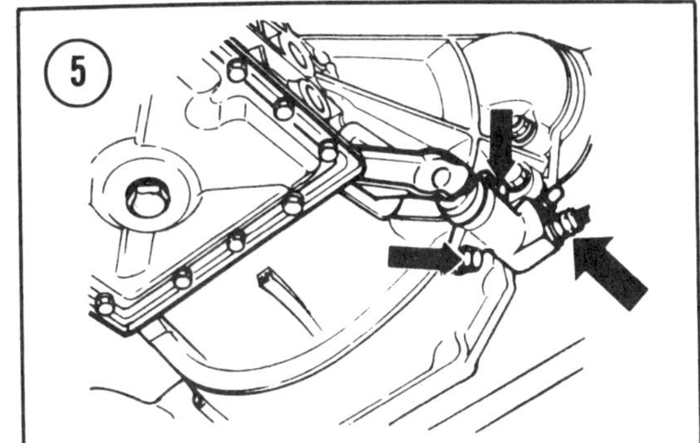

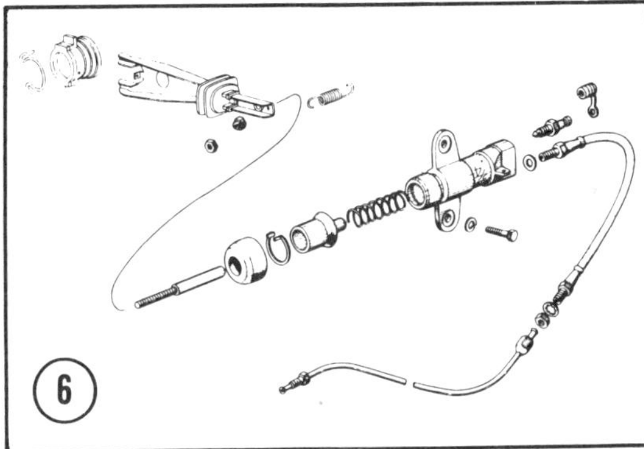

4. As a final check on a suspect cylinder and piston, measure the outside diameter of the piston and inside diameter of the cylinder. If the difference between these 2 figures exceeds 0.006 in. (0.15mm), replace the master cylinder.
5. Check the dust cover for wear, cracks, or signs of deterioration. Replace if these are detected. Check the fluid reservoir, filler cap, and hydraulic line for wear or damage. Replace as needed.

Assembly

1. Coat the cylinder bore with hydraulic fluid.
2. Install the piston return spring assembly.
3. Soak the piston cup with hydraulic fluid, then install it on the piston. The lip of the cup faces the front of the truck when the piston is installed.
4. Coat the piston with hydraulic fluid and insert it into the cylinder. Be careful not to bend back the lip of the piston cup.
5. Place the dust cover on the pushrod. Insert the pushrod and stopper into the cylinder. Install the stopper ring and push the lip of the dust cover over the cylinder.

OPERATING CYLINDER

Early cylinders use external and internal return springs and an adjustable pushrod. Later models use a non-adjustable pushrod and an internal return spring.

Removal/Installation

1. Unhook and remove the external spring (if so equipped).
2. With a container handy to catch dripping hydraulic fluid, disconnect the flexible clutch line from the metal tube. See **Figure 5**.
3. Disconnect the fluid hose from the operating cylinder.
4. Remove 2 cylinder mounting bolts. Separate the pushrod from the clutch withdrawal lever. Take the cylinder out.
3. Installation is the reverse of these steps. Adjust withdrawal lever play (if applicable). Bleed the clutch as described later in this chapter.

Disassembly and Inspection

Figure 6 shows an early operating cylinder. **Figure 7** shows the late type.

1. Remove the dust cover.
2. Remove the snap ring (if so equipped), then take out the piston end cup. Discard the cup.
3. Remove the internal spring (if so equipped).
4. Remove the bleed valve.
5. Thoroughly clean all parts in brake fluid. Do not use gasoline or kerosene.
6. Check the piston for excessive or uneven wear, scoring, cracks, or corrosion. Replace the piston if these conditions are found.
7. Check the cylinder bore for the defects described in Step 6. Replace the entire cylinder if any of these are found.

Assembly

Assembly is the reverse of the disassembly procedure, plus the following:

1. Soak the piston cup in brake fluid before installation. Make sure the lip of the cup faces into the cylinder before installing.
2. On cylinders with an internal spring, assemble the spring to the piston before installing the spring and piston.

9

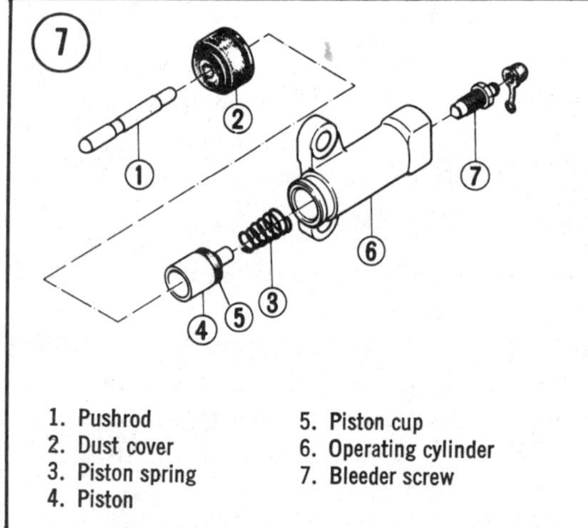

1. Pushrod
2. Dust cover
3. Piston spring
4. Piston
5. Piston cup
6. Operating cylinder
7. Bleeder screw

3. Coat the cylinder bore and piston with brake fluid before installing the piston.

WITHDRAWAL LEVER PLAY

Withdrawal lever play is regulated by the length of the operating cylinder pushrod. On adjustable pushrod models, adjustment is necessary whenever the operating cylinder is removed. On models without adjustable pushrods, withdrawal lever play is not adjustable.

Figure 8 is a cutaway of the operating cylinder, withdrawal lever, and release bearing. Refer to it as needed for this procedure.

1. Loosen the locknut. Rotate the adjusting nut until the top of the withdrawal lever contacts the release bearing inside the clutch housing. All withdrawal lever play should be eliminated.
2. Back off the adjusting nut 1 3/4 turns and secure it with the locknut.

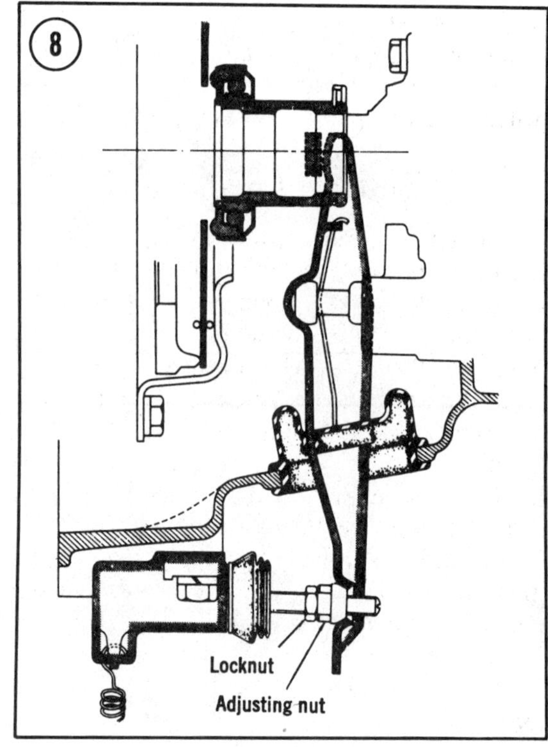

BLEEDING THE CLUTCH

Bleeding air out of the clutch hydraulic system is necessary whenever air enters the system. This occurs when the hydraulic line is disconnected at either end. It can also result from a very low clutch fluid level, or from defective master or operating cylinders. Air in the system can make shifting gears very difficult.

NOTE
This procedure requires 2 people, one to operate the clutch pedal and the other to open and close the bleed valve.

1. Remove the dust cap from the bleed valve on the operating cylinder.
2. Attach a plastic tube to the bleed valve. Place the other end of the tube in a clear glass jar containing several inches of clear brake fluid.

NOTE
Do not allow the end of the tube to come out of the brake fluid during bleeding. If this happens, air may be sucked into the system and the procedure will have to be repeated.

3. Top up the clutch master cylinder reservoir with fluid.
4. Have an assistant pump the clutch pedal 2 or 3 times, then hold it to the floor.
5. While the pedal is down, open the bleed valve to let air escape. Close the valve before letting the pedal up.

6. Repeat Steps 4 and 5 until the fluid entering the jar is free of air bubbles. Remove the tube, put the dust cover on the bleed valve, and top up the master cylinder.

CLUTCH REMOVAL

The engine and clutch housing must be separated to remove the clutch. This can be done either by removing the engine and transmission and separating them (Chapter Five) or by removing only the transmission (Chapter Ten). The release mechanism is incorporated in the clutch housing (front part of the transmission).

Once the engine and transmission have been separated, do the following:

1. Mark the edges of the pressure plate and flywheel so they may be reassembled in the same relative positions.
2. Remove the clutch cover bolts gradually in a diagonal pattern to prevent warping the pressure plate.

CLUTCH INSPECTION

Clutch Disc

Check the clutch disc for the following:

a. Oil or grease on the facings
b. Glazed facings
c. Warped facings
d. Loose or missing rivets
e. Facings worn to within 0.012 in (0.3 mm) of any rivet
f. Broken springs
g. Loose fit or rough movement on transmission main drive shaft splines

Small amounts of oil or grease may be removed from the disc with non-petroleum solvent and the facings dressed with a wire brush. However, if the facings are soaked with oil or grease, the disc must be replaced. The disc must also be replaced if any other defects are present, or if facings are worn and a new pressure plate is being installed.

Pressure Plate

Check the pressure plate for:

a. Scoring
b. Burn marks (blue-tinted areas)
c. Cracks

Replace the pressure plate if these are evident. If the clutch trouble is still not apparent, take the pressure plate and disc to a competent garage. Have disc and pressure plate checked for excessive runout and the diaphragm spring for incorrect finger height. Do not attempt to readjust the fingers or dismantle the pressure plate without proper tools and experience.

CLUTCH INSTALLATION

1. Be sure your hands are clean.
2. Inspect the disc facings, pressure plate, and flywheel to be sure they are free of grease, oil, or other foreign material.
3. Clean the clutch pilot bushing and fill it with multipurpose grease.
4. Place the clutch disc and pressure plate in position on the flywheel. The long side of the disc hub faces the rear of the truck. Line up the alignment marks made during removal.
5. Center the disc and pressure plate with an aligning bar such as the one shown in **Figure 9**. A main drive shaft from a junk transmission can be substituted if the special tool is not available. Inexpensive aligning bars can be purchased at some imported car parts stores. Some tool rental dealers and parts stores rent universal aligning bars which are suitable.

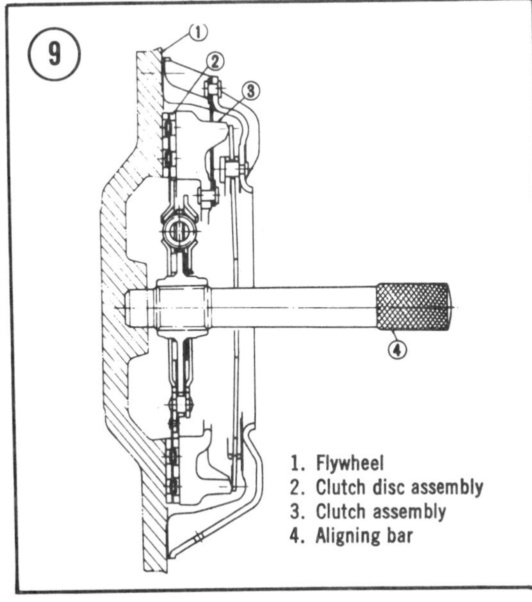

9

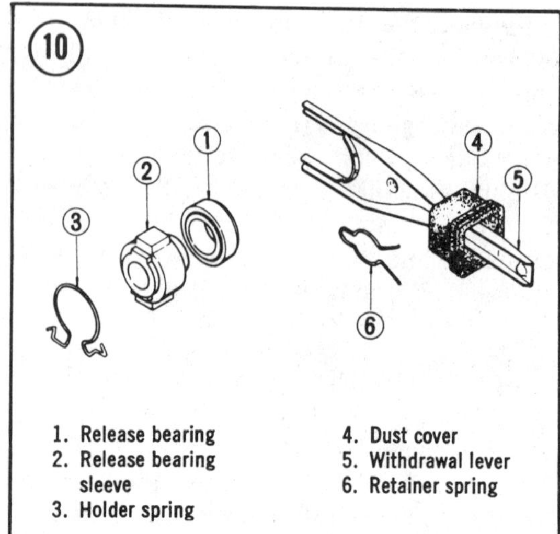

1. Release bearing
2. Release bearing sleeve
3. Holder spring
4. Dust cover
5. Withdrawal lever
6. Retainer spring

6. Install the clutch cover bolts, tightening gradually in a diagonal pattern. Tighten to specifications given at the end of the chapter.

RELEASE MECHANISM

Removal

As with the clutch release mechanism removal requires that the engine and transmission be separated first. The release mechanism is mounted in the clutch housing. Either remove the engine and transmission and separate them (Chapter Five) or remove only the transmission (Chapter Ten).

Disassembly

1. Referring to **Figure 10**, remove the dust cover from the clutch housing.
2. Remove the holder spring. Take out the release bearing and sleeve.
3. If the operating cylinder has an external return spring, unhook it from withdrawal lever.
4. Detach the retainer spring from withdrawal lever. Remove the withdrawal lever from its ball pin.
5. Remove the release bearing from its sleeve with a puller (**Figure 11**). The bearing is a press fit on the sleeve.

Inspection

Check release mechanism for the following:

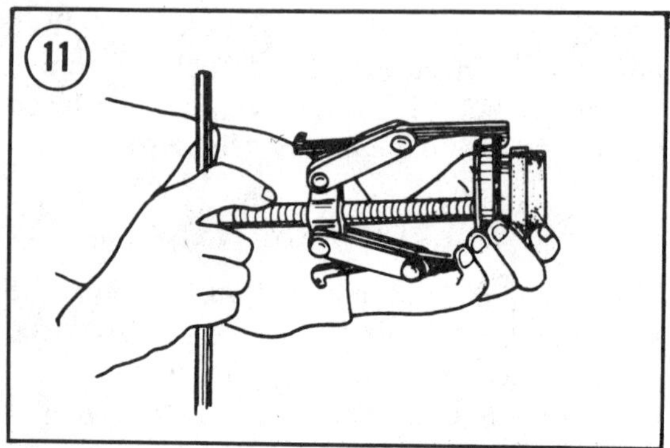

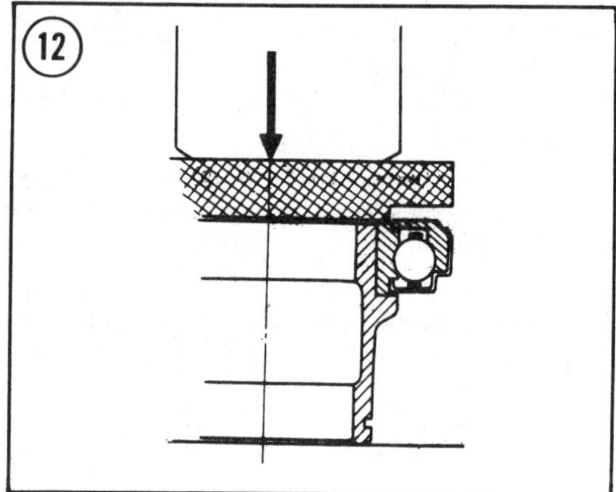

1. *Wear at the contact point of the withdrawal lever and release bearing sleeve.* Replace the sleeve if worn.
2. *Grease leaking from the release bearing.* Replace the bearing if this evident.

CAUTION

Do not clean the release bearing in solvent, since it is prelubricated at the factory. Clean with a lint-free cloth.

3. *A worn release bearing.* To check, hold the inner race with fingers and rotate the outer race while applying light pressure to it. If the bearing feels rough or makes noise, replace it.

Assembly

1. Press the release bearing onto the sleeve (**Figure 12**). When it is in place, rotate the bearing to make sure it operates smoothly.
2. Referring to **Figure 13**, apply a *light* coat of multipurpose grease to the following:
   a. Contact points of withdrawal lever and release bearing sleeve

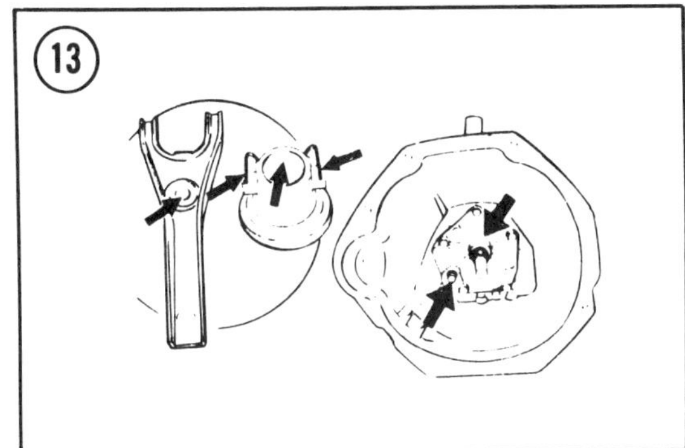
13

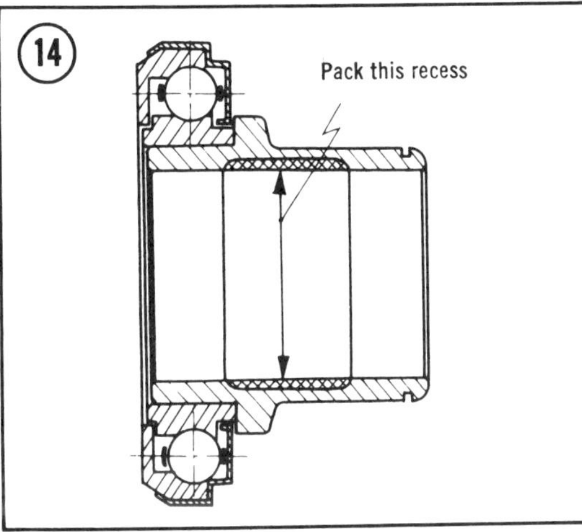

14

b. Contact points of withdrawal lever and ball pin

c. Contact points of release bearing sleeve and transmission front cover

3. Pack the recess inside the bearing sleeve with multipurpose grease. See **Figure 14**.

4. Apply a small amount of molybdenum disulphide grease to the transmission main drive shaft splines.

5. Place the withdrawal lever in position over the transmission main drive shaft, with the operating cylinder end through the hole in the clutch housing.

6. Position the release bearing and sleeve on the withdrawal lever. Install the holder spring.

7. Install the dust cover in the clutch housing.

8. If operating cylinder uses an external return spring, attach it to the withdrawal lever.

9. Install the transmission as described in Chapter Ten.

10. Bleed the air from the clutch hydraulic system as described earlier in this chapter.

11. Check and adjust pedal height as described earlier.

12. On trucks with adjustable operating cylinders, adjust withdrawal lever play as described earlier.

9

Table 1 CLUTCH SPECIFICATIONS

Disc diameter	
1970-1973	7.87 in. (200mm)
1974-on	8.86 in. (225mm)
Master cylinder bore diameter	5/8 in. (15.87mm)
Operating cylinder bore diameter	3/4 in. (19.05mm)

Table 2 TIGHTENING TORQUES

Fastener	Ft.-lb.	Mkg
Clutch cover bolts	12-15	1.6-2.1
Master cylinder mounting bolts/nuts	6-9	0.8-1.2
Operating cylinder mounting bolts		
1970-1979	18-25	2.5-3.5
1980-on	22-30	3.1-4.1
Bleed valve	5-6.5	0.7-0.9

CHAPTER TEN

TRANSMISSION

Standard equipment on the 1970-1973 models is the F4W63 four-speed transmission. From 1974 on, the standard transmission is the F4W71B. The model 3N71B automatic became optional in mid-1972, with the introduction of the PL620 pickup. The five-speed model FS5W71B became optional in 1977.

This chapter provides removal, overhaul, and installation procedures for the manual transmissions. It also includes inspection, removal, and installation procedures for the automatic.

Manual transmission overhaul is not the best starting point for the beginning mechanic. However, it doesn't require special training, and the special tools shown in this chapter can easily be duplicated. Overhaul does require patience and the ability to concentrate. The work area must be clean, free of distractions, and inaccessible to pets and small children. Before starting, read the procedure carefully. Obtain the necessary special tools or substitutes. Check parts availability with local suppliers.

A few special tools are used in this chapter. All are available through your dealer. A few are manufactured by Kent-Moore Tool Division, 29784 Little Mack, Roseville, Michigan, 48066 and may be ordered direct from them.

Automatic transmission overhaul requires special skills, many expensive special tools, and

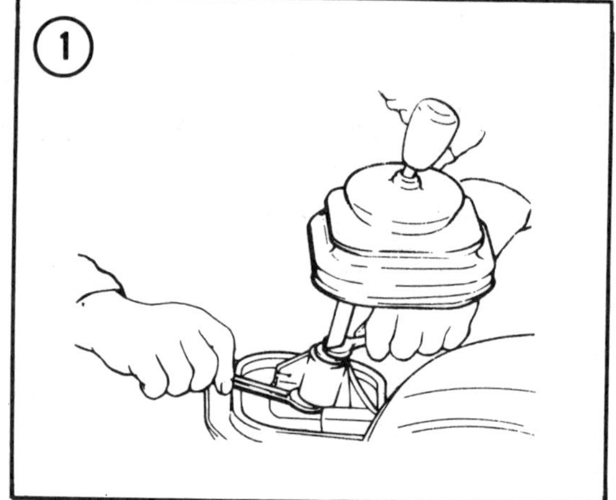

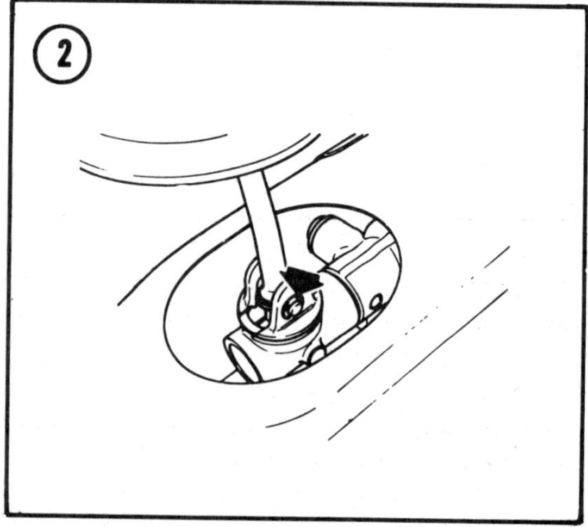

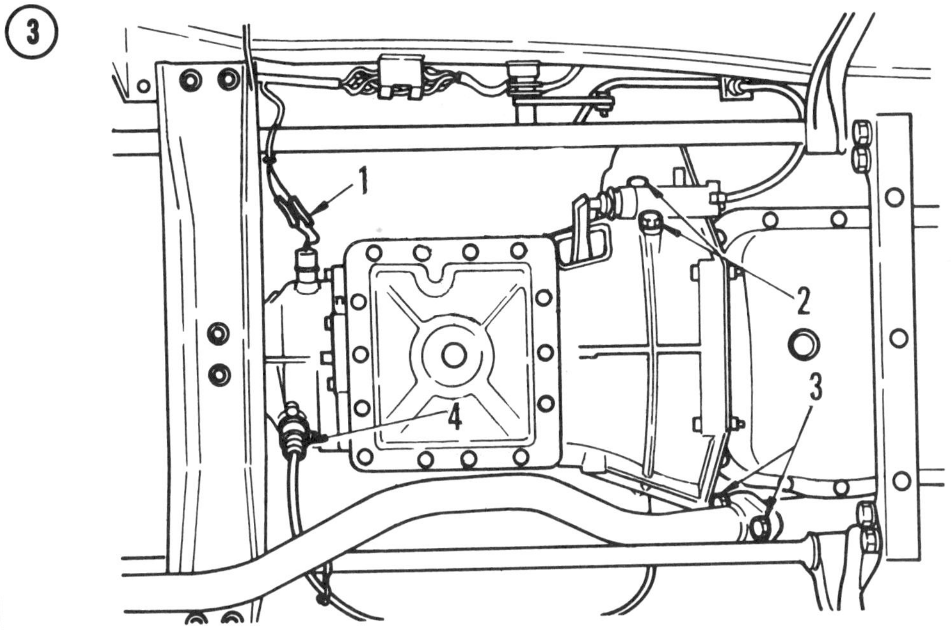

3

1. Back-up lamp switch (third gear and neutral switches similar)
2. Clutch operating cylinder bolts
3. Exhaust pipe bolts
4. Speedometer cable

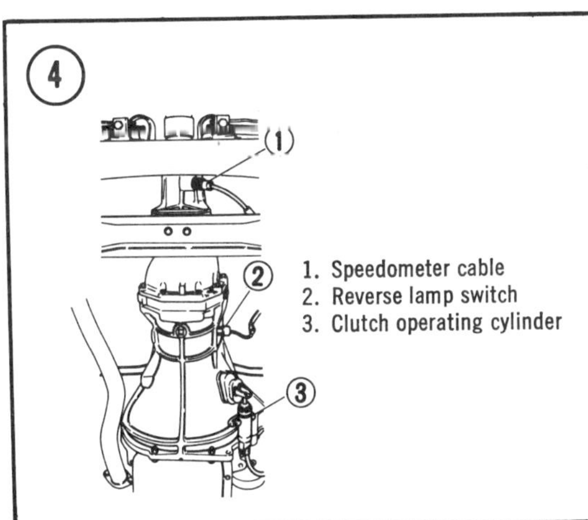

1. Speedometer cable
2. Reverse lamp switch
3. Clutch operating cylinder

extreme cleanliness. For these reasons, overhaul should be left to a Datsun dealer or other competent professional.

The testing and adjustment procedures in this chapter will help you locate and solve many automatic transmission problems. The removal and installation procedures will help you reduce labor costs if major overhaul is necessary.

MANUAL TRANSMISSION

Removal/Installation

1. Disconnect the negative cable from battery.
2. Remove the shift lever hole cover from the floor.
3. On 1970-1973 transmissions remove the nut from the base of the shift lever (**Figure 1**). On 1974 and later models remove the snap ring and pivot pin securing the shift lever (**Figure 2**). Lift lever out.
4. Jack up all 4 corners of the vehicle and place it on jackstands. Be sure the stands are securely positioned.
5. Drain the transmission oil. If this is not done, the oil will run onto the floor when the transmission is removed.
6. Remove the drive shaft (Chapter Eleven).
7. Disconnect the wires from the reverse lamp switch, third gear switch, and neutral switch (if so equipped).
8. Detach the speedometer cable from the rear extension. See **Figure 3** or **Figure 4**.

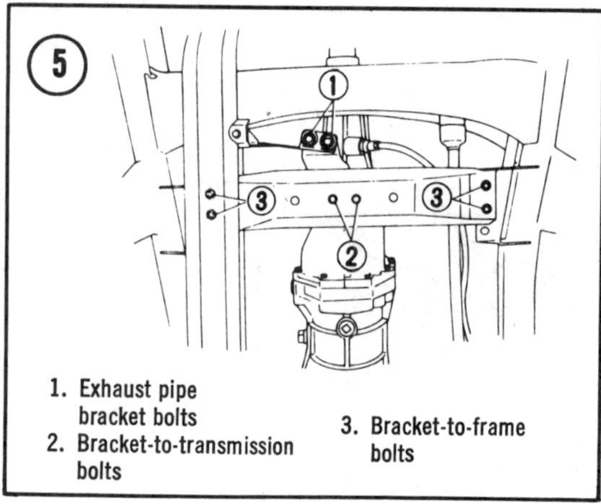

5

1. Exhaust pipe bracket bolts
2. Bracket-to-transmission bolts
3. Bracket-to-frame bolts

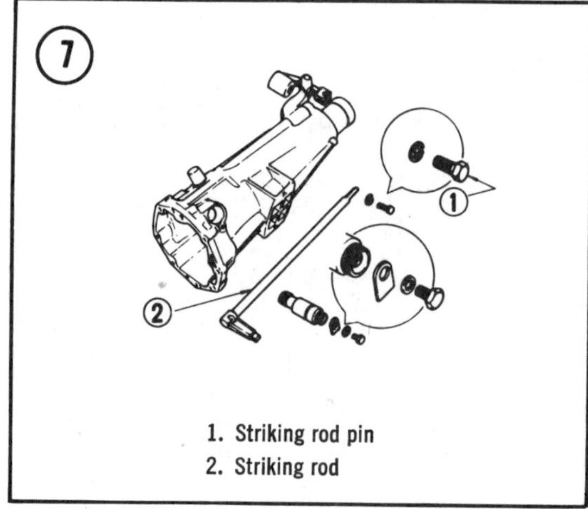

7

1. Striking rod pin
2. Striking rod

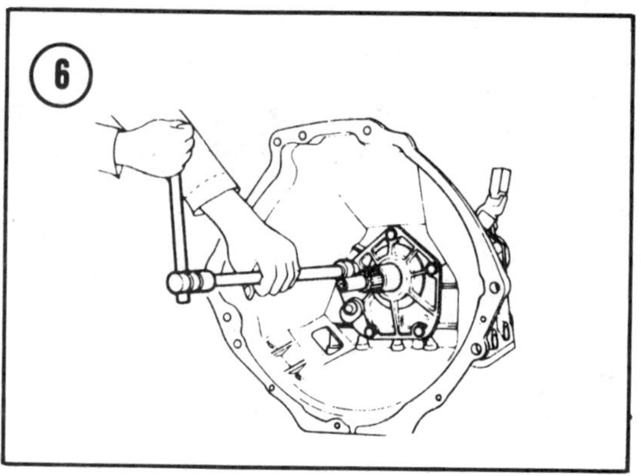

6

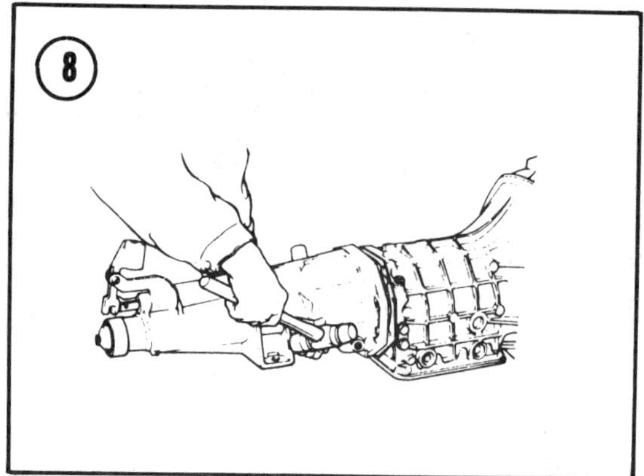

8

9. Remove the clutch operating cylinder (Chapter Eight).

10. Remove the starter (Chapter Seven).

11. On 1975 and later models, disconnect the front exhaust pipe from the manifold. See Chapter Five, *Exhaust System* section.

12. On late California models, disconnect the exhaust pipe bracket from the transmission. See **Figure 5**.

13. Place a jack beneath the engine. Use a block of wood beneath the jack and oil pan to prevent damage.

14. Place a transmission jack beneath the transmission. These are available from rental dealers.

15. Detach the mounting member from the vehicle frame, then from the transmission. **Figure 5** shows a typical mounting member.

16. Remove the engine-to-transmission bolts.

17. Lower the jacks beneath the engine and transmission. Slide the transmission backward and down until it is clea of the engine. Lower transmission and take it out from under the car.

CAUTION

To prevent damage to the transmission input shaft, never remove the transmission partway. Be sure the input shaft separates completely from the engine when removing transmission.

18. Install by reversing Steps 1-17. Tighten nuts and bolts to specifications (**Table 1**, end of chapter). Fill the transmission with an oil recommended in Chapter Three. Fill and bleed the clutch hydraulic system. If the vehicle has an adjustable pushrod operating cylinder, adjust withdrawal lever play. See Chapter Eight.

Disassembly (F4W63)

1. Thoroughly clean the outside of the transmission before disassembly. Place it on a workbench or stand.

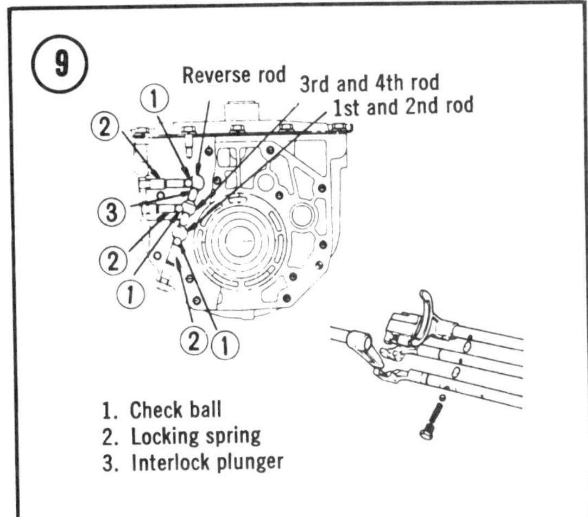

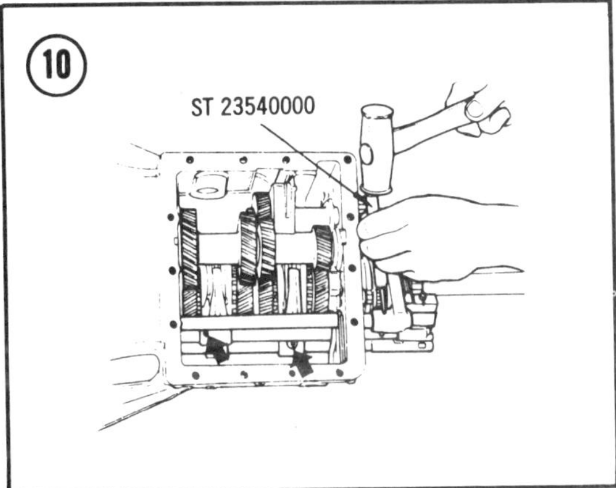

2. Remove the clutch release mechanism (see Chapter Eight).

3. Remove 5 bolts securing the front cover (**Figure 6**). Remove the front cover and gasket.

4. Remove the bottom cover and gasket from the transmission case.

5. On 521 pickups, slide each synchronizer sleeve over a balk ring and the clutch teeth on a gear. This engages 2 gears at once, locking the main shaft. Remove the nut that secures the flange at the rear end of the transmission.Take the flange out, then slide the synchronizer sleeves back to the neutral position.

6. Remove the electrical switches from the rear extension. Tag each switch so it can be reinstalled correctly.

7. Remove the striking rod pin (1, **Figure 7**). Disengage the shift lever bracket from the striking rod (2).

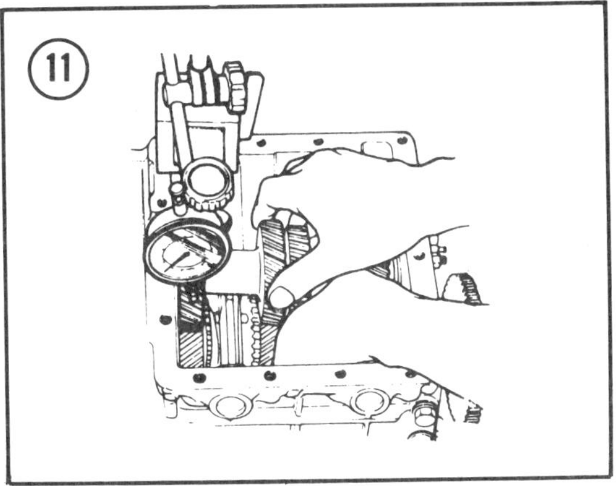

8. Remove the bolt and lock plate securing the speedometer pinion (**Figure 7**). Withdraw the pinion from the extension.

9. Unbolt the rear extension from the transmission case. Tap it free with a soft-faced mallet, then take it off the main shaft. See **Figure 8**.

10. Remove the striking rod (2, **Figure 7**).

11. Remove 3 check ball plugs from the transmission case. Take out the locking springs (2, **Figure 9**) and check balls (1).

12. Drive the retaining pins from all 3 shift forks (**Figure 10**).

13. Carefully pull the shift rods out of the transmission case. Be careful not to lose interlock plungers (3, **Figure 9**).

14. Mount a dial gauge as shown in **Figure 11** and measure gear backlash. To measure, hold the main shaft from turning. Turn the countershaft against the dial gauge plunger as far as possible without turning the main shaft. The reading on the dial gauge is gear backlash. Repeat the procedure for the remaining gears. Compare with specifications (end of chapter). If backlash is excessive, replace driving and driven gears as a set.

15. Slide main shaft reverse gear forward to mesh with the reverse idler gear. Slide a synchronizer sleeve over a balk ring and the clutch teeth on a gear. This engages reverse and a forward gear, locking the main shaft.

16. Bend the lockwasher away from the main nut. Loosen the nut, but don't remove it yet. Slide the main shaft reverse gear out of mesh. Place the synchronizer sleeve in neutral (between gears).

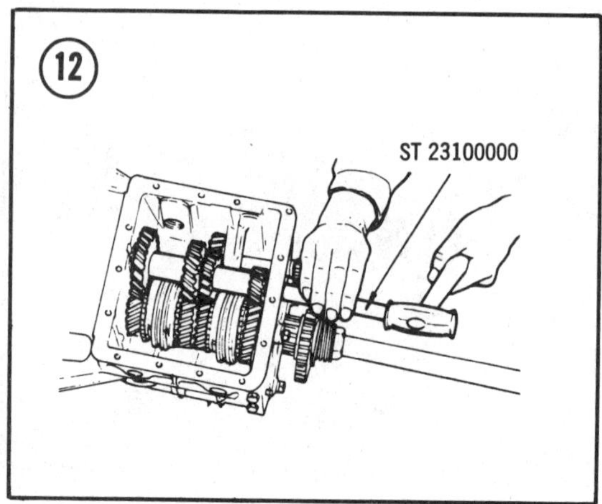

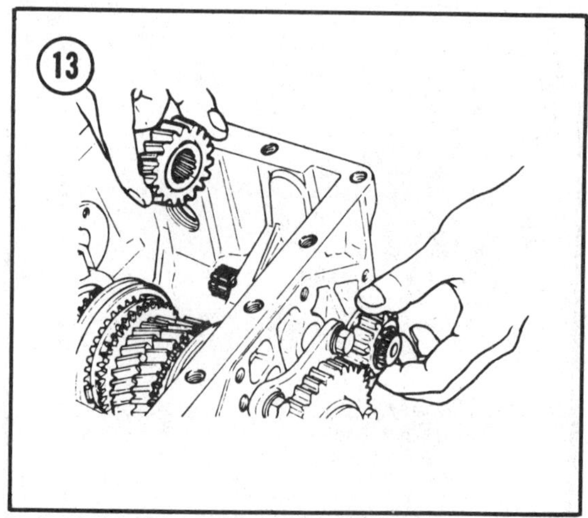

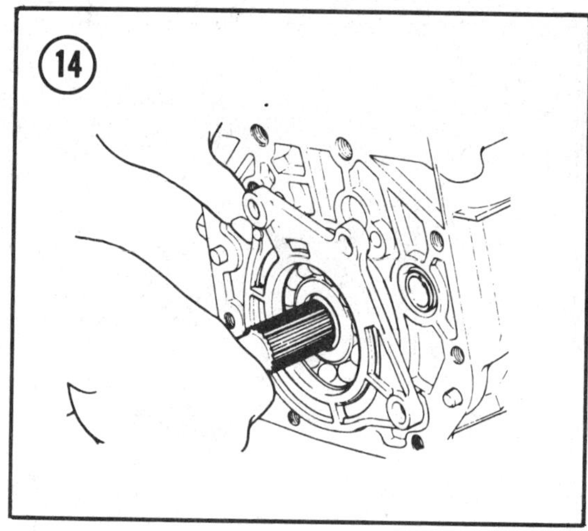

17. Carefully push the countershaft from the transmission case, using a dummy countershaft such as Datsun ST 23100000 or Kent-Moore J25685 (**Figure 12**). If the special tool isn't available, use a metal dowel the same thickness as the countershaft and the same length as the countershaft gear.

CAUTION
Be sure the dummy countershaft fits inside the needle roller bearings when pushing the countershaft out.

18. Lift the countershaft gear from the transmission case, together with its needle roller bearings. Be sure to remove the thrust washers that fit between the transmission case and the countershaft gear.
19. Remove the snap ring securing the reverse idler gear. Pull the reverse idler shaft out of the transmission case. See **Figure 13**.
20. Unbolt the main shaft bearing retainer from the rear side of the transmission case. Pull the main shaft assembly out (**Figure 14**).
21. Remove the small pilot bearing that supports the front end of the main shaft. After removing the main shaft, the bearing will be on the front end of the main shaft, inside the rear end of the input shaft, or will have fallen into the transmission case.
22. Push the main drive gear out of the transmission case. Use a wooden hammer handle as shown in **Figure 15**.
23. Measure the end play of first, second, and third gears (**Figure 16**). Compare with specifications at the end of the chapter.
24. Referring to **Figure 17**, remove the following parts in order from the front end of the main shaft: snap ring, third-fourth gear synchronizer assembly, and third gear. Don't disassemble the synchronizer yet.
25. Remove the nut and lockwasher from the rear end of the main shaft. Remove reverse gear, the reverse hub, and the speedometer drive gear. Be careful not to loose the speedometer gear drive ball.
26. Place a press tool against the front side of first gear (**Figure 18**). Press first gear, the main shaft ball bearing, and bearing retainer off the main shaft.

CAUTION
Do not place the press tool against second gear. This may damage the first gear bushing.

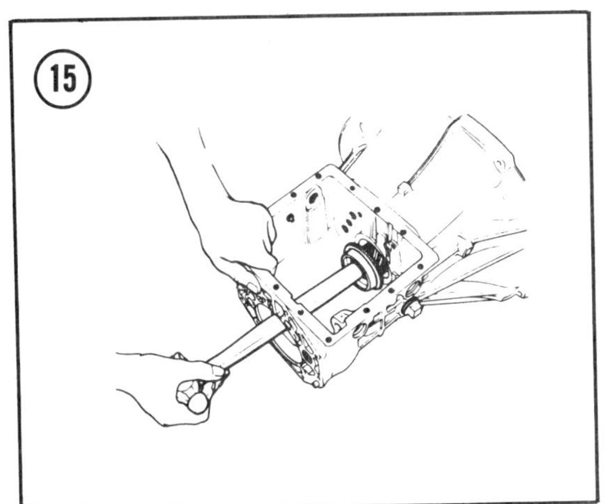

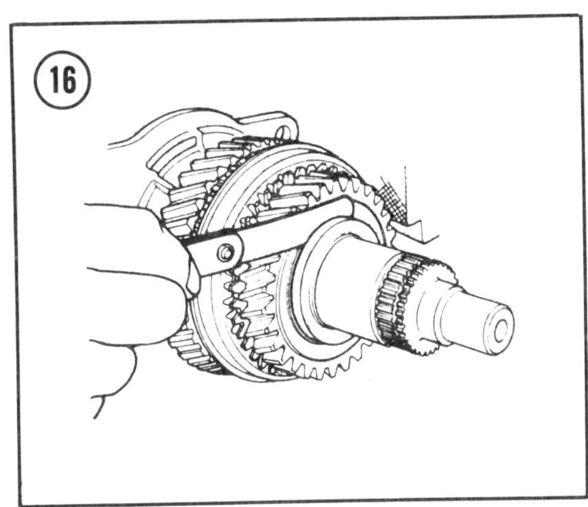

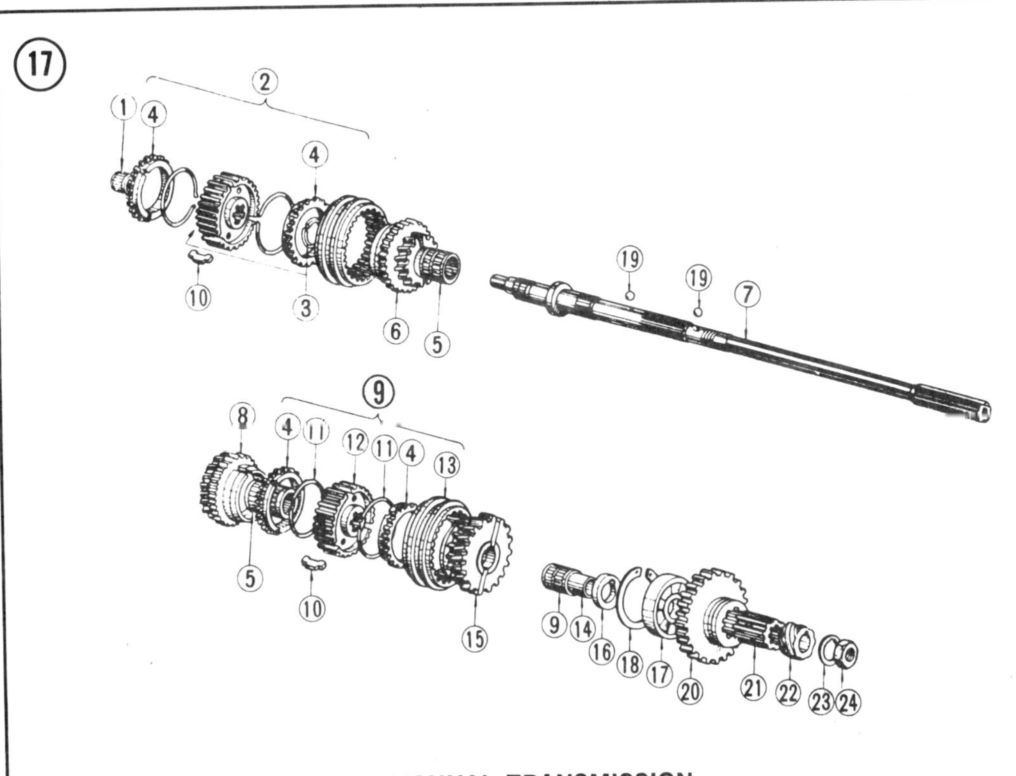

MANUAL TRANSMISSION

1. Pilot bearing
2. 3rd and 4th synchromesh assembly
3. Snap ring
4. Balk ring
5. Needle bearing
6. 3rd gear
7. Main shaft
8. 2nd gear
9. 1st and 2nd synchromesh assembly
10. Shifting insert
11. Spread ring
12. Synchronizer hub
13. Coupling sleeve
14. 1st gear bushing
15. 1st gear
16. Thrust washer
17. Main shaft bearing
18. Snap ring
19. Steel ball
20. Reverse gear
21. Reverse hub
22. Speedometer drive gear
23. Lock plate
24. Nut

27. Place a press tool against the front side of second gear. Press second gear, the first-second gear synchronizer and first gear bushing off the main shaft.

28. Disassemble both synchronizers, referring to **Figure 19**. Keep each synchronizer's parts separate from the other's.

Inspection (F4W63)

1. Thoroughly clean all parts in solvent. Remove all traces of old gasket and sealer. Inspect all parts while cleaning and replace any with obvious wear or damage.

2. Check the transmission case and rear extension for cracks. Check all gasket surfaces for gouges or roughness which could cause an oil leak. Replace if these conditions are found.

3. Inspect bearings for wear and damage. Hold the outer race with one hand and rotate the inner race with the other. See **Figure 20**. Check for excessive noise, roughness, or looseness. Replace any suspect bearings.

4. If the main drive gear bearing is defective, remove the snap ring and spacer **(Figure 21)**, then press the bearing off. A machine shop can do this if you don't have a press.

5. Check the bushing and oil seal at the back of the rear extension. Replace the bushing if worn unevenly. Replace the oil seal whenever the transmission is overhauled. Replace the O-ring and oil seal on the speedometer pinion sleeve.

6. Check the bushing and oil seal at the back of the rear extension. Replace the bushing if worn unevenly. Replace the oil seal if the lip is worn or damaged. Replace the O-ring and oil seal on the speedometer pinion sleeve.

7. Check the front oil seal for wear or damage. Replace the oil seal if there is any doubt about its condition.

8. Check the shafts for signs of bending, twisting, or damaged splines. **Figure 22** shows examples of defective splines.

9. Inspect all gears for chipped, broken, or badly worn teeth. Replace any gears with these conditions.

10. Check balk rings for wear and damage. Place each balk ring on its gear cone. Measure the gap between balk ring teeth and gear clutch

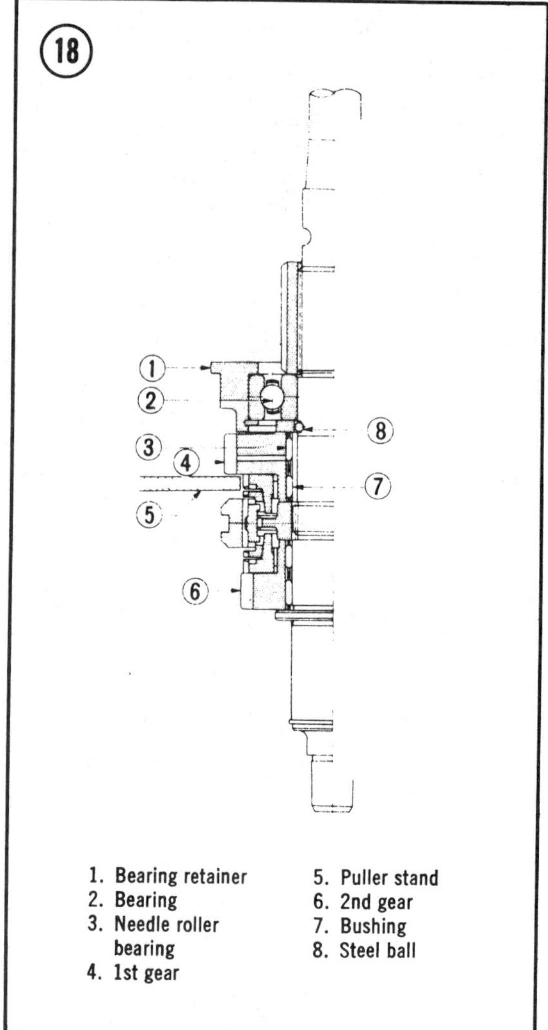

1. Bearing retainer
2. Bearing
3. Needle roller bearing
4. 1st gear
5. Puller stand
6. 2nd gear
7. Bushing
8. Steel ball

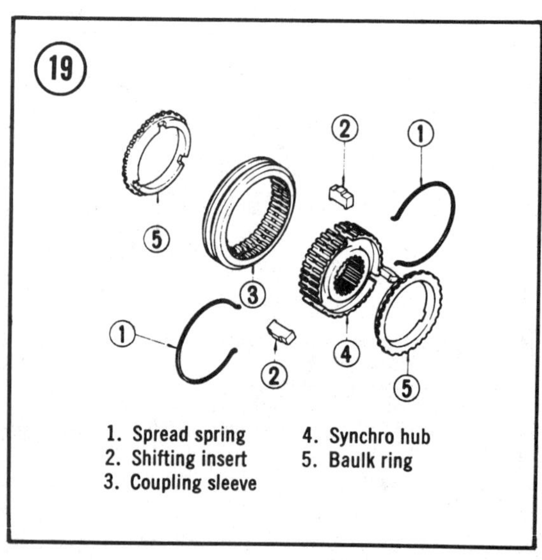

1. Spread spring
2. Shifting insert
3. Coupling sleeve
4. Synchro hub
5. Baulk ring

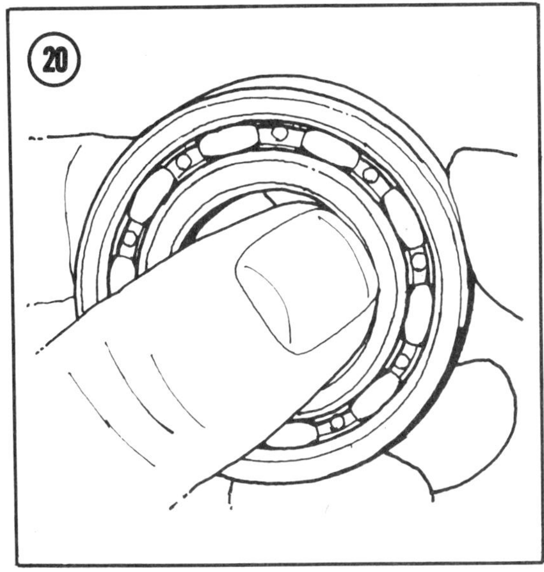

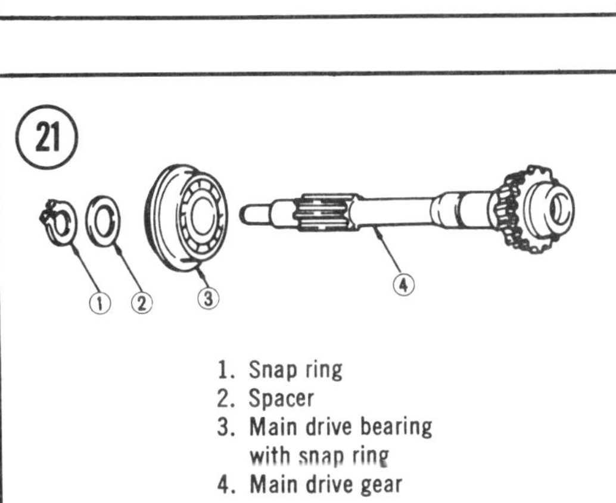

1. Snap ring
2. Spacer
3. Main drive bearing with snap ring
4. Main drive gear

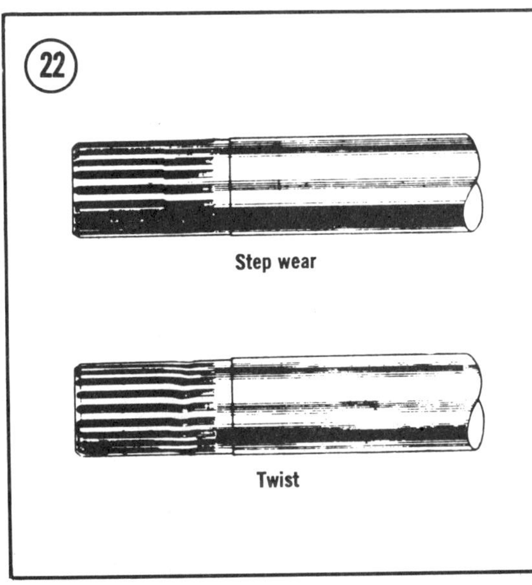

Step wear

Twist

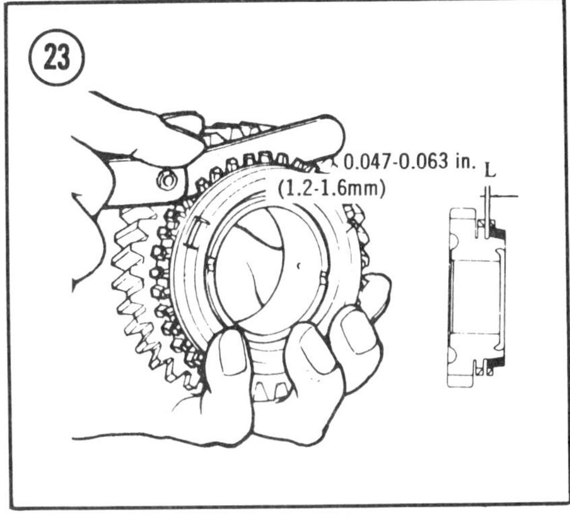

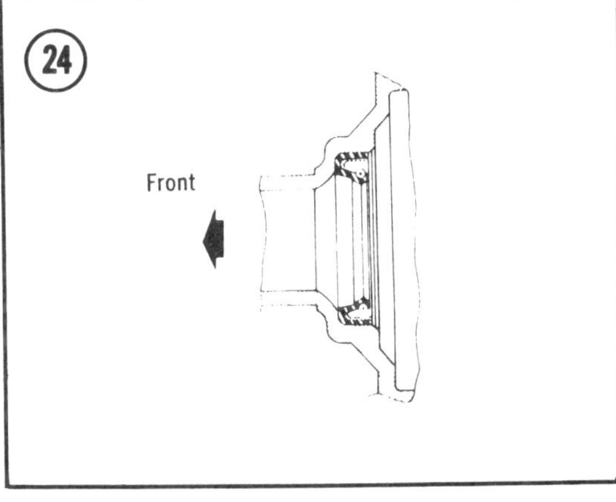

teeth with a feeler gauge. See **Figure 23**. If the gap is too small, replace the balk ring.

Assembly (F4W63)

Cleanliness is essential for transmission assembly. Work in a dust-free area and handle parts with clean, bare hands only. Do not wear gloves or use rags.

During assembly, coat all friction points with gear oil.

1. If the front oil seal was removed, install a new one with a press or suitable drift. See **Figure 24**. Be sure the seal mounting surface in the front cover is clean before installing the seal.

2. If the rear extension oil seal was removed, install a new one. See **Figure 25**.

3. Coat the striking rod with gear oil, then install it in the rear extension. See **Figure 7**.

4. Assemble the synchronizers, referring to **Figure 19**. Install the spread springs as shown in **Figure 26**. Be sure the gaps in the springs are not directly opposite each other.

5. Install the following parts in order on the rear end of the main shaft: second gear needle roller bearing, second gear, second gear balk ring, and first-second gear synchronizer. The long side of the synchronizer hub faces the rear (**Figure 27**).

6. Press the first gear bushing onto the main shaft, using a suitable brass drift. Have a machine shop do this if you don't have the necessary equipment.

7. Install the following parts in order on the rear end of the main shaft: first gear balk ring, first gear needle roller bearing, first gear, drive ball, and thrust washer. See **Figure 28**.

8. Position a press tool as shown in **Figure 29**. Press the main shaft ball bearing, bearing retainer, and reverse hub onto the main shaft.

9. Install the following parts in order from the front end of the main shaft: third gear needle roller bearing, third gear, third gear balk ring, and third-fourth gear synchronizer assembly. The long side of the synchronizer hub faces the rear.

10. Secure the third-fourth gear synchronizer with a snap ring (**Figure 30**). Use the thickest snap ring that will fit in the groove. Snap rings are available in several thicknesses.

11. Install the following parts in order from the rear end of the main shaft: reverse gear, drive ball, speedometer drive gear, lockwasher, and main shaft nut. Tighten the main shaft nut slightly. It will be torqued to specifications later.

12. Install the main shaft in the transmission case (**Figure 14**). Install the bearing retainer bolts. Tighten to 6-7 ft.-lb. (0.9-1.2 mkg).

13. If the bearing was removed from the input shaft, install the new bearing. Use a press or a standard gear puller.

14. Secure the main drive gear bearing with a spacer and snap ring (**Figure 31**). Use the thickest spacer that will fit between the bearing and snap ring. Spacers are available in several thicknesses.

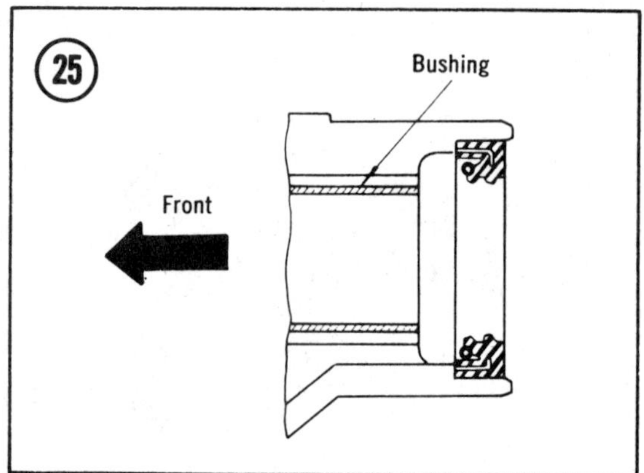

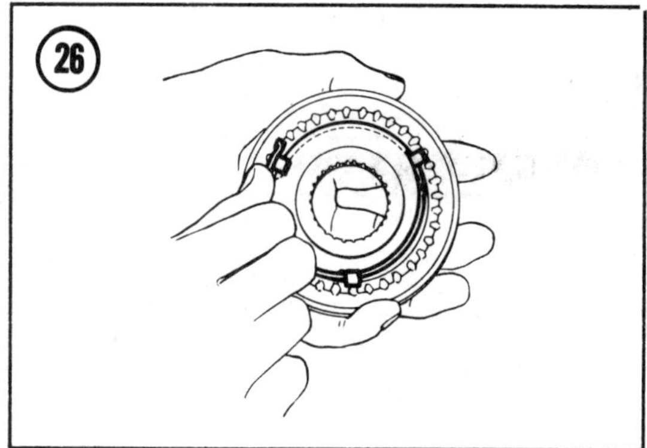

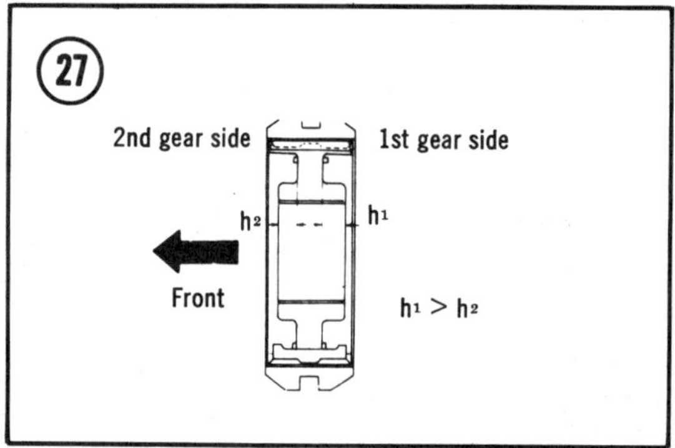

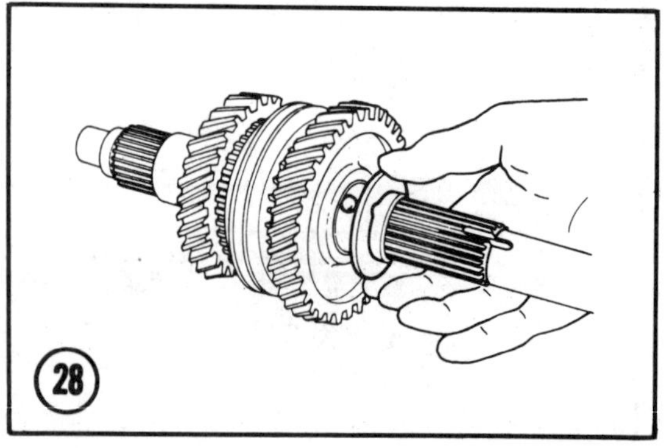

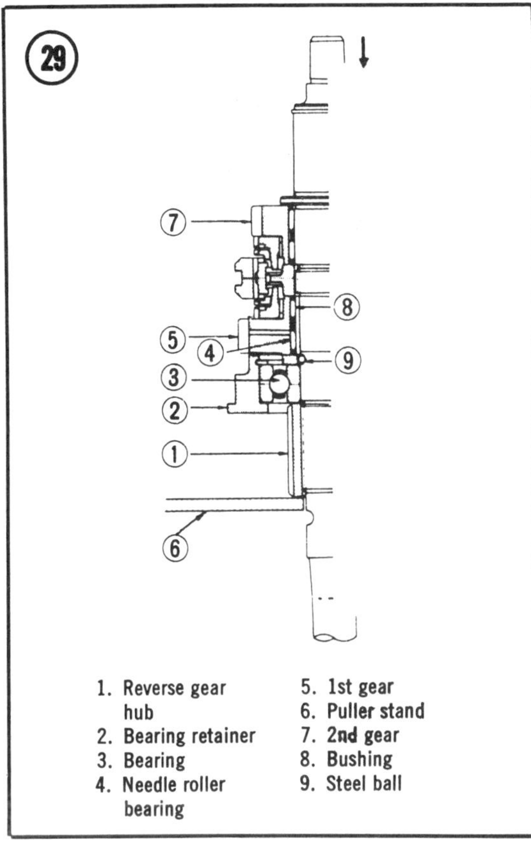

1. Reverse gear hub
2. Bearing retainer
3. Bearing
4. Needle roller bearing
5. 1st gear
6. Puller stand
7. 2nd gear
8. Bushing
9. Steel ball

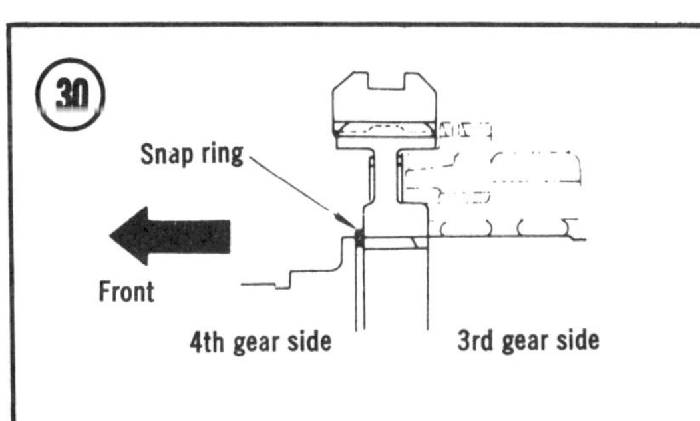

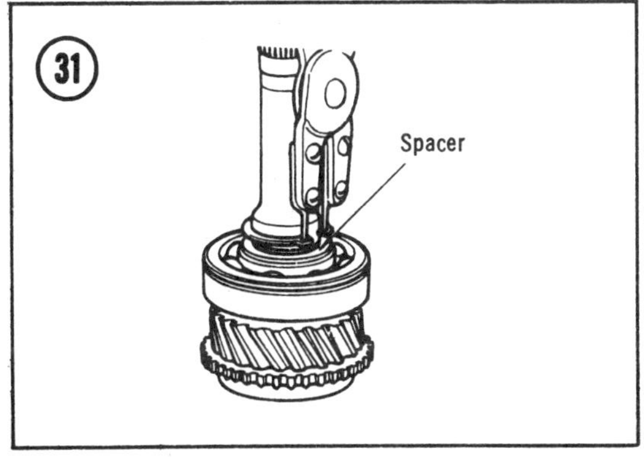

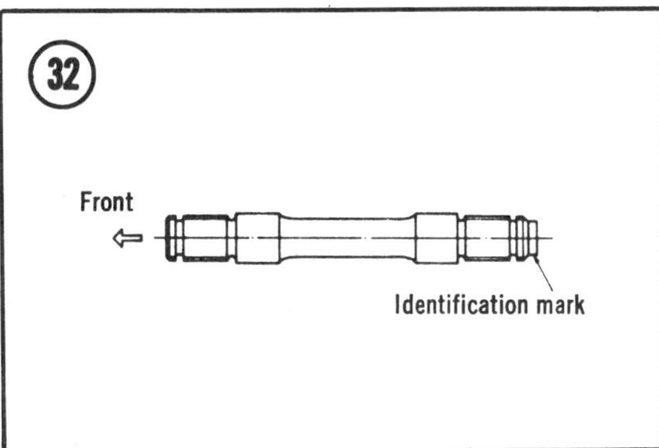

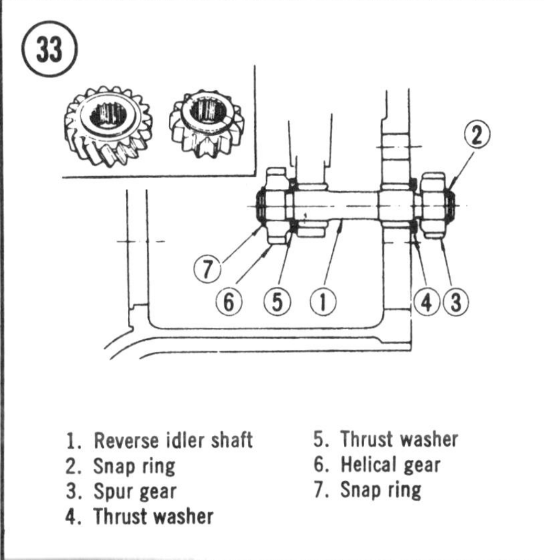

1. Reverse idler shaft
2. Snap ring
3. Spur gear
4. Thrust washer
5. Thrust washer
6. Helical gear
7. Snap ring

15. Install the pilot bearing (1, **Figure 17**) on the front end of the main shaft.

16. Install the input shaft in the transmission case.

17. Insert the reverse idler shaft into the transmission case from the rear. Be sure the identification mark (**Figure 32**) is toward the rear.

18. Install the thrust washers and helical gear (the gear with angled teeth) on the reverse idler shaft. See **Figure 33**. Secure the gear with a snap ring.

19. Insert an 0.004 in. (0.1mm) feeler gauge between the thrust washer and helical gear. Push the reverse idler shaft as far to the rear as it will go.

20. With the feeler gauge still in place, install the rear thrust washer and spur gear (the gear with straight-cut teeth).

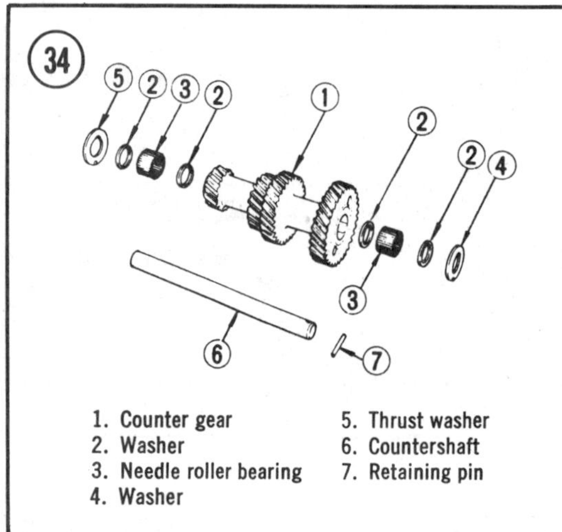

1. Counter gear
2. Washer
3. Needle roller bearing
4. Washer
5. Thrust washer
6. Countershaft
7. Retaining pin

21. Install a snap ring on the rear end of the reverse idler shaft. Select a snap ring of a thickness that will bring the idler shaft end play within specifications. Snap rings are available in several thicknesses.

22. Insert a dummy countershaft into the countershaft gear. See **Figure 34**. Install the inner bearing washers.

23. Install the needle roller bearings in the countershaft **(Figure 35)**. Install the outer bearing washers.

24. Position the countershaft gear and its thrust washers in the transmission case. Carefully push the countershaft into the countershaft gear, pushing the dummy countershaft out at the same time. Be careful not to displace washers or needle roller bearings.

> NOTE: *Select a rear counteshaft thrust washer that will bring countershaft end play within specifications. Rear thrust washers are available in several thicknesses.*

25. Install the retaining pin in the front end of the countershaft.

26. Slide reverse gear into mesh with the reverse idler gear. Slide one synchronizer sleeve over a balk ring and the clutch teeth on a gear. This engages 2 gears at once, locking the main shaft.

27. Tighten the main shaft nut. If you are near a dealer, the easiest method is simply to take the transmission in and have the nut tightened. If

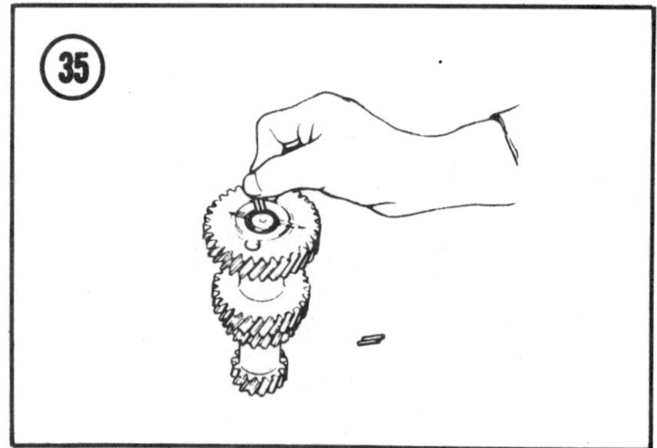

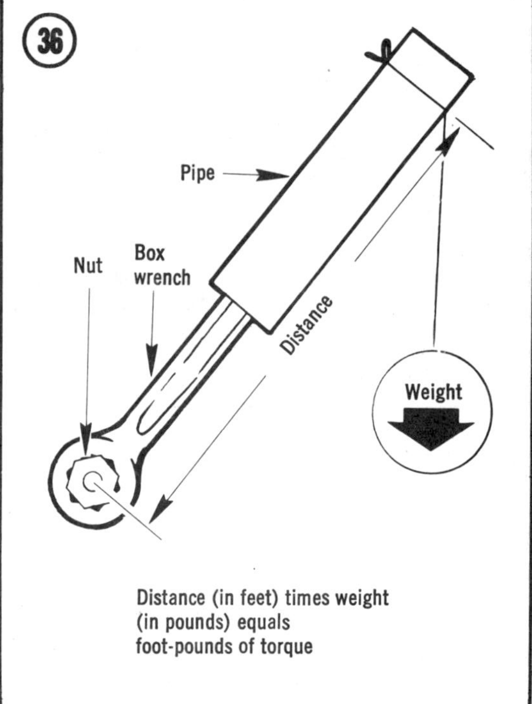

Distance (in feet) times weight (in pounds) equals foot-pounds of torque

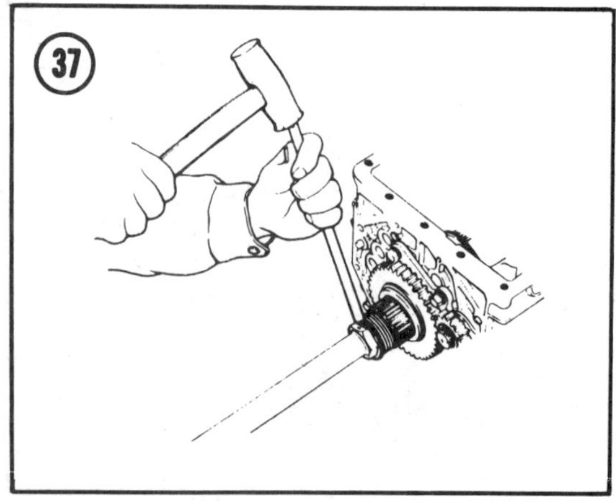

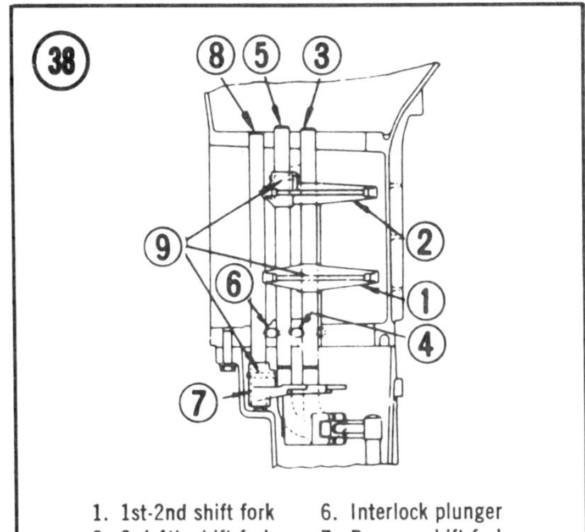

1. 1st-2nd shift fork
2. 3rd-4th shift fork
3. 1st-2nd shift rod
4. Interlock plunger
5. 3rd-4th shift rod
6. Interlock plunger
7. Reverse shift fork
8. Reverse shift rod
9. Retaining pin

39

3. 1st-2nd shift rod
4. Interlock plunger
5. 3rd-4th shift rod
6. Interlock plunger
8. Reverse shift rod

40

1. Striking rod pin
2. Striking rod

not, there is another method. Place a box wrench on the nut. Slip a pipe about 3 ft. long over the wrench. See **Figure 36**. To tighten the nut, hang a 35 lb. weight on the pipe at a distance of 2 ft. from the center of the nut. Let the weight pull the pipe down as far as it will go. The weight (35 lb.) times the distance (2 ft.) gives a torque of 70 ft.-lb. This is within the specified range of 65-80 ft.-lb. (9-11 mkg).

28. After tightening the nut, bend the lockwasher over it (**Figure 37**).

29. Slide reverse gear out of mesh. Slide the synchronizer sleeve back to the neutral position (between gears).

30. Place the first-second and third-fourth shifting forks on synchronizer sleeves (**Figure 38**).

31. Slide the first-second shift rod through the transmission case into the first-second shifting fork. Secure the rod with a retaining pin.

32. Install an interlock plunger next to the first-second shift rod. See **Figure 38** and **Figure 39**.

33. Install the third-fourth shift rod and secure it with a retaining pin.

34. Install an interlock plunger next to the third-fourth shift rod.

35. Install the reverse shift fork. Insert the reverse shift rod and secure it with a retaining pin.

36. Install a check ball and locking spring in each of the 3 holes in the transmission case. Coat the plug threads with gasket sealer, then install all 3 plugs. Tighten all 3 plugs to 12-15 ft.-lb. (1.7-2.1 mkg).

37. Make sure all friction points are coated with gear oil. Make sure gears mesh smoothly.

38. Make sure all gears are in their neutral positions. This occurs when both synchronizer sleeves are centered evenly between their gears, and main shaft reverse gear is out of mesh with the reverse idler gear.

39. Install the rear extension. Use a new gasket, coated on both sides with gasket sealer. As the rear extension is being installed, line up the front end of the striking rod (2, **Figure 40**) with the brackets on the rear ends of the shift rods.

10

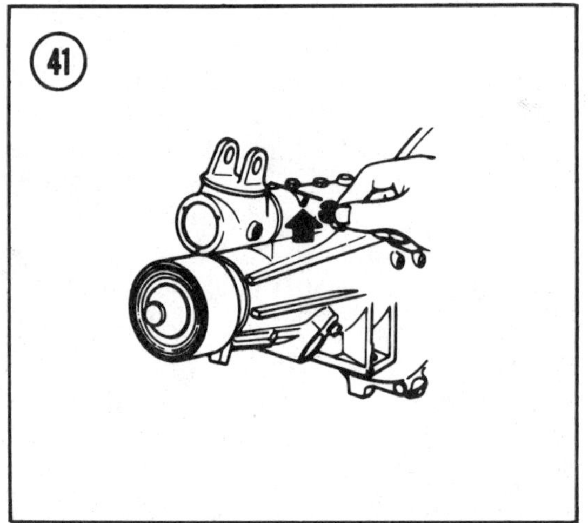

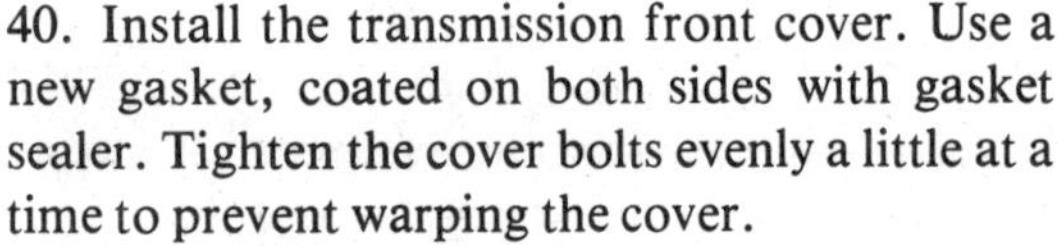

40. Install the transmission front cover. Use a new gasket, coated on both sides with gasket sealer. Tighten the cover bolts evenly a little at a time to prevent warping the cover.

41. On 521 pickups, slide each synchronizer sleeve over a balk ring and the clutch teeth on a gear. This locks the main shaft. Install the flange at the rear end of the transmission and tighten the nut to 72-101 ft.-lb. (10-14 mkg). Return the synchronizer sleeves to the neutral positions (between gears).

42. Install the clutch release mechanism (see Chapter Eight).

43. Install the striking rod pin (1, **Figure 40**).

44. Check again to make sure all friction points are coated with gear oil. Be sure there is nothing in the transmission that doesn't belong there. Temporarily install the shift lever. Move it through all gear positions, checking for smooth movement. Be sure the input shaft turns the main shaft when the transmission is in gear. Remove the shift lever.

45. Install the bottom cover. Use a new gasket, coated on both sides with gasket sealer. Tighten the bolts evenly a little at a time to prevent warping the cover.

46. Install the speedometer pinion in the rear extension. Install the electrical switch(es). Use gasket sealer on the switch threads.

Disassembly (F4W71B)

1. Clean the outside of the transmission with solvent.

2. Remove the dust cover from the clutch housing. Remove the clutch release mechanism (Chapter Eight).

3. Unscrew the back-up lamp switch from the side of the transmission.

4. Make sure the transmission is still in neutral. Remove the speedometer pinion clamp bolt from the rear extension, then take the speedometer pinion out.

5. Remove the snap ring and pin from the striking rod. See **Figure 41**.

6. Unscrew the return spring plug (**Figure 42**).

7. Take out the reverse check spring, return spring, and return spring plunger. See **Figure 43**.

8. Turn the striking guide (4, **Figure 43**) counterclockwise (viewed from rear of transmission). Referring to **Figure 44**, unbolt the rear extension from the adapter plate and transmission case. Tap the extension loose with a soft-faced mallet, then remove it.

9. Unbolt the front cover from the transmission case. Remove the input shaft bearing shim, then remove the bearing snap ring with snap ring pliers. See **Figure 45**.

10. Tap the transmission case with a soft-faced mallet to free it from the adapter plate. Then take the transmission case off.

11. Position the gear assembly in a holding fixture such as Datsun tool ST23810001 (**Figure 46**). **Figure 47** gives dimensions of the tool, which can easily be made from plywood.

43

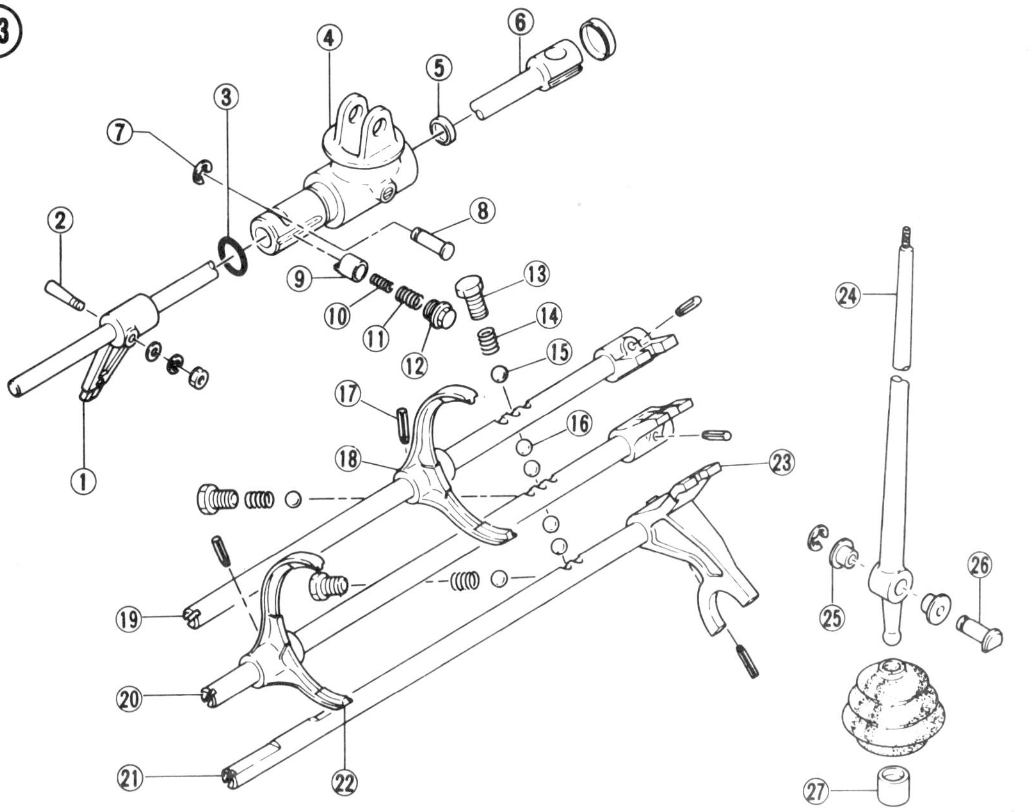

SHIFT CONTROL COMPONENTS (F4W71B)

1. Striking lever
2. Lock pin
3. O-ring
4. Striking guide
5. Oil seal
6. Striking rod
7. E-ring
8. Stopper guide pin
9. Return spring plunger
10. Return spring
11. Reverse check spring
12. Return spring plug
13. Check ball plug
14. Check spring
15. Check ball
16. Interlock ball
17. Retaining pin
18. 1st and 2nd shift fork
19. 1st and 2nd fork rod
20. 3rd and 4th fork rod
21. Reverse fork rod
22. 3rd and 4th shift fork
23. Reverse shift fork
24. Control lever
25. Control lever bushing
26. Control lever pin
27. Control lever bushing

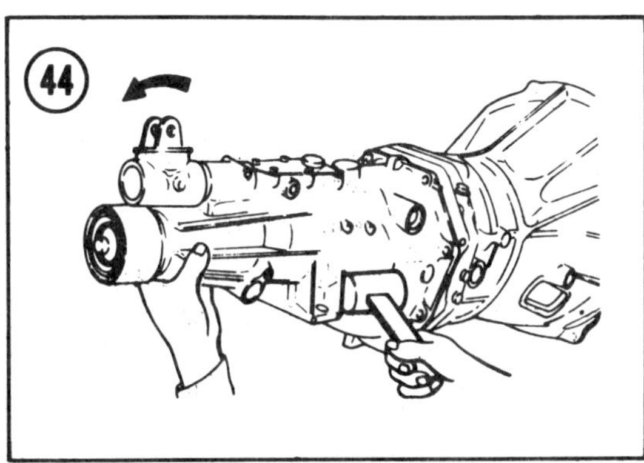

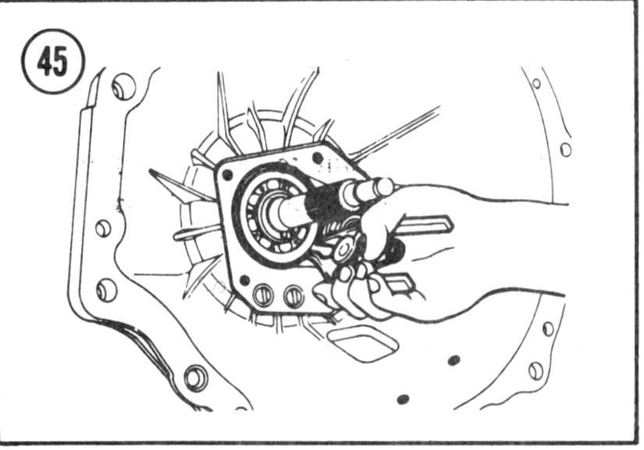

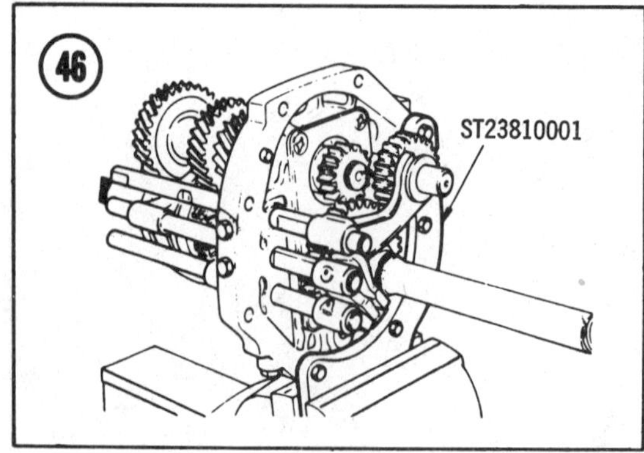

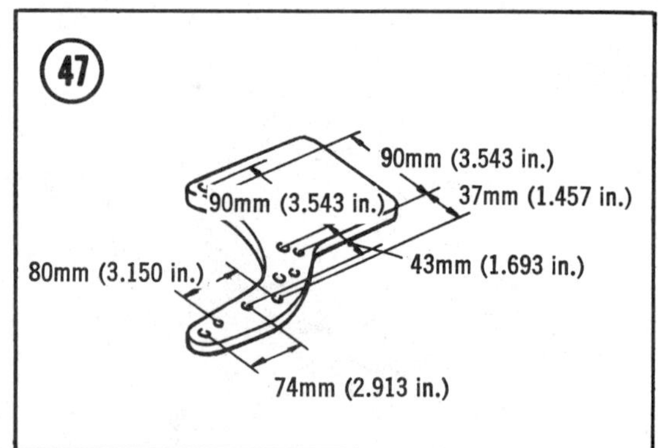

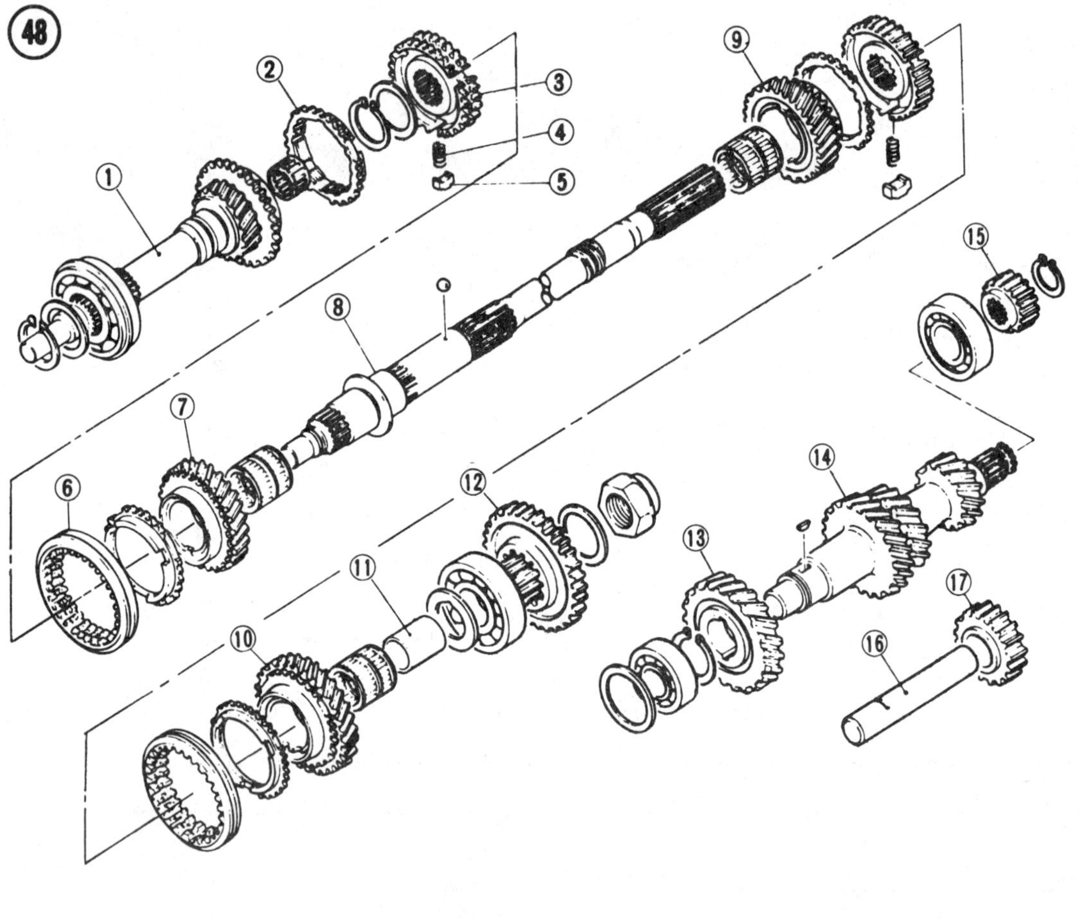

48

GEAR ASSEMBLY (F4W71B)

1. Main drive gear
2. Baulk ring
3. Synchronizer hub, 3rd and 4th
4. Shifting insert spring
5. Shifting insert
6. Coupling sleeve
7. 3rd main gear
8. Main shaft
9. 2nd main gear
10. 1st main gear
11. 1st gear spacer
12. Reverse main gear
13. Counter drive gear
14. Counter gear
15. Reverse counter gear
16. Reverse idler shaft
17. Reverse idler gear

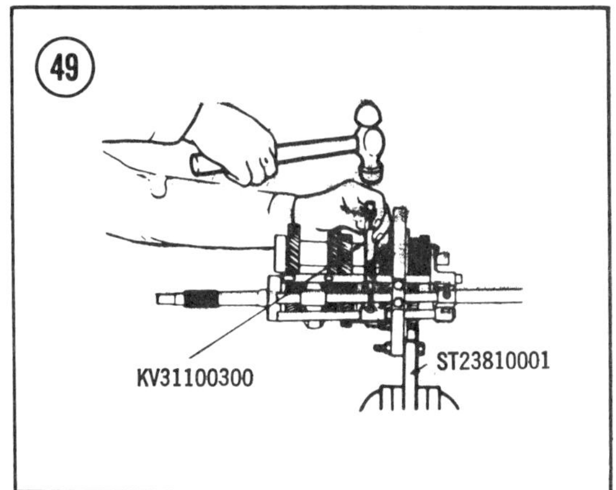

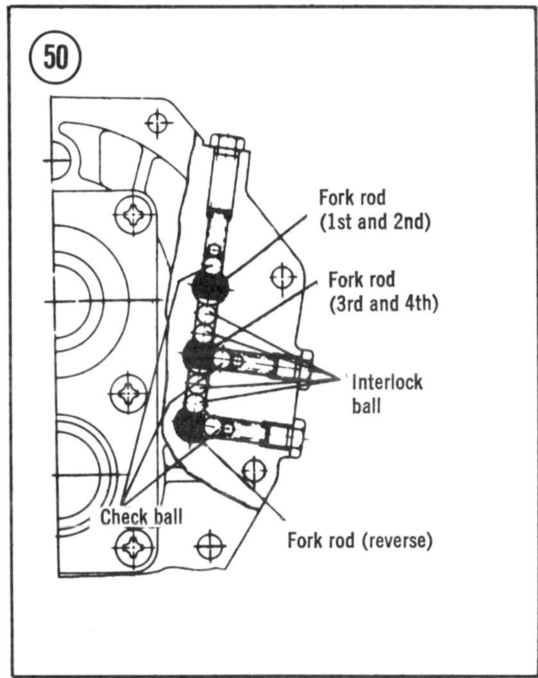

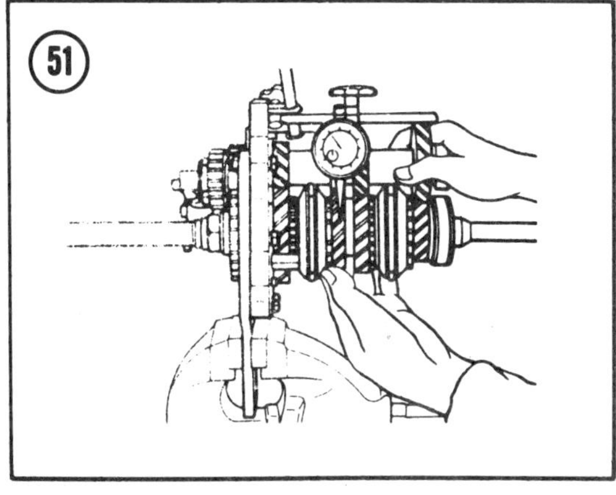

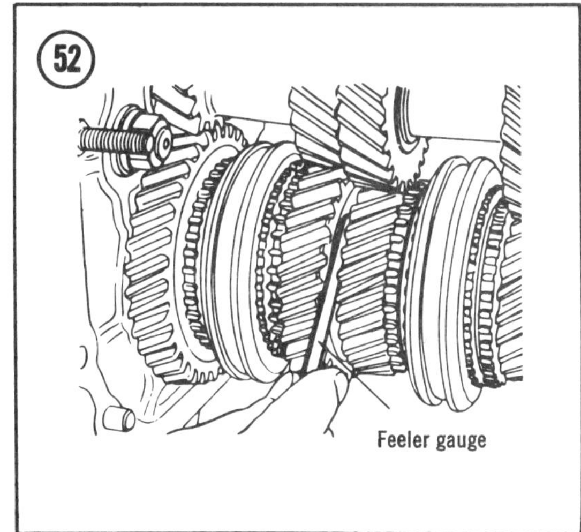

NOTE: ***Figure 48*** *is an exploded view of the gear assembly. Refer to it as needed for the following steps.*

12. Drive the roll pins out of the shift forks and rods. Use Datsun tool KV31100300 (Kent-Moore J-25689-A), as shown in **Figure 49**, or an ordinary pin punch.

13. Remove all 3 check ball plugs. **Figure 50** is a cross-section view of the adapter plate which shows the check ball plugs, check and interlock balls, and shift fork rods.

14. Tap the shift fork rods out of the adapter plate, then remove the check and interlock balls.

NOTE: *Perform the following inspection steps before continuing with disassembly.*

15. Measure gear backlash with a dial gauge as shown in **Figure 51**. Hold the countershaft from turning with one hand and turn each main shaft gear as far as possible against the dial gauge without turning the countershaft. The reading on the dial gauge should be 0.002-0.004 in. (0.05-0.10mm) on the input shaft gear, and 0.002-0.008 in. (0.05-0.20mm) on all others. If backlash is excessive, replace driving and driven gears as a set.

16. Measure gear end play with a feeler gauge (**Figure 52**). It should be 0.013-0.015 in. (0.32-0.39mm) for first gear; 0.005-0.007 in. (0.12-0.19mm) for second gear; 0.005-0.014 in. (0.13-0.37mm) for third gear; and 0.0004-0.0079 in.

10

(0.01-0.20mm) for countershaft reverse rings. Excessive end play can be corrected with oversize snap rings. The main shaft thrust washers should also be checked closely for wear.

NOTE: *Continue with disassembly as follows.*

17. Engage 2 gears at once. To do this, slide each synchronizer sleeve over the small teeth on one of the gears next to it. This locks the main shaft and gears so they won't turn.

18. Remove the countershaft gear front bearing with a gear puller (**Figure 53**). Gear pullers can be rented from tool rental outlets and some auto parts stores.

19. Pull off the countershaft drive gear with a gear puller. Remove the input shaft at the same time. See **Figure 54**.

CAUTION
Do not let the needle roller bearing fall out of the input shaft onto the floor.

20. Remove the snap ring, thrust washer, third-fourth gear synchronizer, and third gear from the front end of the main shaft.

21. Carefully file away the lip of the main shaft nut where it is punched into the main shaft. Remove the nut with a 1½ in. (38mm) box wrench and throw it away. See **Figure 55**.

NOTE: *The nut is tightened to 101-123 ft.-lb. (14-17 mkg). If you don't have the correct wrench, take the gear assembly to a Datsun dealer to have the nut removed.*

22. Remove the snap ring from the rear end of the countershaft, then remove the countershaft reverse gear.

23. Tap the main shaft with a soft-faced mallet to free it **(Figure 56)**. Then remove the main shaft and countershaft from the adapter plate.

24. Remove 6 machine screws securing the bearing retainer to the adapter plate. These screws have been punched in place, so an impact screwdriver is necessary to remove them.

25. Remove the reverse idler shaft and main shaft bearing from the adapter plate.

26. Remove the thrust washer, its steel ball, first gear, and first gear's needle bearing from the rear end of the main shaft.

53

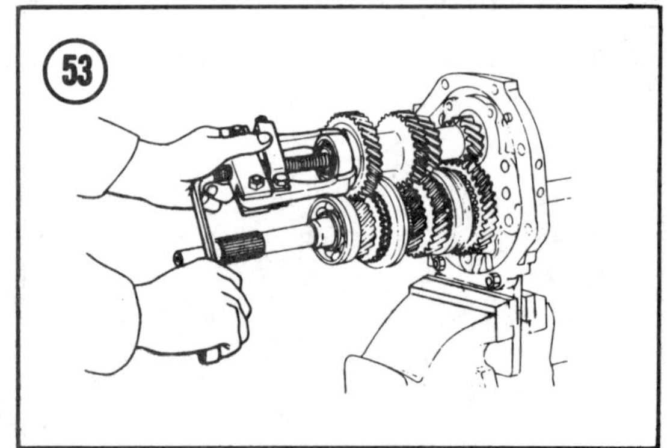

54

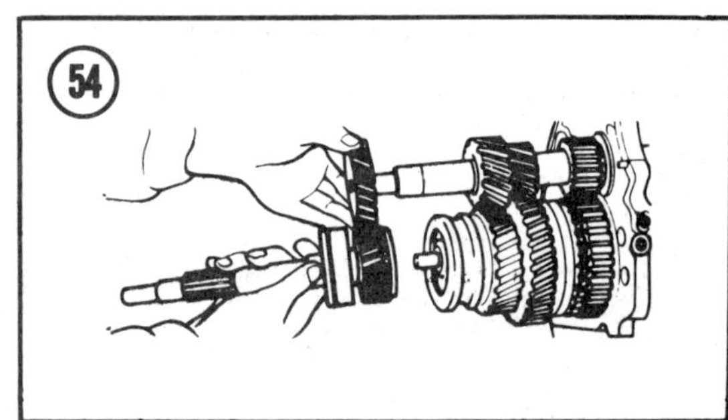

55

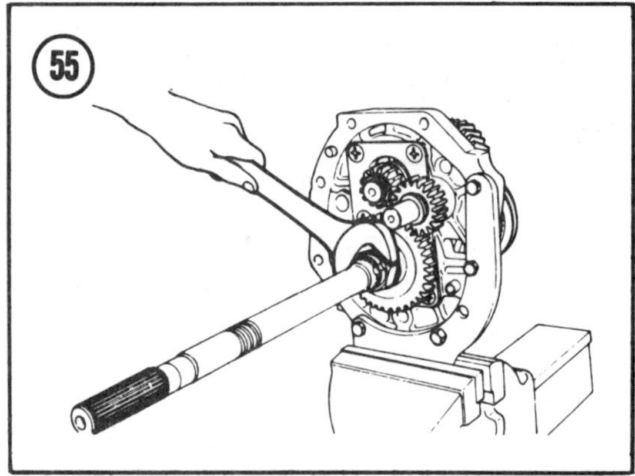

56

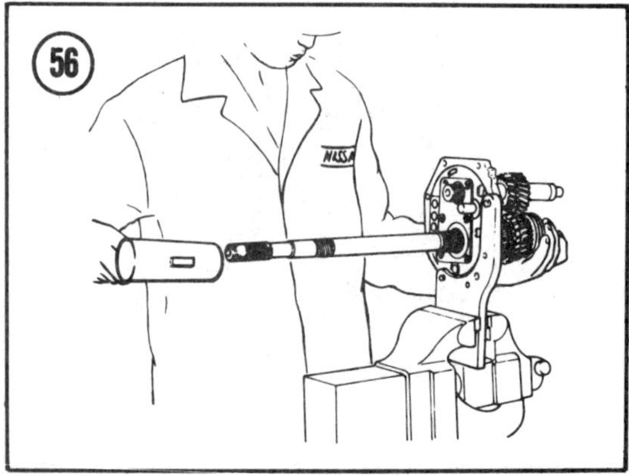

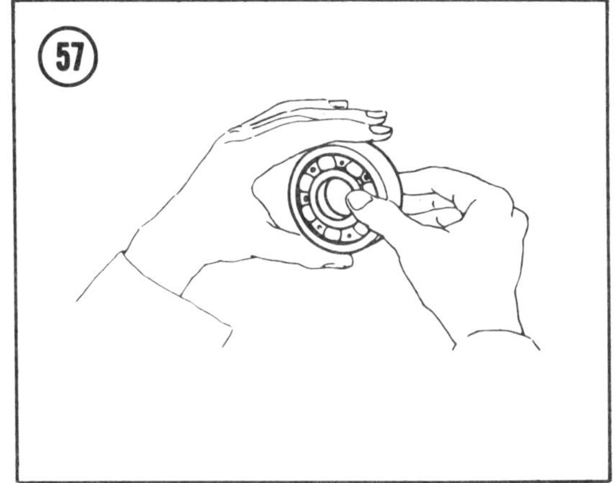

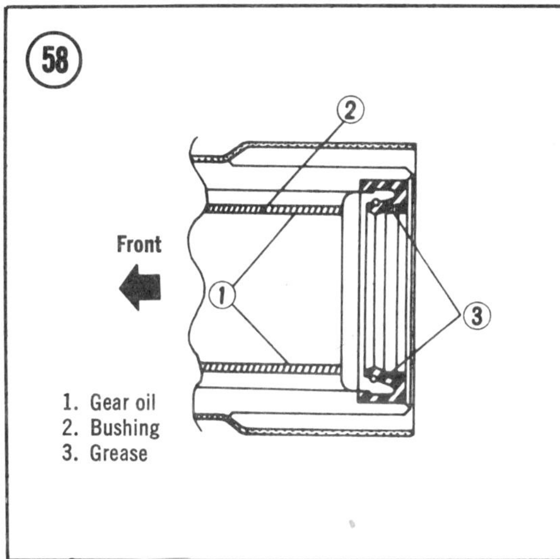

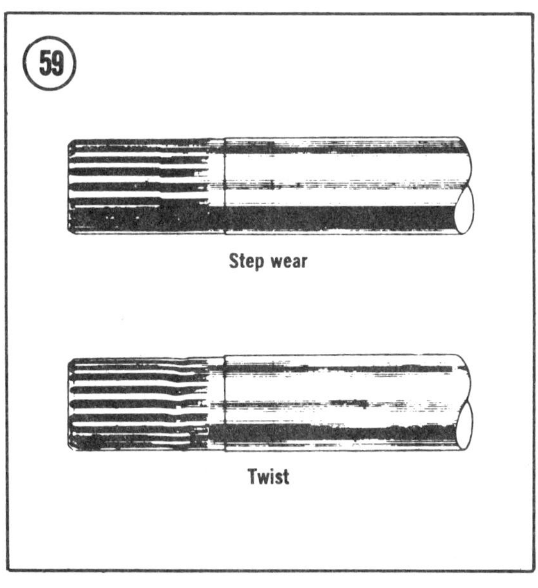

27. Have the first gear bushing, first-second gear synchronizer, and second gear pressed off the main shaft by a machine shop.

Inspection (F4W71B)

1. Thoroughly clean all parts in solvent. Remove all traces of old gasket and sealer. Inspect all parts while cleaning and replace any with obvious wear or damage.

2. Check the transmission case and rear extension for cracks. Check all gasket surfaces for gouges or roughness which could cause an oil leak. Replace if these conditions are found.

3. Check all bearings for wear or damage. Hold the outer race with one hand and rotate the inner race with the other. See **Figure 57**. Check for noise, roughness, and wear. Replace any suspect bearings.

> NOTE: *If the input shaft bearing or countershaft bearing needs to be replaced, have the old one pressed off and a new one pressed on by a machine shop.*

4. Since needle roller bearing wear is hard to see, the needle roller bearings should be replaced whenever the transmission is overhauled.

5. Inspect the bushing at the back of the rear extension. If worn or damaged, the rear extension must be replaced.

6. Carefully pry the oil seal out of the rear extension. Tap in a new one. Use a block of wood to spread the hammer's force, so the seal won't tilt sideways and jam. Coat the seal lip and rear extension bushing with gear oil.

> NOTE: *The lip of the seal faces into the transmission. See **Figure 58**.*

7. Replace the front cover oil seal in the same manner as the rear extension oil seal.

8. Check the main shaft for bending, twisting, cracks, or other damage. Check the splines for the types for wear and damage shown in **Figure 59**. Replace if any of these conditions are found.

9. Check gears for chipped, broken, or badly worn teeth. Replace gears with these conditions.

10

10. Slip a balk ring onto the cones of first, second, third, and input shaft gears. Measure the gap between balk ring and the small teeth on the gear (**Figure 60**). Normal gap is 0.047-0.063 in. (1.2-1.6mm). Minimum is 0.031 in. (0.8mm). If the gap is less than the minimum, replace the balk ring.

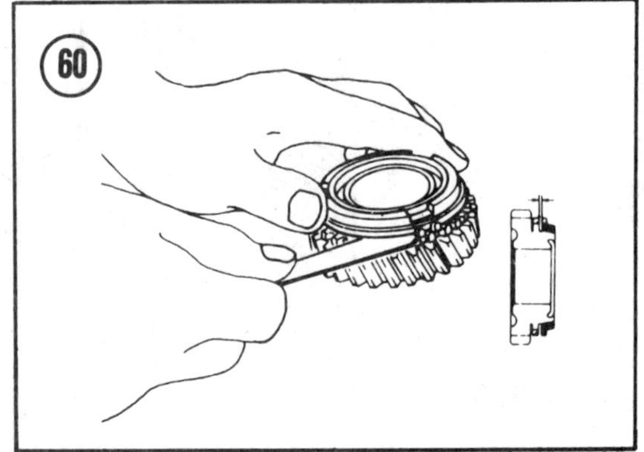

Assembly (F4W71B)

Transmission assembly should be done in a dust-free area.

> NOTE: *Dip each bearing, gear, and synchronizer in new gear oil just before installing.*

1. If the oil gutter was removed from the adapter plate, install it as shown in **Figure 61**.
2. If the main shaft bearing was removed from the adapter plate, tap it into position with a soft-faced mallet.
3. Install the reverse idler shaft in the adapter plate. Make sure the cutout in the shaft faces toward the center of the adapter plate.
4. Install the adapter plate. Make sure the cutout in the reverse idler shaft lines up with the adapter plate. Tighten the adapter plate screws to 14-18 ft.-lb. (1.9-2.5 mkg). Stake each screw at 2 points with a hammer and punch. See **Figure 62**.
5. Install the following parts in order from the rear end of the main shaft: Needle bearing, second gear, balk ring, first-second gear synchronizer, balk ring, first gear bushing, needle bearing, and first gear.
6. Coat the steel ball with grease and install it next to first gear (**Figure 63**). Slip the thrust washer over it.
7. Have the main shaft pressed into the adapter plate by a machine shop (**Figure 64**). A support tool such as KV31100400 (**Figure 65**) is necessary to prevent damage to the adapter plate.
8. Install new Woodruff keys in the countershaft gear. Tap the keys in gently with a soft-faced hammer.
9. Have the countershaft gear pressed into the adapter plate by a machine shop. See **Figure 66**.
10. Install the following parts in order from the front end of the main shaft: needle bearing,

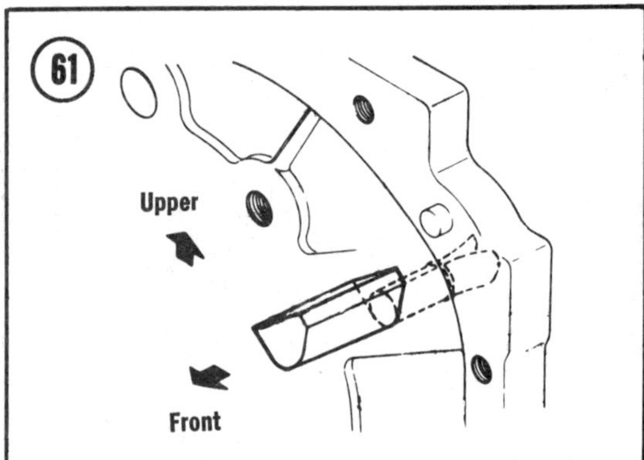

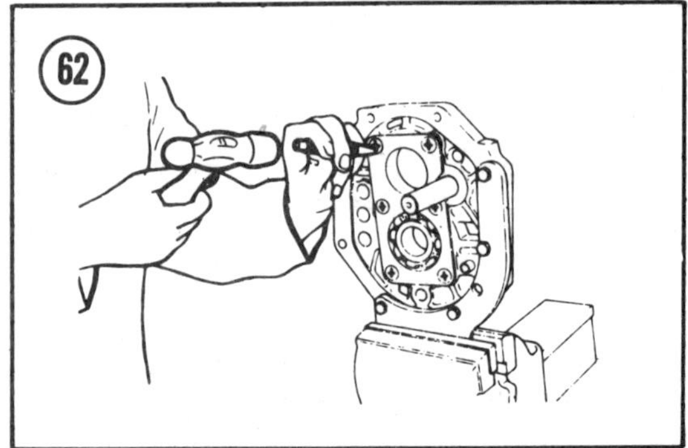

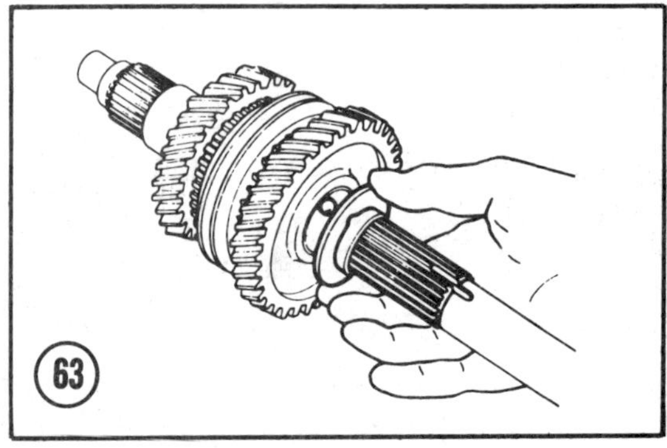

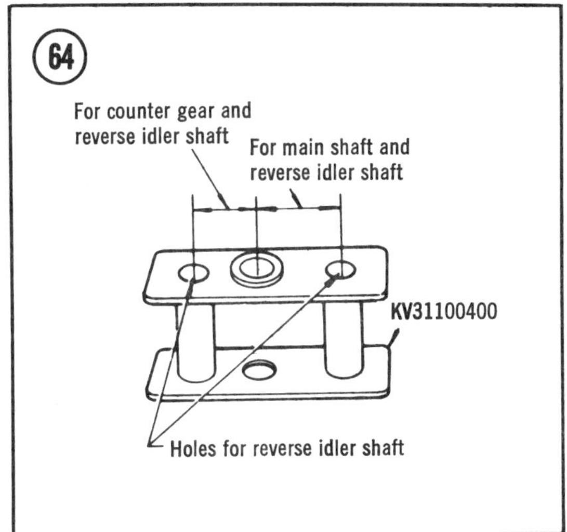

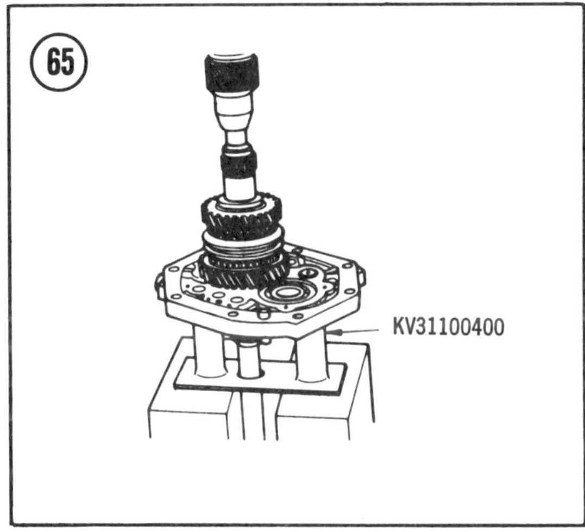

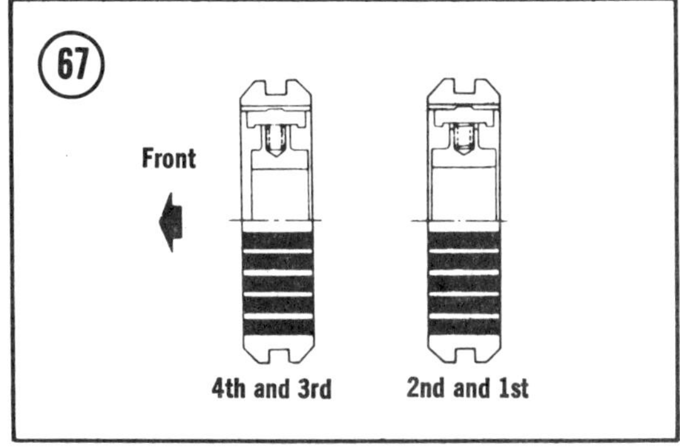

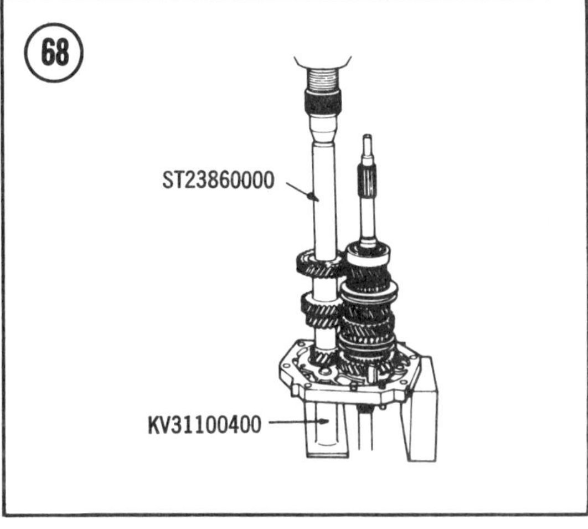

third gear, balk ring, and third-fourth gear synchronizer.

> NOTE: *The third-fourth gear synchronizer hub is offset toward the rear of the main shaft (**Figure 67**). The first-second synchronizer hub is not offset.*

11. Place a thrust washer against the synchronizer, then secure it with a snap ring. Use the thickest snap ring that will fit in the groove. Snap rings are available in thicknesses of 0.055 in. (1.4mm); 0.059 in. (1.5mm); and 0.063 in. (1.6mm).

12. Place a balk ring on the third-fourth gear synchronizer.

13. Place the input shaft pilot bearing on the end of the main shaft.

14. Mesh the countershaft drive gear with the input shaft gear. Position the gears as shown in **Figure 68**, and press the countershaft drive gear onto the countershaft. At the same time, guide the input shaft onto the main shaft.

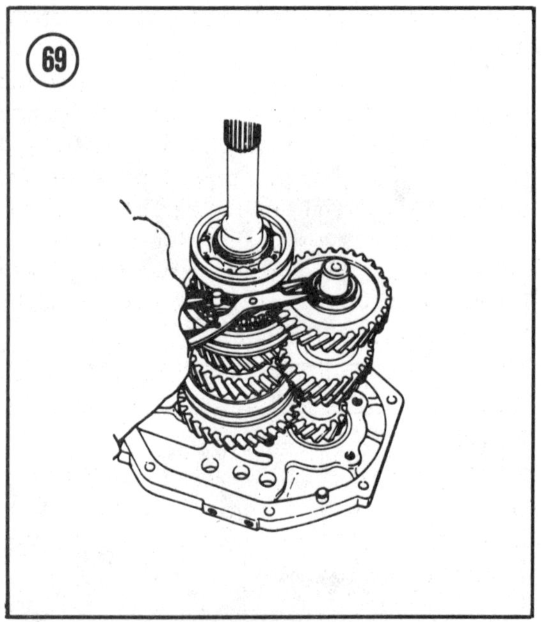

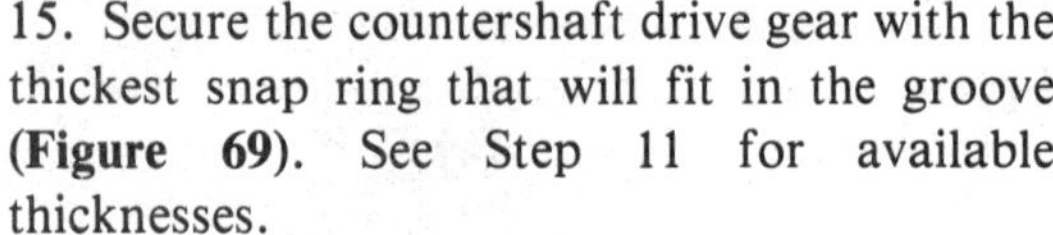

15. Secure the countershaft drive gear with the thickest snap ring that will fit in the groove (**Figure 69**). See Step 11 for available thicknesses.

16. Press the countershaft front bearing onto the countershaft, next to the countershaft drive gear.

17. Install reverse main gear on the main shaft. Install the plain washer next to the gear, then install the main shaft nut. Don't torque the nut yet.

18. Install countershaft reverse gear on the rear end of the countershaft. Secure with the thickest snap ring that will fit in the groove (**Figure 70**). See Step 11 for available thicknesses.

19. Install reverse idler gear on the reverse idler shaft.

20. Slide the third-fourth gear synchronizer sleeve over the small teeth on third gear. Slide the first-second synchronizer sleeve over the small teeth on first or second gear. This engages 2 gears at once, so the main shaft won't turn.

21. Tighten the main shaft nut to 101-123 ft.-lb. (14-17 mkg). If you are near a Datsun dealer, the easiest way to do this is to take the gear assembly to the dealer and have the nut tightened. If not, you will need a 1½ in. (38mm) box wrench and a piece of pipe large

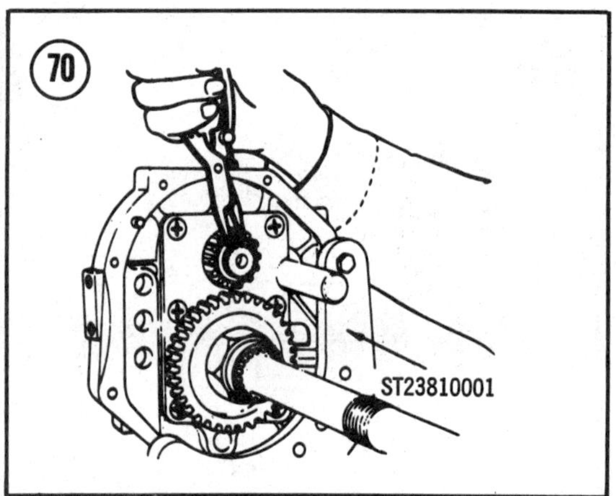

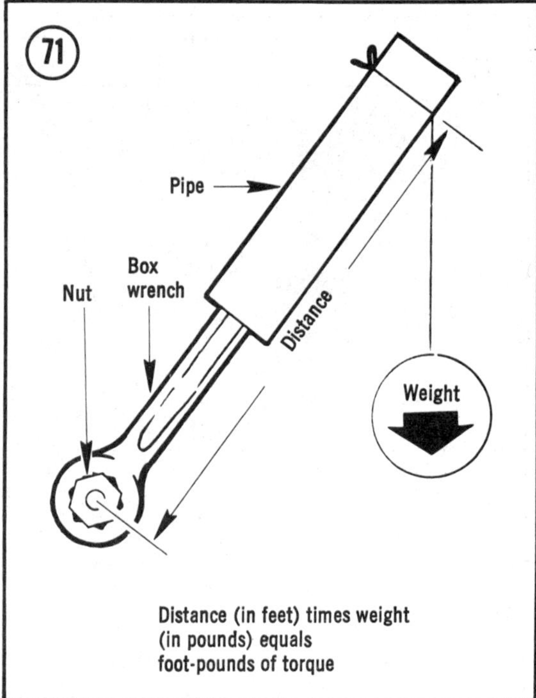

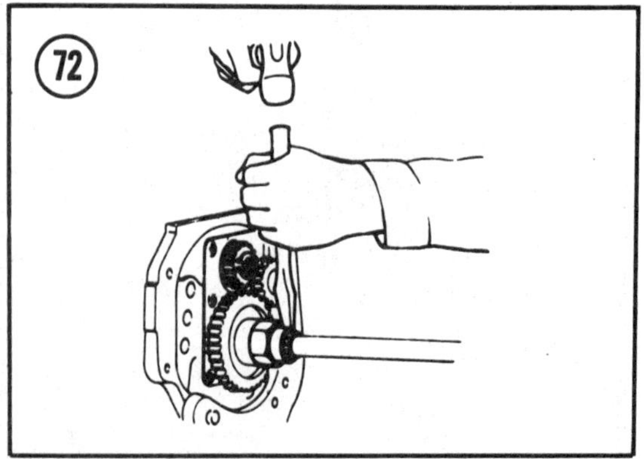

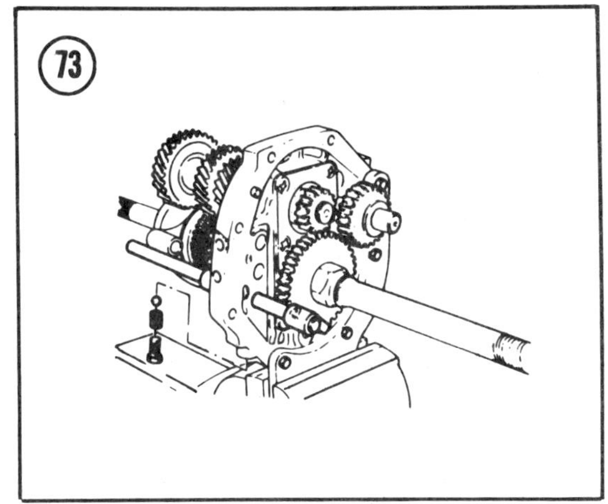

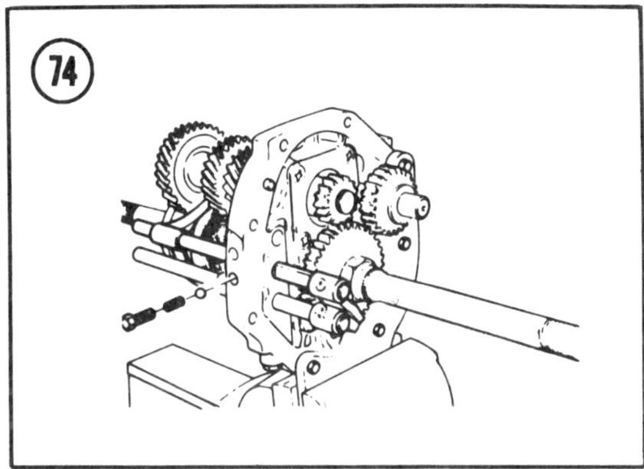

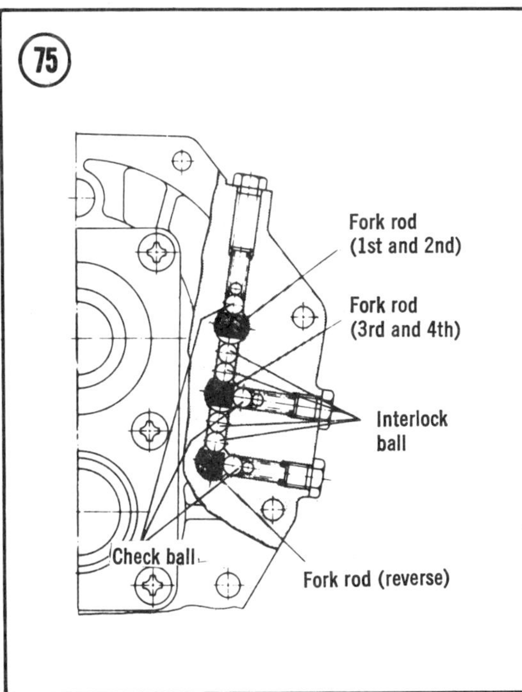

enough to fit over it. The pipe should be about 3 ft. long.

To tighten, place the box wrench over the nut, and slip the pipe over the wrench. Measure 2 ft. out from the center of the main shaft, and mark this point on the pipe. See **Figure 71**. Hang a 55 lb. weight on the pipe at this point, and let it turn the wrench as far as it will go. The distance (2 ft.) times the weight (55 lb.) equals 110 ft.-lb. of torque. This is within the specified range of 101-123 ft.-lb.

22. Once the main shaft nut is tightened, punch its lip into the groove in the main shaft. See **Figure 72**.

23. Place the first-second gear shifting fork in its groove on the first-second gear synchronizer. This is the synchronizer closest to the adapter plate.

> NOTE: *The first-second and third-fourth gear shifting forks are interchangeable. The first-second gear fork is installed with its longer leg toward the countershaft gear.*

24. Place the third-fourth gear shifting fork on the third-fourth gear synchronizer sleeve. The longer leg faces away from the countershaft gear.

25. Slide the first-second gear shift rod through the adapter plate into the first-second gear shifting fork. Secure the rod to the fork with a new roll pin.

26. Coat the threads of the longest check ball plug with gasket sealer. Install a check ball, spring, and the plug in the adapter plate. See **Figure 73**.

27. Install 2 interlock balls in the adapter plate, on top of the first-second shift rod. See **Figure 50**.

28. Slide the third-fourth gear shift rod through the adapter plate into the third-fourth gear shifting fork. Secure with a new roll pin.

29. Apply gasket sealer to the threads of one of the check ball plugs. Install a check ball, spring, and the plug. See **Figure 74**.

30. Install 2 more interlock balls in the adapter plate (**Figure 75**).

31. Position the reverse shifting fork on the reverse idler gear. Install the reverse shift rod,

Table 2 SHIM SIZES

Distance Measured	Shim Thickness
0.135-0.138 in. (3.42-3.51mm)	0.004 in. (0.1mm)
0.130-0.134 in. (3.32-3.41mm)	0.008 in. (0.2mm)
0.127-0.130 in. (3.22-3.31mm)	0.012 in. (0.3mm)
0.123-0.126 in. (3.12-3.21mm)	0.016 in. (0.4mm)
0.119-0.122 in. (3.02-3.11mm)	0.020 in. (0.5mm)
0.115-0.118 in. (2.92-3.01mm)	0.024 in. (0.6mm)

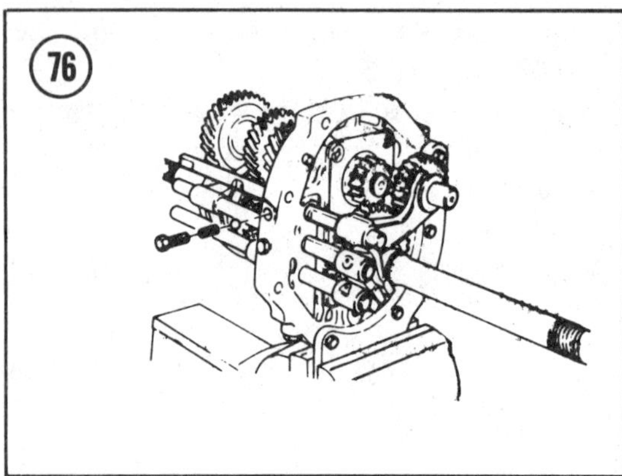

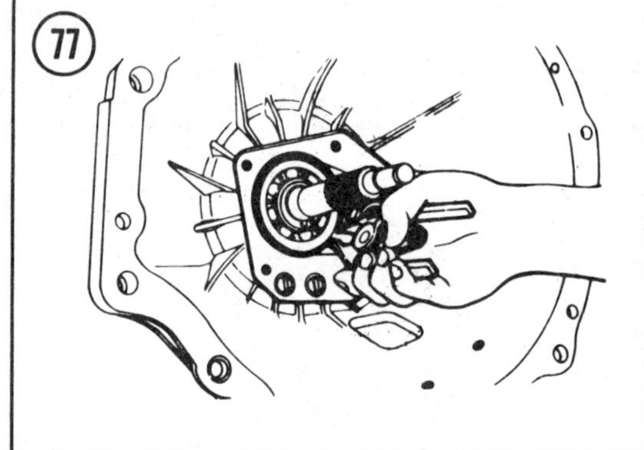

check ball, spring, and check ball plug. See **Figure 76**. Once again, use gasket sealer on the plug threads.

32. Tighten the check ball plugs to 14-18 ft.-lb. (1.9-2.5 mkg).

33. Make sure the transmission is in neutral. The synchronizer sleeves should be midway between the small teeth on the gears. Reverse idler gear should be disengaged from reverse main gear and reverse idler gear.

34. Make sure all bearings, gears, synchronizers, and shift rods are coated with gear oil.

35. Apply gasket sealer to the mating surfaces of transmission case and adapter plate.

36. Install the transmission case on the adapter plate. Tap it into position with a soft-faced mallet.

37. Make sure the main shaft and input shaft rotate freely. Secure the input shaft bearing with a snap ring (**Figure 77**).

38. Apply gasket sealer to the mating surfaces of adapter plate and rear extension. Install the rear extension on the adapter plate. Make sure the striking lever engages the shift rod brackets.

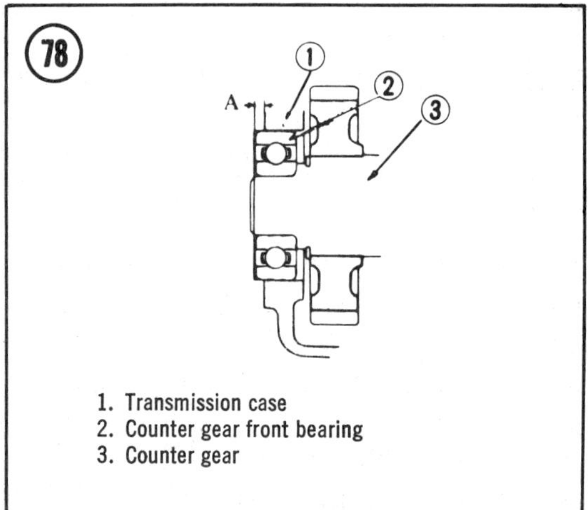

1. Transmission case
2. Counter gear front bearing
3. Counter gear

39. Tighten the rear extension bolts to 12-15 ft.-lb. (1.6-2.1 mkg).

40. Select a shim for the countershaft front bearing. Measure bearing protrusion from the front of the transmission case (distance "A," **Figure 78**), and select a shim according to **Table 2**.

41. Stick the shim to the front cover with multipurpose grease.

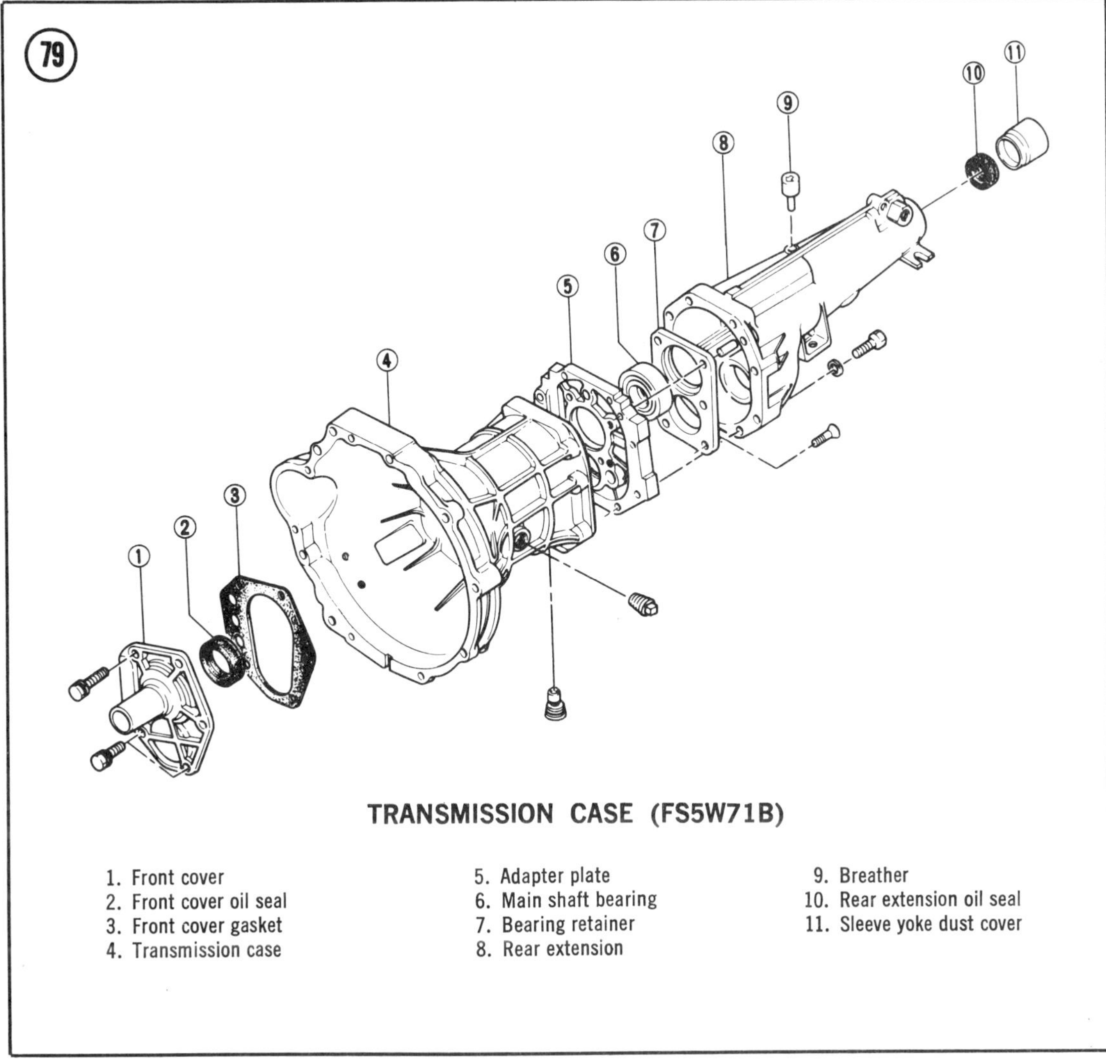

TRANSMISSION CASE (FS5W71B)

1. Front cover
2. Front cover oil seal
3. Front cover gasket
4. Transmission case
5. Adapter plate
6. Main shaft bearing
7. Bearing retainer
8. Rear extension
9. Breather
10. Rear extension oil seal
11. Sleeve yoke dust cover

42. Install the front cover on the transmission case. Use a new gasket, coated on both sides with gasket sealer. Smear gasket sealer on the bolt threads. Tighten the front cover bolts to 12-15 ft.-lb. (1.6-2.1 mkg).

43. Install the speedometer pinion in the rear extension.

44. Coat the threads of the back-up lamp switch with gasket sealer. Install the switch and tighten to 14-22 ft.-lb. (2-3 mkg).

45. Install the clutch release mechanism (Chapter Eight).

46. Temporarily install the shift lever. Move it through the gear positions. Turn the input shaft at each position and make sure the main shaft turns smoothly. In neutral, it should be possible to hold the main shaft still while turning the input shaft.

47. Install the drain plug. Use gel-type gasket sealer on the plug threads.

Gear Disassembly (FS5W71B)

This is the five-speed version of the F4W71B transmission. It has been optional since 1977. The transmission is very similar to the F4W71B. The following sections cover the differences. Any information not included will be found in the F4W71B section preceding this section.

Figure 79 shows the transmission case. **Figure 80** shows the gear assembly. **Figure 81** shows the shift mechanism.

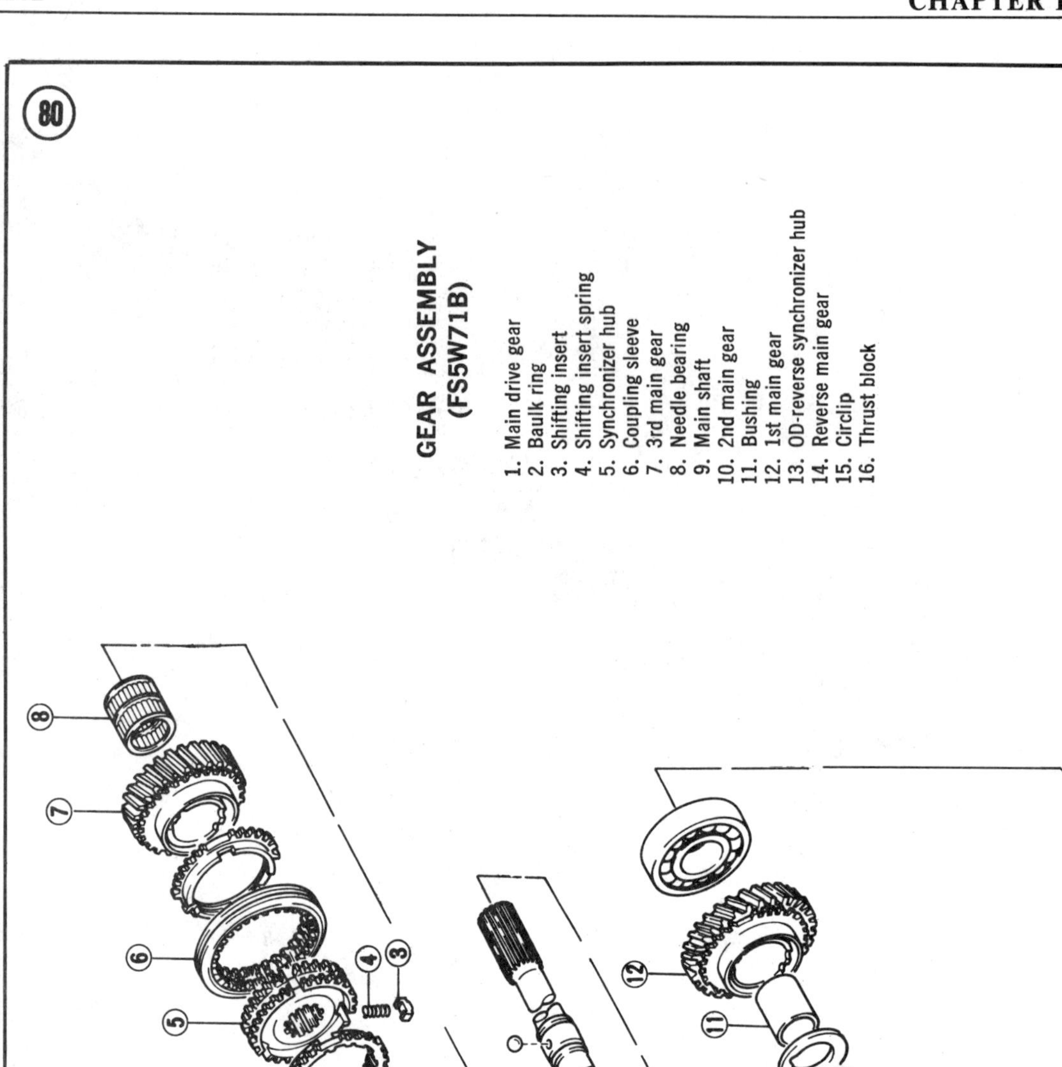

GEAR ASSEMBLY (FS5W71B)

1. Main drive gear
2. Baulk ring
3. Shifting insert
4. Shifting insert spring
5. Synchronizer hub
6. Coupling sleeve
7. 3rd main gear
8. Needle bearing
9. Main shaft
10. 2nd main gear
11. Bushing
12. 1st main gear
13. OD-reverse synchronizer hub
14. Reverse main gear
15. Circlip
16. Thrust block

17. Brake band
18. Synchronizer ring
19. Overdrive main gear
20. Overdrive gear bushing
21. Washer
22. Main shaft nut
23. Main shaft rear bearing
24. Speedometer drive gear
25. Counter gear front bearing shim
26. Counter gear front bearing
27. Counter drive gear
28. Counter gear
29. Counter gear bearing
30. Reverse counter gear spacer
31. Reverse counter gear
32. Overdrive counter gear
33. Counter gear rear bearing
34. Counter gear nut
35. Reverse idler shaft
36. Reverse idler thrust washer
37. Reverse idler gear
38. Reverse idler gear bearing
39. Reverse idler thrust washer

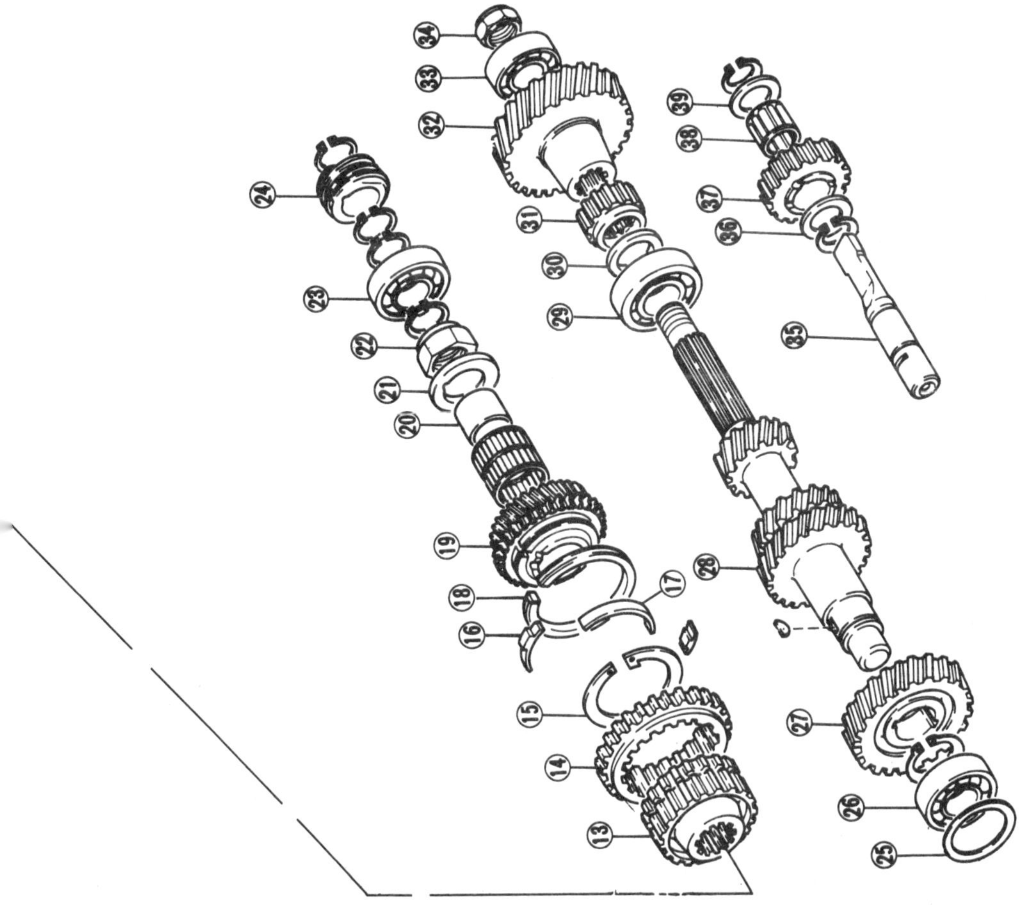

81

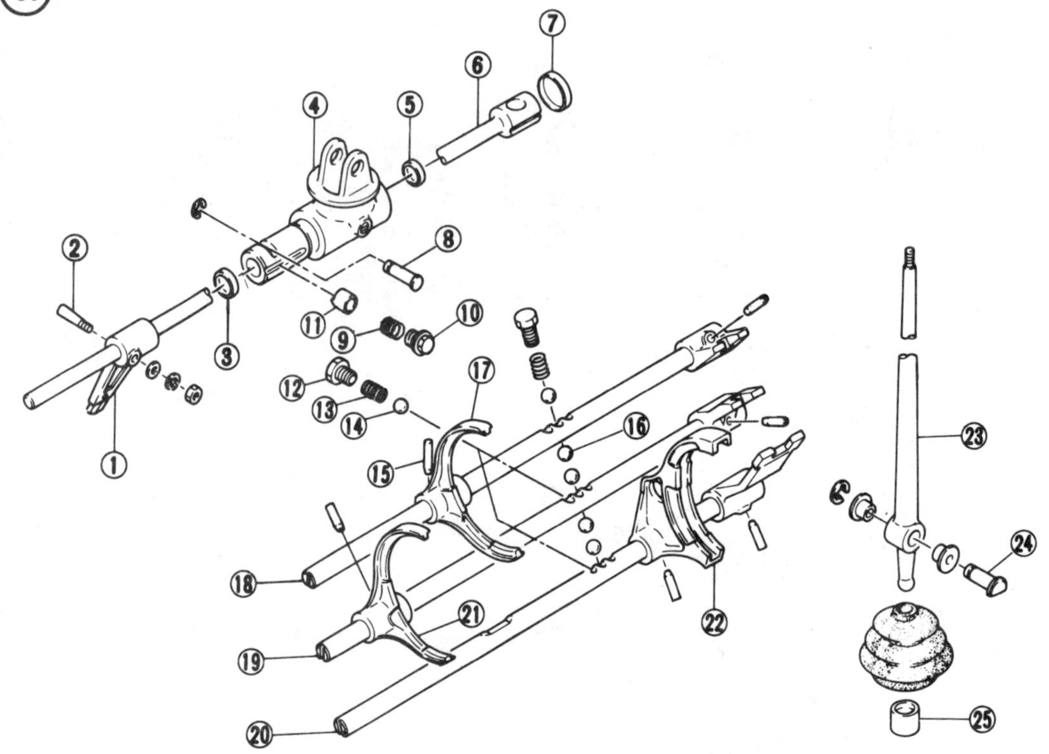

SHIFT MECHANISM (FS5W71B)

1. Striking lever
2. Lock pin
3. Oil seal
4. Striking guide
5. Oil seal
6. Striking rod
7. Expansion plug
8. Stopper guide pin
9. Return spring
10. Return spring plug
11. Return spring plunger
12. Check ball plug
13. Check spring
14. Check ball
15. Retaining pin
16. Interlock ball
17. 1st and 2nd shift fork
18. 1st and 2nd fork rod
19. 3rd and 4th fork rod
20. Reverse and OD fork rod
21. 3rd and 4th shift fork
22. Reverse and OD shift fork
23. Control lever
24. Control lever pin
25. Control lever bushing

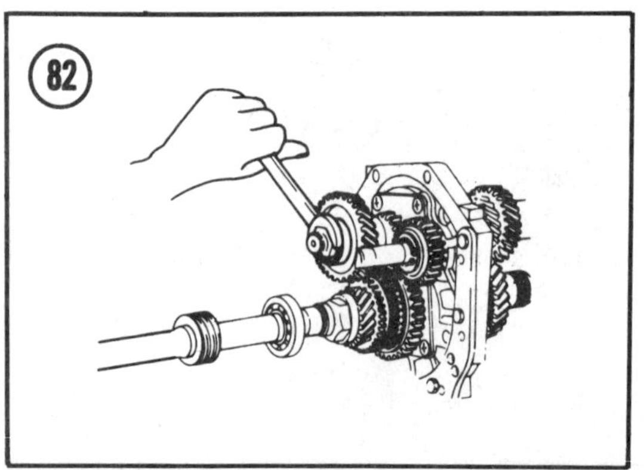

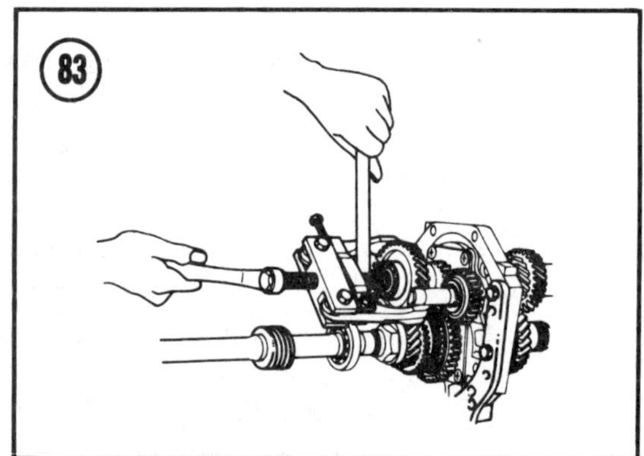

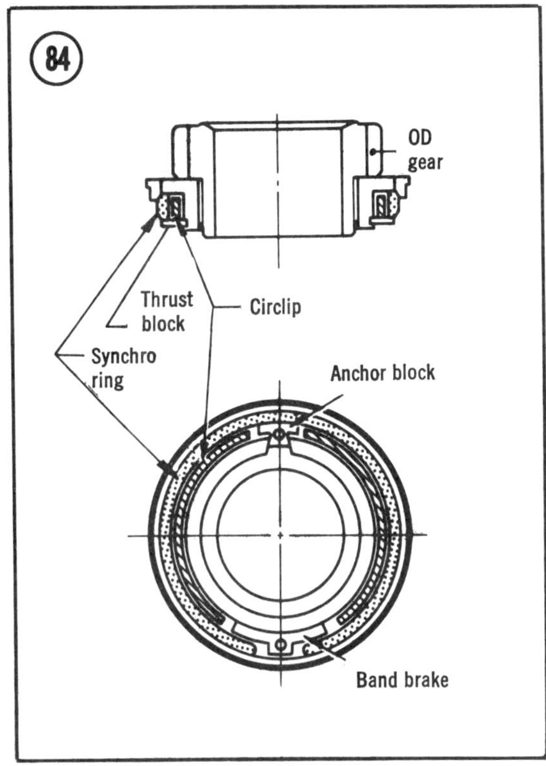

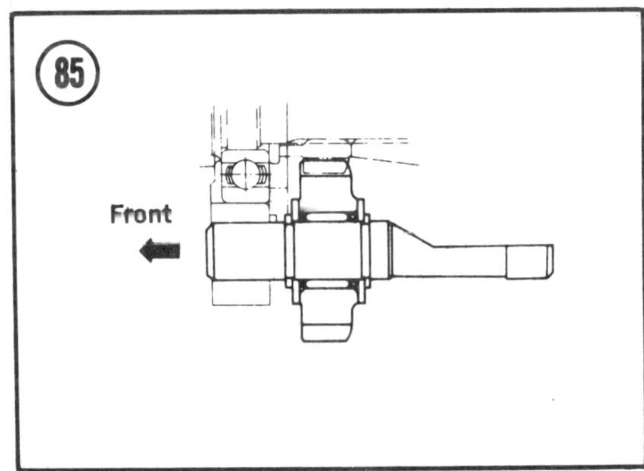

1. Before disassembling, check gear end play and backlash. Refer to *Transmission Disassembly (F4W71B)* earlier in this chapter. Specifications are the same, with 2 exceptions: fifth gear end play is 0.005-0.007 in. (0.12- 0.19mm); and reverse idler gear end play is 0.002-0.020 in. (0.05-0.50mm). Countershaft reverse gear end play is not measured.

2. Remove the front bearing and snap ring from the countershaft gear.

3. Remove the countershaft drive gear and input shaft simultaneously.

4. Slide the third-fourth gear synchronizer sleeve over the small teeth on third gear. Slide the first-second synchronizer sleeve over the small teeth on one of the gears next to it. This engages 2 gears at once, which prevents the main shaft from turning.

5. Carefully file away the punched portions of the main shaft nut and countershaft gear nut. Loosen both nuts with a 1 ½ in. (38mm) wrench (**Figure 82**). Take the countershaft gear nut off. Leave the main shaft nut on for now.

NOTE: *If you don't have the correct wrench, take the gear assembly to a Datsun dealer and have the nut removed.*

6. Remove the countershaft overdrive gear and bearing with a gear puller (**Figure 83**).

7. Remove reverse countershaft gear and its spacer.

8. Remove the snap ring from the reverse idler shaft, then remove reverse idler gear.

9. Remove a snap ring, the speedometer drive gear, and 2 more snap rings from the rear end of the main shaft.

10. Have the main shaft rear bearing pressed off by a machine shop.

11. Remove the following parts in order from the rear end of the main shaft: nut, thrust washer, reverse main gear, overdrive synchronizer, and overdrive (fifth) gear.

12. Tap the main shaft loose from the adapter plate with a soft-face mallet. Remove the main shaft and countershaft simultaneously.

13. Remove the following parts in order from the front end of the main shaft: snap ring, thrust washer, balk ring, third-fourth gear synchronizer, balk ring, third gear, and needle bearing.

Gear Assembly (FS5W71B)

Assembly is the reverse of disassembly, plus the following.

1. Dip all gears, bearings, and synchronizers in new gear oil before installing.

2. Assemble the overdrive gear (fifth gear) and its synchronizer as shown in **Figure 84**.

3. Assemble the reverse idler gear and shaft as shown in **Figure 85**.

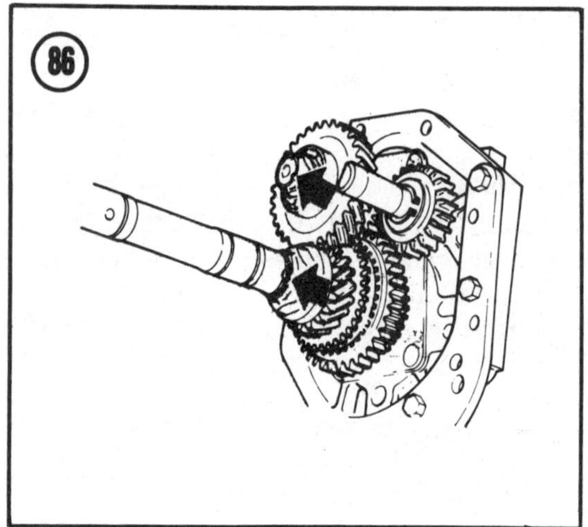

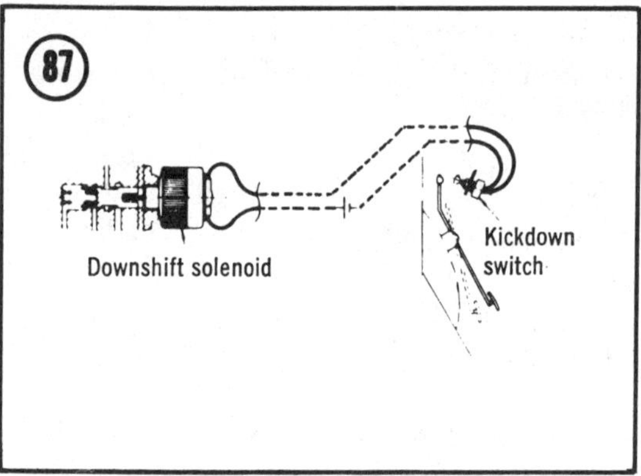

4. Tighten the countershaft and main shaft locknuts. Refer to Step 21, *Transmission Assembly (F4W71B)* for the correct method. Since specified torque for the countershaft nut is 72-94 ft.-lb. (10-13 mkg), use a 45 lb. weight. This will give a torque of 90 ft.-lb., which is within the specified range.

5. After tightening the nuts, stake them in place with a hammer and punch. See **Figure 86**.

TRANSMISSION (3N71B)

This automatic transmission has been optional for all model years since 1972. This section provides testing, removal, and installation procedures.

Checking Procedures

1. With the car on a level surface, start the engine and let it run for approximately 10 minutes to warm the transmission fluid to

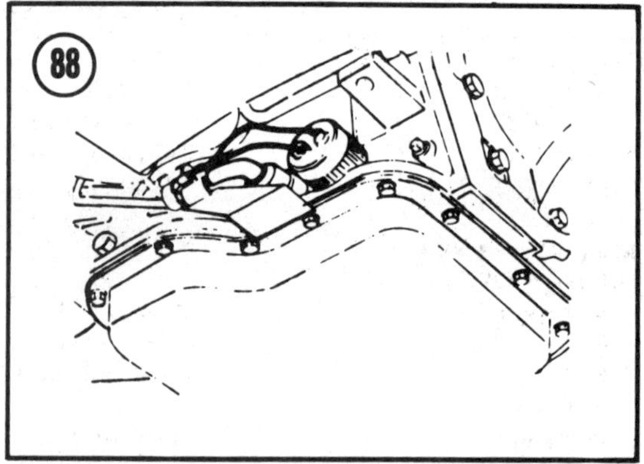

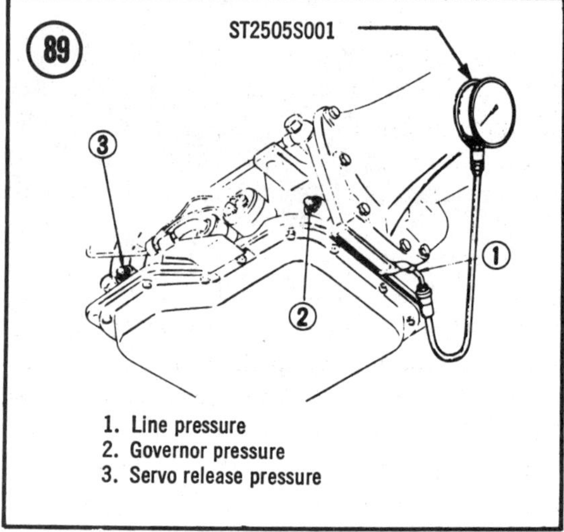

1. Line pressure
2. Governor pressure
3. Servo release pressure

122-176°F (50-80°C). Apply the brakes and move the shift lever through all gear positions to P. Check the transmission fluid level on the dipstick. If necessary, top up to the "F" line, using Dexron type automatic transmission fluid. Do not use Type F or Type A fluid.

> NOTE: *Do not fill the transmission past the "F" line. Overfilling will cause the fluid to foam, resulting in wear and damage.*

Inspect the fluid on the dipstick. Clean transmission fluid is a transparent red. If the fluid has deteriorated to a varnish-like condition, it may cause the control valve to stick. If it is black, it may indicate a burned clutch or brake band.

2. Turn the ignition key to ON (but don't start the engine) and floor the accelerator. Listen for a click from the transmission, indicating that

Table 3 AUTOMATIC TRANSMISSION SPECIFICATIONS

Stall speed	
Through 1974	1,800-2,000 rpm
1975-1977	2,000-2,200 rpm
1978-1979	1,900-2,000 rpm
1980	1,750-2,050 rpm
1981	1,800-2,100 rpm
Idling line pressure	
Through 1977	
In 1 and D	43-57 psi (3-4 kg/cm^2)
In 2	85-171 psi (6-12 kg/cm^2)
In R	43-78 psi (3.0-5.5 kg/cm^2)
1978-on	
In 1 and D	46-54 psi (3.2-3.8 kg/cm^2)
In 2	85-166 psi (6.0-11.7 kg/cm^2)
In R	60-80 psi (4.2-5.6 kg/cm^2)

the downshift solenoid is working. If there is no click, check the kickdown switch, kickdown solenoid, and the wiring between them. See **Figure 87**.

If the solenoid is defective, drain approximately 2⅛ pints (1 liter) of fluid from the transmission, unscrew the solenoid, and install a new one. **Figure 88** shows the solenoid.

3. Move the selector lever through the gears, feeling for the detents in the lever positioning plate. Make sure the selector lever pointer indicates the correct gear at each lever position.

4. Check that the starter operates only in N and P. Make sure the back-up light operates only in R. If a problem is detected, adjust the starter inhibitor switch as described later.

5. Check idle speed as described in Chapter Three, *Tune-up* section. Adjust if necessary.

6. With the engine idling and the brakes applied, move the selector lever through the gears. The shift into gear should be noticeable, but not excessively harsh.

7. With the engine idling, let off the brakes and check for excessive creeping in 1, 2, D, and R.

Stall Test

The stall test is combined with line pressure tests to isolate various problems. The tests require a tachometer and an oil pressure gauge. Connect the tachometer to the engine and connect the pressure gauge to the transmission as shown in **Figure 89**.

1. With the selector lever in P, run the engine at 1,200 rpm for several minutes to warm the transmission fluid to 140-212°F (60-100°C).

2. While the fluid is warming, look up your truck's stall speed in **Table 3**. Mark the tachometer face with small pieces of tape at these points. The tachometer must be read very quickly during this test, and the tape will make it easier.

3. Place the tachometer and oil pressure gauge where they can easily be seen from the driver's seat.

4. Block all 4 wheels so the car can't roll in either direction.

5. Place the selector lever in D. Compare idling line pressure with **Table 3**.

6. Press the accelerator slowly to the floor. Quickly note the rpm reading when engine speed levels off.

CAUTION

Do not run the engine at full load for more than five seconds. The transmission fluid heats very rapidly during this test, and severe damage could result from excessive full-load running.

7. Place the selector lever in N. Run the engine at 1,200 rpm for at least one minute to let the transmission fluid cool.

8. Repeat the line pressure check and stall speed check in 1, 2, and R. Compare results with **Table 3**.

CAUTION

Between each stage of the test, run the engine at 1,200 rpm in N for at least one minute. This is necessary to cool the transmission fluid.

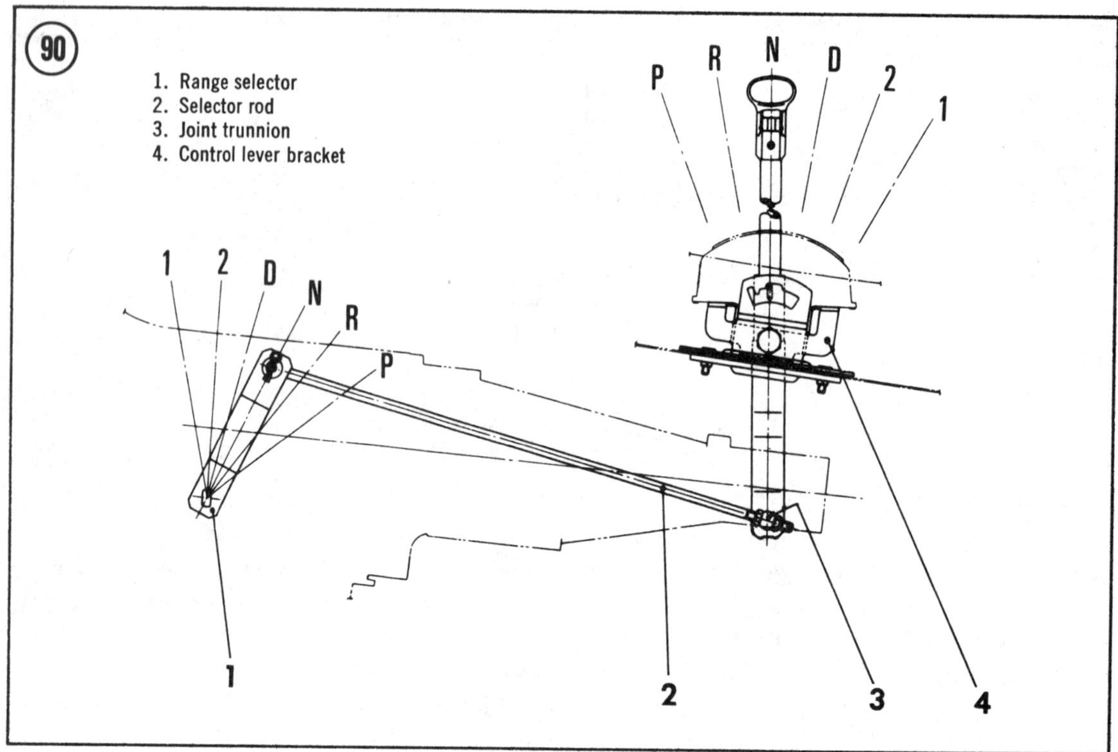

Test Interpretation

1. ***Stall speed within specifications***—This indicates that the engine is delivering full power and the control elements of the transmission are working properly. The torque converter's one-way clutch could possibly be sticking, but if it were, the car would not be able to exceed approximately 50 mph.

CAUTION

If the torque converter's one-way clutch is sticking, the transmission fluid will heat up excessively. The car should not be driven more than absolutely necessary until it can be repaired.

2. ***Stall speed too high in all gears***—One or more of the clutches in the transmission is slipping.

3. ***Stall speed too high in D, 2, and 1***—The rear clutch is slipping.

4. ***Stall speed too high in D and 2, normal in 1***—Torque converter one-way clutch is slipping.

5. ***Stall speed too high in R only***—Either the front clutch or the low and reverse brake is slipping. This problem can be isolated further in the road test, described later in this chapter.

6. ***Stall speed too low***—Either the engine is not delivering full power, or the torque converter one-way clutch is slipping. This can be further isolated in the road test.

7. ***Line pressure too low in all ranges***—This could indicate a worn oil pump, oil pressure leakage in the oil pump, valve body, or case, or a sticking regulator valve.

8. ***Line pressure normal in D, 2, and 1, low in R***—This indicates an oil leak in the low and reverse brake circuit.

9. ***Line pressure normal in R, low in 1, 2, and D***—This indicates an oil leak in the rear clutch and governor.

Road Test

1. If the stall speed was excessive in R only, determine the cause by accelerating, then letting up on the accelerator, while the selector lever is in 1. If the engine slows the car (compression braking), the front clutch is slipping. If there is no engine braking effect, the low and reverse brake is slipping.

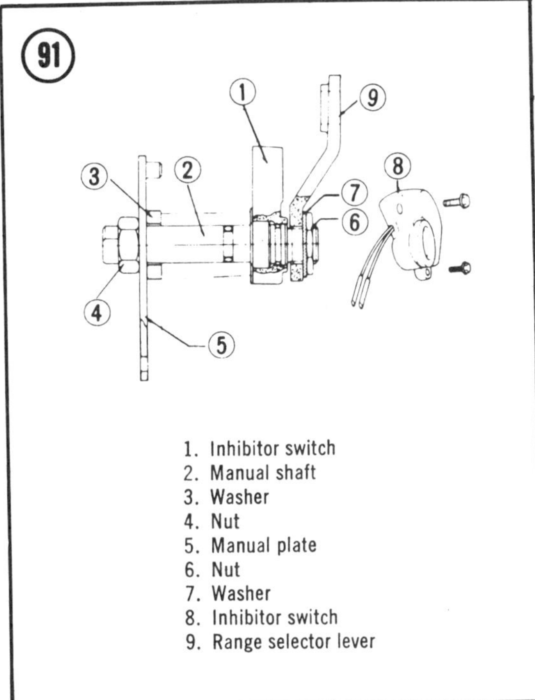

1. Inhibitor switch
2. Manual shaft
3. Washer
4. Nut
5. Manual plate
6. Nut
7. Washer
8. Inhibitor switch
9. Range selector lever

2. If the stall speed was too low, isolate the cause by checking the acceleration. Accelerate to a speed over 30 mph. If acceleration is poor to 30 mph and improves about that speed, the torque converter one-way clutch is slipping. If acceleration does not improve above 30 mph, the engine is not delivering full power and may need a tune-up.

3. While driving at approximately 31 mph, let up the accelerator and pull the selector into 1. The transmission should downshift into second, then into first.

4. While driving at approximately 31 mph, pull the selector lever into 2 without letting up the accelerator. The transmission should shift into second gear. Once in second gear, it should not shift up or down.

5. Park the car on a slope. Apply the brakes and shift to P. Let off the brakes and make sure the transmission holds the car. Check with the car facing up and down the hill.

Linkage Adjustment

1. Move the selector lever back and forth from 1 to P several times. A slight click should be heard and felt at each gear position.

2. Place the selector lever in N. Detach the selector lever from the linkage. See **Figure 90**.

3. Working beneath the car, make sure the range select lever on the side of the transmission is in the N position. This occurs when the slot in the manual shaft, to which the lever is attached, is vertical.

4. Make sure the selector lever inside the car is in N, then reconnect the linkage.

Starter Inhibitor Switch

If the starter operates in any gear other than N or P, or if the reverse light lights in any gear other than R, check the linkage. If the linkage is adjusted correctly, check the inhibitor switch.

1. Detach the range select lever (9, **Figure 91**) from the transmission shift linkage. Move the range select lever to the N position.

2. Attach a continuity tester (such as an ohmmeter or self-powered test lamp) to the black-and-yellow inhibitor switch wires. The tester should indicate continuity (the lamp should light) while the range select lever is within 3° of the N position.

3. Repeat Step 2 with the range select lever in the P position.

4. Move the lever to the R position, and connect the tester to the red and red-and-black wires on the inhibitor switch. Again, the tester should indicate continuity in a 3° range on either side of the R position.

5. If the tester shows continuity when the lever is obviously more than 3° away from the N, R, or P positions in Steps 2, 3, or 4, adjust the inhibitor switch. To do this, first move the range select lever to the N position. Then remove the lever retaining nut (6, **Figure 91**), two inhibitor switch installation bolts, and the machine screw under the switch. Align the machine screw hole with the pinhole in the manual shaft. Check the alignment by insering a piece of wire 1/16 in. (1.5mm) thick through the two holes. Then install the switch bolts, pull out the wire, and install the machine screw. Install the nut on the manual shaft and recheck the switch as described in Steps 2, 3, and 4.

6. If the tester still indicates continuity when the lever is moved from the N, R, or P positions, replace the inhibitor switch.

10

Transmission Removal/Installation

1. Drain the transmission fluid.
2. Jack up the car on both ends and place it on jackstands.
3. Disconnect one cable from the battery.
4. Disconnect and remove the front section of the exhaust system.
5. Disconnect the wires from the starter inhibitor switch and kickdown solenoid.
6. Disconnect the vacuum line from the vacuum diaphragm (located next to the kickdown solenoid). Disconnect the transmission oil cooler lines.
7. Disconnect the shift linkage from the transmission.
8. Disconnect the speedometer cable from the rear extension.
9. Remove the drive shaft (Chapter Eleven).
10. Place a jack beneath the engine to support it. Use a block of wood between the jack and the oil pan.
11. Remove the cover from the torque converter housing. Remove four bolts attaching the torque converter to the drive plate. See **Figure 92**.

> NOTE: *Mark the torque converter and drive plate so they can be reassembled in the same relative positions.*

12. Remove the starter (Chapter Seven).
13. Place a jack beneath the transmission to support it. Remove two bolts attaching the rear mounting member to the transmission, then detach the mounting member from the car.
14. Remove bolts attaching the transmission to the engine.
15. Lower the jack beneath the transmission gradually and remove the transmission toward the rear of the car.
16. Installation is the reverse of these steps. If the torque converter has been separated from the transmission, be sure to align the notch shown in **Figure 93** with the corresponding notch in the transmission oil pump. Also, be sure dimension "A" in **Figure 94** is 0.846 in. (21.5mm).

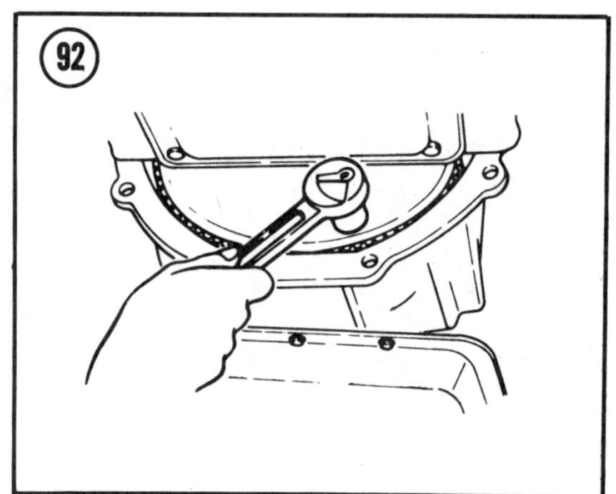

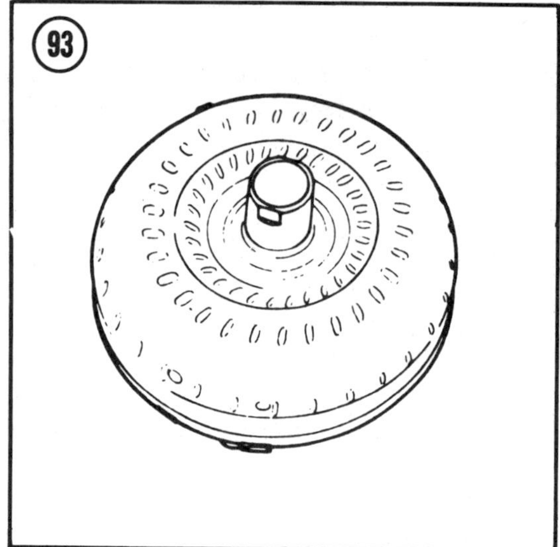

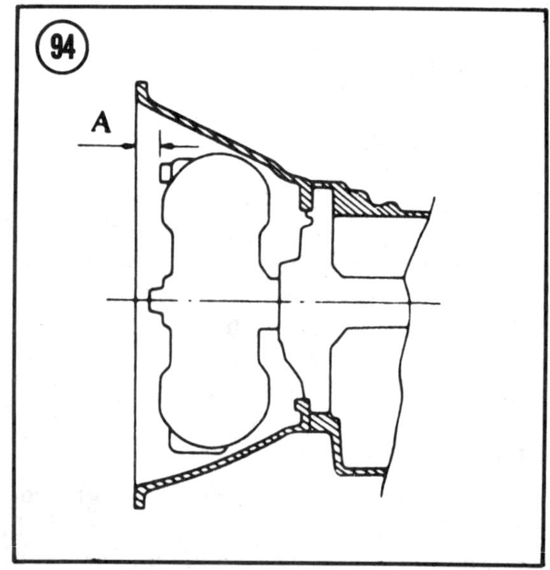

Table 1 TIGHTENING TORQUES, MANUAL TRANSMISSION

Item	Ft.-lb.	Mkg
Removal/Installation		
Engine to transmission bolts		
1970-1973	17-20	2.4-2.8
1974-1976	30-36	4.0-5.0
1977 and later	32-43	4.4-5.9
Shift lever nut (1970-1973 only)	14-16	1.9-2.2
Speedometer pinion bolt or nut		
1970-1973	2-3	0.3-0.4
1974 and later	3-4	0.4-0.5
Inspection cover bolts (1970-1973 only)	6-7	0.8-1.0
Rear bracket-to-transmission bolts	6-8	0.8-1.1
Rear bracket-to-frame bolts		
1970-1973	24-28	3.3-3.8
1974 and later	23-31	3.2-4.3
Overhaul (F4W63)		
Main shaft nut	58-80	8-11
Rear extension bolts	10-13	1.4-1.8
Front cover bolts	6-7	0.8-1.0
Rear flange nut	72-101	10-14
Electrical switches	15-22	2-3
Inspection cover bolts	6-7	0.8-1.0
Filler plug	18-25	2.5-3.5
Drain plug	15-22	2-3
Overhaul (F4W71B, FS5W71B)		
Bearing retainer machine screws	14-18	1.9-2.5
Main shaft nut	101-123	14-17
Check ball plugs	14-18	1.9-2.5
Rear extension bolts	12-15	1.6-2.1
Front cover bolts	12-15	1.6-2.1
Electrical switches	14-22	2-3
Filler and drain plugs	18-25	2.5-3.5
Clutch withdrawal lever pivot	14-25	2.0-3.5
Return spring plug	6-7	0.8-1.0
Rear extension upper cover bolts	3-4	0.4-0.5
Striking lever pin and nut	6-9	0.9-1.2
Countershaft gear nut (FS5W71B)	72-94	10-13

NOTE: If you own a 1982 or later model, first check the Supplement at the back of the book for any new service information.

CHAPTER ELEVEN

BRAKES

The 1970-1977 models use drum brakes at all four wheels. Front disc brakes have been used since 1978. A vacuum booster (power brakes) is used on late models. The 1976 and later trucks use a load sensing valve. This senses the amount of weight in the truck bed and proportions fluid pressure to the front and rear brakes accordingly. The handbrake on all models is a mechanical type that operates the rear brakes.

Specifications (**Table 1**) and tightening torques (**Table 2**) are listed at the end of the chapter.

FRONT DRUM BRAKES

Figure 1 shows the front brake assembly.

Removal

1. Loosen the front wheel nuts, jack up the front end of the truck, place it on jackstands, and remove the front wheels.

2. Pull the brake drum off. If the drum does not come off easily, remove the boot from the adjuster (**Figure 2**). Turn the adjuster wheel upward to loosen the shoes.

3. Remove hub assembly. See Chapter Twelve.

4. Unhook all 3 shoe return springs, then remove the brake shoes.

5. If wheel cylinder overhaul is planned, disconnect the hose from the wheel cylinder (**Figure 2**). Remove the cylinder attaching nut and take the cylinder out of the backing plate.

6. Remove the retaining spring, shim, and lock plate securing the adjuster. Take adjuster out.

7. If necessary, remove 4 bolts and lift the brake backing plate off the spindle. Backing plate removal is rarely necessary for normal brake service.

Inspection

1. Clean all parts except the wheel cylinder in rubbing alcohol or brake fluid. Do not use gasoline or kerosene.

CAUTION

If cleaning with brake fluid, keep it off the brake linings. Brake fluid will ruin the linings and they will have to be replaced.

2. Check drums for visible scoring, excessive or uneven wear, and corrosion. If you have precision measuring equipment, measure the drum for wear and out-of-roundness. If you do not have the equipment, this measurement can be done by a dealer or machine shop. Maximum permissible out-of-roundness is 0.0008 in. (0.02mm). If the drum is out-of-round or otherwise defective, it can be turned to correct it. However, the inside diameter must not exceed

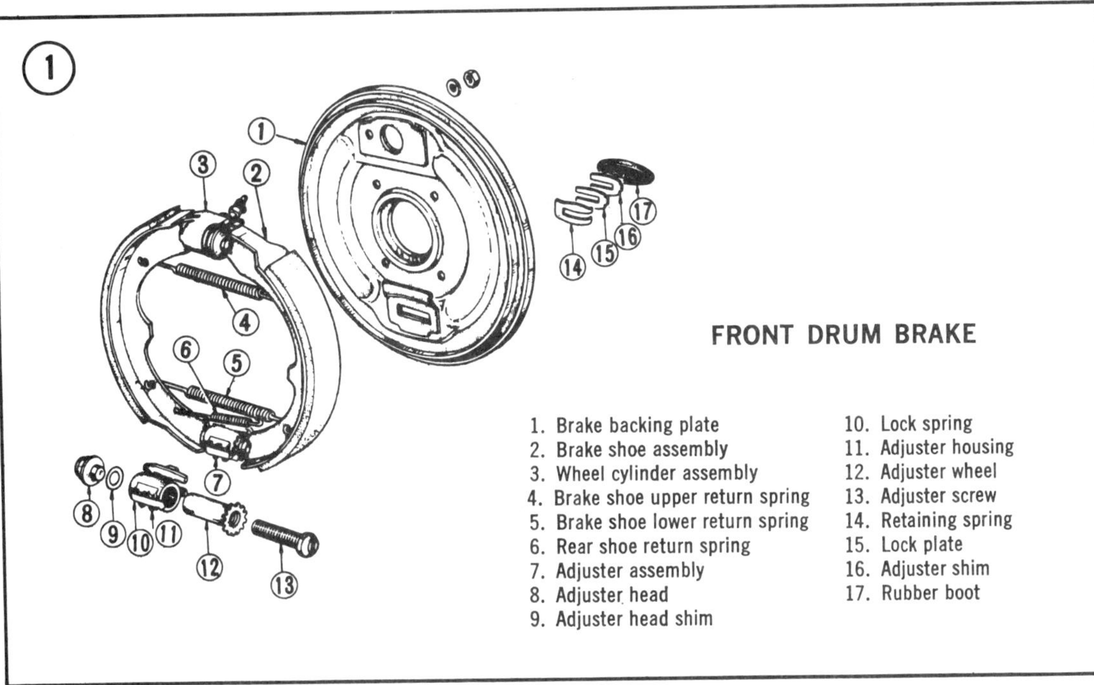

FRONT DRUM BRAKE

1. Brake backing plate
2. Brake shoe assembly
3. Wheel cylinder assembly
4. Brake shoe upper return spring
5. Brake shoe lower return spring
6. Rear shoe return spring
7. Adjuster assembly
8. Adjuster head
9. Adjuster head shim
10. Lock spring
11. Adjuster housing
12. Adjuster wheel
13. Adjuster screw
14. Retaining spring
15. Lock plate
16. Adjuster shim
17. Rubber boot

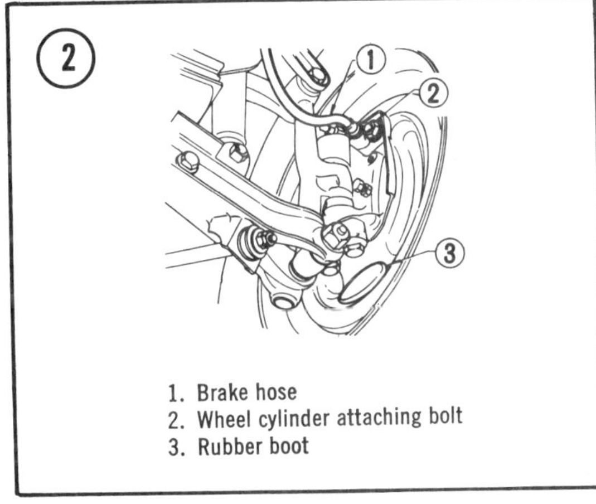

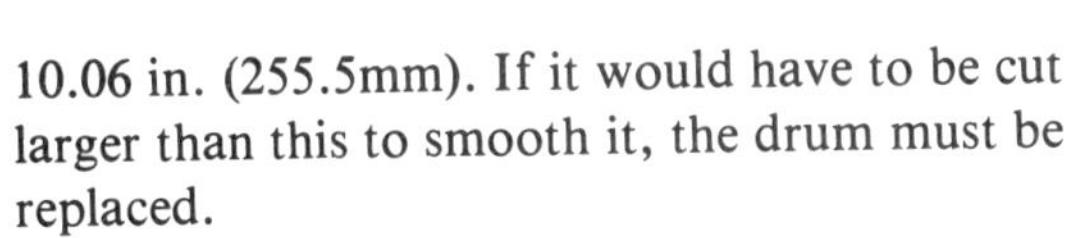

1. Brake hose
2. Wheel cylinder attaching bolt
3. Rubber boot

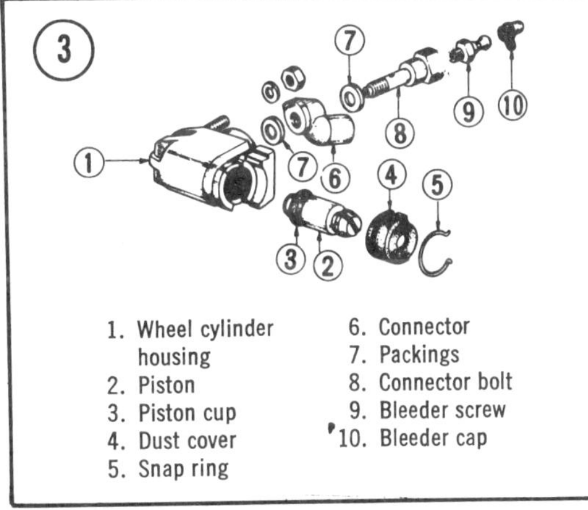

1. Wheel cylinder housing
2. Piston
3. Piston cup
4. Dust cover
5. Snap ring
6. Connector
7. Packings
8. Connector bolt
9. Bleeder screw
10. Bleeder cap

10.06 in. (255.5mm). If it would have to be cut larger than this to smooth it, the drum must be replaced.

3. Inspect the lining material on the brake shoes. Make sure it is not cracked, unevenly worn, or separated from the shoes. If linings are only slightly oily or greasy, and not excessively worn, they may be cleaned in non-petroleum based solvent and reused. If linings are saturated with oil or grease, or contaminated with brake fluid, they must be replaced. Linings must also be replaced if worn thinner than 1/16 in. (1.5mm).

4. Check the anti-rattle pins, adjuster mechanism, and handbrake operating arm for worn or damaged parts. Replace as needed.

5. Check return springs for weakness or deformation. Replace if these conditions are detected.

Wheel Cylinder Overhaul

Figure 3 shows the wheel cylinder parts.

1. Remove the snap ring and dust cover.
2. Carefully remove the piston and cup. Take the cup off the piston and discard it.

3. Remove the bleed valve, connector bolt, and connector.
4. Clean all parts in alcohol or brake fluid. Do not immerse rubber parts in alcohol for more than 30 seconds. Do not clean with kerosene or gasoline.
5. Check the cylinder bore and piston for scoring, cracks, corrosion, dirt, or excessive wear. Check cylinder body and piston for wear in their brake shoe slots. Replace cylinder and piston if any of these conditions are found.
6. As a final check on a suspect cylinder and piston, measure diameter of the piston and cylinder bore. If the difference between these measurements is more than 0.006 in. (0.15mm), replace the cylinder and piston.
7. Apply rubber grease to a new piston cup. Install it on the piston. The lip of the cup faces into the cylinder.
8. Coat the piston and cylinder bore with brake fluid. Install the piston, then the dust cover and snap ring.
9. Install the connector and bolt. Tighten the bolt to 14-18 ft.-lb. (1.9-2.5 mkg).

Installation

Installation is the reverse of the removal procedure, plus the following:

1. Apply brake grease to the adjuster housing bore, adjuster wheel, and adjuster screw. Also apply grease to the points shown in **Figure 4**.

CAUTION
Do not let grease touch brake linings.

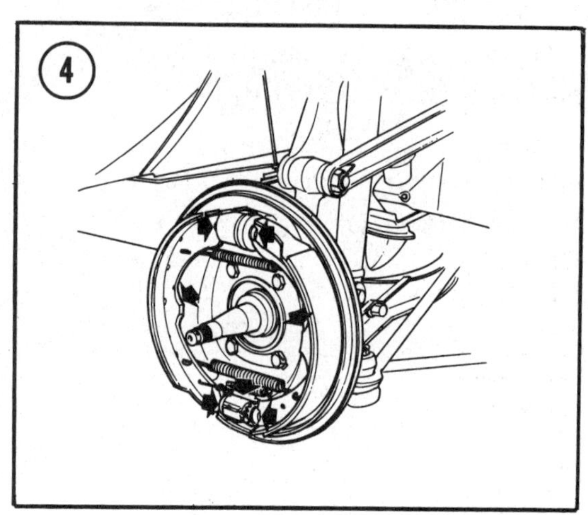

5

FRONT DISC BRAKE

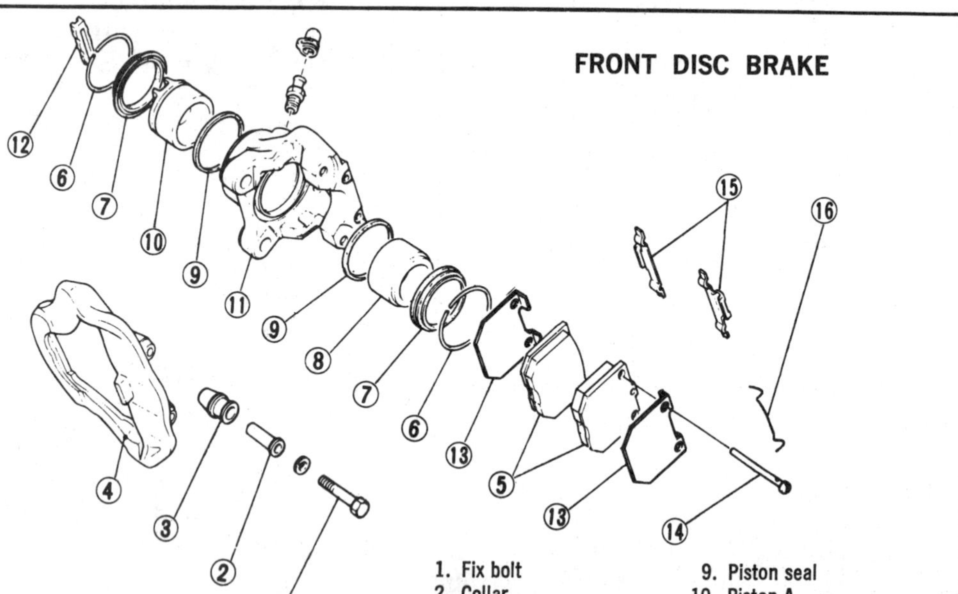

1. Fix bolt
2. Collar
3. Gripper
4. Yoke
5. Pad
6. Retaining ring
7. Dust seal
8. Piston B
9. Piston seal
10. Piston A
11. Cylinder body
12. Yoke holder
13. Shim
14. Pad pin
15. Anti-squeal spring
16. Clip

2. Be sure the wheel cylinder marked "L" goes on the left side, and the cylinder marked "R" goes on the right. Tighten the wheel cylinder nut to 39-48 ft.-lb. (5.4-6.6 mkg).

3. If the hub was removed, adjust front wheel bearings (Chapter Twelve).

4. After installation, adjust and bleed brakes as described later in this chapter.

FRONT DISC BRAKES

Figure 5 shows the front disc brake assembly.

Pad Replacement

Pads must be replaced whenever the friction material is worn to 0.08 in. (2mm) or less.

1. Loosen the front wheel nuts, jack up the front of the truck, place it on jackstands, and remove the front wheels.

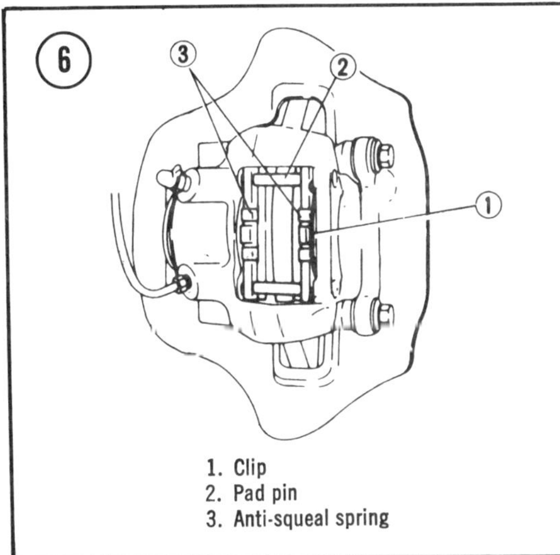

1. Clip
2. Pad pin
3. Anti-squeal spring

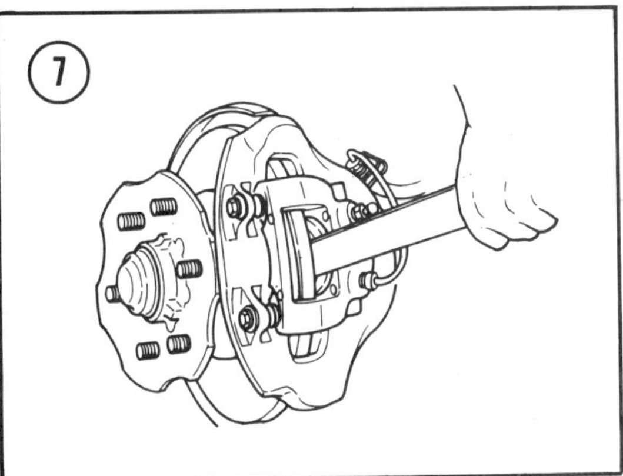

2. Remove the clips (**Figure 6**).

3. Pull out the pad pins.

4. Pull the pads out with pliers.

CAUTION
Do not press the brake pedal with the pads removed. This will cause the pistons to fall out. The caliper will then have to be rebuilt.

5. Carefully clean and inspect the area which holds the pads. Clean with alcohol or brake fluid. Do not use gasoline, kerosene, or solvent.

6. Check the pads for wear or for damage caused by overheating.

7. Inspect the pads for wear and damage caused by overheating. Check for grease, oil, or brake fluid on the friction material. If the pads are only slightly oily or greasy, and not excessively worn, they can be cleaned in trichloroethylene and reused. If they are saturated with oil or grease, wet with brake fluid, or damaged from overheating, replace the pads. Always replace pads in full sets.

8. Place rags beneath the master cylinder in case it overflows. Open the caliper bleed valve far enough to let brake fluid escape. Lever the pistons into the cylinder (**Figure 7**) and install the outer brake pad.

CAUTION
*Do not push the pistons in past the point shown in **Figure 8**. If they are pushed past this point, the pistons will hang up on the seal. The caliper will then have to be rebuilt.*

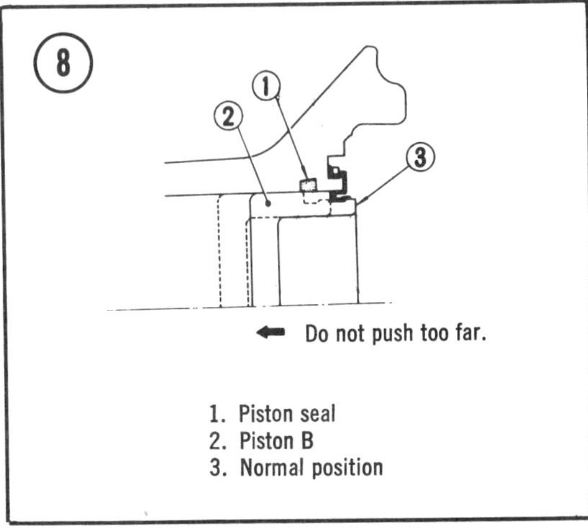

1. Piston seal
2. Piston B
3. Normal position

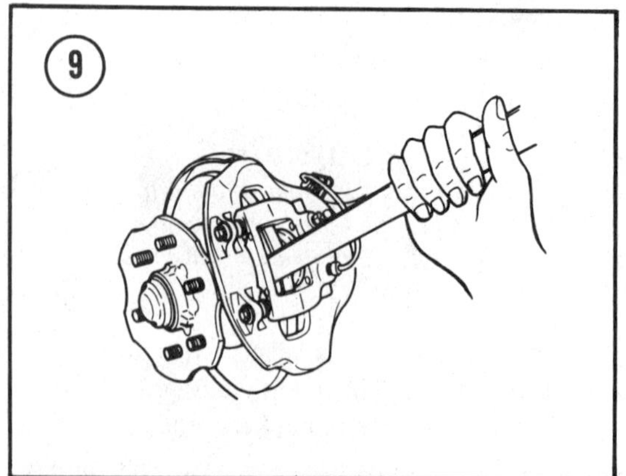

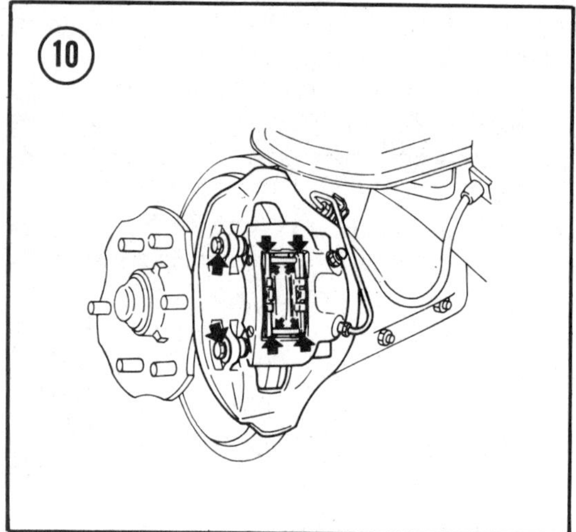

9. Pry the yoke away from the disc **(Figure 9)** and install the inner pad.

10. Apply brake grease to the points shown in **Figure 10**.

CAUTION

Do not let grease touch the friction material on the brake pads.

11. Install the anti-squeal spring and pad pins. Secure with the clips.

12. Press the brake pedal several times to seat the pads.

13. Check brake fluid level. Top up as needed. If the pedal feels mushy, bleed the brakes as described under *Brake Bleeding*.

Caliper Removal/Installation

1. Remove the pads as described earlier.

2. Disconnect the caliper brake line. The factory recommends using tube wrench GG94310000. Do not use an adjustable wrench.

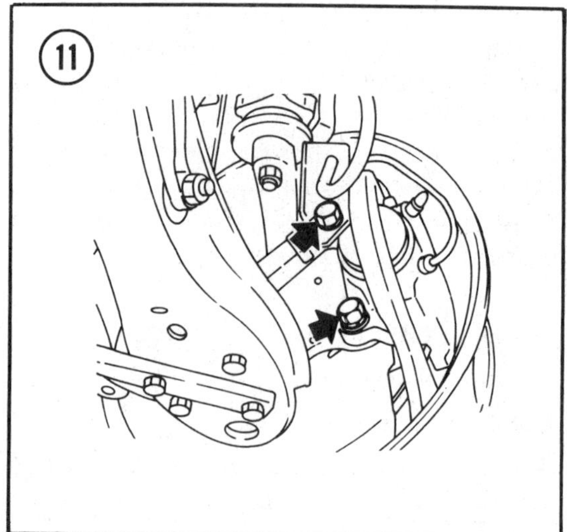

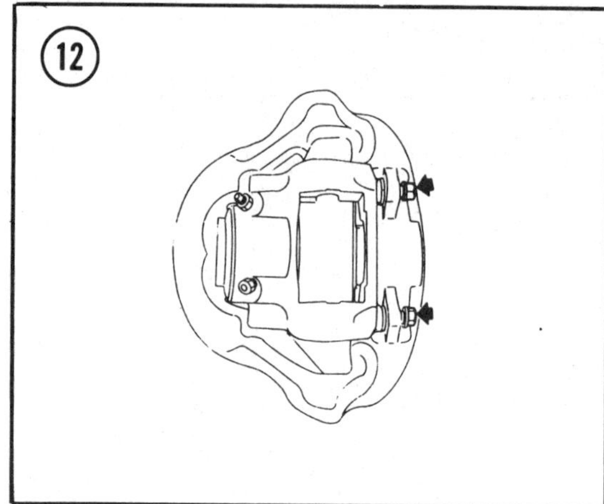

NOTE: *Plug the brake line so it doesn't siphon fluid from the master cylinder.*

3. Remove the caliper mounting bolts **(Figure 11**. Take the caliper off.

4. Installation is the reverse of removal. Tighten caliper bolts to 53-72 ft.-lb. (7.3-9.9 mkg). Bleed the brakes as described under *Brake Bleeding*.

Caliper Overhaul

1. Remove the caliper as described earlier. Pour out the brake fluid.

2. Thoroughly clean the outside of the caliper.

3. Remove the fixing bolts **(Figure 12)**.

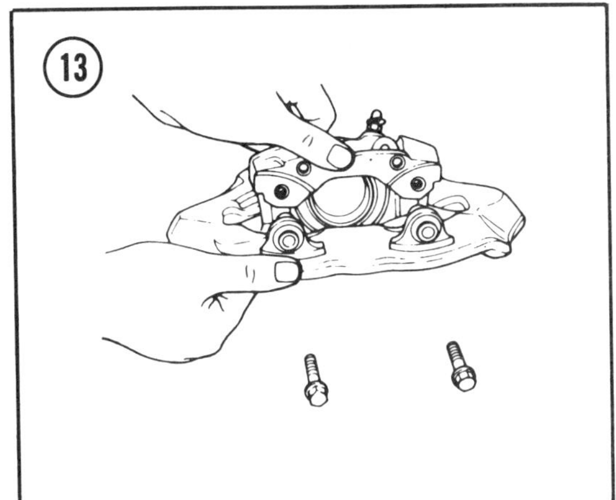

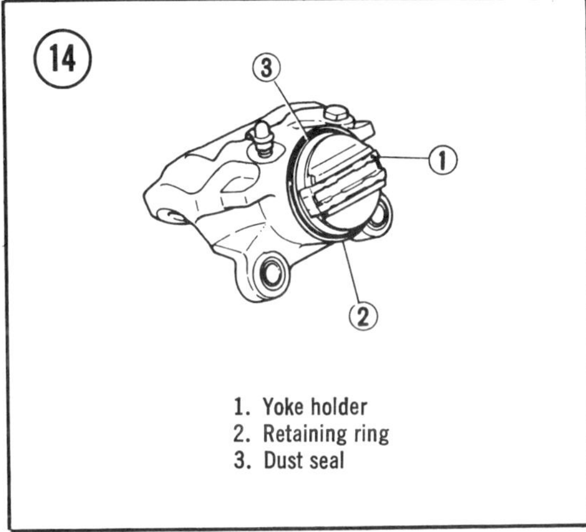

1. Yoke holder
2. Retaining ring
3. Dust seal

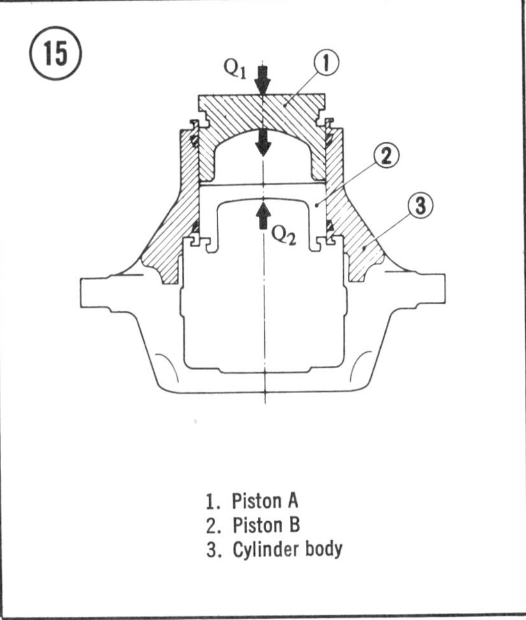

1. Piston A
2. Piston B
3. Cylinder body

4. Separate the cylinder body from the yoke (**Figure 13**).

5. Remove the retaining ring and dust seal from each end of the cylinder body. See **Figure 14**.

6. Apply compressed air to the brake line hole to blow the pistons out of the cylinder. Use a service station air hose if you don't have a compressor.

WARNING

The pistons may shoot out with extreme force. Apply air pressure gradually. Hold the cylinder body inside a sturdy wooden box. Be sure the pistons are pointed at the sides of the box.

7. Remove the piston seals from inside the cylinder. Use fingers only so the cylinder bore won't be scratched.

8. Thoroughly clean the cylinder body and pistons in alcohol or brake fluid. Do not use gasoline, kerosene, or solvent. These may leave residue that will damage the piston seals.

9. Check the cylinder bore for wear and damage. If these conditions are apparent, replace the cylinder body. The cylinder body must also be replaced if the bore is corroded.

10. Check the yoke for cracks or other damage. Replace if these can be seen. If the yoke is rusted, clean it with fine emery paper.

11. Check the piston for scratches, wear, pits, corrosion, or dirt. Since the piston is plated, it cannot be cleaned with emery paper. If the piston cannot be cleaned with chrome cleaner and a rag, replace it.

12. Discard the piston seals. These must be replaced whenever the caliper is disassembled.

13. Coat new piston seals with rubber grease or brake fluid. Install the seals in the cylinder bore.

14. Coat the cylinder bore and pistons with brake fluid. Install the pistons.

NOTE: *Be sure to install the pistons from the directions shown in* **Figure 15**.

15. Make sure the groove in piston A will align with the yoke when the cylinder body is installed in the yoke.

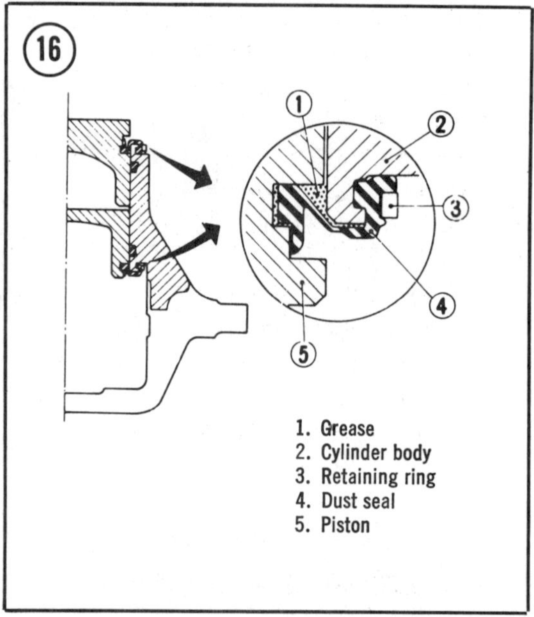

1. Grease
2. Cylinder body
3. Retaining ring
4. Dust seal
5. Piston

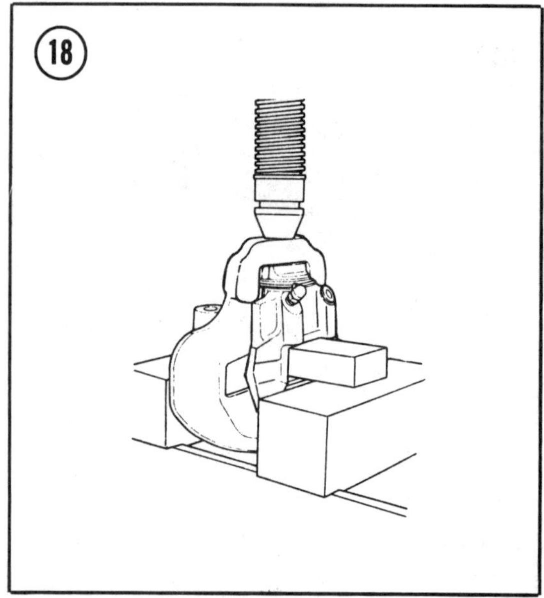

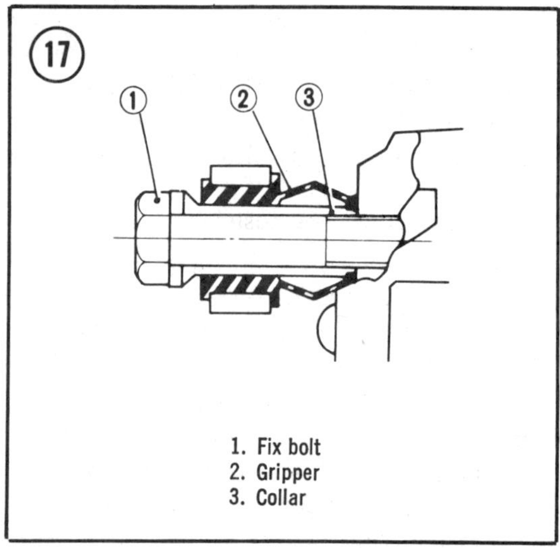

1. Fix bolt
2. Gripper
3. Collar

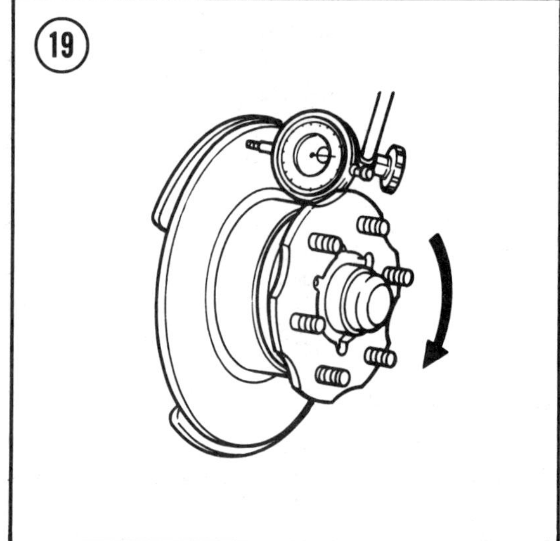

16. Apply rubber grease to the sealing surface of the dust seals (**Figure 16**). Install the dust seals and secure with the retainer rings.

NOTE: *Wipe off any excess grease with alcohol.*

17. Install the yoke holder in piston A's groove.

18. Install the grippers in the yoke. Apply a one percent soap solution (one teaspoon in 2 cups of water) to the inner walls of the grippers, then drive in the collars. See **Figure 17**.

NOTE: *Do not use a stronger soap solution.*

19. Align the yoke with the yoke holder. Support the cylinder body and press the yoke into the yoke holder. See **Figure 18**. If you don't have a press, a machine shop can do this inexpensively.

CAUTION

The yoke must be vertical when pressing, or the yoke holder will be damaged. If pressing force is not 44-66 lb. (20-30 kg), replace the yoke holder.

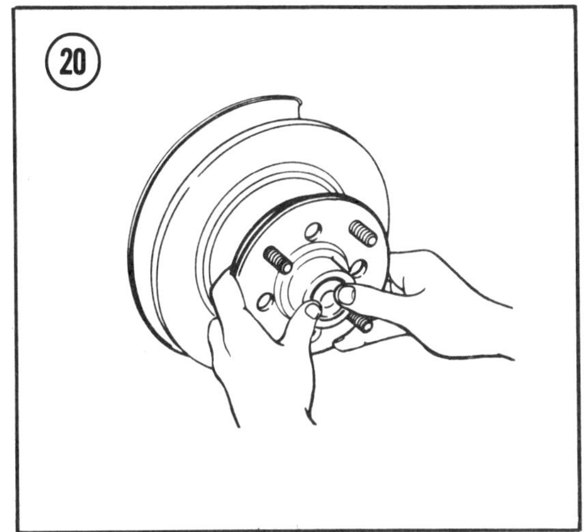

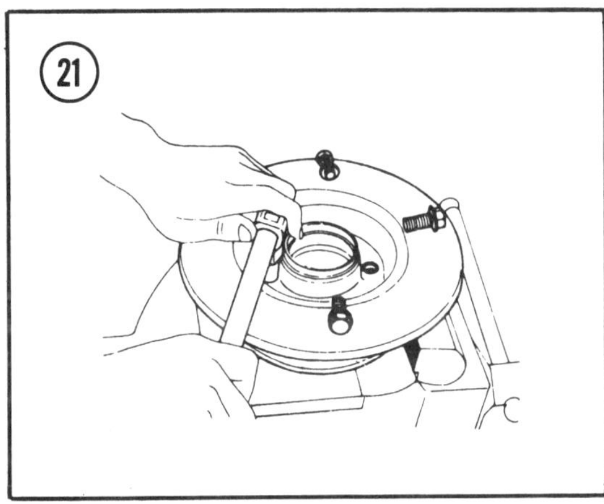

Disc Inspection

1. Check the disc for rust, burn marks (blue-tinted areas), or scratches. If these can be seen, the disc should be turned by a machine shop. Standard disc thickness is 0.492 in. (12.5mm). Minimum is 0.413 in. (10.5mm). If it would have to be cut thinner than the minimum to repair it, the disc must be replaced.
2. Set up a dial indicator as shown in **Figure 19**. Rotate the disc one full turn and measure runout. If it exceeds 0.006 in. (0.15mm), have the disc turned by a machine shop.

Disc Removal/Installation

1. Loosen the front wheel nuts, jack up the front end of the truck, place it on jackstands, and remove the front wheels.
2. Remove the caliper as described earlier.
3. Remove the wheel bearing grease cap and locknut as described in Chapter Twelve.
4. Remove the brake disc together with the wheel hub (**Figure 20**).
5. Remove 4 bolts and separate the brake disc from the hub (**Figure 21**).
6. Bolt the disc to the hub. Tighten the bolts to 28-38 ft.-lb. (3.9-5.3).
7. Repack and adjust the wheel bearings as described in Chapter Twelve.
8. Install the caliper.
9. Install the front wheels, lower the truck, and bleed brakes as described later in this chapter.

REAR DRUM BRAKE

Figure 22 shows the rear drum brakes.

Removal

1. Loosen the rear wheel nuts, jack up the rear end of the truck, place it on jsckstands, and remove the rear wheels.
2. Make sure the handbrake is off, then remove the brake drum. If the drum is difficult to remove, turn the adjuster wheel upward to loosen the shoes.
3. Turn the anti-rattle springs 90° with pliers. Remove the pins, retaining collars, springs, and spring washers.
4. Spread the brake shoes and remove the extension link.
5. Remove the return springs, then the brake shoes. The rear shoe must be pulled partway off, then separated from toggle link (**Figure 23**).
6. Disconnect the toggle lever from the handbrake cable.
7. Remove the lock plate, adjuster shim, and adjuster spring. Take the adjuster out.
8. If wheel cylinder overhaul is planned, disconnect the brake line and remove the cylinder attaching nuts. Take the cylinder out of the backing plate.
9. Backing plate removal — rarely necessary for normal brake service — requires removal of the rear axle shaft and wheel bearing. See Chapter Eleven for removal procedures.

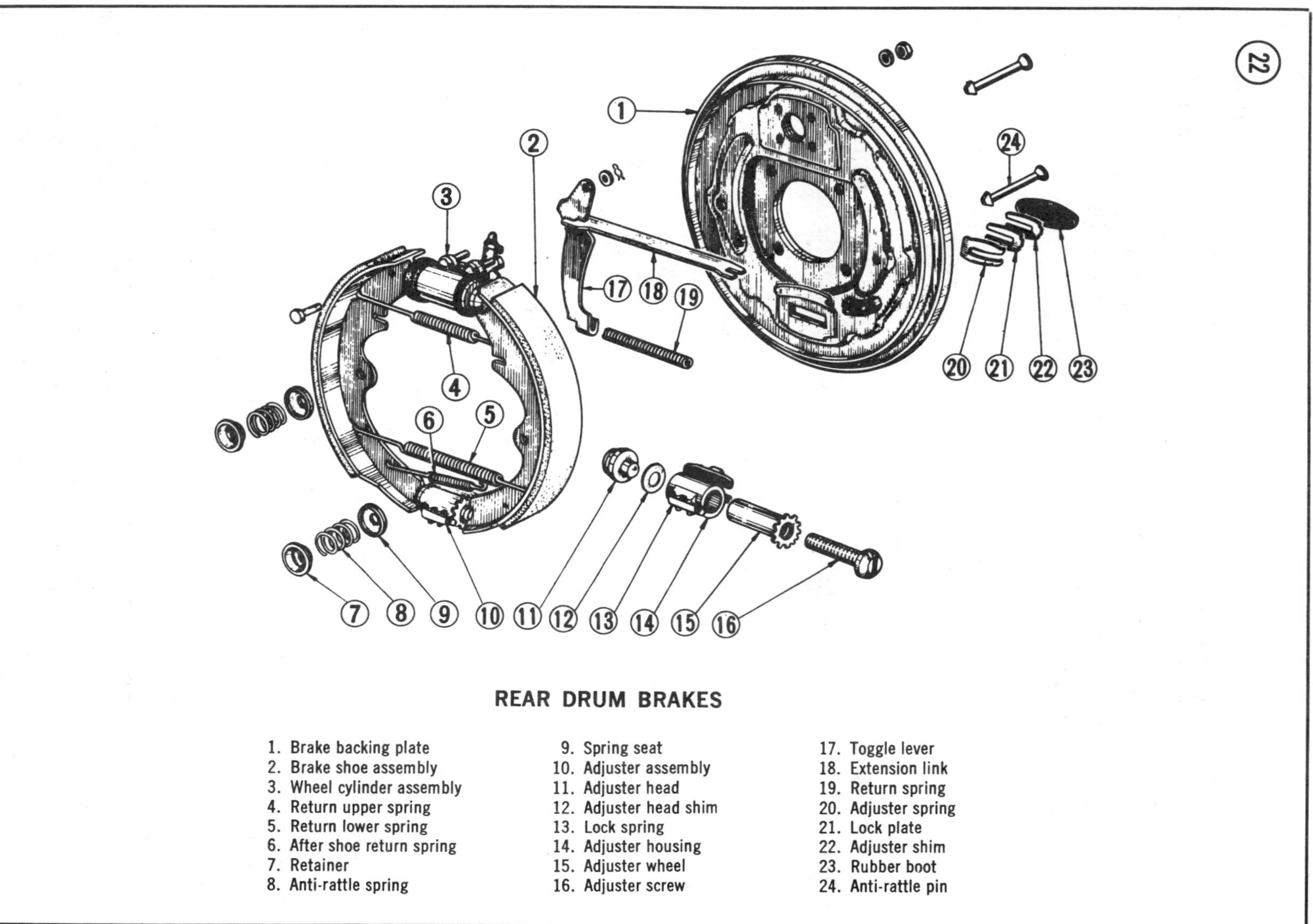

REAR DRUM BRAKES

1. Brake backing plate
2. Brake shoe assembly
3. Wheel cylinder assembly
4. Return upper spring
5. Return lower spring
6. After shoe return spring
7. Retainer
8. Anti-rattle spring
9. Spring seat
10. Adjuster assembly
11. Adjuster head
12. Adjuster head shim
13. Lock spring
14. Adjuster housing
15. Adjuster wheel
16. Adjuster screw
17. Toggle lever
18. Extension link
19. Return spring
20. Adjuster spring
21. Lock plate
22. Adjuster shim
23. Rubber boot
24. Anti-rattle pin

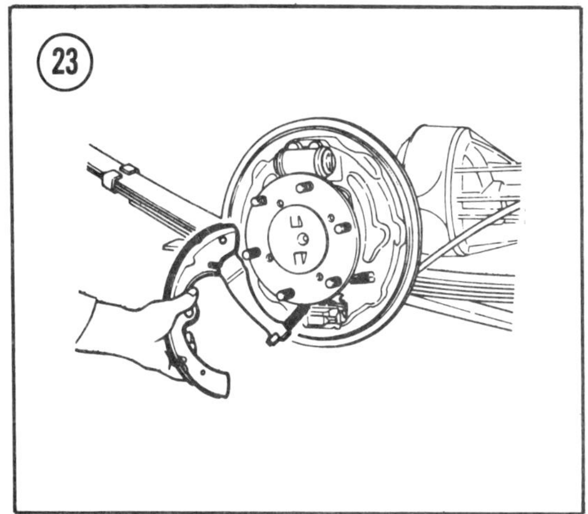

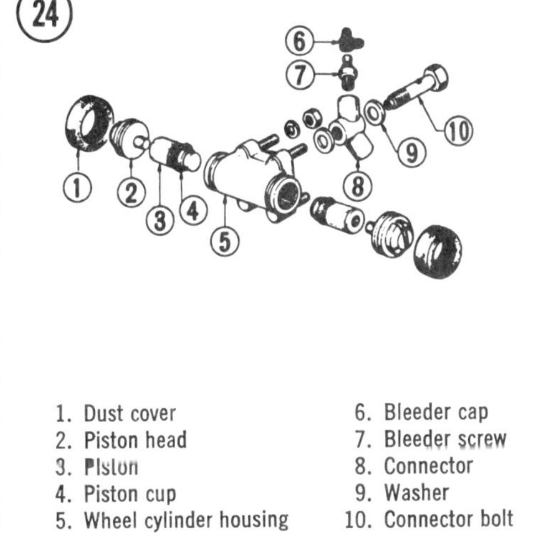

1. Dust cover
2. Piston head
3. Piston
4. Piston cup
5. Wheel cylinder housing
6. Bleeder cap
7. Bleeder screw
8. Connector
9. Washer
10. Connector bolt

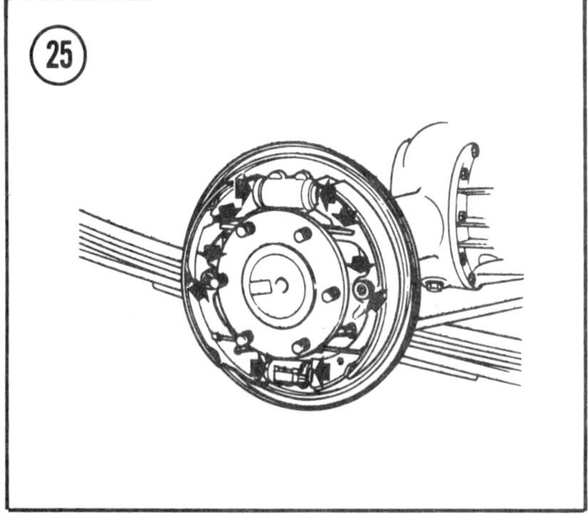

Inspection

Inspection is basically the same as for front brakes, described earlier in this chapter. Maximum permissible drum diameter is 10.06 in. (255.5mm). Minimum lining thickness is 0.04 in. (1mm).

Wheel Cylinder Overhaul

Figure 24 shows the rear wheel cylinder parts. Overhaul procedures are basically the same as for front wheel cylinders, described earlier in this chapter.

Installation

Installation is the reverse of the removal procedure, plus the following:

1. Clearance between the rearward brake shoe and toggle lever must range from zero to 0.012 in. (0-0.3mm). If necessary, adjust by installing a thicker or thinner washer on the toggle lever pivot pin.
2. Apply brake grease to the adjuster housing bore, adjuster wheel, and adjuster screw. Also apply grease to the points shown in **Figure 25**.

CAUTION
Do not let grease touch brake linings.

3. Tighten the wheel cylinder attaching nuts to 11-13 ft.-lb. (1.5-1.8 mkg).
4. After installation, adjust and bleed the brakes as described later in this chapter.

11

MASTER CYLINDER

Late model pickups use dual-piston master cylinders. Early pickups use single-piston master cylinders. **Figure 26** shows the early design; **Figure 27** shows the type used through 1980; **Figure 28** shows the 1981 design.

NOTE: *Tokico and Nabco brand master cylinders are used in production. Although they are very similar, parts are not interchangeable between the brands. When you buy a rebuild kit, be sure it is the right brand.*

Removal/Installation

1. On cars without brake boosters, disconnect the pushrod from the brake pedal.

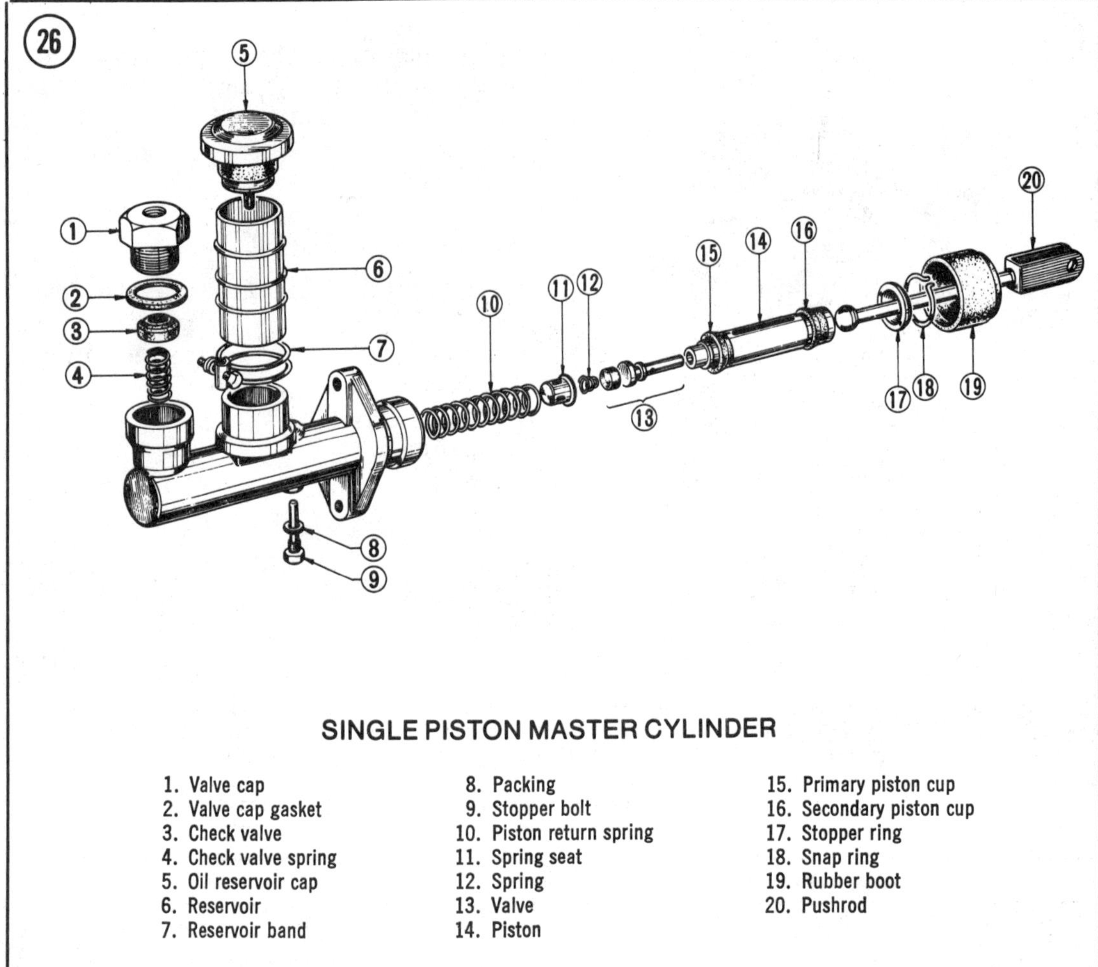

SINGLE PISTON MASTER CYLINDER

1. Valve cap
2. Valve cap gasket
3. Check valve
4. Check valve spring
5. Oil reservoir cap
6. Reservoir
7. Reservoir band
8. Packing
9. Stopper bolt
10. Piston return spring
11. Spring seat
12. Spring
13. Valve
14. Piston
15. Primary piston cup
16. Secondary piston cup
17. Stopper ring
18. Snap ring
19. Rubber boot
20. Pushrod

2. Disconnect the brake lines from the master cylinder.

CAUTION

Place rags beneath the master cylinder to keep brake fluid off the paint.

3. Remove 2 master cylinder installation nuts. **Figure 29** shows a typical installation. Lift the master cylinder out.
4. Installation is the reverse of these steps.

Disassembly

Refer to the appropriate exploded view for this procedure.

1. Remove the stopper bolt(s) and drain the brake fluid from the cylinder.
2. Remove the snap ring. Take out the stopper, piston assemblies, and return springs.

CAUTION

Remove the piston(s) carefully to prevent damaging the piston and cylinder friction surfaces.

3. Remove the cap screw(s). Take out the check valve(s) and spring(s).

NOTE

Do not remove the brake fluid reservoirs unless installing new ones.

Inspection

1. Thoroughly clean all parts in alcohol or brake fluid. Do not use gasoline or kerosene.
2. Discard the piston cups, check valves, and packing rings.
3. Check the cylinder bore and piston(s) for excessive or uneven wear, scoring, or

(27)

DUAL PISTON MASTER CYLINDER (THROUGH 1980)

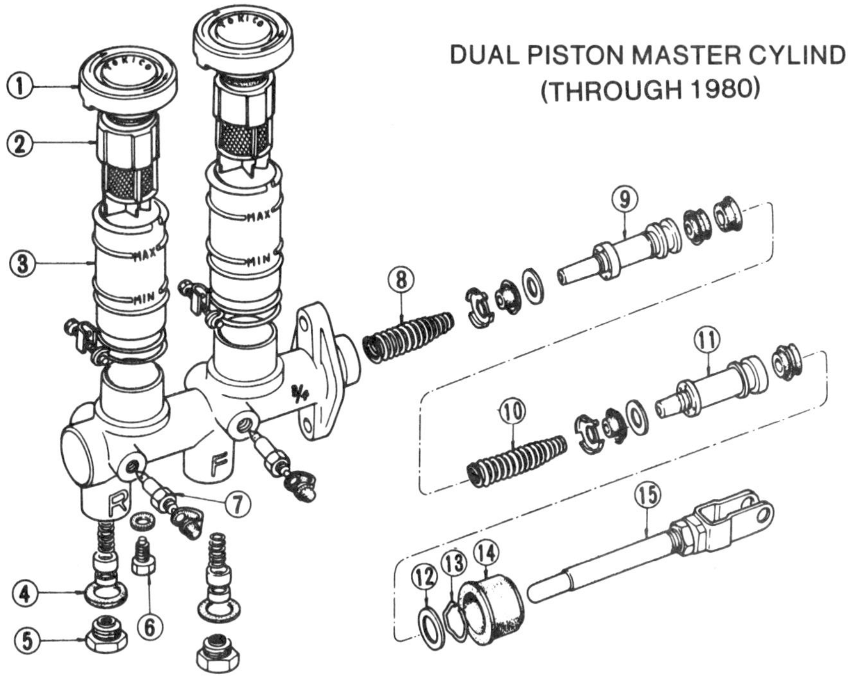

1. Reservoir cap
2. Oil filter
3. Oil reservoir
4. Packing
5. Valve cap
6. Secondary piston stopper
7. Bleeder screw
8. Secondary return spring
9. Secondary piston
10. Primary return spring
11. Primary piston
12. Piston stopper
13. Piston stopper ring
14. Dust cover
15. Pushrod assembly (non-power brakes)

(28)

MASTER CYLINDER (1981)

T: (ft.-lb., mkg)

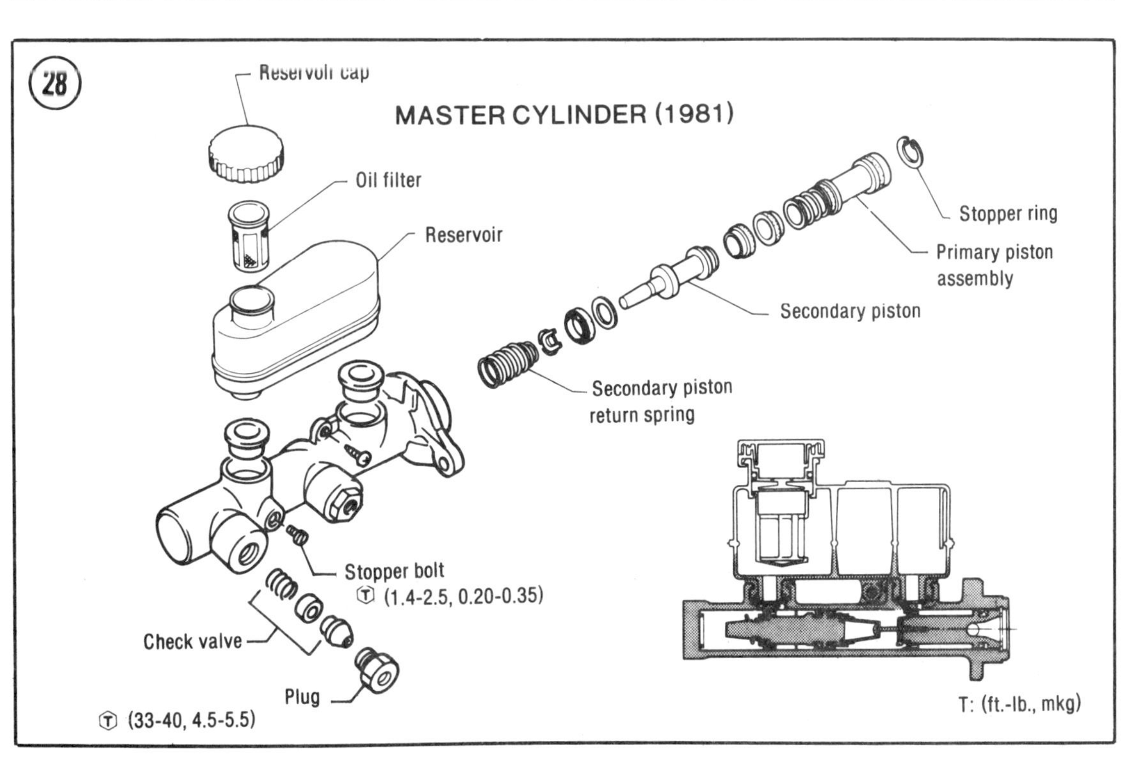

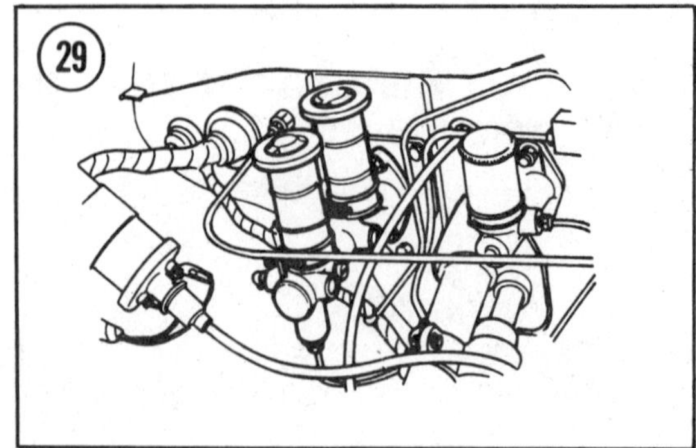

corrosion. Wear is excessive if clearance between cylinder walls and pistons exceeds 0.006 in. (0.15 mm). Replace cylinder and piston if these conditions are evident.
4. Check spring for wear, damage, or weakness. Replace as needed.
5. Inspect the bleed valves, stopper screw, check valve cap screws, and fluid reservoirs for wear or damage. Replace as needed.

Assembly

Assembly is the reverse of the disassembly procedure plus the following:
1. Coat the cylinder bore, piston, and cups with brake fluid before assembly.

CAUTION
Do not scratch the cylinder bore or piston(s) when installing.

2. After installation, bleed the brakes and check for brake fluid leaks.
3. Check pedal pad height. If necessary, adjust as described later in this chapter.

BRAKE BOOSTER

The Master-Vac brake booster uses intake manifold vacuum to reduce braking effort. The booster is used on late model 620 and all 720 pickups. The booster and its check valve should be tested at intervals specified in Chapter Three.

Check Valve Test

1. Remove the check valve from its clip on the firewall (**Figure 30**).
2. Disconnect the hose from the brake booster side of the valve. Connect a vacuum gauge in its place.

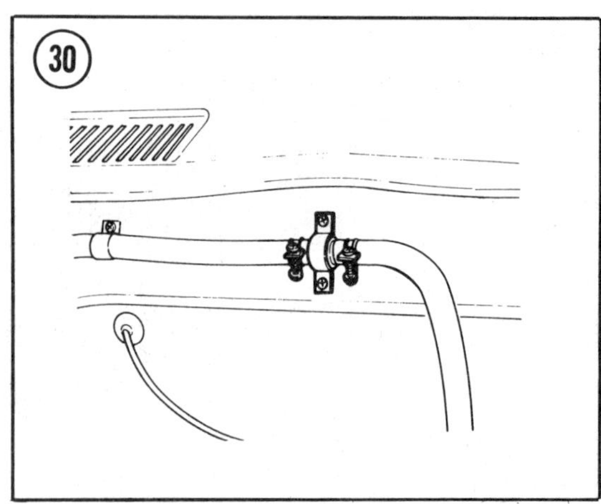

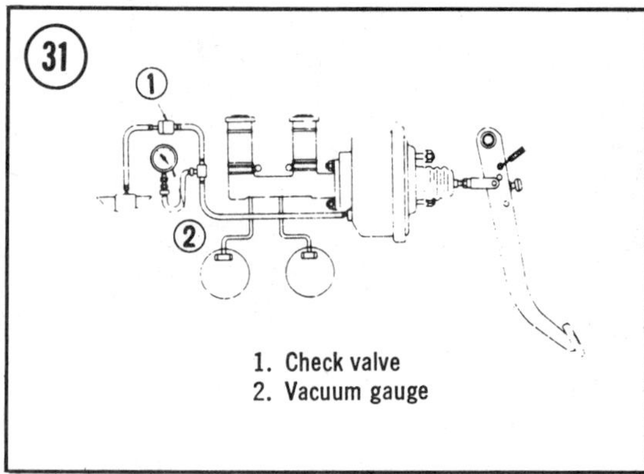

3. Run the engine at a fast idle. Turn the engine off when vacuum reaches approximately 20 in. Hg (500 mm Hg).
4. With the engine off, watch the vacuum gauge for 15 seconds. Any vacuum drop, even a slight one, indicates a defective check valve or vacuum line. If no defect can be seen in the vacuum line, replace the check valve.

Airtightness Test (No Load)

1. Using a T-fitting, connect a vacuum gauge into the line between check valve and brake booster. See **Figure 31**.
2. Run the engine at a fast idle. Turn the engine off when vacuum reaches approximately 20 in. Hg (500 mm Hg).
3. With the engine off, watch the vacuum gauge for 15 seconds. Any vacuum drop indicates a defective vacuum line or brake booster. If no defects can be found in the vacuum line, replace or rebuild the brake booster as described later.

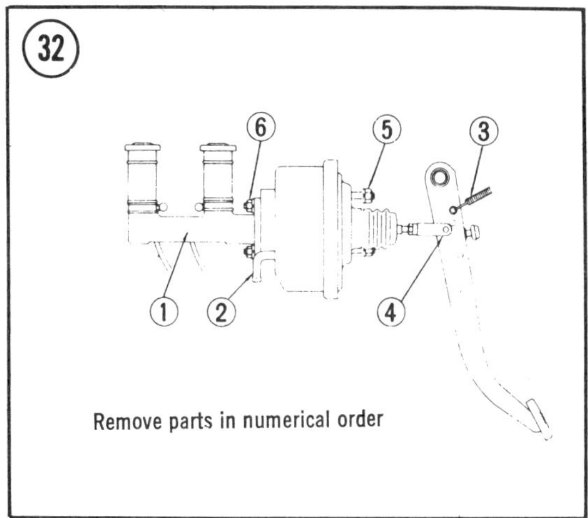

Remove parts in numerical order

Airtightness Test (Under Load)

1. Connect a vacuum gauge as described in Step 1 of the previous procedure. Place the gauge where it can be seen from the driver's seat, or have an assistant watch it for you.
2. With the engine running, press the brake pedal as far as it will go.
3. When vacuum reaches approximately 20 in. Hg (500 mm Hg), shut the engine off. Keep the brake pedal down.
4. Watch the vacuum gauge for 15 seconds after the engine is shut off. Any vacuum drop indicates a defective brake booster. Replace or overhaul as described later in this chapter.

Booster Removal/Installation

Refer to **Figure 32** for this procedure.

1. Disconnect the brake lines (1, **Figure 32**) from the master cylinder.
2. Detach the vacuum line from the fitting on the brake booster (2).
3. Detach the return spring (3) and booster pushrod (4) from the pedal.
4. Remove the nuts attaching the booster to firewall (5). Lift the booster out of the engine compartment.
5. Remove the nuts attaching the master cylinder to the booster (6). Separate the master cylinder and booster.
6. Installation is the reverse of these steps. After installation, bleed the brakes, test the brake booster as described earlier, and check pedal height. If necessary, adjust the pedal height as described later in this chapter.

Disassembly

NOTE

The following sections apply to 1978 and earlier models only. The factory recommends against overhauling 1979 and later brake boosters.

Refer to **Figure 33** for this procedure. During disassembly, lay the parts in a bench in order of removal, even if they are going to be replaced. Having the parts in order will ease reassembly.

1. Thoroughly clean the outside of the booster before disassembly. Be sure your working area is *clean.*
2. Paint or scribe mating marks on the front shell, rear shell, and stud assembly. This ensures that the parts will be reassembled in their original positions.
3. Place the booster in a soft-jawed vise as shown in **Figure 34**. Remove the pushrod, locknut, and valve body guard.
4. Separate the front and rear shells. Use the Datsun special tool shown in **Figure 35** or improvise a substitute.
5. Carefully pry the seal retainer loose with a screwdriver (**Figure 36**). Remove the seal and discard it.
6. Remove the diaphragm from the diaphragm plate (**Figure 37**). Throw the diaphragm away.
7. Carefully pry the air silencer retainer loose from the valve body (**Figure 38**).

CAUTION

Do not tap on the screwdriver with a hammer, or the valve body may be damaged.

8. Press in the valve operating rod and take out the stop key. See **Figure 39**.
9. Pull the valve plunger assembly, together with the air silencer filter and air silencer, out of the valve body. See **Figure 40**. Take the air silencer filter and air silencer off the valve operating rod.
10. Remove the reaction disc (**Figure 41**).
11. Detach the flange from the front shell (**Figure 42**).
12. Remove the plate and seal assembly from beneath the flange.

33

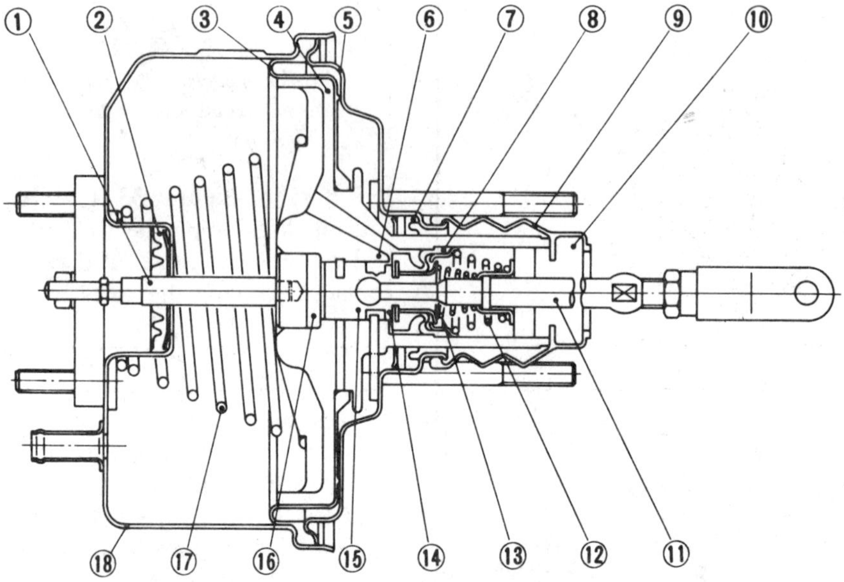

BRAKE BOOSTER

1. Pushrod
2. Plate and seal
3. Diaphragm
4. Diaphragm plate
5. Rear shell
6. Vacuum valve
7. Seal
8. Poppet assembly
9. Valve body guard
10. Air silencer filter
11. Valve operating rod
12. Valve return spring
13. Poppet return spring
14. Exhaust valve
15. Valve plunger
16. Reaction disc
17. Diaphragm return spring
18. Front shell

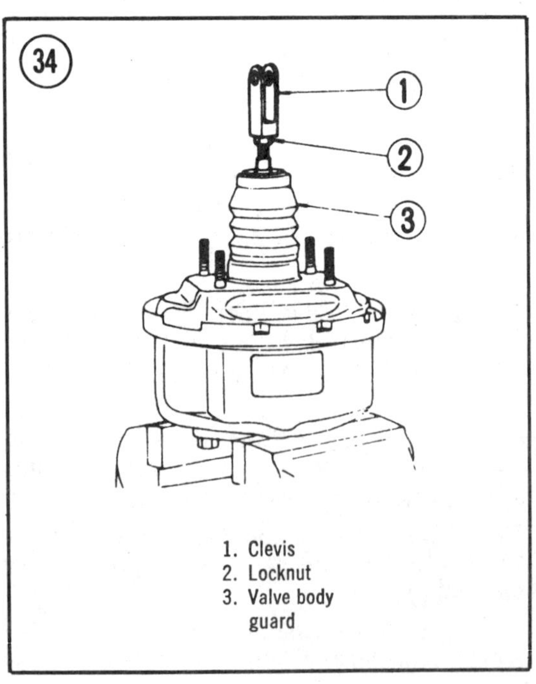

1. Clevis
2. Locknut
3. Valve body guard

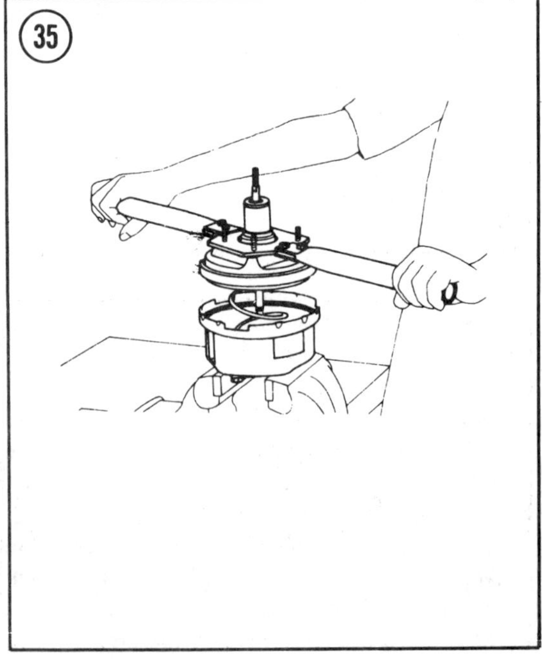

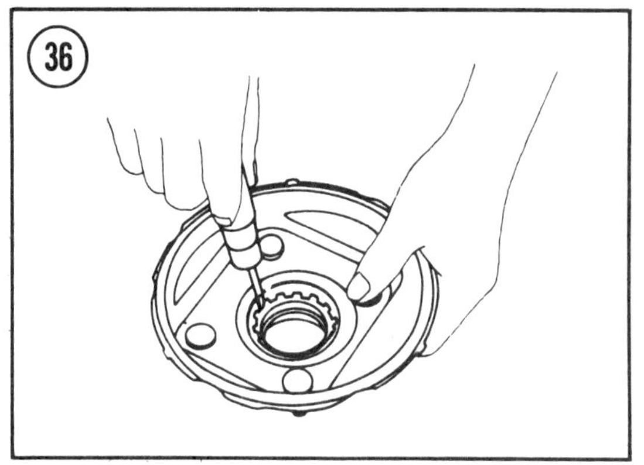

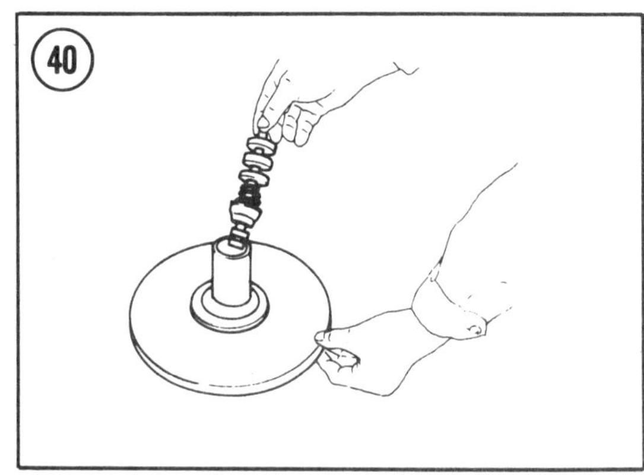

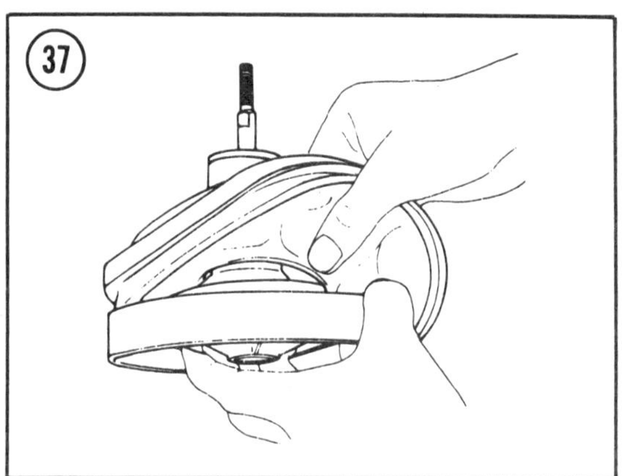

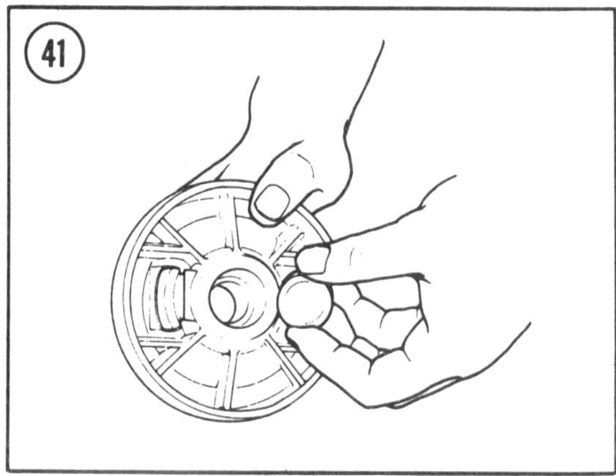

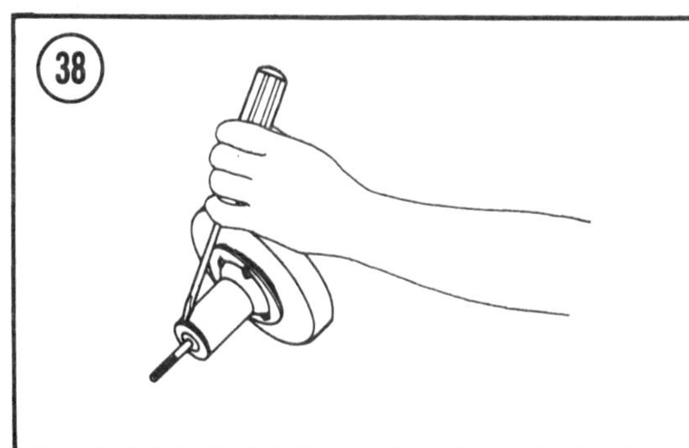

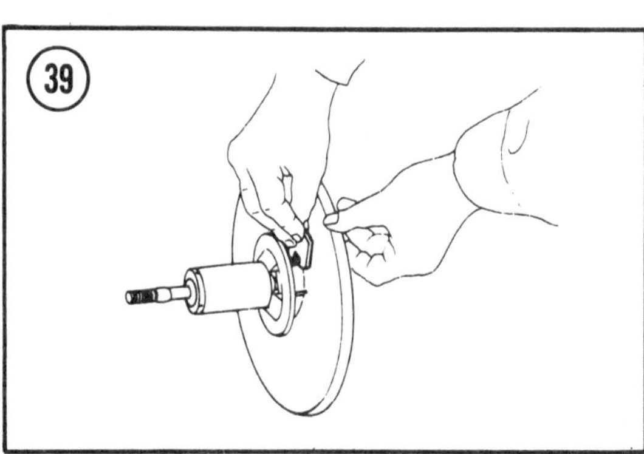

Inspection

1. Thoroughly clean all parts with alcohol before inspection.
2. Check front and rear shells for wear or damage. Replace if these conditions are found.
3. Examine stud threads. Repair lightly damaged threads with a die. Replace parts with severely damaged threads. Check welds at bases of the studs for cracks. Replace cracked parts.
4. Check for corrosion on the areas marked "D" in **Figure 43**. Clean off light corrosion with emery paper. Replace heavily corroded parts.
5. Inspect the outer surface of the valve body (E, **Figure 44**). Any visible damage, including slight scratches, is cause for replacement.
6. Check bearing movement on the valve body. Replace bearing if it does not move smoothly.
7. Check the diaphragm plate and valve body for cracks. Replace if cracks can be found.

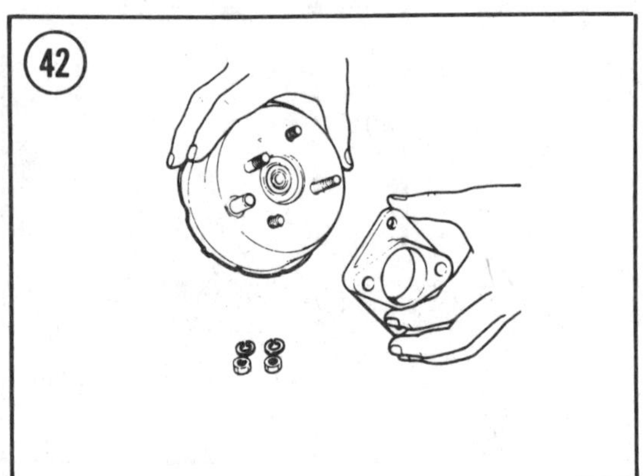
42

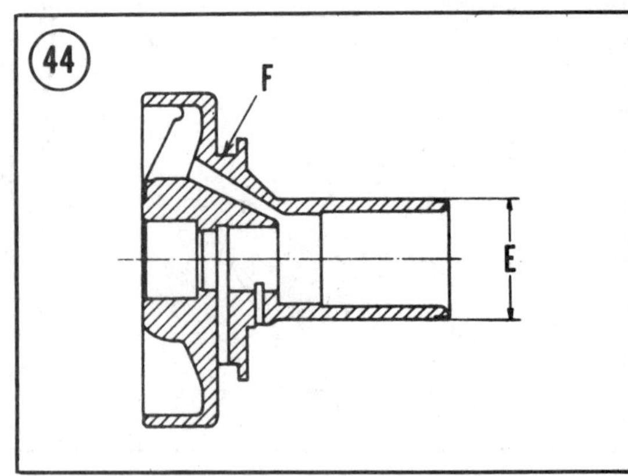

44

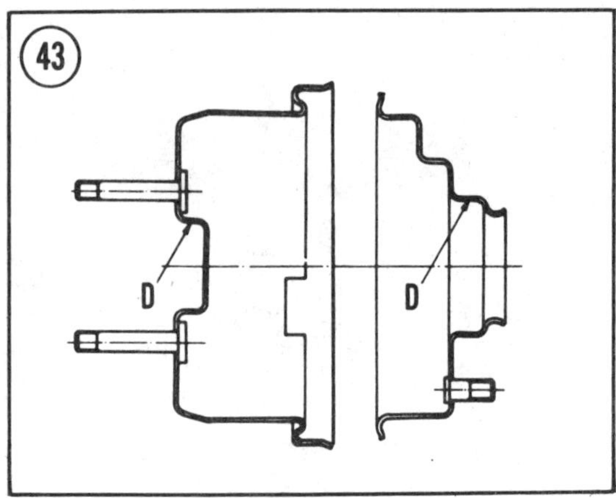

43

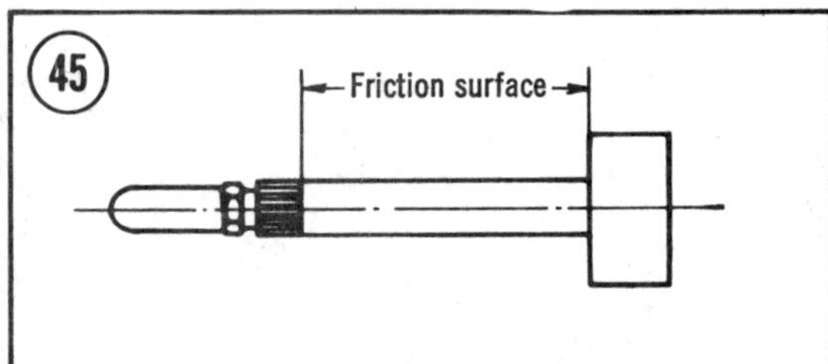

45

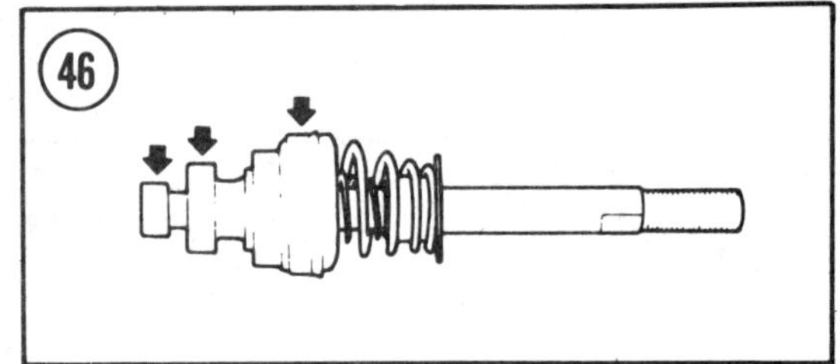
46

8. Carefully examine the groove in the diaphragm plate (F, **Figure 44**). Replace the diaphragm plate if wear or damage can be seen.
9. Check the flange for cracks or rust. Replace if these can be found.
10. Check the diaphragm spring for weakness, rust, or deformation. Replace as needed.
11. Check the pushrod for rust. Remove light rust with emery paper. Replace heavily rusted pushrods. The pushrod must also be replaced if the friction surface (**Figure 45**) is scored.
12. Check the stop key and pedal-to-booster clevis for wear and damage. Replace as needed.

Assembly and Adjustment

Assembly is the reverse of the disassembly procedure, plus the following steps.

1. Replace the following parts whenever the booster is disassembled:
   a. Bearing and valve body seal
   b. Diaphragm
   c. Air silencer retainer, silencer, and filter
   d. Valve plunger assembly
   e. Reaction disc
   f. Plate and seal assembly
   g. Valve and body seal
2. Apply a light coat of silicone grease (contained in the repair kit) to the following:
   a. On the seal (7, **Figure 33**), the lip and face contacting the rear shell
   b. Friction surfaces of the valve plunger assembly (**Figure 46**)
   c. Both surfaces of the reaction disc
   d. The edge of the diaphragm where it makes contact with the front and rear shells
   e. The surfaces on the plate and seal assembly (2, **Figure 33**) that contact the front shell and pushrod

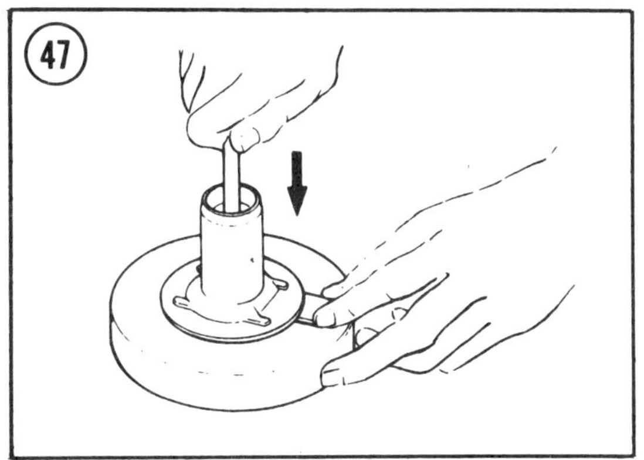

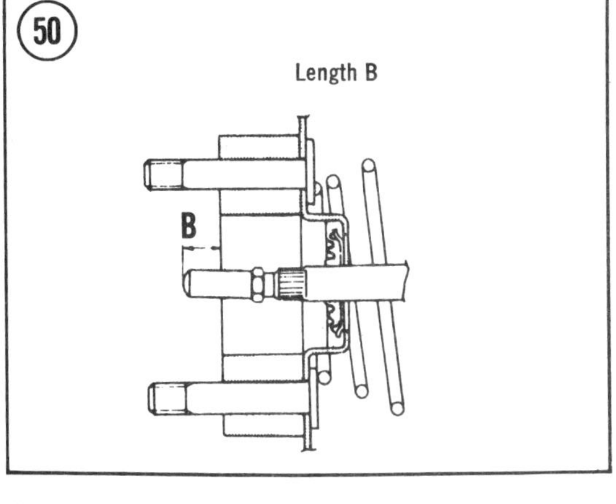

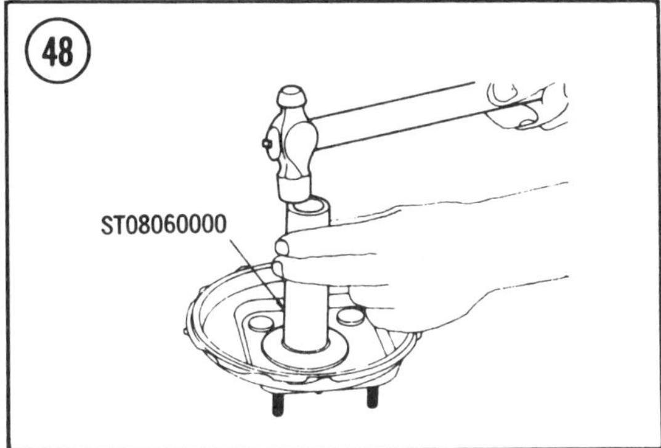

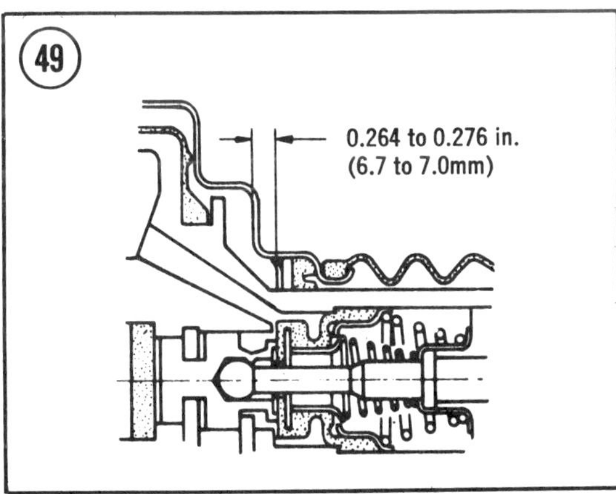

f. The pushrod surface that contacts the diaphragm plate

3. Apply a thin coat of mica powder to the diaphragm. Do not get any powder on outer edge.

4. When inserting the valve operating rod in the valve body, be sure the rod goes straight in and is not tilted to either side. When the rod is in, press it down against its spring and insert the stop key. See **Figure 47**.

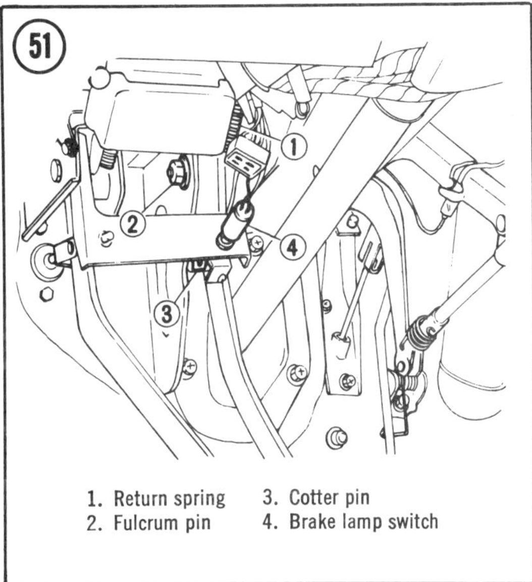

1. Return spring
2. Fulcrum pin
3. Cotter pin
4. Brake lamp switch

5. When installing bearing and seal retainer on the rear shell, use a drift such as ST 08060000 (**Figure 48**). Tap the retainer in until the flange on the drift contacts the rear shell. If you cannot get the special tool, tap the retainer in until it is 0.26-0.28 in. (6.7-7.0 mm) deep in its recess. See **Figure 49**.

6. After assembly, adjust pushrod protrusion (B, **Figure 50**). Correct protrusion on models through 1977 is 0.39-0.41 in. (10.0-10.5 mm). On 1978 models protusion is 0.38-0.39 in. (9.75-10.0mm).

STOPLIGHT SWITCH REPLACEMENT

The stoplight switch is located on the pedal bracket (**Figure 51**). To remove it, disconnect

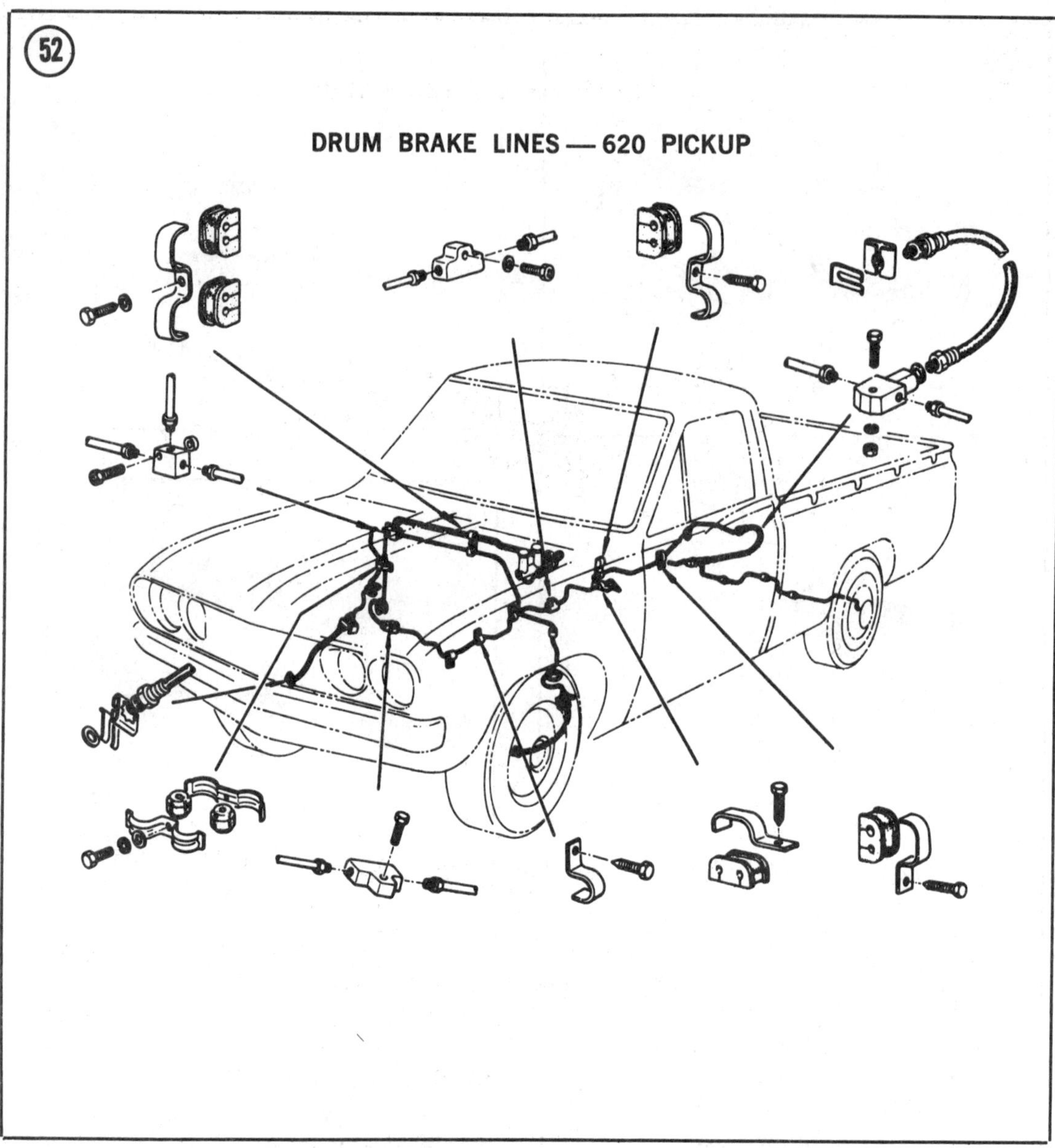

the wires, loosen the locknut, and unscrew the switch. Screw the new switch in far enough so the brakelights go on when the pedal is moved slightly. Secure with the locknut.

BRAKE LINES

Figure 52 shows the brake lines used on drum-brake 620 pickups. The 521 pickup brake lines are similar. **Figure 53** shows the brake lines on disc-brake 620 pickups. **Figure 54** shows the 720 pickup brake lines.

Brake Line Inspection

Check brake lines for the following:

a. Cracks or wear
b. Leakage at connections
c. Warped or twisted rubber brake hoses
d. Sufficient clearance between brake lines and other parts of the vehicle to prevent wear and damage to the lines

The factory recommends that a tube wrench be used to loosen brake line connections and a preset torque wrench such as GG94310000 (**Figure 55**) be used for tightening.

53

DISC BRAKE LINES — 620 PICKUP

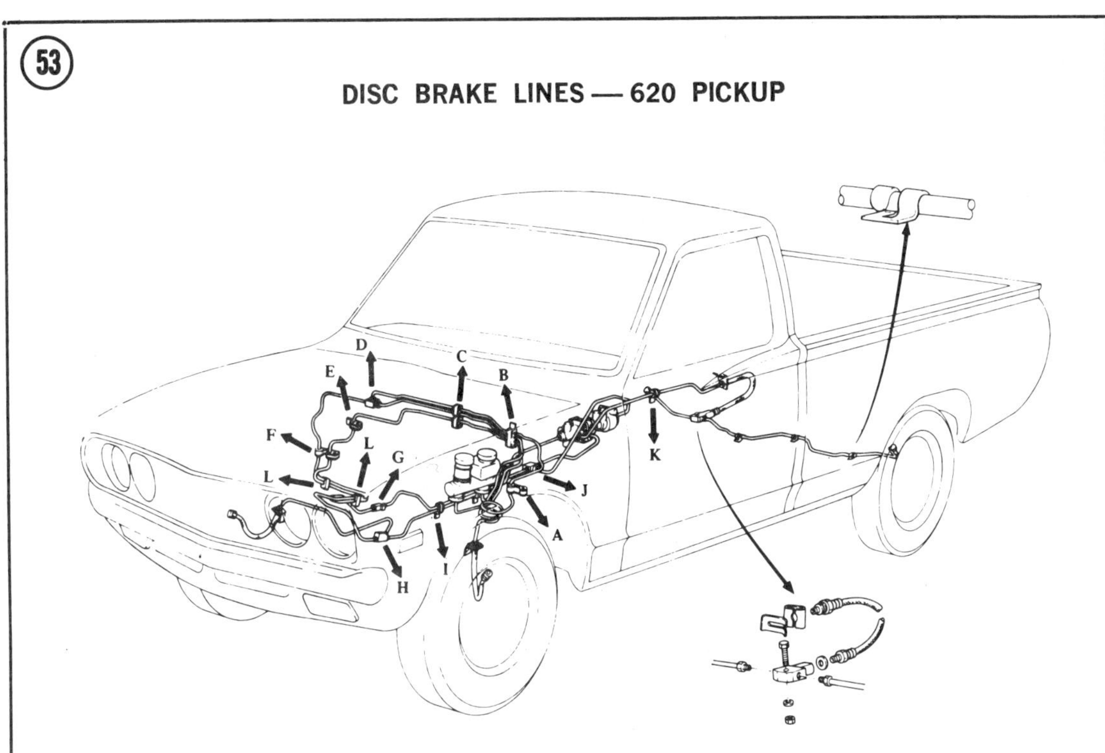

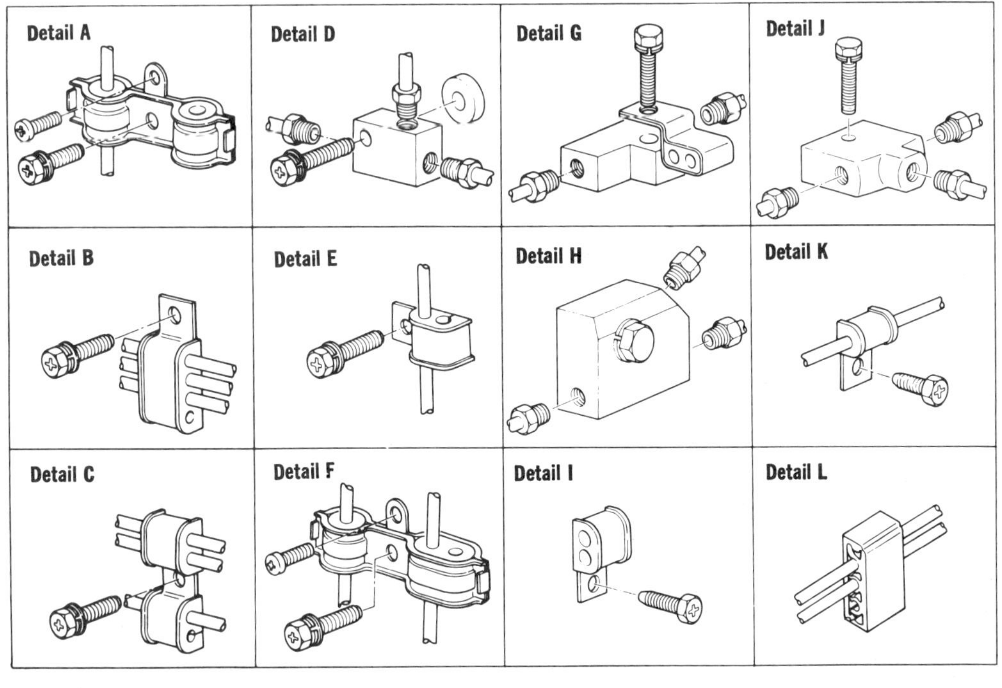

11

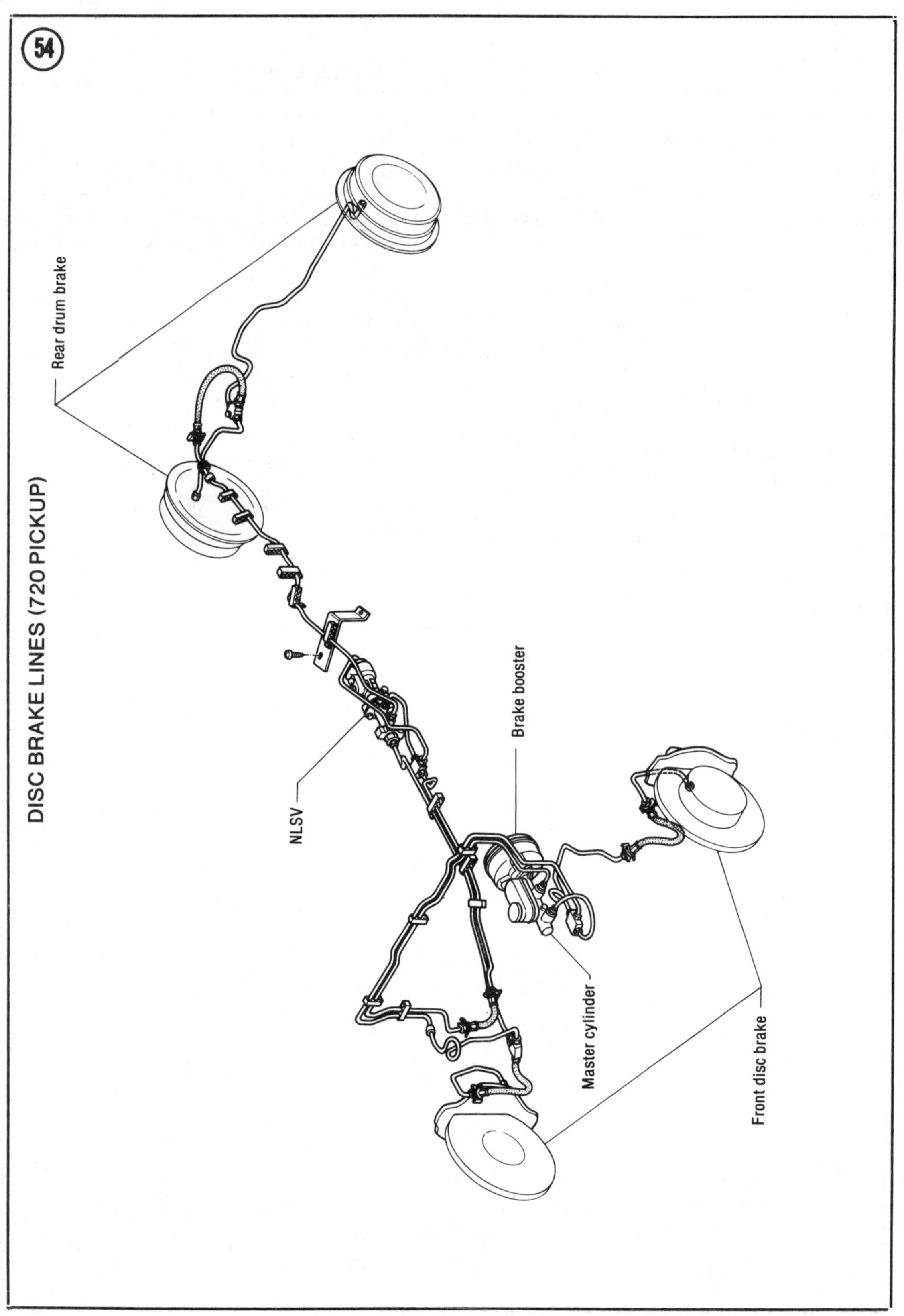

54

DISC BRAKE LINES (720 PICKUP)

LOAD SENSING VALVE

This valve, used on 1976 and later models, prevents premature rear wheel lockup by regulating pressure to the front and rear brakes. When the truck is lightly loaded, pressure to the rear brakes is reduced. As the load increases, pressure to the rear brakes increases accordingly. **Figure 56** shows the valve.

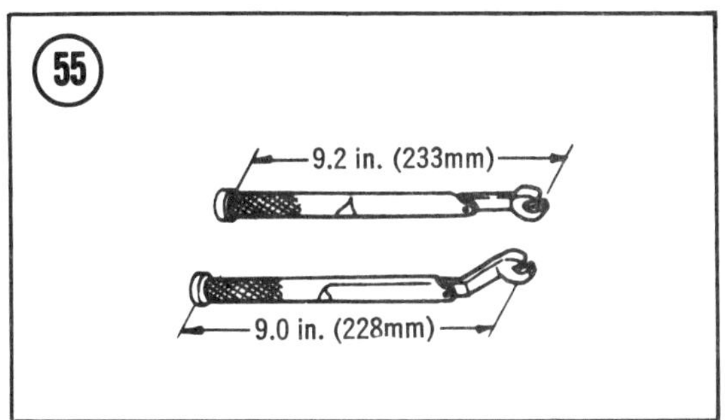

Valve Test

The braking system must be in good condition to test the valve accurately. Make any necessary repairs before testing.

1. Drive at 30 mph (1976) or 25 mph (1977-on) with truck unloaded and apply the brakes hard enough to lock the wheels *slightly*. Stopping distance must be 43 ft. (13.1 meters) or less and the front wheels must lock before or at the same time as the rear wheels.
2. Repeat the test with a load in the truck's bed. Again, stopping distance should be less than 43 ft. (13.1 meters) and the rear wheels must not lock before the front wheels.
3. If the valve fails either part of this test, replace it.

BRAKE BLEEDING

The hydraulic system should be bled whenever air enters it and reduces braking

56

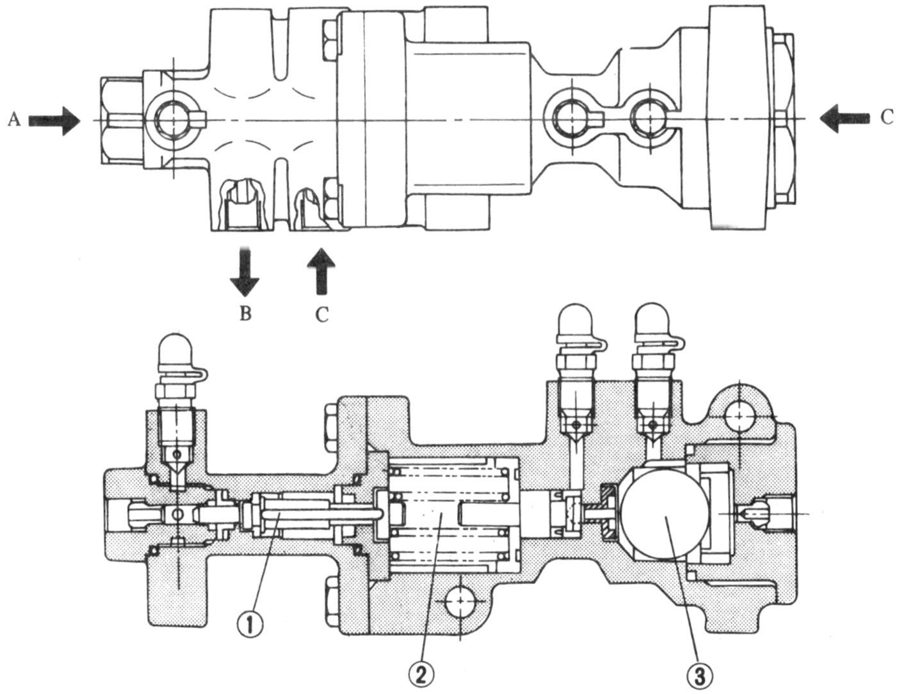

A C B C

A: From brake master cylinder front side oil pressure
B: To rear brake wheel cylinder oil pressure
C: From brake master cylinder rear side oil pressure

1. Plunger
2. Spring
3. Retainer ball

LOAD SENSING VALVE

effectiveness. If the pedal feels spongy, or if pedal travel increases considerably, brake bleeding is usually called for. Bleeding is also necessary whenever a hydraulic line is disconnected or the system is repaired.

This procedure requires handling brake fluid. Be careful not to get any fluid on brake shoes or drums. Clean all dirt from bleed valves before beginning. Two people are required, one to operate the brake pedal and the other to open and close the bleed valves.

Bleeding should be conducted in the following order: master cylinder, load sensing valve; right rear, left rear, right front, left front.

1. Clean away any dirt around the master cylinder. Top up the reservoir with brake fluid marked DOT 3 or DOT 4.
2. Attach a plastic tube to the bleed valve. Dip the end of the tube in a jar containing several inches of clean brake fluid.

NOTE
Do not allow the end of the tube to come out of the brake during bleeding. This could allow air into the system, requiring that the bleeding procedure be done over.

3. Press the brake pedal as far down as it will go 2 or 3 times, then hold it down.
4. With the brake pedal down, open the bleed valve until the pedal goes to the floor, then close the bleed valve. Do not let the pedal up until the bleed valve is closed.
5. Let the pedal back up slowly.
6. Repeat Steps 3-5 until the fluid entering the jar is free of air bubbles.
7. Repeat the process for the other bleed valves.

NOTE
Keep an eye on the brake fluid level in the master cylinder throughout the bleeding process. If the reservoirs are allowed to become empty, air will be sucked into the hydraulic system and the procedure will have to be repeated.

ADJUSTMENTS

Brake Pedal (521 Pickup)

1. Back off the stoplight switch until it is clear of the pedal. See **Figure 57**.

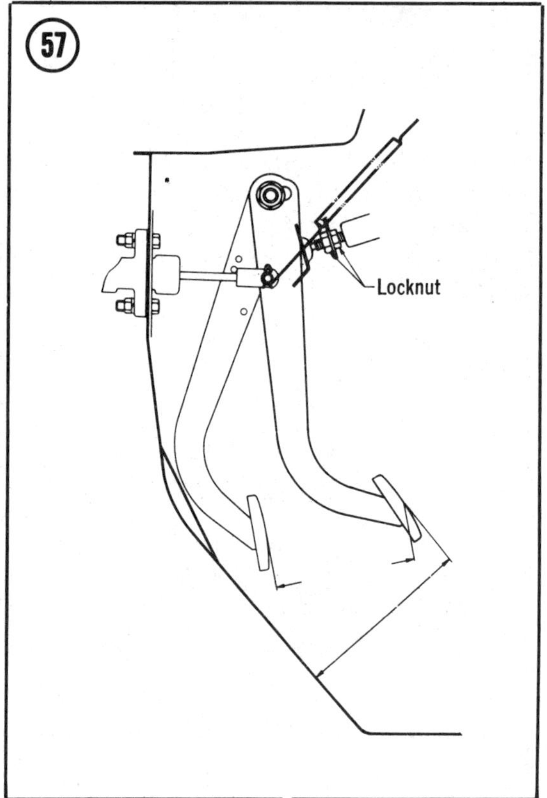

2. Measure pedal pad height from the floor. It should be 5.45 in. (138.5 mm). If pedal height is incorrect, remove or install shims between the master cylinder and firewall to change it. Be sure to use shims of the same thickness above and below the cylinder.
3. Lower the pedal to 5.33 in. (135.5 mm) by turning the stoplight switch. Tighten the locknuts.

Brake Pedal (620 and 720 Pickups)

1. Check pedal pad height from the floor. See **Figure 58**. Compare with specifications (**Table 1**).
2. If pedal height is incorrect, loosen the stoplight switch locknuts. Turn the stoplight switch to change pedal height, then tighten tthe locknuts.
3. Push the pedal by hand until resistance abruptly increases. This is pedal free play. Compare with **Table 1**. If free play is incorrect, loosen the pushrod locknut. Turn the pushrod to adjust free play, then tighten the locknut.

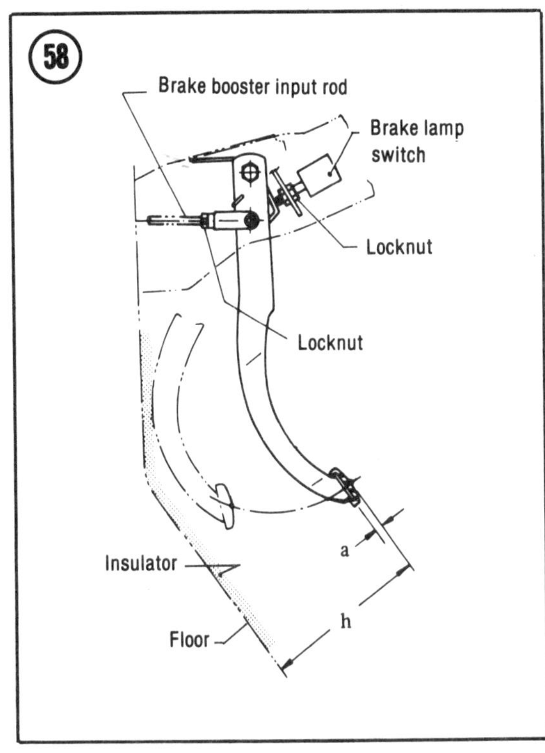

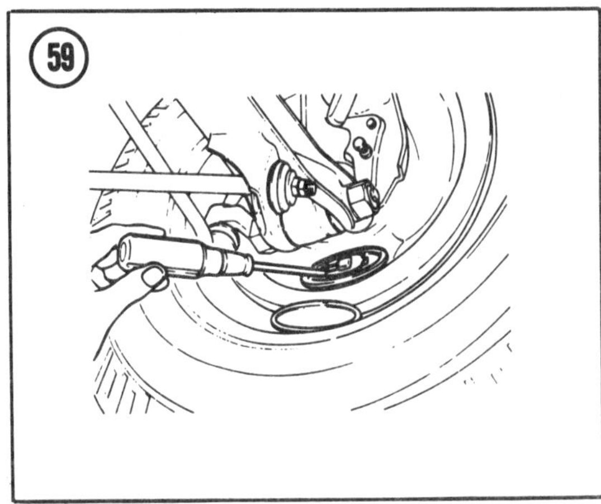

Front and Rear Drum Brakes

Figure 59 shows the adjusting hole for front brakes. The rear adjusting hole is similar.

1. Jack up the end of the truck on which the brakes are being adjusted. Place jackstands beneath the frame.
2. Remove the rubber boot from each of the adjusting holes.
3. Reach through the hole with a screwdriver (front brakes) or brake adjusting tool (rear brakes). Tap the adjuster lightly to free it, then push it foward.

NOTE

Since the adjusting hole is narrow, it may be necessary to grind the sides of the adjusting tool.

4. Turn the adjuster wheel downward to spread the brake shoes. At the same time, spin the tire by hand until a strong drag is felt. At this point, stop spinning the tire. Keep turning the adjuster wheel until the brake drum is locked.
5. Turn the adjuster wheel upward 12 notches. This gives the correct clearance between brake shoes and drum.
6. Spin the tire. Make sure it spins smoothly without excessive brake drag. If necessary, back the adjuster off further to lessen drag.
7. Install adjusting hole boot and lower truck.

Front Disc Brakes

Front disc brakes are self-adjusting. No means of manual adjustment is necessary or provided.

Handbrake

521 Pickup

Figure 60 shows the 521 pickup handbrake mechanism.

1. Before adjusting the handbrake, adjust thc rear brakes as described in this chapter.
2. Loosen the locknut on the cable equalizer link (A, **Figure 61**). Screw the equalizer rod in or out of the link to adjust its length. After adjustment, the rod should protrude 1.16 in. (29.5 mm) forward of the frame member (dimension L, **Figure 61**).
3. Check handbrake control stem stroke. A pull of 44-66 lb. (20-30 kg) should give a stroke of 3-1/4-4 in. (95-102 mm). If necessary, adjust the length of the front cable to change stroke length. The front cable is adjusted at the turnbuckle (B, **Figure 61**).

620 Pickup (Through 1974)

Figure 62 shows the handbrake mechanism used on 620 pickups from mid-1972 through 1974.

1. Before adjusting the handbrake, adjust the rear brakes as described earlier in this chapter.

60

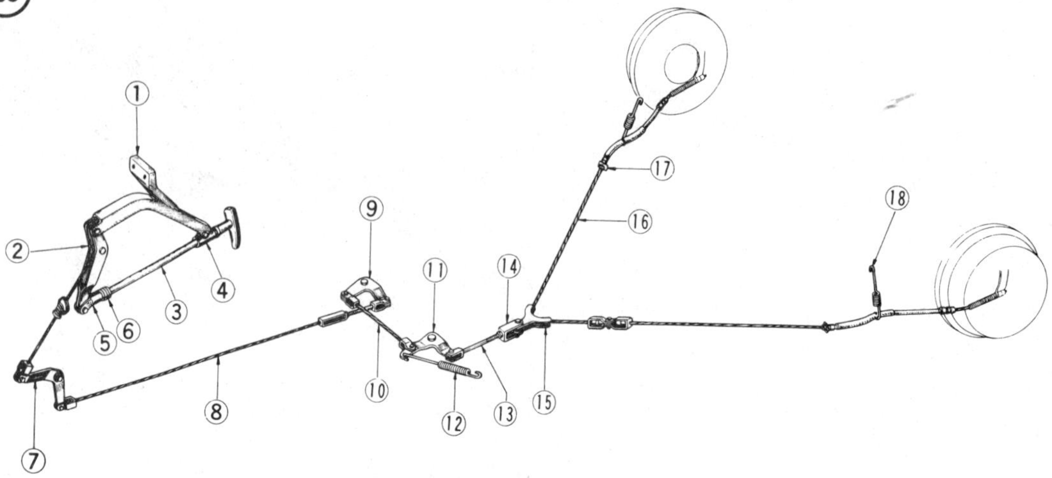

HANDBRAKE (521)

1. Control bracket
2. Control lever
3. Control stem
4. Control guide
5. Control yoke
6. Set spring
7. Front lever
8. Front cable
9. Outer lever
10. Center cable
11. Inner lever
12. Arm spring
13. Center link rod
14. Equalizer link
15. Equalizer
16. Rear cable
17. Lock plate
18. Cable spring

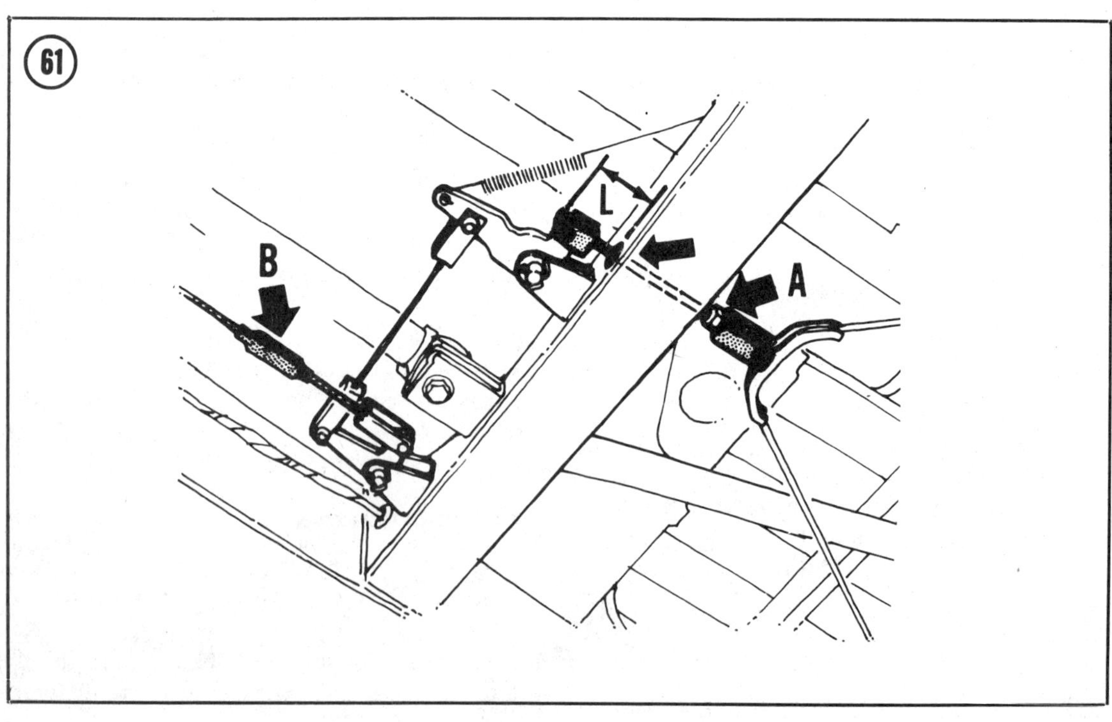

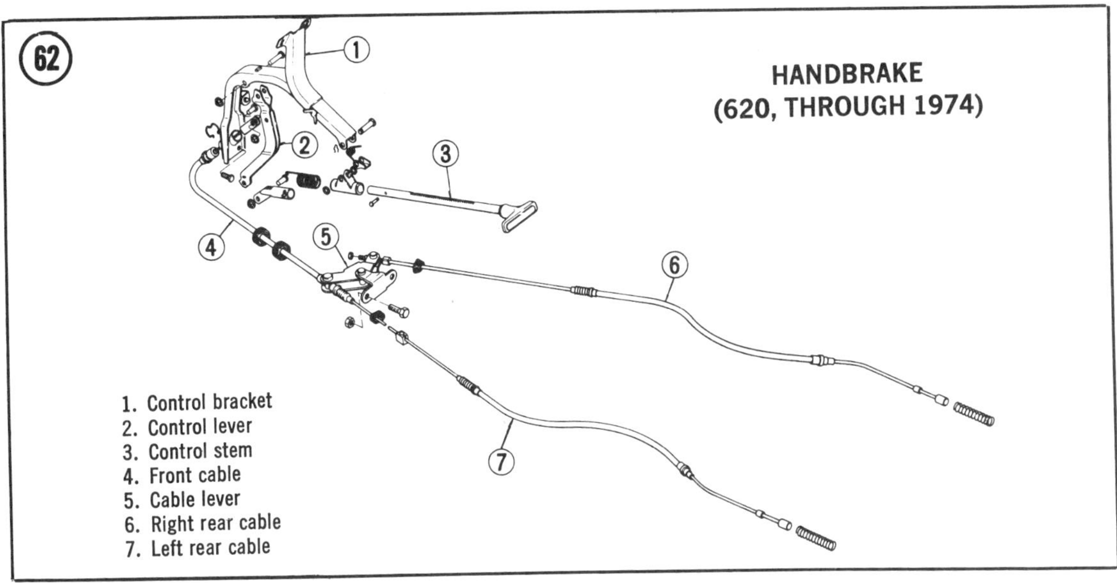

2. Check handbrake control stem stroke. A 44 lb. (20 kg) pull should give a stroke of 3-1/4-4 in. (95-102 mm).

3. If adjustment is necessary, loosen the locknut (**Figure 63**). Rotate the adjusting nut to change cable length, then tighten the locknut.

620 Pickup (1975-on)

Figure 64 shows the handbrake mechanism used on 1975 and later 620 pickups.

1. Before adjusting, check rear brake adjustment as described earlier in this section.
2. Pull the handbrake control stem. A pull of 44-66 lb. (20-30 kg) should give a stroke of 3-1/8 to 4 in. (80-100 mm).
3. If adjustment is necessary, loosen the turnbuckle adjusting nuts (**Figure 65**). Turn the nuts to take up cable slack, then secure the turnbuckle.

720 Pickup

Figure 66 shows the handbrake mechanism used on 720 pickups.

1. Pull the handbrake handle with a force of 44 lb. (20 kg). It should move 6-10 notches.
2. If adjustment is necessary, loosen the locknut (**Figure 67**). Turn the adjusting nut to adjust handbrake play, then tighten the locknut.

64

HANDBRAKE
(620, 1975 AND LATER)

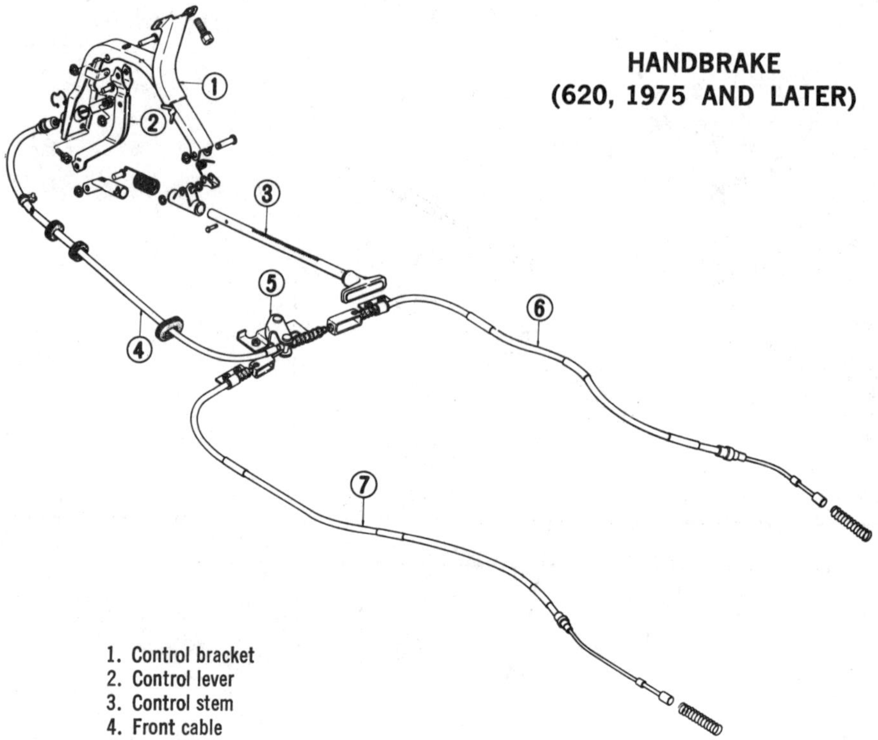

1. Control bracket
2. Control lever
3. Control stem
4. Front cable
5. Balance lever
6. Right rear cable
7. Left rear cable

65

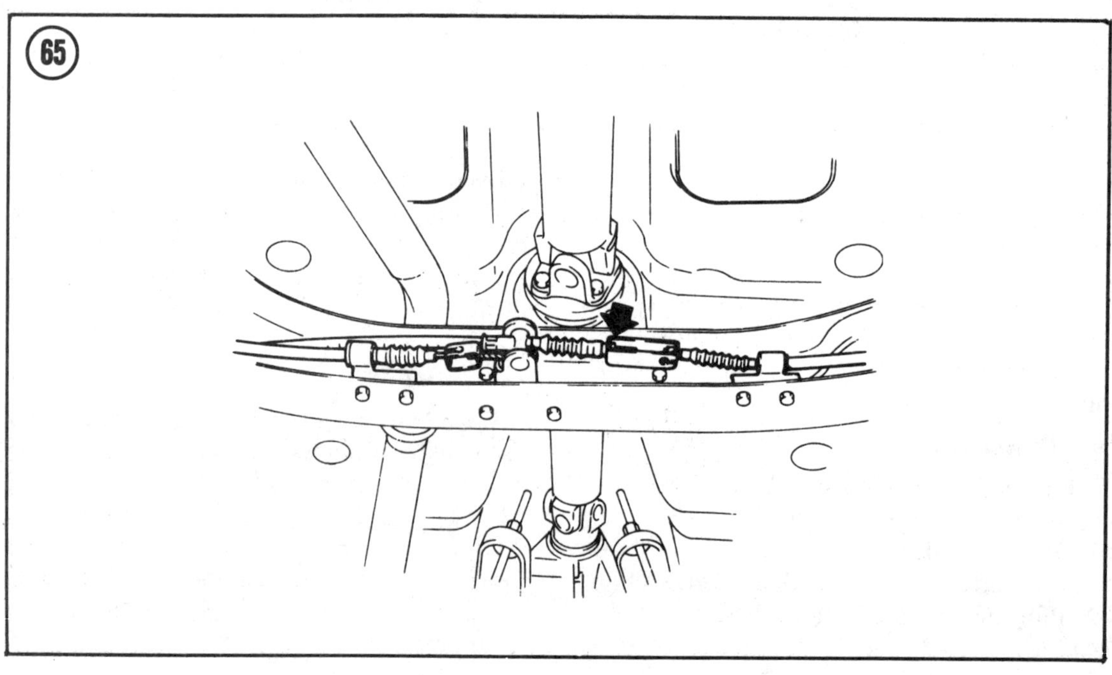

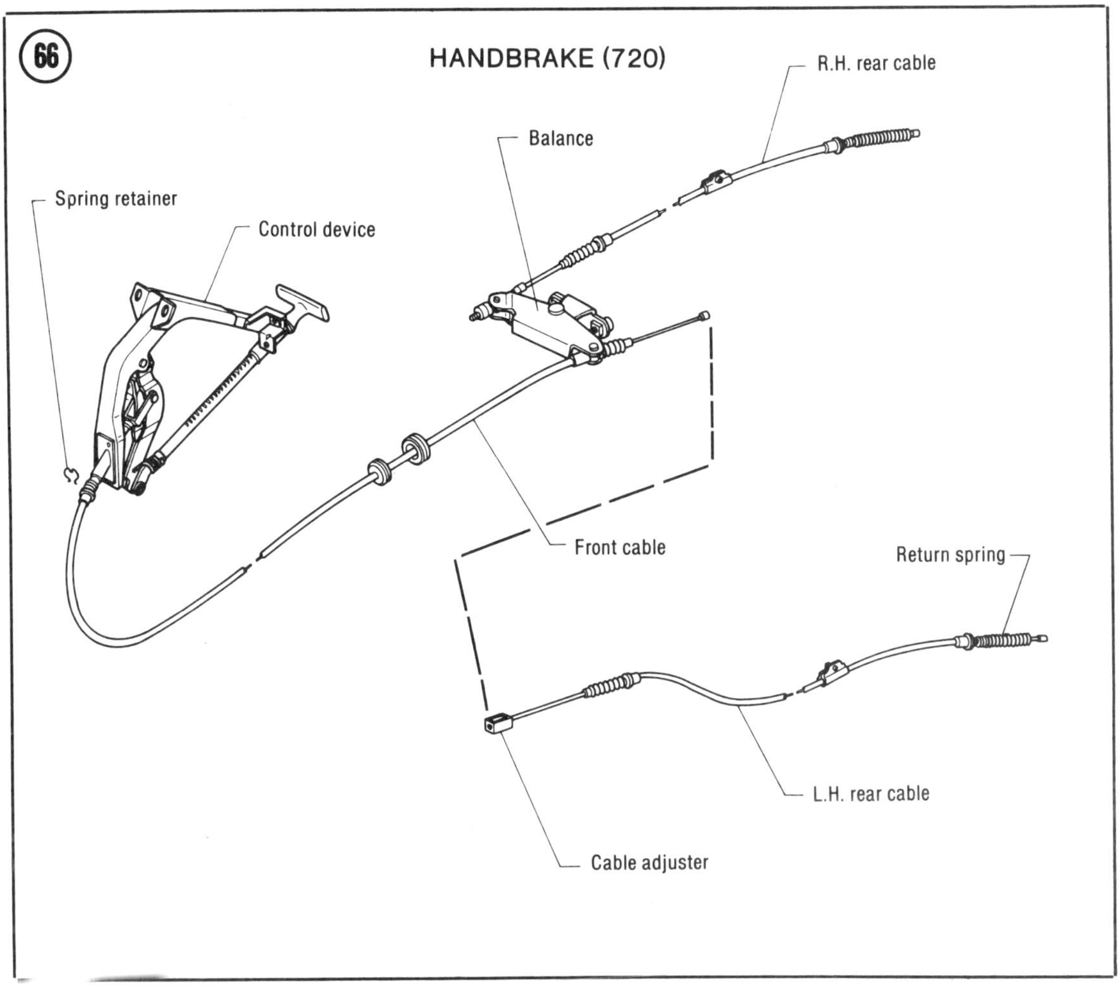

66
HANDBRAKE (720)
R.H. rear cable
Balance
Spring retainer
Control device
Front cable
Return spring
L.H. rear cable
Cable adjuster

67
Locknut

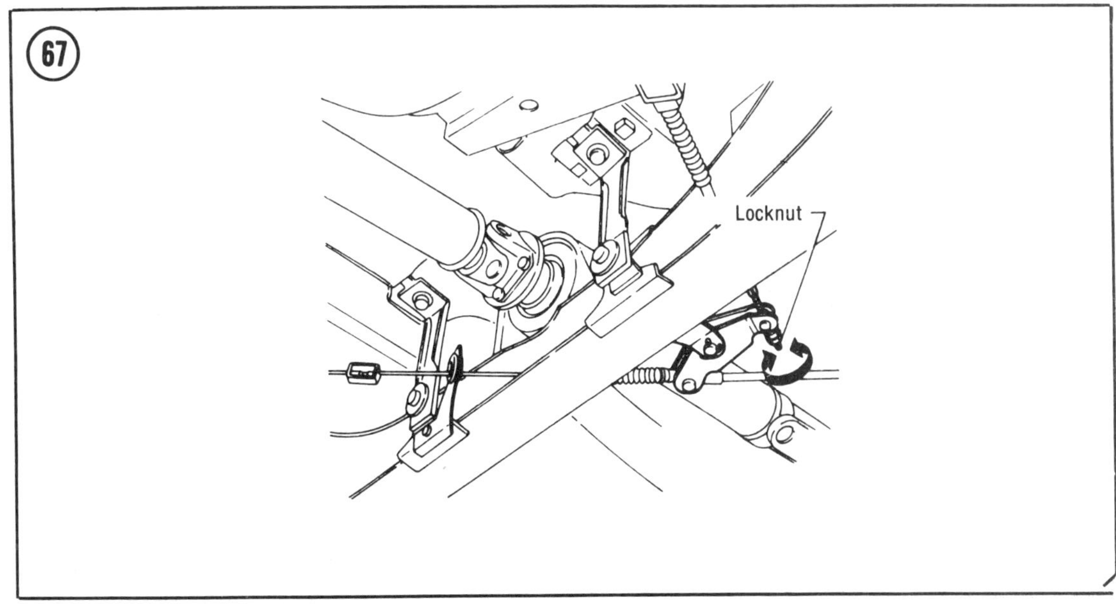

Table 1 BRAKE SPECIFICATIONS

Pedal height	
521 pickup	5 1/3 in. (135.5mm)
620 pickup	
1972-1976	5 1/2 in. (148mm)
1977	5 7/8 in. (148mm)
1978-1979	6 in. (154mm)
720 pickup	6 5/8-6 7/8 in. (168-174mm)
Drum diameter	10 in. (254mm)
Disc thickness	
Standard	0.492 in. (12.5mm)
Minimum	0.413 in. (10.5mm)
Master cylinder diameter	
With front drum brakes	3/4 in. (19.05mm)
With front disc brakes	
1970-1979	13/16 in. (20.64mm)
1980-on	7/8 in. (22.23mm)
Wheel cylinder diameter	
521 pickup	13/16 in. (20.64mm)
620 pickup	
Drum brakes	3/4 in. (19.05mm)
Disc brakes	5/8 in. (15.88mm)
720 pickup	5/8 in. (15.88mm)
Caliper bore diameter	2 1/8 in. (53.98mm)

Table 2 TIGHTENING TORQUES

	Ft.-lb.	Mkg
Brake lines, 521 pickup	12-14	1.7-2.0
Brake lines, 620 and 720 pickups	11-13	1.5-1.8
Flexible brake hoses, 620 and 720 pickups	12-14	1.7-2.0
Front backing plate bolts, drum brakes		
521 pickup	29-39	4.0-5.4
620 pickup	30-36	4.2-5.0
Master cylinder (non-power brakes)	15-18	2.1-2.5
Master cylinder (power brakes)	6-8	0.8-1.1
Load sensing valve to body	6-8	0.8-1.1

CHAPTER TWELVE

DRIVE SHAFT, DIFFERENTIAL, AND REAR SUSPENSION

Datsun pickups use a rigid rear axle supported by leaf springs and conventional tube shock absorbers. The drive shaft is a 2-piece, 3-joint type, supported in the center by a bearing.

A few special tools are used in this chapter. All are available through your dealer. A few are manufactured by Kent-Moore Tool Division, 29784 Little Mack, Roseville, Michigan, 48066 and may be ordered direct from them.

DRIVE SHAFT

Removal/Installation

1. Securely block both front wheels so the truck will not roll in either direction. Jack up the rear end and place it on jackstands.

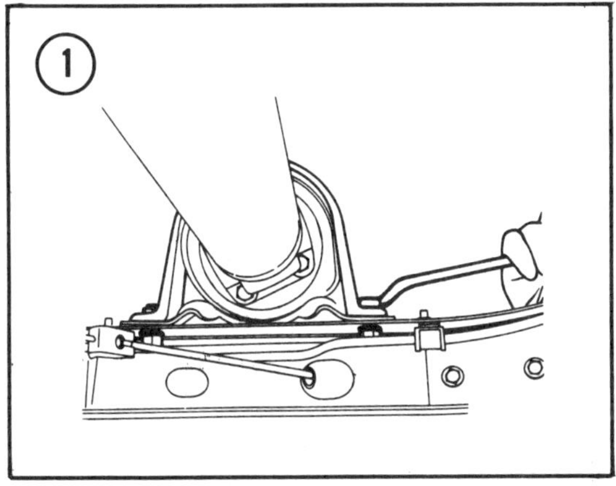

2. Make match marks on the drive shaft and differential flanges so they can be reassembled in the same relative positions. On 521 pickups, mark the transmission flange as well.
3. Unbolt the center bearing bracket from the truck. See **Figure 1**.
4. Remove 4 bolts attaching the drive shaft to the differential.
5. On 521 pickups, unbolt the drive shaft from the transmission flange. On 620 pickups, slide the drive shaft rearward out of the transmission.
6. Installation is the reverse of these steps. Tighten all nuts and bolts to specifications (end of chapter).

12

Universal Joint Repair

The drive shaft should not be disassembled unless the universal joints are worn. Center bearing replacement requires special equipment and should be left to a Datsun dealer.

1. Before disassembly, mark all parts so they can be reassembled in the same relative positions.
2. Remove the 4 snap rings from each universal joint.
3. Place the drive shaft in a vise as near the U-joint as possible. Be careful not to distort the shaft.

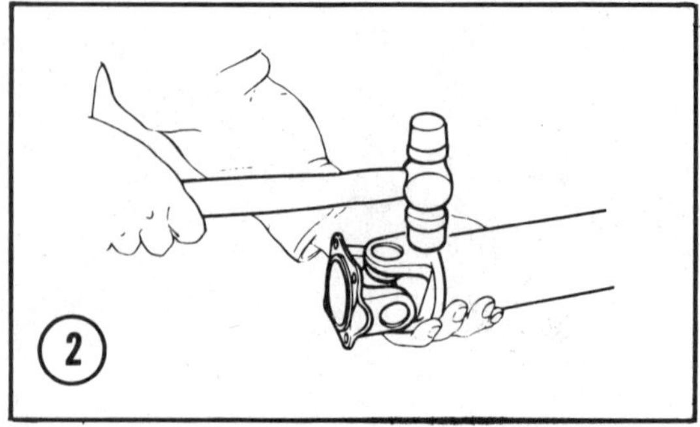

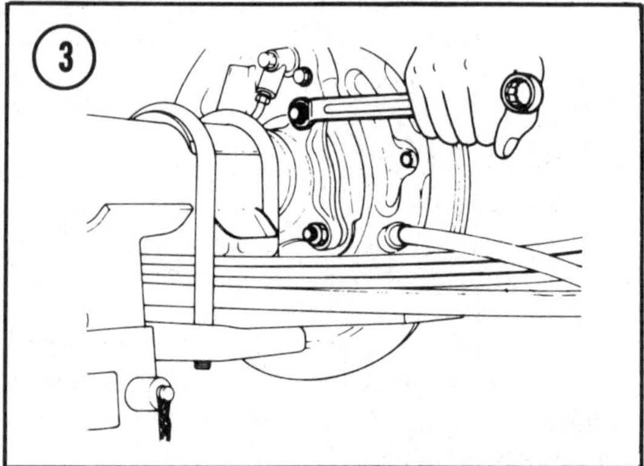

4. Lightly tap the base of the yoke with a hammer (**Figure 2**). Withdraw the opposite bearing race. Do the same for the remaining bearing races. Carefuly separate the crosses and yokes.

5. Check universal joint components for wear, damage, pitting, rust or distortion. Replace as needed. If the drive shaft shows signs of damage, have it checked for balance by a dealer.

6. Assemble by reversing Steps 1-4. Apply grease liberally to the bearings and races.

REAR AXLE

Axle Shaft Removal

1. Loosen the rear wheel nuts, jack up the rear end of the truck, place it on jackstands, and remove the rear wheel(s).

2. Remove the brake drum (Chapter Ten). Disconnect the the brake line and handbrake cable at the wheel.

3. Remove 4 nuts securing the bearing cage to the brake backing plate. See **Figure 3**.

4. Remove the axle shaft, together with the brake backing plate. Use a slide hammer and adapter like the ones shown in **Figure 4**. Similar tools are available from rental dealers.

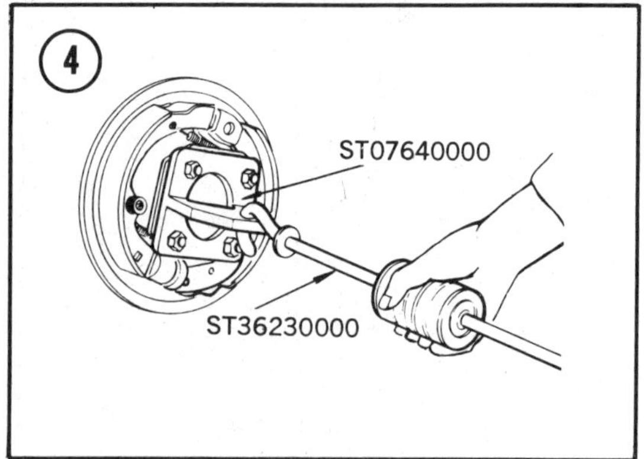

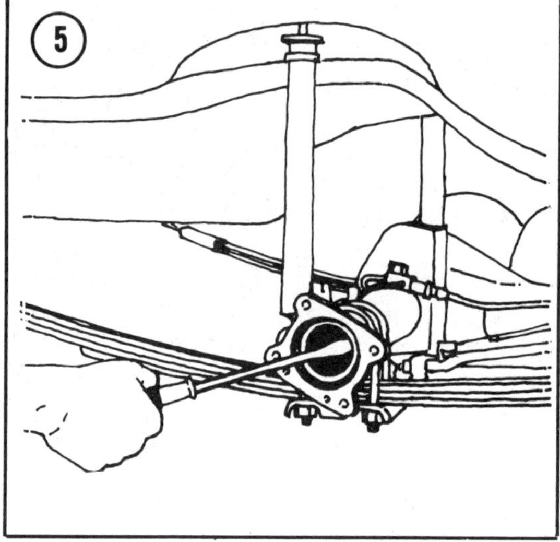

Rear Axle Shaft Inspection

1. Carefully examine the machined surfaces of the axle shaft and housing for wear. Check the shaft for bending, twisting, or damaged splines.

2. Inspect the rear wheel bearing. Rotate it and check for noise, roughness, or excessive play. If in doubt about the bearing, replace it.

Axle Oil Seal Replacement

1. Remove the axle shaft as described earlier.

2. Pry out the old oil seal with a screwdriver (**Figure 5**).

3. Drive the new seal in with a suitable drift.

4. Pack the space between the seal lips with multipurpose grease.

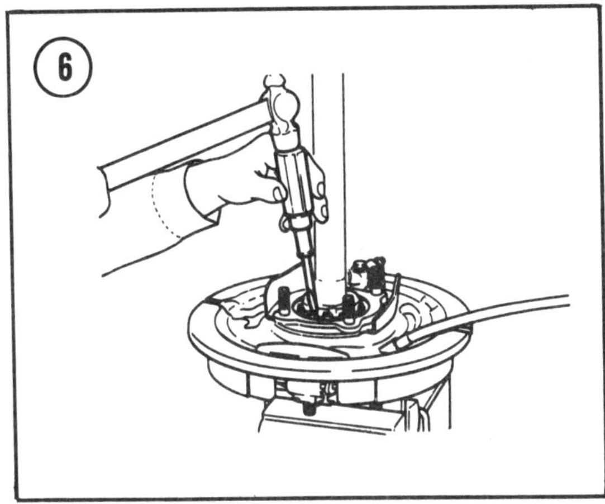

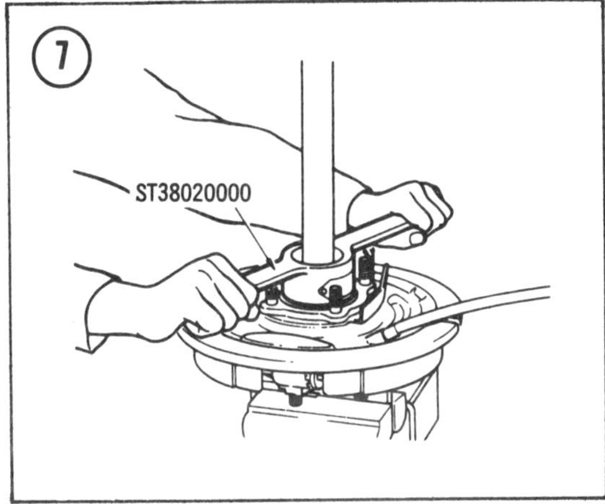

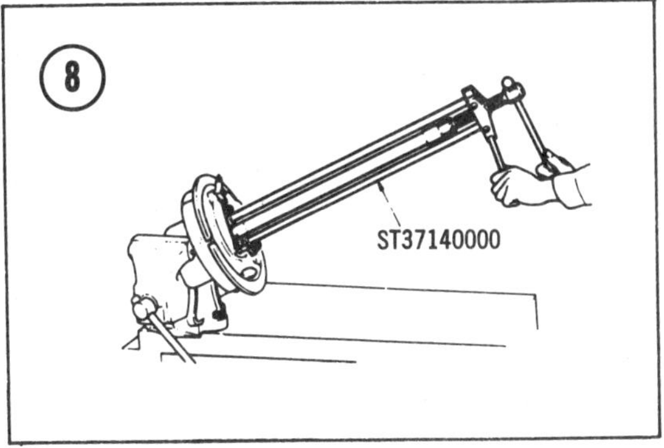

Rear Wheel Bearing Replacement

This procedure requires special equipment and should be left to a dealer or automotive machine shop. It is included in case you are not near a dealer and your local machine shop is not familiar with the Datsun pickup. Much of the cost can be saved by removing the axle shaft yourself and taking it to a shop for bearing replacement.

1. Remove the rear axle shaft as described previously.

2. Bend back the tabs on the wheel bearing lockwasher (**Figure 6**).

3. Remove wheel bearing locknut (**Figure 7**).

> NOTE: *The nut is tightened to 108-145 ft.-lb.(15-20mkg). A wrench like the one shown in* ***Figure*** *7 must be used to remove it. Use Datsun Tool ST38020000 or Kent-Moore J-25864-01.*

4. Remove the wheel bearing, bearing cage, and brake backing plate. Use a puller like the one shown in **Figure 8**: Datsun Tool ST37140000 or Kent-Moore J-25852-B.

5. Inspect the oil seal in the bearing cage. Replace if necesary.

6. Drive the bearing outer race from its seat with a brass drift. Install a new outer race with the same tool.

7. Carefully drive a new seal into place in the bearing cage. Fill the space between the seal lips with multipurpose grease.

8. Place the bearing cage and brake backing plate on the axle shaft. Position a new bearing cone, then tap it into place with a brass drift. See **Figure 9**.

9. Install a *new* lockwasher. Install the bearing locknut with its beveled side toward the washer. Tighten the locknuts to 108-145 ft.-lb. (15-20 mkg) using the tool shown in **Figure 7**. Bend up the lockwasher to secure the nut.

10. Pack the bearing with grease. Apply grease to the bearing recess in the axle housing.

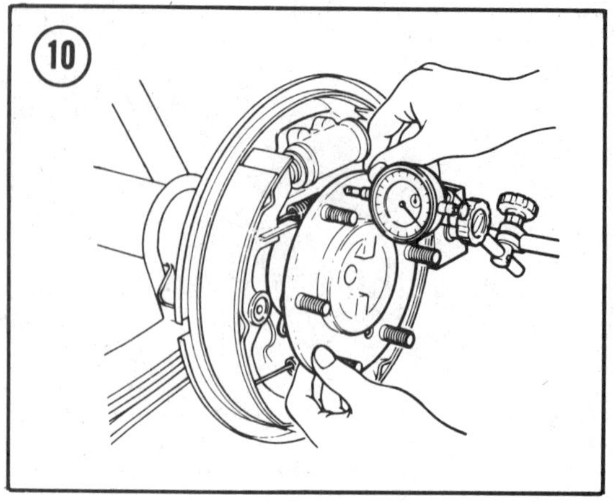

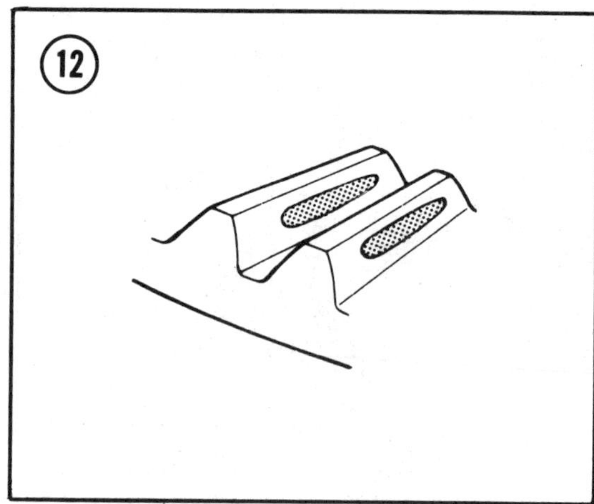

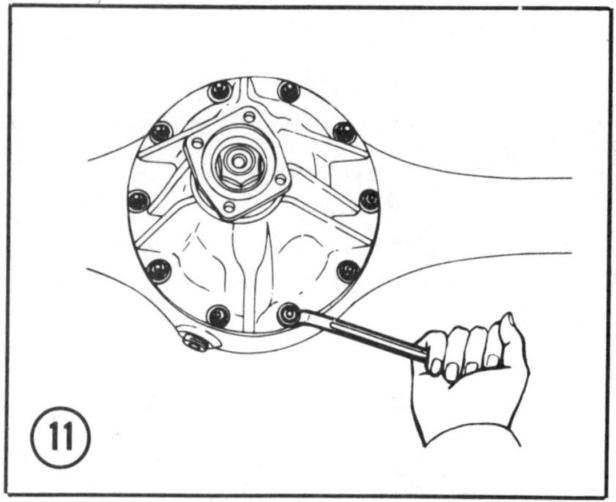

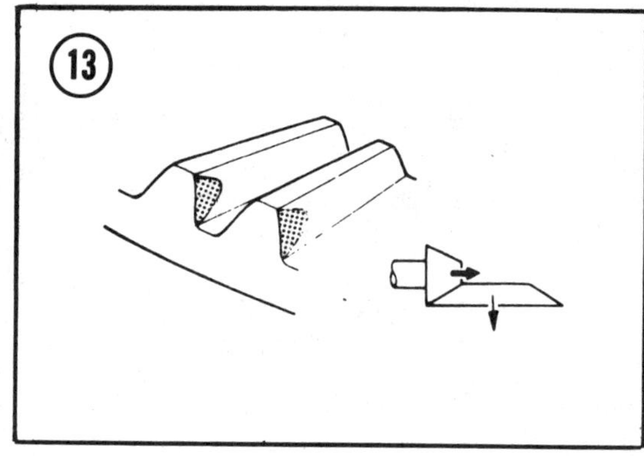

Axle Shaft Installation

1. Install a new axle housing oil seal as described earlier. Make sure the wheel bearing is packed with grease.
2. Install the axle shaft in the housing. Be careful not to damage the oil seal.
3. Install the axle shaft on one side and measure its end play (**Figure 10**). It should range from 0.012-0.035 in. (0.3-0.9mm). If necessary, add or remove shims between axle housing and bearing cage to adjust.

The other axle shaft's end play should now be 0.0008-0.0059 in. (0.02-0.15mm). If necessary, adjust by adding or removing shims between bearing cage and axle housing.

4. Tighten the axle shaft nuts or bolts to specifications (**Table 1**, end of chapter).
5. Install the brake drum and wheel. Connect the brake line and handbrake cable. Install the wheels and lower the car.

DIFFERENTIAL

This section includes removal, inspection. and installation procedures. Differential repair requires special skills and tools and should be left to a dealer. The inspection procedures will tell you if repair is necessary.

Removal/Installation

1. Securely block both front wheels so the truck will not roll in either direction. Jack up the rear end and place it on jackstands.
2. Disconnect the drive shaft from the differential. Mark the drive shaft and differential flanges so they may be reassembled in the same relative positions.
3. Remove the rear axle shafts as described prevously.
4. Remove the differential attaching nuts. See **Figure 11**. Lift the differential out.
5. Installation is the reverse of these steps. Use a new gasket between differential and axle

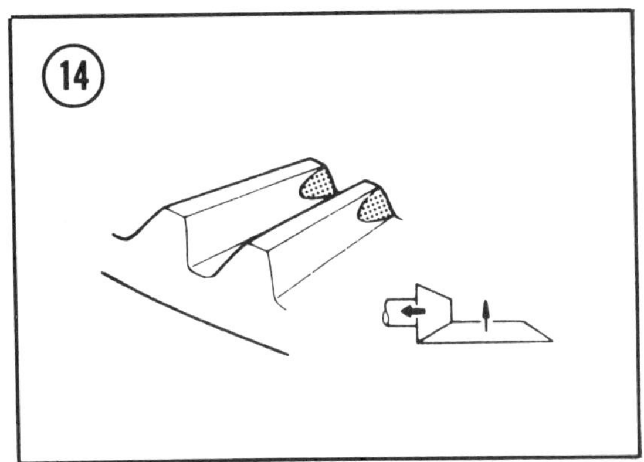

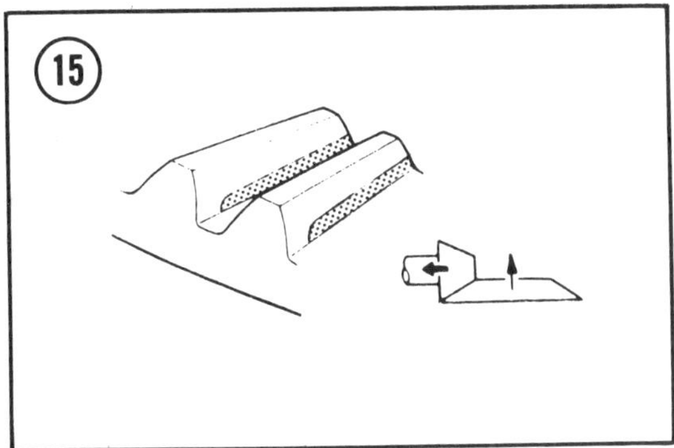

housing. Tighten all nuts and bolts to specifications at the end of the chapter.

Inspection

1. Drain the gear oil from the differential.
2. Place the differential on a workbench.
3. Look for visible wear or damage and check the gears for chipped or missing teeth.
4. Check the tooth contact pattern of the ring gear. To do this, apply a thin, even coat of red lead oxide to 4 or 5 ring gear teeth a 2 or 3 positions on the gear. Turn the gear several turns in both directions so the contact pattern of the teeth is pressed into the coat of lead oxide. Compare the contact pattern with the following illustrations to determine differential condition.

Figure 12—Correct contact pattern.

Figure 13—Heel contact. Indicates that the thickness of the pinion adjusting shim and washer should be increased to move the pinion closer to the ring gear.

Figure 14—Toe contact. Indicates that thickness of the pinion adjusting shim and

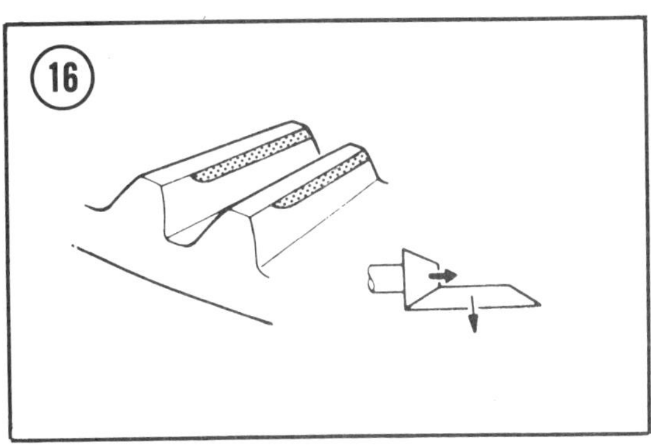

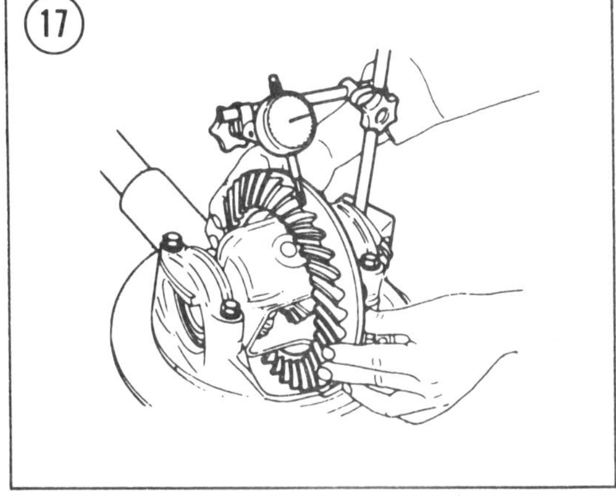

washer should be reduced to move the pinion away from the ring gear.

Figure 15—Flank contact. Adjusted in the same manner as toe contact.

Figure 16—Face contact. Adjusted in the same manner as heel contact.

Connect a dial gauge as shown in **Figure 17** and measure backlash of the pinion and ring gear. To measure, hold the pinion from turning and move the ring gear while noting the reading on the gauge. It should be 0.005-0.007 in. (0.13-0.18mm) on 521 pickups, or 0.006-0.008 in. (0.15-0.20mm) on 620 pickups. Excessive or insufficient backlash requires disassembly and adjustment of the differential.

REAR SUSPENSION

Rear Shock Absorber Replacement

1. Securely block both front wheels so the truck will not roll in either direction. Jack up the rear end and place jackstands beneath the frame.

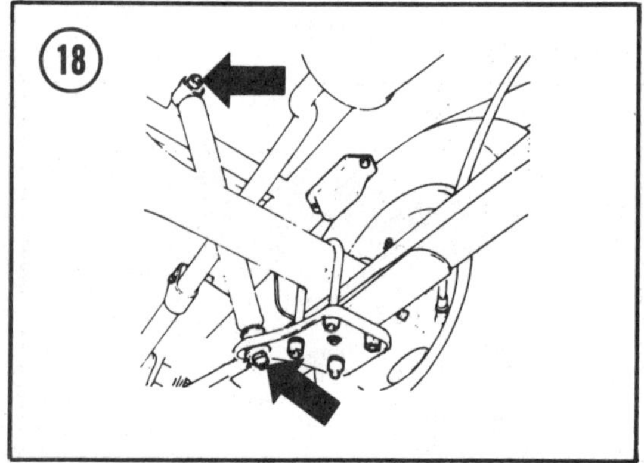

2. Place a jack beneath the axle. The jack is used to raise or lower the axle.

3. Detach the lower end of the shock absorber **(Figure 18)**, then the upper end. Remove it from the truck.

4. Installation is the reverse of these steps. Tighten all nuts and bolts to specifications (end of chapter). The truck's weight must be on the wheels before either end of the shock is tightened.

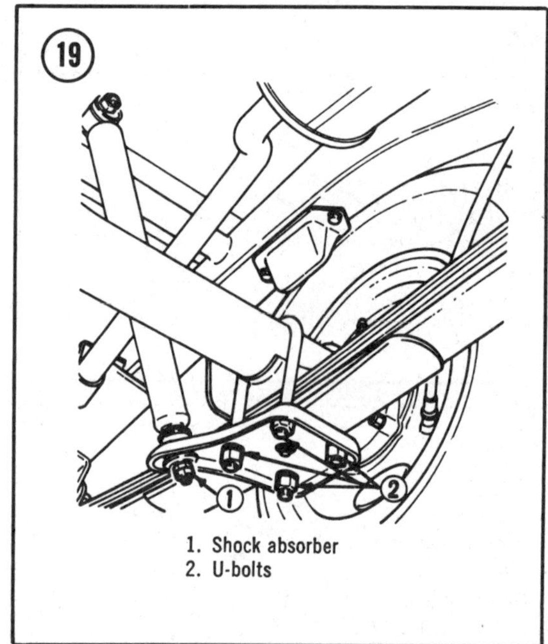

1. Shock absorber
2. U-bolts

Leaf Spring Removal

1. Securely block both front wheels so the truck will not roll in either direction. Jack up the rear end, place it on jackstands, and remove the rear wheels.

2. Place a jack beneath the center of the axle to support it.

3. Remove the nuts from U-bolts and shock absorber lower end. See **Figure 19**.

4. Remove the bolts from the rear shackle. See **Figure 20**.

5. Detach the front end of the spring **(Figure 21)**. Lower the spring away from the truck.

6. Check all parts for rust, wear, or damage. Replace as needed.

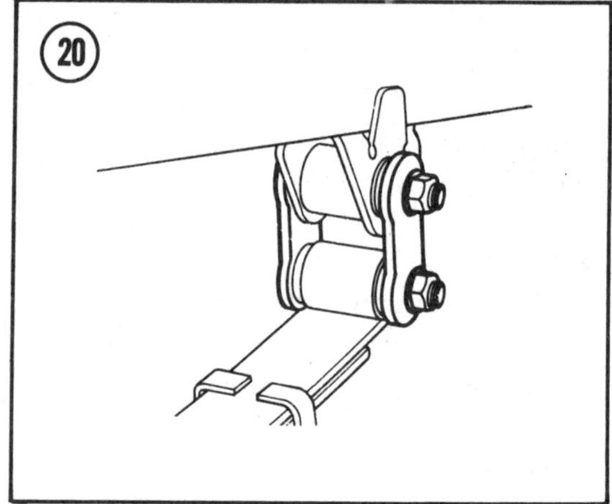

Leaf Spring Installation

Installation is the reverse of the removal procedure, plus the following.

1. Coat rubber bushings with soapy water before installation.

2. Tighten U-bolt nuts evenly in a diagonal pattern. Be sure U-bolts are vertical, not tilted to one side.

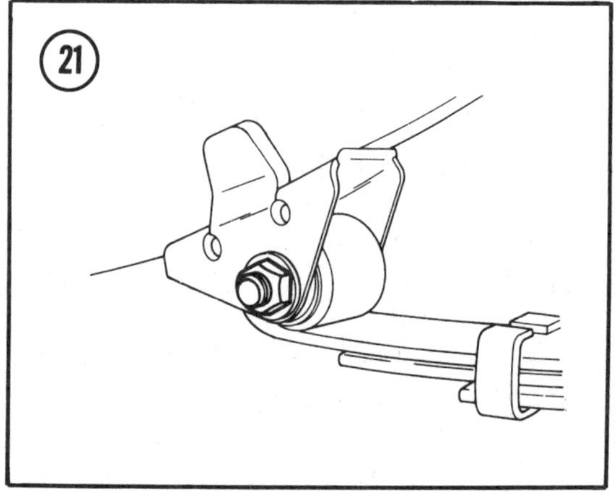

Table 1 TIGHTENING TORQUES

Fastener	Ft.-lb.	Mkg
Drive shaft		
521 pickup		
Flange bolts	18-22	2.5-3.0
Center bearing bracket bolts	17-20	2.4-2.7
620 and 720 pickups		
Center flange bolts	17-24	2.4-3.3
Rear flange bolts	17-24	2.4-3.3
Bearing bracket bolts	12-16	1.6-2.2
Axle shafts		
Bearing cage nuts		
1970-1973	27-35	3.7-4.8
1974 and later	39-46	5.4-6.4
Wheel bearing locknut	108-145	15-20
Differential attaching nuts		
521 pickup	12-17	1.6-2.4
620 and 720 pickups	12-18	1.6-2.5
Shock absorbers*		
521 pickup		
Upper nuts	26-31	3.6-4.3
Lower nuts	10-12	1.4-2.6
620 and 720 pickups		
Upper nuts	22-30	3.1-4.1
Lower nuts	12-16	1.6-2.2
Springs*		
521 pickup		
Front pin and shackle	83-94	11.5-13.0
U-bolts	62-72	8.5-10.0
620 pickup		
Front pin (through 1977)	83-94	11.5-13.0
Front pin (1978-1979)	37-50	5.1-6.9
Rear shackle	83-94	11.5-13.0
U-bolt nuts	53-72	7.3-9.9
720 pickup		
Front pin	37-50	5.1-6.9
Rear shackle	37-50	5.1-6.9
U-bolt nuts	65-72	9-10

*Tighten with the truck's weight on the wheels.

12

NOTE: If you own a 1982 or later model, first check the Supplement at the back of the book for any new service information.

CHAPTER THIRTEEN

FRONT SUSPENSION, WHEEL BEARINGS AND STEERING

Datsun pickups use upper and lower suspension links (A-arms), tube shock absorbers, and torsion bar springs. The wheel hub is supported by a knuckle spindle. On 1970-1977 models (drum brakes), the knuckle spindle pivots on a kingpin. On 1978 and later models (front disc brakes), the knuckle spindle pivots on upper and lower ball-joints.

Steering on all models is recirculating ball type. Specifications (**Table 1**) and tightening torques (**Table 2**) are listed at the end of the chapter.

A few special tools are used in this chapter. All are available through your dealer. A few are manufactured by Kent-Moore Tool Division, 29784 Little Mack, Roseville, Michigan, 48066 and may be ordered direct from them.

WHEEL ALIGNMENT

Several front suspension angles affect the running and steering of the front wheels. These angles must be properly aligned to prevent excessive wear, as well as to maintain directional stability ease of steering. The angles are as follows:

a. Caster
b. Camber
c. Toe-in
d. Kingpin or steering axis inclination
e. Steering lock angles

Caster, steering angle, camber, and toe-in are adjustable. However, all but toe-in require a front end rack. Take the job to a dealer or front end specialist.

Pre-alignment Check

Adjustment of the steering and various suspension angles is affected by several factors. Perform the following steps before any adjustments are attempted.

1. Check tire pressure and wear. See *Tire Wear Analysis,* Chapter Two.
2. Check play in front wheel bearings. Adjust if necessary.
3. Check play in kingpins.
4. Check for broken springs.
5. Remove any excessive load.
6. Check shock absorbers.
7. Check steering gear adjustments.
8. Check play in steering linkage.
9. Check wheel balance.
10. Check rear suspension for looseness.

Front tire wear patterns can indicate several alignment problems. These are covered under *Tire Wear Analysis,* Chapter Two.

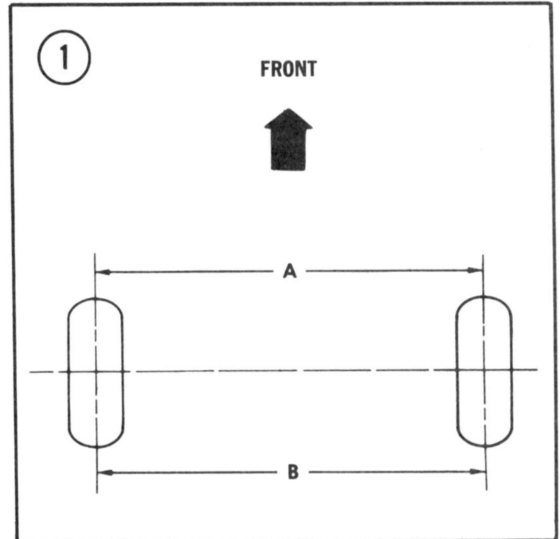

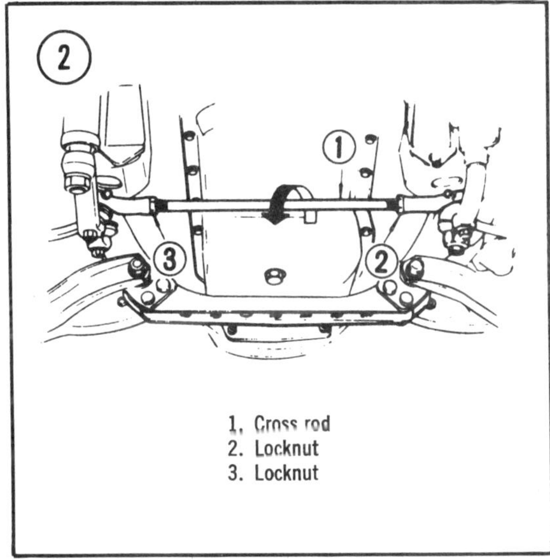

1. Cross rod
2. Locknut
3. Locknut

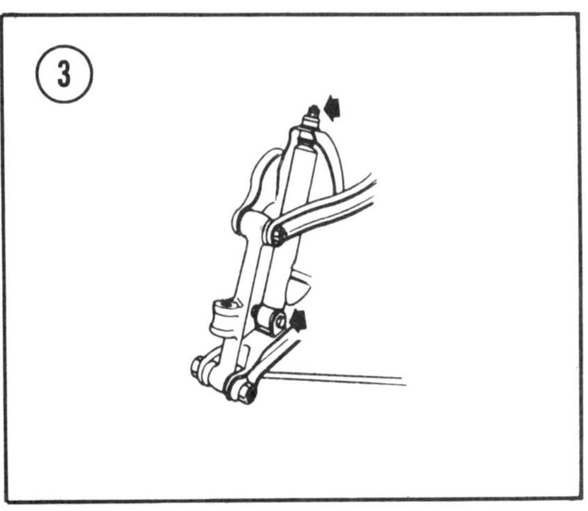

Caster and Camber

Caster is the inclination from vertical of the line through the kingpins. Positive caster shifts the wheel forward; negative caster shifts the wheel rearward. Caster causes the wheels to return to the straight ahead position after a turn. It also prevents the wheels from wandering due to wind, potholes, or uneven road surfaces.

Camber is the inclination of the wheel from vertical. With positive camber, the top of the tire leans outward. With negative camber, the top of the tire leans inward.

Toe-in

Since the front wheels tend to point outward when the vehicle is moving forward, the distance between the front edges of the tire (A, **Figure 1**) is slightly less then the distance between the rear edges (B) when the vehicle is at rest.

To adjust, loosen the locknuts on the cross rod (**Figure 2**). Rotate the cross rod forward to reduce toe-in, or back to increase it.

Kingpin or Steering Axis Inclination

This is the inward or outward lean of the kingpin (1970-1977) or of the line through the ball-joints (1978 on). It is not adjustable.

Steering Lock Angles

When a vehicle turns, the inside wheel makes a smaller circle than the outside wheel. Because of this, the inside wheel turns at a greater angle than the outside wheel. Steering lock angle is adjustable on all models, but the job should be left to a dealer or front end specialist.

FRONT SHOCK ABSORBER REPLACEMENT

1. Loosen the front wheel nuts, jack up the front end of the truck, place it on jackstands, and remove the front wheels.

2. Spray the shock absorber nuts and bolts with penetrating oil. See **Figure 3** (1970-1977) or **Figure 4** (1978 on).

3. Hold the shock absorber stem from turning and remove upper nuts, washers, and bushings.

4. Remove the nut and bolt from the lower end of the shock absorber. Lift it out.

5. Inspect bushings and attaching hardware. Replace as needed.

6. Installation is the reverse of these steps. Install the lower bolt with its head toward the front of the truck. Tighten bolts and nuts to specifications at the end of the chapter.

STABILIZER

At their front ends, the torsion bars are attached to torque arms, which in turn are attached to the lower suspension links. At the rear, the torsion bars are attached through anchor arms to a crossmember. As the suspension links move up and down, they twist the torsion bars. This provides a spring effect. **Figure 5** shows a torsion bar and related parts.

Removal

1. Loosen the front wheel nuts, jack up the front end of the truck, place it on jackstands, and remove the front wheels.

2. Remove anchor bolt from anchor arm.

3. Remove the dust cover and snap ring from the rear side of the anchor arm. Throw the snap ring away. It must not reused.

4. Slide the anchor arm off the torsion bar. Slide torsion bar rearward out of torque arm.

Inspection

Check torsion bars for wear, twisting, bending, or damaged splines. Replace if any of these conditions are found.

4

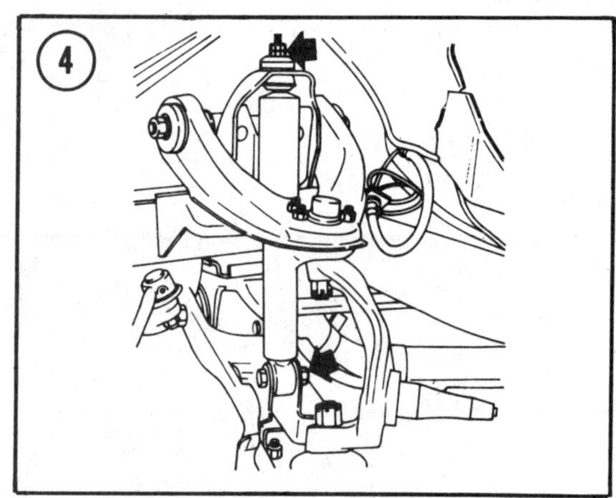

5

TORSION BAR

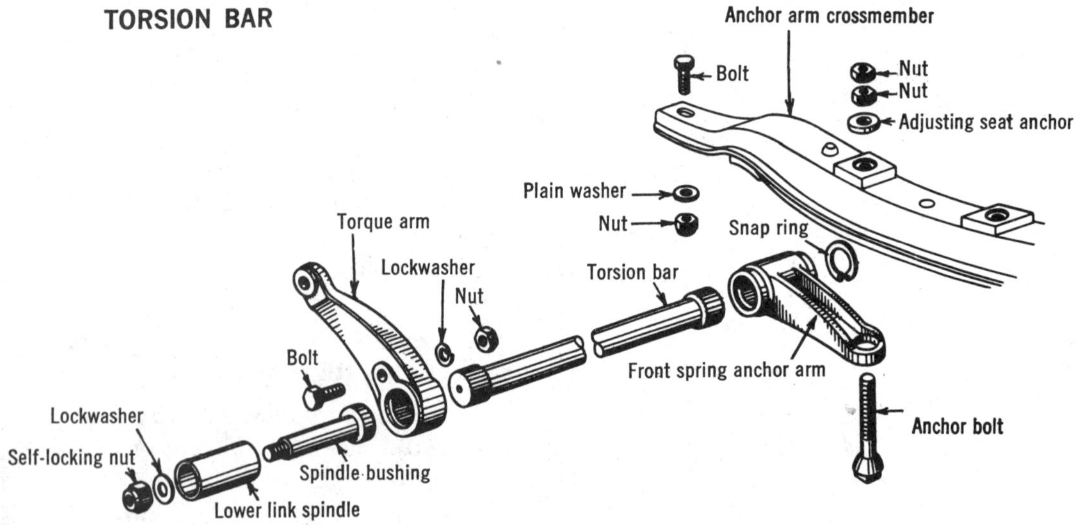

Anchor arm crossmember
Bolt
Nut
Nut
Adjusting seat anchor
Plain washer
Nut
Snap ring
Torque arm
Lockwasher
Nut
Torsion bar
Front spring anchor arm
Bolt
Lockwasher
Self-locking nut
Spindle bushing
Lower link spindle
Anchor bolt

Installation and Adjustment

1. Make sure the lower suspension link is resting on its rubber rebound bumper.

2. Grease the splines at both ends of the torsion bar. Install it in the torque arm.

> NOTE: *Left and right torsion bars are not interchangeable. They can be identified by "L" and "R" marks stamped on the ends.*

3. Install the bolt in the anchor arm.

> NOTE: *Steps 4-7 apply to 521 pickups only. If you have a 620 pickup, skip these steps.*

4. Install the anchor arm on the torsion bar. The anchor arm is pointed in the right direction when dimension "A" (**Figure 6**) is 3.5 in. (90mm).

5. Install a new snap ring and the dust cover in the rear side of the anchor arm.

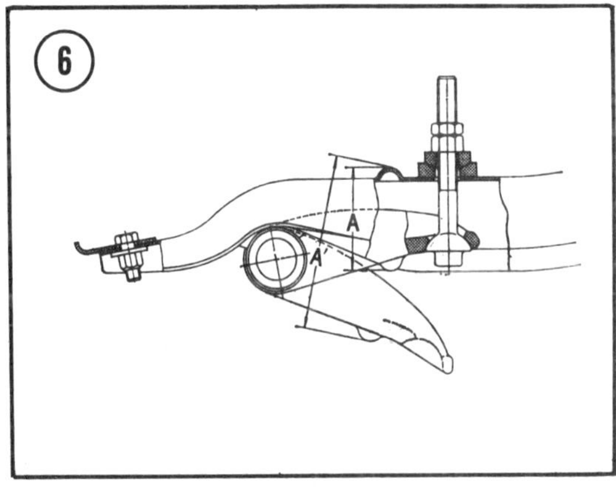

6. Place a jack beneath the anchor arm. Raise it until dimension "A" is reduced to 2.70 in. (68.5mm). This preloads the torsion bar, causing it to push the lower suspension link downward. When the truck is lowered onto the wheels, the preloaded torsion bar holds it as its normal ride height.

7. Install the anchor bolt adjusting nut and locknut. Hold the adjusting nut steady and tighten the locknut against it to 29-36 ft.-lb. (4-5mkg).

> NOTE: *Steps 8-10 apply to 620 pickups only. If you have a 521 pickup, skip these steps.*

8. Install the anchor arm on torsion bar. On standard-bed trucks, the anchor bolt should protrude 0.2-0.6 in. (5-15mm) from the top of the crossmember (dimension "A," **Figure 7**). On long-bed pickups, dimension "A" should be 0.6-1.0 in. (15-25mm).

9. Install a new snap ring in the rear side of the anchor arm.

10. Install the adjusting nut on the anchor bolt. Tighten until dimension "B" (**Figure 7**) is 2.36-2.75 in. (60-70mm). Install the locknut and tighten to 23-30 ft.-lb. (3.1-4.1mkg).

> NOTE: *The next steps apply to all pickups.*

11. Install the wheels and lower the truck.

12. Check truck height. On 1970-1977 models, measure the distance between the centerlines of the lower suspension link pivots (dimension "H," **Figure 8**). On 1978 and

13

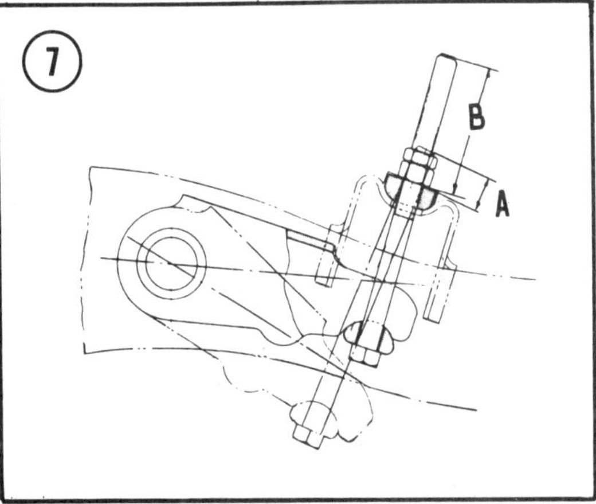

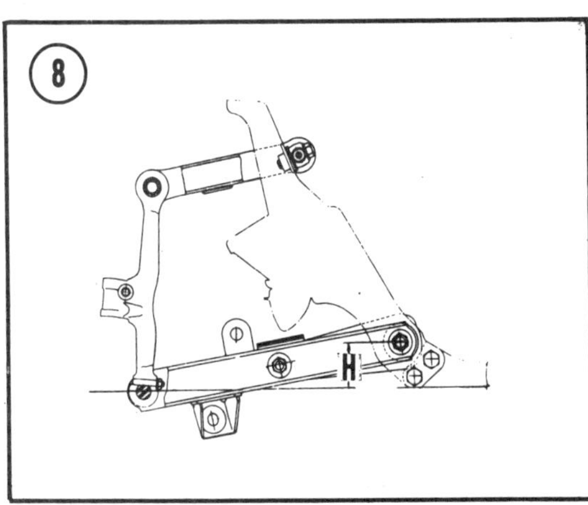

later models, measure the distance between the lower link spindle center and tension rod bolt (dimension "H," **Figure 9**). Compare with **Table 1**.

> NOTE: *Check truck height with the gas tank full, the spare tire and jack in their stowed positions, and no other weight in the truck.*

13. If dimension "H" is incorrect, tighten or loosen anchor bolt adjusting nut to change it.

SWAY BAR

Removal

1. Jack up the front end of the truck and place it on jackstands.
2. Detach the stabilizer brackets from the truck frame.
3. Detach the stabilizer from the transverse links or lower suspension links, then take it out.
4. Check the rubber mounting bushings for wear, cracks, or general deterioration. Replace as needed.

Installation (1970-1977)

1. Make sure the sway bar is centered in the brackets.
2. Tighten the sway bar connecting rod nuts until the distance from bracket to stabilizer is 3.84 in. (97.6mm). See **Figure 10**. Secure with the locknut. See **Table 2** for tightening torques.

Installation (1978 On)

Installation is the reverse of removal. Be sure the white paint mark (**Figure 11**) is on the left side of the truck, and to the inside of the mounting bracket.

TENSION RODS

Removal/Installation (1970-1977)

1. Jack up the front end of the truck and place it on jackstands.
2. Remove the nuts from both ends of the tension rod (1, **Figure 12**).
3. Remove the tension rod bracket bolts (2, **Figure 12**). Remove the tension rod and bracket.

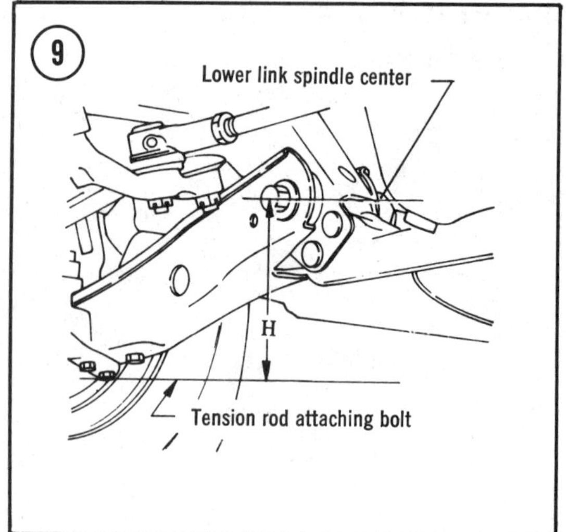

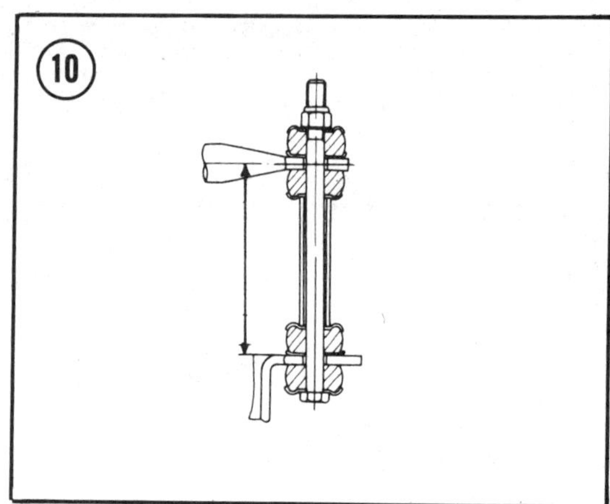

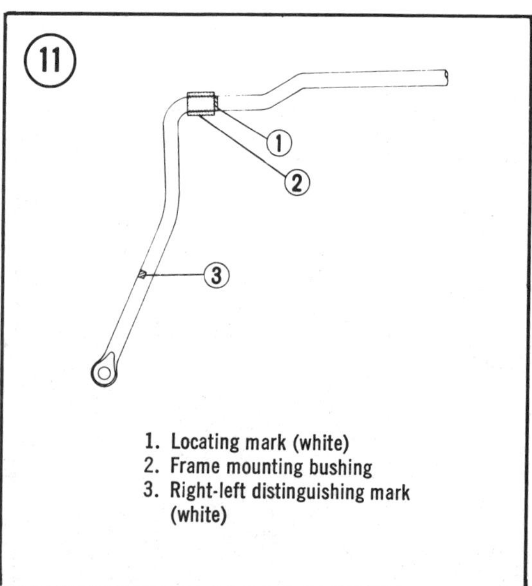

1. Locating mark (white)
2. Frame mounting bushing
3. Right-left distinguishing mark (white)

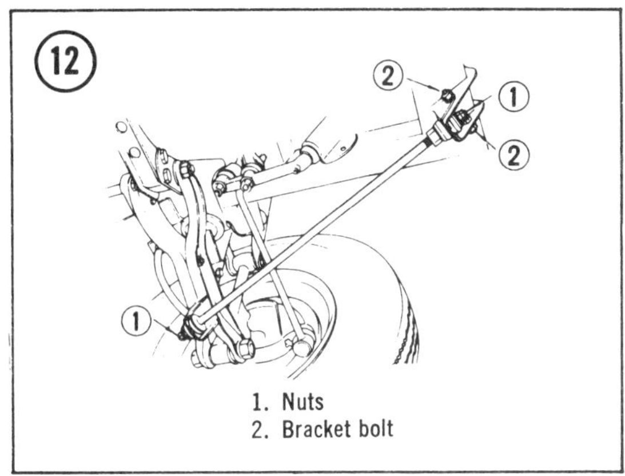

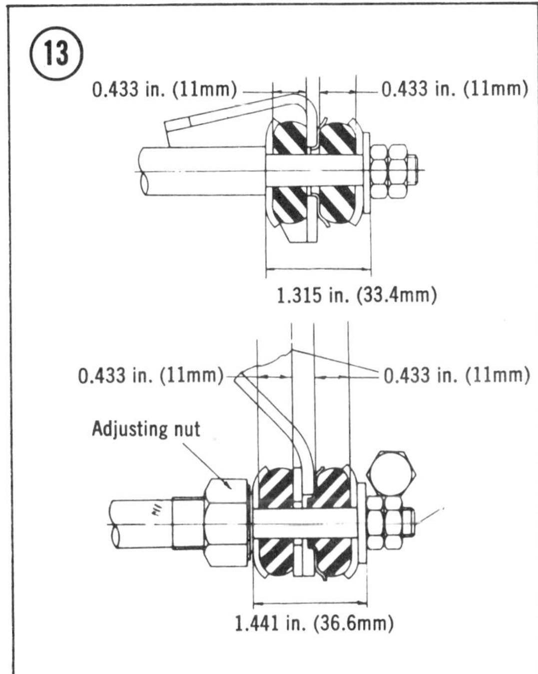

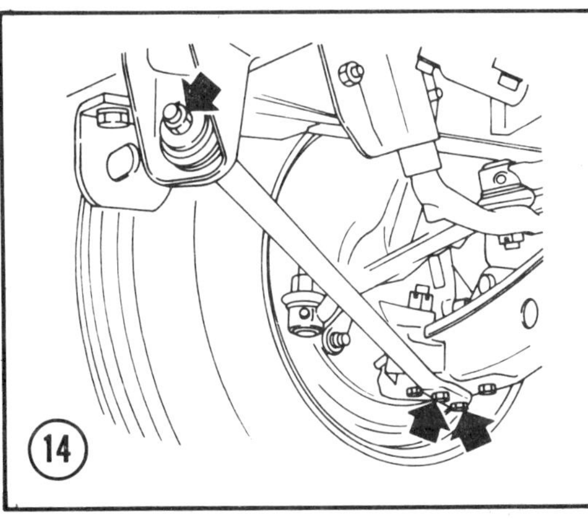

4. Installation is the reverse of these steps. Be sure the tension rod bushings are compressed to the dimension shown in **Figure 13**. Tighten locknuts and bracket bolts to 11-15 ft.-lb. (1.5-2.1 mkg) on 521 pickups; 12-16 ft.-lb. (1.6-2.2 mkg) on 620 pickups.

Removal/Installation (1978 On)

1. Remove the tension rod nut and bolts **(Figure 14)**. Take the tension rod out.
2. Check the bushings for wear or deterioration. Replace as needed.
3. Installation is the reverse of removal. Tighten the nut to 22-30 ft.-lb. (3.0-4.2 mkg). Tighten the bolts to 28-38 ft.-lb. (3.9-5.3 mkg).

KINGPINS AND KNUCKLE SPINDLES (1970-1977)

Figure 15 shows the suspension parts for one side. Refer to it as needed for the following procedures.

Removal

1. Loosen the front wheel nuts, jack up the front end of the truck, place it on jackstands, and remove the front wheels.
2. Disconnect the brake hose from the wheel cylinder. Remove the brake drum as described in Chapter Ten.
3. Remove the wheel bearings and related parts as described later in this chapter.
4. Remove 4 bolts securing the brake backing plate to the knuckle spindle. Remove the front brake assembly. See Chapter Ten for details.
5. Remove bolts securing the knuckle arm to the bottom of the knuckle spindle **(Figure 16)**. It is not necessary to detach the knuckle arm from the tie rod.
6. Remove the kingpin locknut and bolt. See **Figure 17**.
7. Drive a pointed tool into the upper kingpin plug and pry it out **(Figure 18)**. As an alternative, drill and tap the plug, thread in a bolt, and pull on the bolt to remove the plug.
8. Using a hammer and drift, drive the kingpin and its lower plug out of the knuckle spindle. See **Figure 19**.

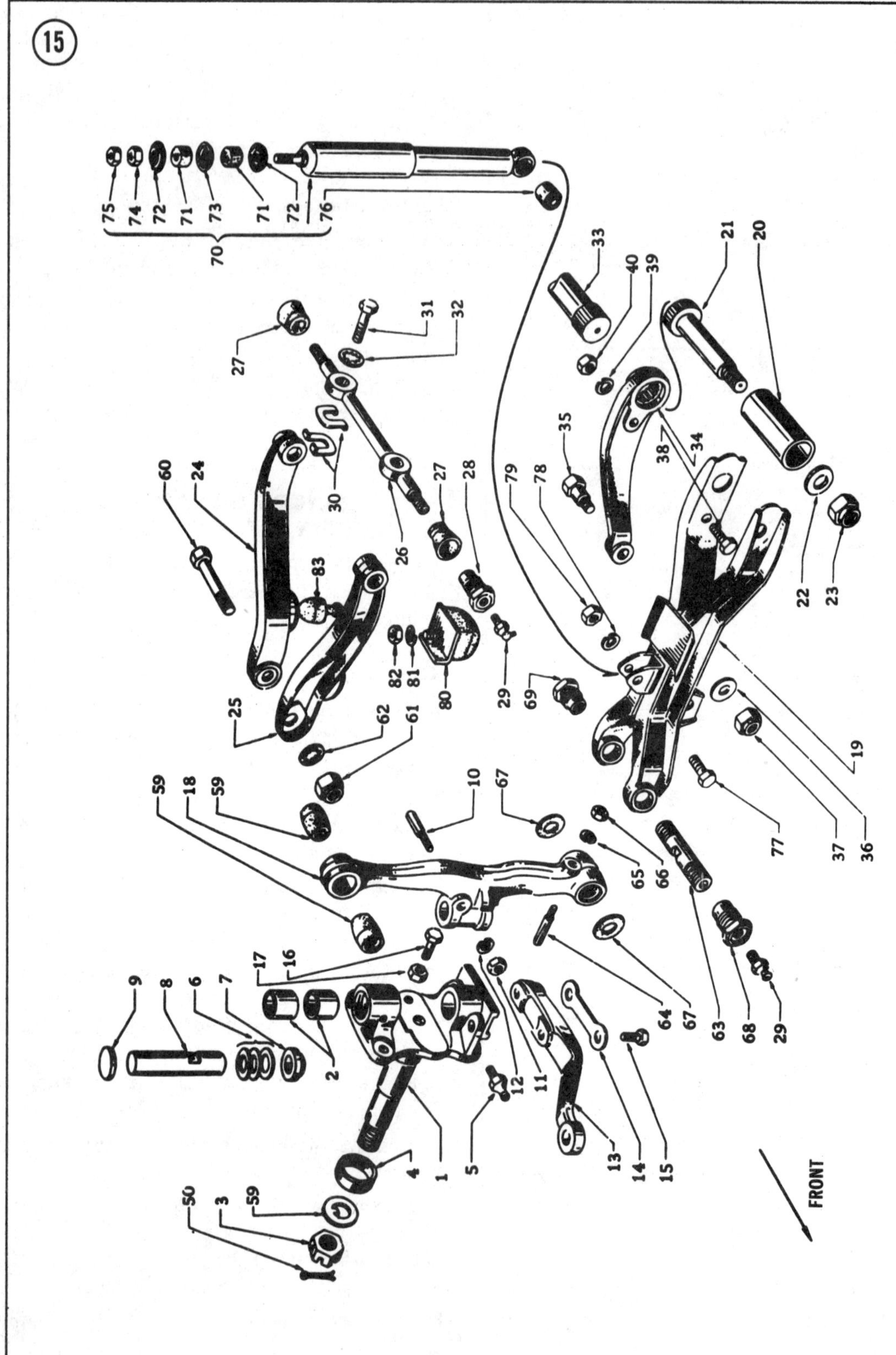
15
FRONT

KINGPINS AND KNUCKLE SPINDLE

1. Knuckle spindle assembly with nut
2. Front spindle bushing
3. Knuckle spindle nut
4. Front spindle collar
5. Grease plug or nipple
6. Front spindle shims
7. Front spindle thrust washer assembly
8. King pin
9. Front spindle plug
10. Bolt
11. Nut
12. Lockwasher
13. Knuckle arm
14. Lock plate
15. Knuckle arm bolt
16. Bolt
17. Nut
18. Knuckle spindle support
19. Front suspension lower link assembly
20. Front suspension lower link bushing assembly
21. Front suspension lower link spindle
22. Special lower link washer
23. Self-locking nut
24. Front suspension upper link assembly (rear)
25. Front suspension upper link assembly (front)
26. Front suspension upper link spindle
27. Upper link bushing dust seal
28. Front suspension upper link bushing assembly
29. Grease plug or nipple
30. Camber shim A
31. Upper link spindle bolt
32. Lockwasher
33. Front spring
34. Front spring torque arm
35. Front suspension torque arm bolt
36. Plain washer
37. Self-locking nut
38. Bolt
39. Lockwasher
40. Nut
59. Upper link bushing assembly
60. Upper link fulcrum bolt
61. Self-locking nut
62. Lockwasher
63. Front suspension lower link fulcrum pin
64. Taper pin
65. Lockwasher
66. Nut
67. Lower link fulcrum pin ring
68. Front suspension lower link bushing assembly (front)
69. Front suspension lower link bushing assembly (rear)
70. Front shock absorber kit
71. Shock absorber rubber bushing
72. Shock absorber special washer
73. Special washer
74. Nut
75. Locknut
76. Front shock absorber bushing assembly
77. Front shock absorber clamp bolt
78. Lockwasher
79. Nut
80. Front suspension rebound bumper assembly
81. Lockwasher
82. Nut
83. Front suspension rebound bumper

13

9. Gently tap the knuckle spindle loose from the knuckle spindle support (**Figure 20**).

Inspection

1. Check the kingpin and bushings for visible wear or damage. Replace if these conditions are found.

> NOTE: *Steps 2-6 can be done by a dealer or machine shop if you do not have the necessary equipment.*

2. If there is any doubt about kingpin and bushing condition, measure bushing bore and kingpin diameter. Maximum clearance between kingpin and bushings is 0.006 in. (0.15mm). Normal kingpin diameter is 0.7866-0.7874 in. (19.979-20.000mm). Normal bushing bore is 0.7878-0.7888 in. (20.010-20.035mm). Replace worn parts.
3. If the bushings are worn, drive them out with a hammer and drift such as Datsun tool ST 35380000 (Kent-Moore J-25387). See **Figure 21**. On 620 pickups, drive out the upper bushing grease seal at the same time.
4. Press new bushings in with the drift used for removal. If the new bushings have grease holes, line them up with knuckle spindle grease nipples. If there are no holes, drill new ones after installing the bushings. Use a 0.12 in. (3mm) drill. Clean away all shavings and burrs after drilling.
5. Ream new bushings to specifications. Use the lower bushing as a pilot while reaming the upper bushing; use the upper bushing as a pilot while reaming the lower bushing. This keeps the bushing centers aligned.
6. On 620 pickups, install a new upper bushing grease seal. Use a tool such as Datsun ST 35390000 (Kent-Moore J26069). See **Figures 22 and 23**.
7. Inspect wheel bearing as described later in this chapter.

Installation

Apply multipurpose grease to all friction points during assembly.

1. Grease an O-ring and install it on the lower

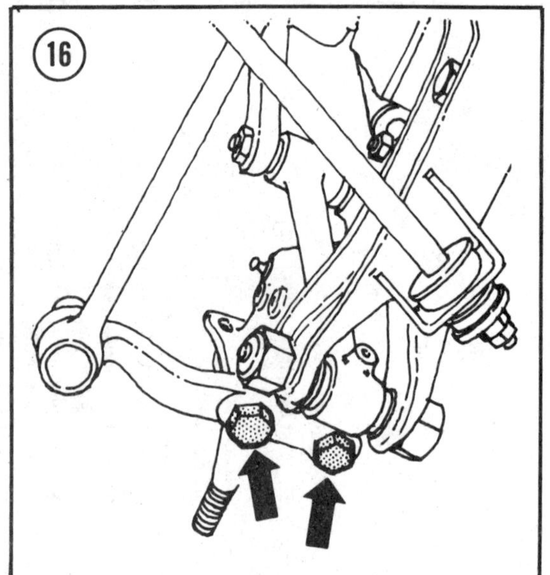

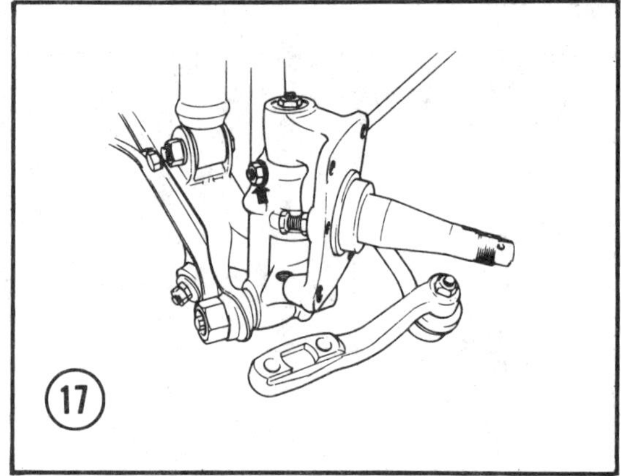

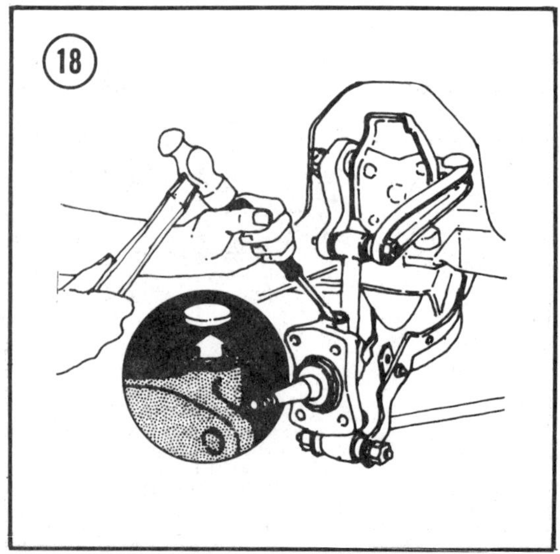

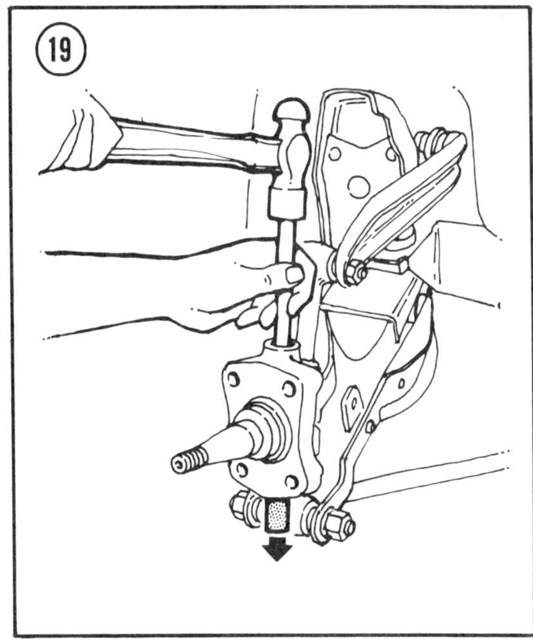

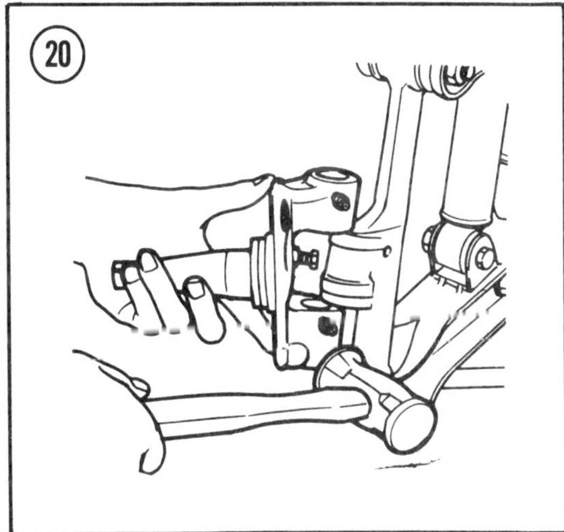

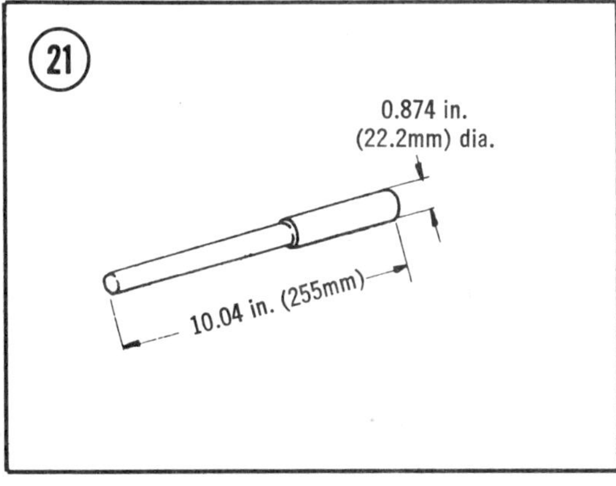

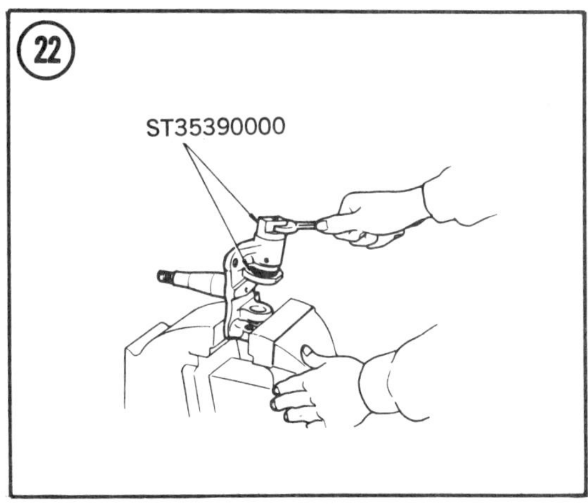

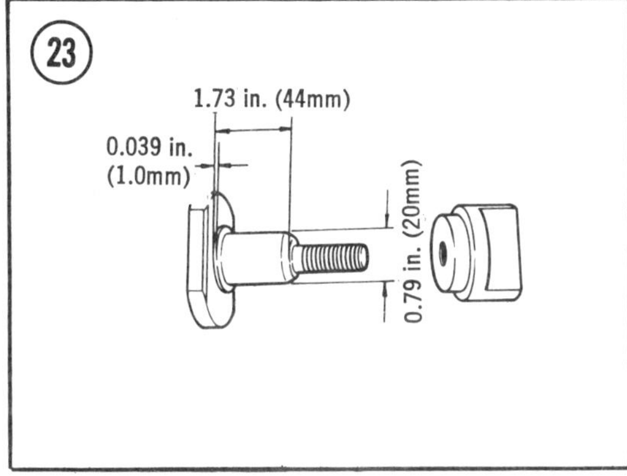

side of the knuckle spindle support. The grease will keep the O-ring in place.

2. Temporarily install the knuckle spindle and thrust bearing on the knuckle spindle support. Be sure the covered side of the bearing faces up. Place a jack beneath the knuckle spindle and raise it slightly. Measure the gap between the knuckle spindle support and knuckle spindle with a feeler gauge. Select shims to reduce this gap to 0.004 in. (0.1mm) or less.

3. Remove the knuckle spindle and thrust bearing, install the shims, then reinstall the knuckle spindle and thrust bearing.

4. Insert the kingpin into the knuckle spindle and support. Line up the lock bolt notch with the holes in the knuckle spindle support. Install the lock bolt and nut. Tighten to 15-18 ft.-lb. (2.1-2.5mkg).

5. Make sure the knuckle spindle moves smoothly back and forth. If necessary, add or remove knuckle spindle shims.

6. Coat the outer edges of the upper and lower plugs in the knuckle spindle with the gasket sealer, then install them. On 521 pickups, stake the plugs into place with a hammer and punch.

7. Bolt the knuckle arm to the knuckle spindle, using a new lock plate. Tighten bolts to 81-95 ft.-lb. (11.2-13.1 mkg) on 521 pickups; 75-88 ft.-lb. (10.4-12.2 mkg) on 620 pickups.

8. Install the grease nipples on the knuckle spindle. Inject multipurpose grease until it is forced out between the knuckle spindle and knuckle spindle support.

9. Install the brake assembly as described in Chapter Ten.

10. Install and adjust the wheel bearings as described later in this chapter.

11. Install the brake drum and wheel. Lower the truck.

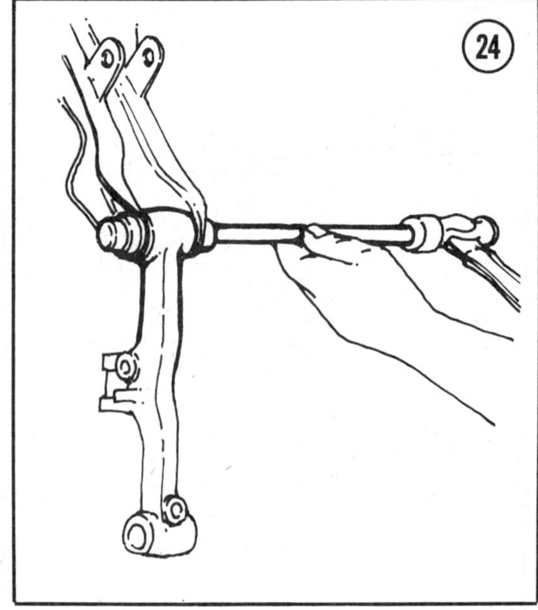

SUSPENSION LINKS (1970-1977)

See **Figure 15** for the following procedures.

> NOTE: *Some of the following steps require unusually tight torque settings. Read through the procedure and determine whether you can obtain the necessary tools before starting.*

1. Loosen the front wheel nuts, jack up the front end of the truck, place it on jackstands, and remove the front wheels.

2. Remove the brake drum (Chapter Ten).

3. Remove the wheel bearings and hub as described later in this chapter.

4. Remove front brake assembly (Chapter Ten).

5. Unbolt the knuckle arm from the bottom of the knuckle spindle (**Figure 16**).

6. Remove the torsion bar as described earlier.

7. Disconnect the stabilizer from the lower suspension link.

8. Remove the shock absorber and tension rod as described earlier.

9. Remove the nut and bolt attaching the knuckle spindle support to the upper suspension link. Pull the knuckle spindle support outward, away from the link. Remove the bushings from the upper end of the knuckle spindle support.

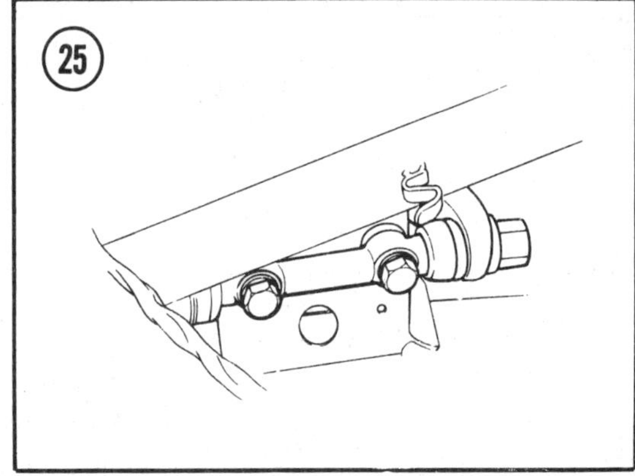

10. Remove the screw bushings (68 and 69, **Figure 15**) from the lower link fulcrum pin. These bushings are torqued to 174-181 ft.-lb. (24.1-25.0 mkg) on 521 pickups; 145-217 ft.-lb. (20.1-30.0 mkg) on 620 pickups. Brace the lower link by placing a jack beneath it. Use a socket and breaker bar to loosen the bushings. If necessary, place a pipe over the breaker bar to increase leverage.

11. Remove the nut and lock pin (64 and 66, **Figure 15**) from the lower link fulcrum pin.

12. Drive the fulcrum pin out with a hammer and drift (**Figure 24**). Separate the knuckle spindle support from the lower link. Remove 2

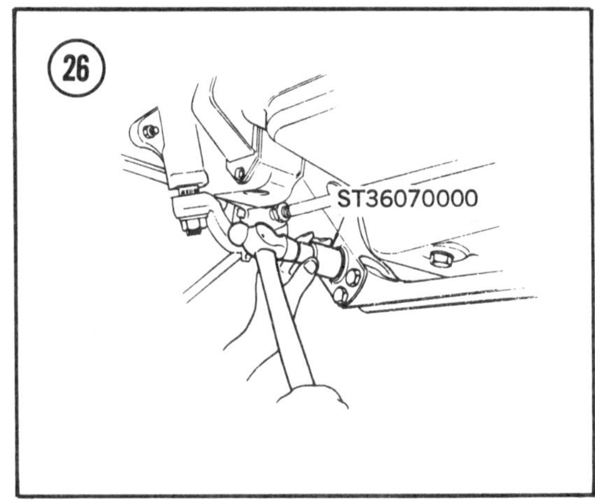

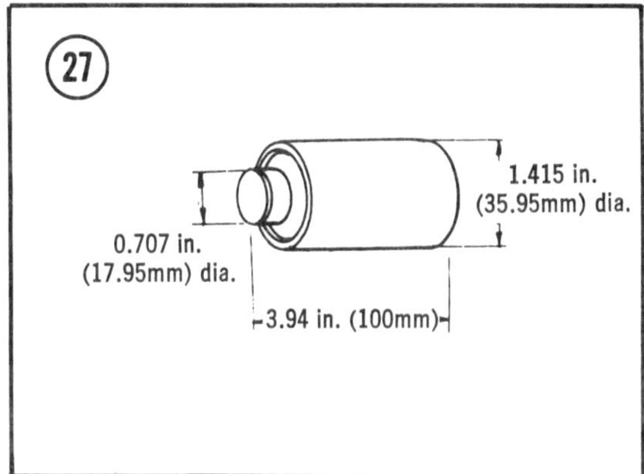

dust seals (67, **Figure 15**) from the bottom end of the knuckle spindle support.

13. Remove 2 bolts securing the upper link spindle (**Figure 25**). Remove the upper link, spindle, and wheel alignment shims.

> NOTE: *Record the locations and positions of all shims. They must be reinstalled exactly as they were.*

14. Remove the self-locking nut and washer from the lower link spindle (21, **Figure 15**). Remove the spindle and lower link.

15. Separate the upper suspension link halves from the link spindle. Place the link halves in a vise and remove the screw bushings.

> NOTE: *These bushings are torqued to 174-181 ft.-lb. (24.1-25 mkg) on 521 pickups; 253-398 ft.-lb. (35-55 mkg) on 620 pickups. If you do not have the equipment necessary for removal, have this step done by a Datsun dealer.*

16. After removing the screw bushings, remove and discard the dust covers and dust seals.

Inspection

1. Clean all metal parts in solvent. While cleaning, check for obvious wear or damage. Replace parts with these conditions.

2. Carefully check suspension links, spindles, and the knuckle spindle support for bends, cracks, or wear. Replace if these conditions can be detected.

3. Check all bushings for wear or damage. Replace bushings if there is any doubt about their condition. If the lower link spindle bushing must be replaced, drive it out with a hammer and a drift such as ST36070000. **Figure 26** shows the drift in use; **Figure 27** gives its dimensions. Remove any rust from the bushing hole before installing the bushing.

4. Inspect all threaded parts. Clean dirty or rusty threads. Slightly damaged threads may be cleaned with a tap or die. Replace parts that have badly damaged threads.

Installation

1. Place the upper link halves in a vise and install the screw bushings.

> NOTE: *These bushings are tightened to unusually high torques in Step 10. If you do not have the equipment necessary for installation, have the screw bushings installed by a Datsun dealer.*

2. Coat the insides of the screw bushings and the upper link spindle threads with mutipurpose grease. Install the upper link halves on the upper link spindle. Center the link halves on the spindle as shown in **Figure 28**. 13

3. Coat the lower link spindle with multipurpose grease. Position the lower link on its mounting bracket and insert the spindle. Secure with the washer and a new self-locking nut. Tighten the nut to specifications (end of chapter).

4. Bolt the upper link spindle to its mounting bracket. Be sure to install the wheel alignment shims in their original locations and positions.

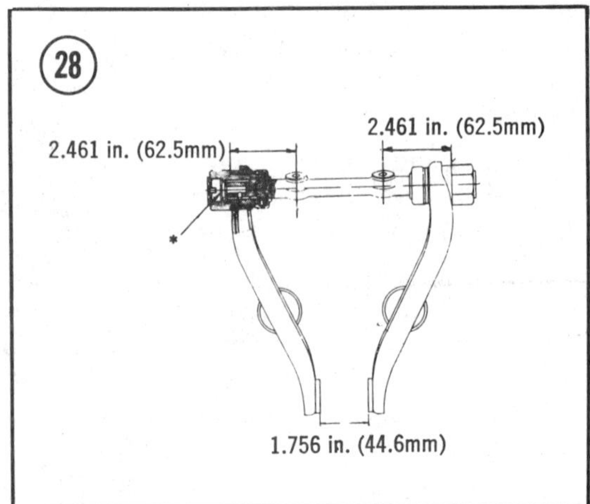

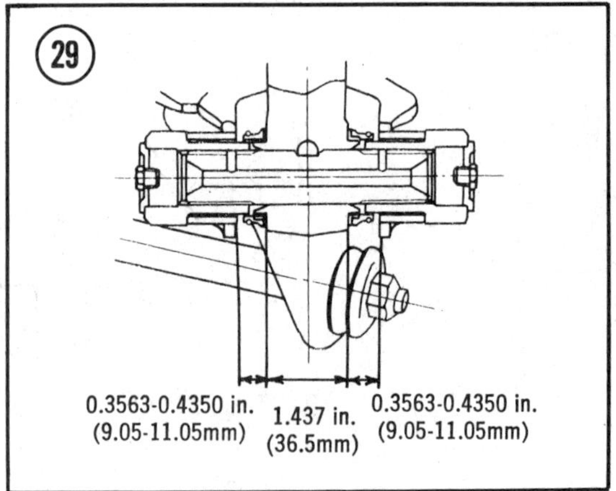

Tighten the bolts to specfications (end of chapter).

5. Remove the grease filler plugs from the upper link screw bushings. Install a grease nipple in place of each plug, then inject multipurpose grease into the bushings. Remove the grease nipples and reinstall the plugs.

6. Install the dust seals in the bottom end of the knuckle spindle support.

7. Position the knuckle spindle support in the outer end of the lower link.

8. Start the lower link fulcrum pin into the lower link. Line up the taper pin notch in the fulcrum pin with the taper pin hole in the knuckle spindle support. Tap the fulcrum pin through the knuckle spindle support and the lower link.

9. Insert the taper pin into the knuckle spindle support and fulcrum pin. Install the nut and lockwasher on the taper pin. Tighten the nut to 3-4 ft.-lb. (0.41-0.55 mkg) on 521 pickups; 6-8 ft.-lb. (0.83-1.11 mkg) on 620 pickups.

10. Coat the lower link screw bushing threads with multipurpose grease. Remove the grease filler plugs from the bushings. Thread the bushings in by hand. Make sure the knuckle spindle support is centered in the lower link (**Figure 29**), then tighten the screw bushings to 174-181 ft.-lb. (24.1-25.0 mkg) on 521 pickups or 145-217 ft.-lb. (20.1-30.0 mkg) on 620 pickups. Use a 150 ft.-lb. torque wrench and a range extender to tighten the screw bushings.

11. Install a grease nipple in place of each grease filler plug. Inject multipurpose grease into the bushings until it is forced out past the seals. Remove the grease nipples and reinstall the filler plugs.

12. Install the upper link bushings in the knuckle spindle support.

13. Position the upper end of the knuckle spindle support between the upper link halves. Insert the fulcrum bolt into the upper link halves and knuckle spindle support.

> NOTE: *Insert the fulcrum bolt from the rear side of the truck.*

14. Secure the fulcrum bolt with a washer and a new self-locking nut. Tighten the nut to specifications (end of chapter).

15. Install the shock absorber and tension rod as described earlier in this chapter.

16. Attach stabilizer to lower suspension link.

17. Install the torsion bar as described earlier in this chapter.

18. Bolt the knuckle arm to the bottom of the knuckle spindle (**Figure 16**). Tighten the bolts to specifications (end of chapter).

19. Install front brake assembly (Chapter Ten).

20. Install the wheel bearings and hub as described later in this chapter.

21. Install the brake drum. Install the wheel and lower the truck.

UPPER BALL JOINT (1978 ON)

Figure 30 is an exploded view of the suspension parts for one side of the truck. Refer to it as needed.

(30)

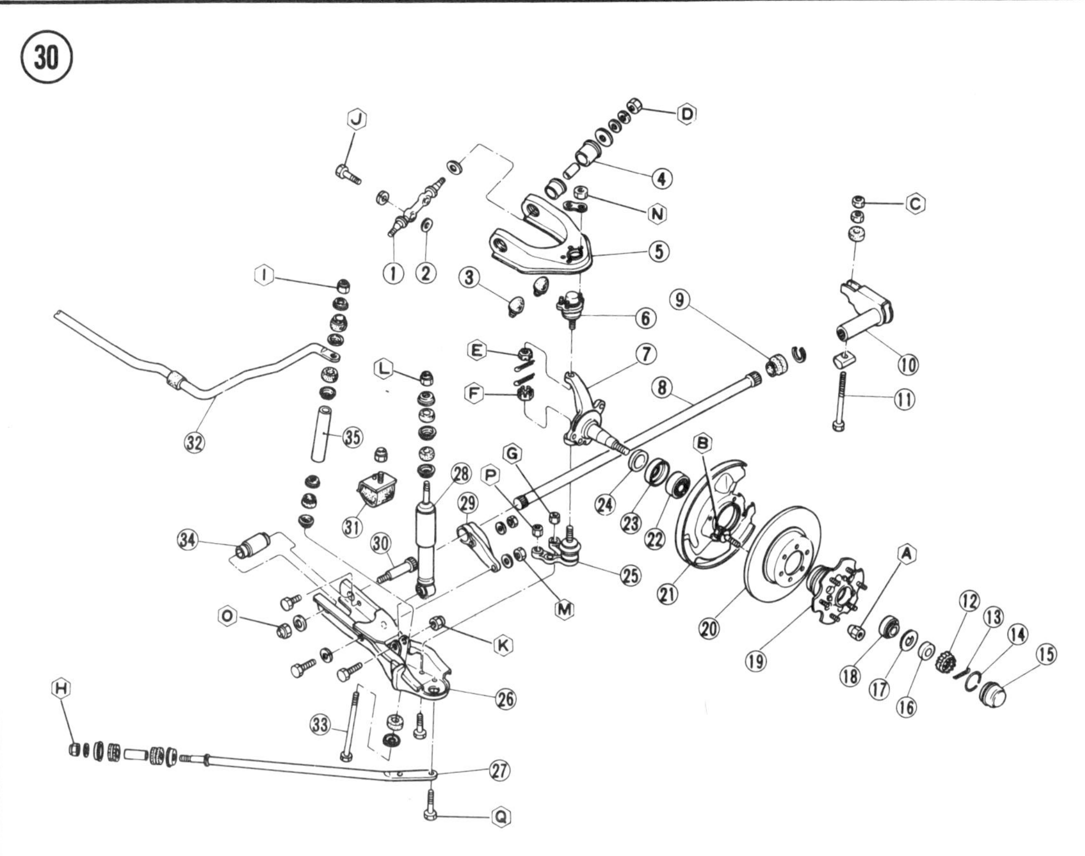

SUSPENSION (1978-ON)

1. Upper link spindle
2. Camber adjusting shim
3. Rebound bumper
4. Upper link bushing
5. Upper link
6. Upper ball-joint
7. Knuckle spindle
8. Torsion bar spring
9. Dust cover
10. Anchor arm
11. Anchor arm adjusting bolt
12. Adjusting cap
13. Cotter pin
14. O-ring
15. Hub cap
16. Spindle nut
17. Washer
18. Outer wheel bearing
19. Wheel hub
20. Rotor
21. Baffle plate
22. Inner wheel bearing
23. Grease seal
24. Spacer
25. Lower ball-joint
26. Lower link
27. Tension rod
28. Shock absorber
29. Torque arm
30. Lower link spindle
31. Bound bumper
32. Stabilizer
33. Stabilizer connecting bolt
34. Lower link bushing
35. Stabilizer collar

Tightening torque mkg (ft.-lb.)

A. 8.0 to 10.0 (58 to 72)
B. 3.9 to 5.3 (28 to 38)
C. 3.1 to 4.1 (22 to 30)
D. 7.7 to 10.5 (56 to 76)
E. 8.0 to 10.0 (58 to 72)
F. 17.2 to 19.5 (124 to 141)
G. 3.9 to 5.3 (28 to 38)
H. 3.0 to 4.2 (22 to 30)
I. 1.6 to 2.2 (12 to 16)
J. 11.1 to 15.0 (80 to 108)
K. 3.1 to 4.1 (22 to 30)
L. 1.6 to 2.2 (12 to 16)
M. 2.7 to 3.7 (20 to 27)
N. 1.7 to 2.2 (12 to 16)
O. 11.1 to 15.0 (80 to 108)
P. 3.6 to 4.6 (26 to 33)
Q. 3.9 to 5.3 (28 to 38)

13

Removal

1. Set the handbrake. Place the transmission in first gear (manual) or PARK (automatic).
2. Loosen the front wheel nuts. Jack up the front end of the truck, place it on jackstands, and remove the front wheels.
3. Loosen the nuts on the anchor arm adjusting bolt (11, **Figure 30**). This relieves torsion bar tension.
4. Remove the cotter pin and nut from the ball-joint.
5. Separate the ball-joint from the knuckle spindle. Use a puller (**Figure 31**) or fork-type separator (**Figure 32**). These are available from rental dealers.
6. Remove the ball-joint mounting nuts. Take the ball-joint out of the suspension link.

Inspection

1. Check the dust cover, retainer, and clip for wear or damage. Replace the ball-joint if these can be seen.
2. Place the ball-joint in a vise with the stud pointing upward. See **Figure 33**. Thread the nut onto the stud. Turn the ball-joint with a torque wrench and note the amount of torque necessary to turn it. It should be at least 8.7 in.-lb. (10 cmkg). If it is less than the minimum, replace the ball-joint.

Installation

Installation is the reverse of removal, plus the following.

1. Remove the plug from the top of the ball-joint and install a grease nipple (Zerk fitting). Inject multipurpose grease with a grease gun, then reinstall the plug.
2. Have wheel alignment checked by a dealer or front end shop.

UPPER SUSPENSION LINK (1978 ON)

Refer to **Figure 30** for this procedure.

Removal

1. Remove the upper ball-joint as described earlier.

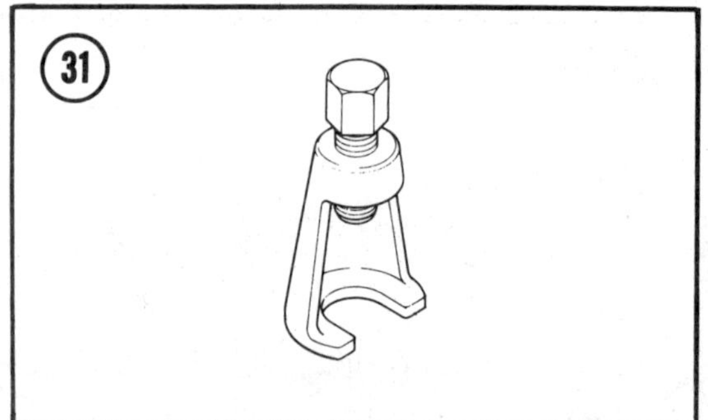

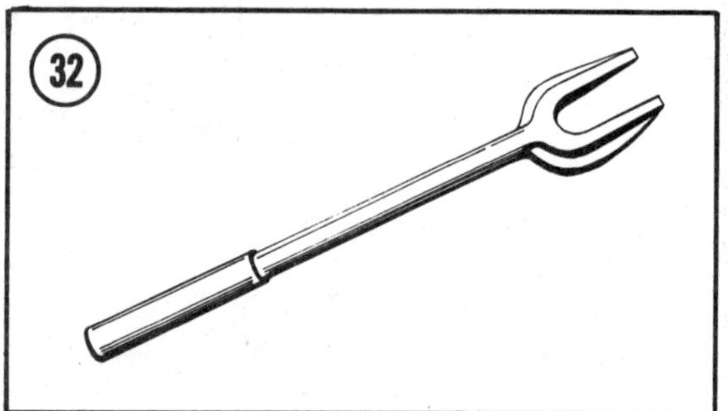

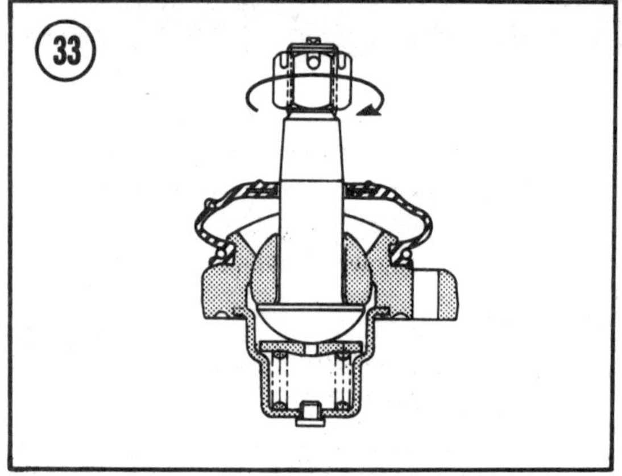

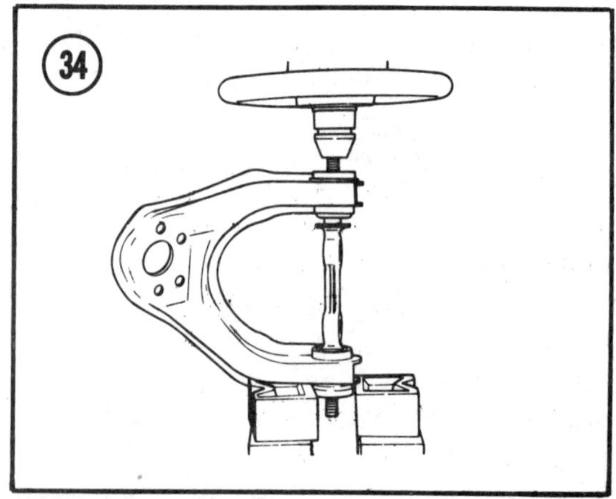

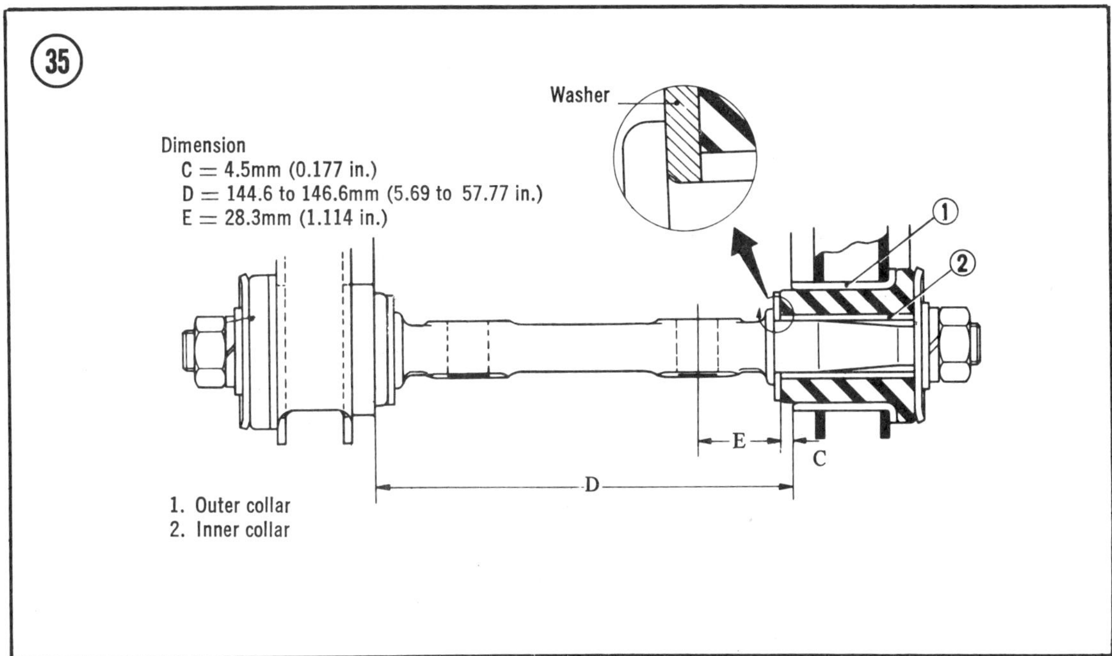

2. Unbolt the upper suspension link spindle (1, **Figure 30**) from the frame. Take the suspension link off.

> NOTE: *There are camber shims between the spindle and frame. Label these so they can be returned to their original locations.*

Disassembly

1. Remove the nut and washers from each end of the upper link spindle.

2. Press the spindle in one direction and remove the bushings from one end **(Figure 34)**. Then press it in the other direction and remove the bushings from the other end. The spindle can then be removed from the link.

> NOTE: *Pressing can be done by a machine shop if you don't have a press.*

Inspection

1. Check the link for bending or cracks. Replace if these conditions are found. If the link is slightly rusty, clean and paint it. If the rust is severe, replace the link.

2. Check the spindle for wear or damage. Replace if these can be seen.

3. Check the rubber bushings for wear, damage, or deterioration. Replace the bushings if there is any doubt about their condition.

Assembly

1. Coat one of the bushings with soapy water. Press it into the link until it protrudes at least 0.177 in. (4.5mm) toward the center (dimension "C," **Figure 35**).

2. Position the inner washer on the bushing and insert the spindle into the bushing.

> NOTE: *Be sure the rounded corner of the washer is toward the center of the spindle (inset,* ***Figure 35****).*

3. Press the other bushing into the link.

4. Position the spindle as shown in **Figure 36**. Tighten the spindle nuts to 56-76 ft.-lb. (7.7-10.5 mkg).

5. Attach the ball-joint to the link. Tighten the attaching nuts to 12-16 ft.-lb. (1.7-2.2 mkg).

Installation

Installation is the reverse of removal, plus the following.

1. Adjust truck height. See *Torsion Bar Installation* earlier in this chapter.

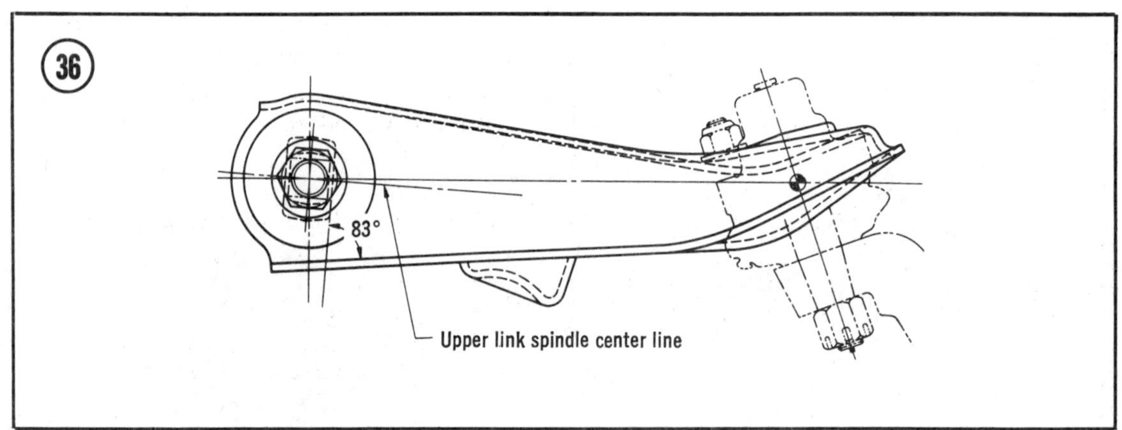

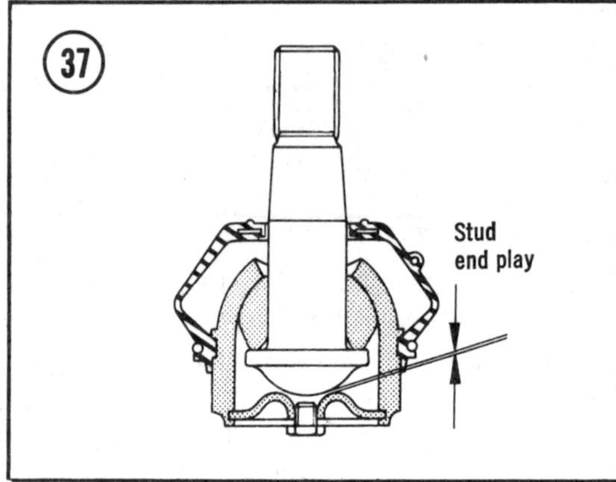

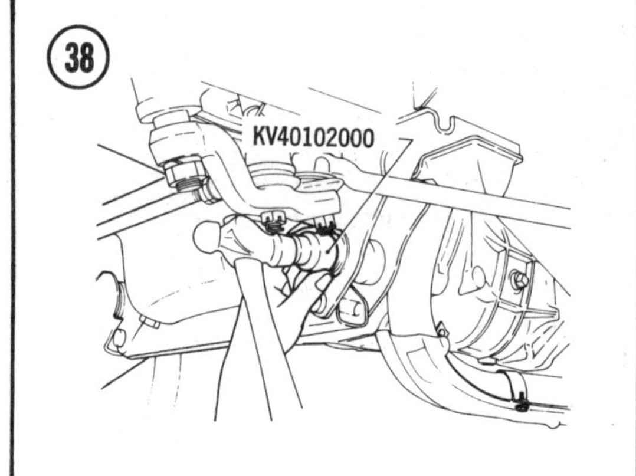

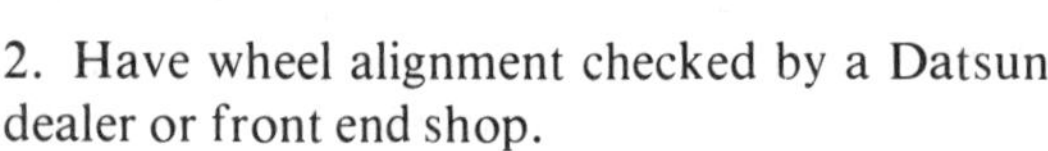

2. Have wheel alignment checked by a Datsun dealer or front end shop.

LOWER BALL-JOINT (1978 ON)

Removal

Refer to **Figure 30** for this procedure.

1. Set the handbrake. Place the transmission in first gear (manual) or PARK (automatic).
2. Loosen the front wheel nuts. Jack up the front end of the truck, place it on jackstands, and remove the front wheels.
3. Remove the shock absorber lower bolt. See *Shock Absorber Replacement* earlier in this chapter.
4. Remove the torsion bar. See *Torsion Bar Removal* earlier in this chapter.
5. Unbolt the sway bar (if so equipped) and tension rod from the lower link.
6. Remove the cotter pin and nut from the lower ball-joint stud.
7. Separate the lower ball-joint from the knuckle spindle. Use a puller (**Figure 31**) or a fork-type separator (**Figure 32**). These are available from rental dealers.
8. Unbolt the ball-joint from the lower link and take it out.

Inspection

1. Check the dust cover, retainer, and clip for cracks or other damage. Replace the ball-joint if these conditions can be seen.
2. Place the ball-joint in a vise with the stud pointing upward (**Figure 37**). Pull the stud up and down and measure the amount of play. It should range from 0.004-0.039 in. (0.1-1.0mm). If play exceeds the maximum, replace the ball-joint.

Installation

Installation is the reverse of removal, plus the following.

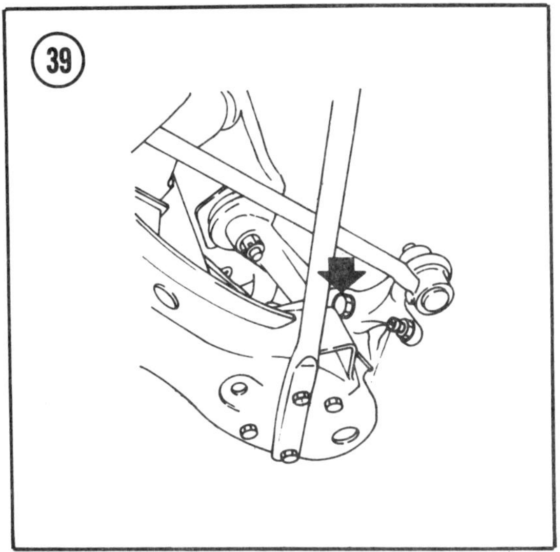

1. Adjust truck height. See *Torsion Bar Installation* earlier in this chapter.

2. Have wheel alignment checked by a Datsun dealer or front end shop.

LOWER SUSPENSION LINK (1978 ON)

Removal

Refer to **Figure 30** for this procedure.

1. Remove the lower ball-joint as described earlier.

2. Remove the nut and washer from the front end of the lower link spindle. Gently tap the spindle out, then remove the lower link.

3. Check the lower link spindle bushing for wear or damage. If its condition is in doubt, drive it out with a drift as shown in **Figure 38**. If you don't have a special tool, use a piece of pipe the same diameter as the bushing.

Inspection

1. Check the lower link for cracks or bending. Replace it if these can be seen. If the link is slightly rusty, clean and paint it. If rust is severe, replace the link.

2. Check the lower link spindle for wear or damage. Replace if these can be seen.

Installation

Installation is the reverse of removal, plus the following.

1. Adjust truck height. See *Torsion Bar Installation* earlier in this chapter.

2. Have wheel alignment checked by a Datsun dealer or front end shop.

KNUCKLE ARM AND SPINDLE (1978 ON)

Removal

1. Set the handbrake. Place the transmission in first gear (manual) or PARK (automatic).

2. Loosen the front wheel nuts. Jack up the front end of the truck, place it on jackstands, and remove the front wheels.

3. Remove the brake caliper (Chapter Ten).

4. Remove the hub and brake disc. See *Wheel Bearings* later in this chapter.

5. Loosen the nuts on the torsion bar anchor arm bolt. See *Torsion Bar Removal* earlier in this chapter.

6. Unbolt the knuckle arm from the knuckle spindle. See **Figure 39**.

7. Remove the cotter pin and nuts from each ball-joint. Separate the ball-joints from the knuckle spindle. Use a puller **(Figure 31)** or fork-type separator **(Figure 32)**. These are available from rental dealers.

Inspection

Check the knuckle spindle for wear, rust, or cracks. If its condition is in doubt, have it Magnafluxed by a machine shop. This will detect hidden cracks. Replace the knuckle spindle if any defects are found.

Installation

Installation is the reverse of removal, plus the following.

1. Adjust truck height. See *Torsion Bar Installation* earlier in this chapter.

2. Have wheel alignment checked by a Datsun dealer or front end shop.

WHEEL BEARINGS

1. Loosen the front wheel nuts, jack up the front end of the truck, place it on jackstands, and remove the front wheels.

40

41

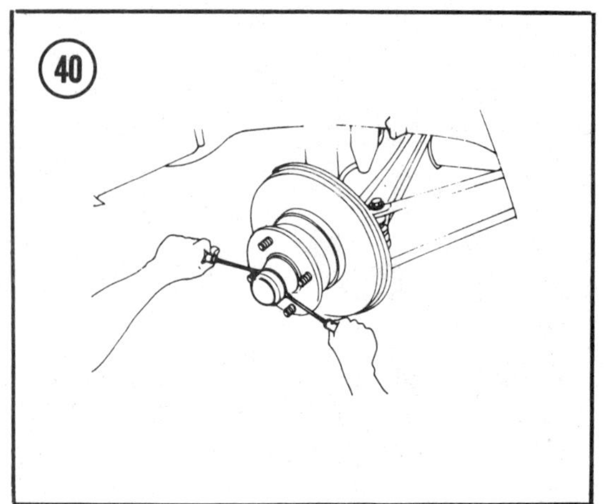

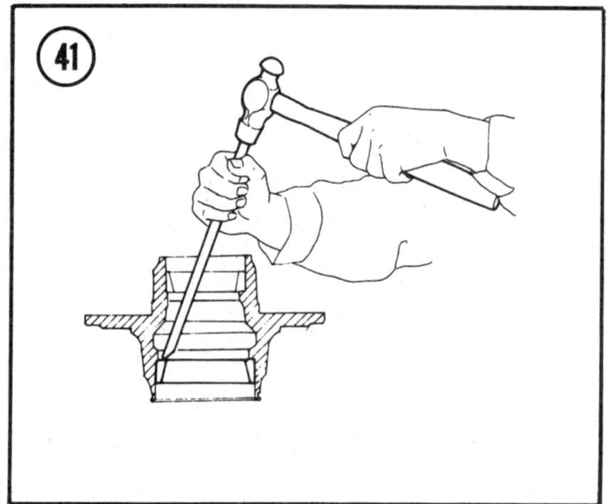

42

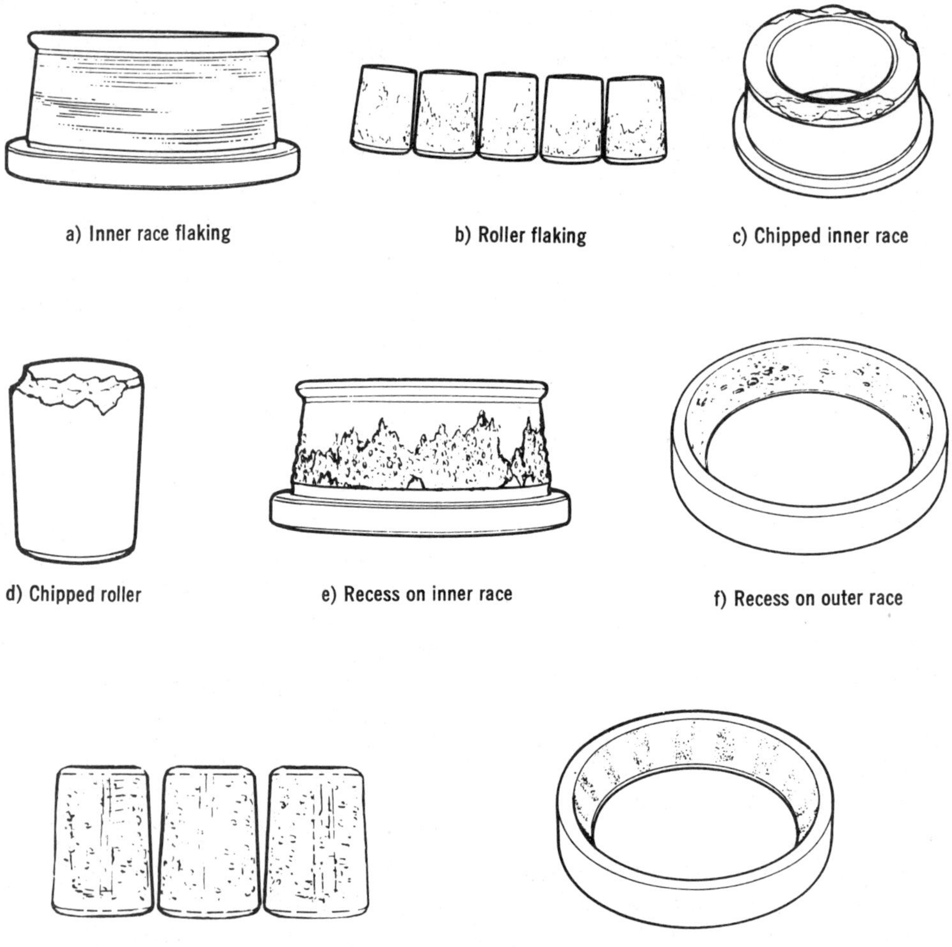

a) Inner race flaking

b) Roller flaking

c) Chipped inner race

d) Chipped roller

e) Recess on inner race

f) Recess on outer race

g) Recess on roller

h) Rust on outer race

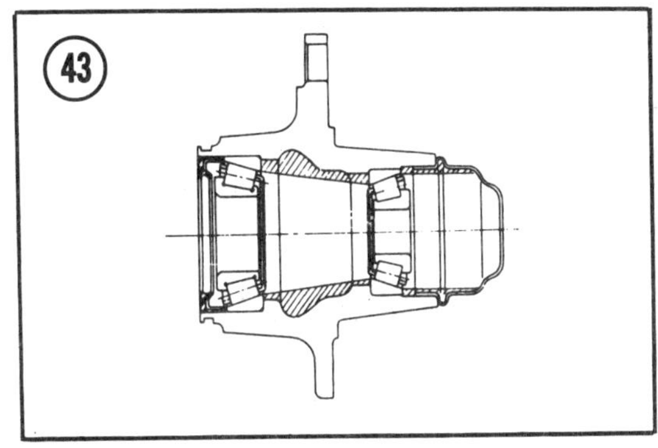

43

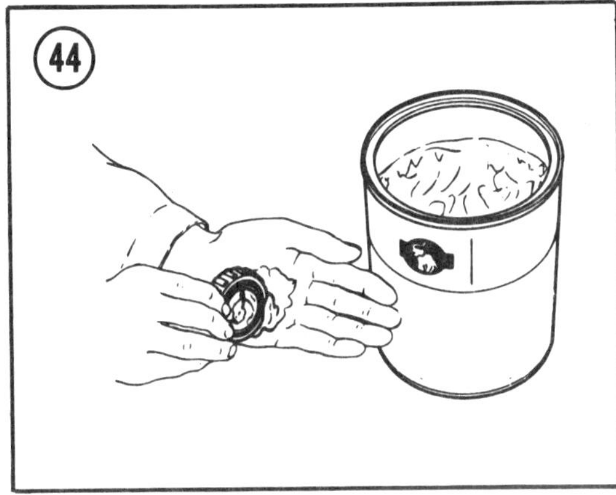

44

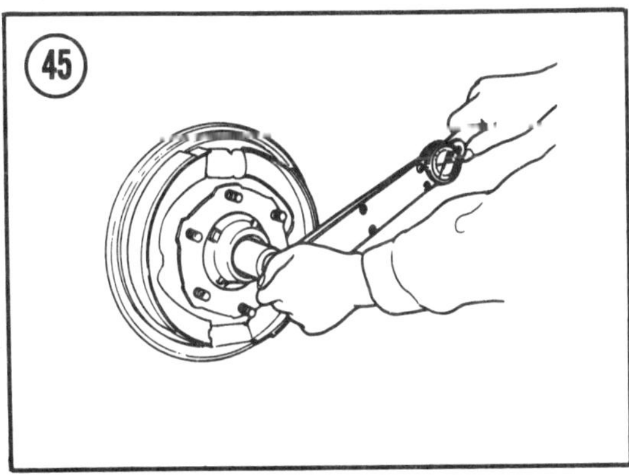

45

2. On 1970-1977 models, remove the brake drum (Chapter Ten).

3. Remove the grease cap from the wheel hub (**Figure 40**).

4. Remove the cotter pin from the wheel bearing locknut (early models) or stamped metal nut lock (later models). Remove the wheel bearing nut from the spindle.

5. Grasp the hub with both hands and pull it off the spindle.

6. Pry the grease seal out of the hub with a screwdriver. Remove the bearing cones.

7. Using a hammer and brass bar, tap the bearing outer races out of the hub (**Figure 41**).

Inspection

1. Thoroughly clean the wheel bearings and hub in solvent.

2. Inspect inner and outer races for rust, galling, and the bluish tint that indicates overheating. Rotate the bearings and check for roughness and excessive noise. Compare the races and rollers to the defective bearing parts shown in **Figure 42**. Replace any bearings that have similar defects.

Installation

1. Tap the outer bearing races into place in the hub. Use a drift (such as a piece of pipe) with the same diameter as the outer race.

2. Fill the hub and grease cap (shaded areas in **Figure 43**). Use multipurpose lithium grease.

3. Work as much grease as possible between the wheel bearing rollers (**Figure 44**).

4. Install the inner wheel bearing in the hub, then install the grease seal. Coat the grease seal lips with grease.

5. Apply a light coat of grease to the bearing spindle, including the threaded area. Install the hub (together with the brake disc on cars).

6. Install the outer wheel bearing. Lightly grease the bearing washer and the spindle nut threads. Install the washer and nut.

7. Adjust wheel bearings as described in the following procedure.

13

Adjustment (Drum Brakes)

1. Tighten the spindle nut to 22-25 ft.-lb. (3.0-3.5 mkg). See **Figure 45**.

2. Rotate the hub several turns in both directions, then retighten to specifications.

3. Back off the spindle nut 40-70°, until the cotter pin holes in nut and spindle are aligned.

> NOTE: *Later models use a plain nut and a stamped metal nut lock. The adjustment procedure is the same as for castellated locknuts.*

4. Rotate the hub. Check for noise or rough movement. If these are present, remove the wheel bearings and check for foreign material. If the hub rotates smoothly, attach a spring scale (**Figure 46**) and measure the force necessary to turn the hub. With new bearings, it should be 4.6 lb. (2.1 kg) or less. With used bearings, it should be 2.2 lb. (1 kg) or less. If within specifications, install a cotter pin and spread it. See **Figure 47**.
5. Install the grease cap in the hub.
6. Install the brake drum. See Chapter Ten.
7. Install the wheel(s) and lower the truck.

Adjustment (Disc Brakes)

1. Tighten the spindle nut to 25-29 ft.-lb. (3.5-4.0 mkg).
2. Turn the hub several turns in both directions to seat the bearings. Then retighten the spindle nut to 25-29 ft.-lb. (3.5-4.0 mkg).

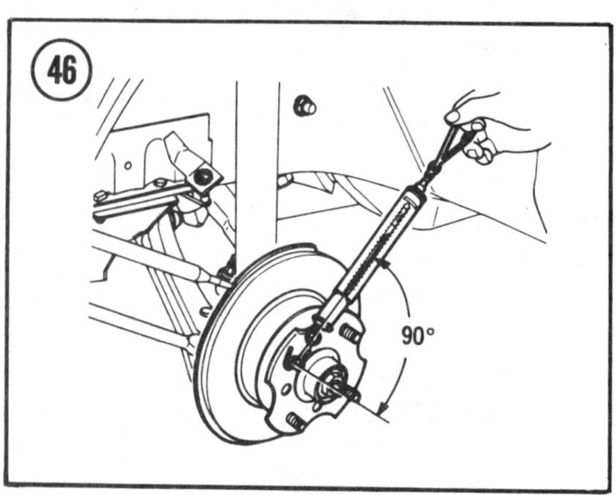

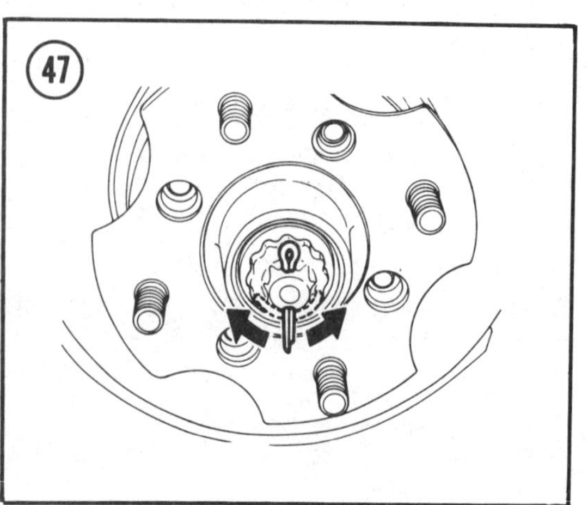

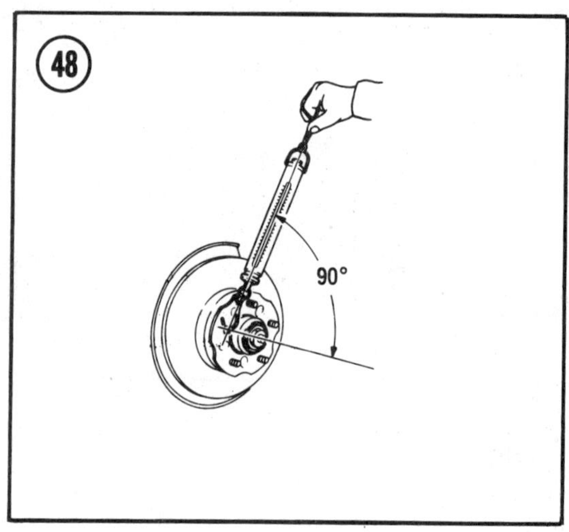

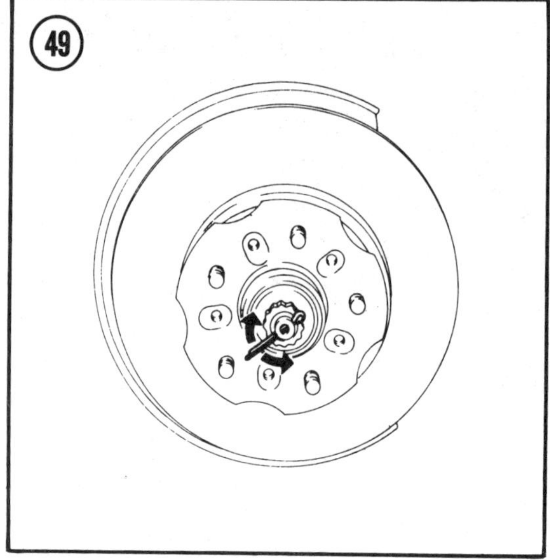

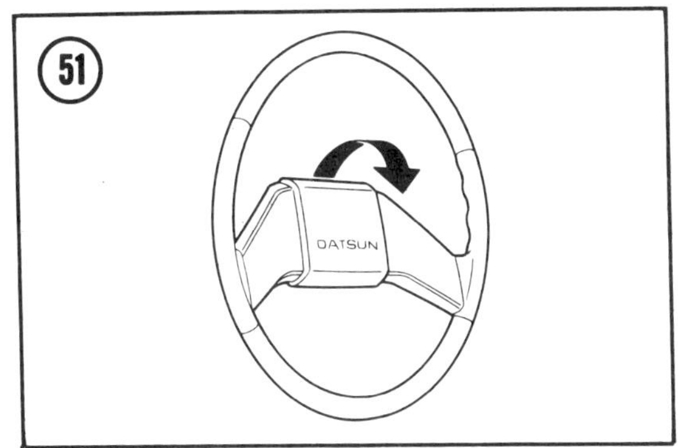

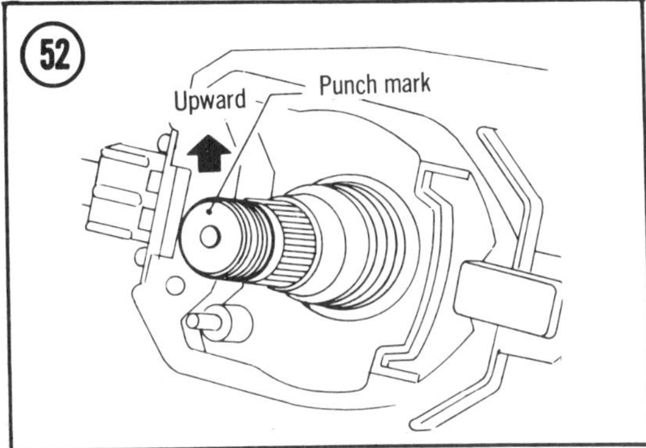

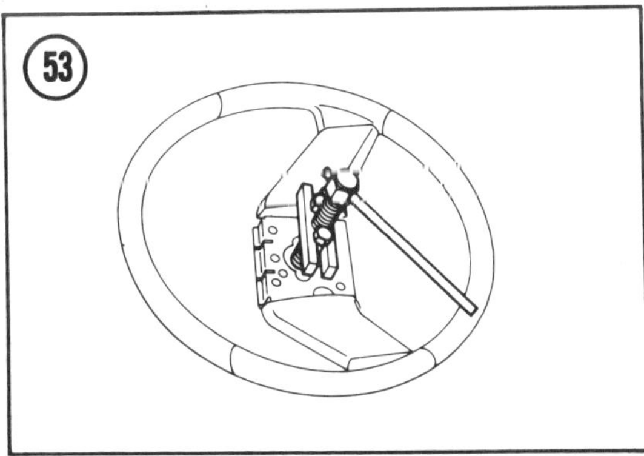

3. Back off the spindle nut 45°. Install the adjusting cap on the nut. Tighten until one of its slots aligns with the cotter pin hole.

NOTE: *Do not tighten more than 15°.*

4. Rotate the hub. Check for noise or rough movement. If these are present, remove the wheel bearings and check for foreign material. If the hub rotates smoothly, attach a spring scale **(Figure 48)** and measure the force necessary to turn the hub. With new bearings, it should be less than 6.4 lb. (2.9 kg). With used bearings, it should be less than 2.6 lb. (1.2 kg). If within specifications, install a cotter pin and spread it **(Figure 49)**.

STEERING (521 and 620)

Steering Wheel Removal/Installation

1. Disconnect negative cable from battery.
2. Turn the steering wheel to the straight ahead position.
3. Remove the horn pad. On 521 pickups, push down, turn clockwise, and pull up. On 620 pickups, remove the screws from the back of the steering wheel.
4. Remove the steering wheel nut.
5. Make alignment marks on steering wheel and column, then remove the wheel. It should be possible to remove the wheel by pulling gently on alternate sides. If not, use a puller like the one shown in **Figure 50**.

CAUTION

Do not pound on the wheel or use an impact puller. This could damage the steering column.

6. Install in the reverse order. Be sure to align the match marks on steering wheel and column. Tighten the steering wheel nut to 51-54 ft.-lb. (7.0-7.5 mkg).

Steering Wheel Removal/Installation (720)

1. Disconnect the negative cable from the battery.
2. Remove the horn pad as shown in **Figure 51**.
3. Make sure the punch mark in the end of the steering column (**Figure 52**) is straight up.
4. Remove the steering wheel nut.
5. Remove the steering wheel with a puller as shown in **Figure 53**. These are available inexpensively at auto parts stores.

CAUTION

Do not pound on the wheel or use an impact puller. This may damage the steering column.

6. Installation is the reverse of removal. Make sure the column punch mark is straight up,

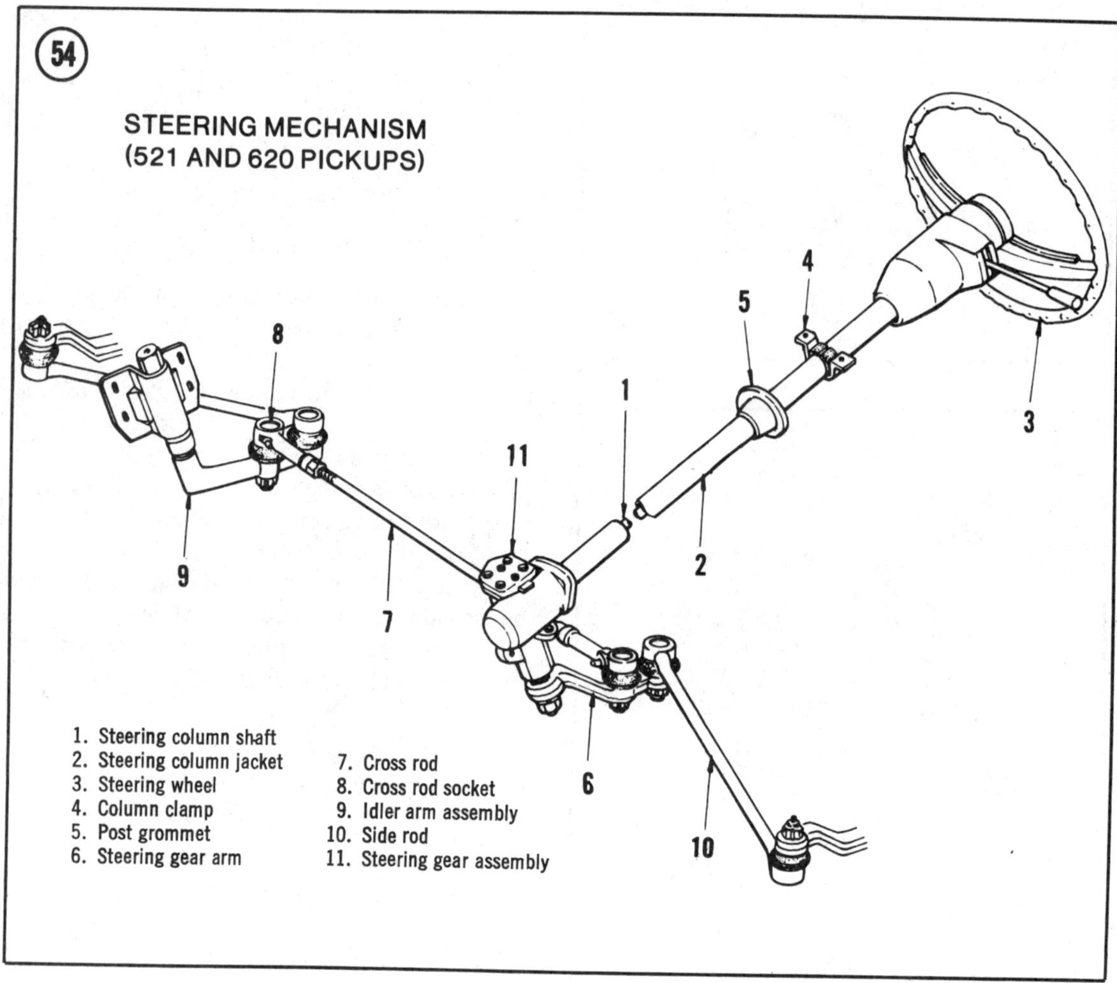

and the steering wheel is in the straight-ahead position. Tighten the steering wheel nut to 29-36 ft.-lb. (4-5 mkg).

Steering Column Removal/Installation (521 and 620)

Figure 54 shows a typical steering mechanism. Refer to it as needed for this procedure.

1. Remove the steering wheel as described previously.
2. Remove the steering column shell (**Figure 55**).
3. Remove 2 screws securing the turn signal switch. Take it off the steering column (**Figure 56**).
4. Remove 4 screws or bolts securing the steering column to the floor (**Figure 57**).
5. Remove 2 bolts or screws from the steering column clamp (**Figure 58**).
6. Detach the gear arm from the steering gear (**Figure 59**). Use a puller such as Datsun ST 27200000 (**Figure 60**). Use a small gear puller if the special tool is not available.
7. Remove 3 nuts and bolts securing the steering gear to the frame.
8. Remove the steering column and steering gear into the passenger compartment.
9. Installation is the reverse of these steps. Tighten all nuts and bolts to specifications (end of chapter). Check steering gear oil as described in Chapter Three.

Steering Column Removal/Installation (720)

1. Remove the steering wheel as described in this chapter.

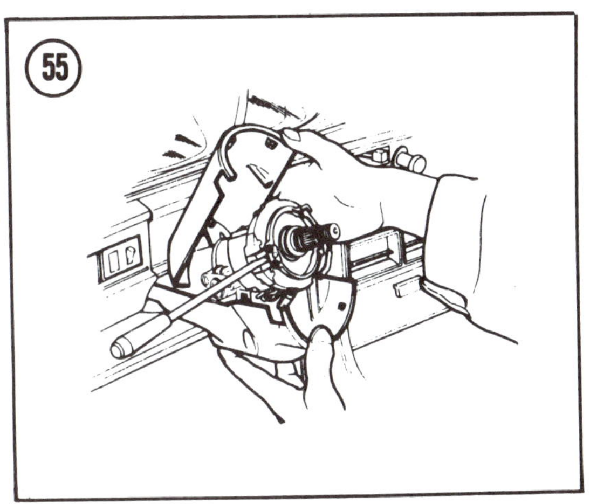
55

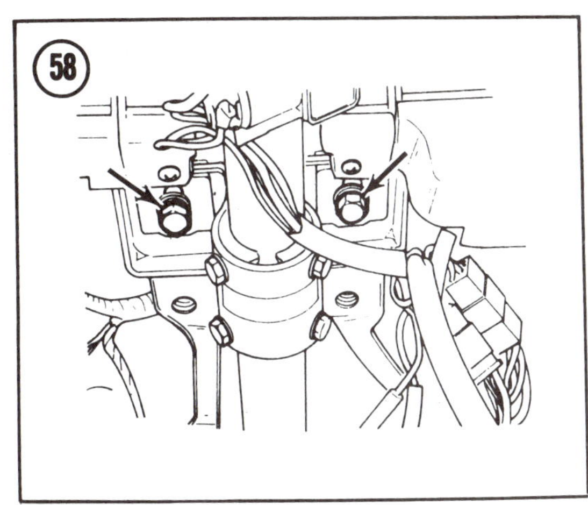
58

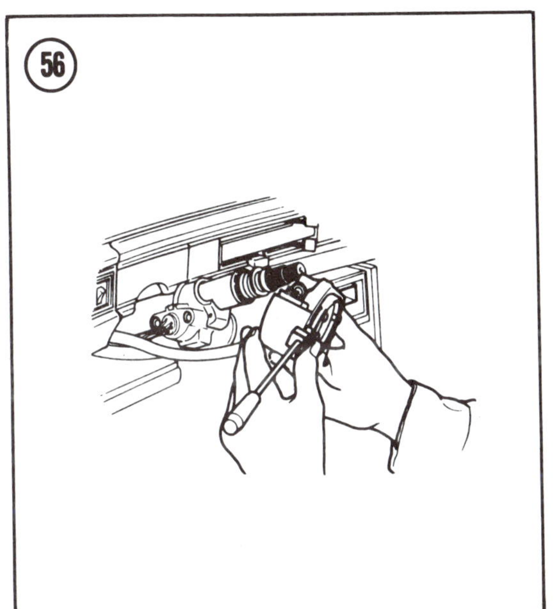
56

59

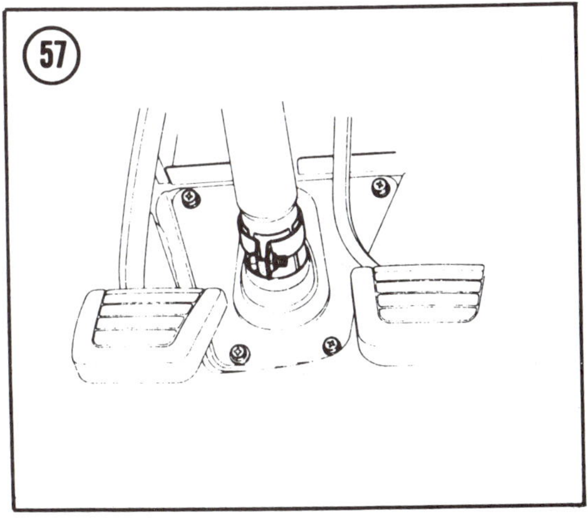
57

60

2. Remove the steering column shell (**Figure 61**).
3. Disconnect the combination switch wiring connectors. Remove the switch mounting screw (**Figure 62**), then take the switch off the column.
4. Remove the bolt securing the end of the steering column to the steering gear. See **Figure 63**.

NOTE
The bolt passes through a notch in the steering gear shaft, so it must be removed, not just loosened.

5. Remove the heater duct (**Figure 64**).
6. Detach the steering column grommet from the floor. See **Figure 65**.
7. Unbolt the column bracket (**Figure 66**). Lower the column, then pull it into the passenger compartment.
8. Installation is the reverse of removal. Make sure the punch mark on the end of the steering column is straight up, and that the

63

64

61

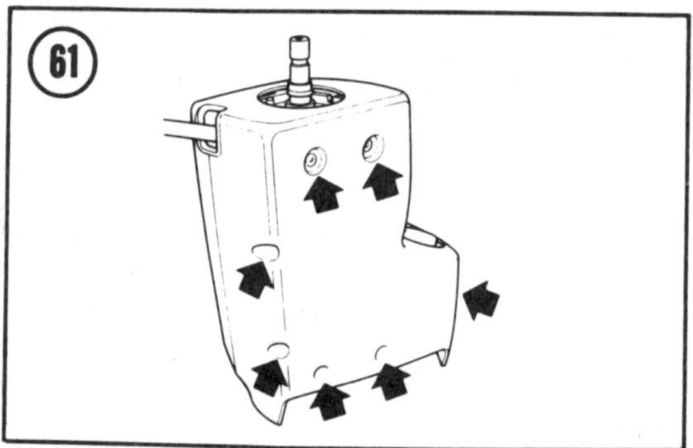

65

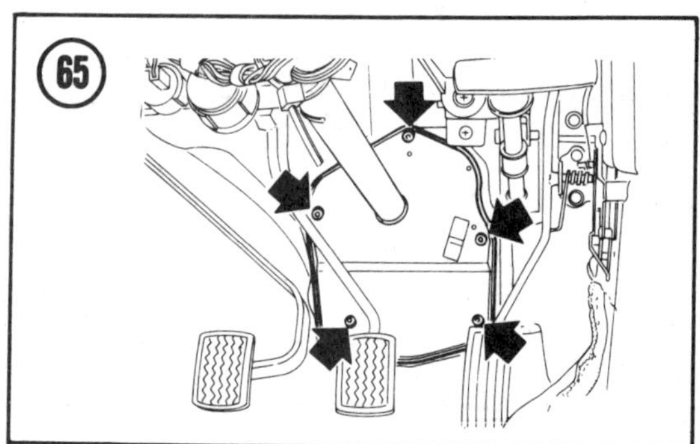

62

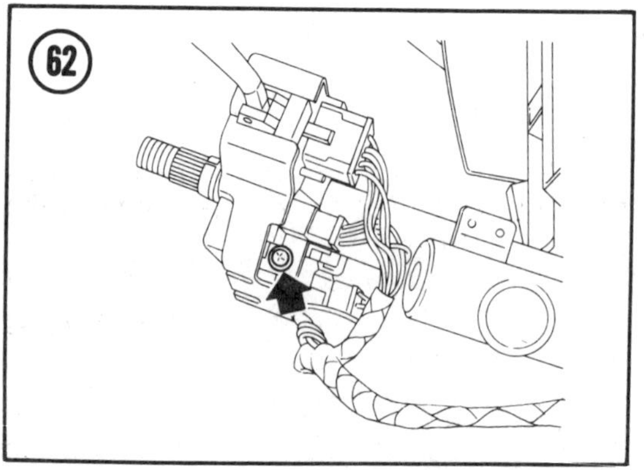

66

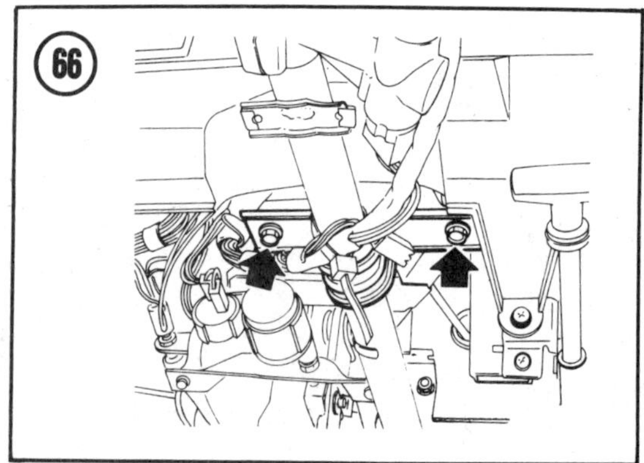

67

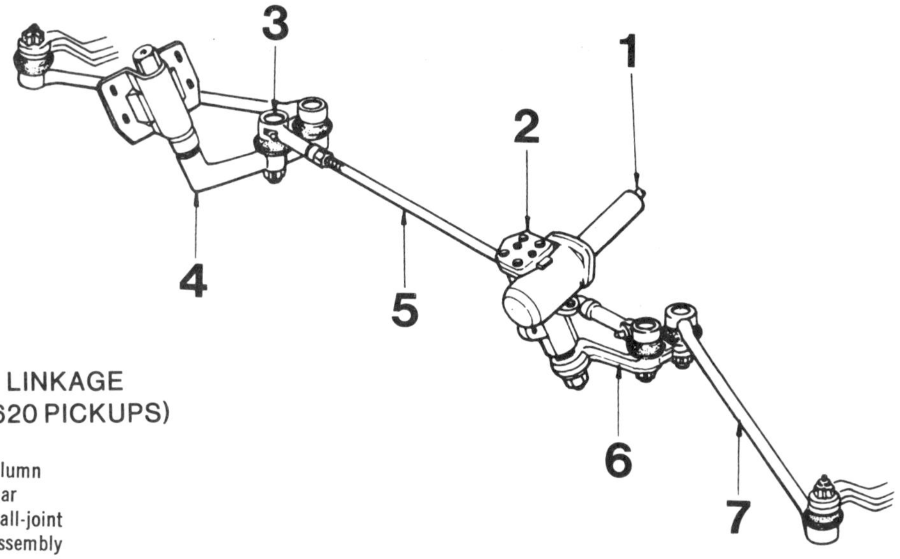

STEERING LINKAGE
(521 AND 620 PICKUPS)

1. Steering column
2. Steering gear
3. Cross rod ball-joint
4. Idler arm assembly
5. Cross rod
6. Steering gear arm
7. Tie rod

steering wheel is in the straight-ahead position.

Steering Linkage Overhaul (521 and 620)

Figure 67 shows the 521 and 620 steering linkage. If the linkage shows signs of looseness, it should be overhauled as follows.

1. Set the parking brake. Place the transmission in FIRST (manual) or PARK (automatic).
2. Loosen the front wheel nuts, jack up the front end of the truck, place it on jackstands, and remove the front wheel.
3. Remove the cotter pins and locknuts from the outer tie rod ball-joints.
4. Detach the tie rod ball-joints from the knuckle arms. If available, use a fork-type separator such as Datsun ST 27850000 (Kent-Moore J-25730-A). See **Figure 68**. If the special tool is not available, hold a large hammer or heavy steel body tool against the knuckle arm boss (the part that the ball-joint stud goes through) and tap the other side of the boss with a hammer. Do not tap the ball-joint stud, ball-joint socket, or tie rod.

68

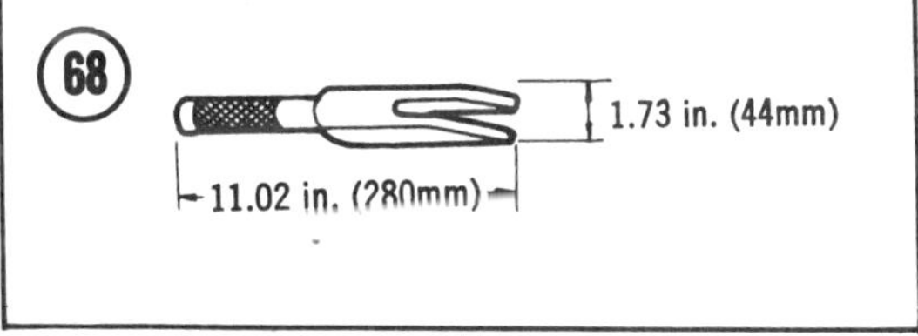

5. Scribe match marks on the steering gear arm and steering gear. Detach the gear arm from the gear with a puller such as ST 27200000 (**Figure 60**). Use a small gear puller if the special tool is not available.
6. Remove 2 bolts securing the idler arm assembly to the frame.
7. Remove the steering linkage as an assembly.
8. Separate the remaining steering linkage ball-joints as described in Step 4. Remove the screw bushing from the idler arm assembly.
9. Clean metal parts in solvent. Do not immerse ball-joints. Wipe them with a rag dipped in solvent.
10. Check tie rods and the cross rod for bends, cracks, or damaged threads. Replace if

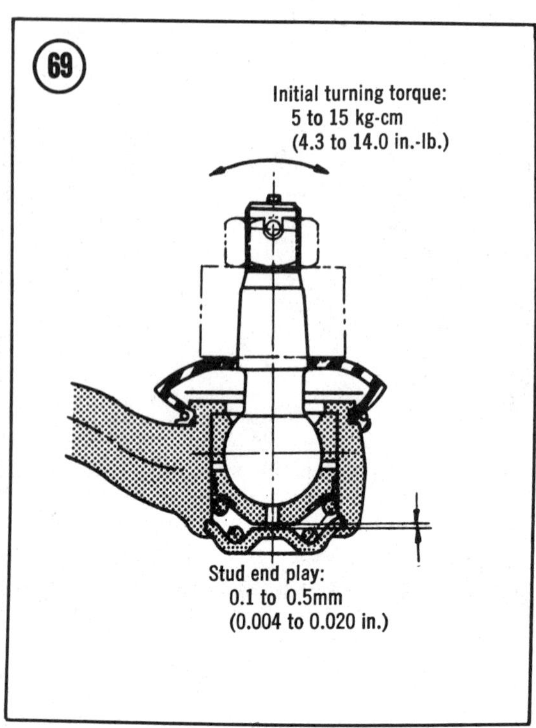

these conditions are found.

11. Check the idler arm bushings for wear or damage. Replace as needed.

12. Place each ball-joint in a vise with the stud upward (**Figure 69**). Set up a dial gauge with its pointer contacting the end of the stud. Pull the stud up and down and measure the movement. This is axial play. Permissible play is 0.004-0.020 in. (0.1-0.5 mm). Replace any ball-joints with play outside this range.

13. Assemble and install by reversing Steps 1-8. Tighten all nuts and bolts to specifications (end of chapter).

Steering Linkage Overhaul (720)

If the linkage shows signs of looseness, it should be overhauled. Refer to **Figure 70**.

1. Set the handbrake. Place the transmission in FIRST (manual) or PARK (automatic).

2. Loosen the front wheel nuts. Jack up the front end of the truck, place it on jackstands, and remove the front wheels.

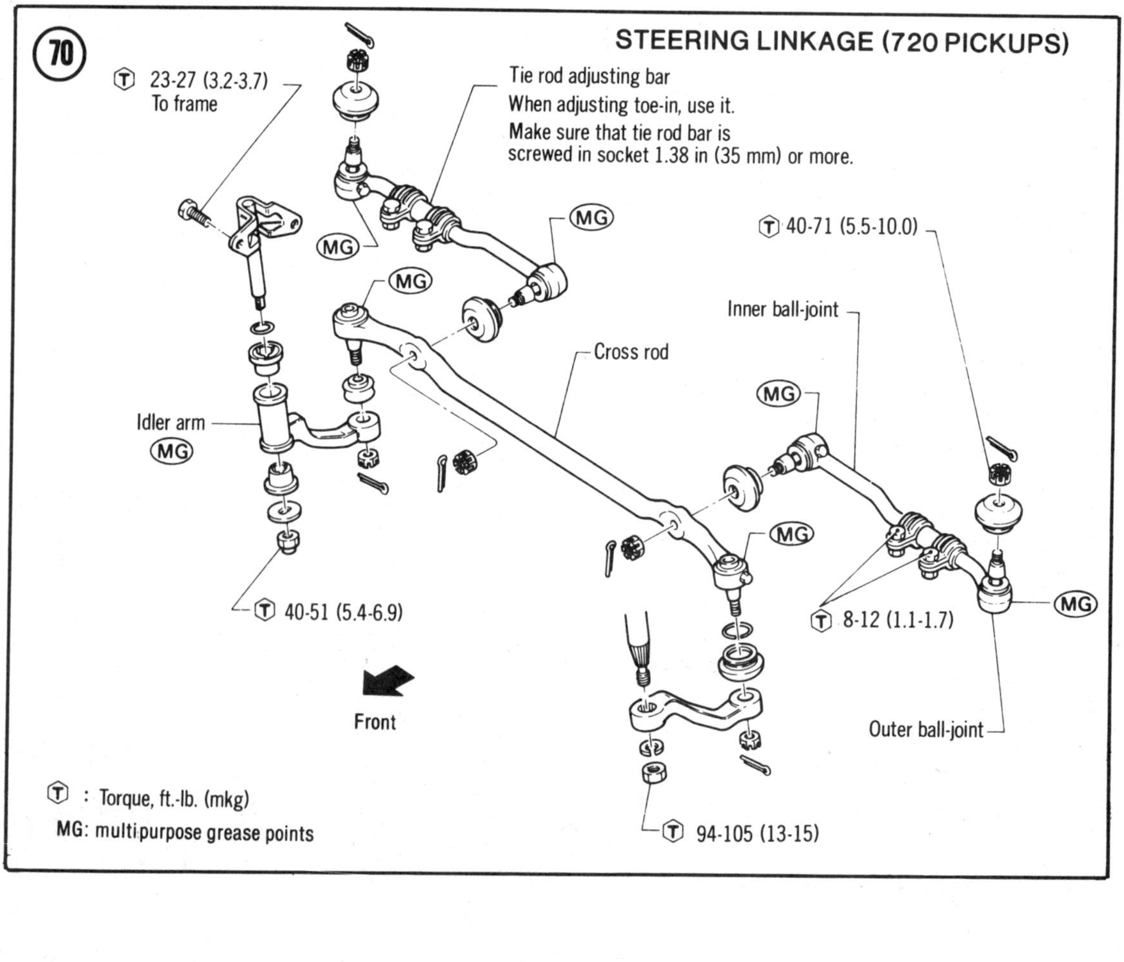

70

STEERING LINKAGE (720 PICKUPS)

T 23-27 (3.2-3.7)
To frame

Tie rod adjusting bar
When adjusting toe-in, use it.
Make sure that tie rod bar is
screwed in socket 1.38 in (35 mm) or more.

MG

MG

T 40-71 (5.5-10.0)

MG

Inner ball-joint

Cross rod

MG

Idler arm
MG

MG

MG

T 8-12 (1.1-1.7)

T 40-51 (5.4-6.9)

Front

Outer ball-joint

T : Torque, ft.-lb. (mkg)
MG: multipurpose grease points

T 94-105 (13-15)

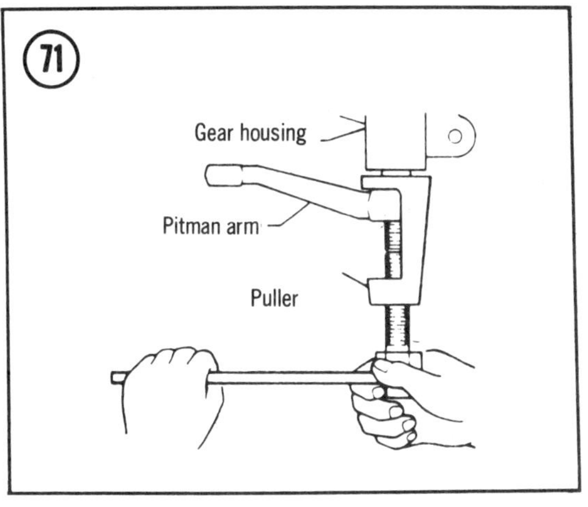

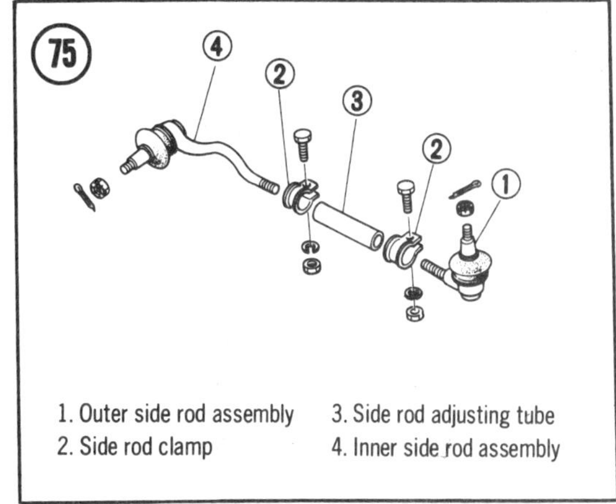

1. Outer side rod assembly
2. Side rod clamp
3. Side rod adjusting tube
4. Inner side rod assembly

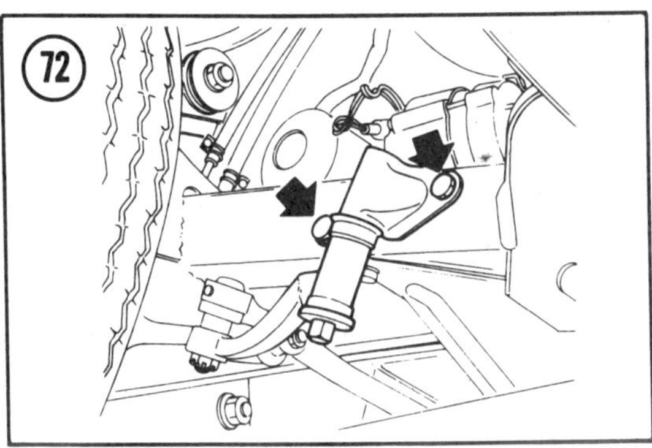

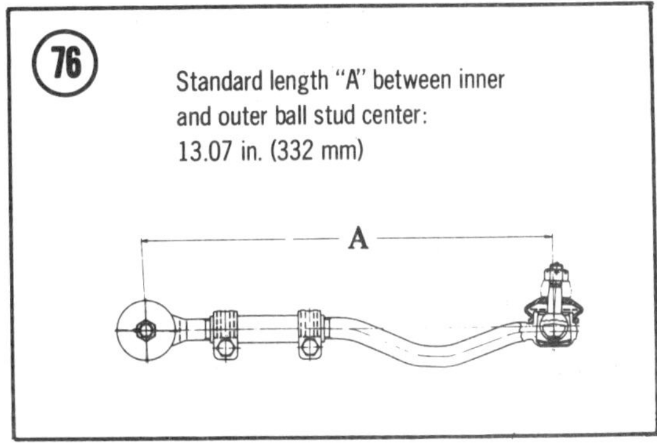

Standard length "A" between inner and outer ball stud center: 13.07 in. (332 mm)

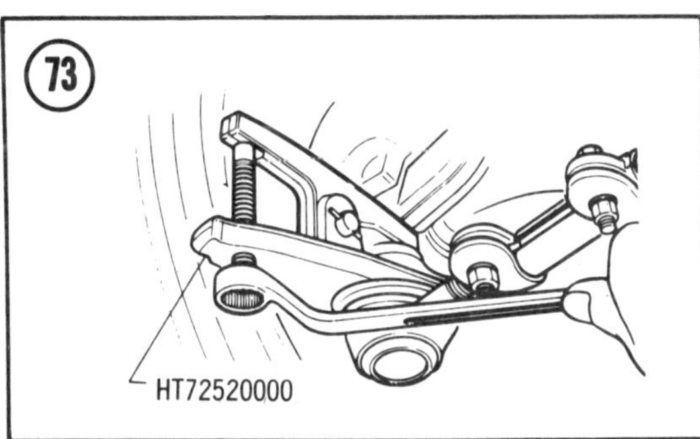

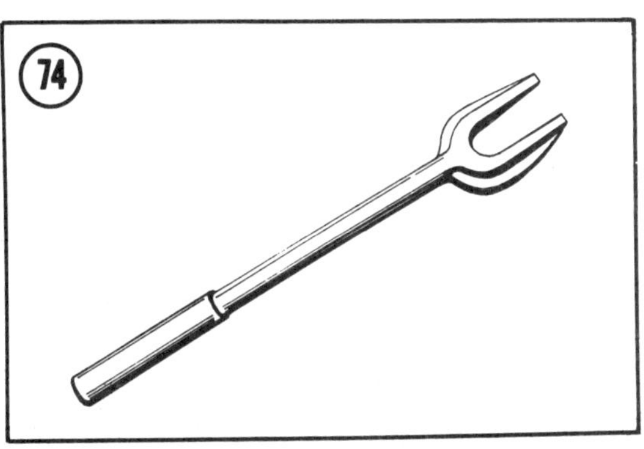

3. Remove the nut securing the pitman arm to the steering gear. Detach the pitman arm from the steering gear with a pitman arm puller (**Figure 71**). These are available from tool rental dealers.
4. Unbolt the idler arm assembly from the frame. See **Figure 72**.
5. Remove the nuts securing the tie rods to the knuckle arms. Detach the tie rod ends from the knuckle arms. Use a puller as shown in **Figure 73**, or a fork-type separator (**Figure 74**). These are available from rental dealers.
6. Take the steering linkage out from under the truck.
7. Check tie rod ends for looseness or damaged dust covers. If these are found, replace the tie rod ends.
8. To remove tie ends, loosen the clamps, then unscrew the tie rod ends. See **Figure 75**.
9. When installing new tie rod ends, position the ends at 90° from each other. Tie rod length should be 13.07 in. (332mm) between stud centerlines. See **Figure 76**.

13

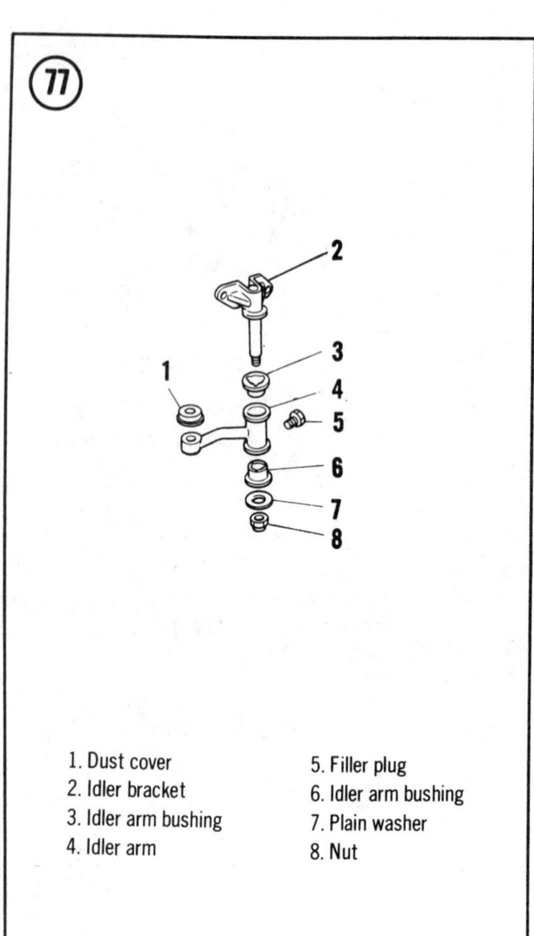

1. Dust cover
2. Idler bracket
3. Idler arm bushing
4. Idler arm
5. Filler plug
6. Idler arm bushing
7. Plain washer
8. Nut

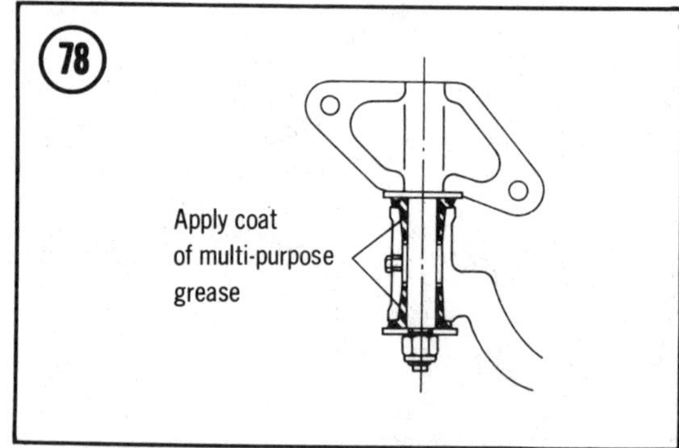

10. Disassemble the idler arm assembly, referring to **Figure 77**. Check all parts, especially rubber bushings, for wear or damage. Replace as needed.

11. Reassemble the idler arm assembly. Apply multipurpose grease to the points shown in **Figure 78**.

12. Reassemble the linkage, referring to **Figure 70**. At points labeled "MG," remove the filler plugs and install grease nipples. Inject multipurpose lithium grease into the grease nipples, then remove them and install the plugs.

13. Installation is the reverse of removal. Tighten all fasteners to specifications shown in **Figure 70**. Have wheel alignment checked by a Datsun dealer or front end shop.

Table 1 SPECIFICATIONS

Camber	
1970-1977	15'-2° 15'
1978-1979	15'-1° 15'
1980-on	0 +/- 1°
Caster	
1970-1977	1° 5'-2° 35'
1978-1979	35'-2° 35'
1980-on	50'-1° 50'
Kingpin inclination	6° 15'
Steering axis inclination	8° 30'-9° 30'
Toe-in	
1970-1976	0.04-0.57 in. (1-5mm)
1977	0.08-0.12 in. (2-3mm)
1978-on	5-7 mm (0.20-0.28 in.)
Steering lock angles, 1970-1977	
Inside wheel	35-37°
Outside wheel	30-32°
Steering lock angles, 1978-1979	
Inside wheel	34-36°
Outside wheel	29 1/2-31 1/2°
Steering lock angles, 1980-on	
Inside wheel	34-36°
Outside wheel	30-32°
Truck height dimension "H"	
521 pickup	2.99-3.19 in. (76-81mm)
620 pickup (through 1976)	3.07-3.23 in. (78-82mm)
620 pickup (1977)	3.11-3.31 in (79-84mm)
620 pickup (1978- 1979)	4.92 in.(125mm)
720 pickup (1980-on)	4.88-5.08 in. (124-129mm)

13

Table 2 TIGHTENING TORQUES

Fastener	Ft.-lb.	Mkg
Shock absorber upper end		
521 pickup	11-15	1.5-2.1
620 and 720 pickups	12-16	1.6-2.2
Shock absorber lower end		
521 pickup	26-31	3.6-4.3
620 and 720 pickups	22-30	3.1-4.1
Stabilizer brackets		
521 pickup	11-15	1.5-2.1
620 and 720 pickups	12-16	1.6-2.2

(continued)

Table 2 TIGHTENING TORQUES (continued)

Tension rod nuts and bracket bolts		
521 pickup	11-15	1.5-2.1
620 pickup (1972-1977)	12-16	1.6-2.2
Tension rod front nut (1978-1979)	22-30	3.1-4.1
Tension rod front nut (1980-on)	87-116	12-16
Tension rod bolts (1978-on)	28-38	3.9-5.2
Torque arm outer end		
521 pickup	18-22	2.5-3.1
620 and 720 pickups	20-27	2.7-3.7
Torque arm inner end		
521 pickup	6-9	0.8-1.2
620 pickup (through 1977)	13-19	1.8-2.6
620 and 720 pickups (1978-on)	26-33	3.6-4.6
Anchor bolt locknut		
521	29-36	4-5
620 and 720 pickups	22-30	3.1-4.1
Rubber bumper		
521 pickup	8-12	1.1-1.6
620 and 720 pickups	6-8	0.8-1.1
Kingpin lockbolt (1970-1977)	15-18	2.1-2.5
Ball-joint stud nut (1978-on)		
Upper	58-72	8-10
Lower (1978-1979)	124-141	17.2-19.5
Lower (1980-on)	87-123	12-17
Knuckle arm		
521 pickup	81-95	11.2-13.2
620 pickup (through 1977)	74-88	10.3-12.1
620 and 720 pickups (1978-on)	53-72	7.3-9.9
Lower link spindle nut		
521 pickup	62-69	8.5-9.5
620 pickup (through 1977)	54-58	7.4-8.0
620 and 720 pickups (1978-on)	80-108	11.1-15.0
Lower link screw bushings (through 1977)		
521 pickup	174-181	24-25
620 pickup	145-217	20-30
Upper link spindle bolts		
521 pickup	40-45	5.5-6.2
620 pickup (through 1977)	51-65	7-9
620 and 720 pickups (1978-on)	80-108	11.1-15.0
Upper link screw bushings (through 1977)		
521 pickup	174-181	24-25
620 pickup	253-398	35-55
Upper link bushing nuts (1978-on)	56-76	7.7-10.5
Steering gear housing to body		
521 pickup	23-27	3.2-3.7
620 and 720 pickups (through 1980)	33-38	4.6-5.3
720 pickup (1981)	62-71	8.6-9.8

(continued)

Table 2 TIGHTENING TORQUES (continued)

Pitman arm nut		
521 pickup	101	14
620 and 720 pickups	94-108	13-15
Cross rod and tie rod ball-joints		
521 pickup	44-51	6-7
620 pickup (through 1974)	40-55	5.5-7.6
620 and 720 pickups (1975-on)	40-72	5.5-10.0
Steering wheel nut		
521 and 620 pickups	51-54	7.0-7.5
720 pickup	29-36	4-5
Brake disc to hub	38-52	28-38

CHAPTER FOURTEEN

BODY

This chapter includes service procedures for the seats, bumpers, grille, hood, fenders, tailgate, bed, and cab. Door window replacement is also covered. Other repairs require special skills and equipment. These should be left to a dealer or body shop.

SEATS

Removal/Installation (521)

To remove seat, remove four mounting nuts and take it out. See **Figure 1**. Installation is the reverse of removal.

Removal/Installation (620)

To remove, undo the nuts securing the front ends of the frame rails. Then remove the bolts securing the rear ends. See **Figure 2** (bench seats) or **Figure 3** (bucket seats). Installation is the reverse of removal.

Front Seat Removal/Installation (720)

1. Slide the seat back and remove its front mounting bolts. See **Figure 4**.
2. Slide the seat forward and remove its rear mounting bolts. See **Figure 4**.
3. Installation is the reverse of removal.

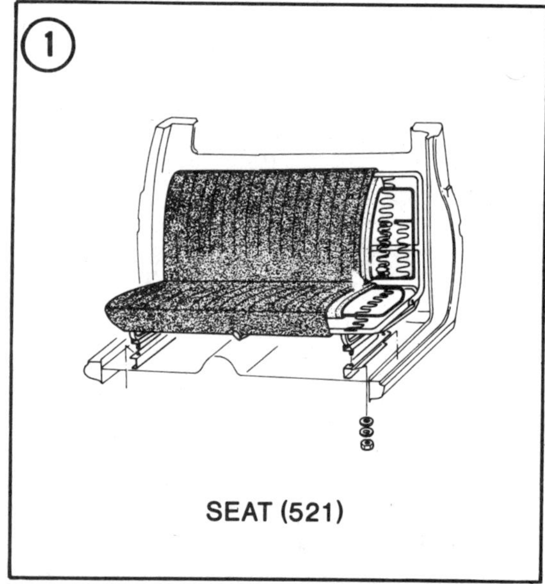

SEAT (521)

Jump Seat Removal/Installation (King Cab)

1. Lift up the seat cushion, remove its mounting screws, and take the cushion out.
2. Remove the mounting screws securing the lower edge of the seatback. Lift the seatback up and out.
3. Installation is the reverse of removal.

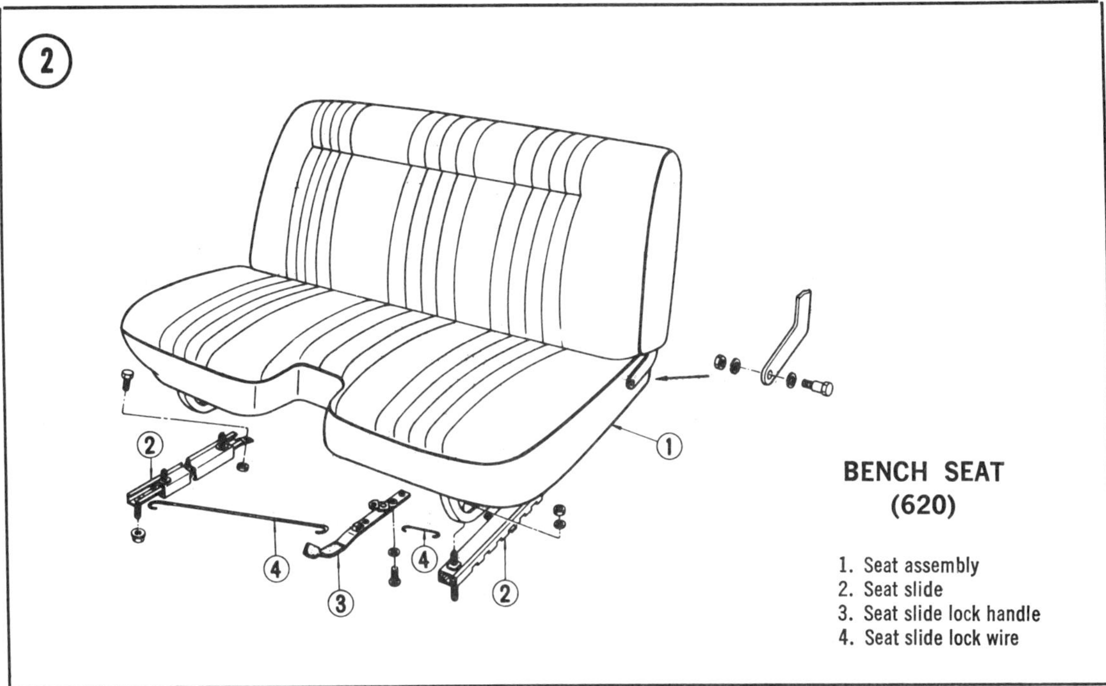

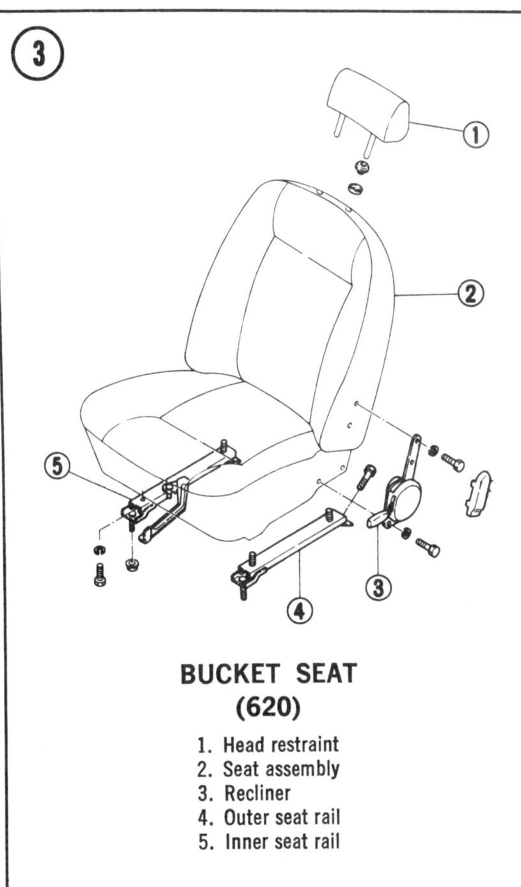

GRILLE

Removal/Installation (521 and 620)

To remove, open the hood, remove the grille attaching screws, and take the grille out. See **Figure 5** (521) or **Figure 6** (620). Installation is the reverse of removal.

Removal/Installation (720)

1. Referring to **Figure 7**, turn the grille fasteners 1/4 turn with a standard screwdriver. Detach the fasteners and lift the grille out.
2. Installation is the reverse of removal. Insert the fasteners into the grille from the rear.

BUMPERS

Removal/Installation (521 and 620)

1. Remove the bumper-to-fender nuts or bolts. See **Figure 8** (521) or **Figure 9** (620).
2. Remove the bumper-to-frame bolts. Pull the bumper straight forward.
3. Installation is the reverse of removal.

Front Bumper Removal/Installation (720)

1. Disconnect the negative cable from the battery.

4

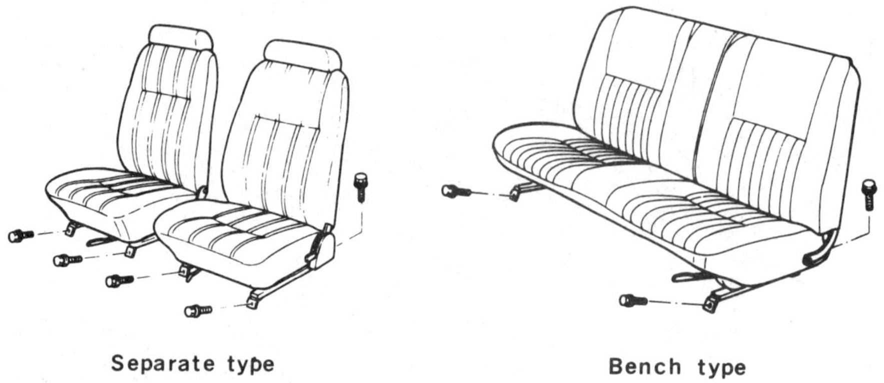

FRONT SEATS (720)

5

GRILLE — 521

1. Upper radiator grille surrounding
2. Radiator grille
3. Headlamp rim
4. Side radiator grille surroundings
5. Lower radiator grille surroundings

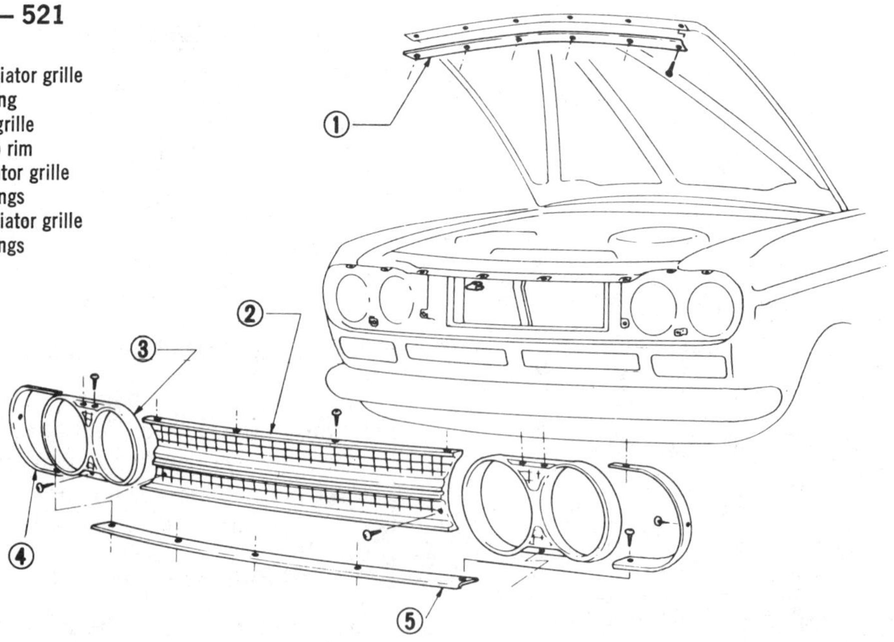

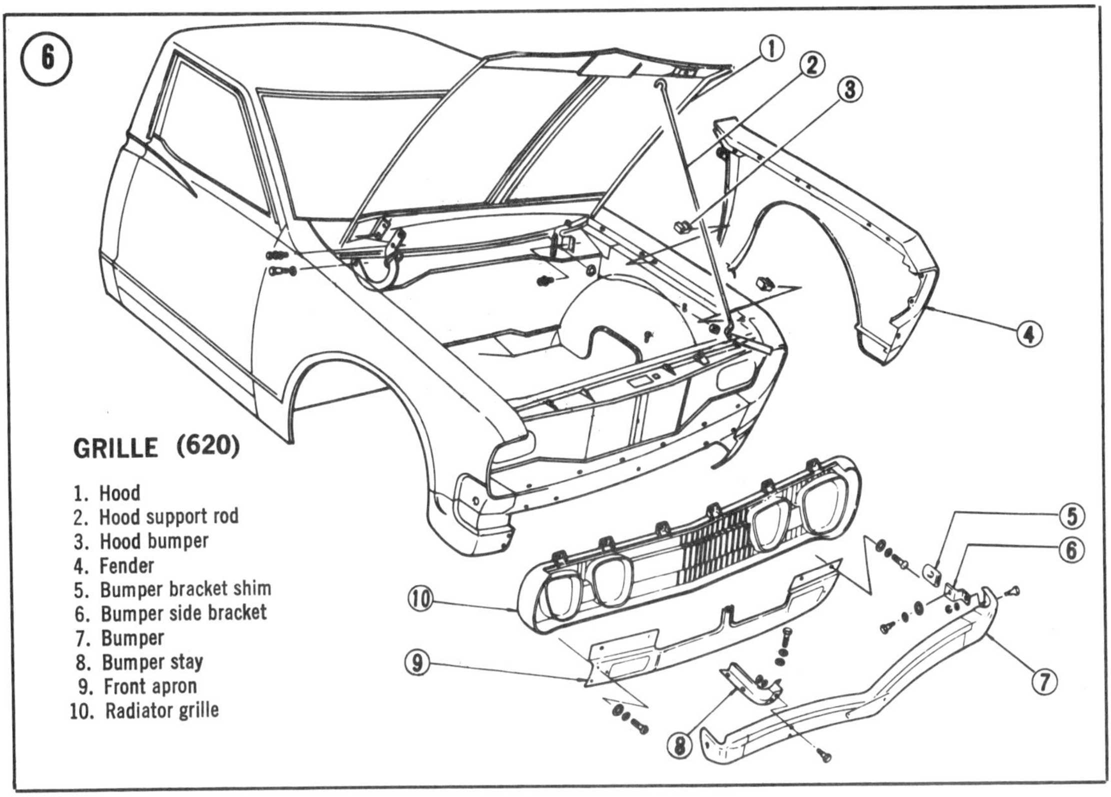
6
1
2
3
4
5
6
7
8
9
10
GRILLE (620)
1. Hood
2. Hood support rod
3. Hood bumper
4. Fender
5. Bumper bracket shim
6. Bumper side bracket
7. Bumper
8. Bumper stay
9. Front apron
10. Radiator grille

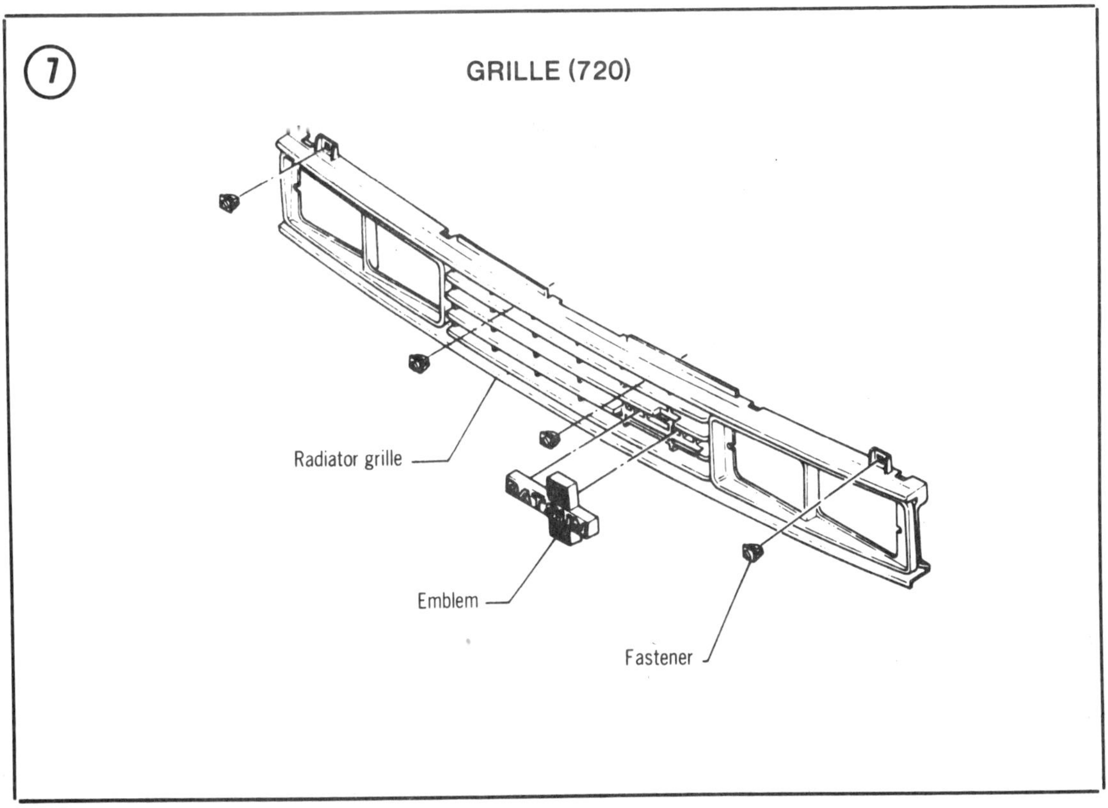
7
GRILLE (720)
Radiator grille
Emblem
Fastener

2. Remove the bumper mounting bolts (**Figure 10**). Take the bumper partway out, disconnect the wiring for the front combination lamps, then remove the bumper.
3. Installation is the reverse of removal.

Rear Bumper Removal/Installation (720)

To remove the rear bumper, remove its mounting bolts and take it out. See **Figure 11**.

Installation is the reverse of removal.

HOOD

Adjustment

1. If the hood moves forward, back, or to one side when closed, adjust the hood latch. On 521's, the male side is adjustable front to rear, and the female side from side to side. See **Figures 12** and **13**. On 620's and 720's, the male side is adjustable in front-to-rear and side-to-side directions. See **Figure 14**.

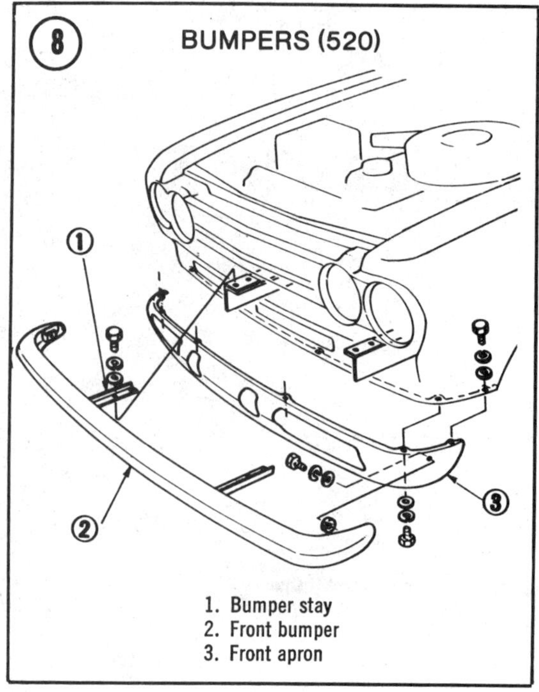

BUMPERS (520)

1. Bumper stay
2. Front bumper
3. Front apron

9

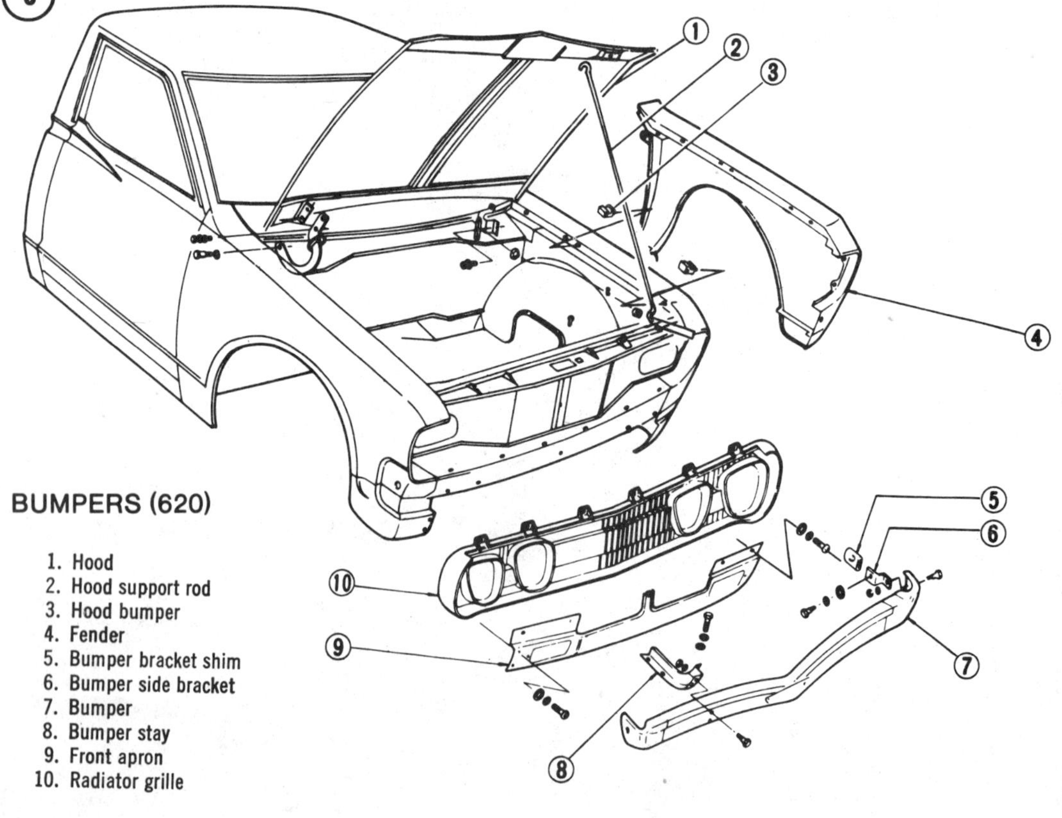

BUMPERS (620)

1. Hood
2. Hood support rod
3. Hood bumper
4. Fender
5. Bumper bracket shim
6. Bumper side bracket
7. Bumper
8. Bumper stay
9. Front apron
10. Radiator grille

(10)

BUMPERS (720)

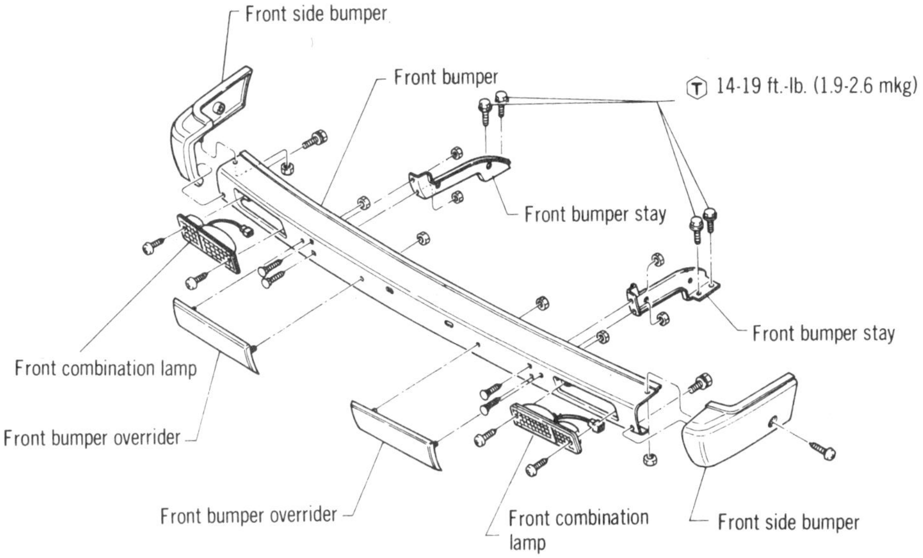

Front side bumper
Front bumper
Ⓣ 14-19 ft.-lb. (1.9-2.6 mkg)
Front bumper stay
Front bumper stay
Front combination lamp
Front bumper overrider
Front bumper overrider
Front combination lamp
Front side bumper

(11)

REAR BUMPER (720)

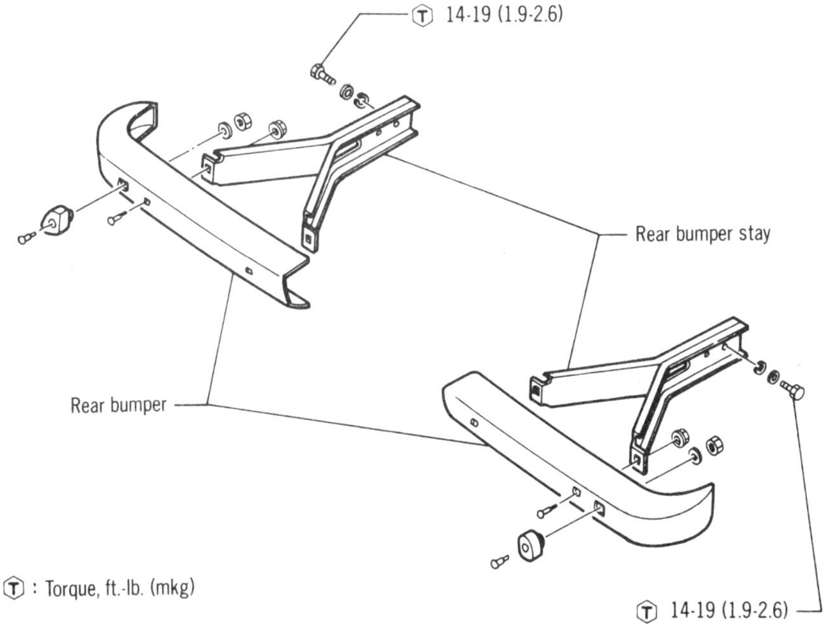

Ⓣ 14-19 (1.9-2.6)
Rear bumper stay
Rear bumper
Ⓣ : Torque, ft.-lb. (mkg)
Ⓣ 14-19 (1.9-2.6)

2. To adjust hood tightness, loosen the dovetail bolt locknut (**Figure 15**). Turn the dovetail bolt in or out with a screwdriver.
3. To align the rear edge of the hood, loosen the hinge bolts just enough so the hood will move. Close the hood, position it, then open the hood and tighten the hinge bolts.
4. To adjust hood height, loosen the locknuts securing the rubber bumpers. Turn the bumpers to raise or lower them, then tighten the locknuts.

Removal/Installation

1. Open the hood. Place a thick rag between the rear edge and the cowl top grille.
2. While an assistant supports one side of the hood, unbolt the hinges.
3. Lift the hood off.
4. Installation is the reverse of removal.

FENDER REMOVAL/INSTALLATION

1. If the inside of the fender is dirty, hose it out so you can see the mounting bolts.
2. Remove the front bumper, grille, front apron, and cowl top grille.
3. Disconnect the wires for side marker and turn signal lights.
4. On 521's, remove 2 bolts securing the headlamp assembly to the fender. See **Figure 16**.
5. Remove the fender's mounting bolts. See **Figure 17** (521), **Figure 6** (620), or **Figure 18** (720).

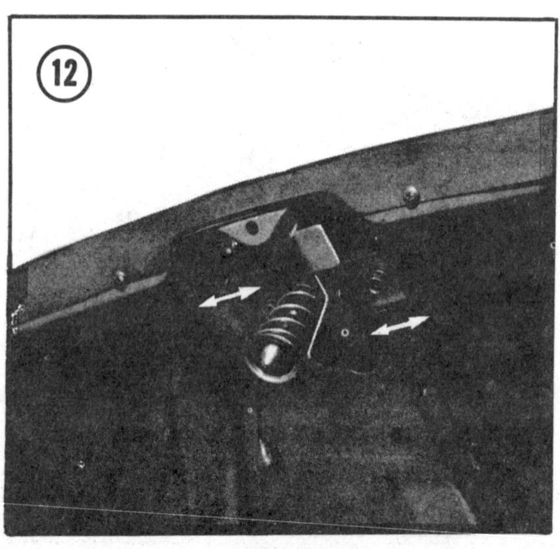

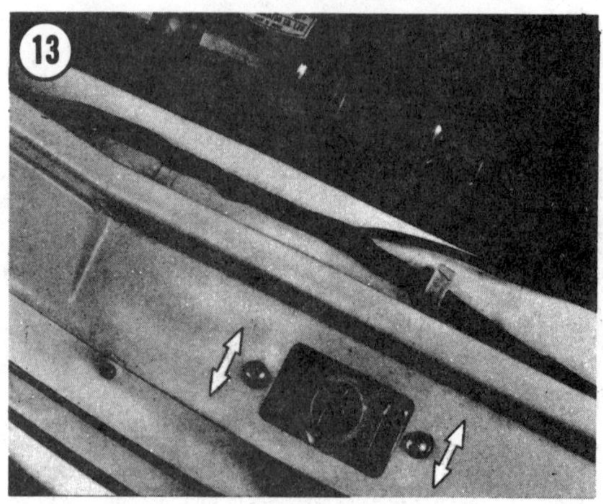

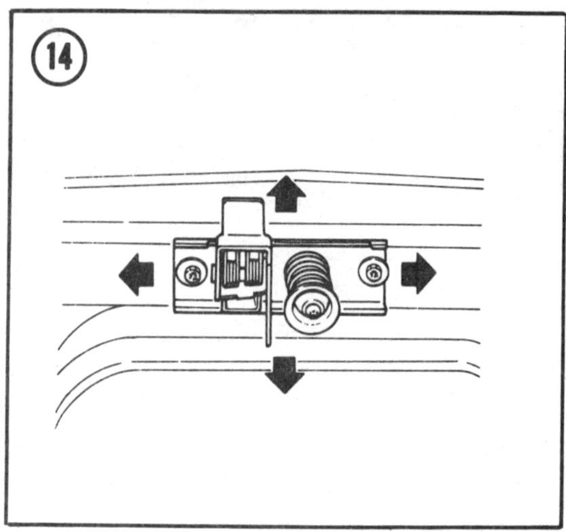

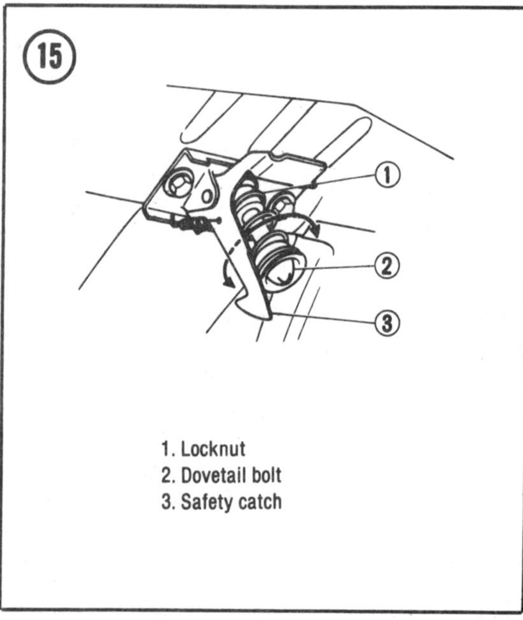

1. Locknut
2. Dovetail bolt
3. Safety catch

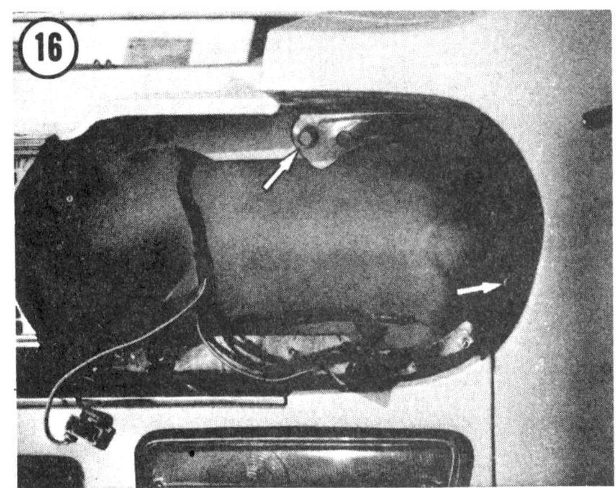

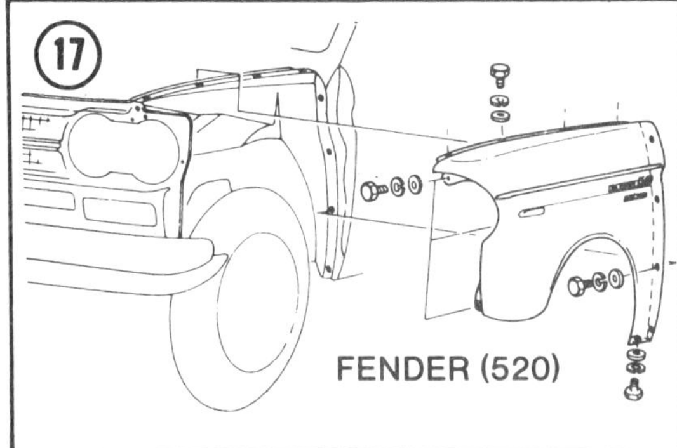
FENDER (520)

TAILGATE REMOVAL/INSTALLATION

1. Unbolt the tailgate chains or stays. **Figure 19** shows the 620 installation. The 521 installation is basically the same. **Figure 20** shows the 720 installation.
2. Unbolt the tailgate and take it off.
3. Installation is the reverse of removal.

DOORS

Trim Panel Removal/Installation (521)

1. Note the positions of the door handle and window crank.
2. Remove the handle and crank screws (**Figure 21**) and take them off.
3. Insert a wide-bladed screwdriver or similar tool between panel and door. Carefully pry the panel up until its clips pull out of the door.
4. Installation is the reverse of removal.

Trim Panel Removal/Installation (620)

1. Note the position of the window crank. Push the panel toward the door, pull out the crank clip, and take the crank off. See **Figure 22**.

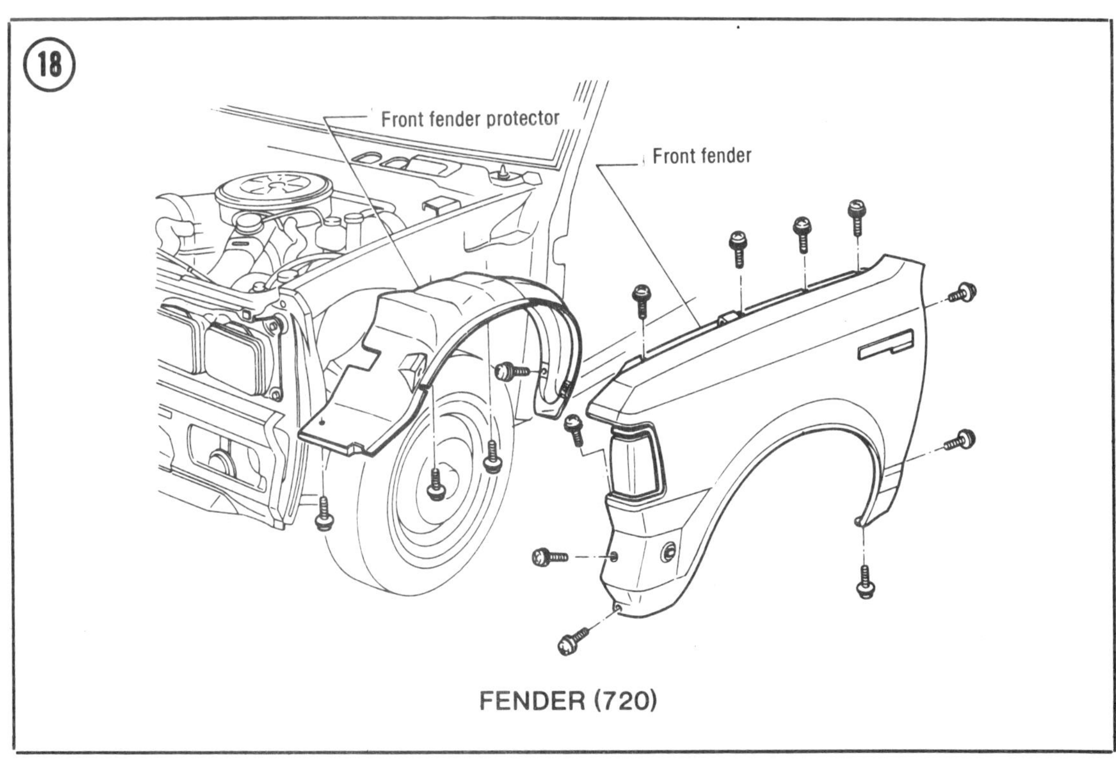

FENDER (720)

(19)

1
2
3
4
5
6

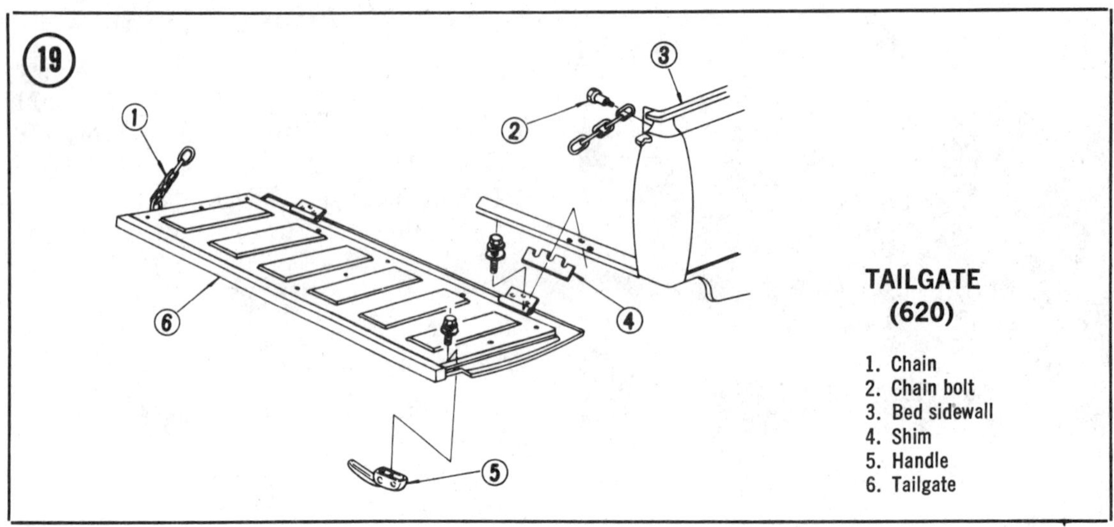

TAILGATE (620)

1. Chain
2. Chain bolt
3. Bed sidewall
4. Shim
5. Handle
6. Tailgate

(20)

TAILGATE (720)

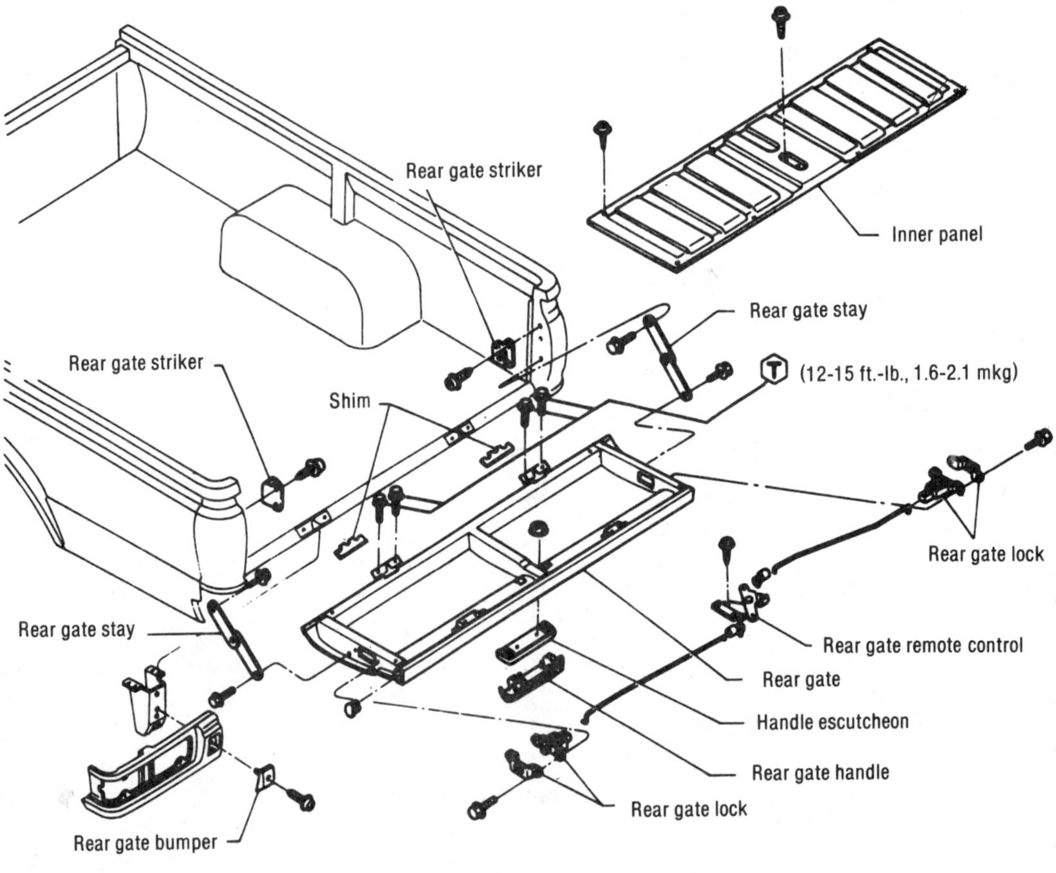

Rear gate striker
Inner panel
Rear gate stay
Rear gate striker
(12-15 ft.-lb., 1.6-2.1 mkg)
Shim
Rear gate lock
Rear gate stay
Rear gate remote control
Rear gate
Handle escutcheon
Rear gate handle
Rear gate lock
Rear gate bumper

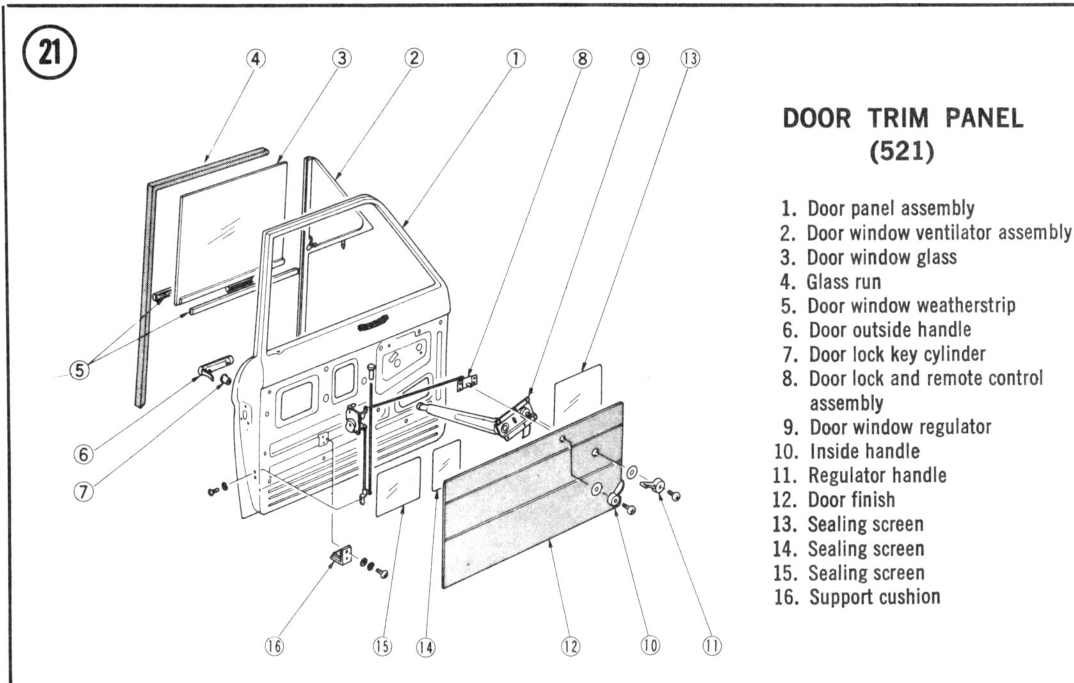

DOOR TRIM PANEL (521)

1. Door panel assembly
2. Door window ventilator assembly
3. Door window glass
4. Glass run
5. Door window weatherstrip
6. Door outside handle
7. Door lock key cylinder
8. Door lock and remote control assembly
9. Door window regulator
10. Inside handle
11. Regulator handle
12. Door finish
13. Sealing screen
14. Sealing screen
15. Sealing screen
16. Support cushion

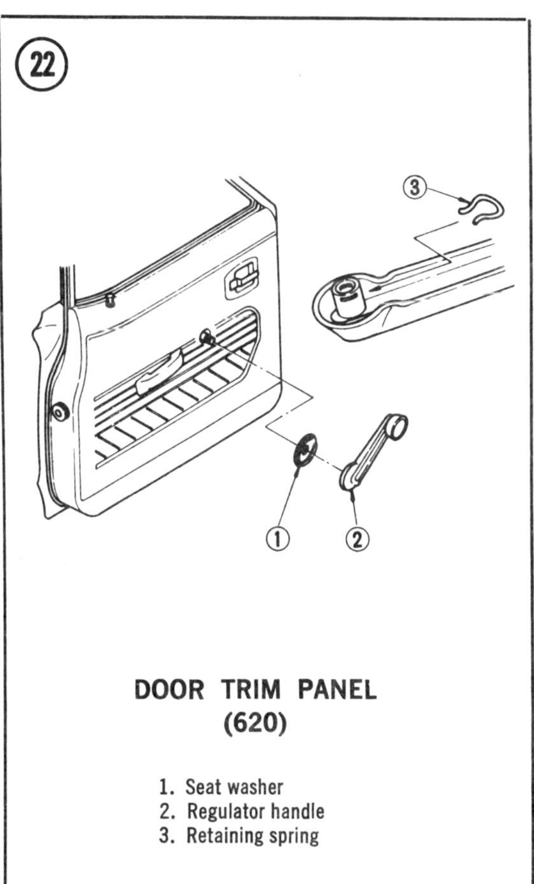

DOOR TRIM PANEL (620)

1. Seat washer
2. Regulator handle
3. Retaining spring

2. Remove the screw securing the door handle trim piece. Slip the trim piece over the door handle and take it off.
3. Remove the armrest mounting screws. Take the armrest off.
4. Insert a wide-bladed screwdriver or similar tool between panel and door. Carefully pry the panel away from the door until its retaining clips pull out.
5. Installation is the reverse of removal.

Trim Panel Removal/Installation (720)

1. Remove the armrest, lock knob, and door handle trim. See **Figure 23**.
2. Make a wire hook. Press in on the door panel around the window crank and pull the clip out. See **Figure 24**.
3. Insert a wide-bladed screwdriver between door panel and door. Carefully pry the panel clips out of the door, then take the panel off.
4. If necessary, peel the plastic sealing screen away from the door. Be careful not to let the sealing screen adhesive stick to surrounding parts.
5. If necessary, carefully pry out the door outside weatherstripping. Use a screwdriver wrapped with a rag to protect the paint.
6. Installation is the reverse of removal.

Lock Mechanism Removal/Installation (521)

Refer to **Figure 25** for this procedure.

1. Remove the trim panel as described earlier. Carefully peel the plastic sealing screens off the door.
2. Unscrew the lock knob.
3. Pry out the rod attaching the key cylinder to the lock.
4. Take the lock assembly out through the rear access hole. See **Figure 26**.
5. Installation is the reverse of removal. Be sure the gap between the outside handle lever and locking lever is 0.039-0.118 in. (1-3 mm). If not, reposition the outside door handle.

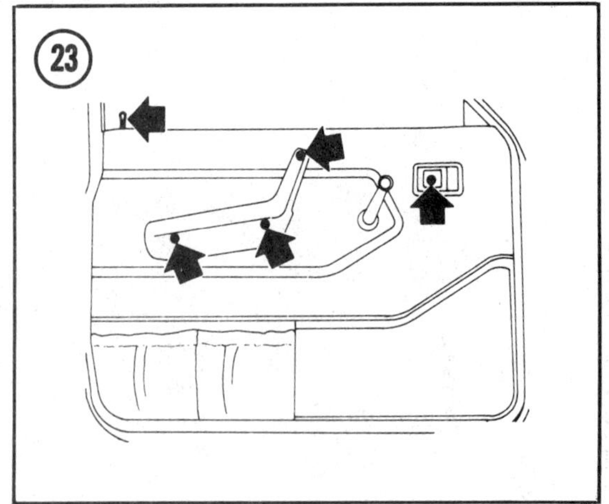

Lock Mechanism Removal/Installation (620)

Refer to **Figure 27** for this procedure.

1. Remove the door trim panel as described earlier. Carefully peel the sealing seams from the access holes.
2. Raise the window.
3. Unscrew the lock knob.
4. Remove the attaching bolts from the rear window guide.
5. Disconnect the rods from key cylinder and outside door handle.
6. Remove 3 lock assembly mounting screws.

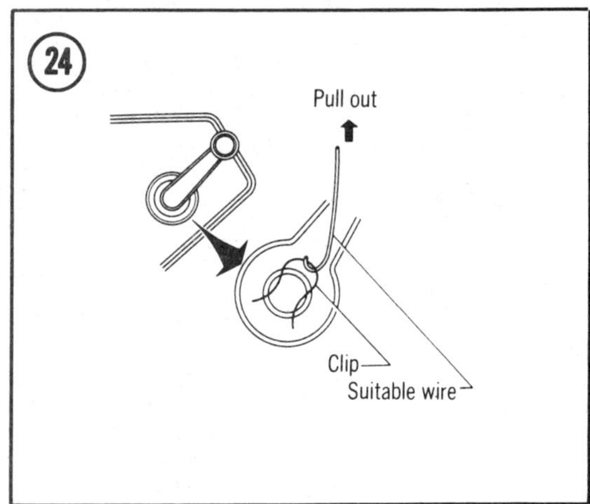

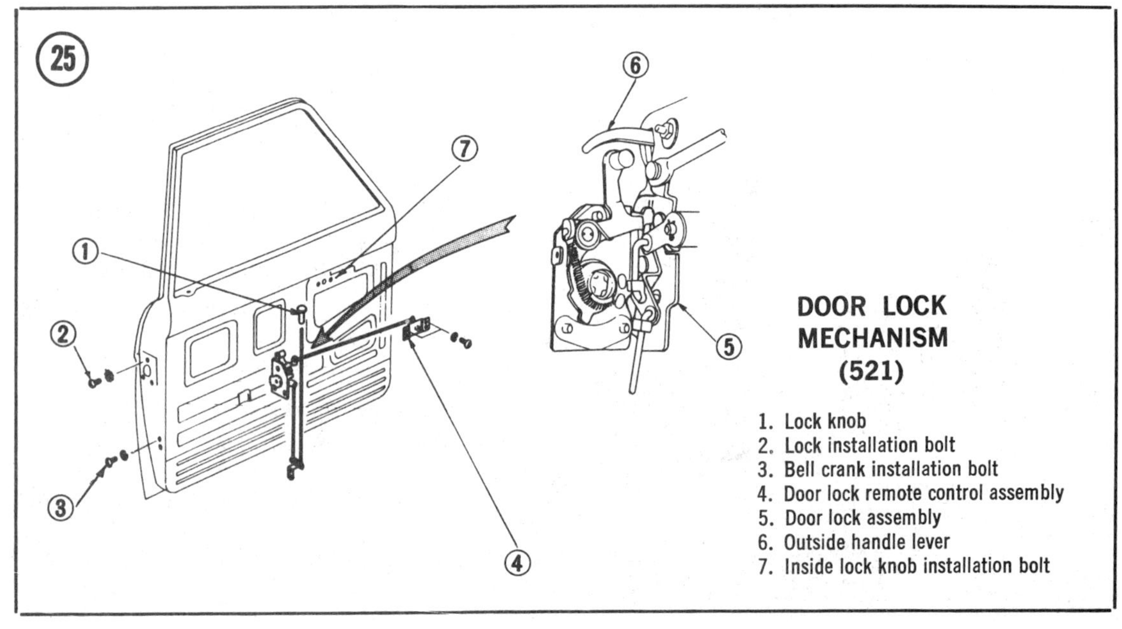

DOOR LOCK MECHANISM (521)

1. Lock knob
2. Lock installation bolt
3. Bell crank installation bolt
4. Door lock remote control assembly
5. Door lock assembly
6. Outside handle lever
7. Inside lock knob installation bolt

27

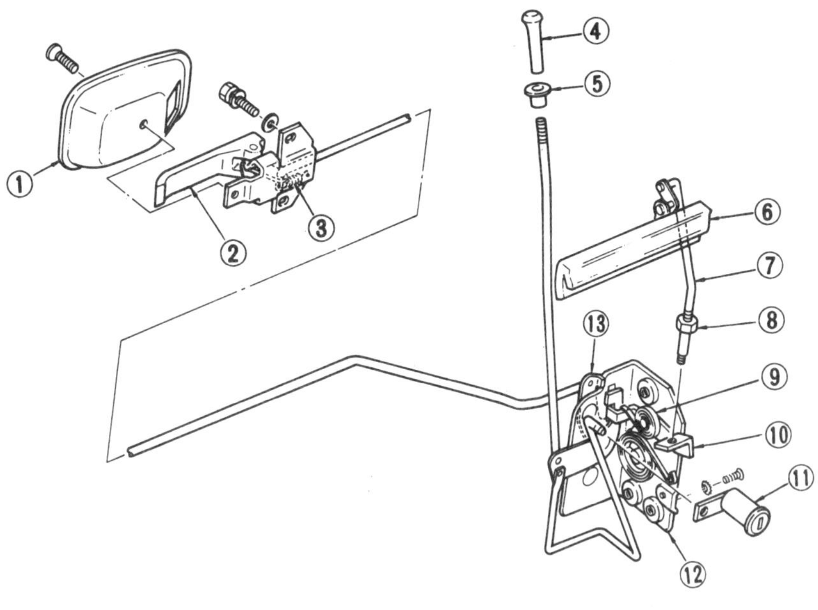

DOOR LOCK
MECHANISM (620)

1. Escutcheon	8. Nylon nut
2. Inside handle	9. Locking plate spring
3. Spring	10. Locking plate
4. Door lock knob	11. Door lock cylinder
5. Knob grommet	12. Door lock
6. Outside handle	13. Stopper
Outside handle rod	

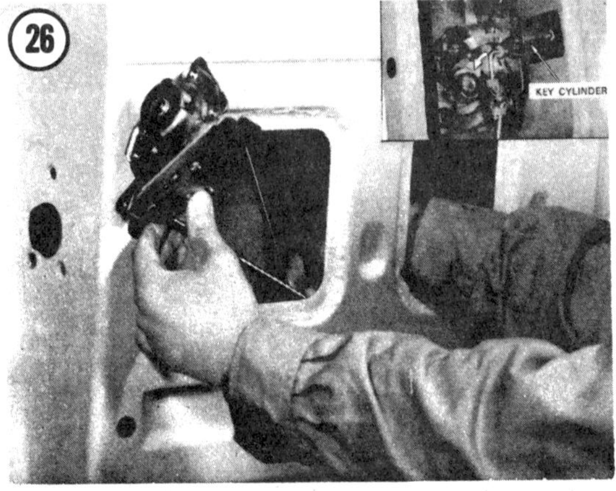

7. Remove 2 screws securing the inside door handle.
8. Remove the lock assembly, together with the inside door handle, through the large access hole.
9. Installation is the reverse of removal.

Lock Mechanism Removal/Installation (720)

1. Remove the door panel as described in this chapter.
2. Detach the clip from the inside handle rod (**Figure 28**).

3. Remove the inside door handle.
4. Pull out the lock cylinder retaining clip, then take out the lock cylinder.
5. Detach the rod holder from the door lock rod. See **Figure 29**.
6. Remove the lock assembly mounting screws, then take the lock assembly out.
7. Remove the outside handle.
8. Installation is the reverse of removal. Apply multipurpose grease to all friction points.

Window Removal/Installation (521)

1. Remove the lock mechanism as described earlier.
2. Remove 5 screws (**Figure 30**) and take the window support cushions out.
3. Slip a piece of string under the glass. This will be used later to pull it up.
4. Detach the roller on the end of the regulator (9, **Figure 21**) from the glass channel. Lower the window to the bottom of the door.
5. Remove 4 ventilator securing screws (**Figure 31**).
6. Carefully pry the window weatherstripping loose from its clips.
7. Remove 2 screws securing the vent window's vertical frame piece. Lift the vent window out (**Figure 32**).
8. Lift the window up and out of the door.

29

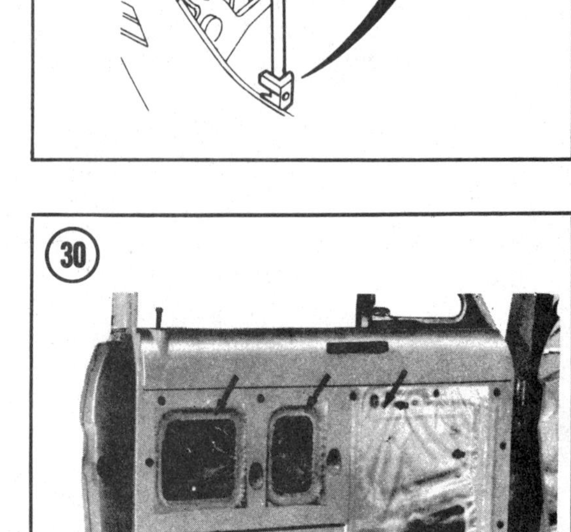

30

28

31

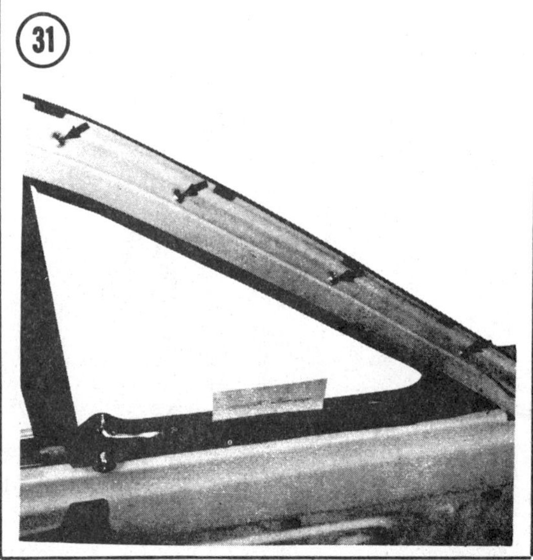

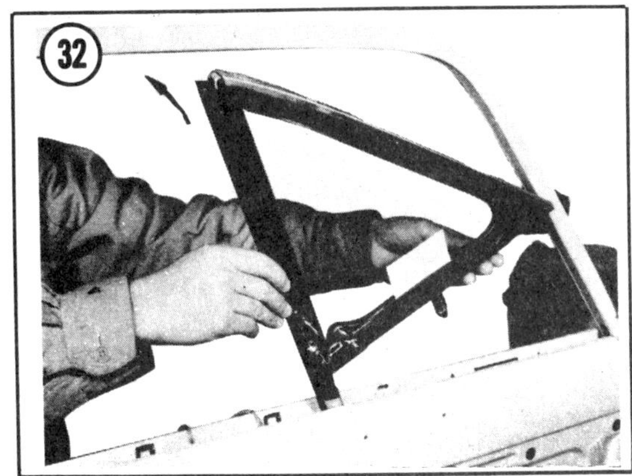

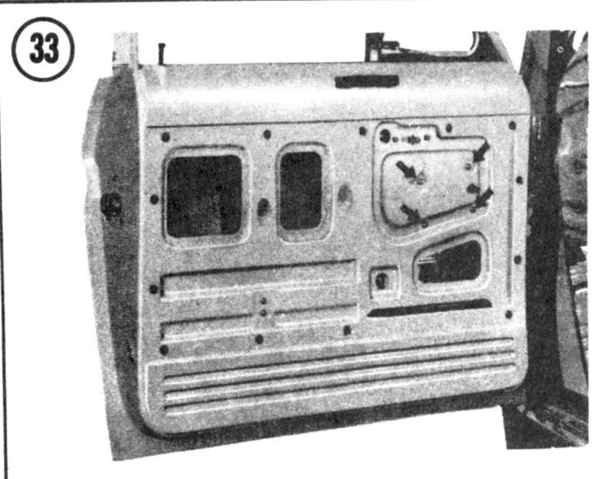

9. If necessary, remove 4 screws (**Figure 33**) and take the regulator out through the rear access hole.
10. Installation is the reverse of removal.

Window Removal/Installation (620)

If equipped with the optional vent window, refer to **Figure 34**. If not, see **Figure 35**.

1. Lower the window. Remove the door trim panel as described earlier, then peel off the plastic sealing screens.
2. Carefully pry the window weatherstripping out of its clips. See **Figure 36**.
3. Remove 3 bolts securing the window's bottom channel. On trucks without vent windows, lift the window out. On trucks with vent windows, perform the next 2 steps.
4. Lower the window to the bottom of the door.
5. Unbolt the vent window frame from the door. Lift out the vent window frame, then the door window.
6. Installation is the reverse of removal.

Window Removal (720)

1. Remove the door trim panel as described in this chapter.

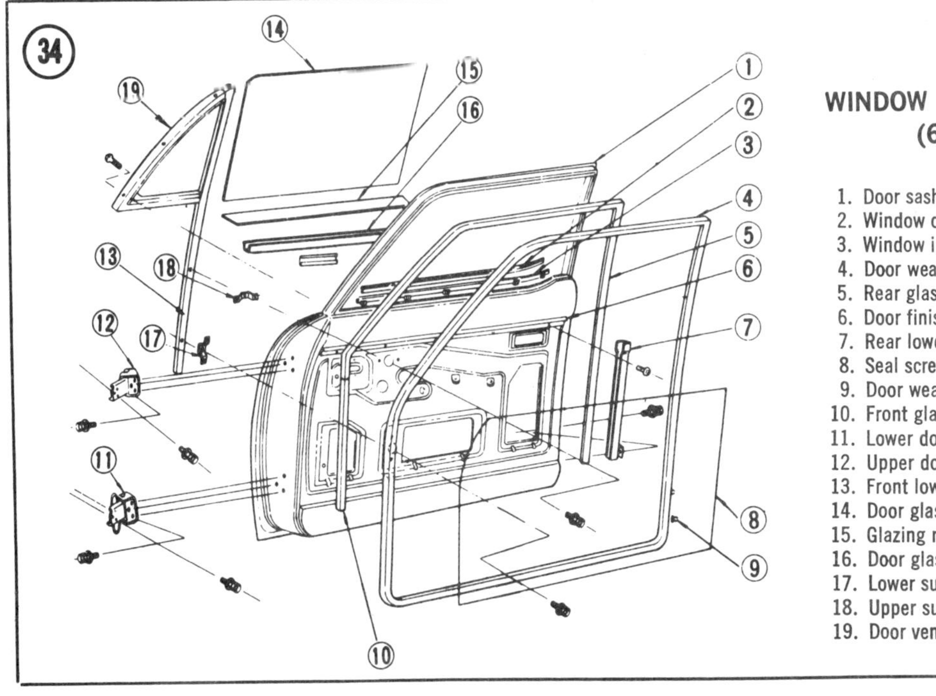

WINDOW AND VENT (620)

1. Door sash
2. Window outside weatherstrip
3. Window inside weatherstrip
4. Door weatherstrip
5. Rear glass run rubber
6. Door finish holder
7. Rear lower sash
8. Seal screen
9. Door weatherstrip clip
10. Front glass run rubber
11. Lower door hinge
12. Upper door hinge
13. Front lower sash
14. Door glass
15. Glazing rubber
16. Door glass bottom channel
17. Lower support
18. Upper support
19. Door ventilator assembly

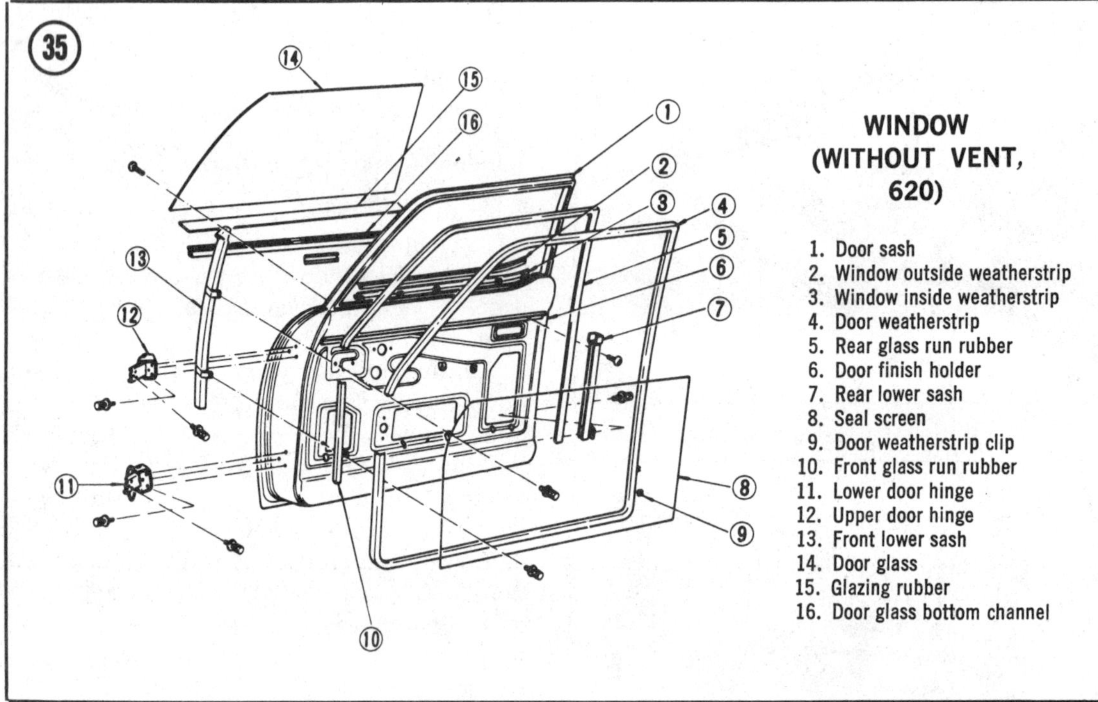

2. If equipped with vent windows, remove the vent window frame. If not equipped with vent windows, remove the lower sash (**Figure 37**).
3. Detach the window from the regulator (**Figure 38**).
4. Lift the window up and out of the door.
5. If necessary, detach the regulator from the door and remove it through the access hole.

Window Installation (720)

Installation is the reverse of removal, plus the following.
1. To adjust glass tilt, loosen the nuts securing guide channel B (**Figure 39**). Tilt the guide channel to straighten the glass, then tighten the nuts.
2. To slide the glass to front or rear, loosen guide channel A. Push the window up and back into its run, then tighten guide channel A.
3. If the window doesn't slide easily, loosen the vent window frame or lower sash. Reposition the vent window frame or lower sash as needed, then tighten it.

Door Adjustment (521 and 620)

1. Remove the striker plate from the door jamb. Close the door and check its alignment with the body.
2. To adjust door position, remove the trim panel from the footwell. Loosen the hinge bolts (**Figure 40**) and position the door. Then tighten the bolts.
3. Reinstall the striker plate. Position it so the door closes easily, without moving up or down when the latch is engaged.

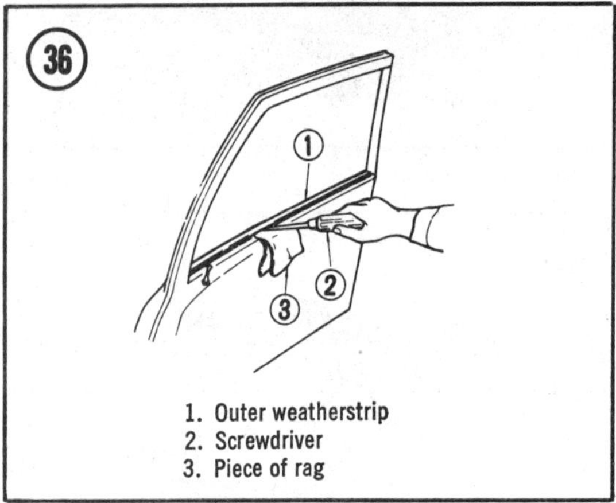

Door Adjustment (720)

1. Remove the door striker plate (**Figure 41**).

37

40

38

41

39
DOOR WINDOWS (720)
A
B
1
2
3
4
A. Tilt adjustment
B. Fore and back adjustment
1. Guide channel A
2. Guide channel B
3. Front door lower sash
4. Front door ventilator frame

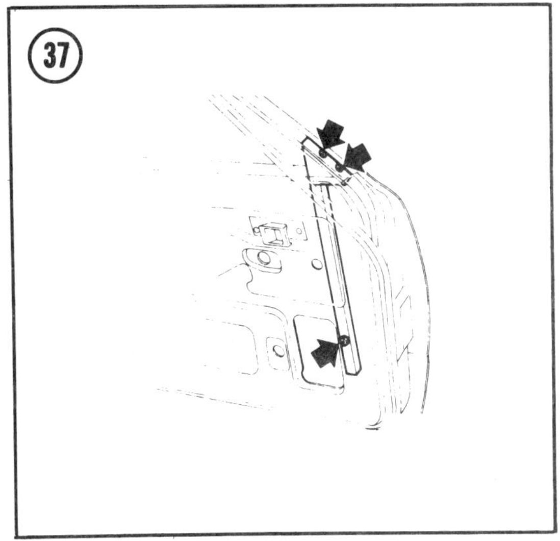

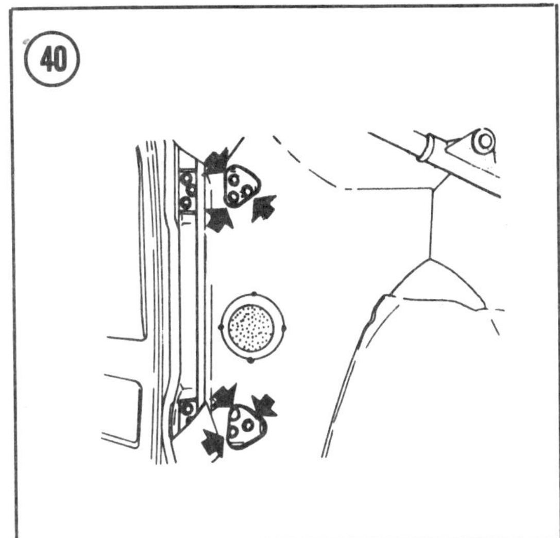

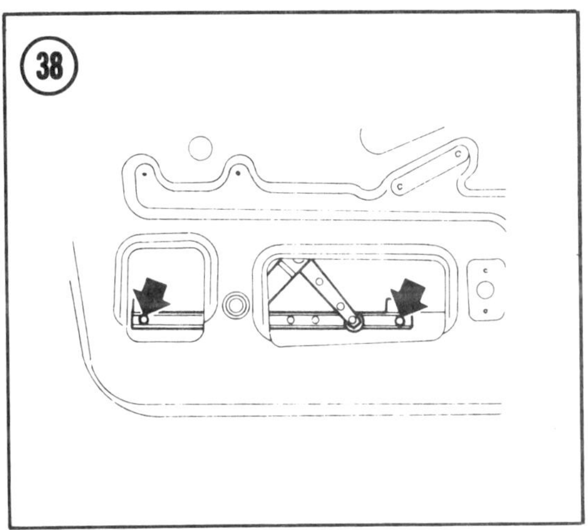

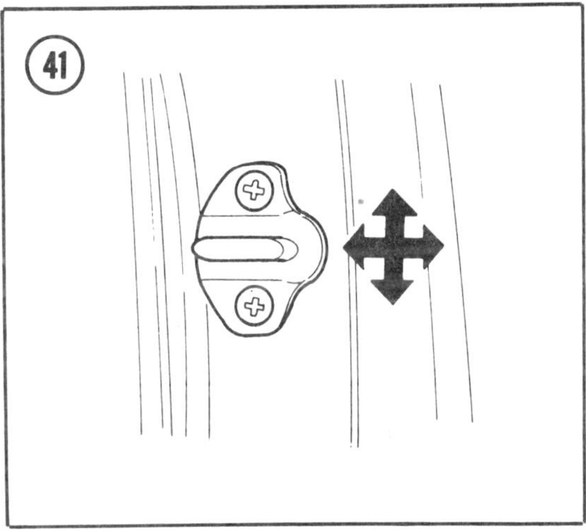

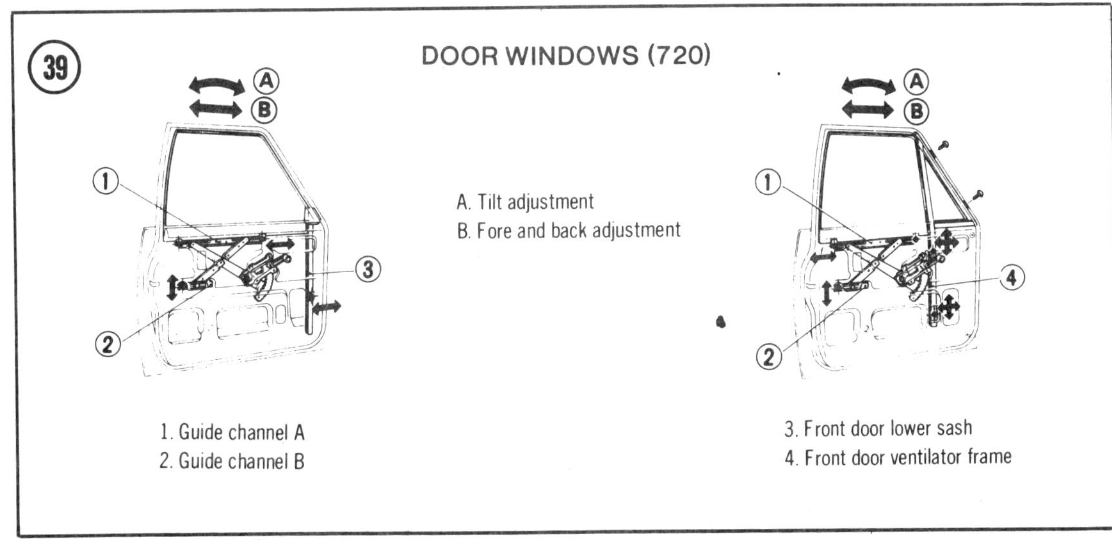

14

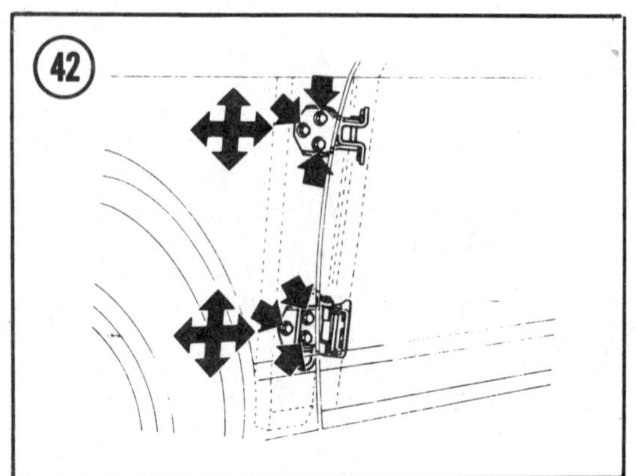

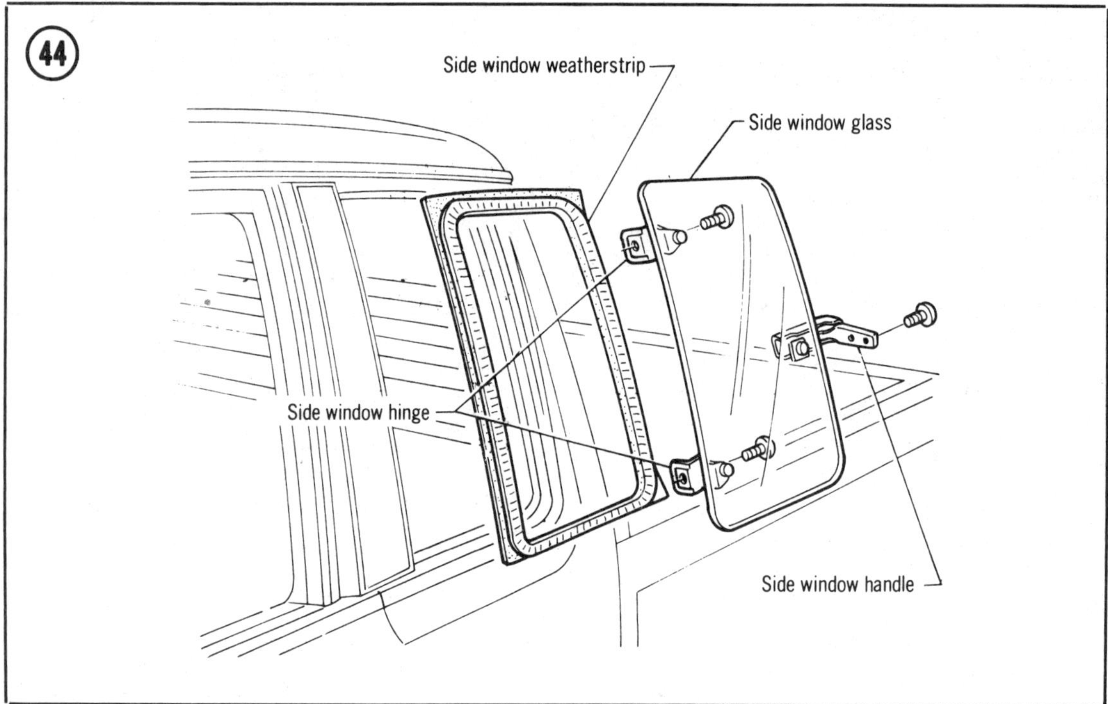

2. Remove the fender protector. Refer to *Fender Removal/Installation* in this chapter.
3. Loosen the hinge-to-pillar bolts (**Figure 42**). Align the door with the body, then tighten the bolts.
4. Install the striker plate. Position the striker plate so the door closes evenly, then tighten its mounting screws.

Door Removal/Installation

1. Remove the trim panel from the footwell.
2. Place a jack beneath the door. Use a rag between jack and door to protect the paint.
3. While an assistant holds the door, unbolt the hinges (**Figure 40** or **Figure 42**). Lift the door off.
4. Installation is the reverse of removal. Adjust the door as described in the preceding section.

SIDE WINDOW REMOVAL/INSTALLATION (KING CAB)

1. Undo the mounting screws (**Figure 43**).
2. Take out the window and weatherstripping (**Figure 44**).

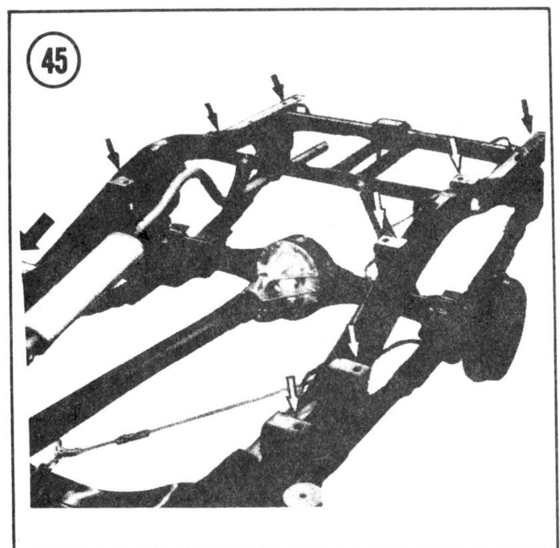

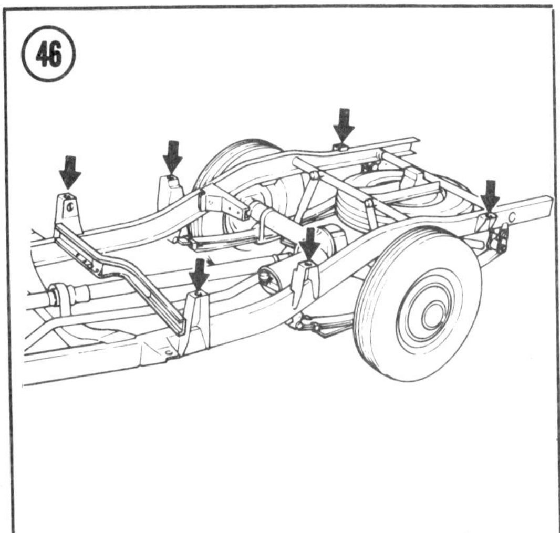

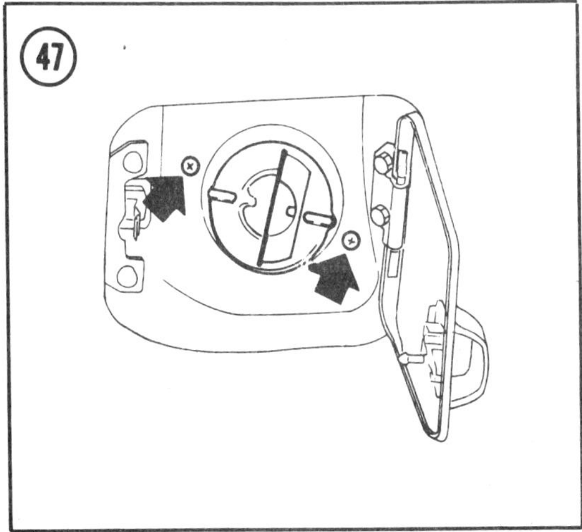

3. Installation is the reverse of removal. Replace the weatherstripping if deteriorated or damaged.

BED

Removal/Installation (521 and 620)

1. Disconnect the negative cable from the battery.
2. Disconnect rear combination lamp wiring.
3. On 620 pickups, remove the fuel tank. See Chapter Six, *Fuel Tank* section.
4. Unbolt the bed from the frame. See **Figure 45** (521) or **Figure 46** (620).
5. Attach a hoist to the tie-down hooks and lift the bed off. The bed weighs approximately 300 lb. (140 kg), so be sure the hoist is attached to a sturdy support.

NOTE
Shims are used at some of the mounting points. Tag them so they can be returned to the correct locations.

6. Installation is the reverse of removal.

Removal/Installation (720)

1. Disconnect the negative cable from the battery.
2. Disconnect the wiring for rear combination lamps and license plate lights.
3. Remove the fuel filler neck screws (**Figure 47**).
4. Detach the bed from the frame. See **Figure 48**.

NOTE
Mark the locations of all shims for reinstallation.

5. Attach a hoist to the bed and lift it off (**Figure 49**).
6. Installation is the reverse of removal. **Figure 48** shows the arrangements of mounting fasteners and bushings.

14

CAB

Removal/Installation (521)

1. Disconnect the battery cables. Remove the battery from the engine compartment.
2. Disconnect the speedometer cable from the side of the transmission.

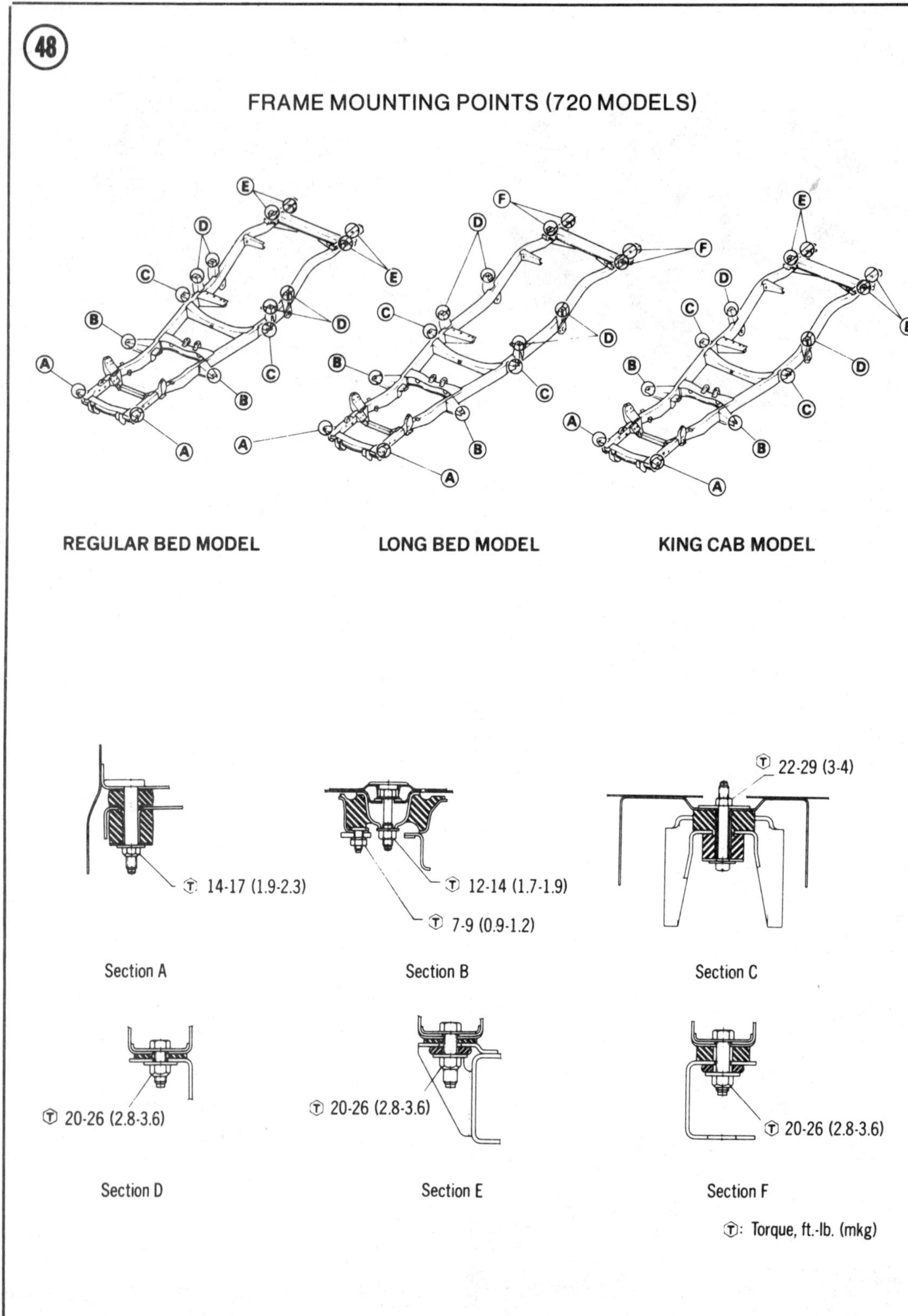
48
FRAME MOUNTING POINTS (720 MODELS)
A
B
C
D
E
F
REGULAR BED MODEL
LONG BED MODEL
KING CAB MODEL
14-17 (1.9-2.3)
12-14 (1.7-1.9)
7-9 (0.9-1.2)
22-29 (3-4)
Section A
Section B
Section C
20-26 (2.8-3.6)
20-26 (2.8-3.6)
20-26 (2.8-3.6)
Section D
Section E
Section F
T: Torque, ft.-lb. (mkg)

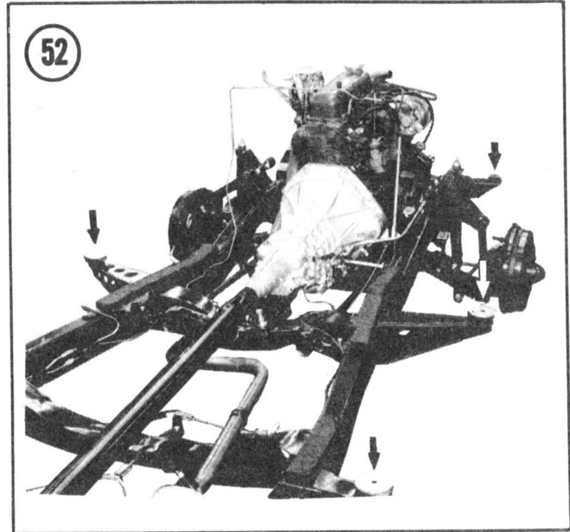

3. Remove the steering column. See Chapter Twelve, *Steering* section.
4. Disconnect the front brake hoses at their brackets. See **Figure 50**.
5. Disconnect the brake line running to the rear brakes (**Figure 51**).
6. Disconnect the choke cable (if so equipped) and throttle linkage.
7. Disconnect the lines from the fuel filter and carburetor. Plug the lines so they won't drip and create a fire hazard.
8. Disconnect the heater hoses. See Chapter Seven, *Heater* section.
9. Disconnect the handbrake cable. See *Adjustments*, Chapter Eleven.
10. Remove the shift lever from the transmission. See *Transmission Removal/ Installation*, Chapter Ten.
11. Disconnect the wiring harnesses for engine compartment and instrument panel.
12. Remove 6 mounting bolts (**Figure 52**).
13. Attach a hoist to the cab and lift it off. Since the cab weighs approximately 440 lb. (200 kg), be sure the hoist is attached to a sturdy support.
14. Installation is the reverse of removal. If the rubber mounting insulators are worn or deteriorated, replace them. Bleed the brakes and clutch. Adjust the handbrake.

Removal/Installation (620)

1. If the truck is air conditioned, have the system discharged by a dealer or air conditioning shop.

WARNING
Do not disconnect air conditioning hoses until the system has been discharged. They contain refrigerant under high pressure which can cause frostbite if it touches skin and blindness if it touches the eyes. If discharged near an open flame, the refrigerant forms poisonous gas.

2. Remove the battery cables. Remove the battery from the engine compartment.
3. Remove the radiator (Chapter Seven).
4. Remove the grille, front bumper, and hood as described earlier in this chapter.
5. Remove the steering gear and column. See Chapter Thirteen, *Steering* section.
6. Disconnect the speedometer cable from the transmission.
7. Disconnect the handbrake cable. See *Adjustment*, Chapter Eleven.
8. Disconnect the hoses from the carbon canister. See *Evaporative Emission Control System*, Chapter Six.
9. On 1975 and later models, disconnect the hoses from the air pump air cleaner. See *Air Injection System*, Chapter Six.
10. If equipped with air conditioning, disconnect the hoses from the compressor.
11. If equipped with an air cleaner duct, remove it.
12. Disconnect the brake booster vacuum hose from the intake manifold.
13. On manual transmissions, remove the shift lever. On automatics, disconnect the shift linkage from the transmission.
14. Disconnect the lines from the fuel filter and carburetor. Plug the lines so they won't drip and create a fire hazard.
15. Disconnect the throttle cable from the carburetor.
16. Disconnect the fluid lines from the brake and clutch master cylinders.
17. Detach the fuel and hydraulic lines from their clips on the body.
18. Disconnect the handbrake cable. See *Adjustments*, Chapter Eleven.
19. Disconnect the heater hoses from the engine.
20. Disconnect the wiring harnesses for engine compartment and instruments.
21. Remove 6 body-to-frame bolts. See **Figure 53**.
22. Attach a hoist to the cab and lift it off. Since the cab weighs approximately 485 lb. (220 kg), be sure the hoist is attached to a sturdy support.
23. Installation is the reverse of removal. If the rubber mounting insulators are worn or deteriorated, replace them. Bleed the brakes and clutch. Adjust the handbrake.

Removal/Installation (720)

1. If equipped with air conditioning, have the system discharged by a Datsun dealer or air conditioning shop.

WARNING
Do not disconnect air conditioning hoses until the system has been discharged. They contain refrigerant under high pressure which can cause frostbite if it touches skin and blindness if it touches the eyes. If discharged near an open flame, the refrigerant forms poisonous gas.

2. Remove the hood and front bumpers as described in this chapter.
3. Remove the battery.
4. Remove the air cleaner.
5. Detach the emission control lines from the engine compartment sidewalls. See *Vacuum Lines*, Chapter Six.
6. Disconnect the brake booster vacuum hose from the intake manifold.
7. Disconnect all wiring from the engine.
8. Disconnect the throttle linkage.
9. Detach the steering column from the steering gear at the rubber coupling. See **Figure 54**.
10. Remove the radiator mounting bolts. Tie the radiator and shroud back against the engine.
11. Disconnect the brake and clutch lines in the engine compartment (**Figure 55**).
12. Disconnect the brake lines under the truck (**Figure 56**).
13. Disconnect the speedometer cable from the transmission.
14. On manual transmissions, remove the shift lever. On automatics, disconnect the shift linkage from the transmission.

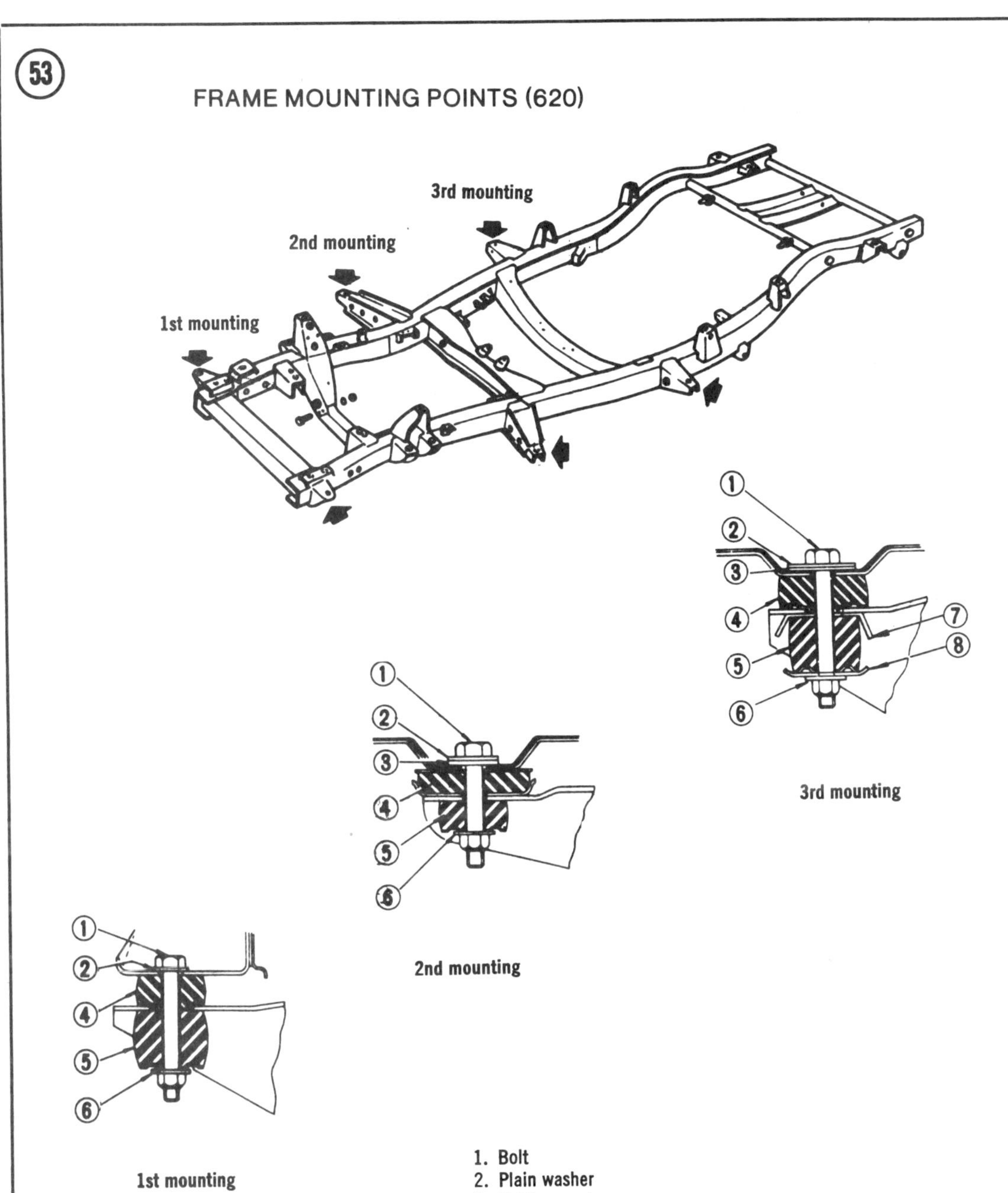

1. Bolt
2. Plain washer
3. Rubber washer
4. Upper rubber
5. Bottom rubber
6. Plain washer
7. Upper washer
8. Lower washer

15. Disconnect the handbrake lever and cable. Refer to *Handbrake*, Chapter Eleven.
16. Disconnect all wiring harnesses securing the cab to the frame.
17. Attach a hoist to the cab as shown in **Figure 57**.
18. Detach the cab from the frame. See **Figure 57**.
19. Hoist the cab off.
20. Installation is the reverse of removal. **Figure 48** shows the arrangement of mounting fasteners and bushings.

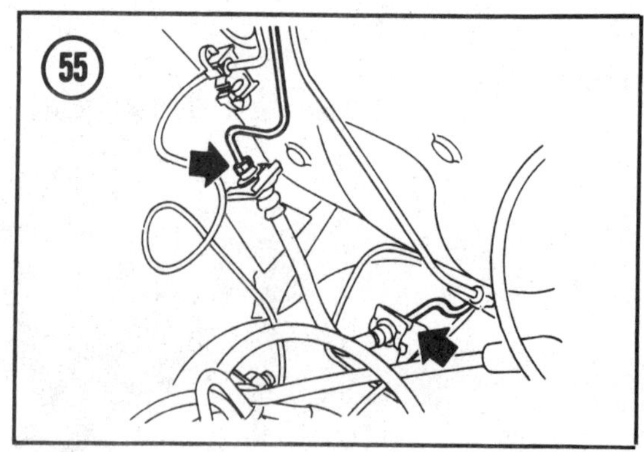

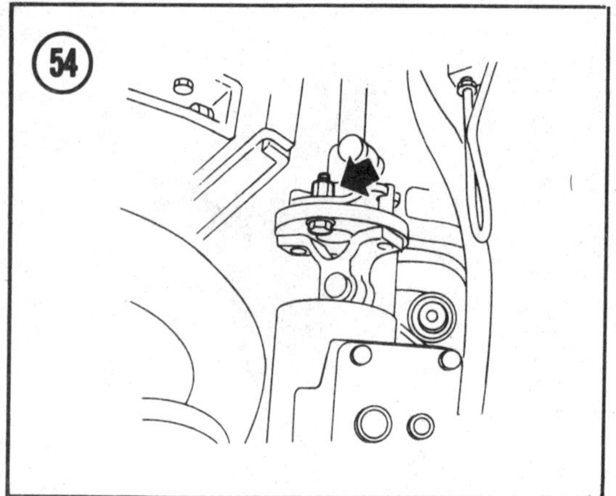

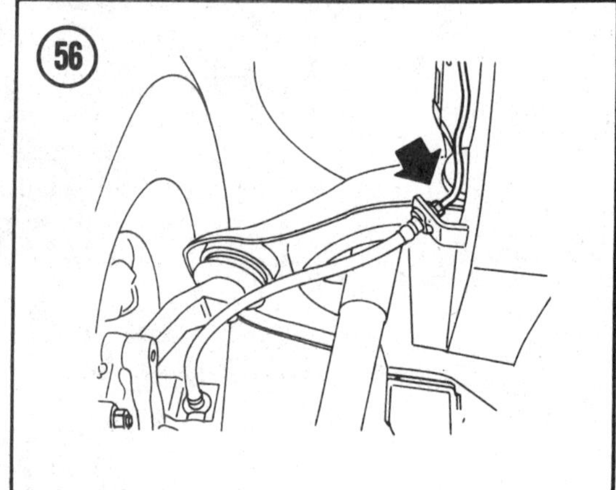

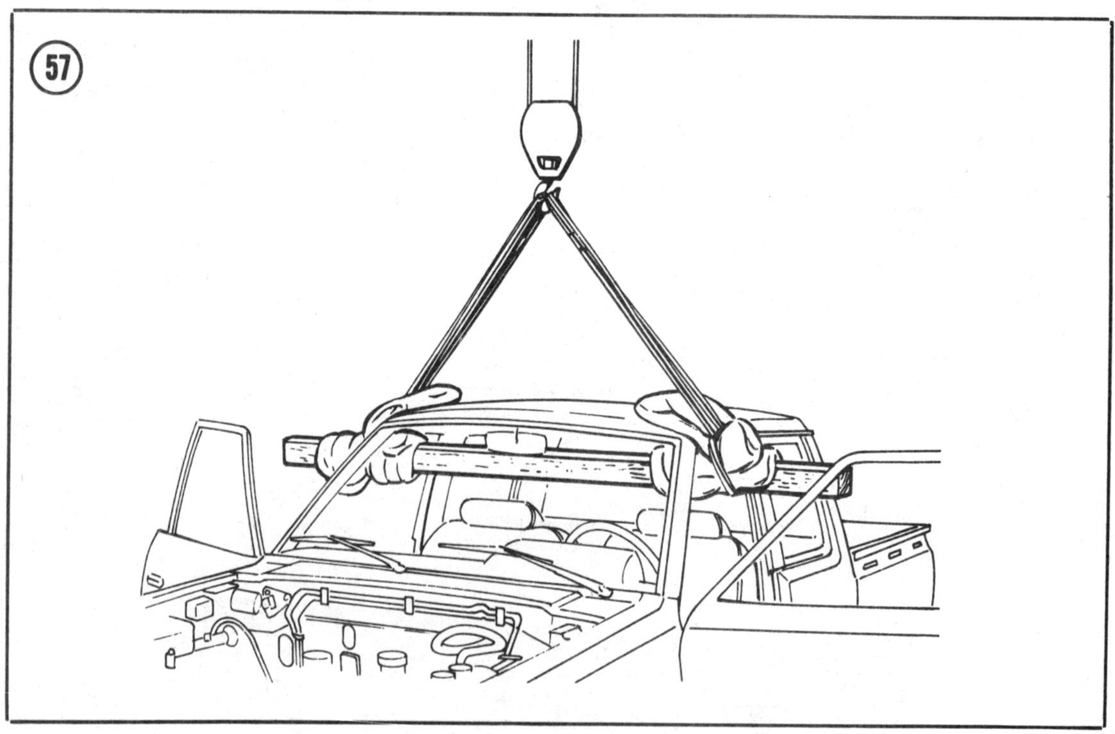

SUPPLEMENT

1982 AND LATER SERVICE INFORMATION

This supplement provides service procedures unique to 1982 and 1983 models. All procedures not covered in this supplement are the same as for 1981 models.

The chapter headings in this supplement correspond to those in the main body of this book. If a procedure is not included in the supplement, there are no changes affecting 1982 and later models.

CHAPTER THREE

LUBRICATION, MAINTENANCE AND TUNE-UP

Some maintenance intervals differ from 1981. **Table 1** lists scheduled maintenance intervals for trucks given normal use. **Table 2** lists intervals for severe service conditions.

Engine Oil and Filter Change

API service SE oil is recommended for 1982 models. API service SE or SF oil is recommended for 1983. Viscosity recommendations for SE oil are the same as for 1981. Viscosity recommendations for SF oil are listed in **Table 3**.

Drive Belts

Adjustment procedures are the same as for 1981 models, except for the addition of the power steering pump belt on 1982 and later models so equipped. Belt deflection specifications are listed in **Table 4**.

To adjust the power steering belt, loosen the idler pulley locknut (**Figure 1**). Turn the adjusting bolt as needed to change belt tension, then tighten the locknut.

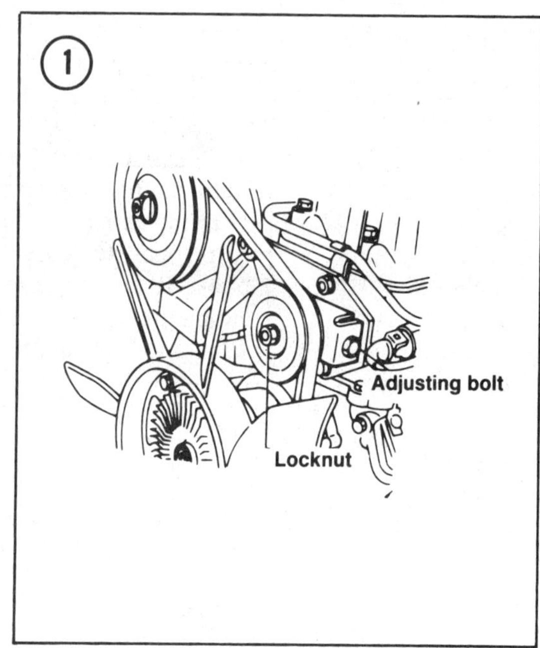

Power Steering

Check fluid level and look for leaks as described in the Chapter Thirteen section of this supplement.

TUNE-UP

Tune-up procedures are the same as for 1981 models, except for valve adjustment on 1983 trucks. Periodic idle speed adjustment is recommended but not required.

Some tune-up specifications differ from those for 1981 models. These are listed in **Table 5**.

Valve Adjustment (1983)

1. Warm the engine until the temperature needle points to the middle of the gauge.
2. Remove the air cleaner, spark plug wires and valve cover.
3. Turn the engine until No. 1 piston is at top dead center on its compression stroke. When this occurs, the 0 degree mark on the timing pointer will align with the notch in the crankshaft pulley (**Figure 2**). In addition, the distributor rotor will point to No. 1 terminals in the distributor cap. See **Figure 3**.

NOTE
Be sure to remove the distributor cap and check rotor position. The timing marks also line up when No. 4 cylinder is at TDC on its compression stroke.

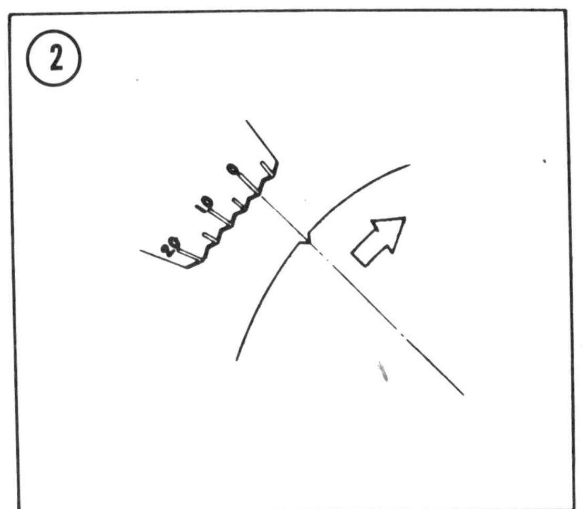

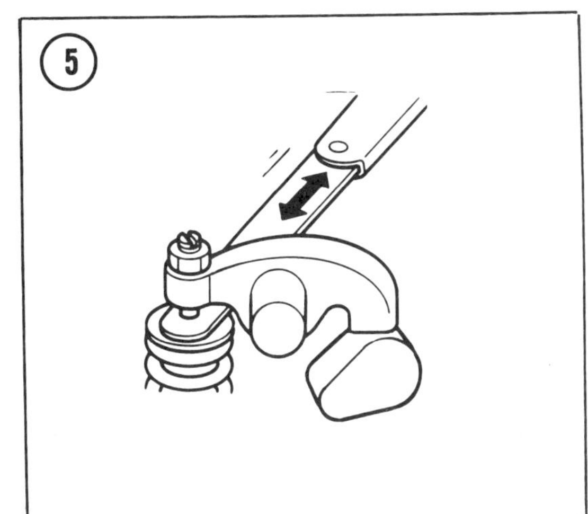

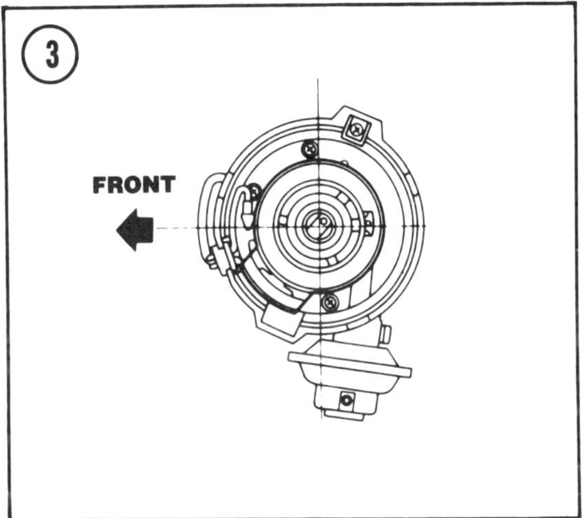

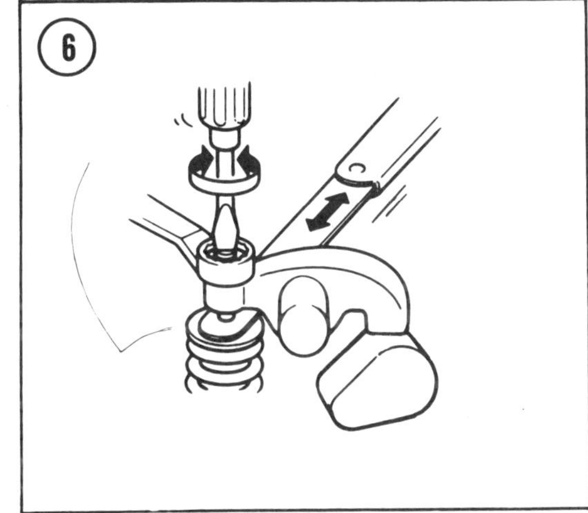

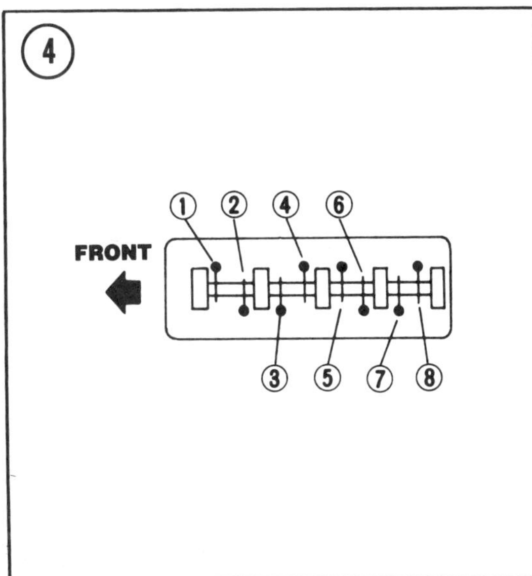

4. Measure the clearances of valves 1, 2, 4 and 6 (counting from the front of the engine). See **Figure 4**. To measure, insert a feeler gauge between the rocker arm adjusting screw and valve stem as shown in **Figure 5**.

5. If clearance is incorrect, loosen the adjusting screw locknut (**Figure 6**). Turn the adjusting screw as shown to change clearance, then tighten the locknut.

6. Once valves 1, 2, 4 and 6 are adjusted properly, turn the crankshaft one full turn, so the 0 degree mark on the timing scale aligns with the notch in the crankshaft pulley again. This places No. 4 piston at top dead center on its compression stroke.

7. With No. 4 piston at TDC on its compression stroke, adjust valves 3, 5, 7 and 8 (**Figure 4**).

Table 1 SCHEDULED MAINTENANCE

Every 7,500 miles (6 months)	• Engine oil and filter
Every 15,000 miles (12 months)	• Brakes • Brake fluid change (1982) • Power steering fluid, lines and hoses • Manual transmission oil check • Automatic transmission fluid check • Differential oil check • Drive shaft (1982) • Wheel alignment (1982) • Hinges, latches, locks
Every 30,000 miles (24 months)	• Air cleaner element • Air induction valve filter • Evaporative emission system lines • Fuel lines • Coolant • Spark plugs • Ignition wires • Automatic temperature control air cleaner
Every 60,000 miles (48 months)	• Drive shaft (1983) • Suspension and steering linkage ball-joints

Table 2 SEVERE SERVICE MAINTENANCE

Every 3,000 miles (3 months) **Every 7,500 miles (6 months)**	• Engine oil and filter[1, 2, 3, 5] • Air filter inspection[4] • Brake inspection[1, 3, 5, 6, 7] • Steering inspection[7] • Suspension and steering linkage ball-joint inspection[3, 4, 6, 7] • Hinges, latches, locks[6] • Exhaust system[1, 5, 6, 7]
Every 15,000 miles (12 months) **Every 60,000 miles (48 months)**	• Brake fluid change[8] • Manual transmission oil change[5] • Automatic transmission fluid change[5] • Differential oil change[5]

1. Frequent short trips.
2. Prolonged idling.
3. Heavy dust.
4. Extremely high or low temperatures.
5. Trailer towing.
6. Road salt or other corrosive materials.
7. Rough or muddy roads.
8. High humidity or mountainous areas.

Table 3 RECOMMENDED VISCOSITY (SF ENGINE OIL)

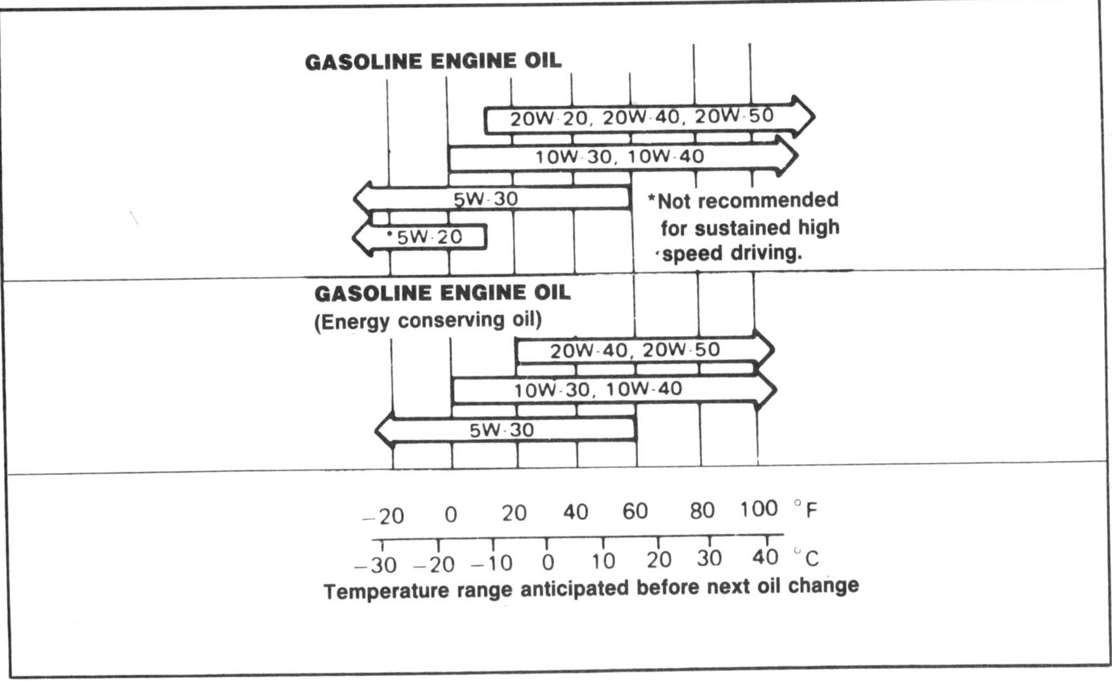

Table 4 BELT DEFLECTION SPECIFICATIONS

Fan belt	
New	8-11 mm (5/16-7/16 in.)
Used	12-15 mm (1/2-5/8 in.)
Air conditioning compressor belt	
New	5-8 mm (3/16-5/16 in.)
Used	7-10 mm (1/4-1/3 in.)
Power steering pump belt	
New	12-15 mm (1/2-5/8 in.)
Used	15-18 mm (5/8-3/4 in.)

Table 5 TUNE-UP SPECIFICATIONS

Spark plug type (NGK brand)	
Intake side	
Standard	BPR6ES
Hot type	BPR5ES
Cold type	BPR7ES
Exhaust side	
Standard and hot type	BPR5ES
Cold type	BPR6ES, BPR7ES
Ignition timing and idle speed*	3 +/-2° BTDC at 650 +/-100 rpm
*Automatic transmissions in DRIVE.	

CHAPTER FIVE

NAPS-Z ENGINE

ENGINE REMOVAL

This is the same as for 1981 models. On trucks equipped with power steering, unbolt the power steering pump from the engine and tie it back out of the way. It is not necessary to disconnect the pump hoses.

VALVES AND VALVE SEATS

Valve seat dimensions differ from 1981 models. See **Figures 7-10**.

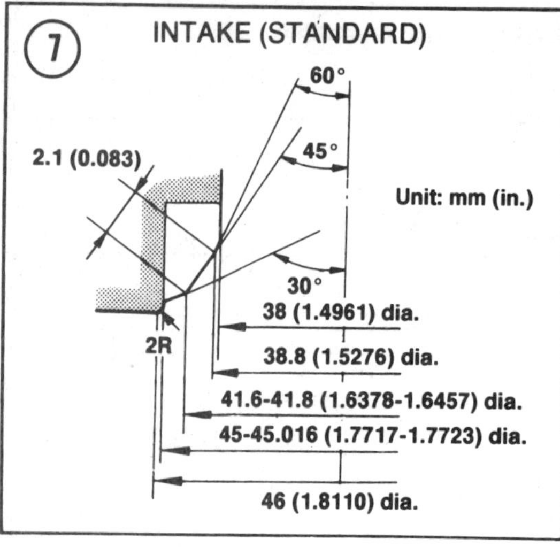

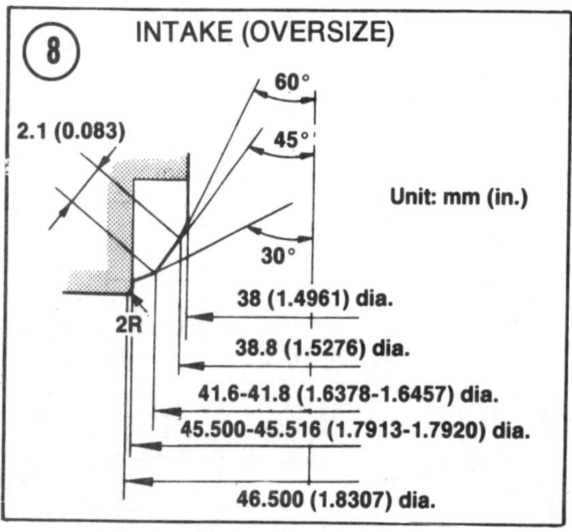

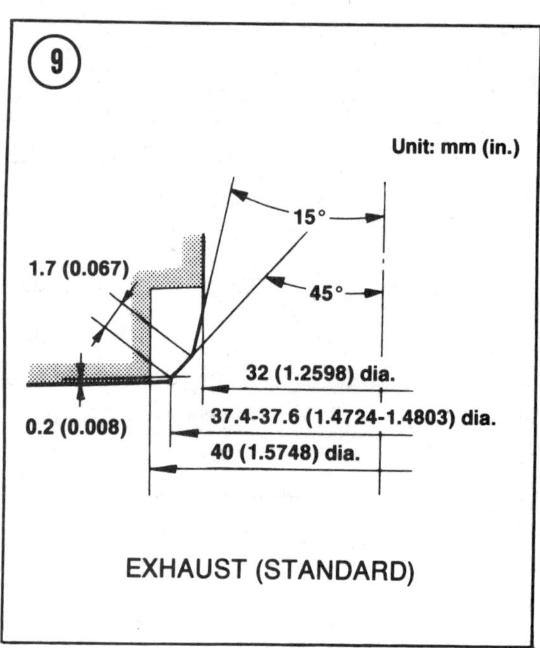

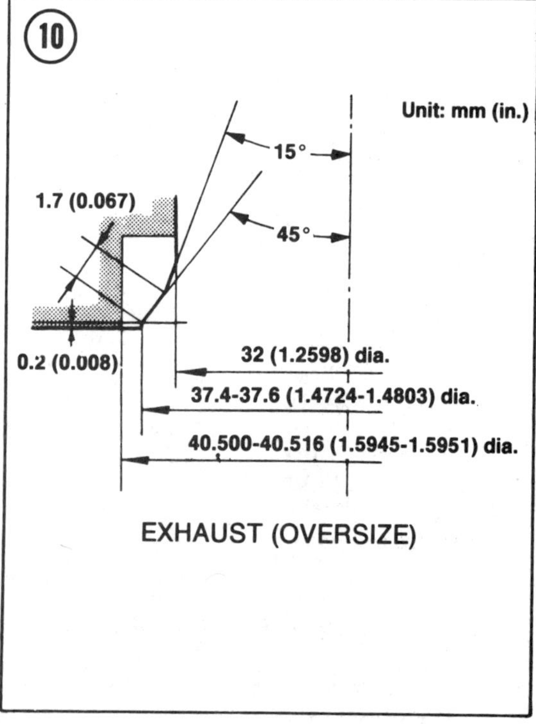

CHAPTER SIX

FUEL, EXHAUST AND EMISSION CONTROL SYSTEMS

CARBURETOR

Service procedures are the same as for 1981 trucks. Some specifications differ. See **Table 6**.

VACUUM LINES

Vacuum lines for all models except non-California high altitude trucks are the same as for 1981. The 1982 and later non-California high altitude vacuum lines are shown in **Figure 11**.

EVAPORATIVE EMISSION CONTROL SYSTEM

System inspection procedures are the same as for 1981. The system layout used on 1982 and later non-California high altitude models differs from that on earlier models. See **Figure 12**.

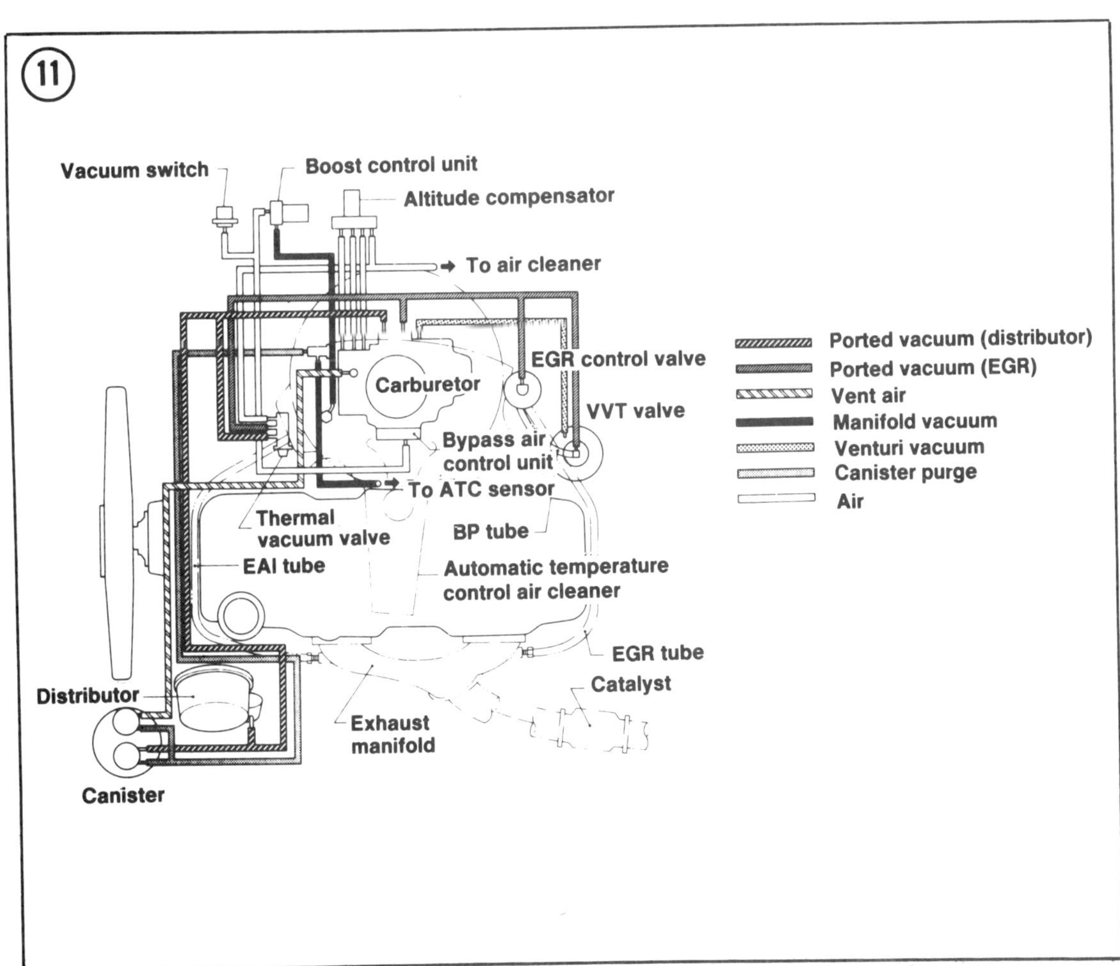

15

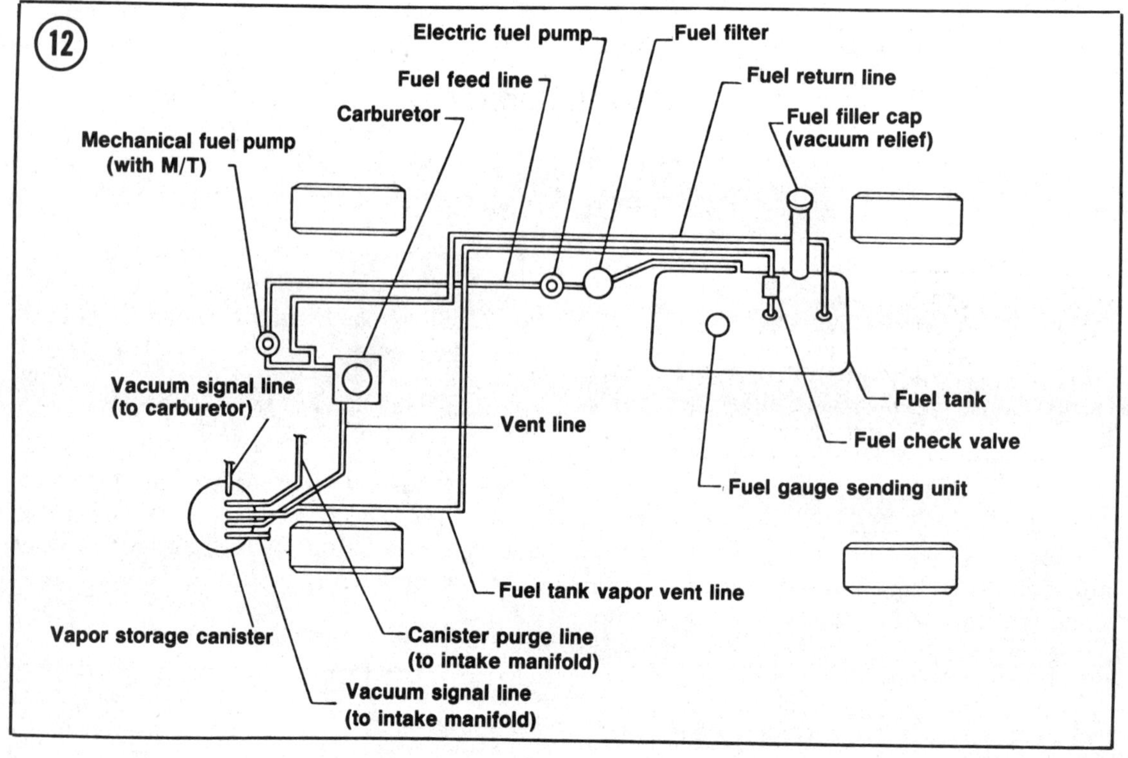

Table 6 CARBURETOR SPECIFICATIONS

Jets and air bleeds	
Primary main jet	
California standard	113
California heavy duty	112
49-state and Canada	
1982	105
1983	107
Secondary main jet	
California standard	155
California heavy duty	145
49-state and Canada	155
Primary main air bleed	80
Secondary main air bleed	60
Primary slow jet	47
Secondary slow jet	
California standard	100
California heavy duty	80
49-state and Canada	100
Power valve	
California	35
49-state and Canada	40
Float adjustment	
Dimension "h" (needle valve stroke)	0.051-0.067 in. (1.3-1.7 mm)
	0.91 in. (23 mm)
Dimension "H" (float level)	
Fast idle cam adjustment (second step)	
Manual transmission	0.032-0.037 in. (0.81-0.95 mm)
Automatic transmission	0.038-0.044 in. (0.97-1.11 mm)
Dashpot adjusting speed	1,400-1,600 rpm

CHAPTER EIGHT

ELECTRICAL SYSTEM

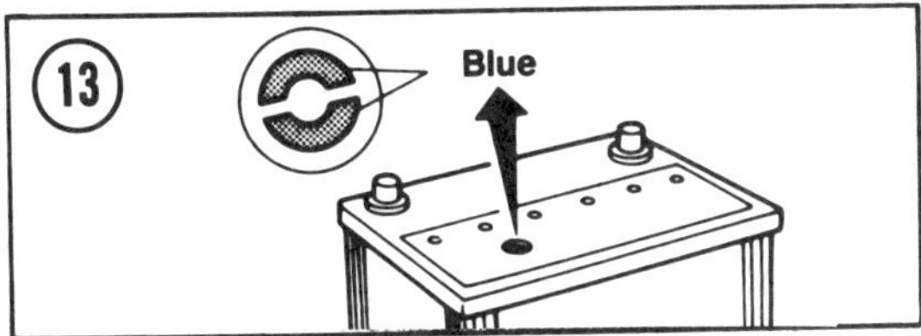

The 1982 and later models use a sealed, maintenance-free battery with a built-in condition indicator. A blue indicator (**Figure 13**) indicates that the battery is in good condition. If the indicator is transparent, the battery needs to be recharged.

CHAPTER NINE

CLUTCH AND TRANSMISSION

Service procedures are the same as for 1981. Specifications are the same as for 1981, except clutch pedal height on 1983 trucks which is 6 1/2-7 in. (166-176 mm).

CHAPTER TEN

TRANSMISSION

Service procedures and specifications are the same as for 1981 models. On 1982 and later 5-speed manual transmissions, the center steel ball on the main shaft has been replaced by a steel roller. See **Figure 14**.

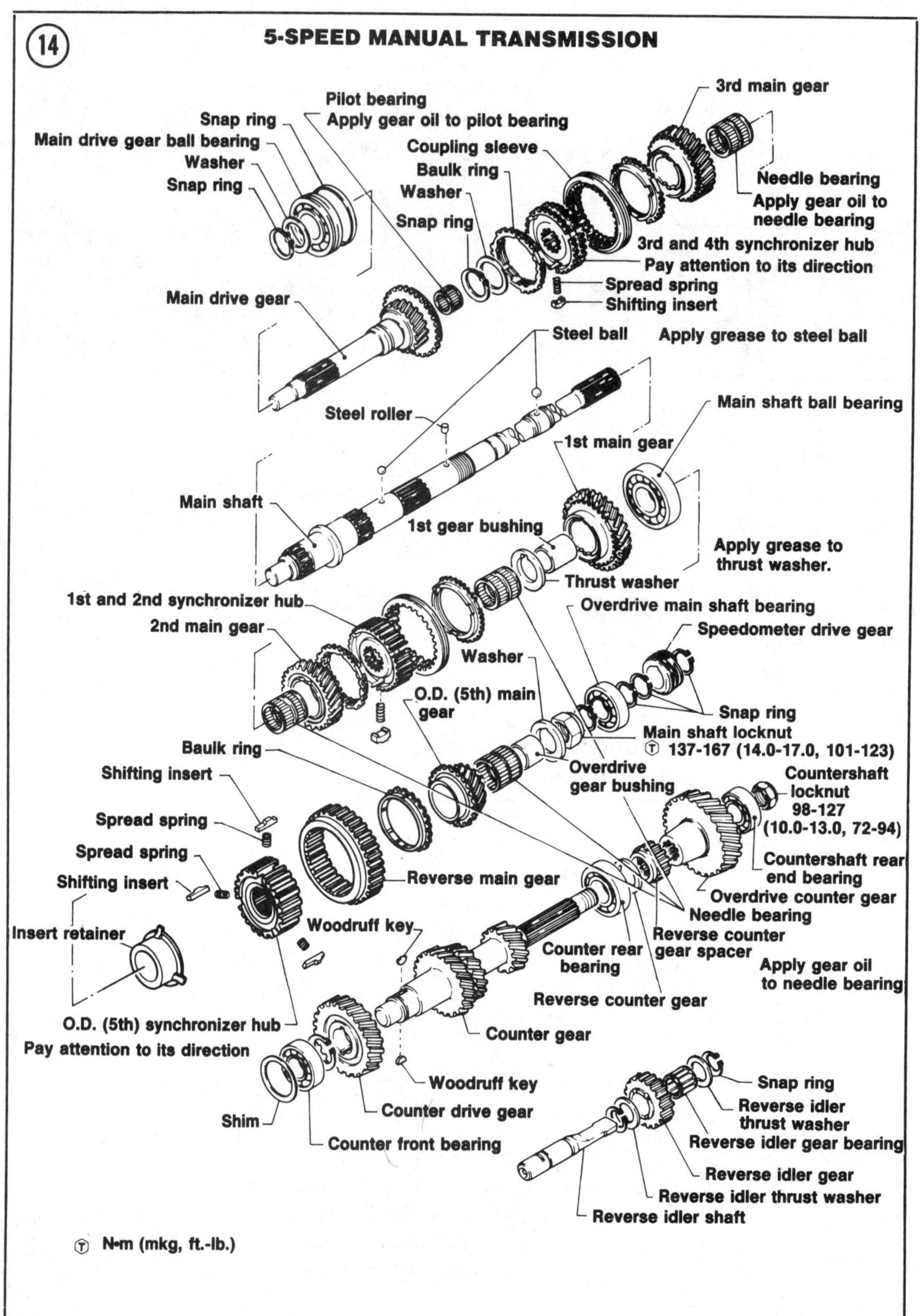
14
5-SPEED MANUAL TRANSMISSION
3rd main gear
Pilot bearing
Snap ring
Apply gear oil to pilot bearing
Main drive gear ball bearing
Coupling sleeve
Washer
Baulk ring
Snap ring
Washer
Needle bearing
Apply gear oil to needle bearing
Snap ring
3rd and 4th synchronizer hub
Pay attention to its direction
Spread spring
Main drive gear
Shifting insert
Steel ball
Apply grease to steel ball
Main shaft ball bearing
Steel roller
1st main gear
Main shaft
1st gear bushing
Apply grease to thrust washer.
Thrust washer
1st and 2nd synchronizer hub
Overdrive main shaft bearing
2nd main gear
Speedometer drive gear
Washer
O.D. (5th) main gear
Snap ring
Main shaft locknut
137-167 (14.0-17.0, 101-123)
Baulk ring
Overdrive gear bushing
Countershaft locknut 98-127 (10.0-13.0, 72-94)
Shifting insert
Spread spring
Spread spring
Countershaft rear end bearing
Reverse main gear
Shifting insert
Overdrive counter gear
Needle bearing
Insert retainer
Woodruff key
Reverse counter gear spacer
Counter rear bearing
Apply gear oil to needle bearing
Reverse counter gear
O.D. (5th) synchronizer hub
Pay attention to its direction
Counter gear
Woodruff key
Snap ring
Reverse idler thrust washer
Counter drive gear
Shim
Reverse idler gear bearing
Counter front bearing
Reverse idler gear
Reverse idler thrust washer
Reverse idler shaft
N•m (mkg, ft.-lb.)

CHAPTER ELEVEN

BRAKES

Service procedures are the same as for 1981 models, with 2 exceptions. The 1982 and later front brakes use pad shims (**Figure 15**). Brake pedal adjustment on 1983 trucks differs from earlier procedures.

ADJUSTMENTS

Brake Pedal

1. Check brake pedal height from the floor (**Figure 16**). It should be 6 1/2-6 3/4 in. (163-173 mm). To adjust, loosen the locknut on the brake booster input rod. Turn the input rod to change pedal height, then tighten the locknut.

2. Measure clearance between the pedal stopper and the end of the stoplight switch. It should be 0-0.040 in. (0-1 mm). To adjust, loosen the stoplight switch locknut. Turn the stoplight switch to change the clearance, then tighten the locknut.

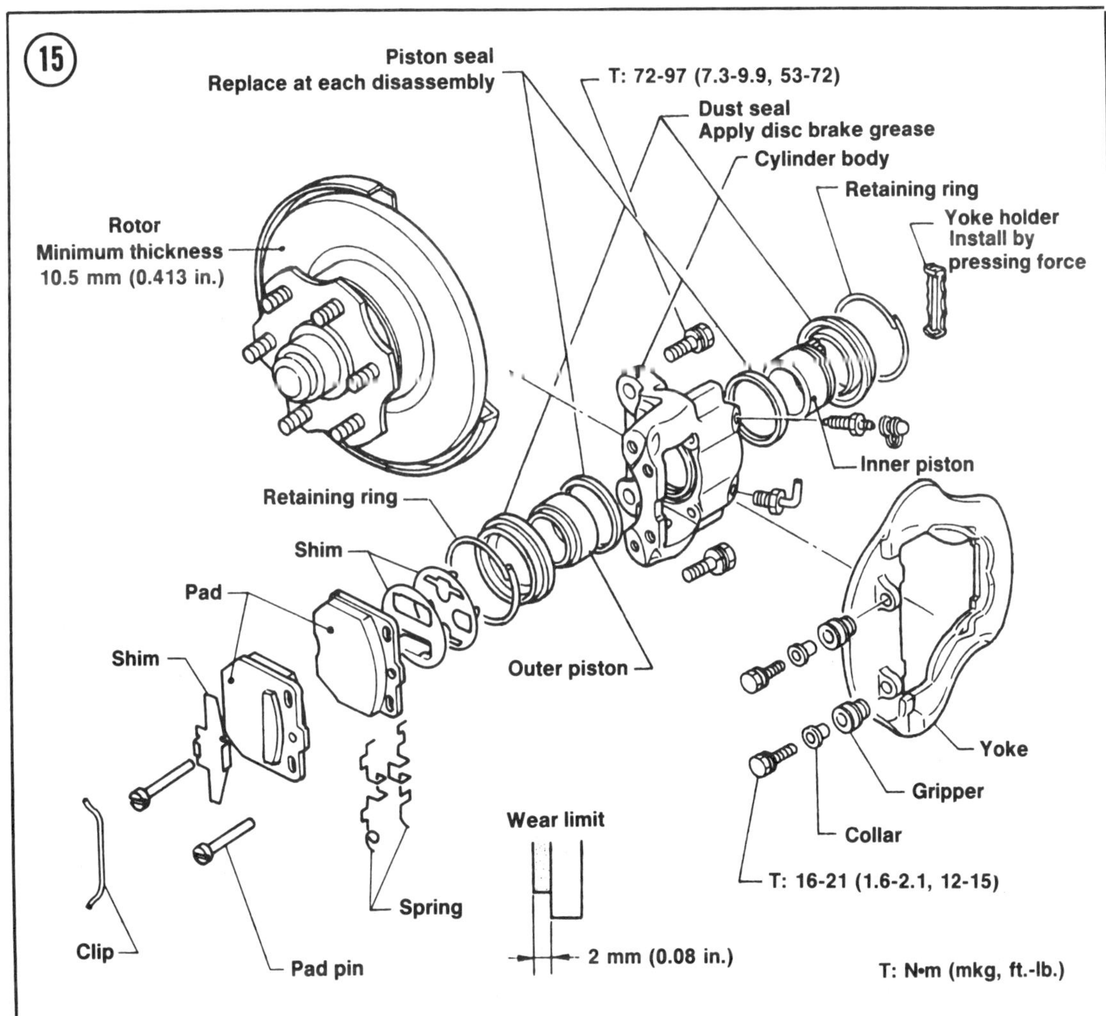

15

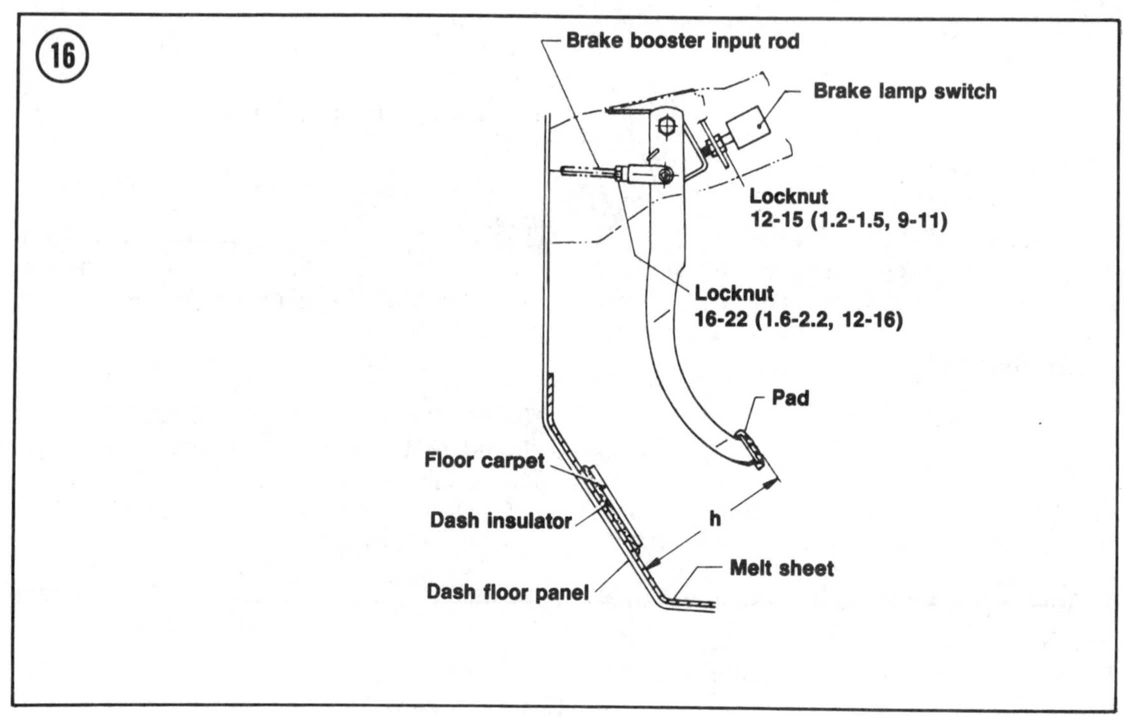

CHAPTER THIRTEEN

FRONT SUSPENSION, WHEEL BEARINGS AND STEERING

Service procedures for non-power steering are the same as for 1981 models. Power steering is optional on 1982 and later trucks.

POWER STEERING SYSTEM

Fluid Level and Leak Inspection

1. With the engine cold, unscrew the reservoir cap and check fluid level on the dipstick. See **Figure 17**. Top up if necessary with DEXRON type automatic transmission fluid. Do not use any other type of fluid.
2. Warm the engine to normal operating temperature. With a thermometer, make sure the power steering fluid is at operating temperature (104-176° F; 40-60° C).
3. Run the engine at idle. Do not run it over 1,000 rpm.

CAUTION
During the next step, turn the wheel slowly to prevent scrubbing damage to the tires.

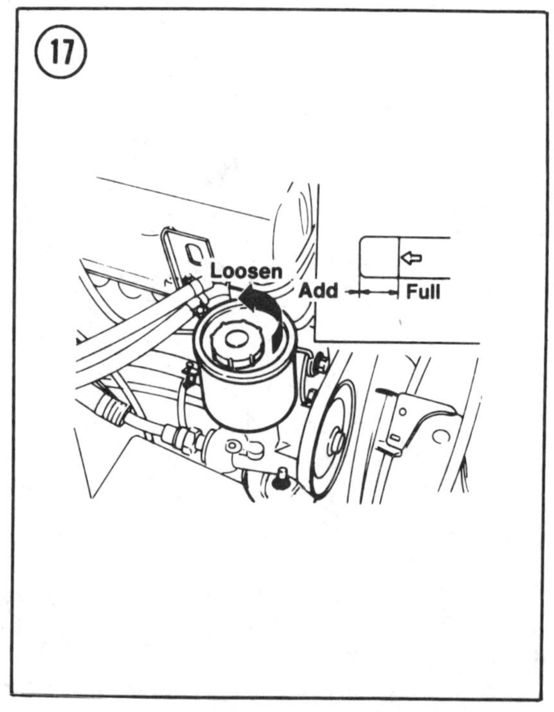

4. Have an assistant turn the steering wheel from full left lock to full right lock several times.

CAUTION
During the next step, do not hold the steering wheel at full lock for more than 15 seconds at a time.

5. Hold the steering wheel at each lock position for 5 seconds. Carefully check the power steering pump gaskets, seals and hose connections for fluid leaks. See **Figure 18**.

System Bleeding

1. With the engine cold, check fluid level on the dipstick (**Figure 17**). Top up if necessary with DEXRON type automatic transmission fluid. Do not use any other type of fluid.
2. Securely block both wheels so the truck will not roll in either direction. Jack up the front end of the truck and place it on jackstands.

CAUTION
During the next step, make sure the linkage contacts the stops lightly. Do not turn the steering hard against the stops.

3. With the engine off, quickly turn the steering wheel from full left to full right lock 10 times.

4. Recheck fluid level and top up if necessary.

5. Warm the engine to normal operating temperature. With a thermometer, make sure fluid temperature is 104-176° F (40-60° C).

6. Turn off the engine and recheck fluid level. Top up if necessary.

7. Run the engine for 3-5 seconds.

8. Turn off the engine and recheck fluid level. Top up if necessary.

CAUTION
During the next step, make sure the linkage contacts the stops lightly. Do not turn the steering hard against the stops.

9. With the engine off, quickly turn the steering wheel from full left to full right lock 10 times.

10. Check the power steering fluid. It should be free of bubbles. If not, repeat Steps 6-9.

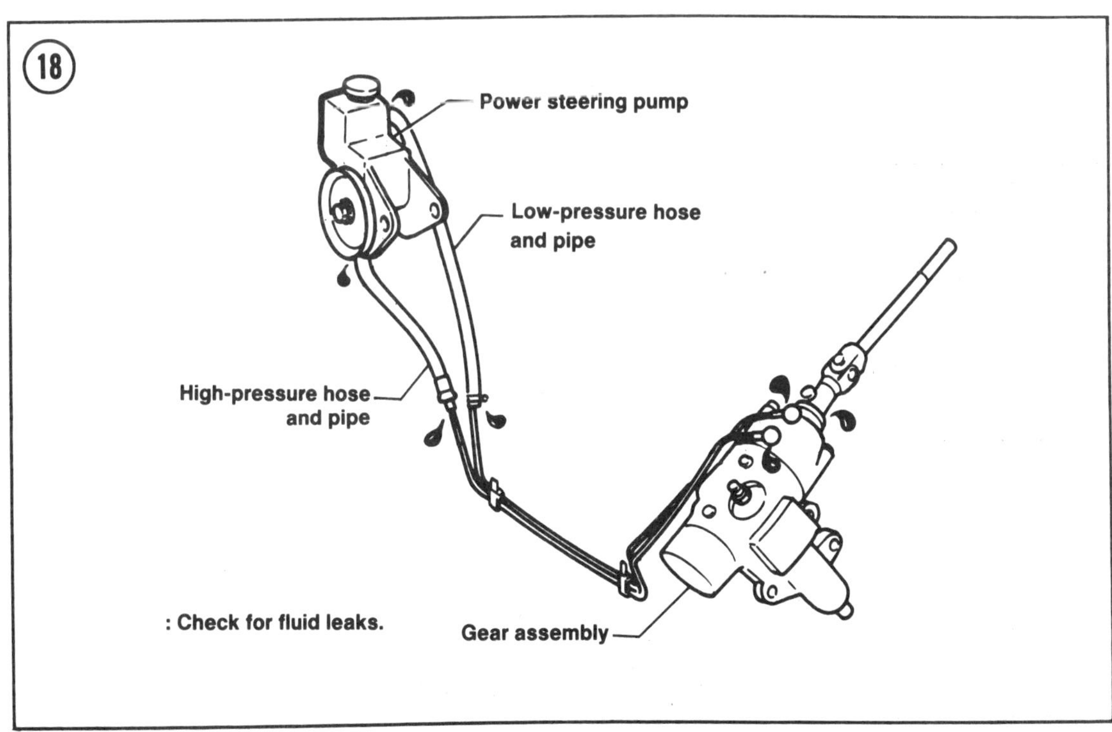

11. If there are still bubbles in the fluid after repeating Steps 6-9, check the system for leaks.

Pump Removal/Installation

1. Before removal, steam clean the pump and surrounding area, then let dry completely. Blow dry with an air compressor if available.
2. Loosen the idler pulley locknut (**Figure 19**). Turn the adjusting bolt counterclockwise to loosen the drive belt, then take the belt off.
3. Loosen the hoses at their connections to the pump (**Figure 20**). Do not remove the hoses.
4. Remove the pump mounting nuts and bolts (**Figure 21**). Disconnect the hoses, then take the pump off.
5. Installation is the reverse of removal. Tighten fasteners to specifications in **Figure 20** and **Figure 21**. Add fluid if the pump was drained or a new pump is being installed. Capacity is 900-1,000 ml (30-33 fl. oz.). Check fluid level, check for leaks and bleed the system as described in this supplement.

Steering Gear Removal/Installation

1. Before removal, steam clean the steering gear and surrounding area, then allow to dry thoroughly. Blow dry with a compressor if available.
2. Disconnect the gear at the points shown in **Figure 22**, then lift it out.
3. Installation is the reverse of removal. Tighten all fasteners to specifications in **Figure 22**. Check fluid level, look for leaks and bleed the system as described in this supplement.

Steering Linkage Overhaul

Refer to **Figure 23** for this procedure.

1. Set the handbrake. Place the transmission in FIRST (manual) or PARK (automatic).
2. Loosen the front wheel nuts. Jack up the front end of the truck, place it on jackstands and remove the front wheels.
3. Remove the cotter pins and locknuts from the outer tie rod ball-joints.
4. Detach the tie rod ball-joints from the knuckle arms. Use a puller of the type shown

19

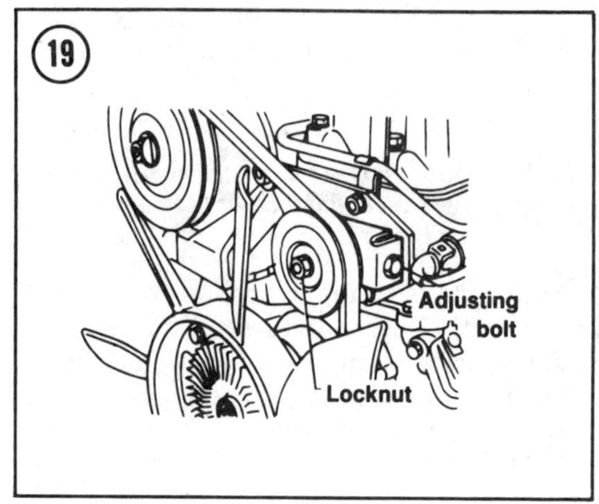

20

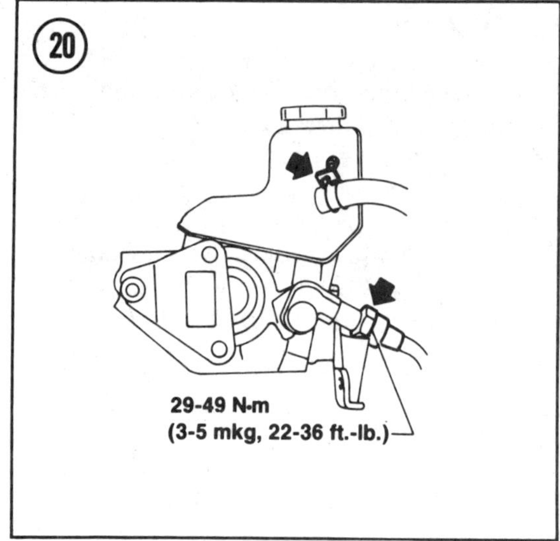

21

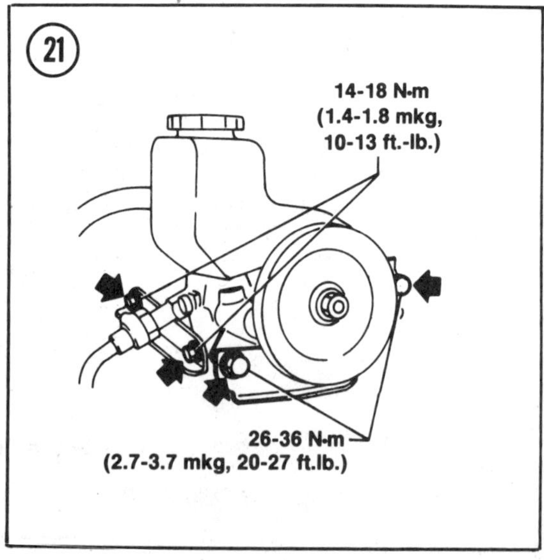

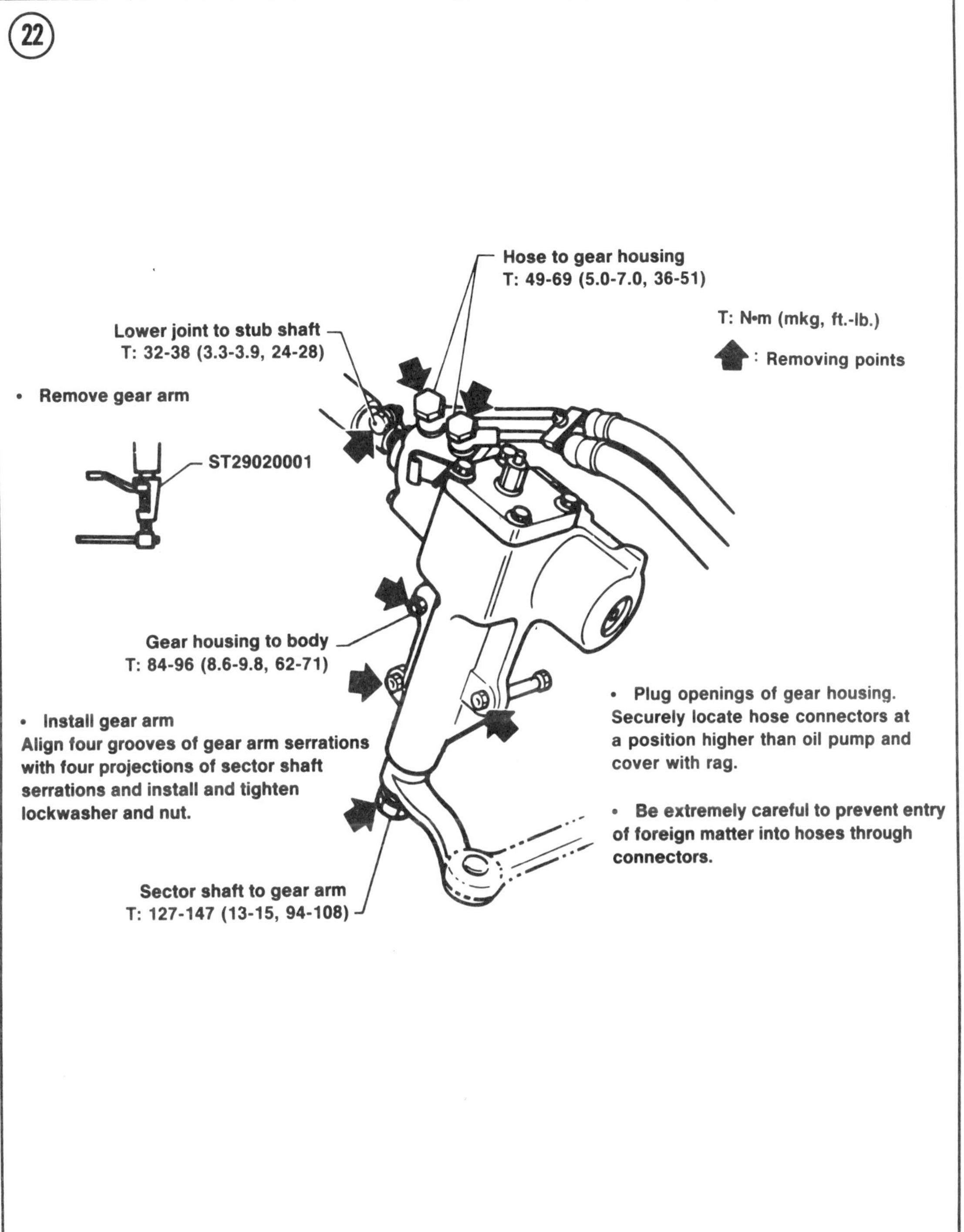
22
Hose to gear housing
T: 49-69 (5.0-7.0, 36-51)
T: N•m (mkg, ft.-lb.)
: Removing points
Lower joint to stub shaft
T: 32-38 (3.3-3.9, 24-28)
• Remove gear arm
ST29020001
Gear housing to body
T: 84-96 (8.6-9.8, 62-71)
• Install gear arm
Align four grooves of gear arm serrations with four projections of sector shaft serrations and install and tighten lockwasher and nut.
• Plug openings of gear housing. Securely locate hose connectors at a position higher than oil pump and cover with rag.
• Be extremely careful to prevent entry of foreign matter into hoses through connectors.
Sector shaft to gear arm
T: 127-147 (13-15, 94-108)

23

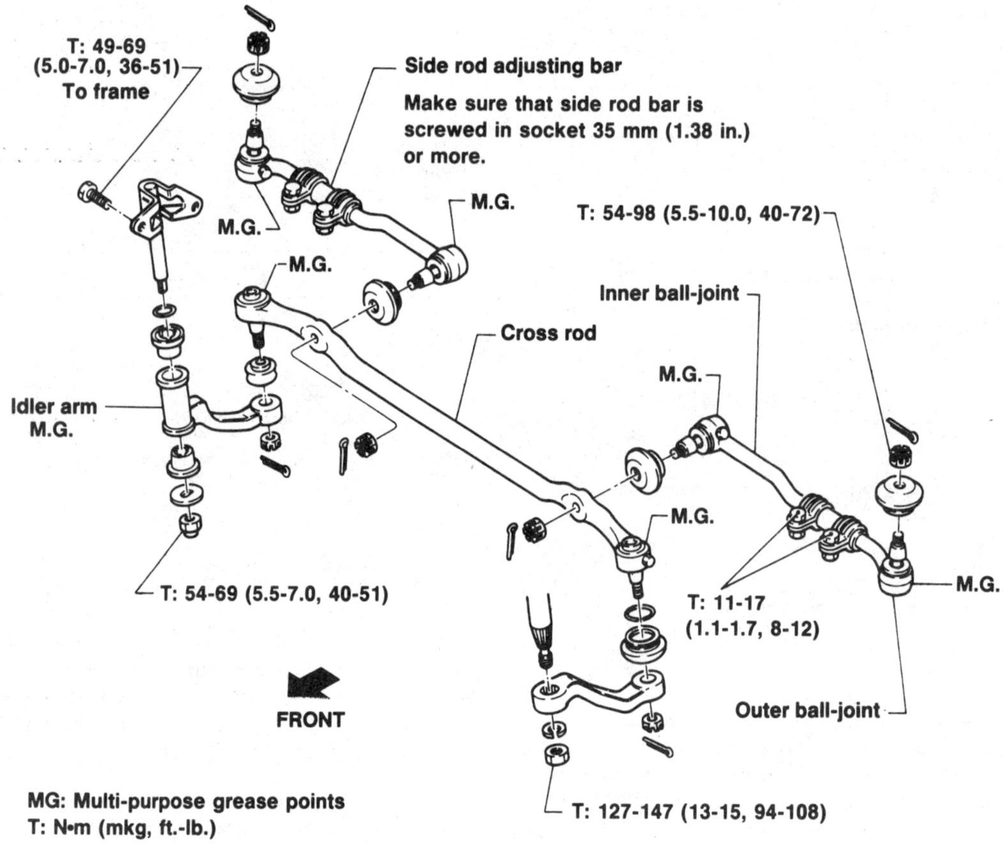

in **Figure 24** or a fork-type separator (**Figure 25**). These are available from rental dealers.

5. Detach the pitman arm from the shaft with a pitman arm puller such as Datsun tool part No. ST29020001 (Kent-Moore part No. J 25725). See **Figure 26**. These are available from rental dealers.

6. Detach the idler arm assembly from the frame.

7. Remove the steering linkage as an assembly.

8. Separate the remaining steering linkage ball-joints as described in Step 4. Remove the nut from the idler arm assembly.

24

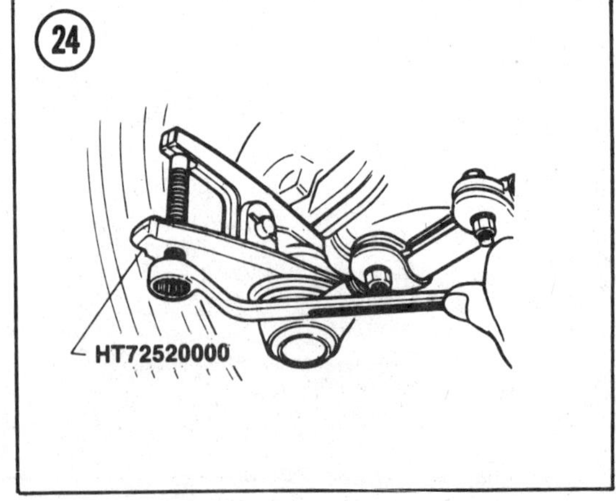

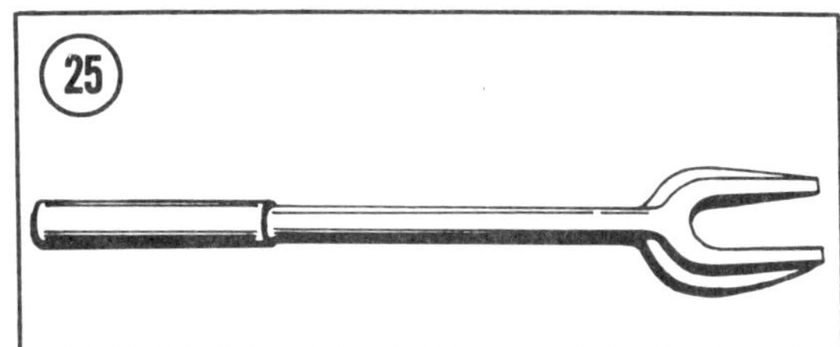

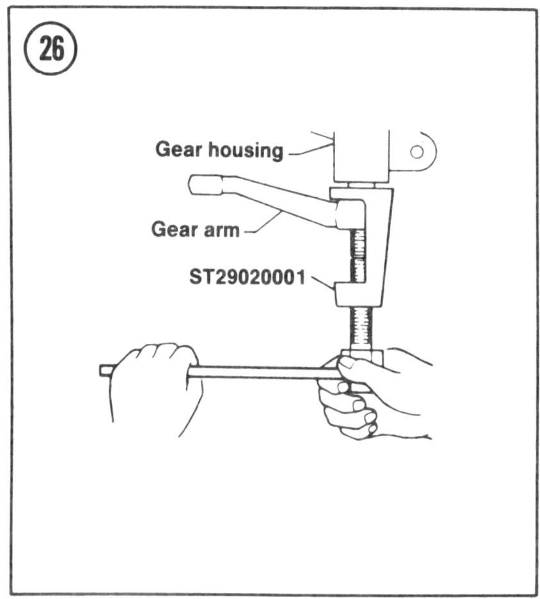

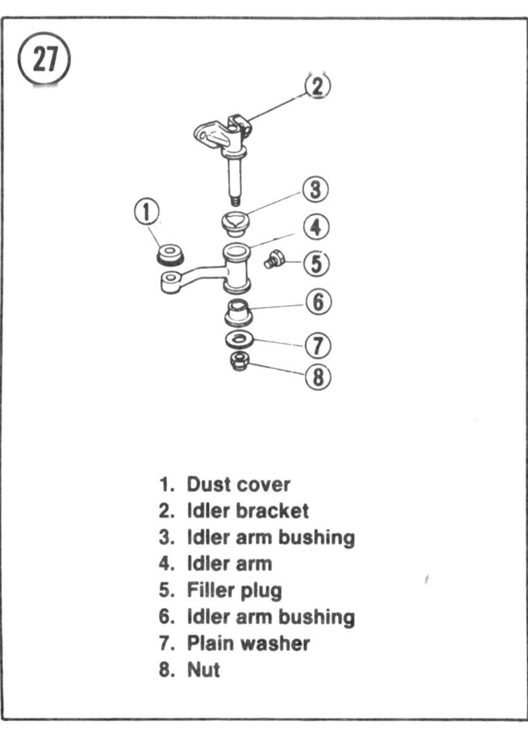

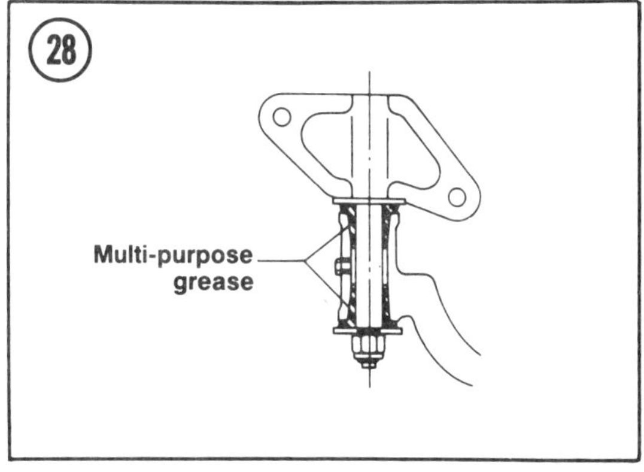

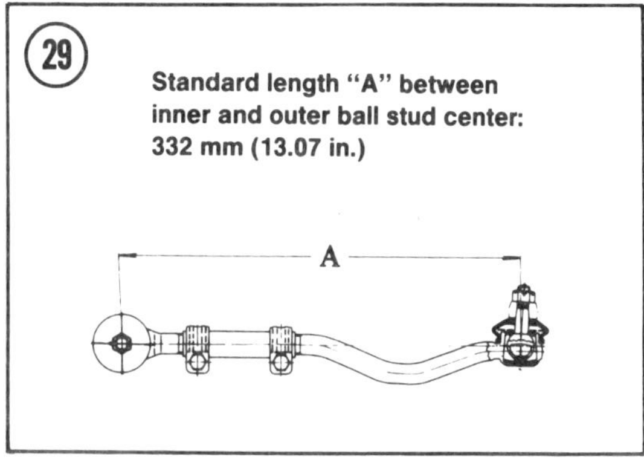

9. Clean metal parts in solvent. Do not immerse ball-joints. Wipe them with a rag dipped in solvent.
10. Check tie rods and the cross rod for bends, cracks or damaged threads. Replace if these conditions are found.
11. Check the idler arm bushings (**Figure 27**) for wear or damage. Replace as needed.
12. Check tie rod and cross rod ball-joints for worn studs. Place each ball-joint in a vise with the stud facing upward. Try to pull the stud up and down. If any play can be felt, replace the ball-joint.
13. Assemble and install by reversing Steps 1-8. Apply multipurpose grease to idler arm bushings, then assemble the idler arm as shown in **Figure 28**. Tighten all nuts and bolts to specifications (**Figure 23**).

NOTE
*If tie rod ball-joints are removed, make sure the tie rod is the correct length when installing the new balljoints. Dimension A, **Figure 29**, should be 13.07 in. (332 mm).*

INDEX

F

G

H

I

K

L

M

NOTES

NOTES